# Health, Happiness, and Well-Being

# Health, Happiness, and Well-Being

## Better Living Through Psychological Science

**Steven Jay Lynn**
*Binghamton University (SUNY)*

**William T. O'Donohue**
*University of Nevada, Reno*

**Scott O. Lilienfeld**
*Emory University, USA*

Editors

Los Angeles | London | New Delhi
Singapore | Washington DC

Los Angeles | London | New Delhi
Singapore | Washington DC

FOR INFORMATION:

SAGE Publications, Inc.
2455 Teller Road
Thousand Oaks, California 91320
E-mail: order@sagepub.com

SAGE Publications Ltd.
1 Oliver's Yard
55 City Road
London EC1Y 1SP
United Kingdom

SAGE Publications India Pvt. Ltd.
B 1/I 1 Mohan Cooperative Industrial Area
Mathura Road, New Delhi 110 044
India

SAGE Publications Asia-Pacific Pte. Ltd.
3 Church Street
#10-04 Samsung Hub
Singapore 049483

Printed in the United States of America

*Library of Congress Cataloging-in-Publication Data*

Lynn, Steven J.

Health, happiness, and well-being : better living through psychological science / Steven J. Lynn, State University of New York, Binghampton, William T. O'Donohue, State University of Nevada, Reno, Scott O. Lilienfeld, Emory University, USA.

pages cm
Includes bibliographical references and index.

ISBN 978-1-4522-0317-1 (pbk.)

1. Happiness. 2. Health. 3. Well-being. I. O'Donohue, William T. II. Lilienfeld, Scott O., 1960-III. Title.

BF575.H27L96 2015
158.1—dc23        2014020163

This book is printed on acid-free paper.

Acquisitions Editor:  Reid Hester
Editorial Assistant:  Lucy Berbeo
Production Editor:  Kelly DeRosa
Copy Editor:  Michelle Ponce
Typesetter:  C&M Digitals (P) Ltd.
Proofreader:  Sarah J. Duffy
Indexer:  Rick Hurd
Cover Designer:  Bryan Fishman
Marketing Manager:  Shari Countryman

SUSTAINABLE FORESTRY INITIATIVE

Certified Chain of Custody
Promoting Sustainable Forestry
www.sfiprogram.org
SFI-01268

SFI label applies to text stock

14 15 16 17 18 10 9 8 7 6 5 4 3 2 1

# Table of Contents

About the Editors      vii

1. Health, Happiness, and Well-Being:
   Better Living Through Psychological Science      1
   *Steven Jay Lynn, William O'Donohue,*
   *and Scott O. Lilienfeld*

PART I: ESSENTIAL SKILLS FOR BETTER LIVING

2. Emotion Regulation: Staying in Control      14
   *Lorie A. Ritschel and Cynthia L. Ramirez*

3. Effective Problem Solving      41
   *Christine Maguth Nezu, Arthur M. Nezu,*
   *and Sarah Ricelli*

4. Understanding and Enhancing Psychological Acceptance      62
   *James D. Herbert and Lynn L. Brandsma*

PART II: COPING AND RESILIENCE

5. Stress, Coping, and Resilience in the Face of Trauma      90
   *Anthony Papa, Julie Kahler, and Clair Rummel*

6. Coping With Chronic Pain      117
   *Joshua R. Dyer, Merry Sylvester, Emily K. Traupman,*
   *Jessica L. Mackelprang, and David R. Patterson*

7. Chilling Out: Meditation, Relaxation, and Yoga      142
   *Anne Malaktaris, Peter Lemons, Steven Jay Lynn,*
   *and Liam Condon*

PART III: STAYING HEALTHY
        AND BECOMING HEALTHIER

8. Sleeping Well                                                        168
   *Richard R. Bootzin, Elaine Blank, and Tucker Peck*

9. Science Weighs in on Obesity                                         195
   *Adria Pearson and Linda W. Craighead*

10. Exercise: A Path to Physical and Psychological Well-Being           223
    *Reed Maxwell and Steven Jay Lynn*

PART IV: HAPPINESS AND SPIRITUALITY

11. What Psychological Science Knows
    About Achieving Happiness                                           250
    *S. Katherine Nelson, Jaime L. Kurtz,*
    *and Sonja Lyubomirsky*

12. Integrating Religion and Spirituality Into
    Treatment: Research and Practice                                    272
    *Emily A. Padgett, Katherine G. Kusner,*
    *and Kenneth I. Pargament*

13. Building Wisdom and Character                                       296
    *Robert J. Sternberg*

PART V: ENRICHING RELATIONSHIPS,
        MANAGING MONEY

14. Making Marriage (and Other Relationships) Work                     318
    *Matthew D. Johnson*

15. The Joys of Loving: Enhancing Sexual Experiences                   341
    *Rachael Ann Fite*

16. Raising Our Kids Well: Guidelines for Positive Parenting           369
    *Keith D. Allen, Mark D. Shriver, and Cy Nadler*

17. Financial Skills                                                    405
    *William O'Donohue and Alexandros Maragakis*

Author Index                                                           425

Subject Index                                                          443

# About the Editors

**Steven Jay Lynn, PhD** is a Distinguished Professor of Psychology (SUNY) and director of the Psychological Clinic at Binghamton University. He is the inaugural editor and editor of *Psychology of Consciousness: Theory, Research, and Practice* (APA), and he is the recipient of numerous professional awards, including the Chancellor's Award, State University of New York for Excellence in Scholarship and Creative Activities. He has published over 300 articles and chapters on psychotherapy, hypnosis, memory, dissociative disorders, and trauma, and he has written or edited 20 books. The National Institute of Mental Health has supported his research.

**William T. O'Donohue** is professor of psychology at the University of Nevada, Reno. He received a doctorate in psychology from SUNY at Stony Brook. For the past 19 years, he has directed a clinic supported by the Victims of Crime Act that provides free therapy to child sexual abuse victims and adult sexual abuse victims. He has published over 75 books and 300 journal articles and book chapters.

**Scott O. Lilienfeld** is professor of psychology at Emory University in Atlanta. He received his PhD in psychology (clinical) from the University of Minnesota. Dr. Lilienfeld is associate editor of the *Journal of Abnormal Psychology*, past president of the Society for a Science of Clinical Psychology, and current president of the Society for the Scientific Study of Psychopathy. He has published over 300 manuscripts on personality disorders, dissociative disorders, psychiatric classification, pseudoscience in psychology, and evidence-based practices in clinical psychology.

# 1

# Health, Happiness, and Well-Being

## Better Living Through Psychological Science

*Steven Jay Lynn*

*William O'Donohue*

*Scott O. Lilienfeld*

E ach day the popular media churns out a multitude of tidbits of advice about how to stay healthy and lead the good life. From Oprah, to Dr. Oz, to Dr. Phil, we hear about what and what not to eat, how to improve our sex lives, whom to hang out with and to avoid, and what berry provides the richest source of antioxidants to ward off disease and infirmity. In a mere 1 or 2 hours of television viewing we can listen to Bill Maher and Jenny McCarthy wax negative about the dangers of routine vaccinations and Suzanne Somers pooh-pooh standard chemotherapy for breast cancer. In strolling through the local bookstore or cruising Amazon.com, we may be intrigued by books that promise to reveal "the secret" to achieve success and realize our wildest fantasies on the same shelf as tomes that hawk upbeat strategies to overcome any obstacle to fulfillment in love and marriage. The

Internet offers an incredible storehouse of scientifically supported advice for enhancing the quality of life, yet it also provides indiscriminate access to potentially dangerous pseudoscience and nonsense. In short, let the consumer beware.

Unfortunately, it is not only the popular media that pedal misinformation. Professionals, including mental health professionals, are also responsible for a lot of this noise. Prevention programs like Critical Incident Stress Debriefing (Mitchell & Everly, 1995), widely employed to reduce posttraumatic reactions, are touted despite evidence that not only do they not perform their intended preventative functions but may actually cause harm. Universities endow chairs and have centers for junk therapies such as facilitated communication, which claim to permit severely autistic children to communicate normally (Biklen & Schubert, 1991). Similar problems occur with putative drug abuse prevention programs like Project Dare (Ennett, Tobler, Ringwalt, & Flewelling, 1994; West & O'Neal, 2004). Yet a wide variety of professionals continue to subject children and adolescents to these ineffective or potentially iatrogenic programs. Adults and children are all too often given psychotropic medications in ways in which they are not fully informed of problems with their safety and efficacy (Antonuccio, Danton, & DeNelsky, 1995). Too much practice in wellness, prevention, and treatment fails to be evidence based.

The question of how can we slog through the morass of information and misinformation we encounter in popular sources to glean precious nuggets of reliable information is complicated by the fact that (a) the recommendations for living the good life and the health fad du jour may become the risky or dubious practices of tomorrow, (b) the advice offered is often contradictory, and (c) all too often there is precious little sound research available to guide good health decisions and practices. The grapefruit and cabbage diets have met the fate of the Edsel, yet we can still encounter daily debate regarding the value of the Atkins versus the Mediterranean diets. At one time or another, people have made diet and vitamin supplement choices based on the ideas that vitamin C could nip colds (or even cancer) in the bud, shark cartilage could cure some cancers, the herb St. John's Wort could alleviate the symptoms of severe depression, and vitamin E could reduce the risk of Alzheimer's disease. Today, there is good evidence from the research literature to doubt each of these "facts" promoted by the popular media. In fact, high doses of vitamin E may increase the risk of death from many causes (Miller, et al., 2005), and some herbal preparations contain dangerous amounts of lead and even the poison arsenic (Ernst, 2002). Some experts suggest that when it comes to exercise, we should adopt the *no pain, no gain* slogan as a mantra, and exercise vigorously for at least 30 minutes a day, whereas other experts suggest that gardening and cleaning our rooms is sufficient (Blair, Kohl, Gordon, & Paffenberger, 1992; Pate et al., 1995). Is it possible that experts on both sides of the exercise divide are correct? Or consider advice about expressing our righteous anger. Should we uncork our indignation and even aggression in the name of emotional honesty or instead learn to accept our feelings while practicing forgiveness and forbearance? When a relationship begins to go south, should we directly confront our partner when we're upset or just learn to deal with it? And what about how to express grief? Is one way of grieving better than another? Should we cry a lot and let mundane activities come to a standstill until we work through the grieving process, or will we fare just as well in the long run if we resume our normal lives soon after our loved one dies? In the absence of scientifically supported information, answering such questions and making healthy choices becomes a risky guessing game for most of us. Each year, Americans shell out about $34 billion to complementary and alternative medical (CAM) practitioners, on the sidelines of traditional medical care, to purchase CAM products, such as vitamin supplements, untested herbal remedies, and homeopathic products (Nahin, Barnes, Strussman, & Bloom, 2009). In the National Health Interview Survey, 38% of adults and 12% of children reported using some form of CAM such as acupuncture, chiropractic medicine, or homeopathic medicine over the preceding year (Barnes, Bloom, & Nahin, 2008). Each of these methods is popular, yet there are serious questions about whether they are more effective than a placebo. With so many choices about mental and physical health care available, on what basis do we choose CAM approaches versus traditional medical treatments?

Staying afloat in this vast ocean of information and misinformation is daunting: Most of us lack reliable authorities to depend on for accurate, state-of-the-science advice for achieving health and well-being. Our book assists readers in acquiring a panoramic view of what the best psychological science has to offer with regard to how to attain physical health and optimum psychological functioning. Health, Happiness, and Well-Being (HHWB) is premised on the idea that valid health information derived from controlled studies, provided by credible experts, is vital to achieving the good life, acquiring up-to-date information, and side-stepping lost opportunities associated with pursuing ineffective treatments.

We are not the first to suggest that clinical psychology has focused too much on treating problems instead of preventing these problems in the first place (Rappaport, 1987). Community psychologists historically were among the first to suggest that more attention ought to be given to prevention. They also advocated a level of analysis in which some of the strongest but perhaps distal putative causes of mental health problems could be changed:

unemployment, poverty, discrimination, and homelessness are key examples. In an important sense, they were advocating at a public health level, and this is important as historians of medicine have agreed that public health measures such as improved sanitation, clean drinking water, inoculations, and improved nutrition have accounted for a large amount of the improvements in the health of the U.S. population (Thomas, Quinn, Butler, Fryer, & Garza, 2011). However, unfortunately, decades later the evidence regarding similar gains for these sorts of community health changes on mental or behavioral health is much less clear. This can be due to a number of problems:

1. We possess much less information regarding the causal pathways that lead to mental health problems.

2. We are much less clear on how to define exactly what is meant by mental or behavioral health, as compared to physical health. For example, what exactly constitutes a healthy sex life? It also may be the case that this is not entirely a scientific question, but rather values play an important role.

3. Relatedly, even if we settle this definitional issue, again, little is known regarding the causal pathways to these desired end states.

4. Some of these issues involve complex religious, moral, and political dimensions that are not only controversial but also may be interpreted as protected under the U.S. Constitution. For example, when considering what one's sex life ought to look like, many people take into account their moral or religious views, and some also need to take into account legal constraints.

5. The pragmatics of these issues are also largely unknown. How well does prevention program $x$ work to produce result $y$? In what populations? How cost-effective is this or that prevention program? If we spend $x$ dollars what do we save—on what? Does one need the time and money of the relatively affluent in order to live a particular lifestyle?

In part, our book can be seen as a response to the following practical question. Imagine if a client or a loved one were to ask the following: "I'd like to be mentally healthy and lead a good life. What ought I do each day or each week to maximize the likelihood that I will achieve this? What does the best science say about this?" This seems to be an important and practical question but also a very tough one—a question also that has been relatively neglected by our profession. President Barack Obama has made a central component of healthcare reform a shift from the old focus on waiting until people are sick and then attempting to remove this state of ill health, to the new orientation to keep people healthy and even to enhance health in the already healthy. The Affordable Care Act (ACA) attempts to correct some of this imbalance by reemphasizing prevention. The underlying rationale for this is that it is preferable certainly from a humanitarian point of view and perhaps from a financial point of view to prevent suffering and disability in the first place. The ACA takes a number of steps to enhance prevention and the promotion of health, including:

1. The promotion of patient-centered medical homes (PCMHs) in which a patient's care is coordinated and prevention services are mandated.

2. The promotion of evidence-based care, including evidence-based preventative care.

3. The ACA creates a new agency housed in the U.S. Department of Health and Human Services called the National Prevention, Health Promotion, and Public Health Council. This new agency is charged with the coordination of prevention, wellness, and health promotion strategies.

4. It creates the Prevention and Public Health Fund with $15 billion in additional funding for prevention and health promotion activities.

5. Small businesses can receive financial benefits for worksite wellness programs.

6. Community transformation grants will be funded to aid large-scale health promotion activities such as tobacco cessation, active living, and nutritional improvement.

The ACA also creates a sizeable research agenda. More research is needed on how to define mental/behavioral health and regarding cost-effective strategies for improving health. Key questions involve to what extent are external agencies responsible for these activities, and what needs to take place in the context of other institutions such as the family or the neighborhood or the school? To the extent that these basic societal agencies are in a time of crisis—and to the extent that the distress of these are a function of a number of variables and trends—none of these answers will be easy. Right now if we as clinical psychologists are invited to the table to participate in these initiatives, we believe that we have too little systematic information to rely on. This book is an attempt to bring together what we do know, while underlining the critical need for a research agenda.

Our book capitalizes on the fact that maintaining and enhancing health has several advantages. First, people don't want to be merely "not sick" but rather to be healthy and lead a good life. Second, it may be less costly, on a personal and societal basis, to keep people healthy rather than to attempt to fix them when they are not. Third, health maintenance and enhancement attempts to not be satisfied with "not sick" but continually strives to enhance life potential. Proponents of positive psychology (e.g., Seligman & Csikszentmihalyi, 2000) have likewise observed that the mental health professions have traditionally been oriented toward finding and modifying disorder instead of promoting health and optimizing human potential.

We conceived HHWB with broad goals in mind. First, we conceptualized HHWB as a standard or supplementary textbook in courses on health psychology, positive psychology, and adjustment. Second, HHWB provides readers with essential tools to become knowledgeable consumers of information related to their psychological and physical health and well-being. In HHWB, we assist readers with evaluating claims and appreciating the influence of popular yet unsubstantiated beliefs in shaping opinions about behavioral health and psychological well-being. Many chapters illustrate these concepts with lively examples drawn from the popular media as well as scholarly works.

Each chapter (a) defines and illustrates key concepts (e.g., mindfulness, coping), (b) reviews research relevant to psychological or physical health and well-being, (c) discusses the roles and applications of personal enhancement and health promotion methods in the healthcare delivery system, and (d) points to directions for future developments in research and understanding regarding how to prevent illness and enhance health and well–being. We wrote HHWB to appeal to (a) advanced undergraduates and graduate students in clinical psychology, counseling psychology, health psychology, nursing, social work, and other mental health professions; (b) clinicians and their clients; (c) researchers and academics; and (d) educated laypersons. In short, our objective is to provide readers with a one-stop shop resource for information derived from psychological science and conveyed by top experts regarding the optimization of health and well-being. Unlike many volumes with a narrow focus on getting fit and slim or learning how to meditate, for example, our text offers a comprehensive and scholarly approach to health and wellness. In fulfilling our mission, we are grateful for the support of eminent authorities at the forefront of scientific knowledge who have contributed the following chapters (summarized below) in their areas of expertise.

Emotions ranging from peaks of ecstasy, to the agony of a broken bone, to the depths of depression, color virtually all aspects of our lives. Regulating emotions, especially in the face of stressors, is often no easy task, yet it is essential to effective coping on an everyday basis. In Chapter 2, "Emotion Regulation: Staying in Control," which begins the first section, "Essential Skills for Better Living," Lorie Ritschel and Cynthia Ramirez discuss how we can regulate our feelings and develop strategies to get and stay in control on psychological, physical, and interpersonal levels and thereby maximize opportunities for an emotionally rich, healthy life. A life without problems to solve is almost certain to be dull and dreary, lacking in vigor and meaningful challenges to surmount. Still, for most of us, there is no dearth of problems to solve. Accordingly, how we negotiate the problems and obstacles we encounter often shapes our level of psychological health, happiness, and ability to get things done effectively. In Chapter 3, "Effective Problem Solving," Christine Maguth Nezu, Arthur Nezu, and Sarah Ricelli provide an in-depth view of their decades-long quest to learn about problem solving and how it can best be accomplished through a rich toolkit of adaptive and planful strategies.

Despite our best efforts, some problems are intractable. Sometimes acceptance of what cannot be changed, and the ability to take refuge in the present moment, is crucial to avoiding the trap of getting mentally stuck in a past we cannot rewrite and a future we cannot predict with certainty. The ability to ride with the tide of our emotions, allow thoughts to come and go, and not act reflexively on our impulses is at the heart of acceptance-based approaches that James Herbert and Lynn Brandsma describe in Chapter 4, "Understanding and Enhancing Psychological Acceptance." The authors review the increasingly popular use of techniques and strategies to promote psychological acceptance to promote well-being, improved functioning, and quality of life, as well as the potential of acceptance-based approaches to prevent psychological and perhaps physical disorders.

If stressful circumstances are an inevitable part of life, then the ability to cope with them is an essential aspect of well-being. In Chapter 5, "Stress, Coping, and Resilience in the Face of Trauma," which leads the second section, "Coping and Resilience," Anthony Papa, Julie Kahler, and Clair Rummel, view stressors through the lens of their detrimental effects on the ability to maintain a valued and stable sense of self. The authors discuss effective ways to cope with stress and provide a review of science-based treatments that can be used proactively to manage stress on a daily basis.

Pain is one of the most significant and costly public health problems in the United States and around the world. In Chapter 6, "Coping With Chronic Pain," Josh Dyer, Merry Sylvester, Emily Traupman, Jessica Mackelprang, and David Patterson describe how a contemporary biopsychosocial model that emphasizes a multidisciplinary approach can steer pain assessment and interventions based on education, cognitive behavioral strategies, activation and increasing activity, relaxation and imagery, hypnosis, and mindfulness and acceptance. Combined in an encompassing integrative treatment, these approaches can prevent acute pain from becoming chronic and, more broadly, foster pain relief.

Meditation, relaxation techniques, and yoga have been used for millennia in cultures around the world to achieve physical and mental calmness, relieve stress, and promote well-being. In recent decades, these approaches have caught the eye of researchers and clinicians and have begun to move into the mainstream of scientific investigation. In Chapter 7, "Chilling Out: Meditation, Relaxation, and Yoga," Anne Malaktaris, Peter Lemons, Steven Jay Lynn, and Liam Condon review the empirical basis for using meditation, relaxation, and yoga in treating and possibly preventing an array of psychological (e.g., depression, anxiety) and physical (e.g., chronic pain, essential hypertension) conditions.

Richard Bootzin, Elaine Blank, and Tucker Peck's Chapter 8, "Sleeping Well," leads the third section of the book, "Staying Healthy and Becoming Healthier." To sleep, perchance to be happier and healthier, is the theme of their instructive contribution, which addresses popular myths about sleep and provides many empirically supported recommendations for how to sleep well and optimize our ability to function during the daytime. Their chapter covers pharmacological and psychological interventions and spans a wide range of topics, including the benefits of naps, the effects of exercise and alcohol and drugs on sleep, caffeine and energy drinks, and the use of herbal preparations and prescription sleeping pills.

In Chapter 9, "Science Weighs in on Obesity," Adria Pearson and Linda Craighead present a down-to-earth, talk-to-the-reader account of "the science behind dieting and weight loss and describe some helpful strategies to implement amidst the onslaught of promises for a quick fix." The authors consistently highlight the importance of preventing the development of obesity and underline the point that a worthy goal for readers is health with happiness, not achieving a particular weight on a scale. The authors argue that successful weight loss involves lifestyle changes and offer an illustration of healthy eating through mindfulness practice.

In Chapter 10, "Exercise: A Path to Physical and Psychological Well-Being," Reed Maxwell and Steven Jay Lynn trace the recognition of the role of exercise in promoting well-being from antiquity to the present-day scientific approach to the evaluation of the short and long-term effects of exercise to prevent disease, promote health, and calm the mind. The authors review the evidence for the effectiveness of different types of exercise (e.g., isometric, isotonic) and focus on the well-researched findings pertaining to aerobic exercise with respect to psychological (e.g., depression, anxiety) and physical (e.g., heart disease, neurogenerative diseases) outcomes, with enormous public health consequences for the prevention and treatment of disease and infirmity.

Katherine Nelson, Jaime Kurtz, and Sonja Lyubomirsky's Chapter 11, "What Psychological Science Knows About Achieving Happiness," starts off the fourth section of the book, "Happiness and Spirituality." Achieving happiness is surely a prominent goal, if not a preoccupation, of people in modern cultures. Although happiness is often ephemeral and elusive, it has been the subject of considerably recent scientific inquiry, which the authors review in their consideration of empirically supported ways to become happier. The authors evaluate popular claims about happiness (e.g., money can buy happiness) and delineate which happiness-increasing practices should—and should not—be implemented in everyday life.

In Chapter 12, "Integrating Religion and Spirituality Into Treatment: Research and Practice," Emily Padgett, Katherine Kusner, and Kenneth Pargament discuss how religion and spirituality can play important roles in the physical and mental healthcare systems, often enriching programs geared to enhance health and well-being. The chapter underlines the importance of assessment of spirituality, provides strategies and guidelines for integrating spirituality into treatment, and describes a spiritually focused intervention to address spiritual struggle in a person facing a difficult medical diagnosis.

In Chapter 13, "Building Wisdom and Character," Robert Sternberg argues that "having intelligence is not tantamount to being wise or ethical." Sternberg further contends that wisdom can be measured and taught by using procedures encompassing reflection, project-based learning, ethical values, flexible thinking, thinking about ends, and role modeling. The chapter presents a model of ethical behavior and wisdom that builds character and fosters the common good by "balancing intrapersonal, interpersonal, and extrapersonal interests."

Matthew Johnson's Chapter 14, "Making Marriage (and Other Relationships) Work," launches the fifth and final section of the book, "Enriching Relationships, Managing Money." Johnson makes a strong case for a close tie between positive intimate relationships and well-being across many aspects of our lives. Johnson uses marriage as a prototype of an intimate relationship to discuss intrapersonal (e.g., values, beliefs) and interpersonal (e.g., communication, social support) predictors of relationship satisfaction, the role of thoughts and behaviors in preventing and treating relationship discord, and empirically supported interventions to promote relationship satisfaction and minimize discord.

In Chapter 15, "The Joys of Loving: Enhancing Sexual Experiences," Rachael Fite separates facts from the many fictions (e.g., women experience sex as men do) regarding human sexuality—propagated by popular media and by some early scientific findings—which can interfere with the ability to enjoy sexual relationships. As a research-trained clinical psychologist who specializes in sexual health, Fite relies on a wealth of information, drawn from the scientific literature and her clinical experience, to present healthy concepts (e.g., healthy sexuality is your own responsibility) that set the stage for enjoying sexual relations, and she reviews empirically supported skills and interventions found to be related to enhanced sexual functioning.

In Chapter 16, "Raising Our Kids Well: Guidelines for Positive Parenting," Keith Allen, Mark Shriver, and Cy Nadler review a large body of evidence that documents the importance of effective parenting, especially with children who are challenging or difficult. The chapter presents many useful guidelines and parenting techniques that illustrate best parenting practices derived from the empirical literature and parenting programs with demonstrated success. The authors review applied controversies in the field (e.g., spanking, timeout), recommend potentially useful self-help books on parenting, and provide a case example that illustrates positive parenting practices.

In the concluding Chapter 17, "Financial Skills," William O'Donohue and Alexandros Maragakis suggest that money matters: Research points to a potential causal link between socioeconomic status and numerous indicators of quality of life. Accordingly, the authors argue that the ability to use knowledge and skills to manage financial resources effectively (i.e., financial literacy) is essential to maximizing well-being. The chapter includes a list of 25 irrational or problematic thoughts about finances that stand in the way of acquiring financial literacy and provides recommendations for therapists to assist clients in managing their financial resources. In conclusion, we are pleased to present this compendium of chapters regarding what psychological science can contribute to achieving optimum health, happiness, and well-being.

# References

Antonuccio, D. O., Danton, W. G., & DeNelsky, G. Y. (1995). Psychotherapy versus medication for depression: Challenging the conventional wisdom with data. *Professional Psychology: Research and Practice, 26*(6), 574.

Barnes, P. M., Bloom, B., & Nahin, R. (2008). *CDC national health statistics report # 12—Complementary and alternative medicine use among adults and children: United States, 2007*. Atlanta, GA: National Center for Health Statistics.

Biklen, D., & Schubert, A. (1991). New words: The communication of students with autism. *Remedial and Special Education, 12*(6), 46–57. doi:10.1177/0741 93259101200607

Blair, S. N., Kohl, H. W., Gordon, N. F., & Paffenbarger, R. S., Jr. (1992). How much physical activity is good for health? *Annual Review of Public Health, 13*(1), 99–126.

Ennett, S. T., Tobler, N. S., Ringwalt, C. L., & Flewelling, R. L. (1994). How effective is drug abuse resistance education? A meta-analysis of Project DARE outcome evaluations. *American Journal of Public Health, 84*(9), 1394–1401.

Ernst, E. (2002). Toxic heavy metals and undeclared drugs in Asian herbal medicines. *Trends in Pharmacological Sciences, 23*(3), 136–139.

Miller, E. R., Pastor-Barriuso, R., Dalal, D., Riemersma, R. A., Appel, L. J., & Guallar, E. (2005). Meta-analysis: High-dosage vitamin E supplementation may increase all cause mortality. *Annals of Internal Medicine, 142*(1), 37–46.

Mitchell, J.T., & Everly, G.S., Jr. (1995). Critical incident stress debriefing (CISD) and the prevention of work-related traumatic stress among high risk occupation groups. *Psychotraumatology: The Springer Series on Stress and Coping, Part IV.* pp. 267–280. doi:10.1007/978–1–4899–1034–9_16

Nahin, R. L., Barnes, P. M., Strussman, B. J., & Bloom, B. (2009). *National health statistics reports costs of complementary and alternative medicine (CAM) and frequency of visits to CAM practitioners: United States 2007.* Atlanta, GA: National Center for Health Statistics.

Pate, R. R., Pratt, M., Blair, S. N., Haskell, W. L., Macera, C. A., Bouchard, C., . . . Wilmore, J. H. (1995). Physical activity and public health: A recommendation from the Centers for Disease Control and Prevention and the American College of Sports Medicine. *Journal of the American Medical Association, 273*(5), 402–407.

Rappaport, J. (1987). Terms of empowerment/exemplars of prevention: Toward a theory for community psychology. *American Journal of Community Psychology, 15*(2), 121–148.

Seligman, M. E., & Csikszentmihalyi, M. (2000). *Positive psychology: An introduction* (Vol. 55, No. 1). Washington, DC: American Psychological Association.

Thomas, S.B., Quinn, S.C., Butler, J., Fryer, C.S., & Garza, M.A. (2011). Toward a fourth generation of disparities research to achieve health equity. *Annual Review of Public Health, 32,* 399–416. doi:10.1146/annurev-publhealth-031 210-101136

West, S. L., & O'Neal, K. K. (2004). Project D.A.R.E. Outcome effectiveness revisited. *American Journal of Public Health 94*(6), 1027–1029.

# PART I

## Essential Skills for Better Living

# 2

# Emotion Regulation

## Staying in Control

*Lorie A. Ritschel*

*Cynthia L. Ramirez*

Emory University School of Medicine

*"You cannot make yourself feel something you do not feel, but you can make yourself do right in spite of your feelings."*

Pearl S. Buck

Humans are fundamentally emotional creatures, and emotional experience is an inherent part of human existence. Our feelings drive us to engage in particular behaviors and are hallmark features of many aspects of human existence. Certain types of experiences prompt similar reactions across people and cultures, thereby knitting a common fabric of human experience. For example, loss is typically associated with sadness, whereas goal blockage often prompts anger. While meta-analytic findings reveal some subtleties in emotion recognition between members of different cultural groups (Elfenbein & Ambady, 2002), findings show that facial expressions that are associated with the six basic emotions—sadness, anger, surprise, disgust, happiness, and fear—are recognizable in every country and culture worldwide (Ekman, Friesen, & Ellsworth, 1972; but see Russell, 1994, for alternative views and interpretations on this topic).[1]

Complex emotional reactions often occur in response to life situations. A promotion at work may be associated with both pride and happiness in our accomplishment as well as anxiety and excitement in beginning a new role; similarly, significant disagreements with longtime friends may prompt feelings of disappointment and even anger, which are mixed with and often balanced by feelings of loyalty, commitment, and warmth that have developed from years of positive interactions with our friends. Through all these experiences, a common thread emerges. No matter what we feel or when we feel it, a fundamental task inherent in the process of growing and maturing is to learn to recognize our emotions, express them in appropriate times and ways, and use them as a springboard to motivate and impel future action.

Although a considerable amount of the published literature in psychology focuses on the downside of emotions (e.g., psychopathology), this chapter—like this book *in toto*—focuses on how we can best leverage our emotions to our advantage so that we can become better, stronger, and wiser individuals within our own emotional spheres.

## What Are Emotions?

First, it is important to note what emotions *are not*. As John and Gross (2007) pointed out, emotions are not stress (a more general, negative affective response), mood (which lasts longer than affect and is less reactive to specific stimuli), or biobehavioral impulses (i.e., hunger, thirst, sex, and pain). Rather, emotions are multifaceted experiences that involve cognitive, behavioral, and physiological components (Gross & Thompson, 2007; Hooff, Schouten, & Simonovski, 2012; Mauss, Levenson, McCarter, Wilhelm, & Gross, 2005).

Emotion theorists and researchers are divided on the concept of *response coherence,* which suggests that the components of the emotional experience should be correlated and are defined by the intensity of the emotion (Ekman, 1992). Thus, low-grade emotional responses should prompt minor alterations in thoughts, behaviors, and physiology, whereas heightened or intense emotions should produce correspondingly more intense changes across these systems (Davidson, 1992). According to the response coherence theory, a mild fear response would result in slight changes in thoughts ("I hope that spider doesn't get any closer"), behaviors (scooting away from the spider), and physiology (slight increases in heart rate and breathing). A specific phobia of spiders, in contrast, would result in intense changes in thoughts ("It's probably poisonous—if it bites me, I'll die!"), behaviors (running away), and physiology (extremely rapid heart rate and breathing, facial expression that is easily identifiable as fear).

To date, the empirical evidence on response coherence is mixed (for a summary, see Mauss et al., 2005). Some studies have shown positive associations between emotions and interoceptive awareness (Pollatos, Gramann, & Schandry, 2007), behaviors (Mauss et al., 2005), facial expressions (Ekman, Davidson, & Friesen, 1990), and neural activity (Critchley et al., 2005). Other studies, however, have found weak or even nonexistent relationships between emotion intensity and the components of emotion (e.g., Edelmann & Baker, 2002). Although findings from these studies may not yet be clear, we can say definitively that emotions are associated with changes in thoughts, behaviors, and physiology, regardless of the intercorrelations among these three components.

Emotions serve three basic functions (Kennedy-Moore & Watson, 1999). First, emotions provide us with feedback about ourselves and the world around us. They may signal danger, or they may alert us that an event is pleasurable and worth continuing. Second, emotions and emotional displays (e.g., crying, slumping, smiling) communicate how we feel to other people, thereby influencing how they respond to us. Ultimately, this reciprocity enables (and sometimes hinders) human relationships. Third, we often use the information learned from an emotional response to compel future behavior. For example, a snorkeler who looks up and realizes that she has floated far from the dive boat probably feels fear, because there is some danger that she will be left behind or that if she needs help nobody will hear her cries. Her fear impels her to discontinue snorkeling and start moving back toward the dive boat. As the threat of danger decreases, so does her fear, which indicates that her behavioral choice was effective in returning to emotional homeostasis.

Emotional experiences can occur in response to internal stimuli, external stimuli, or both (Gross & Thompson, 2007). At times, emotions also include subjective interpretations of prompting stimuli, which may further alter our physiology and behaviors (A. Beck, Rush, Shaw, & Emery, 1979). Thus, emotions are subjective in that we assess situations and attribute meaning to them, and these attributions can vary based on a wide variety of factors. For example, individuals suffering from major depression make distorted, negative interpretations of even the most benign circumstances (J. Beck, 1995); in fact, cognitive behavior therapy (CBT) for depression was designed to help correct these distortions (A. Beck et al., 1979). Thus, a relatively benign stimulus, such as a friend not returning a phone call for several days, can be interpreted differentially based on our current emotional status and well-being. For example, whereas a euthymic individual may interpret this event by saying to herself, "My friend must be really busy," a depressed person may say, "I knew she didn't like me. I'll never make friends in this city." The euthymic individual may have little or no emotional reaction in response to her thought, whereas the depressed individual is likely to feel increasing sadness in response to the interpretation that she will be friendless forever.

Even people who are not suffering from depression may interpret situations differently based on their emotional equilibrium at any particular moment. We become more vulnerable to our emotions when, for example, we sleep or eat poorly, are sick, neglect our medication regimens, abuse drugs or alcohol, or live in chronically stressful environments (see Linehan, Bohus, & Lynch, 2007, for a review of biological and contextual factors that increase emotional vulnerability). Ergo, we stand a higher likelihood of maximizing our emotional functioning when we reduce our emotional vulnerability. In this way, we are more resilient to stressors and triggers that occur in our lives (Sapolsky, 2007).

## Emotion Regulation Defined

One of the best ways to observe the various ways (and success rates) of a group of unrelated people attempting to regulate emotion in response to a common stimulus is to go to the airport and observe passenger reactions when a flight is cancelled. Motivating factors behind purchasing an airline ticket certainly differ; some people are flying for work, others for weddings, funerals, vacations, or visits with friends. But everyone has a common trigger for emotion when they learn that they are not going to get where they planned to go (at least in the way and on the timeline they originally chose). A few themes emerge in watching these passengers. First, the type and extremity of the reactions will vary widely, running the gamut from minor reactions to rage. Some will be sad, others angry; some may even be relieved. At some point after the news has sunk in (and this time frame will vary across passengers), most people will begin to engage in some sort of strategy to regulate their emotions. Strategies will range from effective problem solving (e.g., getting listed on another flight, renting a car in preparation to drive, calling the people who would be waiting at the other airport) to acceptance (e.g., a shrug of the shoulders and return to checking email while awaiting the next departure) to ineffective problem solving (e.g., yelling at the gate agent and demanding the flight leave as scheduled). Finally, the extent to which these various problem-solving strategies mitigate the initial emotional response will vary widely as well.

Emotion regulation refers to the ability to influence both positive and negative emotions in response to salient stimuli (John & Gross, 2007). The ability to regulate one's emotions is a major component of staying in control of one's life and of maximizing emotional opportunities. Emotions that are out of control or too intense often are related to problematic consequences in a variety of life domains; in addition, failure to respond to positive stimuli can be similarly problematic. Although the majority of research on emotion regulation has focused on mitigating negative affect, an excess of positive affect can also be problematic, as in the case of mania in bipolar disorder (Gruber, 2011).

The inability to regulate emotions effectively is associated with physical illness, interpersonal difficulties, and various forms of psychopathology (McLaughlin, Hatzenbuehler, Mennin, & Nolen-Hoeksema, 2011). Conversely, effective emotion regulation has been associated with a decrease in mental and physical illness as well as increased social and general well-being (Gross & Thompson, 2007; Kemeny et al., 2012; Singh & Mishra, 2011; Smyth & Arigo, 2009). Well-adjusted people are able to down-regulate negative emotion (e.g., sadness, shame, anger) in order to behave in ways that are effective and in line with their goals and values *and* know how to savor pleasant events when they occur.

The ability to successfully regulate emotion is associated with overall emotional intelligence, or EI (Mayer, DiPaolo, & Salovey, 1990; Mayer & Salovey, 1997; Salovey & Grewal, 2005). Salovey and Mayer (1990) articulated four branches of emotional intelligence: (1) perceiving emotions in self and others (i.e., via verbal and nonverbal emotional expressions); (2) using emotions (i.e., leveraging information from emotions to engage in intra- and interpersonal problem solving); (3) understanding emotions (i.e., grasping how emotions are nuanced and how they are related to each other); and (4) managing emotions (i.e., regulating emotion in self and others). These abilities are interrelated, and it is likely that emotion knowledge is a necessary component of successful emotion regulation (Wranik, Barrett, & Salovey, 2007). Although the role of emotion regulation in the social context is clearly an important branch of EI, in this chapter we focus on (1) the ability to regulate emotions in the self and (2) how different emotion regulation strategies affect an individual's well-being on psychological, physical, and interpersonal levels.

# The Process Model of Emotion Regulation

The study of emotion regulation is related to a large historical literature on *coping* (see Folkman & Lazarus, 1988). Coping is defined as managing stress-inducing internal or external demands. By extension, coping strategies are the mechanisms employed to mitigate stress and solve problems with the goal of downregulating negative affect. Thus, there is considerable overlap in coping and emotion regulation strategies. These two constructs can be differentiated, however, in two important ways: (1) coping is generally employed to downregulate negative affect, whereas emotion regulation is used both to downregulate negative affect and to upregulate positive affect; and (2) coping typically covers a longer period of time, rather than the moment-to-moment process encompassed in emotion regulation (Gross & Thompson, 2007).

Gross and Thompson (2007) constructed a framework of emotion regulation known as the process model, which includes five consecutive time points at which individuals can choose to regulate emotions. We describe each of these strategies in turn, and we reference parallel constructs from the coping literature where appropriate. We illustrate each aspect of the process model using the example of Erin, a woman with a fear of the ocean (and specifically, shark attacks).

The first emotion regulation strategy in the process model is termed *situation selection*. In general, one way to stay in control emotionally is to select situations that are likely to result in positive emotions and to avoid situations that are likely to result in negative emotions. Of course, this is not always possible; although Erin may generally opt for vacations in Colorado, at times she may have to join her family for trips to the beach. In these situations, we are required to choose other emotion regulation strategies that become available once we are already in the situation.

The second emotion regulation strategy is *situation modification*, in which an individual modifies a situation with the goal of decreasing negative emotional responses or increasing positive responses. In using this strategy, Erin has several options; she may sit on the beach but never enter the water; she may go into shallow water but not go swimming in deeper water; or she may only enter the water in a shark-proof cage.

The third strategy is *attentional deployment*, which refers to how individuals direct their attention to influence their emotions. This strategy is particularly useful when a situation cannot be changed, and it generally involves moving attention away from the situation itself or away from the emotionally distressing aspects of a situation. Attentional deployment is similar to Folkman and Lazarus's (1988) distancing strategy, in which an individual works to forget or not think much about a distressing situation. To illustrate this point, consider that Erin's daughter wants to play in the ocean but is too young to swim by herself (negating Erin's ability to use the situation modification strategy). To engage the strategy of attentional deployment, Erin can (1) distract herself from her fears by thinking about something else entirely (e.g., the movie she saw the night before) or (2) distract herself from thoughts of being attacked by a shark (the distressing aspect of the situation) by concentrating on less distressing elements of the situations (e.g., the soothing feeling of the warm water, the joy she feels as she sees her daughter play in the water).

The fourth emotion regulation strategy is *cognitive change,* in which an individual modifies his or her appraisal of a situation in order to alter its emotional significance. Cognitive change is similar to Folkman and Lazarus's (1988) strategy of positive reappraisal, in which an individual looks at a stressful situation as an opportunity for personal growth and self-improvement; by finding the beneficial aspects of a stressful situation, the emotional impact of the stressor is mitigated. Using this strategy, Erin might remind herself that shark attacks are actually quite rare, and that the likelihood that she or her daughter would be injured or killed is very low. She might also remind herself of the numerous times she has gone swimming in the ocean previously, all without incident. Alternatively, Erin may consider her trip to the beach as an opportunity to overcome an irrational childhood fear or to demonstrate bravery and strength to her daughter.

The final emotion regulation strategy is *response modulation,* which encompasses a set of strategies that might be used to alter the physiological and behavioral components of the emotional response after it has already occurred. If Erin in fact experiences fear as a result of her trip to the beach, she may still need to use relaxation techniques to calm herself further, even after she is safely out of the water and, therefore, perceived danger. Alternatively, she may elect to engage in expressive suppression and hide her fear response from her daughter or other family members. In this latter case, Erin may still experience fear internally (e.g., increased heart rate and respiration, sweating), but she masks the outward expression of emotion by inhibiting facial expressions of fear or anxiety, avoiding discussing her fears, or even actively denying her emotion if she is questioned about it.

These five emotion regulation strategies are divided into two categories: antecedent-focused strategies, which occur earlier in the emotion-generative cycle, and response-focused regulation, which occurs later in the cycle. The first four classes of strategies (i.e., situation selection, situation modification, attentional deployment, and cognitive change) are antecedent-focused strategies; response modulation is a response-focused strategy. As Lazarus (1998) notes, coping serves one of two functions; coping strategies are either problem focused or emotion focused. In the former, a distressed individual would work to modify the environmental context as a way to remediate subsequent emotional distress; thus, situation selection and situation modification strategies can be thought of as problem-focused coping strategies. Conversely, emotion-focused strategies are designed to change how the person responds emotionally to the distressing stimulus without necessarily impacting or changing the distressing stimulus itself. Emotion-focused coping would therefore incorporate the strategies of attentional deployment, cognitive change, and response modulation. Two aspects of the process model should be noted: (1) these strategies become available in sequence (i.e., it is unlikely that Erin would engage in attentional deployment to mitigate fear of the ocean if she were not at the ocean), and (2) individuals can use several different emotional regulation strategies in any given situation.

## What Are Effective Emotion Regulation Strategies?

The use of effective emotion regulation strategies has been linked to mental and physical health, interpersonal satisfaction, and productivity (Singh & Mishra, 2011). The majority of research on the process model of emotion regulation has focused on cognitive reappraisal and expressive suppression strategies (John & Gross, 2007). Importantly, cognitive reappraisal is the mechanism of change that underpins cognitive behavioral therapy (Clark, 1995; DeRubeis, Tang, & Beck, 2001; but for dissenting opinions, see Dimidjian et al., 2006; Longmore & Worrell, 2007), which enjoys a vast literature supporting its use as an effective treatment for numerous psychological difficulties (for a review, see Butler, Chapman, Forman, & Beck, 2006).

Most published studies indicate that cognitive reappraisal works more effectively and uses fewer cognitive resources than expressive suppression to downregulate negative emotions. In large part, suppression is believed to modulate only emotional expression (Cheavens et al., 2005); thus, individuals who engage in suppression still experience negative emotions as indicated by subjective report and increased cardiovascular and electrodermal activation (John & Gross, 2004). Suppression also appears to contribute to a discrepancy between inner emotional experience and outward expression. This process ultimately—and paradoxically—often leads to a rebound effect (Wegner, Schneider, Carter, & White, 1987), wherein the unwanted thought occurs with greater, not less, frequency (Abramowitz, Tolin, & Street, 2001). This emotional inauthenticity leads to increased negative affect. Moreover, suppression requires considerable cognitive resources, which detracts from the ability to attend to other environmental stimuli. As a result, suppressors tend to have difficulty attending to interpersonal cues needed to respond appropriately to others (Gross & John, 2003).

Individuals use both strategies to varying degrees (Gross & John, 2003). Reappraisal, however, is associated with a host of favorable psychosocial outcomes, whereas suppression is associated with multiple deleterious consequences. Reappraisers, for example, report that they experience and express more positive emotions and fewer negative emotions. They are less vulnerable to depressive symptoms and report higher levels of optimism, life satisfaction, and self-esteem (Gross & John, 2003). They also tend to be more successful interpersonally than suppressors, in that they have more relationships in general and are better liked by others. Reappraisers are more satisfied with life in general and are psychologically healthier than those who use suppression strategies (Gross, Richards, & John, 2006). Conversely, suppressors experience and express fewer positive and more negative emotions, which may be due in part to the negative impact associated with emotional inauthenticity (i.e., a mismatch between the experience and expression of emotion, as in smiling when angry). High suppressors report less social closeness and support, as well as greater levels of depression and lower levels of life satisfaction, optimism, and self-esteem. It should be noted that studies examining how emotion regulation strategies (i.e., the tendency to use reappraisal versus suppression) relate to long-term individual outcomes generally have used cross-sectional and correlational designs, limiting the ability to infer directional causality of effects (John & Gross, 2004). Longitudinal designs and intervention-based studies would help clarify how emotion regulation strategies influence psychological and physical well-being and vice versa.

A couple of additional caveats about these findings bear mentioning. First, the benefits of reappraisal over suppression hold true in Western cultures but do not necessarily extend to other cultures. In particular, Asian cultures place a higher value on suppression (Singh & Mishra, 2011). Correspondingly, findings regarding the psychological and interpersonal consequences of suppression in Western cultures do not hold in cultures that value suppression as an emotion regulation strategy (Soto, Perez, Kim, Lee, & Minnick, 2011). Again, causal directionality cannot be inferred, and longitudinal experimental designs would shed some light on how and why the benefits and detriments of emotion regulation strategies vary by culture.

Likewise, we cannot conclude that suppression is categorically ineffective. Côté, Gyurak, and Levenson (2010) pointed out that some situations may require suppression of emotional expression, whereas other situations require an increase in emotional expression. One can imagine several interpersonal situations in which suppressing an emotion, at least initially, is effective. For example, quickly suppressing anger during a difficult interaction with an employer may ultimately save one's job. In a laboratory paradigm (Côté et al., 2010), undergraduates who successfully downregulated emotionally expressive behavior by suppressing a fear response had higher scores on a measure of well-being, suggesting that the ability to suppress the expression of fear may in some cases be adaptive. These cultural and situational differences highlight the likelihood that the relationship between emotion regulation strategies and well-being are complex and likely bidirectional.

In another study, Schutte, Manes, and Malouff (2009) found that antecedent-focused emotion regulation strategies were generally associated with higher life satisfaction and positive mood and lower negative mood. Specifically, reappraisal was associated with higher life satisfaction, positive mood, and higher emotional intelligence. In terms of response-focused strategies, this study examined both suppression and behavior modulation, which includes talking with others about positive emotional experiences, resolving the conflict or problem that prompted the initial emotion, and behaving in ways that strengthen positive emotions and weaken negative emotions. Whereas behavior modulation was associated with higher life satisfaction and positive mood and was unrelated to negative mood, suppression was associated with lower life satisfaction, fewer positive and more negative affective experiences, and lower overall emotional intelligence. The authors concluded that antecedent-focused regulation strategies are a better predictor of subjective well-being than are response regulation strategies, but that the predictive algorithm is nuanced; that is, it is erroneous to conclude that antecedent-focused strategies are uniquely and consistently superior to response-focused strategies.

Identifying effective emotion regulation strategies may depend on the function of the chosen strategy. Koole (2009) categorized emotion regulation strategies into three classes according to function: (1) hedonically oriented strategies function to minimize negative emotion and maximize positive emotion, (2) goal-oriented strategies function to move toward behavioral end points and include balancing multiple goals, and (3) person-oriented strategies function to improve intra- and interpersonal functioning. Hedonic strategies (e.g., comfort seeking) are linked to more immediate emotional relief, which sometimes occurs at the expense of long-term well-being. Goal-oriented strategies include cognitive reappraisal (i.e., thought modification) and distraction techniques (e.g., thought disruption, attentional movement). In contrast to the hedonic and goal-oriented strategies, person-oriented strategies require the ability to be open to both positive and negative emotions in that they are not designed to move away from negative affect; rather, they require the individual to experience whatever emotion arises in the moment, regardless of its valence. Examples include mindfulness, expressive writing, and relaxation techniques (e.g., progressive muscle relaxation). According to Koole, cognitive strategies are more effective than bodily strategies in goal-oriented emotion regulation; however, bodily strategies like relaxation can be quite effective in person-oriented emotion regulation.

Most research on emotion regulation focuses on the downregulation of negative emotions. Our well-being, however, also depends on our ability to upregulate positive emotions, such as love, joy, and amusement. Positive emotions have short-term hedonic value; however, they also have long-term value by improving well-being via intra- and interpersonal growth (Fredrickson, 2000; Fredrickson & Joiner, 2002). In general, less research has been conducted on the *regulation* of positive emotional experiences. Rather, researchers have tended to focus on how individuals prolong or enhance positive emotional experiences (e.g., Tugade & Fredrickson, 2007). One example of maintaining a positive emotional experience is by savoring (Bryant, 1989), or deliberately attending to that experience. Savoring is enacted both intrapersonally, such as by thinking about the experience using anticipation and reminiscence, and interpersonally, such as by talking to others directly about the experience. Savoring is positively correlated with subjective well-being, including optimism, internal locus of control, self-control behaviors, life satisfaction, and self-esteem; it correlates negatively with symptoms of depression and hopelessness (Bryant, 2003). Another strategy that enhances or increases positive emotional experience is finding positive meaning in a negative event, or *benefit finding* (Helgeson, Reynolds, & Tomich, 2006).

The link between positive emotions and well-being is most obvious in the literature on resilience. Resilience, or our ability to adapt successfully to changing and even stressful circumstances, increases when we capitalize on positive emotions while going through a negative emotional experience (Tugade & Fredrickson, 2004). Resilient individuals recover more quickly from stressful events by using positive emotions to dampen the impact of negative emotion. They are also more likely to use the strategy of meaning making in response to the stressful event; that is, even if an event is overtly negative, resilient individuals are better able to make lemonade out of lemons by finding some positive angle or slant on the situation. In the example of the cancelled flight, these are the passengers who say, "Too bad the flight was cancelled; at least I can finish watching this football game!"

A reciprocally beneficial relationship exists between positive affect and cognitive functioning as well. Specifically, positive emotions may help individuals think and behave in more flexible ways, making them more effective at problem solving (Fredrickson, 2000). This is the inverse of the relationship between negative affect and rumination, in which individuals think repetitively about a problem in unhelpful ways that leave them feeling stuck, ultimately resulting in little shift in the problem itself or the negative affect experienced by the ruminator (Nolen-Hoeksema, 2000). Positive appraisal of an upcoming event—that is, perceiving an event as a challenge rather than a threat—also is linked to the effective down-regulation of negative emotions (Fredrickson, 2000). Importantly, the link between positive emotions and positive meaning making is iterative: finding positive meaning in a situation increases positive emotions, which in turn increases cognitive flexibility, which makes it easier to find positive meaning in stressful situations, and so on. Both result in higher levels of resilience and, ultimately, improved physical and psychological well-being (Fredrickson, 2000).

Quoidbach, Berry, Hansenne, and Mikolajczak (2010) examined several strategies that individuals use to either savor or dampen positive emotional experiences. Savoring strategies included behavioral displays (nonverbal behaviors including facial expression), being present (deliberately attending to positive experience), communicating positive experiences to others, and positive mental time travel (mentally anticipating or remembering positive experiences). Dampening strategies included suppression, distraction (via worrying or engaging in other activities that are unrelated to the positive event), fault finding (paying attention to negative aspects of positive situations), and negative mental time travel (negative reminiscence on causes of positive events or anticipation of negative future consequences). Being present and engaging in positive mental time travel were associated with higher positive affect, whereas distraction was associated with lower levels of positive affect. Fault finding and negative mental time travel were associated with lower life-satisfaction ratings. Interestingly, the authors found that using a wider range of savoring strategies resulted in higher levels of reported happiness.

## Ineffective Emotion Regulation and Its Role in Psychological and Physical Well-being

Emotion regulation strategies can be effortful, automatic, or both, and each strategy has both costs and benefits. Ineffective emotion regulation occurs when individuals are not successful at reducing unwanted emotion or they do so at the expense of long-term costs that outweigh short-term relief (Campbell-Sills & Barlow, 2007). Effective emotion regulation strategies minimize negative subjective and physiological distress while increasing the probability of achieving both short- and long-term goals.

We can examine the process model of emotion regulation through the lens of ineffective coping strategies. For example, people who are anxious, depressed, or both may ineffectively use attentional deployment by engaging in rumination, in which an individual thinks repetitively about an emotionally distressing situation (Nolen-Hoeksema, 2000). Rumination typically leads to a prolonged maintenance of the negative emotion and detracts from the individual's ability to attend to more positive stimuli. Alternatively, situation avoidance and social withdrawal could be classified as maladaptive situation selection strategies, particularly if they are used to excess. Anxious individuals may avoid situations that prompt anxiety but that in actuality are relatively safe (e.g., work gatherings in the case of social anxiety). Over the long term, this strategy actually maintains or even *increases* the strength of the unjustified fear response, because the person never learns that there is nothing to fear by attending the work party (see Tryon, 2005, for a discussion of the mechanisms that underlie exposure therapy for anxiety disorders). Additionally, the avoidance is likely to result in negative consequences for psychosocial functioning and overall quality of life; individuals who chronically avoid work gatherings miss out on inside jokes and shared experiences, which often leads to maintained or increased feelings of exclusion or isolation. Thus, avoidant-spectrum behaviors effectively downregulate fear in the short term but often produce negative long-term consequences.

Perhaps one of the more common examples of maladaptive emotion regulation strategies is substance abuse, which potentially falls under several categories in the process model. For example, individuals may use substances to alter a situation or to modulate an emotional response; a socially anxious person might use substances to facilitate a social interaction and prevent anxiety (e.g., drinking before going out with friends). Likewise, substance use provides immediate relief from negative emotions after they occur, as in the case of an individual who goes out drinking to mitigate sadness after a relationship breakup. If this strategy becomes habitual (i.e., substance abuse or dependence), situation selection becomes an increasingly common strategy in that people who struggle with addiction generally choose situations and environments that allow them to use alcohol or drugs and avoid situations in which using is not possible. This strategy functions to avoid the negative affect associated with withdrawal. Unfortunately, substance use is a highly reinforcing strategy for some people as it is quickly effective in downregulating affect; however, excessive or prolonged drug use often leads to short- and long-term legal, social, health, and occupational problems.

Human beings appear to engage in more voluntary, or effortful, emotion regulation strategies than any other animal, including other primates (Davidson, Fox, & Kalin, 2007). Our flexibility to choose among different emotion regulation strategies may be both a strength and a weakness, rendering us more susceptible to psychopathology when we select ineffective emotion regulation strategies. Unsuccessful attempts to regulate emotions, or a general tendency toward emotion dysregulation, are linked to psychopathology across the lifespan (Shipman, Schneider, & Brown, 2004). In children, the inability to modulate emotional reactivity using cognitive and behavioral processes has been linked to externalizing behavior problems, including hyperactivity, impulsivity, and aggression; in turn, these behavior problems have been linked to diagnoses such as attention deficit hyperactivity disorder, oppositional defiant disorder, and conduct disorder (Mullin & Hinshaw, 2007). In adults, the inability to effectively downregulate negative emotions has been linked to both anxiety and mood disorders (Campbell-Sills & Barlow, 2007) and personality pathology (Carpenter & Trull, 2013).

Pervasive and severe emotion dysregulation that occurs across emotions and circumstances is associated with the development of borderline personality disorder (BPD; Linehan, Bohus, & Lynch, 2007). According to Linehan (1993a), individuals with BPD demonstrate heightened baseline emotional sensitivity, greater emotional reactivity, and a slower return to baseline emotional arousal compared with non-BPD individuals (see Carpenter & Trull, 2013, for a review). In addition to the emotion regulation strategies outlined in the process model of emotion regulation (John & Gross, 2007), Linehan and colleagues (2007) identified additional times when an individual can regulate emotions. Specifically, and of particular relevance to individuals who are emotionally sensitive, an individual can engage in emotion regulation by decreasing vulnerability to emotional arousal. This goal is accomplished by engaging antecedent-focused strategies to modulate the physiological component of emotions; for example, preemptive emotion regulation can occur by ensuring sufficient sleep, taking care of physical illness, exercising regularly, and avoiding drugs and alcohol. In Linehan's (1993b) model, respondent-focused strategies include additional skills, such as distress tolerance strategies and mindfulness.

From a physiological standpoint, positive emotions and effective emotion regulation are associated with psychological and physical health benefits, whereas ineffective emotion regulation is linked to psychological stress and, in turn, psychological and physical health problems (Rozanski & Kubzansky, 2005). Moreover, ineffective emotion regulation and pervasive negative affect can activate a chronic physiological stress response (Sapolsky, 2007). Although acute stress responses to physiological stressors are essential to survival (e.g., the fight or flight response), chronic stress responses are not necessarily adaptive and may ultimately result in stress-related disease, such as adult-onset diabetes, obesity, cardiovascular and cerebrovascular disease, risk of ulcers, impaired fertility, and infectious disease as a result of immune system suppression (Rozanski & Kubzansky, 2005; Sapolsky, 2007). Additionally, maladaptive emotion regulation strategies employed to reduce negative affect may result indirectly in physiological disease (e.g., habitual alcohol consumption may produce alcohol-related illnesses). Conversely, other research (van Middendorp et al., 2005) demonstrates that effective emotion regulation may be related indirectly to physical health; for example, successful emotion regulation results in psychological well-being, which in turn results in behaviors that promote better health (e.g., increased physician visits, treatment adherence).

## Can Individuals Become More Effective at Emotion Regulation?

Ultimately, overall well-being depends significantly on our ability to effectively downregulate our negative emotions *and* enhance our positive emotions, especially during stressful life events. We know that some individuals lack these skills and suffer a host of negative physical, psychological, and interpersonal consequences. This leads us to the obvious question: Can individuals learn more effective ways to regulate their emotions, and does learning these strategies result in an improvement in well-being?

Fortunately, the available evidence suggests that individuals can improve their ability to regulate their emotions more effectively. Nevertheless, significantly more research has been conducted on this topic among individuals with psychiatric illnesses than among healthy individuals. Successful therapies for anxiety and mood disorders include teaching patients effective cognitive reappraisal skills, modifying emotional action tendencies, and preventing emotional avoidance (Campbell-Sills & Barlow, 2007). In the treatment of major depression, for example, two therapeutic approaches have received considerable empirical support and are commonly used in clinical practice. Perhaps the best known is CBT (Beck, Rush, Shaw, & Emery, 1979; see also Chambless & Ollendick, 2001; Dobson, 1989), which focuses almost exclusively on two goals: (1) teaching the patient to recognize maladaptive, distorted thought processes that lead to negative emotions, and (2) restructuring those cognitions and challenging underlying beliefs that contribute to distorted thinking (Beck et al., 1979). Although developed to treat depressed patients, CBT has been used successfully with a wide range of mood, anxiety, and behavioral disorders (Butler et al., 2006). In a review of meta-analyses contrasting outcomes for CBT with outcomes for control groups, Butler and colleagues (2006) concluded that there are large effect sizes for CBT for unipolar depression and a variety of anxiety disorders in both adults and children. An overwhelming body of evidence supports the use of CBT for these types of patients, supporting the idea that cognitive reappraisal is an effective way to downregulate negative affect.

Another type of therapy used to treat major depression is behavioral activation (BA; Dimidjian et al., 2006). In BA, the therapist works with the patient to reduce maladaptive avoidance behaviors and increase goal-directed physical activity. BA therapists help patients change the contextual factors that maintain or exacerbate depressive symptoms by creating a system of tasks, assignments, and activities that increase activation and opportunities for positive reward while decreasing the tendency to engage in avoidant behaviors (Ritschel, Ramirez, Jones, & Craighead, 2011). Thus, BA helps patients effectively reengage in appropriate situation selection by initially selecting tasks that are likely to yield emotional benefits while minimizing exposure to situations likely to produce negative affect. BA also helps patients with attentional deployment strategies; in particular, BA teaches patients to recognize and disengage from the process of ruminative thinking by moving their attention purposefully to a more rewarding stimulus. When comparing BA to control conditions in depressed individuals, BA is associated with large effect sizes (Mazzucchelli, Kane, & Rees, 2009, 2010; Sturmey, 2009).

Psychotherapy for other disorders (e.g., generalized anxiety disorder, posttraumatic stress disorder) or behavioral problems (e.g., addictions) similarly focuses on teaching emotion regulation at various points along the process model continuum. Over the last couple of decades a treatment called dialectical behavior therapy (DBT) has gained considerable traction in the psychological literature (Rizvi, Steffel, & Carson Wong, 2013). Although it is most often associated with the treatment of borderline personality disorder, DBT was designed to treat underlying problems with emotion regulation that are mitigated by dysfunctional coping strategies (e.g., self-harm, suicide attempts, drug use). Across a variety of studies, DBT has been associated with moderate effect sizes in the treatment of individuals engaging in suicidal and self-injurious behaviors (Kliem, Kröger, & Kosfelder, 2010). DBT teaches patients several antecedent- and response-focused skills across all points in the process model to assist in more effective emotion regulation (Linehan et al., 2007). For example, patients learn to decrease vulnerability to negative or distressing emotions and increase their exposure to situations that are likely to result in positive emotions. On a biological level, this may include taking care of or preventing physical illness, balancing nutrition, exercising regularly, getting adequate sleep, and not abusing prescription or nonprescription medication. Increasing positive events and engaging in activities likely to result in a general sense of mastery also reduces vulnerability to negative emotions and builds positive emotion.

DBT improves skills related to situation selection and modification by teaching effective problem solving and interpersonal effectiveness skills. Using distraction and crisis survival skills may help with attentional deployment away from aversive internal and external stimuli, especially when problem solving is not a viable option. Patients are taught to cognitively appraise situations more accurately by checking the facts and noting how thoughts impact their emotions. In addition, patients learn to discriminate assumptions, interpretations, ruminative thoughts, and worries from the observed facts of the situation. DBT also teaches individuals to reduce impulsive emotional responses (e.g., self-harm, suicide attempts) by teaching patients how to tolerate distress. Patients are taught to acknowledge and accept rather than suppress their emotions. Behavioral response modulation is illustrated in the skill known as opposite action (Rizvi & Linehan, 2005). Patients learn to act opposite to their emotional urges when those emotions are not justified or are ineffective. For example, the urge that accompanies anger is to attack; opposite action involves being kind or gently avoiding. The urge that accompanies sadness is to isolate; opposite action involves becoming active. Opposite action decreases emotional intensity by interrupting the destructive feedback loop among the behavioral, cognitive, and physiological experiences of emotion; that is, disrupting one part of the system generally impacts other parts of the emotional system as well.

Individuals without ostensible mental illness can also improve their capacity for effective emotion regulation. Using an 18-hour intervention, Nelis and colleagues (2011) taught individuals to understand emotions, identify and regulate emotions in self and others, and use positive emotions to enhance well-being. Sessions comprised short lectures, role-plays, and group discussions. Participants also kept diaries in which they recorded and analyzed emotional experiences based on theories learned in group sessions. Outside of session, participants engaged in readings and practical exercises. Compared with a control group, the intervention group significantly improved emotion understanding and regulation. These skills were linked to lasting changes in personality, including increased extraversion and agreeableness and decreased neuroticism. The authors found that developing emotional competence led to several positive consequences, including subjective improvement of physical health, happiness, life satisfaction, and global social functioning as well as employability.

Other studies have revealed that positive emotionality in general is associated with psychological resilience, overall happiness, and generally better outcomes on a variety of physical and mental health outcomes (Tugade, Fredrickson, & Feldman Barrett, 2004). The positive psychology rubric encompasses a number of constructs that have been investigated extensively, including self-efficacy, optimism, hope, resilience, and self-esteem (for a review, see Snyder & Lopez, 2002). Of these, the hope construct is of particular relevance to the idea of improving emotion regulation.

Individuals who have high levels of hope demonstrate significantly better adjustment on a host of outcomes (Cheavens & Ritschel, 2014). According to Snyder (1994), hope is a cognitive construct that comprises three components: goals, pathways thinking (planning to meet goals), and agency thinking (energy to move toward goals). While sharing some similarities with other constructs (e.g., self-efficacy, self-esteem, optimism, problem-solving theory), tests of divergent validity demonstrate that hope is a unique construct in the lexicon of positive psychology (see Snyder, Rand, & Sigmon, 2002). High hopers are people who set well-defined goals that are challenging but achievable and are consistent with their personal values.[2] In addition, high hopers are able to generate multiple routes to achieve their goals such that they are resilient when they encounter obstacles or goal blockages. Finally, high hopers engage in positive self-talk both about specific goals and pathways ("If I study hard enough, I'll get an A in this class") and about global goal attainment ("I can do it!"). When compared to their low hope counterparts, high hopers endorse better overall well-being (Magaletta & Oliver, 1999); hedonic (i.e., well-being derived from pleasure), eudaimonic (i.e., well-being derived from meaning, life purpose, and personal growth), and social well-being (Gallagher & Lopez, 2009); more positive and less negative affect (Snyder et al., 1991; Steffen & Smith, 2012); overall life satisfaction (Bailey, Eng, Frisch, & Snyder, 2007; Valle, Huebner, & Suldo, 2004); perceived physical health (Wrobleski & Snyder, 2005); and overall life meaning (Feldman & Snyder, 2005; Mascaro & Rosen, 2005; Michael & Snyder, 2005). Moreover, high hopers with medical complications such as end-stage renal failure (Billington, Simpson, Unwin, Bray, & Giles, 2008) and spinal cord injuries (Kortte, Gilbert, Gorman, & Wegener, 2010) have better psychological outcomes after taking physical functioning into account. Finally, in terms of coping with stressors, hope is positively correlated with engaged coping and negatively correlated with avoidant coping (Chang & DeSimone, 2001; Roesch, Duangado, Vaughn, Aldridge, & Villodas, 2010).

Like other areas of emotion regulation, hope is malleable, and the important principles of hopeful thought can be taught. Curry, Maniar, Sondag, and Sandstedt (1999) developed a 15-week hope-building curriculum for use with college athletes and found that hope scores increased significantly over time, and that these gains were maintained after 1-year follow-up. Similarly, Rolo and Gould (2007) developed a 6-week hope curriculum and showed that hope scores increased over time. Berg, Snyder, and Hamilton (2008) recruited a low-hope sample of college students who received a 15-minute hope coaching intervention and who were then asked to participate in a pain induction task. Those in the hope condition had higher hope scores and were better able to tolerate the pain task compared with those in the control condition, suggesting that even very brief interventions might be helpful in raising hope. Hope interventions also reduce depression, hopelessness, and anxiety in psychiatric populations (Cheavens et al., 2005; Klausner et al., 1998). In sum, evidence suggests that the tenets of hopeful thinking can be taught and, by extension, can be leveraged to improve emotion regulation and overall well-being.[3]

## Conclusion

Abraham Lincoln said, "People are just as happy as they make up their minds to be." As we have seen in this chapter, making up our minds is often an effortful endeavor, requiring a complex intra- and interpersonal skill set involving recognizing, naming, evaluating, harnessing, and often changing our emotions in order to maximize happiness and minimize suffering. We are not born with emotion regulation skills; we learn them throughout development (Izard et al., 2011). Fortunately, the evidence suggests that we can always fine tune our ability to modulate our emotional experiences and improve our capacity for joy. In this way, we can continually strive to be better, stronger, and wiser.

## References

Abramowitz, J. S., Tolin, D. F., & Street, G. P. (2001). Paradoxical effects of thought suppression: A meta-analysis of controlled studies. *Clinical Psychology Review, 21,* 683–703. doi: 10.1016/S0272–7358(00)00057-X

Bailey, T. C., Eng, W., Frisch, M. B., & Snyder, C. R. (2007). Hope and optimism as related to life satisfaction. *Journal of Positive Psychology, 2,* 168–175. doi:10.1080/17439760701409546

Beck, A.T., Rush, A.J., Shaw, B.F., & Emery, G. (1979). *Cognitive therapy of depression.* New York, NY: Guilford Press.

Beck, J. (1995). *Cognitive therapy: Basics and beyond.* New York, NY: Guilford Press.

Berg, C. J., Snyder, C. R., & Hamilton, N. (2008). The effectiveness of a hope intervention in coping with cold pressor pain. *Journal of Health Psychology, 13,* 804–809. doi:10.1177/1359105308093864

Billington, E., Simpson, J., Unwin, J., Bray, D., & Giles, D. (2008). Does hope predict adjustment to end-stage renal failure and consequent dialysis?

*British Journal of Health Psychology, 13,* 683–699. doi:10.1348/13591070 7X248959

Bryant, F. B. (1989). A four-factor model of perceived control: Avoiding, coping, obtaining, and savoring. *Journal of Personality, 57,* 773–797. doi:10.1111/j.14 67–6494.1989.tb00494.x

Bryant, F. B. (2003). Savoring beliefs inventory (SBI): A scale for measuring beliefs about savoring. *Journal of Mental Health, 12,* 175–196. doi:10.1080/09 63823031000103489

Butler, A. C., Chapman, J. E., Forman, E. M., & Beck, A. T. (2006). The empirical status of cognitive-behavioral therapy: A review of meta-analyses. *Clinical Psychology Review, 26,* 17–31. doi:10.1016/j.cpr.2005.07.003

Campbell-Sills, L., & Barlow, D. H. (2007). Incorporating emotion regulation into conceptualizations and treatments of anxiety and mood disorders. In J. J. Gross (Ed.), *Handbook of emotion regulation* (pp. 542–559). New York, NY: Guilford Press.

Carpenter, R. W., & Trull, T. J. (2013). Components of emotion dysregulation in borderline personality disorder: A review. *Current Psychiatry Reports, 15,* 335–343. doi:10.1007/s11920–012–0335–2

Chambless, D. L., & Ollendick, T. H. (2001). Empirically supported psychological interventions: Controversies and evidence. *Annual Review of Psychology, 52,* 685–716. doi:10.1146/annurev.psych.52.1.685

Chang, E. C., & DeSimone, S. L. (2001). The influence of hope on appraisals, coping, and dysphoria: A test of hope theory. *Journal of Clinical and Social Psychology, 20,* 117–129. doi:10.1521/jscp.20.2.117.22262

Cheavens, J. S., & Ritschel, L. A. (2014). Hope theory. In M. Tugade, M. Shiota, & L. Kirby (Eds.), *Handbook of positive emotions* (pp. 396–412). New York, NY: Guilford Press.

Cheavens, J. S., Rosenthal, M. Z., Daughters, S. B., Nowak, J., Kosson, D., Lynch, T. R., & Lejuez, C. W. (2005). An analogue investigation of the relationships among perceived parental criticism, negative affect, and borderline personality disorder features: The role of thought suppression. *Behaviour Research and Therapy, 43,* 257–268. doi:10.1016/j.brat.2004.08.006

Clark, D. A. (1995). Perceived limitations of standard cognitive therapy: A reconsideration of efforts to revise Beck's theory and therapy. *Journal of Cognitive Psychotherapy, 9,* 153–172.

Côté, S., Gyurak, A., & Levenson, R. W. (2010). The ability to regulate emotion is associated with greater well-being, income, and socioeconomic status. *Emotion, 10,* 923–933. doi:10.1037/a0021156

Critchley, H. D., Rotshtein, P., Nagai, Y., O'Doherty, J., Mathias, C. J., & Dolan, R. (2005). Activity in the human brain predicting differential heart rate responses to emotional facial expressions. *Neuroimage, 24,* 751–762. doi:10.1016/j .neuroimage.2004.10.013

Curry, L. A., Maniar, S. D., Sondag, K. A., & Sandstedt, S. (1999). *An optimal performance academic course for university students and student-athletes.* Unpublished manuscript, University of Montana, Missoula, Montana.

Davidson, R. J. (1992). Prolegomenon to the structure of emotion: Gleanings from neuropsychology. *Cognition and Emotion, 6,* 245–268. doi:10.1080/02699 939208411071

Davidson, R. J., Fox, A., & Kalin, N. H. (2007). Neural bases of emotion regulation in nonhuman primates and humans. In J. J. Gross (Ed.), *Handbook of emotion regulation* (pp. 47–68). New York, NY: Guilford Press.

DeRubeis, R. J., Tang, T. Z., & Beck, A. T. (2001). Cognitive therapy. In K. S. Dobson (Ed.), *Handbook of cognitive behavioral therapies* (pp. 349–392). New York, NY: Guilford Press.

Dimidjian, S., Hollon, S. D., Dobson, K. S., Schmaling, K. B., Kohlenberg, R. J., Addis, M. E., . . . Jacobson, N. S. (2006). Randomized trial of behavioral activation, cognitive therapy, and antidepressant medication in the acute treatment of adults with major depression. *Journal of Consulting and Clinical Psychology, 74,* 658–670. doi:10.1037/0022–006X.74.4.658

Dobson, K. S. (1989). A meta-analysis of the efficacy of cognitive therapy for depression. *Journal of Consulting and Clinical Psychology, 57,* 414–419. doi:10.10 37/0022–006X.57.3.414

Edelmann, R. J., & Baker, S. R. (2002). Self-reported and actual physiological responses in social phobia. *British Journal of Clinical Psychology, 41,* 1–14. doi: 10.1348/014466502163732

Ekman, P. (1992). An argument for basic emotions. *Cognition and Emotion, 6,* 169–200. doi:10.1080/02699939208411068

Ekman, P. (1999). Basic emotions. In T. Dalgleish & M. Power (Eds.), *Handbook of cognition and emotion* (pp. 45–60). Sussex, UK: John Wiley & Sons.

Ekman, P., Davidson, R. J., & Friesen, W. V. (1990). The Duchenne smile: Emotional expression and brain physiology, II. *Journal of Personality and Social Psychology, 58,* 342–353. doi:10.1037/0022–3514.58.2.342

Ekman, P., Friesen, W. V., & Ellsworth, P. (1972). *Emotion in the human face: Guidelines for research and an integration of findings.* Oxford, UK: Pergamon Press.

Elfenbein, H. A., & Ambady, N. (2002). On the universality and cultural specificity of emotion recognition: A meta-analysis. *Psychological Bulletin, 128,* 203–235. doi:10.1037//0033–2909.128.2.203

Feldman, D. B., & Snyder, C. R. (2005). Hope and the meaningful life: Theoretical and empirical associations between goal-directed thinking and life meaning. *Journal of Social and Clinical Psychology, 24,* 401–421. doi:10.1521/jscp .24.3.401.65616

Folkman, S., & Lazarus, R. S. (1988). Coping as a mediator of emotion. *Journal of Personality and Social Psychology, 54,* 466–475.

Fredrickson, B. L. (2000). Cultivating positive emotions to optimize health and well-being. *Prevention & Treatment, 3,* 1a. doi:10.1037/1522–3736.3.1.31a

Fredrickson, B. L., & Joiner, T. (2002). Positive emotions trigger upward spirals toward emotional well-being. *Psychological Science, 13,* 172–175. doi:10.111 1/1467–9280.00431

Gallagher, M. W., & Lopez, S. J. (2009). Positive expectancies and mental health: Identifying the unique contributions of hope and optimism. *Journal of Positive Psychology, 4*, 548–556. doi:10.1080/17439760903157166

Gross, J. J., & John, O. P. (2003). Individual differences in two emotion regulation processes: Implications for affect, relationships, and well-being. *Journal of Personality and Social Psychology, 85*, 348–362. doi:10.1037/0022–3514.85.2.348

Gross, J. J., Richards, J. M., & John, O. P. (2006). Emotion regulation in everyday life. In D. K. Snyder, J. Simpson, & J. N. Hughes (Eds.), *Emotion regulation in couples and families: Pathways to dysfunction and health* (pp. 13–35). Washington, DC: American Psychological Association. doi:10.1037/11468–001

Gross, J. J., & Thompson, R. A. (2007). Emotion regulation: Conceptual foundations. In J. J. Gross (Ed.), *Handbook of emotion regulation* (pp. 3–24). New York, NY: Guilford Press.

Gruber, J. (2011). Can feeling too good be bad? Positive emotion persistence (PEP) in bipolar disorder. *Current Directions in Psychological Science, 20*, 217–221. doi:10.1177/0963721411414632

Helgeson, V. S., Reynolds, K. A., & Tomich, P. L. (2006). A meta-analytic review of benefit finding and growth. *Journal of Consulting and Clinical Psychology, 74*, 797–816. doi:10.1037/0022–006X.74.5.797

Hooff, B., Schouten, A. P., & Simonovski, S. (2012). What one feels and what one knows: The influence of emotions on attitudes and intentions towards knowledge sharing. *Journal of Knowledge Management, 16*, 148–158. doi:10.1108/13673271211198990

Izard, C. E., Woodburn, E. M., Finlon, K. J., Krauthamer-Ewing, E. S., Grossman, S. R., & Seidenfeld, A. (2011). Emotion knowledge, emotion utilization, and emotion regulation. *Emotion Review, 3*(1), 44–52. doi:10.1177/1754073910380972

John, O. P., & Gross, J. J. (2004). Healthy and unhealthy emotion regulation: Personality processes, individual differences, and life span development. *Journal of Personality, 72*(6), 1301–1333. doi:10.1111/j.1467–6494.2004.00298.x

John, O. P., & Gross, J. J. (2007). Individual differences in emotion regulation. In J. J. Gross (Ed.), *Handbook of emotion regulation* (pp. 351–372). New York, NY: Guilford Press.

Kemeny, M. E., Foltz, C., Cavanagh, J. F., Cullen, M., Giese-Davis, J., Jennings, P., . . . Ekman, P. (2012). Contemplative/emotion training reduces negative emotional behavior and promotes prosocial responses. *Emotion, 12*(2), 338–350. doi:10.1037/a0026118

Kennedy-Moore, E., & Watson, J. C. (1999). *Expressing emotion: Myths, realities, and therapeutic strategies.* New York, NY: Guilford Press.

Klausner, E. J., Clarkin, J. F., Spielman, L., Pupo, C., Abrams, R., & Alexopoulas, G. S. (1998). Late-life depression and functional disability: The role of goal-focused group psychotherapy. *International Journal of Geriatric Psychiatry, 13*, 707–716. doi:10.1002/(SICI)1099–1166(1998100)13:10<707::AID-GPS856>3.0.CO;2-Q

Kliem, S., Kröger, C., & Kosfelder, J. (2010). Dialectical behavior therapy for borderline personality disorder: A meta-analysis using mixed-effects modeling. *Journal of Consulting and Clinical Psychology, 78* (6), 936–951.

Koole, S. L. (2009). The psychology of emotion regulation: An integrative review. *Cognition and Emotion, 23*(1), 4–41. doi:10.1080/02699930802619031

Kortte, K. B., Gilbert, M., Gorman, P., & Wegener, S. T. (2010). Positive psychological variables in the prediction of life satisfaction after spinal cord injury. *Rehabilitation Psychology, 55,* 40–47. doi:10.1037/a0018624

Lazarus, R. S. (1998). Coping theory and research: Past, present, and future. *Fifty years of the research and theory of RS Lazarus: An analysis of historical and perennial issues* (pp. 366–388). Mahwah, NJ: Lawrence Erlbaum.

Linehan, M. M. (1993a). *Cognitive-behavioral treatment of borderline personality disorder.* New York, NY: Guilford Press.

Linehan, M. M. (1993b). *Skills training manual for treating borderline personality disorder.* New York, NY: Guilford Press.

Linehan, M. M., Bohus, M., & Lynch, T. R. (2007). Dialectical behavior therapy for pervasive emotion dysregulation: Theoretical and practical underpinnings. In J. J. Gross (Ed.), *Handbook of emotion regulation* (pp. 581–605). New York, NY: Guilford Press.

Longmore, R. J., & Worrell, M. (2007). Do we need to challenge thoughts in cognitive behavior therapy? *Clinical Psychology Review, 27*(2), 173–187. doi:10.1 016/j.cpr.2006.08.001

Magaletta, P. R., & Oliver, J. M. (1999). The hope construct, will, and ways: Their relations with self-efficacy, optimism, and general well-being. *Journal of Clinical Psychology, 55,* 539–551.

Mascaro, N., & Rosen, D. H. (2005). Existential meaning's role in the enhancement of hope and prevention of depressive symptoms. *Journal of Personality, 73,* 985–1013.

Matsumoto, D. (1992). More evidence for the universality of a contempt expression. *Motivation and Emotion, 16,* 363–368. doi:10.1007/BF00992972

Mauss, I. B., Levenson, R. W., McCarter, L., Wilhelm, F. H., & Gross, J. J. (2005). The tie that binds? Coherence among emotion experience, behavior, and physiology. *Emotion, 5,* 175–190. doi:10.1037/1528-3542.5.2.175

Mayer, J. D., DiPaolo, M., & Salovey, P. (1990). Perceiving affective content in ambiguous visual stimuli: A component of emotional intelligence. *Journal of Personality Assessment, 54*(3–4), 772–781. doi:10.1207/s15327752jpa5403&4_29

Mayer, J. D., & Salovey, P. (1997). What is emotional intelligence? In P. Salovey & D. J. Sluyter (Eds.), *Emotional development and emotional intelligence: Educational implications* (pp. 3–34). New York, NY: Basic Books.

Mazzucchelli, T., Kane, R., & Rees, C. (2009). Behavioral activation treatments for depression in adults: A meta-analysis and review. *Clinical Psychology: Science and Practice, 16*(4), 383–411. doi:10.1111/j.1468-2850.2009.01178

Mazzucchelli, T. G., Kane, R. T., & Rees, C. S. (2010). Behavioral activation interventions for well-being: A meta-analysis. *Journal of Positive Psychology, 5*(2), 105–121. doi:10.1080/17439760903569154

McLaughlin, K. A., Hatzenbuehler, M. L., Mennin, D. S., & Nolen-Hoeksema, S. (2011). Emotion dysregulation and adolescent psychopathology: A prospective study. *Behaviour Research and Therapy, 49*(9), 544–554. doi:10.1016/j.brat.2011.06.003

Michael, S. T., & Snyder, C. R. (2005). Getting unstuck: The roles of hope, finding meaning, and rumination in the adjustment to bereavement among college students. *Death Studies, 29,* 435–458. doi:10.1080/07481180590932544

Mullin, B. C., & Hinshaw, S. P. (2007). Emotion regulation and externalizing disorders in children and adolescents. In J. J. Gross (Ed.), *Handbook of emotion regulation* (pp. 523–541). New York, NY: Guilford Press.

Nelis, D., Kotsou, I., Quoidbach, J., Hansenne, M., Weytens, F., Dupuis, P., & Mikolajczak, M. (2011). Increasing emotional competence improves psychological and physical well-being, social relationships, and employability. *Emotion, 11*(2), 354–366. doi:10.1037/a0021554

Nolen-Hoeksema, S. (2000). The role of rumination in depressive disorders and mixed anxiety/depressive symptoms. *Journal of Abnormal Psychology, 109*(3), 504–511. doi:10.1037/0021-843X.109.3.504

Pollatos, O., Gramann, K., & Schandry, R. (2007). Neural systems connecting interoceptive awareness and feelings. *Human Brain Mapping, 28*(1), 9–18. doi:10.1002/hbm.20258

Quoidbach, J., Berry, E. V., Hansenne, M., & Mikolajczak, M. (2010). Positive emotion regulation and well-being: Comparing the impact of eight savoring and dampening strategies. *Personality and Individual Differences, 49*(5), 368–373. doi:10.1016/j.paid.2010.03.048

Ritschel, L. A., Ramirez, C. L., Jones, M., & Craighead, W. E. (2011). Behavioral activation for depressed teens: A pilot study. *Cognitive and Behavioral Practice, 18*(2), 281–299. doi:10.1016/j.cbpra.2010.07.002

Rizvi, S. L., & Linehan, M. M. (2005). The treatment of maladaptive shame in borderline personality disorder: A pilot study of "Opposite Action." *Cognitive and Behavioral Practice, 12,* 437–447. doi:10.1016/S1077-7229(05)80071-9

Rizvi, S. L., Steffel, L. M., & Carson Wong, A. (2013). An overview of Dialectical Behavior Therapy for professional psychologists. *Professional Psychology: Research and Practice, 44*(2), 73–80. doi:10.1037/a0029808.

Roesch, S. C., Duangado, K. M., Vaughn, A. A., Aldridge, A. A., & Villodas, F. (2010). Dispositional hope and the propensity to cope: A daily diary assessment of minority adolescents. *Cultural Diversity and Ethnic Minority Psychology, 16,* 191–198. doi:10.1037/a0016114

Rolo, C., & Gould, D. (2007). An intervention for fostering hope, athletic, and academic performance in university student-athletes. *International Coaching Psychology Review, 2,* 44–61.

Rozanski, A., & Kubzansky, L. D. (2005). Psychologic functioning and physical health: A paradigm of flexibility. *Psychosomatic Medicine, 67*(Supplement 1), S47–S53. doi:10.1097/01.psy.0000164253.69550.49

Russell, J. A. (1994). Is there universal recognition of emotion from facial expression? A review of the cross-cultural studies. *Psychological Bulletin, 115,* 102–141. doi:10.1037/0033–2909.115.1.102

Salovey, P., & Grewal, D. (2005) The science of emotional intelligence. *Current Directions in Psychological Science, 14,* 281–285. doi:10.1111/j.0963–721 4.2005.00381.x

Salovey, P., & Mayer, J. D. (1990). Emotional intelligence. *Imagination, Cognition, and Personality, 9,* 185–211. doi:10.2190/DUGG-P24E-52WK-6CDG

Sapolsky, R. M. (2007). Stress, stress-related disease, and emotional regulation. In J. J. Gross (Ed.), *Handbook of emotion regulation* (pp. 606–615). New York, NY: Guilford Press.

Schutte, N. S., Manes, R. R., & Malouff, J. M. (2009). Antecedent-focused emotion regulation, response modulation and well-being. *Current Psychology: A Journal for Diverse Perspectives on Diverse Psychological Issues, 28*(1), 21–31. doi:10.1007/s12144–009–9044–3

Shipman, K., Schneider, R., & Brown, A. (2004). Emotion dysregulation and psychopathology. In M. Beauregard (Ed.), *Consciousness, emotional self-regulation and the brain* (pp. 61–85). Amsterdam, Netherlands: John Benjamins.

Singh, S. S., & Mishra, R. C. (2011). Emotion regulation strategies and their implications for well-being. *Social Science International, 27*(2), 179–198.

Smyth, J. M., & Arigo, D. (2009). Recent evidence supports emotion-regulation interventions for improving health in at-risk and clinical populations. *Current Opinion in Psychiatry, 22*(2), 205–210. doi:10.1097/YC0.0b013e328 3252d6d

Snyder, C. R. (1994). *The psychology of hope: You can get there from here.* New York, NY: Free Press.

Snyder, C. R., Harris, C., Anderson, J. R., Holleran, S. A., Irving, L. M., Sigmon, S. T., . . . Harney, P. (1991). The will and the ways: Development and validation of an individual-differences measure of hope. *Journal of Personality and Social Psychology, 60,* 570–585. doi:10.1037/0022–3514.60.4.570

Snyder, C. R., & Lopez, S. J. (2002). *Handbook of positive psychology.* New York, NY: Oxford University Press.

Snyder, C. R., Rand, K. L., King, E. A., Feldman, D. B., & Woodward, J. T. (2002). "False" hope. *Journal of Clinical Psychology, 58,* 1003–1022. doi:10.1002/jclp.10096

Snyder, C. R., Rand, K. L., & Sigmon, D. S. (2002). Hope theory: A member of the positive psychology family. In C. R. Snyder, & S. J. Lopez (Eds.), *Handbook of positive psychology* (pp. 257–276). New York, NY: Oxford University Press.

Soto, J. A., Perez, C. R., Kim, Y. H., Lee, E. A., & Minnick, M. R. (2011). Is expressive suppression always associated with poorer psychological functioning? A cross-cultural comparison between European Americans and Hong Kong Chinese. *Emotion, 11*(6), 1450. doi:10.1037/a0023340

Steffen, L. E., & Smith, B. W. (2012). *The relationship of dispositional hope with daily stress and affect in fire service.* Manuscript submitted for publication.

Sturmey, P. (2009). Behavioral activation is an evidence-based treatment for depression. *Behavior Modification, 33*(6), 818–829. doi:10.1177/0145445509350094

Tryon, W. W. (2005). Possible mechanisms for why desensitization and exposure therapy work. *Clinical Psychology Review, 25,* 67–95. doi:10.1016/j.cpr.2004.08.005

Tugade, M. M., & Fredrickson, B. L. (2004). Resilient individuals use positive emotions to bounce back from negative emotional experiences. *Journal of Personality and Social Psychology, 86*(2), 320–333. doi:10.1037/0022–3514.86.2.320

Tugade, M. M., & Fredrickson, B. L. (2007). Regulation of positive emotions: Emotion regulation strategies that promote resilience. *Journal of Happiness Studies, 8*(3), 311–333. doi:10.1007/s10902–006–9015–4

Tugade, M. M., Fredrickson, B. L., & Feldman Barrett, L. (2004). Psychological resilience and positive emotional granularity: Examining the benefits of positive emotions on coping and health. *Journal of Personality, 72*(6), 1161–1190. doi:10.1111/j.1467–6494.2004.00294.x

Valle, M. F., Huebner, E. S., & Suldo, S. M. (2004). Further evaluation of the Children's Hope Scale. *Journal of Psychoeducational Assessment, 22,* 320–337. doi:10.1177/073428290402200403

van Middendorp, H., Geenen, R., Sorbi, M. J., Hox, J. J., Vingerhoets, A. M., van Doornen, L. P., & Bijlsma, J. J. (2005). Styles of emotion regulation and their associations with perceived health in patients with rheumatoid arthritis. *Annals of Behavioral Medicine, 30*(1), 44–53. doi:10.1207/s15324796abm3001_6

Wegner, D. M., Schneider, D. J., Carter, S., & White, T. (1987). Paradoxical effects of thought suppression. *Journal of Personality and Social Psychology, 53,* 5–13. doi:10.1037/0022–3514.53.1.5

Wranik, T., Barrett, L., & Salovey, P. (2007). Intelligent emotion regulation: Is knowledge power? In J. J. Gross (Ed.), *Handbook of emotion regulation* (pp. 393–407). New York, NY: Guilford Press.

Wrobleski, K. K., & Snyder, C. R. (2005). Hopeful thinking in older adults: Back to the future. *Experimental Aging Research, 31,* 217–233. doi:10.1080/0361073 0590915452

# Notes

1. More recently, Ekman and others (e.g., Matsumoto, 1992) have determined that contempt may be a seventh universally recognized emotion, although the data remain equivocal. Ekman (1999) also has proposed a much broader expanded list of positive and negative emotions that may be universally applicable, although more research in this area is needed.

2. Some have argued that excessive hope can be maladaptive under certain situations, such as when goals are truly unattainable or are based on distorted views of reality, or when the pathways chosen are not viable. The available evidence to date

suggests that these criticisms have little to no empirical support, however. For a review, see Snyder, Rand, King, Feldman, and Woodward (2002).

3. As noted, however, the benefits of hope may be related to a higher-order construct of general positive emotionality, rather than being specific to the hope construct. Future studies should thus assess both hope (a lower-order construct) with the higher-order construct of general positivity and should evaluate whether hope demonstrates incremental validity over and above general positivity.

# 3

# Effective Problem Solving

*Christine Maguth Nezu*

*Arthur M. Nezu*

*Sarah Ricelli*

Drexel University

O ur journey through life produces constant challenges and obstacles to overcome. Consider a quote from the poet Emily Dickinson, "Low as my problem bending, another problem comes," suggesting that life can be thought of as a "series of problems." In fact, stress is ubiquitous in day-to-day life, typically presenting itself in the form of daily hassles, such as financial struggles, difficult problems with coworkers, or relationship or family problems. Stress also takes the form of potentially traumatic or grief-inducing major life events, such as divorce, rape, combat trauma, or loss of a loved one. When such problems become stressful and exceed our personal resources and capabilities to cope, they may lead to a wide array of negative consequences. More specifically, when individuals experience stress, handling problems and making effective decisions can become very difficult, often resulting in ineffective coping efforts, inadequate problem resolution, clinical levels of psychosocial distress (e.g., depression, suicidal ideation, anxiety), and even poor physical health (Contrada & Baum, 2011).

However, before we paint too pessimistic a picture, consider another quote, this time from the legendary Helen Keller, who struggled with becoming deaf and blind due to a childhood illness but who eventually came to be viewed as an important role model during the 20th century for her substantial charity work: "All the world is full of suffering, it is also full of overcoming it." It is the second part of her quote that raises our hopes that we can overcome the world's suffering and stress. In fact, research during the past several decades suggests not only that stress can be dealt with effectively but also that doing so leads to positive physical and mental health (D'Zurilla & Nezu, 2007). For example, there is a body of literature that suggests that individuals exposed to even the most traumatic events may perceive some good emerging from their struggles with such tragedy (Tedeschi & Calhoun, 2004). This literature is consistent with the later finding that it is not exposure to daily stressors per se that predicts future chronic health problems, ranging from decreased immune functioning to coronary problems, but rather *how* people respond to such events that makes the crucial difference (Piazza, Charles, Sliwinski, Mogle, & Almeida, 2013).

Another quote is relevant here, this one an ancient Chinese saying, "You can't stop the birds from flying overhead, but you can stop them from making nests in your hair," suggesting that although we often cannot control the world and its associated problems, we *can* prevent these problems from leading to catastrophes and consuming our lives. A more contemporary quote is provided by the musician and singer Dolly Parton, which underscores the same sentiment, "We cannot direct the wind, but we can adjust the sails."

Contemporary problem-solving therapy (PST) is a psychosocial intervention that helps people to learn how to effectively cope with stress, and in doing so, reduce current symptoms of distress and prevent future reoccurrence. This chapter draws heavily from the scientific literature that supports PST as an evidence-based system of psychotherapy to describe what we have learned during the past several decades about effective problem solving and its relation to well-being.

It is also important to state at the onset that PST should be distinguished from more informal problem-solving training approaches. Several principles of effective problem solving such as the use of rational or planful problem-solving steps can be found in many popular psychology approaches as well as a prescriptive strategy in a wide range of other psychotherapies across many theoretic orientations. Although a rational and planful approach of defining problems accurately, coming up with creative solutions, and being able to weigh consequences before carrying out a plan of action represents one part of PST therapy, the suggestion that this represents PST as a system of psychotherapy is an inaccurate oversimplification.

## Definition and Illustration of Key Concepts

We begin by defining the concept of problem solving, which is often referred to as *social problem solving* (SPS) in the literature to distinguish the type of problem solving that takes place in real life compared with more intellectual or academic problems. We have defined SPS as the self-directed process by which individuals attempt to identify adaptive solutions for acute and chronic problems in everyday life (D'Zurilla & Nezu, 2007). Specifically, SPS represents the process whereby people aim their coping efforts at changing (a) the situation itself such that it no longer is problematic (referred to as *problem-focused* goals), (b) their maladaptive reactions to stressful problems (referred to as *emotion-focused* goals), or (c) both. As such, SPS reflects the multidimensional metaprocess of awareness of one's reaction to problems, as well as identifying and selecting a set of coping responses to effectively address the specific features of a given stressful situation (Nezu, Nezu, & D'Zurilla, 2013).

A *problem* is defined as a life situation that requires an adaptive response to prevent negative consequences but for which an effective response is not readily available or apparent to the person experiencing the problem due to the presence of barriers or obstacles. Barriers that make a situation problematic include novelty, ambiguity, unpredictability, conflicting goals, performance skills deficits, and lack of resources. According to this definition, a problem is viewed as a person-environment relationship, characterized by a real or perceived mismatch between the demands of the situation and a person's reactions and coping ability. As such, a problem can be expected to change in importance or difficulty over time, in that a problem for a given time may not be a problem for the same person later. Moreover, problems are idiographic, meaning that the same stressful situation for one person may not be a problem for another person.

A *solution* is a situation-specific coping response or pattern of responses that is the outcome of the problem-solving process when applied to that situation. An *effective* solution accomplishes the problem-solving goal(s), while also maximizing other positive consequences and minimizing negative ones. Important outcomes include the effects on others and oneself, as well as short-term and long-term consequences. Note that the quality or effectiveness of a solution may vary among individuals or situations, depending on such factors as the values and goals of the person confronted with the problem.

D'Zurilla and Goldfried (1971) proposed the original social problem-solving model, but it has undergone significant revisions as a result of decades of continual research (Nezu et al., 2013). According to contemporary social problem-solving theory, attempts at coping with stressful problems are influenced by two general and partially independent dimensions: (a) *problem orientation* and (b) *problem-solving style* (D'Zurilla, Nezu, & Maydeu-Olivares, 2004). This model has been repeatedly validated across numerous populations, cultures, and age groups (D'Zurilla & Nezu, 2007).

*Problem orientation* is the relatively stable set of cognitive-affective schemas that represent a person's emotional reactivity when facing problems, general beliefs about problems in living, and one's ability to cope with them. Research has identified two distinct types of problem orientations, positive and negative, that function orthogonally (Nezu, 2004). A *positive problem orientation* involves the tendency for a person to

- appraise problems as challenges,
- be optimistic in believing that problems are solvable,
- have a strong sense of self-efficacy regarding the ability to cope with problems,
- understand that successful problem solving entails time and effort,
- have a mindful awareness of his or her own emotional reactions, and
- view negative emotions as an essential part of the problem-solving process that can be helpful in coping with stressful problems (i.e., provides information that "a problem exists").

A *negative problem orientation* involves the tendency to

- view problems as threats,
- expect problems to be unsolvable,
- have doubts about one's ability to cope with problems effectively,
- lack awareness of his or her own emotional reactions, and
- become frustrated and upset when faced with problems or negative emotions.

Because a person's orientation can have a strong impact on his or her motivation and ability to engage in focused attempts to solve problems, the importance of assessing and addressing these worldviews and schemas in treatment has continually been underscored (Nezu, 2004; Nezu & Perri, 1989). Note that each orientation involves a general tendency to view a certain type or set of problems from a particular perspective, rather than representing a stable personality trait that is applicable across all life problems. As such, it is possible for a given individual to be characterized as having a positive orientation when addressing a particular problem (e.g., work or career), while having a negative orientation when dealing with another problem (e.g., relationships). For this reason, the assessment of an individual's situation-specific behavior patterns is very important for treatment to be successful.

*Problem-solving style*, the second major problem-solving dimension, refers to the cognitive behavioral activities in which people engage when attempting to solve or cope with stressful problems. Three styles have been identified: (a) *planful problem solving* (previously referred to as "rational problem solving"), (b) *avoidant problem solving*, and (c) *impulsive-careless problem solving* (D'Zurilla et al., 2004).

*Planful problem solving* is the adaptive approach to solving stressful problems that involves the systematic application of the following set of skills: problem definition, generation of alternatives, decision making, and solution implementation and verification. As indicated previously, a common misconception regarding PST has been to equate it solely with training individuals in rational problem solving, erroneously disregarding the important clinical implications of the more complex model that includes the orientation components (Nezu et al., 2013).

In addition to planful problem solving, two other problem-solving styles have been identified, both being maladaptive in nature and generally associated with ineffective problem solving. An *impulsive-careless style* is the problem-solving approach characterized by impulsive or careless attempts at problem resolution (Nezu et al., 2013). Such attempts are hurried and incomplete, and individuals who are characterized as frequently engaging in this type of response pattern typically consider only a few alternative solutions, often impulsively selecting the first idea that comes to mind. An *avoidant style* is characterized by procrastination, passivity, inaction, and dependence on others. A person who engages in this type of problem solving tends to avoid problems rather than confront them, puts off problem solving as long as possible, waits for problems to resolve themselves, and often attempts to shift the responsibility for solving personal problems to other people. Individuals who engage in either or both of these two styles often worsen existing problems or create new ones. As described below, research findings over the past four decades support the role of these styles in both pathology and health.

# Relevance of Effective Problem Solving to Health and Mental Health

The working assumption of this approach is that much of what is typically viewed as "psychopathology" can often be understood as ineffective and maladaptive coping behavior leading to various personal and social consequences, such as depression, anxiety, anger, interpersonal difficulties, and negative physical symptomatology (Nezu & D'Zurilla, 1989; Nezu et al., 2013). This perspective is supported by three lines of research, as described in the next section.

## Social Problem Solving and Psychopathology

The first line of research involves findings regarding various pathology-related differences that have been identified between individuals characterized as *effective* versus *ineffective* problem solvers across differing age groups, populations, and cultures, and using differing measures of SPS (see Nezu, Wilkins, & Nezu, 2004, for an overview of this literature described below). In general, when compared with their effective counterparts, ineffective problem solvers report a greater number of life problems, more health and physical symptoms, more anxiety, more depression, and more psychological maladjustment. Once people experience any of these circumstances, further ineffective problem solving exacerbates their challenges and a vicious cycle ensues. In addition, a negative problem orientation is associated with negative moods under routine and stressful conditions in general, as well as pessimism, negative emotional experiences, and clinical depression. Persons with a negative orientation also tend to worry and complain more about their health. It is important to recognize that there may be specific stressful situations that represent a greater challenge for a given individual. For example a person may demonstrate strong skills in solving business or financial problems while their interpersonal problems are marked by ineffective skills. Problem-solving deficits are also significantly related to poor self-esteem, hopelessness, suicidal risk, self-injury, anger proneness, increased alcohol intake and substance risk taking, personality difficulties, criminal behavior, alcoholism, secondary physical complications among persons with spinal cord injuries, premenstrual and menstrual pain, physical health problems, diminished life satisfaction, physical problems among adult cancer patients, and noncardiac pain severity (Nezu et al., 2004).

## Problem-Solving Model of Stress

A second line of research involves the question of whether SPS moderates the relation between stressful life events and psychopathology. In other words, does the manner in which people cope with stressful events, via effective SPS, influence the degree to which they experience both acute and long-term psychological distress? In general, studies directly asking this question provide evidence that SPS is a significant moderator of the stress-distress relationship.

For example, under similar levels of high stress (e.g., disappointment, rejection, loss, chronic illness), individuals with ineffective or poor SPS experience significantly higher levels of psychological distress, such as depression and anxiety, compared with individuals characterized by effective SPS (see Nezu, 2004, and Nezu et al., 2013, for overviews). This set of findings is particularly important given that these studies provide converging evidence for the mediating and moderating role of problem solving across varying samples (e.g., college undergraduates, adolescent and child populations, clinically depressed patients, adult cancer patients) and differing measures of SPS.

## Efficacy of Problem-Solving Therapy

A third line of research involves studies that evaluate the efficacy of PST. During the past several decades, this psychosocial intervention has been applied, both as the sole intervention strategy, and as part of a larger treatment package, to a wide variety of patient populations and problems. These include major depression, dysthymia, schizophrenia, suicidal ideation and behaviors, social phobia, generalized anxiety disorder, posttraumatic stress disorder, distressed couples, family caregivers, medically ill individuals, substance abuse, sexual offending, primary care patients, persons with intellectual disabilities and a range of comorbid behavioral disorders, AIDS/HIV prevention, obesity, back pain, hypertension, distressed cancer patients, recurrent headaches, personality disorders, and persons with diabetes (see Nezu et al., 2013, for a comprehensive listing of this outcome research literature).

Moreover, meta-analyses support the efficacy of PST across these populations. Specifically, Malouff, Thorsteinsson, and Schutte (2007) conducted a meta-analysis of 32 studies, encompassing close to 3,000 participants, which evaluated the efficacy of PST across a variety of mental and physical health problems. They found that PST was (a) as effective as other psychosocial treatments and (b) significantly more effective than both no treatment and attention placebo conditions. In addition, whether the PST protocol specifically targeted problem orientation and whether homework was assigned were both significant moderators of treatment outcome.

Two additional meta-analyses focused exclusively on PST trials for depression (Bell & D'Zurilla, 2009; Cuijpers, van Straten, & Warmerdam, 2007). The earlier study included 13 randomized controlled trials (RCTs) that included over 1,100 participants. The second study included seven additional studies. Both sets of authors concluded that PST is equally effective for the treatment of depression compared with alternative psychosocial therapies, such as cognitive therapy and antidepressant medication, and more efficacious than supportive therapy and attention-control conditions. In addition, Bell and D'Zurilla (2009) found that significant moderators of treatment effectiveness included whether the PST program included problem-orientation training and whether all four planful problem-solving skills were included in the therapy protocol.

In addition to the versatility of PST with regard to its applicability across psychological problems and clinical populations, it has proven flexible with regard to its treatment and method of implementation. With regard to the first issue, PST has been applied to help decrease distress and psychopathology, to improve overall quality of life, to improve ability to be an effective caregiver, to foster a medical patient's ability to adhere to treatment prescriptions, and to prevent emotional distress and problems among individuals who are vulnerable as a result of exposure to significant stressors (e.g., service members/veterans).

In terms of the varied methods by which this intervention has been implemented, PST has been provided individually, in groups, with couples, over the telephone, via videoconferencing, over the Internet, and in combination with psychiatric medication (for a comprehensive overview of both these bodies of literature, see Nezu et al., 2013). As a result of its strong evidence base, a problem solving metamodel of clinical decision making has been proposed and described in which clinicians are viewed as problem solvers, and effective treatments are framed as problems to be solved (Nezu, Nezu, & Cos, 2007). Nevertheless, research regarding the effectiveness of this approach to case formulation requires further investigation.

## PST: Teaching One to Become an Effective Problem Solver

Given the aforementioned model, we can define *effective problem solving* as composed of a combination of a positive problem orientation and a planful problem-solving style. Thus, the goals of PST include the adoption of an adaptive worldview or orientation toward problems in living and the effective implementation of specific problem-solving behaviors. We suggest that several major obstacles may exist for a given individual when attempting to reach these goals, including (a) brain overload, especially when under stress; (b) limited or deficient ability to engage in effective emotional regulation; (c) biased cognitive processing of emotion-related information, such as negative thoughts or poor self-efficacy beliefs; (d) feelings of hopelessness resulting in limited motivation; and (e) an ineffective or maladaptive problem-solving style. To overcome these obstacles, PST trains individuals in four major problem-solving "toolkits" or sets of clinical strategies: (a) *Problem-Solving Multitasking*, (b) the *"Stop, Slow Down, Think, and Act" (S.S.T.A.) Method of Approaching Problems*, (c) *Healthy Thinking and Positive Imagery*, and (d) *Planful Problem Solving*. The adjunctive techniques of psychoeducation, coaching, modeling, shaping, rehearsal and practice, performance feedback, positive reinforcement, the use of analogies and metaphors, and the provision of handouts are all used to enhance an individual's ability to learn the various problem-solving tools (see Nezu et al., 2013, for a comprehensive description of these four toolkits).

## Problem-Solving Multitasking

This first toolkit provides strategies for individuals to overcome brain overload. Research in cognitive psychology consistently demonstrates that doing more than one task at a time, particularly if they are complex, degrades accuracy and productivity (Rogers & Monsell, 1995). Because the conscious mind is limited in the amount of activity it can perform efficiently at one time, *especially when a person is under stress*, additional tools become necessary to help people better handle such concerns.

In this toolkit, three multitasking strategies are provided. *Externalization* involves the display of information externally as often as possible; for example, writing it down, drawing diagrams or maps to show relationships, or recording information in one's computer, smartphone, or audiotape recorder. *Visualization* emphasizes the use of visual imagery to enhance problem-solving ability, which may include visualizing the problem for clarification purposes (visualizing a current problem situation to begin to clearly define it), visualization for rehearsal (imagining carrying out a solution plan to rehearse and learn a response), or guided imagery (as a relaxation method) to help reduce arousal and maintain focus on any given therapeutic task or activity. Another therapeutic use of visualization is described under Toolkit #3, later in the chapter, and we observe this as having a high clinical potency in reducing hopelessness. The last strategy in this toolkit is *simplification*, which involves attempting to break down a complex problem to make it more manageable by focusing on the most relevant information, breaking it down into more manageable subproblems, and identifying smaller steps to reach one's goal, as well as specifying the goals concretely.

## "Stop, Slow Down, Think, and Act" (S.S.T.A.)

The second problem-solving toolkit, *S.S.T.A.*, comprises a set of strategies geared to help individuals modulate their immediate negative emotional reactions to stressful stimuli, as strong negative emotions can adversely affect problem-solving efforts and decision making. This toolkit teaches individuals to *Stop* when becoming aware of experiencing an emotional reaction such that they may nonjudgmentally observe their emotional reaction, before it evolves into a full-blown and overwhelming negative response. This also involves noticing one's inner experience to stressful triggers when under stress (i.e., emotional, cognitive, physical, and behavioral responses) and identifying unique triggers (i.e., situations, events, people, internal thoughts, or external stimuli that produce potentially strong negative emotional reactions). Individuals are then instructed to *Slow Down* their emotional response, such that they may observe it in a nonjudgmental manner. Recommended strategies to reduce emotional arousal, including counting, deep breathing, guided imagery or visualization, fake smiling, fake yawning, mindful meditation, deep muscle relaxation, exercise, talking to someone, talking out loud while alone, prayer, gum chewing, or other techniques. Once a person is able to "stop and slow down," he or she is instructed to use the information gleaned from emotions to discover what is important and what to change. Finally, individuals are guided to *Think* more planfully about what to do with a lessened degree of interference from the triggered negative emotionality, and then *Act* by carrying out a solution or action plan geared to effectively cope with the stressful situation.

## Healthy Thinking and Positive Imagery

The third problem-solving toolkit is aimed at overcoming negative thinking and feelings of hopelessness for individuals for whom these are concerns that interfere with effective problem solving. The ABC Model of Healthy Thinking is one strategy that draws heavily upon other cognitive behavioral therapies that help individuals to "cognitively restructure" their negative thinking by disputing irrational beliefs (e.g., Ellis, 2003), testing the validity of negative cognitions behaviorally (e.g., Dobson & Hamilton, 2003), and modifying maladaptive dysfunctional beliefs (e.g., Newman, 2003). A person is asked to identify the activating event or stressful problem, beliefs or thoughts about the problem, emotional consequences, and then examine the accuracy of thoughts and dispute inaccuracies with more positive self-statements. The Reversed Advocacy Role-Play, an experiential exercise in which the roles of the therapist and the client are reversed to promote a more adaptive way of thinking, may also be used to overcome negative thinking.

To increase hopefulness and a more positive problem orientation, visualization can be an effective clinical tool. This specific use of visualizing involves guiding the patient to experience having solved the problem (as compared with how to solve the problem). The patient is guided through a visualization in which he or she is on the other side of the problem as a means of developing the motivation to work through the problem. In other words, this strategy helps people to see the light at the end of the tunnel. Additionally, visualizing the simplification of large goals into smaller, more manageable objectives may better engage individuals in planful problem solving.

## Planful Problem Solving

This last toolkit fosters effective problem solving and decision making by teaching individuals four sets of planful problem-solving skills. *Problem Definition* involves seeking the available facts, describing the facts in clear language, separating facts from assumptions, determining a realistic problem-solving goal, and identifying obstacles that prevent one from reaching such a goal. Patients learn how to define problems through the use of strategies designed to help them identify tendencies toward cognitive errors and inaccurate assumptions, so they may practice more accurate problem analysis. *Generation of Alternatives* includes thinking of a range of potential solution strategies aimed at overcoming the identified obstacles by applying the brainstorming principles of quantity, deferment of judgment, and variety. Strategies aimed at engaging patients in creative activities are designed to teach them how to generate alternatives without self-judgment or criticism. *Decision Making* involves four steps to effective decisions, including screening out obviously ineffective solutions, predicting a range of possible consequences (i.e., personal consequences, social consequences, short-term effects, and long-term effects) of the various alternatives, conducting a cost-benefit analysis of these consequences, and identifying effective solutions and developing an action plan to achieve the problem-solving goal. *Solution Implementation and Verification*, the last planful problem-solving skill, involves motivating patients to carry out the action plan, undergoing certain preparations to ensure that the plan can be carried out optimally, implementing the solution, monitoring the actual effects of the plan, self-reinforcing for attempting to solve a problem, and troubleshooting if the solution was not successful.

## Case Example

We present the case of David in this section to illustrate the application of a PST approach to treatment and the positive steps taken by him to achieve his goals that promote physical and psychological health. A summary of his initial assessment is first provided, followed by an overview of his treatment. Handouts are frequently provided to clients throughout PST treatment, although they are not discussed here (for information on the use of client handouts to aid treatment, see Nezu et al., 2013; see also Nezu, Nezu, & D'Zurilla, 2007, for a self-help book based on problem-solving principles).

David is a 30-year-old man who presented for psychotherapy due to "tremendous stress" in both his workplace and personal life. He reported that he had previously been able to manage the stress associated with his position in financial sales, but it had intensified in recent months since he was transferred to another department where his workload was substantially increased. He felt overwhelmed in the new position and frequently stayed late at the office to complete his assignments, stating that almost all of his time was spent working. He was also assigned a new boss who was never satisfied with David's work and frequently "singled him out" and yelled at him in front of other employees. When this occurred, David felt very badly about himself, and he worried constantly about losing his job and not being able to pay bills. He often came home from work very irritable and tired and reported that this often served as a precipitant of arguments with his wife, Kathy. He stated that their arguments centered on Kathy's complaints that he did not make time for her anymore and acted distant when they did have time together. David was frequently angry that she was not more understanding about his work situation and felt that her claims that he did not make time for her were exaggerated. The quarrels had increased in frequency during the previous weeks, which further caused David to keep to himself even more to avoid negative confrontations with his wife, further straining their relationship. Moreover, David experienced severe gastrointestinal symptoms when he was distressed. David believed that all these difficulties were preventing him from living a "good and satisfying life" but felt "stuck" as though "nothing would be able to improve my situation for the better." This is the point where David became hopeless and desperate for help and decided to seek treatment.

David described his childhood as "pretty normal," raised as an only child by both his parents until the age of eight when they divorced. He reported that his mother "always worried about every little thing that could go wrong" and tended to become overwhelmed when faced with stress. His father, in contrast, "was the opposite, a man of few words who often kept to himself." David believed that his father eventually wasn't able to deal with his mother's "nonsense," resulting in their divorce. At that point, David stayed to live with his mother while his father moved away and reported that although they kept in contact over the years, they did not spend much time together. David performed well in school and eventually went on to college, where he first met Kathy. They dated for several years before they married when David was 24 years old, and he reported that they had an excellent relationship until recently. He reported that he started his current job a year after getting married, and although he had ups and downs while working there, his recent transfer to a different department had been "nothing short of awful."

David's response to the Social Problem Solving Inventory-Revised (SPSI-R; D'Zurilla, Nezu, & Maydeu-Olivares, 2002), a psychometrically sound, self-report measure of SPS, revealed a significantly high negative problem orientation, reflective of his excessive worrying and difficulties coping with stress. His avoidant problem-solving score was also elevated, indicative of his tendency to withdraw and avoid dealing with his problems at work and home. Additionally, his positive problem orientation, planful problem solving, and impulsive/careless problem-solving scores were in the low range. Overall, it was determined that David had significant problem-solving deficits and limitations, indicating that a more comprehensive version of PST would likely be most beneficial for him. The scores on the SPSI-R can be extremely clinically useful as they create a picture or profile of one's problem-solving effectiveness across both orientation components as well as the three problem-solving styles described earlier (planful problem-solving style, impulsive problem-solving style, and avoidant problem-solving style). Thus, the measure can be extremely useful in identifying particular areas of strength to reinforce or weakness to target. This contributes to an accurate case formulation and directs the foci in treatment.

In the initial sessions with David, his case formulation was discussed, including his early emotional learning experiences, which had contributed to his learned emotional reactions to current stressors. Treatment goals were discussed, including improved management of stress. Also during the introductory session, there was an emphasis on establishing a positive relationship with David, fostering optimism by reinforcing his strength in seeking treatment, and encouraging participation. Additionally, David was provided with a brief overview of how problem-solving ability is related to stress to better understand the nature and cause of his distress (i.e., ineffective problem solving).

David was initially presented with techniques specific to *Problem-Solving Multitasking* (Nezu et al., 2013) as a means of overcoming brain overload by following the principles of externalization, visualization, and simplification. After learning techniques introduced by his therapist concerning various ways to overcome brain overload, he was given an opportunity to put them into practice as a homework assignment. He externalized by writing his thoughts and feelings in a journal, particularly when he was feeling stressed, and reported "it helped get things off my chest." He also used this technique at work by writing lists of tasks that he needed to complete and prioritizing them, which "made all the work that needed to be done a bit less overwhelming." Additionally, David used guided imagery visualization as a stress-management technique to promote calmness just before returning home from work, which reduced his irritability. This required several weeks of practice and placement of visual cues in his work environment and car to result in noticeable improvement.

David was next trained in the *S.S.T.A. Method* (Nezu et al., 2013) to better manage emotional regulation. He was taught to "stop" when becoming first aware of his emotional reactions, and practice a nonjudgmental awareness of his emotional reactions. It is important to note that his instructions were not to stop his feeling but to become aware so that he could use the techniques provided to him in therapy to "slow down" his emotional response and reduce the intensity to a point where he would be able to "listen to what his emotions were telling him." Only after becoming more aware of his inner experience and what was important for his personal goals or life values to change, was he instructed to "think" planfully with a reduced degree of emotional turmoil and "act" by carrying out a solution plan. David identified his boss yelling at him as a major trigger of negative emotions, and after learning and practicing various methods of slowing down, he determined that deep breathing was most helpful in "bringing down the volume" of these emotions, so that he could learn from them. The moment that his boss confronted him at work and his anxiety was triggered, he would "stop" and notice his reaction and "slow down" by breathing deeply several times until he felt that his body and brain were calm before attempting to handle any problems in the workplace. He also practiced this technique when he noticed himself becoming frustrated with Kathy, reporting that it reduced his irritability at home and even "calmed down my stomach."

David was next trained in the skills comprising the *Healthy Thinking and Positive Imagery* Toolkit (Nezu et al., 2013) in order to overcome negative thinking and feelings of hopelessness. The ABC Model of Healthy Thinking was presented to help David to tackle the problem of his boss "speaking down" to him. He identified the emotional consequences of this problem as sad and anxious feelings, and after discussing this with his therapist, David was able to identify beliefs and worries that he was "not good enough," that he was going to lose his job, and that he would not be able to pay his bills. Through the use of a technique referred to as "separating facts from assumptions," David was taught to evaluate the accuracy of such thoughts, ultimately determining that his interpretation of his boss's behavior events were based upon assumptions rather than accurate information. He and his therapist explored how long-term schemas had influenced his interpretation of events during communications with his boss and were not based upon facts. Indeed, as David and his therapist searched for facts about his communication with his boss, they discovered that his assumptions were often irrational, illogical, and inaccurate. David was then able to modify his original statements to increase their accuracy. For example, when David's boss pressured David to take on more work, it was often because he believed David to be the one that was most competent. David's more accurate thoughts in such a situation changed from "I'm not good enough" to "I'm angry that my boss always comes to me with this." More able to observe his anger without judgment and as an important source of information, David was able to see that he often had taken on jobs that others failed to do, and he began to identify an important problem to target with painful problem solving—not always subjugating his work and well-being by continually taking on new tasks.

The *reverse-advocacy role-play* strategy was also introduced to David as another tool in the *Healthy Thinking and Positive Imagery* Toolkit to help him overcome the negative thinking he experienced regarding his wife. In this exercise, his counselor temporarily adopted David's irrational and maladaptive beliefs that his wife did not support him and that he had been acting the same to her lately. David was asked to play the role of the therapist and argue against such statements by providing reasons why they were incorrect. David was able to eventually reason that his wife did, in fact, support him, as evidenced by her willingness to always be there and listen when he needed to vent about work, her encouraging words when he was feeling down, and all the "little things she does for me to make my life easier." David was also able to acknowledge that he had been acting differently in response to his wife, recognizing that he had not been opening up to her as he once had and that he had been avoiding her. As a result of this exercise, David was able to develop more realistic, balanced thoughts about the situation, resulting in an increased appreciation for his wife and ability to see problems from her perspective, allowing him to increase his understanding of his own role in their arguments.

David was next instructed in *Positive Visualization to Overcome Hopelessness*, an additional tool in the *Healthy Thinking and Positive Imagery* Toolkit, as his sense of hopelessness about his problems at work had been interfering with his ability to improve the situation. First, the rationale was provided, explaining that feelings of hopelessness serve as obstacles to effective problem solving because they decrease motivation to pursue goals. With this visualization exercise, David was able to imagine that he had reached his problem-solving goal, that there was much less conflict at work, and that his job was more manageable. He imagined in his mind's eye what it would feel like after the problem was solved, without thinking about how he got there, and was thus able to experience the positive thoughts and feelings associated with doing so. David reported that after he completed this exercise, he felt much more hopeful and motivated to work toward solving the problem.

After David had developed a good understanding of the first three toolkits and practiced the techniques, the final toolkit, *Planful Problem Solving* (Nezu et al., 2013), was introduced to foster further effective problem solving. Because David's initial assessment demonstrated deficits in planful problem solving, an intensive approach was taken in this type of training. Problem definition was the first set of skills in this toolkit in which he was trained. David was taught to seek the facts of the situation by thinking of himself as a detective, asking specific questions, such as "who," "what," "when," "why," and "how," and answering them objectively. He was then asked to externalize by writing down the information in clear language and then separating facts from assumptions. Applying these principles, he described another situation as, "My boss criticizes my work when the company's sales reports have been low. When this occurs, I become anxious and worry that I may lose my job and won't be able to financially support my family. I also feel depressed when this happens because it seems as though I can't do anything right. I end up taking on more and more work to prove myself but my bad feelings make it more difficult to do my job effectively."

In the next step, problem definition, David was taught to set realistic goals, which included both emotion-focused goals (i.e., decreasing his fears and view of himself as a failure as negative emotional reactions to his boss's criticism) and problem-focused goals (i.e., improving his work performance, not having his boss constantly criticizing him, becoming much more discriminating in the many extra jobs he would be willing to take on, and wanting to complete his work but also have time for his family). By asking himself, "What makes this situation a problem?" he was able to identify three major obstacles. The first was his quick and powerful negative emotional response, which served as an emotional barrier to improved work performance. The second obstacle was that he experienced time pressure, often related to poor estimation of how much time a task or project would actually take. Lastly, he had a tendency to immediately say "yes" to any additional job, even when it was someone else's responsibility.

David was next taught the second planful problem-solving skill, generation of alternatives, which involved brainstorming a variety of potential solutions to his problems. He was taught to generate multiple possible solutions, consider a wide range of both strategies and tactics, and defer judgment of the alternative solutions, writing them down as he went along. These included telling his boss off, meeting with his boss to discuss how he could improve his work, finding another job, going to his boss's supervisor, telling his boss that he did not want to do the work assigned to other people, and changing how he responded to his boss's criticism.

During the decision-making process, the next planful problem-solving skill, David examined these possible solutions by evaluating the likely success of the options and deciding which to carry out. First, he screened out those that were "obviously ineffective," eliminating the solution of "telling his boss off," because there was a clearly unacceptable risk of getting fired and the lack of positive consequences, other than momentarily feeling in control. Next, he predicted the consequences of each of the remaining options, considering the likelihood that a solution would work and the likelihood that it could be carried out, as well as short-term and long-term personal and social consequences. After David rated each solution, he determined that a combination of changing how he responded to his boss's criticism and meeting with him to see how he could improve his work as well as discuss ways to be helpful to other workers without doing the job for them carried a maximum number of positive consequences and minimal negative ones.

The last planful problem-solving activity, solution implementation and verification, involved having David carry out the action plan and assess its outcome. He motivated himself to carry it out by considering the consequences of not doing so, namely that his situation would not change. In preparation of the action plan and consideration of any predicted obstacles that might impact his ability to carry out the plan effectively, he realized that meeting with his boss before being able to successfully regulate his emotions could lead to his feeling badly if his boss was especially harsh and critical of him. Thus, he decided that he should focus on practicing "stopping and slowing down" before meeting with his boss so that he could maintain his composure. He also determined that the best time to arrange the meeting would be at the end of the month before the sales reports were distributed, so he had the best chance of his boss responding favorably. In carrying out the action plan, David first practiced emotional regulation strategies to improve how he reacted to criticism and then mentally rehearsed the meeting with his boss via visualization, before meeting with him. Then, after carrying out the action plan, he monitored and evaluated the outcomes. To David's surprise, his boss had a positive response to the meeting, indicating that he was glad David wanted to improve his performance and came to him to discuss how he could do so. It was actually his boss's suggestion for David to cease taking on the tasks that other people in the office should be expected to do, and his boss was willing to back him up in that regard. David also found this meeting helpful in identifying ways that he could improve his work, particularly enhancing his organizational skills, which eventually helped him to cut down the amount of time it took him to complete a project. The criticism from his boss diminished from that point forward, but when it did occur, David found he was better able to handle it. David determined that his action plan was very helpful in reducing the problem, and he self-reinforced his problem-solving efforts by taking his wife out to a nice dinner.

Following his practice in with the four Problem-Solving Toolkits, David engaged in continual guided practice using the various techniques and tackled the next problem of "getting along better with Kathy." As with learning any type of skill, practice is extremely important to master the skill. In this context, practice served the purpose of applying the entire problem solving model (i.e., S.S.T.A.) under the guidance of the therapist who was able to identify problem-solving vulnerabilities, helped David to recognize long held schemas in which he tended to instantly react to negative feelings by taking on more work in an attempt to fix things, and provided helpful feedback. David's use and increased facility with the model decreased the amount of time and effort necessary to apply the model with new problems and facilitated maintenance and generalization of the skills. Before treatment ended, David and his therapist engaged in future forecasting, or discussing potential problems that could occur in the future and how difficulties could be managed. Overall, David reported that this approach was helpful in decreasing his stress and improving his work situation and marital relationship.

## Summary and Future Directions

This chapter focused on effective problem solving and its relation to well-being. Research has documented that the ability to effectively handle life's stressors leads to improved physical and emotional health. PST teaches individuals how to become more effective problem solvers by helping them to examine their affective and cognitive habits and areas of ineffective problem solving. Once areas of ineffective problem solving are identified, patients are provided with several therapeutic experiences and new skills geared to overcome certain major barriers, including brain overload, difficulties in emotional regulation, negative thinking, low motivation, and ineffective problem-solving patterns. Scores of studies focusing on a variety of populations have clearly demonstrated its efficacy. As such, these skills can be useful in helping one to become more balanced, more resilient, and wiser.

## PST for Positive Functioning

More research is needed, however, on the role of PST in enhancing *optimal* functioning that maximizes one's overall quality of life. Such research could focus on fostering exceptional performance, achievement, creativity, and invention in various areas of one's life, such as business and industry, medicine, public service, sports, and marriage and family.

## Preventive Behavioral Health

A number of behavioral and lifestyle changes have been recommended by medical professionals to *prevent* serious medical conditions such as cancer and cardiovascular diseases. These changes include reducing and managing stress more effectively, changing eating habits, losing weight, stopping smoking, controlling alcohol intake, and increasing physical exercise. Hence, research on PST as a *preventive* intervention to help people overcome these obstacles to a healthy lifestyle is another important area for future research.

## Prevention Training for Vulnerable Populations

As noted earlier, substantial research has documented the deleterious effects of traumatic stress. However, research has also shown that it is not exposure to such stress per se that leads to harm but rather how one reacts to such stress both initially and over time. For persons accepting jobs or roles that place themselves in harm's way, such as service members, police officers, firefighters, and first responders, it would seem logical that learning how to best adapt to such exposure may help to prevent negative consequences. In this context, we advocate that research be conducted to evaluate whether PST provided *before* stressors occur can prevent health problems and emotional distress.

## Exploration of New Methods for Implementing PST in Distressed Populations

Many people who can be helped through PST in important ways, such as reduction of depression or suicide, better management of chronic health conditions, emotional dysregulation, or simply getting closer to valued goals in life, may not seek out psychotherapy due to lack of access, fear, shame, or stigma. Advances in new communication technologies could make PST more accessible and cost-effective, while providing alternatives for the therapy to be delivered through the Internet, telehealth systems, or even smartphone applications. These are important avenues to pursue in that PST offers one potent and evidence-based way out of significant and painful distress by teaching people to embrace their internal experiences as important sources of information, learning new skills to regulate negative feelings and become more accurate at identifying what is important for them to change, and how to achieve life goals. Finally, PST can be a very effective intervention to help people learn to approach life challenges with a sense of optimism, empowerment, and intentionality.

# References

Bell, A. C., & D'Zurilla, T. J. (2009). Problem-solving therapy for depression: A meta-analysis. *Clinical Psychology Review, 29,* 348–353.

Contrada, R. J., & Baum, A. (2011). *The handbook of stress science: Biology, psychology, and health.* New York, NY: Springer.

Cuijpers, P., van Straten, A., & Warmerdam, L. (2007). Problem solving therapies for depression: A meta-analysis. *European Psychiatry, 22,* 9–15.

Dobson, K. S, & Hamilton, K. E. (2003). Cognitive restructuring: Behavioral tests of negative cognitions. In W. O'Donohue, J. E. Fisher, & S. C. Hayes (Eds.), *Cognitive behavior therapy: Applying empirically supported techniques in your practice* (pp. 84–88). New York, NY: Wiley.

D'Zurilla, T. J., & Goldfried, M. R. (1971). Problem solving and behavior modification. *Journal of Abnormal Psychology, 78,* 107–126.

D'Zurilla, T. J., & Nezu, A. M. (2007). *Problem-solving therapy: A positive approach to clinical intervention* (3rd ed.). New York, NY: Springer.

D'Zurilla, T. J., Nezu, A. M., & Maydeu-Olivares, A. (2002). *Manual for the Social Problem-Solving Inventory-Revised.* North Tonawanda, NY: Multi-Health Systems.

D'Zurilla, T. J., Nezu, A. M., & Maydeu-Olivares, A. (2004). Social problem solving: Theory and assessment. In E. C. Chang, T. J. D'Zurilla, & L. J. Sanna (Eds.), *Social problem solving: Theory, research, and training* (pp. 11–27). Washington, DC: American Psychological Association.

Ellis, A. (2003). Cognitive restructuring of the disputing of irrational beliefs. In W. O'Donohue, J. E. Fisher, & S. C. Hayes (Eds.), *Cognitive behavior therapy: Applying empirically supported techniques in your practice* (pp. 79–83). New York, NY: Wiley.

Malouff, J. M., Thorsteinsson, E. B., & Schutte, N. S. (2007). The efficacy of problem solving therapy in reducing mental and physical health problems: A meta-analysis. *Clinical Psychology Review, 27,* 46–57.

Newman, C. F. (2003). Cognitive restructuring: Identifying and modifying maladaptive schemas. In W. O'Donohue, J. E. Fisher, & S. C. Hayes (Eds.), *Cognitive behavior therapy: Applying empirically supported techniques in your practice* (pp. 89–95). New York, NY: Wiley.

Nezu, A. M. (2004). Problem solving and behavior therapy revisited. *Behavior Therapy, 35*, 1–33.

Nezu, A. M., & D'Zurilla, T. J. (1989). Social problem solving and negative affective conditions. In P. C. Kendall & D. Watson (Eds.), *Anxiety and depression: Distinctive and overlapping features* (pp.285–315). New York, NY: Academic Press.

Nezu, A. M., Nezu, C. M., & Cos, T. A. (2007). Case formulation for the behavioral and cognitive therapies: A problem-solving perspectiva. In T. D. Eells (Ed.), *Handbook of psychotherapy case formulation* (pp. 2nd ed. 349–378). New York, NY: Guilford Press

Nezu, A. M., Nezu, C. M., & D'Zurilla, T. J. (2007). Solving life's problems: *A 5-step guide to enhanced well-being.* New York, NY: Springer.

Nezu, A. M., Nezu, C. M., & D'Zurilla, T. J. (2013). *Problem-solving therapy: A treatment manual.* New York, NY: Springer.

Nezu, A. M., & Perri, M. G. (1989). Social problem solving therapy for unipolar depression: An initial dismantling investigation. *Journal of Consulting and Clinical Psychology, 57*, 408–413.

Nezu, A. M., Wilkins, V. M., & Nezu, C. M. (2004). Social problem solving, stress, and negative affective conditions. In E. C. Chang, T. J. D'Zurilla, & L. J. Sanna (Eds.), *Social problem solving: Theory, research, and training* (pp. 49–65). Washington, DC: American Psychological Association.

Piazza, J. J., Charles, S. T., Sliwinski, M. J., Mogle, J., & Almeida, D. M. (2013). Affective reactivity to daily stressors and long-term risk of reporting a chronic health condition. *Annals of Behavioral Medicine, 45*, 110–120.

Rogers, R., & Monsell, S. (1995). The costs of a predictable switch between simple cognitive tasks. *Journal of Experimental Psychology: General, 124*, 207–231.

Tedeschi, R. G., & Calhoun, L. G. (2004). Posttraumatic growth: Conceptual foundations and empirical evidence. *Psychological Inquiry, 15*, 1–18.

# 4

# Understanding and Enhancing Psychological Acceptance

*James D. Herbert*

Drexel University

*Lynn L. Brandsma*

Chestnut Hill College

Psychologists and other mental health professionals can scarcely check their mail these days without receiving yet another announcement for a training workshop, book, or podcast focused on enhancing mindfulness and psychological acceptance, both in their patients and in themselves. Several new psychotherapy models featuring mindfulness, acceptance, metacognition, and related concepts have become very popular over the past decade. Not to be left behind, even versions of traditional treatment models such as psychoanalytic psychotherapy have recently adopted the prefix "mindfulness-based" (e.g., Stewart, 2014; Ventegodt et al., 2007). These concepts have also found their way into the public consciousness, with countless media presentations extolling the virtues of mindfulness. Beautiful, young, serene-looking women with palms held together prayerfully and bodies in graceful yoga poses adorn the covers of magazines and websites. References are made to ancient wisdom and esoteric practices newly imported from the East, couched in a seductively exotic and mysterious aura. Life-changing benefits are touted, and not surprisingly, products are sold.

Scientifically minded professionals and laypersons alike can be forgiven for reacting to these developments with a degree of skepticism. Among those who are weary of passing fashions in popular psychology, the very trendiness of these developments may suggest a lack of deeper substance. Indeed, the value of a theory or technique is not determined by its popularity; to do so would be to commit the logical fallacy known as *argumentum ad populum*. Just because many people embrace an idea does not mean it is true or useful. The fact that a large percentage of Americans do not believe in biological evolution (Alfano, 2009; Pew Research Center, 2013) does not speak to its truth value as a scientific fact.

But it is equally important to avoid knee-jerk cynicism. The popularity of an idea does not speak directly to its truth or utility but neither does it speak against it. The *ad populum reversal* describes a sort of guilt by association, in which a proposition is judged to be invalid merely because it is popular. So, like any other novel development, the value of psychological acceptance and mindfulness as theoretical concepts and intervention techniques must be evaluated in light of the scientific evidence.

As it turns out, the past decade has witnessed tremendous growth in the scientific study of these concepts and treatment strategies. Although a great deal more work remains to be done, the results thus far are quite promising. The evidence to date suggests that psychological (also referred to as experiential) avoidance of thoughts, feelings, memories, and sensations is associated with a wide range of psychopathology, and that fostering a sense of experiential acceptance can have therapeutic benefits (Germer, Siegel, & Fulton, 2013; Herbert & Forman, 2011a).

In this chapter, we begin by reviewing key concepts and their recent evolution, followed by a description of specific techniques and strategies for promoting psychological acceptance in the service of prevention and behavior change, with a particular focus on enhancing well-being and quality of life, and on improving functioning. We then review the research assessing the utility of these approaches and their underlying theoretical mechanisms. Finally, we offer suggestions for future innovation and research.

## Key Concepts: Mindfulness and Psychological Acceptance Explained

One way to begin to approach an appreciation for psychological acceptance and mindfulness is to contrast these concepts with their opposites. The most common reaction to distressing subjective experiences is suppression

(Braams, Blechert, Boden, & Gross, 2012). Just as we automatically recoil when we unexpectedly happen upon a dangerous animal or we instinctively pull our hand away from a hot stove, we naturally try to put upsetting thoughts and feelings out of mind. Hayes, Levin, Plumb, Boulanger, and Pistorello (2013) describe this process as "experiential avoidance," which they define as "the attempt to alter the form, frequency, or intensity of private experiences such as thoughts, feelings, bodily sensations, or memories, even when doing so is costly, ineffective, or unnecessary" (p. 184). In contrast, mindfulness involves actively noticing and accepting the full range of one's subjective experience, including negative or distressing thoughts, feelings, sensations, and memories. Psychological acceptance is the active embracing of subjective experience, particularly distressing experiences. The idea is not merely to grudgingly tolerate negative experiences but to embrace them fully and without defense. As we will see, although a state of mindful awareness and psychological acceptance may accrue benefits in its own right, the primary focus within contemporary psychology is applying practices to achieve these states as a means to an end. That is, fostering acceptance helps one achieve important behavior changes, such as overcoming depression or anxiety, coping with psychotic experiences, or sticking to a diet, which in turn may lead to an enhanced quality of life.

There are a number of related terms that involve psychological acceptance. These include mindfulness, cognitive distancing or defusion, metacognition, experiential or psychological acceptance, psychological flexibility, and meditation. Some of these concepts were originally derived from folk psychology rather than scientific theories, and even those terms that were not borrowed from everyday language are used somewhat differently by different theorists. It is therefore not surprising that consensus has not been reached on precise definitions. Nevertheless, it is possible to appreciate the general way the terms are commonly used by theorists and clinicians.

## Mindfulness

The concept of mindfulness originally derived from ancient Buddhist and Hindu spiritual traditions. It was introduced to the United States by 19th century Chinese immigrants and subsequently adopted by psychoanalytic and then existential psychotherapists beginning in the mid-20th century (Williams & Lynn, 2010). The term was introduced to academic psychology by the social psychologist Ellen Langer (1989), who described it as a state of mind associated with openness to new information and relinquishing preconceptions. The concept of mindfulness began featuring prominently in models of behavior therapy beginning in the 1990s and continuing to today (Herbert & Forman, 2011b, 2014).

The most widely cited definition of mindfulness was offered by Jon Kabat-Zinn (1994): "paying attention in a particular way: on purpose, in the present moment, and nonjudgmentally" (p. 4). This definition nicely describes several key aspects of the term. First, mindfulness is described as an active verb, as something that one does. In contrast to passive relaxation, the process involves an active embracing of the totality of one's ongoing experience. Second, mindfulness involves enhanced conscious contact ("paying attention") with one's experience as it unfolds in real time ("the present moment"). Third, mindfulness involves accepting that experience without avoidance or resistance ("nonjudgmentally"). Other theorists have expanded on Kabat-Zinn's definition in various ways, but they still echo these basic features. A number of measures of mindfulness have been developed, each based on each author's particular conceptualization of the construct. Some theorists describe the concept as unifactorial (e.g., Brown & Ryan, 2003), whereas others described up to five distinct components (e.g., Baer, Smith, Hopkins, Krietemeyer, & Toney, 2006). Our group suggested a middle ground, proposing a two-factor conceptualization. We described mindfulness as consisting of enhanced awareness of one's ongoing experience, and psychological acceptance of that experience, and developed the Philadelphia Mindfulness Scale to measure these two factors. Psychometric research reveals that the factors are indeed distinct (Cardaciotto, Herbert, Forman, Moitra, & Farrow, 2008).

## Cognitive Distancing or Defusion

The first step to changing one's reaction to distressing subjective experience is to become more aware of that experience. Beck, Rush, Shaw, and Emery (1979) describe the ability to see one's experience—and in particular one's thoughts—from a distinct perspective as cognitive decentering or distancing. Developing the ability to observe one's thoughts as being distinct from the self is an early step in cognitive therapy and is a prelude to evaluating the rationality of the thoughts and to restructuring them to be less distorted. Hayes, Strosahl, and Wilson (2012) expanded on the distinction between the content of one's subjective experience and the sense of self that observes that experience, a process they refer to as cognitive defusion. From this perspective, one's thoughts are often akin to automatically programmed reactions, and as such, are artifacts of one's unique history rather than necessarily being conveyers of important information. For example, if native English speakers are presented with the phrase "Mary had a little ____," they

will automatically think "lamb." Likewise, the stimulus "A, B, C, ____"
elicits "D." Yet a person with a different learning history (for example, a
nonnative English speaker who had never encountered these particular
phrases) would not have these reactions. So the thought "Mary had a little
lamb" does not necessarily reference a real state of the world; that is, there
may be neither a Mary nor a lamb anywhere nearby. Similarly, one's ongoing
stream of consciousness may not convey important information demanding
scrutiny. Yet we often react as if it does, and feel compelled to do something
about our thoughts, whether that be evaluating them, changing them, or
eliminating them. Alternatively, one can learn to step back and observe the
stream of consciousness as it unfolds as if it were a series of such programmed reactions, without necessarily needing to do anything with them.
The process of stepping back to gain perspective on one's experience is what
is referred to as distancing or defusion.

## Metacognition

Beginning in the 1990s, some theorists working within the cognitive
therapy tradition noticed that standard cognitive restructuring interventions,
which focus on explicitly changing the content of one's thoughts and their
associated underlying beliefs, were of limited usefulness with certain populations (e.g., patients with multiple recurrent episodes of depression). They
therefore began focusing instead on beliefs about one's thinking, a process
termed metacognition, rather than the specific content of the thoughts themselves. For example, a depressed patient might have the thought, "I just can't
bring myself to get out of bed today." Rather than trying to question the
evidence for that thought directly, the therapist might work to undermine the
belief that such a thought necessarily mattered one way or the other to
whether or not the patient could actually get out of bed. According to these
theorists, changes in metacognition tend to occur less through the explicit
examination of evidence but instead more through experiences. The two
primary models to emerge from this new approach to cognitive therapy are
mindfulness-based cognitive therapy (Segal, Williams, & Teasdale, 2001)
and metacognitive therapy (Wells, 2008).

## Experiential Acceptance

The process of not simply noticing but also embracing one's experience
without judgment or defense is known as experiential (or psychological)
acceptance. It is important to note that this is a distinct type of acceptance,
not to be confused with the common use of the term *acceptance* with respect

to the status quo of one's life situation. A woman in a physically abusive relationship, for example, need not accept that this is her fate; quite the contrary. As she takes steps to change the situation (for example, by leaving her partner) she will likely experience anxiety, self-doubt, and other distressing experiences. It is the acceptance of these experiences, in this case in the service of making positive behavior changes consistent with her goals and well-being, that constitutes experiential acceptance.

There are two other noteworthy points about psychological acceptance. First, the term is antonymic with respect to experiential avoidance. As discussed below, a growing body of research documents the pernicious effects associated with such avoidance. Second, psychological acceptance typically goes hand-in-hand with cognitive distancing or defusion. In fact, some theorists argue that the process of distancing oneself from one's distressing experience automatically leads to acceptance of that experience (Brown & Ryan, 2003). Although it is true that strategies to enhance defusion generally enhance acceptance and vice versa, the two concepts are in fact distinct. That is, defusion from distressing experiences does not necessarily lead to acceptance of those experiences (Herbert & Forman, 2014). For example, an individual with panic disorder may be able to step back and observe his or her rapidly beating heart (distancing). But rather than accepting the experience, he or she may believe that it signals an impending heart attack. We will return to this issue below, when discussing strategies to foster both defusion and acceptance of distressing experiences.

## Psychological Flexibility

A common misunderstanding about psychological acceptance is that it should be applied unquestioningly to the totality of one's experience, at all times. However, reflecting on this proposition reveals its absurdity. In some cases, a thought is a meaningful hypothesis about the world, and its validity matters. For example, if I hear noises in my home while lying in bed late one night, I might have the thought, "It's an intruder!" It makes a real difference for the safety of my family whether this thought is true or if I am simply hearing my dog, the wind, or the settling of an old house. The prudent course of action is to gather data on the truth value of the thought, not simply to accept it as an automatic mental reaction. Likewise, some bodily sensations convey important information that should not be ignored. Athletes must learn to distinguish the normal aches and pains that accompany physical exertion from those that signal injury, and failure to do so can lead to overtraining and exacerbation of an injury. The key issue in both of these cases is whether our subjective experience in any particular instance is really about data that matter in some important way to our well-being. The form or content of our cognitions is not always a good clue, because our thoughts often masquerade as being about meaningful data-based propositions when in fact they are not.

A related point concerns attempts to exert control over distressing feelings, sensations, or memories. Although the habitual tendency to suppress or otherwise change such experiences is problematic, it does not follow that all such efforts are doomed to failure. In fact, one may sometimes be able to divert attention away from a distressing thought or feeling in such a way as to change one's ongoing experience in a positive way, enhancing the ability to pursue meaningful activities. In our work with extreme social anxiety, for example, we help patients learn to gently refocus attention away from self-evaluative thoughts and anxious feelings and toward the social task at hand (e.g., a conversation), all in the context of an overall accepting stance toward the individual's subjective experience (Herbert, Gershkovich, & Forman, 2014). The important issue here is the effectiveness and overall consequences of such efforts. That is, does the effort to change directly one's experience in a given situation actually work, and if so, does it bring about more problems than it solves? If such efforts work and do not entail significant costs, then they need not be discouraged. The sensitivity among proponents of psychological acceptance to problems arising from direct efforts to change the content of one's experience is therefore pragmatic, not dogmatic.

To highlight this important point, some theorists have recently used the term *psychological flexibility* to illustrate the importance of limiting efforts to engage with one's experience in an evaluative or control-oriented way to only those contexts in which such efforts are effective and do not entail negative side effects. Emphasizing the pursuit of behaviors consistent with personally relevant goals, Bond and colleagues (2011) defined psychological flexibility as "the ability to fully contact the present moment and the thoughts and feelings it contains without needless defense, and, depending upon what the situation affords, persisting in or changing behavior in the pursuit of goals and values" (p. 678).

## Meditation

In the popular literature, the term *meditation* is often used synonymously with mindfulness (e.g., Gross, 2014; see also Chapter 7 "Chilling Out: Meditation, Relaxation, and Yoga"). As discussed above, mindfulness refers to a particular psychological state. Meditation is not itself that state but rather a practice aimed at fostering it. Mindfulness meditation most commonly refers to a practice of sitting quietly while simply noticing one's stream of experience without any effort to modify it in any way. As discussed below, other forms of meditation training involve variations on this theme.

## Fostering Psychological Acceptance

In the ancient philosophical and faith traditions in which mindfulness was originally described, achieving a state of mindful detachment from and acceptance of one's experience was linked to spiritual enlightenment. In the present context, however, the purposes are more modest. Psychological acceptance is a means to an end—that is, a way of moving forward with the full range of one's experience, without needless defense or struggle, in the service of behaving in a way that will lead to a fulfilling, meaningful life. In many modern models of cognitive behavior therapy (CBT) such as Acceptance and Commitment Therapy (ACT) and behavioral activation (BA), there is also an emphasis on clarifying and articulating important life values, linking achievable goals to those values, and aligning one's behavior with respect to these values and goals. The process of fostering psychological acceptance is a central part of this effort toward fostering values-directed action.

A comprehensive review of the techniques that have been developed to foster psychological acceptance and related concepts is beyond the scope of this chapter; in fact, no single work fully describes all such techniques. What follows is a sample of commonly used techniques, divided into three overlapping areas: (a) those targeting mindful awareness of and flexible attention toward one's ongoing experience, (b) those aimed at increasing a sense of psychological distance from and acceptance of one's subjective experience (especially distressing experiences), and (c) those aimed at articulating one's values and goals. Although we group these techniques into these three target domains as a matter of convenience, in fact the targets themselves overlap, and most of the techniques can be used to address more than one area.

## Mindful Awareness

A number of approaches have been developed to foster enhanced awareness of one's ongoing experience. The most common approach is mindfulness meditation. Although some formal approaches to meditation involve sitting very still without moving for extended periods of time, there is no single approach. Broadly conceived, mindfulness meditation involves any activity in which one turns attention toward becoming acutely aware of the stream of subjective experience as it unfolds, without trying to alter it in any way. Meditation can be completely unstructured, or guided (e.g., by audio recordings), or structured in another way. For example, in the "leaves on a stream" exercise in ACT, one imagines contemplating a stream in the fall with leaves floating by. The contents of one's experience (e.g., thoughts, images, sensations) are imagined to be placed on the leaves, and one simply watches as they float by. One can meditate while lying prone with eyes closed or while walking, playing a musical instrument, or even exercising. Over time, the goal is not simply to achieve a state of heightened nonjudgmental awareness of experience while in a sheltered setting (e.g., a quiet room) free of distractions, but to be able to carry that state forward as one goes through his or her activities in everyday life. More specific variants of meditation also exist. For example, loving-kindness meditation involves contemplating the connectedness of all living things and a deep sense of empathy toward others (Salzberg, 1995).

Yoga is another common technique used to enhance mindful awareness, especially of one's body in space. Indeed, any physical activities involving structured movements, such as dance or katas from tai chi or other martial arts, can be used to foster a sense of enhanced awareness. The body scan is another approach whereby one systematically and sequentially focuses attention on various parts of one's body.

An important distinction is how these practices overlap with relaxation training. Although relaxation often occurs during meditation or somatic-focused practices, it is viewed as an incidental side effect and not a goal per se. Indeed, proponents of mindful meditation warn against becoming too attached to the state of relaxation, lest one become enmeshed in a struggle to force oneself to relax. Rather, relaxation, like any other feeling, is welcomed but not specifically cultivated.

## Cognitive Defusion and Psychological Acceptance

Most strategies that target enhanced mindful awareness also tend to foster a detached perspective on that experience, as well as an accepting posture toward it. Moreover, although defusion and acceptance are technically distinct, in practice, most activities that target one will also affect the other. The practice of cognitive self-monitoring, in which one records key thoughts on a log and which forms a critical step in cognitive therapy, can serve as a powerful defusion exercise. The simple act of writing down one's negative or upsetting thoughts helps objectify them, creating psychological distance between oneself and one's experience. Likewise, journaling can serve a similar purpose.

A number of verbal conventions and exercises can foster defusion and acceptance. For example, when experiencing a distressing thought, one can repeat it, inserting the phrase "I'm having the thought that . . ." before the thought. Or one can add the phrase, "that's an interesting thought" following the thought, simply acknowledging the thought as a product of the mind and not as necessarily important or even particularly meaningful. One can repeat a key word representing an upsetting thought or idea (e.g., *loser*) rapidly for 30 seconds or so until it begins to lose its emotional impact. One can likewise say the word slowly, in various strange, cartoon-like voices. By focusing on the sound of the word, its semantic properties become weakened.

ACT in particular makes liberal use of metaphors and experiential exercises to encourage defusion and acceptance. Many dozens of both metaphors and exercises have been developed, and innovative clinicians (and their patients) frequently add to this repertoire. A common metaphor is the tug-of-war with a monster. The individual is described as being in an all-out tug-of-war with a powerful monster, which represents his or her particular struggle (e.g., anxiety). Between the individual and the monster is a deep moat, into which falling will result in certain death. Despite the individual's attempts to pull as hard as possible against the monster, he or she is slipping ever closer to the edge of the moat. Trying to defeat the monster by enlisting help in pulling the rope, such as from friends, psychotherapy, alcohol or drug use, proves ineffective, only causing the monster to pull back harder. An alternative is simply to drop the rope. As long as one refrains from touching the rope, the monster cannot impact one's functioning and one is free to pursue any chosen activity. The monster may rear its ugly head from time to time, taunting the individual and daring him or her to pick up the rope and re-engage in the struggle. Indeed, the individual is likely to find himself or herself suddenly with the rope in hand, so the process of dropping it must be repeated many times. The key is learning to recognize when one has inadvertently picked up the rope and then immediately dropping it. Such metaphors are especially powerful when they are not merely explained didactically but rather are acted out, even using props; in this case, an actual rope.

An example of an experiential exercise targeting psychological acceptance is the cards exercise. The therapist and client work together to record various upsetting thoughts on index cards; one can also record distressing beliefs, sensations, or memories, for example. The therapist and patient then engage in a conversation, with the primary goal being to attend to and carry on the conversation. The therapist then tosses the cards at the patient one at a time, while the latter is either instructed to catch them and stack them neatly or to bat them away (representing organizing one's thoughts or deflecting them from consciousness, respectively). After a couple of minutes, the therapist stops the conversation and the dyad discusses how the interaction went, highlighting the inevitable disruption that actively trying to manage the cards had on the conversation. The exercise is then repeated, this time with the patient instructed simply to let the cards fall wherever they might, without any effort to do anything with them at all, representing acceptance of one's thoughts. Inevitably, engaging in the conversation is much easier under these circumstances.

Finally, exposure exercises provide an ideal opportunity to practice psychological acceptance of difficult experiences. In classic anxiety exposures, the individual is systematically exposed to anxiety-provoking stimuli of increasing intensities with the goal of anxiety reduction through habituation. Exposures in the present context are conducted with a different purpose; that is, to practice distancing oneself from and accepting one's distressing experience. Often, some behavior is simultaneously practiced. For example, individuals with social anxiety disorder may engage in a highly anxiety-provoking conversation, perhaps with an attractive individual or an authority figure. The dual goals are practicing engaging fully in the conversation while simply noticing one's anxiety (including anxiety-related thoughts and somatic sensations).

## Values Clarification

The process of becoming aware of, distancing oneself from, and accepting one's distressing experience begs the question of the larger purpose of doing so. Why should one be willing to make such intimate contact with painful experiences? Upon reflection, most people realize their ultimate goals in life involve living a happy, meaningful life. Moreover, *happiness* in this context does not mean the absence of pain but rather a deeper sense of personal fulfillment. One way of conceptualizing this state is having clarity with respect to one's values in life and behaving in a way that is consistent with those values. For example, a man might highly value being a good father to his children. By contemplating this value, he operationalizes it by establishing specific goals such as spending at least a few minutes each day playing with or talking to each of his children one-on-one, working hard at his job to provide resources for them, and maintaining a close relationship with their mother. He then strives to behave consistently with this value and its associated goals. Aggressively pursuing one's values typically means engaging in behavior that will take one outside of one's habitual comfort zone, evoking anxiety or other distress. This is where the tools of psychological acceptance come into play, as a method of coping with any distress that results from this values-consistent behavior.

Many people have not deeply contemplated their values. Moreover, a common assumption is that one's values are already fully formed and somehow dormant, waiting to be uncovered. In fact, it is probably more helpful to think of values as something that one chooses and articulates, rather than discovers. This emphasizes that one's values are freely chosen by and therefore owned by the individual.

Exercises have been developed to help one choose, clarify, and articulate one's values and associated goals. A common exercise used in ACT is imagining that one is witnessing one's own funeral and listening to the key eulogies describing one's life. How would you want the speaker to describe your life? What do you want it to have stood for? What legacy do you want to leave the world? The answers to these questions can point the way toward the overarching themes that matter most to the individual. Once clarified, living in accordance with those values in turn leads to a sense of a fulfilled, meaningful life. Tools such as the Valued Living Questionnaire (Wilson, Sandoz, & Kitchens, 2010) may be used to help clarify the importance of specific areas of life. Clarity with respect to one's values is helpful in justifying the building of tolerance for stressful situations with the overarching goal of enhancing well-being.

## Research on Psychological Acceptance

Fortunately, the proliferation of references to psychological acceptance and related concepts in the popular media has been accompanied by serious scientific research in this area. Existing studies can be roughly grouped into four distinct areas. First, correlational studies have examined the relation between experiential avoidance and psychopathology on the one hand and experiential acceptance and psychological and physical health and well-being on the other. Second, laboratory experiments have examined whether brief interventions targeting acceptance (and related constructs) produce beneficial effects consistent with theoretical predictions under highly controlled conditions. Third, clinical trials have examined the effects of intervention programs that focus—at least in part—on enhancing psychological acceptance. Fourth and finally, many of the latter studies have used sophisticated methodological approaches and statistical techniques in an attempt to understand the specific mechanisms by which the treatments are effective. We now turn to a brief overview of each of these lines of research.

## Correlational Studies

Experiential avoidance is often assessed by self-report measures such as the Acceptance and Action Questionnaire (AAQ; Hayes, Strosahl, et al.,

2004; Bond et al., 2011) or the Multidimensional Experiential Avoidance Questionnaire (Gámez, Chmielewski, Kotov, Ruggero, & Watson, 2011). A body of research has consistently demonstrated that experiential avoidance is associated with various measures of psychopathology (Kashdan, Barrios, Forsyth, & Steger, 2006). For example, Marx and Sloan (2005) found that experiential avoidance was associated with posttraumatic stress symptoms in a sample of trauma survivors. McCracken (1998) found that psychosocial functioning was predicted by psychological avoidance of pain, even more than the level of pain itself. In a meta-analysis of 27 studies, Hayes, Luoma, Bond, Massuda, and Lillis (2006) found experiential avoidance (as assessed by the AAQ) to be associated with various measures of psychopathology (e.g., depression, anxiety) as well as other indices of quality of life (e.g., job satisfaction and performance). Nevertheless, the original AAQ was marked by problematic psychometric properties, including somewhat low internal consistency, probably because some of the items were unnecessarily complex and confusing, as well as an unstable factor structure (Hayes, Masuda, Bisset, Luoma, & Guerrero, 2004). To address these issues, Bond et al. (2011) revised the measure, creating a 7-item version (the AAQ-II) that demonstrated very good psychometric qualities, including internal consistency, test-retest reliability, and concurrent, discriminant, and predictive validity with respect to a range of outcomes. Across multiple samples, the AAQ-II was found to be associated with higher scores on standard measures of anxiety, depression, stress, and overall psychological distress. Moreover, higher scores predicted workplace absenteeism over a 1-year period. Finally, high-risk groups (e.g., individuals seeking treatment for substance abuse) scored significantly higher on the AAQ-II than did healthy nonclinical participants (Bond et al., 2011).

Similarly, a comprehensive review of dozens of studies concluded that measures of mindfulness are correlated with a wide range of psychological variables, including positive associations with quality of life, positive affect, and self-esteem and inverse associations with depression, anxiety, the ability to sustain attention, and self-control (Keng, Smoski, & Robins, 2011). In addition, neuroimaging studies suggest that higher levels of mindfulness are associated with better abilities at emotion regulation, as reflected in greater prefrontal cortical inhibition of amygdala activation (Keng et al., 2011).

## Laboratory Experiments

It is widely accepted that research should evaluate not only the effects of psychotherapy programs in clinical trials but also the theories on which those programs are based (Hayes et al., 2013; Herbert, Gaudiano, & Forman, 2013; Lohr, 2011; Rosen & Davison, 2003). Studies conducted in more highly controlled laboratory environments are especially helpful in testing key propositions of these theories. Laboratory studies afford a level of control that is generally not possible in clinical trials of the therapies themselves. Specific treatment components, or analogues of these components, can be directly tested against inert or theoretically distinct control conditions.

In 1863, Fyodor Dostoevsky observed that if one tries not to think of a white bear it will paradoxically persist at the forefront of awareness. Beginning in 1987, social psychologist Dan Wegner and colleagues began extensively studying this phenomenon. This line of research reveals that attempts to suppress a thought are accompanied by an automatic self-monitoring of the progress of doing so, such that awareness of the thought becomes all but inevitable (Wegner, Schneider, Carter, & White, 1987). Subsequent experiments showed that attempts to suppress depressing thoughts actually result in stronger depressed feelings even than actively attempting to feel sad. Moreover, suppression can result in an increase (rebound) in a thought or feeling immediately following attempts to suppress it, and this can occur whether or not one is explicitly instructed to suppress the experience (Sayers & Sayette, 2013).

A number of laboratory experiments have compared thought suppression or other cognitive control strategies with interventions designed to foster mindful awareness and acceptance of thoughts or feelings. For example, in a study of food cravings, our group evaluated the effects of a brief intervention designed to foster psychological acceptance of cravings relative to an intervention focused on distraction and cognitive reappraisal of cravings; both were also compared with a no-intervention condition (Forman et al., 2007). Following the intervention, 98 undergraduate students carried around a transparent box of Hersey's Kisses for 48 hours, during which time they were asked to refrain from eating chocolate of any kind. Among those reporting trait sensitivity to the food environment, the acceptance condition resulted in lower levels of craving and in less chocolate consumption relative to the other conditions. We replicated this study in a sample of 48 overweight women, who carried a transparent box of mixed sweets for 72 hours. Again, the results revealed that the acceptance condition resulted in lower cravings and consumption, especially for those participants who reported greater susceptibility to the presence of food and a tendency to engage in emotional eating (Forman, Hoffman, Juarascio, Butryn, & Herbert, 2013).

A recent meta-analysis of 66 laboratory studies found ample evidence that interventions designed to foster psychological acceptance tended to outperform various control conditions (Levin, Hildebrandt, Lillis, & Hayes, 2012). Support was also found for defusion, mindfulness, and values-oriented interventions relative to inactive comparison conditions. Moreover, larger effects were found for interventions that included an experiential component (such as an exercise or discussion of a metaphor) relative to those that relied on rational discussion alone.

## Clinical Trials

A rapidly growing body of literature documents the effects of psychotherapy programs that highlight psychological acceptance for a wide range of problems (Herbert, Forman, & Hitchcock, in press). Most of these interventions consist of multicomponent packages and incorporate various combinations of techniques and strategies designed to enhance cognitive distancing, mindful awareness, and psychological acceptance, all in the service of behavior change (Herbert & Forman, 2011a). Over the past two decades, a number of psychotherapy models have emerged within the cognitive behavioral tradition that target these processes, while de-emphasizing direct efforts to change distressing cognitions. These models are often referred to as "third generation" behavior therapies, to distinguish them from "first generation" approaches originating in the 1950s and 60s that tended to de-emphasize cognitive factors and "second generation" models developed in the 1970s and 80s that stressed cognitive restructuring interventions (Hayes, 2004). Among the most popular of these models are Mindfulness-Based Stress Reduction (MBSR; Kabat-Zinn, 1990, 2005), Mindfulness-Based Cognitive Therapy (MBCT; Segal, Williams, & Teasdale, 2001), Meta-Cognitive Therapy (Wells, 2008), Dialectical Behavior Therapy (DBT; Linehan, Armstrong, Suarez, Allmon, & Heard, 1991), Functional Analytic Psychotherapy (FAP; Kohlenberg & Tsai, 1991), Integrated Behavioral Couples Therapy (IBCT; Christensen et al., 2004), and ACT (Hayes et al., 2012). Some of these programs were developed for specific populations, such as MBCT for recurrent depression. Others were originally developed for a specific population but have since been extended in other areas; for example, MBSR was originally developed for chronic pain but has been extended to anxiety disorders (Vøllestad, Sivertsen, & Nielsen, 2011). Still other programs, such as ACT, were developed as transdiagnostic approaches, that is, comprehensive programs that can be applied to a variety of problems.

The amount and quality of research on these approaches varies considerably. For example, there is only a limited amount of research on FAP (Busch et al., 2009; Gifford et al., 2011; Kohlenberg, Kanter, Bolling, Parker, & Tsai, 2002) and IBCT (Christensen, Atkins, Yi, Baucom, & George, 2006;

Doss, Thum, Sevier, Atkins, & Christensen, 2005; Sevier, Eldridge, Jones, Doss, & Christensen, 2008); nevertheless, in each case the data are encouraging (Hayes, Masuda, et al., 2004). More work has been done on the two approaches that incorporate formal mindfulness meditation training: MBCT and MBSR. A recent meta-analysis of 39 clinical trials evaluated the efficacy of these models (Hofmann, Sawyer, Witt, & Oh, 2010). The meta-analysis revealed moderately large effects in the overall sample on measures of mood and anxiety symptoms and even larger effects for patients with mood or anxiety disorders.

Of these novel models of CBT, the one that has received the most attention from therapists and clinical scientists alike is ACT. This approach is based on a clinical model that stresses the goal of psychological flexibility, which is in turn based on an underlying theory of cognition known as relational frame theory (Hayes, Barnes-Holmes, & Roche, 2001; Törneke, 2010). In addition to targeting defusion and acceptance, ACT emphasizes clarification of one's key life values, articulating specific goals consistent with those values, and encouraging behavior that is consistent with those goals and values. ACT incorporates many traditional first-generation behavior therapy techniques (e.g., exposure-based interventions), while also making liberal use of metaphors and experiential exercises (Hayes, Villatte, Levin, & Hildebrandt, 2011; Hayes et al., 2013).

Clinical trials have found positive effects of ACT programs for a wide range of problems, including depression, anxiety disorders, psychotic disorders, health conditions such as chronic pain, obesity, smoking cessation, diabetes management, and even nonclinical problems like workplace productivity and stigma. Several meta-analytic reviews support the overall efficacy of ACT. In a meta-analysis of 24 studies, Hayes and colleagues (2006) concluded that ACT was effective for a wide range of psychopathology. Between-group effect sizes relative to various comparison conditions (e.g., wait-list, treatment as usual, psychoeducation, traditional cognitive therapy, attention placebo, pharmacotherapy) were large both at posttreatment ($d = .66$) and at follow-up ($d = .65$). Similar findings were reported in several subsequent meta-analyses (Öst, 2008; Powers, Vörding, & Emmelkamp, 2009; Pull, 2009; see also commentary by Levin & Hayes, 2009). Ruiz (2012) conducted a meta-analysis of 16 randomized controlled trials comparing ACT with cognitive therapy. On primary outcome measures at posttreatment, the results favored ACT. No differences were found on anxiety symptoms, although trends favoring ACT emerged for measures of depression and quality of life. Smout, Hayes, Atkins, Klausen, and Duguid (2012) concluded that there is strong evidence for the effectiveness of ACT for chronic pain, obsessive-compulsive disorder, and certain anxiety disorders, and that the methodological quality of ACT studies has increased considerably over the past few years.

Overall, the clinical outcome research on third-generation models of CBT is highly promising. Indeed, a recent review suggests that each of the major approaches now meets the criteria set forth by the American Psychological Association as empirically supported treatments (Kahl, Winter, & Schweiger, 2012).

## Treatment Mechanisms

We have already explored the importance of research on basic concepts and theories underlying psychotherapy models, as well as research on the effectiveness of the approaches themselves. A final area of research concerns the mechanisms by which treatments exert their effects. This line of inquiry connects directly both with the basic theory underlying psychotherapy models on the one hand and with treatment outcome research on the other. Building and refining the theoretical scaffolding for psychotherapies requires testing how well processes specifically hypothesized by a given model actually function in the context of clinical trials. Two primary strategies have been used to examine this issue. First, clinical component control studies examine whether the presence of a particular clinical strategy or technique adds incremental effects to an established treatment. Second, sophisticated statistical techniques assess whether the variance in treatment-related changes can be accounted for by mechanisms posited by a theory.

It is important to distinguish laboratory-based experiments of the kind described earlier, in which an analogue of a treatment component is isolated from other components under highly controlled conditions, from clinical component control studies, in which the effects of a specific treatment component are isolated from other components in an actual clinical trial. Clinical component control studies require large samples to afford sufficient statistical power to detect potential effects of interest and are therefore quite expensive to conduct. Not surprisingly, there have been relatively few such studies in the psychotherapy literature. Most component control studies have assessed the role of cognitive restructuring interventions with respect to more basic behavioral programs. For example, two meta-analyses of such studies in social anxiety disorder found no incremental effects of cognitive restructuring with respect to exposure only (Feske & Chambless, 1995; Powers, Sigmarsson, & Emmelkamp, 2008). Similarly, Jacobson et al. (1996), Gortner, Gollan, Dobson, and Jacobson (1998), and Dimidjian et al. (2006) found no evidence of incremental effects of cognitive restructuring beyond behavioral activation in the treatment of depression. These studies raise serious questions about the necessity of directly trying to change the content of one's thinking to effective treatment of mood and anxiety disorders.

To our knowledge, there have not yet been any clinical component control studies of ACT or other acceptance-based models of CBT. As discussed earlier, there is a relatively large literature documenting the effects of specific components in laboratory-based studies. For example, Branstetter, Cushing, and Douleh (2009) found that the addition of a values clarification procedure to the other components of ACT resulted in greater pain tolerance on a laboratory cold pressor task than the same ACT program without the values intervention. Although promising, it is not known if these results would generalize to actual pain patients undergoing clinical treatment.

Statistical mediation refers to a theoretical variable accounting for the variance between an independent variable (e.g., treatment condition) and a dependent variable (e.g., a measure of symptoms or functioning). The methods for conducting such analyses were introduced to the psychological literature only relatively recently, beginning in the late 1980s (Baron & Kenny, 1986), with more sophisticated approaches developed even more recently (e.g., Kraemer, Wilson, Fairburn, & Agras, 2002). Hence, the literature on mediation, although growing, remains limited.

Studies of cognitive mediation (i.e., exploring whether changes in the specific content of cognitions drives treatment effects) have been mixed, with some supportive findings but the majority of studies failing to find evidence of such effects (Longmore & Worrell, 2007). In contrast, most studies that have explored the mediating role of psychological acceptance and related variables in the context of third-generation psychotherapies have been largely supportive. For example, reductions in experimental avoidance have been shown to mediate treatment outcome in studies of test anxiety (Zettle, 2003), trichotillomania (Woods, Wetterneck, & Flessner, 2006), worksite stress (Bond & Bunce, 2000), chronic pain (McCracken, Vowles, & Eccleston, 2005), nicotine addiction (Gifford et al., 2004), epilepsy (Lundgren, Dahl, & Hayes, 2008), psychosis (Bach, Gaudiano, Hayes, & Herbert, 2013; Gaudiano & Herbert, 2006; Gaudiano, Herbert, & Hayes, 2010), and obesity (Forman et al., 2009). There are now approximately two dozen formal mediational studies of variables specified by the ACT model (psychological acceptance, defusion, and values), and the results have been surprisingly consistent in supporting the meditational effects of these factors across a wide range of populations (Hayes et al., 2013).

In summary, a rapidly growing body of evidence from various kinds of research studies is largely supportive of the role of psychological acceptance and related concepts as a target for treating various problems and for enhancing well-being and quality of life. Especially noteworthy is the wide range of problems—ranging from subclinical anxiety and depression to severe psychosis—to which interventions designed to foster psychological acceptance have been shown to be effective. In fact, some evidence is beginning to emerge that such approaches are especially effective with more severe, treatment-resistant problems, and in persons with multiple comorbid diagnoses. Nevertheless, a great deal more research is needed, including studies of the unique effects of acceptance-based treatment components.

## Conclusions and Future Directions

There is now strong evidence that psychological acceptance can be a powerful tool in coping with the inevitable distress that accompanies the human condition. A growing body of scientific research documents the benefits of acceptance and related processes not only in the formal treatment of psychological problems and disorders but also in enhancing well-being. Nevertheless, many questions remain and await further clinical innovation and research. For example, direct attempts to alter one's experience sometimes work, and at other times backfire, only intensifying distress. But it is not always obvious in any given situation when efforts to control versus to embrace one's distressing experiences are most likely to be effective. Further work is needed to clarify how best to foster acceptance in various groups of people. Although there are notable exceptions, most of the work to date has focused on adult outpatients.

We need to understand how best to disseminate these methods to both professional therapists and the public in a responsible way. A great number of self-help books featuring these concepts have been developed, and these are variable in quality. Higher quality books include those that are well grounded in scientific theory and research, offer reasonable expectations, present specific guidance for implementing self-help techniques and for monitoring treatment progress, and avoid potentially harmful prescriptions (Redding, Herbert, Forman, & Gaudiano, 2008). Meeting these criteria, however, is no guarantee of effectiveness, and research is needed to evaluate directly the efficacy of self-help books. Although studies in this area remain limited, preliminary findings are encouraging (e.g., Forsyth et al., 2011; Johnston, Foster, Shennan, Starkey, & Johnson, 2010; Muto, Hayes, & Jeffcoat, 2011). A few noteworthy books that we have found both scientifically sound and clinically useful include *Get Out of Your Mind and Into*

*Your Life: The New Acceptance and Commitment Therapy* (Hayes & Smith, 2005), *Overcoming Depression One Step at a Time: The New Behavioral Activation Approach to Getting Your Life Back* (Addis & Martell, 2004), and *The Mindfulness and Acceptance Workbook for Anxiety: A Guide to Breaking Free from Anxiety, Phobias, and Worry Using Acceptance and Commitment Therapy* (Forsyth & Eifert, 2008).

There seems to be a synergistic relationship between psychological acceptance and values clarification, but research into the latter has lagged well behind the former. For example, in a world of limited time and resources, it can sometimes be challenging to reconcile competing demands, even when all are themselves value consistent.

Most of the scientific research to date has focused on treatment, with little work explicitly focused on the prevention of problems in the first place. Given the broad scope and transdiagnostic nature of the concepts and techniques in this area, as well as their emphasis on enhancing well-being, it is possible that these approaches may be useful in primary prevention. For example, perhaps regular meditative practice, learning to defuse from and embrace routine distressing experiences, or clarifying one's values and goals may prove protective against the development of psychopathology or other problems. Biglan, Hayes, and Pistorello (2008) propose that interventions targeting experiential avoidance might be useful in prevention programs for parent training, adolescent peer influence, substance abuse, depression, and burnout among those in high-stress occupations.

Despite the movement's trendiness, solid scientific research supports the idea that enhancing psychological acceptance can accrue significant benefits, in terms of both treating psychological problems and enhancing overall well-being. The area is ripe for further creative innovations, theoretical developments, and empirical research.

# References

Addis, M. E., & Martell, C. R. (2004). *Overcoming depression one step at a time: The new behavioral activation approach to getting your life back*. Oakland, CA: New Harbinger.

Alfano, S. (2009). *Poll: Majority reject evolution*. Retrieved from www.CBSNews .com

Arch, J. J., Wolitzky-Taylor, K., Eifert, G. E., & Craske, M. G. (2012). Longitudinal treatment mediation of traditional cognitive behavioral therapy and acceptance and commitment therapy for anxiety disorders. *Behaviour Research and Therapy, 50*, 469–478.

Bach, P., Gaudiano, B. A., Hayes, S. C., & Herbert, J. D. (2013). Reduced believability of positive symptoms mediates improved hospitalization outcomes of acceptance and commitment therapy for psychosis. *Psychosis: Psychological, Social, and Integrative Approaches, 5*(2), 166–174.

Baer, R. A., Smith, G., Hopkins, J., Krietemeyer, J., & Toney, L. (2006). Using self-report assessment methods to explore facets of mindfulness. *Assessment, 13,* 27–45.

Baron, R. M., & Kenny, D. A. (1986). The moderator-mediator variable distinction in social psychological research: Conceptual, strategic, and statistical considerations. *Journal of Personality and Social Psychology, 51,* 1173–1182.

Beck, A. T., Rush, A. J., Shaw, B. F., & Emery, G. (1979). *Cognitive therapy of depression.* New York, NY: Guilford Press.

Biglan, A., Hayes, S. C., & Pistorello, J. (2008). Acceptance and commitment: Implications for prevention science. *Prevention Science, 9,* 139–152.

Bond, F. W., & Bunce, D. (2000). Mediators of change in emotion-focused and problem-focused worksite stress management interventions. *Journal of Occupational Health Psychology, 5*(1), 156–163.

Bond, F. W., Hayes, S. C., Baer, R. A., Carpenter, K. C., Guenole, N., Orcutt, H. K., . . . Zettle, R. D. (2011). Preliminary psychometric properties of the Acceptance and Action Questionnaire—II: A revised measure of psychological flexibility and acceptance. *Behavior Therapy, 42,* 676–688.

Braams, B. R., Blechert, J., Boden, M. T., & Gross, J. J. (2012). The effects of acceptance and suppression on anticipation and receipt of painful stimulation. *Journal of Behavior Therapy and Experimental Psychiatry, 43*(4), 1014–1018.

Branstetter, A. D., Cushing, C., & Douleh, T. (2009). Personal values and pain tolerance: Does a values intervention add to acceptance? *Journal of Pain, 10,* 887–892.

Brown, K. W., & Ryan, R. M. (2003). The benefits of being present: Mindfulness and its role in psychological well-being. *Journal of Personality and Social Psychology, 84,* 822–848.

Busch, A. M., Kanter, J. W., Callaghan, G. M., Baruch, D. E., Weeks, C. E., & Berlin, K. S. (2009). A micro-process analysis of functional analytic psychotherapy's mechanism of change. *Behavior Therapy, 40*(3), 280–290.

Cardaciotto, L., Herbert, J. D., Forman, E. M., Moitra, E., & Farrow, V. (2008). The assessment of present-moment awareness and acceptance: The Philadelphia Mindfulness Scale. *Assessment, 15,* 204–223.

Christensen, A., Atkins, D. C., Berns, S., Wheeler, J., Baucom, D. H., & Simpson, L. E. (2004). Traditional versus integrative behavioral couple therapy for significantly and chronically distressed married couples. *Journal of Consulting and Clinical Psychology, 72*(2), 176–191.

Christensen, A., Atkins, D. C., Yi, J., Baucom, D. H., & George, W. H. (2006). Couple and individual adjustment for 2 years following a randomized clinical trial comparing traditional versus integrative behavioral couple therapy. *Journal of Consulting and Clinical Psychology, 74*(6), 1180–1191.

Dimidjian, S., Hollon, S. D., Dobson, K. S., Schmaling, K. B., Kohlenberg, R. J., Addis, M. E., . . . Jacobson, N. S. (2006). Randomized trial of behavioral activation, cognitive therapy, and antidepressant medication in the acute treatment of adults with major depression. *Journal of Consulting and Clinical Psychology, 74*(4), 658–670.

Doss, B. D., Thum, Y. M., Sevier, M., Atkins, D. C., & Christensen, A. (2005). Improving relationships: Mechanisms of change in couple therapy. *Journal of Consulting and Clinical Psychology, 73*(4), 624–633.

Dostoevsky, F. (1988). *Winter notes on summer impressions.* Evanston, IL: Northwestern University Press (Original work published 1863).

Feske, U., & Chambless, D. L. (1995). Cognitive behavioral versus exposure only treatment for social phobia: A meta-analysis. *Behavior Therapy, 26*(4), 695–720.

Forman, E. M., Butryn, M. L., Hoffman, K. L., & Herbert, J. D. (2009). An open trial of an acceptance-based behavioral intervention for weight loss. Cognitive and Behavior Practice, 16, 223–235.

Forman, E. M., Chapman, J. E., Herbert, J. D., Goetter, E. M., Yuen, E. K., & Moitra, E. (2012). Using session-by-session measurement to compare mechanisms of action for acceptance and commitment therapy and cognitive therapy. *Behavior Therapy, 43*(2), 341–354.

Forman, E. M., Herbert, J. D., Moitra, E., Yeomans, P. D., & Geller, P. A. (2007). A randomized controlled effectiveness trial of acceptance and commitment therapy and cognitive therapy for anxiety and depression. *Behavior Modification, 31,* 772–799.

Forman, E. M., Hoffman, K. L., Juarascio, A. S., Butryn, M. L., & Herbert, J. D. (2013). Comparison of acceptance-based and standard cognitive-based coping strategies for craving sweets in overweight and obese women. *Eating Behaviors, 14,* 64–68.

Forman, E. M., Hoffman, K. L., McGrath, K. B., Herbert, J. D., Brandsma, L. L., & Lowe, M. R. (2007). A comparison of acceptance- and control-based strategies for coping with food cravings: An analog study. *Behaviour Research and Therapy, 45*(10), 2372–2386.

Forsyth, J. P., & Eifert, G. H. (2008). *The mindfulness and acceptance workbook for anxiety: A guide to breaking free from anxiety, phobias, and worry using acceptance and commitment therapy.* Oakland, CA: New Harbinger.

Forsyth, J. P., Sheppard, S. C., Hickling, E. J., Berghoff, C. R., Russo, A. R., Lehrbach, M. P., . . . Watson, D. (2011). Development of a measure of experiential avoidance: The Multidimensional Experiential Avoidance Questionnaire. *Psychological Assessment, 23*(3), 692–713.

Gamez, W., Chmielewski, M., Kotov, R., Ruggero, C., & Watson, D. (2011). Development of a measure of experiential avoidance: The Multidimensional Experiential Avoidance Questionnaire (MEAQ). *Psychological Assessment.*

Gaudiano, B. A., & Herbert, J. D. (2006). Believability of hallucinations as a potential mediator of their frequency and associated distress in psychotic inpatients. *Behavioral and Cognitive Psychotherapy, 34,* 497–502.

Gaudiano, B. A., Herbert, J. D., & Hayes, S. C. (2010). Is it the symptom or the relation to it? Investigating potential mediators of change in acceptance and commitment therapy for psychosis. *Behavior Therapy, 41*(4), 543–554.

Germer, C. K., Siegel, R. D., & Fulton, P. R. (Eds.). (2013). *Mindfulness and psychotherapy* (2nd ed.). New York, NY: Guilford Press.

Gifford, E. V., Kohlenberg, B. S., Hayes, S. C., Antonuccio, D. O., Piasecki, M. M., Rasmussen-Hall, M. L., & Palm, K. M. (2004). Acceptance-based treatment for smoking cessation. *Behavior Therapy, 35*(4), 689–705.

Gifford, E. V., Kohlenberg, B. S., Hayes, S. C., Pierson, H. M., Piasecki, M. P., Antonuccio, D. O., & Palm, K. M. (2011). Does acceptance and relationship focused behavior therapy contribute to bupropion outcomes? A randomized controlled trial of functional analytic psychotherapy and acceptance and commitment therapy for smoking cessation. *Behavior Therapy, 42*(4), 700–715.

Gortner, E. T., Gollan, J. K., Dobson, K. S., & Jacobson, N. S. (1998). Cognitive-behavioral treatment for depression: Relapse prevention. *Journal of Consulting and Clinical Psychology, 66*(2), 377–384.

Gross, G. (2014). *New year, new you: The power of meditation*. Retrieved from http://www.huffingtonpost.com.

Hayes, S. C. (2004). Acceptance and commitment therapy, relational frame theory, and the third wave of behavioral and cognitive therapies. *Behavior Therapy, 35*, 639–665.

Hayes S. C., Barnes-Holmes, D., & Roche, B. (2001). *Relational frame theory: A post-Skinnerian account of human language and cognition*. New York, NY: Kluwer Academic/Plenum.

Hayes, S. C., Levin, M., Plumb, J., Boulanger, J., & Pistorello, J. (2013). Acceptance and commitment therapy and contextual behavioral science: Examining the progress of a distinctive model of behavioral and cognitive therapy. *Behavior Therapy, 44*(2), 180–198.

Hayes, S. C., Luoma, J. B., Bond, F. W., Masuda, A., & Lillis, J. (2006). Acceptance and commitment therapy: Model, processes and outcomes. *Behavior Research and Therapy, 44*, 1–25.

Hayes, S. C., Masuda, A., Bissett, R., Luoma, J. L., & Guerrero, F. (2004). DBT, FAP, and ACT: How empirically oriented are the new behavior therapy technologies? *Behavior Therapy, 35*(1), 35–54.

Hayes, S. C., & Smith, S. (2005). *Get out of your mind and into your life: The new acceptance and commitment therapy*. Oakland, CA: New Harbinger.

Hayes, S. C., Strosahl, K. D., & Wilson, K. G. (2012). *Acceptance and commitment therapy: The process and practice of mindful change* (2nd ed.). New York, NY: Guilford Press.

Hayes, S. C., Strosahl, K. D., Wilson, K. G., Bissett, R. T., Pistorello, J., Toarmino, D., . . . McCurry, S. M. (2004). Measuring experiential avoidance: A preliminary test of a working model. *The Psychological Record, 54*, 553–578.

Hayes, S. C., Villatte, M., Levin, M., & Hildebrandt, M. (2011). Open, aware, and active: Contextual approaches as an emerging trend in the behavioral and cognitive therapies. *Annual Review of Clinical Psychology, 7*, 141–168.

Herbert, J. D., & Forman, E. M. (Eds.). (2011a). *Acceptance and mindfulness in cognitive behavior therapy: Understanding and applying the new therapies.* Hoboken, NJ: Wiley.

Herbert, J. D., & Forman, E. M. (2011b). The evolution of cognitive behavior therapy: The rise of psychological acceptance and mindfulness. In J. D. Herbert & E. M. Forman (Eds.), *Acceptance and mindfulness in cognitive behavior therapy: Understanding and applying the new therapies* (pp. 3–25). Hoboken, NJ: Wiley.

Herbert, J. D., & Forman, E. M. (2014). Mindfulness and acceptance techniques. In S. G. Hofmann & D. J. A. Dozois (Eds.), *The Wiley-Blackwell handbook of cognitive behavioral therapy* (pp. 131–156). Hoboken, NJ: Wiley-Blackwell.

Herbert, J. D., Forman, E. M., & Hitchcock, P. (in press). Contextual approaches to psychotherapy: Defining, distinguishing, and common features. In R. Zettle (Ed.), *Handbook of Contextual Behavioral Science*. West Sussex, UK: Wiley.

Herbert, J. D., Gaudiano, B. A., & Forman, E. B. (2013). The importance of theory in cognitive behavior therapy: A perspective of contextual behavioral science. *Behavior Therapy, 44*, 580–591.

Herbert, J. D., Gershkovich, M., & Forman, E. M. (2014). Acceptance and mindfulness-based therapies for social anxiety disorder: Current findings and future directions. In J. Weeks (Ed.), *Wiley-Blackwell handbook on social anxiety disorder* (pp. 588–608). Hoboken, NJ: Wiley-Blackwell.

Hofmann, S. G., Sawyer, A. T., Witt, A. A., & Oh, D. (2010). The effect of mindfulness-based therapy on anxiety and depression: A meta-analytic review. *Journal of Consulting and Clinical Psychology, 78*(2), 169–183.

Jacobson, N. S., Dobson, K. S., Truax, P. A., Addis, M. E., Koerner, K., Gollan, J. K., . . . Prince, S. E. (1996). A component analysis of cognitive-behavioral treatment for depression. *Journal of Consulting and Clinical Psychology, 64*, 295–304.

Johnston, M., Foster, M., Shennan, J., Starkey, N. J., & Johnson, A. (2010). The effectiveness of an acceptance and commitment therapy self-help intervention for chronic pain. *Clinical Journal of Pain, 26*, 393–402.

Kabat-Zinn, J. (1990). *Full catastrophe living: Using the wisdom of your mind to face stress, pain and illness.* New York, NY: Dell.

Kabat-Zinn, J. (1994). *Wherever you go, there you are: Mindfulness meditation in everyday life.* New York, NY: Hyperion.

Kabat-Zinn, J. (2005). *Coming to our senses: Healing ourselves and the world through mindfulness.* New York, NY: Hyperion.

Kahl, K. G., Winter, L., & Schweiger, U. (2012). The third wave of cognitive behavioural therapies: What is new and what is effective? *Current Opinions in Psychiatry, 25*(6), 522–528.

Kashdan, T. B., Barrios, V., Forsyth, J. P., & Steger, M. F. (2006). Experiential avoidance as a generalized psychological vulnerability: Comparisons with coping and emotion regulation strategies. *Behaviour Research and Therapy, 44*, 1301–1320.

Keng, S. L., Smoski, M. J., & Robins, C. J. (2011). Effects of mindfulness on psychological health: A review of empirical studies. *Clinical Psychology Review, 31*, 1041–1056.

Kohlenberg, R. J., Kanter, J. W., Bolling, M. Y., Parker, C. R., & Tsai, M. (2002). Enhancing cognitive therapy for depression with functional analytic psychotherapy: Treatment guidelines and empirical findings. *Cognitive and Behavioral Practice, 9*(3), 213–229.

Kohlenberg, R., & Tsai, M. (1991). *Functional analytic psychotherapy.* New York, NY: Plenum.

Kraemer, H. C., Wilson, G. T., Fairburn, C. G., & Agras, W. S. (2002). Mediators and moderators of treatment effects in randomized clinical trials. *Archives of General Psychiatry, 59,* 877–883.

Langer, E. J. (1989). *Mindfulness.* New York, NY: Addison-Wesley.

Lappalainen, R., Lehtonen, T., Skarp, E., Taubert, E., Ojanen, M., & Hayes, S. C. (2007). The impact of CBT and ACT models using psychology trainee therapists: A preliminary controlled effectiveness trial. *Behavior Modification, 31,* 488–511.

Levin, M., & Hayes, S. C. (2009). Is acceptance and commitment therapy superior to established treatment comparisons? *Psychotherapy and Psychosomatics, 78,* 380.

Levin, M. E., Hildebrandt, M. J., Lillis, J., & Hayes, S. C. (2012). The impact of treatment components suggested by the psychological flexibility model: A meta-analysis of laboratory-based component studies. *Behavior Therapy, 43,* 741–756.

Linehan, M. M., Armstrong, H. E., Suarez, A., Allmon, D., & Heard, H. L. (1991). Cognitive-behavioral treatment of chronically parasuicidal borderline patients. *Archives of General Psychiatry, 48,* 1060–1064.

Lohr, J. M. (2011). What is (and what is not) the meaning of evidence-based psychosocial intervention? *Clinical Psychology: Science and Practice, 18,* 100–104.

Longmore, R. J., & Worrell, M. (2007). Do we need to challenge thoughts in cognitive behavior therapy? *Clinical Psychology Review, 27,* 173–187.

Lundgren, T., Dahl, J., & Hayes, S. C. (2008). Evaluation of mediators of change in the treatment of epilepsy with acceptance and commitment therapy. *Journal of Behavioral Medicine, 31,* 225–235.

Marx, B. P., & Sloan, D. M. (2005). Peritraumatic dissociation and experiential avoidance as predictors of posttraumatic stress symptomatology. *Behaviour Research and Therapy, 43,* 569–583.

McCracken, L. M. (1998). Learning to live with the pain: Acceptance of pain predicts adjustment in persons with chronic pain. *Pain, 74,* 21–27.

McCracken, L. M., Vowles, K. E., & Eccleston, C. (2005). Acceptance-based treatment for persons with complex, long standing chronic pain: A preliminary analysis of treatment outcome in comparison to a waiting phase. *Behavior Research and Therapy, 43*(10), 1335–1346.

Muto, T., Hayes, S. C., & Jeffcoat, T. (2011). The effectiveness of acceptance and commitment therapy bibliotherapy for enhancing the psychological health of Japanese college students living abroad. *Behavior Therapy, 42*(2), 323–335.

Öst, L. G. (2008). Efficacy of the third wave of behavioral therapies: A systematic review and meta-analysis. *Behaviour Research and Therapy, 46*(3), 296–321.

Pew Research Center. (2013, December). *Public's views on human evolution.* Washington, DC: Author.

Powers, M. B., Sigmarsson, S. R., & Emmelkamp, P. M. G. (2008). A meta–analytic review of psychological treatments for social anxiety disorder. *International Journal of Cognitive Therapy, 1*, 94–113.

Powers, M. B., Vörding, M. B. Z. S., & Emmelkamp, P. M. G. (2009). Acceptance and commitment therapy: A meta-analytic review. *Psychotherapy and Psychosomatics, 78*, 73–80.

Pull, C. B. (2009). Current empirical status of acceptance and commitment therapy. *Current Opinion in Psychiatry, 22*, 1, 55–60.

Redding, R. E., Herbert, J. D., Forman, E. M., & Gaudiano, B. A. (2008). Popular self-help books for anxiety, depression and trauma: How scientifically grounded and useful are they? *Professional Psychology: Research and Practice, 39*, 537–545.

Rosen, G. M., & Davison, G. C. (2003). Psychology should list empirically supported principles of change (ESPs) and not credential trademarked therapies or other treatment packages. *Behavior Modification, 27*, 300–312.

Ruiz, F. J. (2012). Acceptance and commitment therapy versus traditional cognitive behavioral therapy: A systematic review and meta-analysis of current empirical evidence. *International Journal of Psychology & Psychological Therapy, 12*(2), 333–357.

Salzberg, S. (1995). *Loving-kindness: The revolutionary art of happiness.* Boston, MA: Shambala.

Sayers, W. M., & Sayette, M. A. (2013). Suppression on your own terms: Internally generated displays of craving suppression predict rebound effects. *Psychological Science, 24*, 1740–1746.

Segal, Z. V., Williams, J. M. G., & Teasdale, J. D. (2001). *Mindfulness-based cognitive therapy for depression: A new approach to preventing relapse.* New York, NY: Guilford Press.

Sevier, M., Eldridge, K., Jones, J., Doss, B. D., & Christensen, A. (2008). Observed communication and associations with satisfaction during traditional and integrative behavioral couple therapy. *Behavior Therapy, 39*(2), 137–150.

Smout, M. F., Hayes, L., Atkins, P. W. B., Klausen, J., & Duguid, J. E. (2012). The empirically supported status of acceptance and commitment therapy: An update. *Clinical Psychologist, 16*, 97–109.

Stewart, J. M. (2014). *Mindfulness, acceptance, and the psychodynamic evolution: Understanding mindfulness and acceptance processes.* Oakland, CA: New Harbinger.

Törneke, N. (2010). *Learning RFT: An introduction to relational frame theory and its clinical application.* Oakland, CA: New Harbinger.

Ventegodt, S., Thegler, S., Andreasen, T., Struve, F., Enevoldsen, L., Bassaine, L., . . . Merrick, J. (2007). Clinical holistic medicine (mindful, short-term psychodynamic psychotherapy complemented with bodywork) in the treatment of experienced physical illness and chronic pain. *The Scientific World Journal, 7,* 310–316.

Vøllestad, J., Sivertsen, B., & Nielsen, G. H. (2011). Mindfulness-based stress reduction for patients with anxiety disorders: Evaluation in a randomized controlled trial. *Behaviour Research and Therapy, 49*(4), 281–288.

Wegner, D. M., Schneider, D. J., Carter, S., & White, T. (1987). Paradoxical effects of thought suppression. *Journal of Personality and Social Psychology, 53,* 5–13.

Wells, A. (2008). *Metacognitive therapy: A practical guide.* New York, NY: Guilford Press.

Williams, J. C., & Lynn, S. J. (2010). Acceptance: An historical and conceptual review. *Imagination, Cognition and Personality, 30*(1), 5–56.

Wilson, K. G., Sandoz, E. K., & Kitchens, J. (2010). The Valued Living Questionnaire: Defining and measuring valued action within a behavioral framework. *The Psychological Record, 60,* 249–272.

Woods, D. W., Wetterneck, C. T., & Flessner, C. A. (2006). A controlled evaluation of acceptance and commitment therapy plus habit reversal for trichotillomania. *Behavior Research and Therapy, 44*(5), 639–656.

Zettle, R. D. (2003). Acceptance and commitment therapy (ACT) vs. systematic desensitization in treatment of mathematics anxiety. *Psychological Record, 53*(2), 197–215.

# PART II

## Coping and Resilience

# 5

# Stress, Coping, and Resilience in the Face of Trauma

*Anthony Papa, PhD*

*Julie Kahler, MA*

*Clair Rummel, PhD*

University of Nevada, Reno

I f people ask you to tell them about yourself, what do you say? If you are like most people, you probably start by listing social roles and relationships ("I am a mother." "I'm a good friend."), group memberships ("I'm Chinese." "I'm a lawyer."), activities that set you apart from others ("I play the saxophone."), and perhaps traits or characteristics ("I'm funny."). These statements reflect the goals and values that are central to one's identity or sense of self (Kashima, Hardie, Wakimoto, & Kashima, 2011). Opportunities to engage in activities related to self-relevant goals or values tend to be self-affirming, promote self-esteem, build self-efficacy, and are central to maintaining mental health. In this chapter, we examine stress in terms of the effects of life events on the ability to maintain a stable and valued sense of self. Further, we evaluate coping in terms of efforts to ameliorate stress that either promote resilience by bolstering our sense of self or engender dysfunction by undermining our sense of self. We next discuss how empirically based treatments for stress-related mental health difficulties can be used proactively to help cope with stressors in everyday life and prevent stress from disrupting one's life. Finally, before our concluding remarks, we present a case example that synthesizes our thoughts about how to treat problems that arise in the wake of highly aversive events.

## Stressors, Stress, and Coping

Stressors are life events that affect people's ability to fulfill goals central to their self-concept ("I am in control of my life."), violate self-defining values or beliefs ("I wouldn't hurt a fly." "People are basically good."), or challenge important aspects of identity ("I'm working toward my MBA."). Stress is the emotional experience related to having to readjust one's goals, values, or beliefs after events, such as losing a job or a loved one or marital discord, affect our ability to fulfill our goals or engage in valued, self-affirming activities. The intensity of a stress response is related to the extent to which (1) the stressor instigates thoughts, feelings, and actions antithetical to the sense of self; (2) many aspects of identity are threatened or challenged by the stressor; (3) the stressor prevents participation in identity-related activities (e.g., sports, academic pursuits); and (4) the stressor precludes engagement in such activities for a lengthy period of time (Crocker & Park, 2004; Vignoles, Regalia, Manzi, Golledge, & Scabini, 2006). For example, researchers have linked the distress from losing a job to how meaningful the job was to the person's self-image (see Papa & Maitoza, 2013). Similarly, adjustment to retirement is related to individuals' ability to engage in alternative meaningful, goal-directed activities that provide a sense of personal control, self-definition, and self-worth (e.g., van Solinge & Henkens, 2008). In the case of bereavement, researchers have linked grief severity to the extent that the death interferes with individuals' sense of security and mastery in the world at large (Bauer & Bonanno, 2001; Currier, Holland, & Neimeyer, 2009).

Moreover, whether people experience symptoms of posttraumatic stress disorder (PTSD) after a potentially traumatic event is often related to their ability to reconcile the reality of their experience and their reactions to the stressor (e.g., running away, not helping others in need) with prior beliefs about the person they are, how the world should be, and how people should treat each other (Dalgleish, 2004). The inability to reconcile pre-event beliefs with postevent perceptions of the self and the world can give rise to feelings of diminished control and increased feelings of guilt, shame, fear, and anger. These feelings can (a) lead to avoidance of people, places, and activities associated with the potentially traumatic event and related emotions and

(b) limit or preclude participation in rewarding, self-defining, goal-directed activities associated with a stable and positive sense of self (Dunmore, Clark, & Ehlers, 1999). In fact, interactions with people, places, and activities that become linked with a stressor may be experienced as punishing and thereby extinguish goal-directed behaviors, fostering a passive, ruminative response to stress in general that contributes to major depression (Dimidjian, Barrera, Martell, Muñoz & Lewinsohn, 2011), PTSD and other anxiety disorders (Foa & Kozak, 1986), and chronic grief (K. Shear et al., 2007). Stress is not just a product of challenging negative life experiences. Stress can also ensue from positive life events. For example, getting the job you always wanted or getting married involves major life changes requiring considerable adjustment in the goals and activities we pursue on a day-to-day basis.

Coping describes what we do to alleviate stress. Coping encompasses efforts to change a stressor itself, manage emotional reactions to a stressor, or reassess the importance of a threatened belief or other aspect of identity. Some situations are easier to cope with than others. For example, if stress is related to limited finances, effective, problem-focused coping could involve getting a higher paying job or asking for a raise. If such problem-focused approaches are not possible, then managing one's emotional reactions or reexamining the importance of money, for example, becomes more important (e.g., Park, Folkman, & Bostrom, 2001). Managing emotions might include blowing off steam to a friend, playing sports to provide distraction, or using alcohol or drugs to suppress disturbing feelings. Over time, though, focusing exclusively on managing emotions can be exhausting and maladaptive because focusing inward and away from a problem doesn't solve it. Nevertheless, when people cannot exert any control over a situation, as in some cases of chronic illness, then trying to problem solve to change the unchangeable may prove to be futile and demoralizing. In this instance, revisiting what is truly important and revising one's goals or finding a proverbial silver lining, such as becoming closer to friends and family or stronger as a person, can be essential (Cheng, 2003).

## Resilience, Flexibility, and Stability

Resilience is not a personality variable. Resilience is maintaining relatively good functioning, positive mood, and mental health across situations—both the good and the bad (see Bonanno, 2012). Still, some people are born with a genetic predisposition to be more or less sensitive to changes in their environment (e.g., Caspi et al., 2003), and some personality variables do predispose individuals to act in ways that promote resilience in some situations

(Bonanno, 2012). For example, the normally noxious characteristic of being overly self-absorbed and self-promoting can be adaptive in circumstances in which stressors are chronic and when little can be done to change the situation, such as after bereavement or experiencing terrorism (e.g., Bonanno, Field, Kovacevic & Kaltman, 2002; Bonanno, Rennicke, & Dekel, 2005). Similarly, habitual avoidance of emotions is adaptive for some people in the immediate aftermath of an adverse event, although this pattern of response may be harmful in the long term (e.g., Fraley & Bonanno, 2004; M. K. Shear, 2010). Still, virtually anyone can learn to be more resilient. Research on the characteristics that distinguish between those who are most resilient to stress versus those who are not suggests several areas people might cultivate in order to help be less reactive to stress. First, having a number of obligations, social roles, and daily routines may be protective in dealing with stressful events (Cohen, 2004; Pat-Horenczyk, Schifff, & Doppelt, 2006). There are a few explanations for this protective effect. People with the greatest range of obligations and roles may simply have larger social networks, more social support resources (people who provide opportunities to vent to, ask for help, or get sympathy), and thus more opportunity to feel supported. Another explanation is that a varied social network—one that includes family, coworkers, and people from the bowling league, church, and a weekly poker game—means that if something stressful happens in one area of life, such as at work, social resources in the nondisrupted parts of the social network are available to help cope. In the case of bereavement, the most resilient individuals typically are able to maintain a sense of stability and meaning, even after the loss of a meaningful relationship, by continuing engagement with other rewarding or meaningful aspects of their lives, such as work, bowling league, or church (e.g., Baruch & Barnett, 1986; Bonanno, 2009). Conversely, disruptions of daily routines and lack of access to rewarding or meaningful activities undermine self-esteem and efficacy and have been linked to psychopathology (e.g., Prigerson, Frank, Reynolds, George, & Kupfer, 1993). Accordingly, one way to promote resilience to stress is to cultivate a sense of self based on a multiplicity or range of social roles and life goals, so that no single event can destabilize all the aspects of life central to one's self-concept (e.g., Brown & Rafaeli, 2007). People with broad-based, complex self-concepts derive their sense of self from diverse reinforcers and are therefore relatively immune to the adverse impact of any single stressor. Consequently, they tend to report more stable and positive mood over time (Koch & Shepard, 2004; Linville, 1987), which enhances their ability to marshal personal resources when coping with stress (e.g., A. B. Burns et al., 2008).

A second characteristic that distinguishes resilient from nonresilient people is the ability to accurately assess which aspects of stressor situations are controllable. This ability allows resilient individuals to tailor effective, problem-focused coping responses that capitalize on what can be changed and identify what cannot be changed. In unpredictable, uncontrollable, and chronically stressful situations (e.g., caring for a loved one with a terminal disease), focusing on aspects of one's self (rather than the situation) that can be changed, such as one's emotions, values, or goals, may promote better adjustment compared with active problem-focused coping approaches (Cheng, 2003). As stated in the serenity prayer, having the wisdom to know what can be changed and working to accept what can't be changed is essential for optimum coping and adjustment. People who flexibly calibrate their coping responses to situational demands tend to experience higher levels of well-being compared with individuals who exhibit inflexible, rigid, avoidant patterns of coping (e.g., Kashdan & Rottenberg, 2010; Park et al., 2001). Thus, another way one might become less reactive to stress is to practice identifying and testing what aspects of situations are under one's control and how one might effect change in the context of different, less pressing situations in order to develop this skill for when the need to cope is more urgent.

For those seeking to build resilience in their daily lives, it is important to note that these two ways to promote resilience may not be mutually exclusive. The ability to flexibly cope with stress is contingent on having enough perspective about one's situation to discern what might realistically be done about it. Having the emotional distance to allow for such perspective taking may be contingent on having already cultivated a sense of self based on a range of social roles involving engagement in a number of goal-related activities. Stability in our environment and decreased reactivity to challenging situations allows us to experience continuity and stability in our self-concept, as our ability to cope is not overwhelmed by the situations we encounter, thus affording a sense of control over our lives, perspective about our situations, and the grounding to flexibly assess and engage with stressor situations (e.g., Bauer & Bonnano, 2001).

## Stress-Related Health Problems in the Healthcare Delivery System

Stress can impair our physical and mental well-being. Although the most common responses to stress are adequate coping and resilience, some people, in some situations, experience long-term problems and psychological disorders that include major depressive disorder, PTSD, adjustment disorder, and other anxiety responses as well as high levels of substance abuse, impulsivity, and aggression (e.g., Benjet, Borges & Medina-Mora, 2010;

Milliken, Auchterlonie, & Hoge, 2007). Most of these stress-related conditions are maintained by avoidance of the stressor or are triggered by reminders of the stressor (e.g., K. Shear et al. 2007). All are associated with high levels of fight-or-flight responding and increased cortisol production, contributing to physical illness and mortality due to cardiovascular disease, hypertension, and compromised immune functioning (McEwan, 1998; Segerstrom & Miller, 2004). High levels of cortisol can also impair hippocampus functioning (associated with memory storage and retrieval), executive brain functioning, and the ability to make decisions and get adequate sleep (e.g., see Chapter 8, "Sleeping Well"; Johnson et al., 2002). Moreover, the severity of stress-related conditions tends to wax and wane depending on daily stress. Accordingly, preexisting problems with anxiety or mood may become more intense and debilitating at the worst possible time, as individuals cope with subsequent stressors.

Generally, psychosocial treatments for stress are designed to help individuals to be less reactive to stress by addressing three interrelated areas: (1) behavioral responding and repertoires; (2) interpretations about people, situations, and the self; and (3) ability to regulate emotional reactivity to events. In the following section, we outline the specific practices and principles of the formal treatment protocols used by healthcare professionals to treat stress reactions and how the treatments may be employed for effective self-management of stress.

## Techniques That Target How People Act or Behave in Events or Situations

In the face of a severe stressor, our instinct may be to disengage from the environment to reduce exposure to other potential stressors, to conserve resources to focus on the problem at hand, or to avoid the aversive feelings associated with engagement with the stressor. At first, avoidance can afford people time and opportunity to think clearly about the causes and consequences of a stressor before they engage in problem solving or emotion-focused coping (Bonanno, Wortman, et al., 2002). Nevertheless, if avoidance is prolonged, it can create greater problems than those caused by the original stressor: Continued avoidance and disengagement can narrow behavioral, cognitive, and emotional repertoires to the point that they lack the flexibility or breadth to meet everyday challenges. The primary goal of behavioral therapies, such as systematic desensitization (Wolpe, 1961), exposure therapy (Foa & Rothbaum, 1998), and behavioral activation (e.g., Dimidjian et al., 2011), is to reduce avoidance by helping people make contact with what provides meaning and purpose in life or by mitigating debilitating reactivity to reminders of the stressful event. If the experience of stress is related to a high-impact, physically dangerous event like assault, it can be adaptive to avoid situations in which assault is particularly risky. But what if the stress is job related? Avoiding work is likely to exacerbate, rather than diminish, stress.

In addition to narrowing coping repertoires, another problem with avoidance is that it tends to generalize: The same adverse reactions that accompanied the original stressor can come to be triggered by cues or reminders of the stressor in a variety of novel and nondangerous situations and thereby promote avoidance of these situations as well. For example, people can begin to avoid not only places or situations associated with a sexual assault (e.g., dating, bars) but also aspects of the assault more generally, such as interacting with individuals that resemble their attacker in some small way, walking down the street, or the feeling of being out of control, thereby constricting their lives so severely that it undermines their ability to function. Generally speaking, maladaptive avoidance and behavioral constriction can cause problems to be magnified, creating a cycle of increased stress and subsequent avoidance. Although assault may seem to be an extreme example, it is similar to everyday procrastination in that merely thinking about what is being avoided engenders stress, which builds with subsequent reminders, until not only the task is avoided but the reminders as well!

Systematic desensitization, exposure therapy, and behavioral activation all help people to overcome avoidance and increase goal-directed activity to facilitate full reengagement with life. Prolonged exposure therapy (PE) accomplishes this by (a) inviting people to engage in imagined or real-life approximations of situations or feelings they avoid in order to overcome debilitating emotional reactions to stressors and (b) assisting people to learn that they can exert control and appreciate that they are not helpless when they confront stress-producing situations and emotions (Foa & Rothbaum, 1998). In short, exposure involves practice facing one's fears and mastering the fear associated with these confrontations in order to promote a sense of mastery and self-control. PE has been found to be an effective treatment for PTSD (e.g., Powers, Halpern, Ferenschak, Gillihan, & Foa, 2010), acute stress disorder (Kornør et al., 2008), and prolonged, unresolved grief (e.g., Boelen & van den Bout, 2007). Exposure is a critical component of most empirically supported treatments for anxiety disorders (Olatunji, Cisler, & Deacon, 2010).

Systematic desensitization (SD; Wolpe, 1961), a variant of PE, involves proactively confronting potentially stressful stimuli in a step-wise manner, often in imagination, as mental preparation in advance of facing real-life stress-producing events like surgery, fighting fires, or combat. In terms of cultivating resilience to stress, self-guided SD is a way to practice experiencing and overcoming feelings of stress in a graduated, manageable way. In fact, an approach that uses the principles of SD called *Stress Inoculation Training* (SIT; Meichenbaum, 1985) is so named because it inoculates or immunizes people to the effects of stress by allowing them to practice overcoming it in various performance situations. Self-guided SD/SIT can be a helpful way to build resilience to an anticipated or recurrent stressor. For instructions, see Chapter 14 ("Coping Skills Training for Fears," pp. 187, 204) of *The Relaxation and Stress Reduction Workbook* by Davis, Eshelman, and McKay (2008).

Although workbooks are available for SD/SIT and for PE for posttraumatic reactions (e.g., *Reclaiming Your Life from a Traumatic Experience Workbook;* Rothbaum, Foa, & Hembree 2007), self-guided exposure techniques can be risky without the guidance of a trained mental health professional. Reducing avoidance and promoting resilience are the goals of these techniques. Nevertheless, if the stressor is related to inherently destructive or dangerous behaviors, like driving aggressively or placing oneself at risk for being assaulted, then the goal is not to reduce avoidance of such activities. Instead, exposure techniques could be used to decrease avoidance that has generalized to other behaviors or feelings that interfere with optimal day-to-day functioning. Self-guided exposure can be problematic because it can be difficult to discern objectively when avoidance is adaptive and when it is destructive. The ability to be objective in deciding when to engage with previously experienced aversive events is further complicated because it is not uncommon for people who have experienced traumatic events to reenact the event, either in an attempt to master it or because they are so avoidant of their reactions (e.g., being fearful), that they ignore signs of danger in the environment that cues them to back away before they get hurt again (e.g., Cloitre & Rosenberg, 2006).

In contrast, self-guided behavioral activation might be accomplished successfully using a good workbook. *Overcoming Depression One Step at a Time* by Michael Addis and Christopher Martell (2004; see also Moss, Scogin, DiNapoli, & Presnell, 2012) and *A Cancer Patient's Guide to Overcoming Depression and Anxiety* by Derek Hopko and Carl Lejuez (2008) present approaches to behavioral activation that have been used to successfully treat anxiety and depression responses in multiple populations (e.g., Mazzucchelli, Kane & Rees, 2009; Papa, Sewell, Garrison-Diehn, & Rummel, 2013). In addition, there is a nascent literature on the efficacy of behavioral activation as an effective treatment for PTSD (e.g., Jakupcak et al., 2010) and pathological grief (e.g., Papa et al., 2013). Although the workbooks mentioned earlier were written for people experiencing depression or coping with cancer, the techniques outlined in both books can be used by anyone to alleviate and master stress.

Behavioral activation can be used to minimize avoidance and expand contact with valued activities in at least two ways. One way is to schedule pleasant events that are rewarding, nondestructive, make one feel good, or contribute to a burgeoning sense of mastery. Another approach targets avoidant behaviors that disrupt positive moods and engender problems in everyday functioning and increases goal-directed coping and behavior. The workbooks listed above focus on the latter approach. Both approaches increase engagement in self-defining activities that bolster self-efficacy and identity stability, consistent with the value placed on promoting self-complexity discussed earlier. In terms of translating these principles to self-help and cultivating resilience to stress, at the core of these approaches is making an effort to do all the things central to one's self-concept, staying engaged with one's troubles (though not directly when the source of the stress might cause you harm!), trying to solve problems proactively, and identifying and reducing avoidance. Sometimes when individuals feel over-whelmed by stress, this could mean having to "fake it until you make it," until activities that were formerly pleasurable feel good again.

Behavioral activation may also involve making sure one is partaking in appropriate self-care (e.g., getting enough sleep, nutrition, exercise, and lei-sure time) and that these self-care activities become part of a daily routine. Regular routines provide a sense of security and control when other aspects of life are hectic and chaotic. Behavioral activation may further involve engaging in activities that not just are enjoyable but also afford a sense of meaning and purpose that bolster feelings of accomplishment that boosts self-efficacy, which affects how ambitious goals are set and whether they are achieved (e.g., Carver & Sheier, 1998). Finally, behavioral activation might entail keeping careful track of day-to-day activities and how mood fluctuates with such activities; identifying situations that engender avoidance and rumination; and practicing adaptive, proactive alternatives to avoidance and rumination.

## Techniques That Target How One Thinks and Interprets Events or Situations

Lazarus and Folkman's (1984) cognitive coping theory is one of the most influential descriptions to date of how people cope with stress. According to this theory, if an event is assessed as self-relevant, because it is likely to affect day-to-day functioning or well-being, it leads individuals to secondarily assess their ability to manage the situation. This assessment encompasses (a) a review of how they coped in similar situations; (b) general beliefs regarding their ability to effect change in life; (c) beliefs regarding the fairness of the world or other people; and (d) the extent to which their social, health, and financial resources are sufficient to manage the situation at hand. Stress is experienced when individuals make the attribution that their ability or resources to address the stressor will be inadequate. Influencing this assessment, and sometimes distorting it, is the fact that people often organize their sense of self around the idea that the world is predictable and that we get what we deserve (Hafer & Begue, 2005). To preserve beliefs that the world is just, predictable, and thus controllable, people often have to work hard to find positive personal implications and minimize negative implications (finding the silver lining) of aversive events. In some cases, stressful events may violate just world beliefs and rock our fundamental assumptions of the world, our place in it, and our future, destabilizing virtually every aspect of our lives.

A basic premise of cognitive therapy (CT; Beck, 1976) is that negative beliefs about the self, the world, and the future related to expectations of unpredictability and uncontrollability of events lead to automatic interpretations about the meaning or consequences of events that in turn influence mood and cause us to act in maladaptive ways. Negative expectations about the ability to predict and control life events lead to self-protective, reflexive, or automatic tendencies to focus on the negative aspects of situations while ignoring positive aspects, think in all-or-nothing or black-and-white terms (e.g., complete success or failure or totally good or bad), or impose feelings or beliefs inappropriately on situations or other people by habitually predicting or focusing on poor or catastrophic possible outcomes. When preexisting beliefs lead to interpretations that are distorted, exaggerated, or inaccurate, the ability to cope effectively is impaired because individuals are not accounting for critical information inherent in each unique situation. Ignoring aspects of a situation can only hamper one's ability to effectively deal with what is happening, making it difficult, if not impossible, to problem solve and cope optimally.

Over time, accumulations of unresolved stressors can increase the sense of helplessness and erode self-efficacy, leading to habitual avoidance and disengagement from goal-directed activities as a primary means to cope with stress. Avoidance can, in turn, reduce reinforcement from engaging in identity-consistent activities, while unresolved pressing problems can spiral out of control, providing fodder for the beliefs that one is helpless, incapable, unlovable, and so forth. Moreover, consistently viewing the self and interactions with the world as negative facilitates the recall of memories congruent with our negative beliefs and inhibits positive memories (e.g., feeling empowered, capable, loved) incongruent with these beliefs (e.g., Hamilton & Gotlib, 2008). The grim expectations emanating from this sense of the world can undermine the ability or motivation to effect change (e.g., Mathews & MacLeod, 2005) and promote rumination about the nature and consequences of the stressor and the inability to change the situation—all framed within the thoughts that contributed to the situation being unresolved in the first place. This trap can be difficult to escape. For example, rumination increases negative thinking, decreases flexible problem solving, and magnifies feelings of hopelessness or powerlessness, leading to withdrawal and avoidance as a way to cope, further amplifying the problem (Nolen-Hoeksema, Wisco, & Lyubomirsky, 2008).

CT challenges these habitual patterns of thinking by inviting individuals to test if predicted and feared negative outcomes occur when they experiment with alternative interpretations of events and means of coping. Challenging maladaptive habitual patterns of thinking in order to develop and substitute more accurate interpretations and attributions is called *cognitive restructuring*. Cognitive restructuring first entails tracking situations that are interpreted as particularly stressful, the actions and feelings that stem from the interpretation, and the consequences of the actions or feelings. Cognitive restructuring then explores alternative interpretations that promote more adaptive resolution of distressing situations. The goal is to reduce suffering by engaging in more accurate, adaptive ways of thinking and acting during and after stress-provoking situations. Research has shown that CT is an effective treatment for depression, PTSD, and many anxiety disorders, including panic disorder and social anxiety disorder (e.g., Butler, Chapman, Forman, & Beck, 2006; Hans & Hiller, 2013; Hollon & Ponniah, 2010; Stewart & Chambless, 2009). Two particularly useful guides to cognitive restructuring are the *Feeling Good Handbook* by David Burns (1999; see Scogin, Welsh, Hanson, Stump, & Coates, 2005) and *Mind Over Mood* by Greenberger and Padesky (1995; see Whitfield, Williams & Shapiro, 2001).

## Techniques Targeting How One Feels in Events or Situations

Ultimately, changing behaviors and automatic interpretations of stressful events improve functioning by ameliorating emotional pain. For example, exposure therapy is hypothesized to reduce avoidance and bolster resilience by diminishing the intensity of emotional distress associated with memories or situations similar to events experienced as aversive or traumatic. Repeated, deliberate re-exposure to distressing aspects of highly traumatic or aversive events associated with intense emotional distress—to the point that the experience comes to be tolerable and the feared consequences of exposure mitigated—is hypothesized to gradually reduce the intensity of distress triggered by stress-related stimuli (see Foa & Kozak, 1986).

Nevertheless, some people's reactions to stressors are so intense, and their patterns of thinking so deeply ingrained, that changing their behavior or challenging their interpretations is neither realistic nor feasible. Similarly, sometimes stress is related to situations that are truly beyond our ability to control and reconcile with our values. Fortunately, in such cases, effective treatment protocols based on mindfulness, nonjudgmental awareness, and acceptance are available to reduce the potency of reactions to stressors (e.g., fear, guilt, shame, hopelessness) and facilitate the ability to examine and modify negative beliefs, interpretations, and avoidance of emotional responses (see Chapter 3, "Effective Problem Solving," acceptance, mindfulness).

In addition to acceptance and nonjudgmental awareness, mindfulness and acceptance-based techniques often encompass practicing being compassionate and expressing gratitude to oneself and others (Coffey, Hartman, & Fredrickson, 2010; Sheldon & Lubormirsky, 2006; see Chapter 11, "What Psychological Science Knows About Achieving Happiness"). Other exercises focus on present-moment mindful awareness, which entails focusing attention on what is happening in the present and not letting expectations, judgments, and memories distract one from being present in the moment (Killingsworth & Gilbert, 2010). All of these exercises contribute to well-being by reducing avoidance, rumination, and distorted, self-fulfilling interpretations of events. In fact, regular meditation has been found to reduce physiological reactivity to stress and improve physical well-being, even in patients undergoing chemotherapy for cancer (e.g., Grossman, Niemann, Schmidt, & Walach, 2004; Ott, Norris, & Bauer-Wu, 2006).

Mindfulness-Based Stress Reduction (MBSR; Kabat-Zinn, 1990; see Chapter 7, "Chilling Out: Meditation, Relaxation, and Yoga") uses relaxation and attentional control techniques, practiced in the context of a mindfulness meditation group, to promote acceptance and nonjudgmental awareness of thoughts and feelings. Mindfulness-Based Cognitive Therapy (MBCT; Teasdale et al., 2000) combines cognitive therapy with mindfulness meditation as a means to promote awareness of automatic thoughts and negative interpretations, restructure ruminative and maladadptive thoughts and decrease their believability, and enhance effective problem solving. Similarly, Acceptance and Commitment Therapy (ACT; Hayes, Strosahl, & Wilson, 1999) views maladaptive responses to stressors as inflexible, ineffective, and excessive attempts to control unwanted/intrusive thoughts and emotions through experiential avoidance (e.g., suppressing or avoiding negative thoughts and feelings). The main goal of ACT is to increase psychological flexibility and fortify resilience by (a) increasing acceptance of the full gamut of human experiences, (b) cultivating present moment awareness skills, (c) decreasing experiential avoidance using verbal metaphors and mindfulness exercises, and (d) teaching behavioral change skills and facilitating behavioral activation and committed action consistent with personal values.

In addition to promoting nonjudgmental awareness, the aforementioned approaches focus on increasing radical acceptance. Radical acceptance entails allowing oneself to experience aversive emotional states without trying to suppress, avoid, or distract oneself from the emotional response or the environmental triggers of that response (Hayes et al., 2004). Practicing radical acceptance allows for greater engagement in life and allows for more contextually appropriate coping responses. Over time, enhanced coping efficacy associated with increased acceptance engenders a number of positive outcomes, including increases in self-esteem and self-efficacy, willingness to confront challenging situations, and decreased attachment to the belief that the world is dangerous or the self is weak (Jain et al., 2007).

Nevertheless, reducing or eliminating experiential avoidance and suppression should not be ends unto themselves. Avoidance becomes problematic when it becomes the de facto means of coping with distressing events. Flexible, strategic use of emotional suppression and avoidance, as well as focusing away or distracting from distressing events, can reduce the subjective experience of negative emotion and increase adaptive adjustment in the immediate aftermath of stressful events, ranging from bereavement to adjusting to college (e.g., Boscarino & Figley, 2009; Galatzer-Levy, Burton, & Bonanno, 2012). Sometimes taking breaks is necessary to recharge and allow people to reengage with problems (e.g., Keltner & Bonanno, 1997). For example, expression of genuine positive emotion during bereavement has been associated with reduced arousal from experiencing negative emotion; more positive, fluid thinking; and increased engagement of social support (Coifman & Bonanno, 2010; Keltner & Bonanno, 1997; Papa & Bonanno, 2008).

Nonetheless, mindfulness-based approaches appear to be an effective means to cope with stress. For example, Mindfulness-Based Cognitive Therapy has been shown to reduce or prevent relapse for those recovering from major depressive disorder (e.g., Hollon & Ponniah, 2010; Piet & Hougaard, 2011). Preliminary evidence suggests that both Mindfulness-Based Stress Reduction and ACT have salubrious effects on mental and physical distress related to depression, anxiety, and adversity (e.g., Bohlmeijer, Prengera, Taala, & Cuijpers, 2010; Grossman et al., 2004; Smout, Hayes, Atkins, Klausen, & Duguid, 2012). Guides to these mindfulness-based treatment protocols include *Get Out of Your Mind and Into Your Life* by Steve Hayes and Spencer Smith (2005; see Jeffcoat & Hayes, 2012), *A Mindfulness-Based Stress Reduction Workbook* by Bob Stahl and Elisha Goldstein (2010), and *Full Catastrophe Living* by Jon Kabat-Zinn (1990).

## Caveat Emptor

A plethora of other therapies exist but have little or no evidential basis to warrant their claim to treat maladaptive stress responses. A limited list of these therapies include Thought Field (Callahan & Callahan, 1996) and Emotional Freedom (Craig, 2010) therapies, which posit that tapping on the points where invisible thought fields intersect with the body remove emotional blockages; equine-assisted therapies (Selby & Smith-Osbourne, 2013); and Traumatic Incident Reduction (Gerbode, 1989), based on principles of Scientology (see Lohr, Devilly, Lilienfeld, & Olatunji, 2006; Norcross, Koocher, & Garofalo, 2006, for more complete lists and critiques of these therapies).

One common approach that is not supported by the empirical literature for use with the general population is post-event psychological debriefing interventions (PD), which are aimed at preventing the onset of PTSD. The most common of such interventions are Critical Incident Stress Debriefing (Mitchell & Everly, 2001) and Critical Incident Stress Management (Everly & Mitchell, 1999). These are group interventions in which individuals' review their experiences, emotional reactions, and coping in the days after potentially traumatic events like mass violence, natural disasters, and traumatic loss of loved ones. In general, in populations in which individuals are not exposed to potentially traumatizing events as a part of their profession, PD is not consistently associated with improvement in adjustment (Litz, Gray, Bryant, & Adler, 2002; McNally, Bryant, & Ehlers, 2003). Research findings are more positive when debriefing interventions are conducted in the context in which exposure to adverse events is a routine part of a profession (e.g., firefighters, military personnel; Battlemind debriefing; Adler, Bliese, McGurk, Hoge, & Castro, 2009). Nevertheless, much of the extant research lacks adequate controls to draw strong inferences regarding effectiveness. In contrast, to treat overwhelming reactions in the aftermath of a trauma, CT and PE have enjoyed considerable empirical support and have a wide range of applications (see Litz et al. 2002). In the case of post-bereavement pathology particularly, watchful waiting is advocated, absent any acute condition such as suicidality or severe substance abuse (Papa & Litz, 2011).

Another approach with a limited scientific foundation for use with stress reactions is Eye Movement Desensitization and Reprocessing (EMDR; F. Shapiro, 2001), which was developed to treat PTSD. EMDR uses exposure and cognitive techniques similar to those used in CT and PE, free association techniques derived from psychoanalysis to aid in recall of events, and a unique dual attention technique to assist in purportedly reprocessing and reducing anxiety associated with memories of traumatic events. The most common dual attention technique is inviting clients to recall traumatic memories while they move their eyes back and forth, tracking a finger or pen the clinician moves across their visual field (alternating tones in earphones or taps on the hand are sometimes substituted for eye movements). Clinical outcome studies have supported the efficacy of EMDR for PTSD (Bisson et al., 2007). Nevertheless, practitioners who use EMDR have expanded its use to other problems, ranging from general anxiety disorders to depression, stress, eating disorders, and body dysmorphic disorder, among others (e.g., R. Shapiro, 2009). Research assessing EMDR's use for anxiety disorders, other than PTSD, consists mainly of case studies and poorly designed clinical trials that provide little to no compelling evidence that EMDR is effective for these problems (see de Jongh & ten Broeke, 2009, for a review). An additional controversy is the clinical utility of the dual attention techniques, which proponents state are the key change mechanism in this therapeutic approach. Dual attention techniques in EMDR are hypothesized to help in the "re-processing" of trauma memories by facilitating the dissociation of emotional distress from memories of traumatic events, as in exposure therapy. The rhythmic nature of these attentional techniques is hypothesized to stimulate loosely defined neural systems related to information processing. Component studies and comparisons of EMDR to exposure therapy have not found these attentional techniques to be an active change agent over and above the elements of exposure therapy in EMDR protocols (see Benish, Imel, & Wampold, 2008; Hembree, Cahill, & Foa, 2003, for reviews). Reviews supporting the use of dual attention techniques have critical flaws that temper any conclusions that can be drawn from them (e.g., Lee & Cuijpers, 2013).

## Case Study Illustrating Best Practices

The following is a de-identified case of a person seen in our clinic for trouble adjusting to life after the loss of a spouse. The primary presenting problems were her inability to control her overwhelming longing for her spouse's return, crying much of the time, and loss of purpose in life. In this case, behavioral activation techniques were used to help the client rebuild a sense of meaning, purpose, and control in her life by promoting more flexible, contextually appropriate responses to changes in her life due to her spouse's death.

Mrs. X was a 49-year-old widow with no children. Beginning 18 months prior to this narrative, she experienced a series of deaths in her family. Her husband, father, and sister all died within 8 months of each other. Her husband, whose death had the greatest impact on her, was diagnosed with terminal cancer the same week her father died unexpectedly, and he passed away 4 months later, followed 3 months later by her sister from breast cancer. Mrs. X was the caregiver for her husband and sister and planned funerals for all three family members. At the time of these deaths, she was unemployed, having given up her administrative assistant job to provide ongoing care for her elderly mother. Mrs. X met diagnostic criteria for major depressive disorder and the DSM-5 (American Psychiatric Association, 2013) criteria for pervasive grief. She had been attending a weekly grief support group for 8 months, but her symptoms had not lessened. Her grief symptoms consisted of feelings of longing and yearning for her husband, father, and sister, which occurred several times a day and interfered with her ability to focus on daily tasks; feeling stunned and dazed by the losses; and experiencing a high level of confusion about her role in life on a daily basis. Her depression symptoms consisted of loss of interest and pleasure in things she used to enjoy and depressed mood; she also suffered from survivor guilt. She had also gained considerable weight while caring for her family, valuing their well-being above her own. However, her main difficulty was making decisions about the future. Rather than problem solve or plan, she ruminated for hours every day about what her husband would have wanted her to do, the question of whether making decisions would mean leaving him behind, and the unfairness of his death and having to face the quandary of decisions on her own.

She had been married 26 years and relied on her husband for financial support and social contact, as he was much more outgoing than she was. In terms of hobbies, her husband had been an old car buff, and she had enjoyed going to antique car meets and meetings of the local enthusiast club but stopped participating after he died. Other hobbies included going to movies with her husband and eating at restaurants, for which they would plan frequent overnight trips. She reported no other strong interests prior to the loss of her husband, other than going out dancing when she was in high school. After her husband's death, Mrs. X lost their home, as she was unable to make the payments due to quitting her job to care for her elderly mother. She had not talked to the friends she had made with her husband since his death, stating it was awkward without him present and that her distress was too burdensome for others to be around. Her other main source of social interaction centered around her job, which she had previously found enjoyable and rewarding, and her niece, whom she had not seen since her sister's funeral. Although she found some meaning in caring for her elderly mother, life felt empty and unfulfilling. Mrs. X avoided reminders of her husband, such as the storage unit filled with their furniture, the church they attended, and contacts with members of their social circle. She had withdrawn from the world and avoided social contact for fear that someone would ask about the deaths and her intense emotional response to their question would be alienating.

She presented with feeling overwhelmed and helpless. Given that significant time had passed since the loss of her husband and that his death was continuing to influence her daily functioning, she and the clinic therapist agreed that addressing the lack of meaning and purpose in her life and the extensive daily rumination in which she engaged was a critical treatment goal. After discussing her options, they decided that behavioral activation would be an appropriate way to build meaningful, reinforcing activities; help her to decide what to do with her life; and address extensive ruminations, which were interfering with engagement in other options. To do this, she was assigned the workbook *Overcoming Depression One Step at a Time* by Addis and Martell (2004) and assigned to a therapist coach to work through the material.

Using the workbook, Mrs. X learned how the series of losses she experienced had affected her daily routine and sense of self and delineated how the direct and indirect changes she had experienced during the loss, coupled with her ongoing grief and depression symptoms, had a profound influence on her ability to meet the daily challenges of life. The workbook also outlined how Mrs. X's symptoms were manifested in behaviors that maintained her symptoms. She then used the workbook to focus on making a series of small, manageable changes in the way she lived her life, identifying and seeking out activities that were meaningful and rewarding by changing the way she responded to people and situations that might be disconnecting her from the things she wanted.

She worked through the workbook over a 14-week period, checking in periodically with her therapist/coach. Mrs. X began by using the daily activity monitoring sheets provided by the workbook. Examination of Mrs. X's daily activity monitoring sheets brought the realization that she was not grieving all day as she thought but instead experienced intense moments of grief at discrete points in the day—mostly when she was ruminating. This finding surprised Mrs. X but highlighted that her symptoms were not constant, arbitrary, or out of control. This realization also highlighted that Mrs. X's daily life mainly consisted of caretaking for her mother, avoiding grief triggers such as old friends, church activities, and sorting through the storage unit of items from her old house, with no activity being particularly rewarding or meaningful. By the third week of treatment, Mrs. X's short-term goals were to explore employment options and how she could reconnect with friends. Meeting these goals entailed using the workbook to pinpoint situations in which her responses to reminders of her losses may have helped to maintain her symptoms and interfered with her ability to achieve her goals. She then used the workbook to develop a series of small manageable steps to change the situations she targeted and her responses to them.

Bedtimes emerged as a particularly hard time as she reviewed the demands of the day in the quiet before bedtime, which led predictably to ruminating about her losses. Sleep-interfering thoughts included a mental review of her sister's and husband's last few weeks of life and her regret at not being able to better alleviate their pain and suffering. These thoughts would remind her of how much her expectations for her life had changed and lead to worry about the future. Her rumination-fueled inability to fall asleep made it difficult for her to think clearly or to meet her responsibilities during the next day, further eroding her self-confidence. Although sleep hygiene was moderately effective (getting up the same time every day, not napping, using the bedroom for sleep only, not allowing herself to lie in bed if unable to sleep due to rumination, etc.), she found that the strength of the association of bedtime with rumination was hard to overcome.

The deleterious effects of rumination on her ability to meet her goals, and especially her ability to make concrete decisions, were not due only to lack of sleep. Rumination also served to distract her from focusing on the demands of her life, and when she did focus on day-to-day demands, it interfered with her ability to concentrate and problem solve. In many cases, her ruminative behavior was triggered by any situation that highlighted how her life had changed or any situation that required planning. Instead of focusing on what her life had become and how she wanted her life to be, she ruminated on the deaths, her inability to alleviate the suffering of her loved ones, the prospect of a less emotionally satisfying future without her husband, her worry of what might happen to her, and the unfairness of it all. Although rumination functioned to help her stay disengaged from the painful reality of her life without the deceased, by focusing on these negative thoughts and memories, she magnified her emotional distress to the point that she felt constantly overwhelmed. Because her feelings of being overwhelmed were associated with specific triggers in her life, she began to avoid them and to think that dealing with these situations was beyond her ability. Using the workbook, she identified small manageable steps toward meeting her short-term goals, which included identifying ways to recognize when she was ruminating and then using rumination as a cue for engaging in an alternative behavior. Mrs. X developed a list of new behaviors to perform at night and at other times of the day in lieu of ruminating to pull her out of her grief loop, including distracting herself from these reminders by getting out of bed and quilting for a prescribed period of time, an activity she always enjoyed.

By the end of the eighth week, Mrs. X had made progress on all of her goals and her emotional state brightened. Mrs. X was going to bed earlier and sleeping more soundly. Although she continued to be confused about the future, she was making small steps and exploring her options. Decisions in general continued to be difficult for her, although not as paralyzing as they had been in the past, as the frequency and intensity of her rumination, grief, and depression had lessened. In weeks 9 and 10, she focused on completing specific tasks, such as cleaning out a storage unit filled with her husband's possessions and items from their home in a series of small graded steps. In week 10, Mrs. X went on a four-day cruise with another sister and her nieces.

In the final 2 weeks she had contact with the clinic, Mrs. X concentrated on incorporating more self-care activities into her life, specifically exercise, and participating in community groups to increase socialization. Mrs. X continued to feel uncertain about the future but felt confident in her ability to make decisions and follow through on tasks. Mrs. X acknowledged that, although the losses she experienced will never go away, she could build a meaningful life that made coping with the losses easier. Mrs. X planned to continue monitoring her moods and behaviors so she would not slip into old patterns of rumination and grief. Although her grief and sadness had not completely gone away, the improvement in her mental state and coping abilities allowed her to face her life and take control of her future.

## Conclusion

We know a great deal about the effects of stress on physical and emotional health. A large toolbox of techniques is available to help people for whom stress adversely affects their daily lives. This chapter has attempted to provide a conceptual framework that encompasses what we know about stress and resilience and what works to help people recover from loss and stressful life events in order to encourage readers to apply these principles to cultivate resilience to stress in their daily lives. The proposed framework suggests that stress resolution and resilience is a product of the ability to maintain or reestablish a stable sense of self through engagement with goal-directed activities consonant with individuals' values. Proactive, goal-directed interactions with the environment to cope with stress can protect against the adverse effects of stress or decrease vulnerability to stressors.

For those already suffering from effects of chronic or uncontrollable stress, it is important to note that although treatments exist for many of the difficulties that arise in the aftermath of stressful events, most people do not avail themselves of effective techniques. One major barrier to obtaining help with reactions to stress is financial burden for those not covered by health insurance. While much could be done on a societal level to make these treatments more affordable, for those that live in urban areas or close to major universities, there are often mental health services available for free or reduced fees. Nevertheless, while cost is an important barrier to seeking help when needed, a more common barrier is shame and stigma, leading many people to suffer in silence, toughing it out on their own. In PTSD, and less extreme reactions to more common stressors, many people blame themselves for what they did or did not do, for weakness in not better regulating their emotions or showing strain, or even for experiencing mental health problems in the wake of the aversive event. Thus, people magnify feelings of stigma and shame by blaming themselves for not controlling the uncontrollable and coming to see themselves as inadequate, which reinforces avoidance and nonengagement—contrary to the techniques described above.

Results from one of the largest epidemiological studies of mental illness and mental health care use in the United States indicated that only 41% of those who reported symptoms of any mental disorder sought care of any kind in the last 12 months, and of those who had sought care, only 33% of the care received was classified as minimally effective based on treatment efficacy research (Wang et al., 2005; see also Substance Abuse and Mental Health Services Administration, 2012). Even when we consider PTSD as an example of a more extreme reaction to a severe stressor, the statistics reported, albeit somewhat higher, are still woefully inadequate (57% sought any kind of care, 40% of which met standards for minimally adequate care). The latest estimates based on data from 1990 put the economic cost of anxiety disorders in the United States at $42.3 billion, based on projected cost of healthcare dollars spent, lost productivity, and absenteeism. Based on the U.S. Bureau of Labor Statistics Inflation Calculator (http://www.bls.gov/data/ inflation_ calculator.htm), this is equivalent to $74.5 billion annually in 2013 (Greenberg et al., 1999). Of this cost, the greatest single contributor to this estimate was PTSD.

Much work remains to be done to promote resilience to stress, in terms of further defining what is different between people who are resilient versus nonresilient but also overcoming barriers to seeking mental health care in those that need it. Recent work on the integration of mindfulness techniques with other treatments has opened a number of exciting areas of inquiry and ways of thinking about posttraumatic responses, which are likely to feed further growth in treatment options as well as our understanding of human interactions with the environment. Nevertheless, these efforts will be largely wasted if the people who could most benefit from advances in conceptual approaches and interventions do not incorporate them into their lives.

# References

Addis, M., & Martell, C. (2004). *Overcoming depression one step at a time.* Oakland, CA: New Harbinger.

Adler, A. B., Bliese, P. D., McGurk, D., Hoge, C. W., & Castro, C. (2009). Battlemind debriefing and battlemind training as early interventions with soldiers returning from Iraq. *Journal of Consulting and Clinical Psychology, 77,* 928–940.

American Psychiatric Association. (2013). *Diagnostic and statistical manual of mental disorders* (5th ed.). Washington, DC: Author.

Baruch, G. K., & Barnett, R. C. (1986). Role quality, multiple role involvement, and psychological well-being in midlife women. *Journal of Personality and Social Psychology, 51,* 578–585.

Bauer, J. J., & Bonanno, G. A. (2001). I can, I do, I am: The narrative differentiation of self-efficacy and other self-evaluations while adapting to bereavement. *Journal of Research in Personality, 35,* 424–448.

Beck, A. T. (1976). *Cognitive therapy and emotional disorders.* New York, NY: International Universities Press.

Benish, S. G., Imel, Z. E., & Wampold, B. E. (2008). The relative efficacy of bona fide psychotherapies for treating post-traumatic stress disorder: A meta-analysis of direct comparisons. *Clinical Psychology Review, 28,* 746–758.

Benjet, C., Borges, G., & Medina-Mora, M. E. (2010). Chronic childhood adversity and onset of psychopathology during three life stages: Childhood, adolescence and adulthood. *Journal of Psychiatric Research, 44,* 732–740.

Bisson, J. I., Ehlers, A., Matthews, R., Pilling, S., Richards, D., & Turner, S. (2007). Psychological treatments for chronic post-traumatic stress disorder systematic review and meta-analysis. *British Journal of Psychiatry, 190,* 97–104.

Boelen, P. A., & van den Bout, J. (2007). Examination of proposed criteria for complicated grief in people confronted with violent or non-violent loss. *Death Studies, 31,* 155–164.

Bohlmeijer, E., Prenger, R., Taal, E., & Cuijpers, P. (2010). The effects of mindfulness-based stress reduction therapy on mental health of adults with a chronic medical disease: A meta-analysis. *Journal of Psychosomatic Research, 68,* 539–544.

Bonanno, G. A. (2009). *The other side of sadness.* New York, NY: Basic Books.

Bonanno, G. A. (2012). Uses and abuses of the resilience construct: Loss, trauma, and health-related adversities. *Social Science and Medicine, 74,* 753–756.

Bonanno, G. A., Field, N. P., Kovacevic, A., & Kaltman, S. (2002). Self-enhancement as a buffer against extreme adversity: Civil war in Bosnia and traumatic loss in the United States. *Personality and Social Psychology Bulletin, 28,* 184–196.

Bonanno, G. A., Rennicke, C., & Dekel, S. (2005). Self-enhancement among high-exposure survivors of the September 11th terrorist attack: Resilience or social maladjustment? *Journal of Personality and Social Psychology, 88,* 984.

Bonanno, G. A., Wortman, C. B., Lehman, D. R., Tweed, R. G., Haring, M., Sonnega, J., . . . Nesse, R. M. (2002). Resilience to loss and chronic grief: A prospective study from preloss to 18 months postloss. *Journal of Personality and Social Psychology, 83,* 1150–1164.

Boscarino, J. A., & Figley, C. R. (2009). The impact of repression, hostility, and post-traumatic stress disorder on all-cause mortality: A prospective 16-year follow-up study. *Journal of Nervous and Mental Disease, 197,* 461–466.

Brown, G., & Rafaeli, E. (2007). Components of self-complexity as buffers for depressed mood. *Journal of Cognitive Psychotherapy, 21,* 310–333.

Burns, A. B., Brown, J. S., Sachs-Ericsson, N., Plant, E. A., Curtis, J. T., Fredrickson, B. L., & Joiner, T. E. (2008). Upward spirals of positive emotion and coping: Replication, extension, and initial exploration of neurochemical substrates. *Personality and Individual Differences, 44,* 360–370.

Burns, D. D. (1999). *The feeling good handbook.* New York, NY: Plume.

Butler, A., Chapman, J., Forman, E., & Beck, A. (2006). The empirical status of cognitive-behavioral therapy: A review of meta-analyses. *Clinical Psychology Review, 26,* 17–31.

Callahan, R., & Callahan, J. (1996). *Thought Field Therapy (TFT) and trauma: Treatment and theory.* Indian Wells, CA: Callahan Techniques.

Carver, C. S., & Scheier, M. F. (1998). *On the self-regulation of behavior.* New York, NY: Cambridge University Press.

Caspi, A., Sugden, K., Moffitt, T. E., Taylor, A., Craig, I. W., Harrington, H., . . . Poulton, R. (2003). Influence of life stress on depression: Moderation by a polymorphism in the 5-HTT gene. *Science Signaling, 301,* 386.

Cheng, C. (2003). Cognitive and motivational processes underlying coping flexibility: A dual-process model. *Journal of Personality and Social Psychology, 84,* 425–438.

Cloitre, M., & Rosenberg, A. (2006). Sexual revictimization: Risk factors and prevention. In V. M. Follette & J. I. Ruzek (Eds.), *Cognitive-behavioral therapies for trauma* (pp. 321–361). New York, NY: Guilford Press.

Coffey, K. A., Hartman, M., & Fredrickson, B. L. (2010). Deconstructing mindfulness and constructing mental health: Understanding mindfulness and its mechanisms of action. *Mindfulness, 1,* 235–253.

Cohen, S. (2004). Social relationships and health. *American Psychologist, 59,* 676–684.

Coifman, K., & Bonanno, G. A. (2010). When distress does not become depression: Emotion context sensitivity and adjustment to bereavement. *Journal of Abnormal Psychology, 119,* 479.

Craig, G. (2010). *The EFT manual* (2nd ed.). Santa Rosa, CA: Energy Psychology Press.

Crocker, J., & Park, L. E. (2004). The costly pursuit of self-esteem. *Psychological Bulletin, 130,* 392–414.

Currier, J. M., Holland, J. M., & Neimeyer, R. A. (2009). Assumptive worldviews and problematic reactions to bereavement. *Journal of Loss and Trauma, 14,* 181–195.

Dalgleish, T. (2004). Cognitive approaches to posttraumatic stress disorder: The evolution of multirepresentational theorizing. *Psychological Bulletin, 130,* 228–260.

Davis, M., Eshelman, E. R, & McKay, M. (2008). *The relaxation and stress reduction workbook.* Oakland, CA; New Harbinger.

de Jongh, A., & ten Broeke, E. (2009). EMDR and the anxiety disorders: Exploring the current status. *Journal of EMDR Practice and Research, 3,* 133–140.

Dimidjian, S., Barrera M., Jr., Martell, C., Muñoz, R. F., & Lewinsohn, P. M. (2011). The origins and current status of behavioral activation treatments for depression. *Annual Review of Clinical Psychology, 7,* 1–38.

Dunmore, E., Clark, D. M., & Ehlers. A. (1999). Cognitive factors involved in the onset and maintenance of posttraumatic stress disorder (PTSD) after physical or sexual assault. *Behavior Research and Therapy, 37,* 809–829.

Everly, G. S., & Mitchell, J. T. (1999). *Critical Incident Stress Management: A new era and standard of care in crisis intervention* (2nd ed.). Ellicott City, MD: Chevron.

Foa, E. B., & Kozak, M. J. (1986). Emotional processing of fear: Exposure to corrective information. *Psychological Bulletin, 99,* 20–35.

Foa, E. B., & Rothbaum, B. (1998). *Treating the trauma of rape: Cognitive-behavioral therapy for PTSD.* New York, NY: Guilford Press.

Fraley, R. C., & Bonanno, G. A. (2004). Attachment and loss: A test of three competing models on the association between attachment-related avoidance and adaptation to bereavement. *Personality and Social Psychology Bulletin, 30,* 878–890.

Galatzer-Levy, I. R., Burton, C. L., & Bonanno, G. A. (2012). Coping flexibility, potentially traumatic life events, and resilience: A prospective study of college student adjustment. *Journal of Social and Clinical Psychology, 31,* 542–567.

Gerbode, F. (1989). *Beyond psychology: An introduction to metapsychology.* Palo Alto, CA: IRM Press.

Greenberg, P. E., Sisitsky, T., Kessler, R. C., Finkelstein, S. N., Berndt, E. R., Davidson, J. R., . . . Fyer, A. J. (1999). The economic burden of anxiety disorders in the 1990s. *Journal of Clinical Psychiatry, 60,* 427–435.

Greenberger, D., & Padesky, C. A. (1995). *Mind over mood.* New York, NY: Guilford Press.

Grossman, P., Niemann, L., Schmidt, S., & Walach, H. (2004). Mindfulness-based stress reduction and health benefits. *Journal of Psychosomatic Research, 57,* 35–44.

Hafer, C. L., & Begue, L. (2005). Experimental research on just-world theory: Problems, developments, and future challenges. *Psychological Bulletin, 131,* 128–167.

Hamilton, J. P., & Gotlib, I. H. (2008). Neural substrates of increased memory sensitivity for negative stimuli in major depression. *Biological Psychiatry, 63,* 1155–1162.

Hans, E., & Hiller, W. (2013). Effectiveness of and dropout from outpatient cognitive behavioral therapy for adult unipolar depression: A meta-analysis of nonrandomized effectiveness studies. *Journal of Consulting and Clinical Psychology, 81,* 75–88.

Hayes, S., & Smith, S. (2005). *Get out of your mind and into your life: The new acceptance and commitment therapy.* Oakland, CA: New Harbinger.

Hayes, S. C., Strosahl, K. D., & Wilson, K. G. (1999). *Acceptance and commitment therapy: An experiential approach to behavior change.* New York, NY: Guilford Press.

Hayes, S. C., Strosahl, K. D., Wilson, K. G., Bissett, R. T., Pistorello, J., Toarmino, D., . . . McCurry, S. M. (2004). Measuring experiential avoidance: A preliminary test of a working model. *Psychological Record, 54,* 553–578.

Hembree, E. A., Cahill, S. P., & Foa, E. B. (2003). Response to "Comment on Hembree and Foa (2003)." *Journal of Traumatic Stress, 16,* 575–577.

Hollon, S. D., & Ponniah, K. (2010). A review of empirically supported psychological therapies for mood disorders in adults. *Depression and Anxiety, 27,* 891–932.

Hopko, D., & Lejuez, C. W. (2008). *A cancer patient's guide to overcoming depression and anxiety: Getting through treatment and getting back to your life.* Oakland, CA: New Harbinger.

Jain, S., Shapiro, S. L., Swanick, S., Roesch, S. C., Mills, P. J., Bell, I., & Schwartz, G. E. (2007). A randomized controlled trial of mindfulness meditation versus relaxation training: Effects on distress, positive states of mind, rumination, and distraction. *Annals of Behavioral Medicine, 33,* 11–21.

Jakupcak, M., Tull, M. T., McDermott, M. J., Kaysen, D., Hunt, S., & Simpson, T. (2010). PTSD symptom clusters in relationship to alcohol misuse among Iraq and Afghanistan war veterans seeking post-deployment VA health care. *Addictive Behaviors, 35*(9), 840–843.

Jeffcoat, T., & Hayes, S. C. (2012). A randomized trial of ACT bibliotherapy on the mental health of K–12 teachers and staff. *Behaviour Research and Therapy, 50,* 571–579.

Johnson, J. D., O'Connor, K. A., Deak, T., Spencer, R. L., Watkins, L. R., & Maier, S. F. (2002). Prior stressor exposure primes the HPA axis. *Psychoneuroendocrinology, 27*(3), 353–365.

Kabat-Zinn, J. (1990). *Full catastrophe living.* New York, NY: Bantam Dell.

Kashdan, T. B., & Rottenberg, J. (2010). Psychological flexibility as a fundamental aspect of health. *Clinical Psychology Review, 30,* 467–480.

Kashima, E. S., Hardie, E. A., Wakimoto, R., & Kashima, Y. (2011). Culture- and gender-specific implications of relational and collective contexts on spontaneous self-descriptions. *Journal of Cross-Cultural Psychology, 42,* 740–758.

Keltner, D., & Bonanno, G. A. (1997). A study of laughter and dissociation: Distinct correlates of laughter and smiling during bereavement. *Journal of Personality and Social Psychology, 73*, 687.

Killingsworth, M. A., & Gilbert, D. T. (2010). A wandering mind is an unhappy mind. *Science, 330*, 932–932.

Koch, E. J., & Shepperd, J. A. (2004). Is self-complexity linked to better coping? A review of the literature. *Journal of Personality, 72*, 727–760.

Kornør, H., Winje, D., Ekeberg, Ø., Weisæth, L., Kirkehei, I., Johansen, K., & Steiro, A. (2008). Early trauma-focused cognitive-behavioural therapy to prevent chronic post-traumatic stress disorder and related symptoms: a systematic review and meta-analysis. *BMC Psychiatry, 8*, 81.

Lazarus, R. S., & Folkman, S. (1984). *Stress, appraisal, and coping.* New York, NY: Springer.

Lee, C. W., & Cuijpers, P. (2013). A meta-analysis of the contribution of eye movements in processing emotional memories. *Journal of Behavior Therapy and Experimental Psychiatry, 44*, 231–239.

Linville, P. W. (1987). Self-complexity as a cognitive buffer against stress-related illness and depression. *Journal of Personality and Social Psychology, 52*, 663–676.

Litz, V. T., Gray, M. J., Bryant, R. A., & Adler, A. B. (2002). Early intervention for trauma: Current status and future directions. *Clinical Psychology: Science and Practice 9*, 112–113.

Lohr, J. M., Devilly, G. J., Lilienfeld, S. O., & Olatunji, B. O. (2006). First do no harm, and then do some good: Science and professional responsibility in the response to disaster and trauma. *Behavior Therapist, 29*, 131.

Mathews, A., & MacLeod, C. (2005). Cognitive vulnerability to emotional disorders. *Annual Review of Clinical Psychology, 1*, 167–195.

Mazzucchelli, T., Kane, R., & Rees, C. (2009). Behavioral activation treatments for depression in adults: A meta-analysis and review. *Clinical Psychology: Science and Practice, 16*, 383–411.

McEwan, B. S. (1998). Protective and damaging effects of stress-mediators. *New England Journal of Medicine, 338*, 171–179.

McNally, R., Bryant, R., & Ehlers, A. (2003). Does early psychological intervention promote recovery from posttraumatic stress? *Psychological Science in the Public Interest, 4*, 45–79.

Meichenbaum, D. (1985). *Stress inoculation training,* Elmsford, NY: Pergamon Press.

Milliken, C. S., Auchterlonie, J. L., & Hoge, C. W. (2007). Longitudinal assessment of mental health problems among active and reserve component soldiers returning from the Iraq war. *Journal of the American Medical Association, 298*, 2141–2148.

Mitchell, J. T., & Everly, G. S., Jr. (2001). *Critical Incident Stress Debriefing: An operations manual for CISD, Defusing and other group crisis intervention services* (3rd ed.). Ellicott City, MD: Chevron.

Moss, K., Scogin, F., Di Napoli, E., & Presnell, A. (2012). A self-help behavioral activation treatment for geriatric depressive symptoms. *Aging & Mental Health, 16*, 625–635.

Nolen-Hoeksema, S., Wisco, B. E., & Lyubomirsky, S. (2008). Rethinking rumination. *Perspectives on Psychological Science, 3,* 400–424.

Norcross, J. C., Koocher, G. P., & Garofalo, A. (2006). Discredited psychological treatments and tests: A delphi poll. *Professional Psychology: Research and Practice, 37,* 515–522.

Olatunji, B. O., Cisler, J. M., & Deacon, B. J. (2010). Efficacy of cognitive behavioral therapy for anxiety disorders: A review of meta-analytic findings. *Psychiatric Clinics of North America, 33,* 557.

Ott M. J., Norris, R. L., & Bauer-Wu, S. M. (2006). Mindfulness meditation for oncology patients. *Integrative Cancer Therapies, 5,* 98–108.

Papa, A., & Bonanno, G. A. (2008). Smiling in the face of adversity: The interpersonal and intrapersonal functions of smiling. *Emotion, 8,* 1–12.

Papa, A., & Litz, B. T. (2011). Grief. In W. T. O'Donohue, Draper & C. (Eds.), *Stepped care and e-health: Practical applications to behavioral disorders.* New York, NY: Springer.

Papa, A., & Maitoza, R. (2013). The role of loss in the experience of grief: The case of job loss. *Journal of Loss and Trauma, 18,* 152–169.

Papa, A., Sewell, M. T., Garrison-Diehn, C., & Rummel, C. (2013). A randomized open trial assessing the feasibility of bhavioral activation for pathological grief responding. *Behavior Therapy, 44,* 639–650.

Park, C. L., Folkman, S., & Bostrom, A. (2001). Appraisals of controllability and coping in caregivers and HIV+ men: Testing the goodness-of-fit hypothesis. *Journal of Consulting and Clinical Psychology, 69,* 481–488.

Pat-Horenczyk, R., Schiff, M., & Doppelt, O. (2006). Maintaining routine despite ongoing exposure to terrorism: A healthy strategy for adolescents? *Journal of Adolescent Health, 39,* 199–205.

Piet, J., & Hougaard, E. (2011). The effect of mindfulness-based cognitive therapy for prevention of relapse in recurrent major depressive disorder: A systematic review and meta-analysis. *Clinical Psychology Review, 31,* 1032–1040.

Powers, M. B., Halpern, J. M., Ferenschak, M. P., Gillihan, S. J., & Foa, E. B. (2010). A meta-analytic review of prolonged exposure for posttraumatic stress disorder. *Clinical Psychology Review, 30,* 635–641.

Prigerson, H. G., Frank, E., Reynolds, C. F., George, C. J., & Kupfer, D. J. (1993). Protective psychosocial factors in depression among spousally bereaved elders. *American Journal of Geriatric Psychiatry, 1,* 296–309.

Rothbaum, B., Foa, E., & Hembree, E. (2007). *Reclaiming your life from a traumatic experience.* New York, NY: Oxford University Press.

Scogin, F., Welsh, D., Hanson, A., Stump, J., & Coates, A. (2005). Evidence-based psychotherapies for depression in older adults. *Clinical Psychology: Science and Practice, 12,* 222–237.

Segerstrom, S. C., & Miller, G. E. (2004). Psychological stress and the human immune system: A meta-analytic study of 30 years of inquiry. *Psychological Bulletin, 130,* 610–630.

Selby, A., & Smith-Osborne, A. (2013). A systematic review of effectiveness of complementary and adjunct therapies and interventions involving equines. *Health Psychology, 32,* 418–432.

Shapiro, F. (2001). *Eye movement desensitization and reprocessing* (2nd ed.). New York, NY: Guilford Press.

Shapiro, R. (2009). *EMDR Solutions II; For depression, eating disorders, performance, and more.* New York, NY: Norton.

Shear, K., Monk, T., Houck, P., Melhem, N., Frank, E., Reynolds, C., & Sillowash, R. (2007). An attachment-based model of complicated grief including the role of avoidance. *European Archives of Psychiatry and Clinical Neuroscience, 257,* 453–461.

Shear, M. K. (2010). Exploring the role of experiential avoidance from the perspective of attachment theory and the dual process model. *OMEGA—Journal of Death and Dying, 61,* 357–369.

Sheldon, K. M., & Lyubomirsky, S. (2006). How to increase and sustain positive emotion: The effects of expressing gratitude and visualizing best possible selves. *Journal of Positive Psychology, 1,* 73–82.

Smout, M. F., Hayes, L., Atkins, P. W., Klausen, J., & Duguid, J. E. (2012). The empirically supported status of acceptance and commitment therapy: An update. *Clinical Psychologist, 16,* 97–109.

Stahl, B., & Goldstein, E. (2010). *A mindfulness-based stress reduction workbook.* Oakland, CA: New Harbinger.

Stewart, R. E., & Chambless, D. L. (2009). Cognitive-behavioral therapy for adult anxiety disorders in clinical practice: A meta-analysis of effectiveness studies. *Journal of Consulting and Clinical Psychology, 77,* 595.

Substance Abuse and Mental Health Services Administration. (2012). *Mental health, United States, 2010.* HHS Pub. No. (SMA) 12–4681.

Teasdale, J. D., Segal, Z. V, Williams, J. M. G., Ridgeway, V. A., Soulby, J. M., Lau, M. A. (2000). Prevention of relapse/recurrence in major depression by mindfulness-based cognitive therapy. *Journal of Consulting and Clinical Psychology, 68,* 615–623.

van Solinge, H., & Henkens, K. (2008). Adjustment to and satisfaction with retirement: Two of a kind? *Psychology and Aging, 23,* 422–434.

Vignoles, V. L., Regalia, C., Manzi, C., Golledge, J., & Scabini, E. (2006). Beyond self-esteem: Influence of multiple motives on identity construction. *Journal of Personality and Social Psychology, 90,* 308–333.

Wang, P. S., Lane, M., Olfson, M., Pincus, H. A., Wells, K. B., & Kessler, R. C. (2005). Twelve-month use of mental health services in the United States: Results from the National Comorbidity Survey Replication. *Archives of General Psychiatry, 62,* 629.

Whitfield, G. E., Williams, C. J., & Shapiro, D. A. (2001). Assessing the take up and acceptability of a self-help room used by patients awaiting their initial outpatient appointment. *Behavioural and Cognitive Psychotherapy, 29,* 333–343.

Wolpe, J. (1961). The systematic desensitization treatment of neuroses. *Journal of Nervous and Mental Disease, 132,* 189–203.

# 6

# Coping With Chronic Pain

*Joshua R. Dyer*

*Merry Sylvester*

*Emily K. Traupman*

*Jessica L. Mackelprang*

*David R. Patterson*

University of Washington School of Medicine

P ain is a great motivator. People expend a great deal of effort, energy, and resources in a battle to eliminate pain. It is the number-one reason people go to the doctor. Pain medications are the most commonly prescribed medications, as estimated annual sales in the United States are $27 billion (Melnikova, 2010). A population motivated to eliminate pain along with the burgeoning recognition that medications are only minimally effective for the large number of individuals with chronic pain has led patients and providers to search for relief with other types of medications (e.g., antidepressants) and to the development of an industry of complementary and alternative medicine. Unfortunately, promises of a pain-free life are typically met with disappointment and continued suffering. Research does indicate, though, that people can continue to lead meaningful, fulfilling lives, often with *decreased* pain, through a variety of means. This chapter provides a brief overview of pain, describes its global, national, and individual consequences, and discusses models that are more or less effective in terms of management. Finally, we describe the evidence for several biopsychosocial interventions that are based on broader, more useful conceptualizations of chronic pain.

## Definitions and Overview of Pain

Pain is defined as "an unpleasant sensory and emotional experience associated with actual or potential tissue damage, or described in terms of tissue damage, or both" (IASP Newsletter, 1986). As is evident from this definition, pain is a multidimensional experience that includes both sensation and emotion. As a result of this, pain is a personal experience, and it is impossible to predict the severity of pain or suffering any one individual will experience based upon characteristics of injury or lesion. As reviewed below in more detail, there are physiological reasons for this as pain is modulated in the spinal cord and the brainstem prior to being recognized by the cortex; psychological influences such as thoughts, attention, and mood can magnify or minimize our perception of pain. Further, social influences such as attention from caring loved ones can unwittingly reinforce our experience of pain or, conversely, societal norms can minimize our experience of pain.

Broadly speaking, pain is usually either acute or chronic. *Acute* pain develops quickly and, although it may be severe, persists for a relatively short duration. The cause of acute pain is often able to be determined, given that it is often induced by medical procedures or trauma, such as in the case of postsurgical pain or throbbing after stubbing a toe. Over time, acute pain may become chronic, a phenomenon termed *chronification* or *hyperalgesic priming*. This refers to the changes that are believed to occur in central nervous system nociceptors (pain receptors) as they become hypersensitive and related vascular damage and inflammation (Pergolizzi, Raffa, & Taylor, 2014; Reichling & Levine, 2009). Chronic pain refers to pain persisting beyond the expected healing time, which is generally for more than 3 months (Harstall & Ospina, 2003). Thus, acute pain is generally associated with a higher degree of pathology than chronic pain, and chronic pain often continues after a wound has healed and when identifiable pathology does not completely explain the presence or severity of the pain experienced (Turk & Okifuji, 2009). Whereas acute pain is considered to be a normal outcome of injuries or procedures that serves an adaptive purpose (e.g., reminding us to stay off the broken leg while it heals), chronic pain is associated with many adverse outcomes; it seldom serves an adaptive or protective purpose, and it typically highly disrupts the day-to-day lives of those who struggle with it.

## Scope of the Problem

Chronic pain is recognized as a significant public health problem by federal agencies and international organizations (Steglitz, Buscemi, & Ferguson, 2011). According to the World Health Organization (WHO) World Mental Health Surveys, the prevalence of chronic pain was 38.4% among a sample of 42,249 adults from 17 countries (Tsang et al., 2008). A recent study of 15 European countries and Israel found that 19% of 46,394 respondents to a telephone survey endorsed moderate-to-severe chronic pain (Breivik, Collett, Ventafridda, Cohen, & Gallacher, 2006).

Estimates of the prevalence of chronic pain in individuals in the United States range from 30% to 40% (Johannes, Le, Zhou, Johnston, & Dworkin, 2010; Tsang et al., 2008). It directly affects approximately 100 million Americans (Gaskin & Richard, 2011), with chronic low back pain being the most prevalent (National Center for Health Statistics, 2010). Studies consistently find that chronic pain is more common among women and becomes increasingly prevalent with age (Ospina & Harstall, 2002; Tsang et al., 2008). Individuals who suffer from pain are more likely to seek out medical care than those who do not (Andersson, Ejlertsson, Leden, & Schersten, 1999; Simpson, 2004); however, they also frequently report that their pain is not sufficiently managed or is even dismissed by their doctors (Breivik et al., 2006).

## Costs to Society

Chronic pain is not just an issue for persons suffering from it; as put by Skinner and colleagues, "The presence of persistent pain carries profound physical, emotional, social, and economic burdens not only for the persons experiencing the symptoms but for their significant others and society as well" (Skinner, Wilson, & Turk, 2012). Recent studies have attempted to quantify the economic cost of pain on healthcare systems and society. Utilizing Medical Expenditure Panel Survey (MEPS) data, Gaskin and Richard (2011) estimated that the medical expense of treating pain is 261 to 300 billion dollars annually. When adding approximations of pain-related costs to society such as diminished productivity (e.g., fewer hours, days worked, lost wages), the estimated cost is between 560 and 635 billion dollars. Given the large number of individuals who struggle with chronic pain, the economic costs on society are more burdensome than cardiovascular diseases; neoplasms, injury and poisoning; endocrine, nutritional, and metabolic diseases; digestive system diseases; or respiratory system diseases (Gaskin & Richard, 2011).

Even more difficult to quantify than the economic burden associated with pain is the psychological and emotional toll that prolonged pain inflicts upon those who suffer from it. Studies have demonstrated repeatedly the existence of a relationship between pain and psychological well-being (Carnes et al., 2007). In a large multicenter study, Gureje, Von Korff, Simon, and Gater (1998) found that individuals who experienced persistent pain were four times more likely to suffer from anxiety or depression than those who did not. Likewise, Arnow and colleagues (2006) found that individuals with major depressive disorder are more likely to endorse a history of chronic pain (66%) than are those without this diagnosis (43%). Concerning the progression from acute to chronic pain, Casey, Greenberg, Nicassio, Harpin, and Hubbard (2008) reported that depression and a history of more traumas predicted that pain would be chronic in the 3 months after new onset neck or back pain. Depressed mood and beliefs that pain would be enduring and not subside over time were most predictive of disability associated with pain. Pain and psychological well-being are closely related and, although it may not always be clear which symptoms emerge first, the strong interplay between the two makes clear the importance of addressing both variables.

Chronic pain takes a toll not only on the individual living with the pain but also on those significant to that person's life. Studies have suggested that family life, including spousal relationships, are disrupted by chronic pain (Lipton et al., 2003), and child pain sufferers are at greater risk of anxiety and depression (Kaasboll, Lydersen, & Indredavik, 2012). Importantly, parents often model pain behaviors to their children, as parents with chronic pain are significantly more likely to have adolescent or young adult children with nonspecific complaints of this nature (Hoftun, Romundstad, & Rygg, 2013). Chronic disabling pain is also associated with low income, low education, and higher rates of divorce (Portenoy, Ugarte, Fuller, & Haas, 2004).

As reviewed above, chronic pain has a far-reaching impact on the lives of individuals. Chronic pain affects emotional, social, vocational, and sexual functioning and often leads to depression and disruptions in marital and family relationships. Due to the broad impact of these conditions, research in the past 40 years has focused on understanding how individuals cope and adapt to chronic illnesses and pain through a comprehensive framework.

# Biomedical Model

Traditional biomedical models focus solely on biological malfunctions as causative factors for chronic illness or pain. Health is determined by the freedom from disease, pain, or defect. According to this perspective, the onset and course of a condition are viewed as irregularities in physiology and assumes that the organism can be explained in terms of its parts. This reductionist philosophy may lead to stereotypes that patients having the same condition are similar, while ignoring psychological, cultural, and social differences among patients with the same diagnosis. Biomedical approaches may not recognize the whole person and can fail to evaluate and treat in a comprehensive fashion. This approach emphasizes a cure or a fix for chronic pain; as such, few guidelines exist for the management of this problem, which often leads to primary care physicians, anesthesiologists, neurologists, and surgeons all approaching managing chronic pain differently. Occasionally the focus from a biomedical perspective, centered on identifying and treating a causative etiology for pain, can bring a patient relief, but more often than not, this approach overlooks the more comprehensive diagnostic picture.

Treatment from a solely biomedical model shows modest results. Under the best circumstances, medications only reduce pain by 30% to 40% in fewer than one half of patients (Turk, 2002). The most common treatment is opioid management; indeed, retail sales of opioid analgesics increased by 176% between 1997 and 2006 (Turk, Wilson, & Cahana, 2011), making them the most common class of drug prescription in the United States. This is in spite of the fact that they result in only small improvements in chronic pain and carry with them significant side effects and risks. Across a similar time frame (1995 to 2005), emergency room visits involving opioid analgesics increased 274%, and over a 5-year period (1999 to 2004) deaths from methadone increased 390%. Opioid analgesics also cause considerable side effects, such as nausea, constipation, somnolence, and among a small percentage of long-term users, opioid induced hyperalgesia, in which patients become hypersensitive to nociception.

In spite of the bombardment of commercials touting medications that target "painful depression," antidepressant medications, particularly tricyclic antidepressants and selective serotonin and norepinephrine reuptake inhibitors (SNRIs), are similarly modestly effective for a minority of patients; they decrease pain by 30% or more in roughly 40% of patients (compared to 30% of those receiving placebo reporting similar pain reductions); (Derry, Gill, Phillips, & Moore, 2012).

Surgery shows similarly modest results. A review of surgery for one of the most common causes of low back pain (nonradicular low back pain with common degenerative changes) found that less than one half of patients achieve "optimal outcomes" (e.g., sporadic pain, slight reduction in function, and sporadic analgesics were typically seen instead), and that surgery is no better than intensive rehabilitation with a cognitive behavioral focus (Chou et al., 2009). Importantly, surgery is not benign in terms of side effects, as between 30% and 46% of back surgeries result in failed back surgery syndrome in which patients experience persistent or recurring chronic pain after surgery (Chan & Peng, 2011). Other strictly medical interventions, such as nerve blocks, anticonvulsant medications, muscle relaxants, topical agents, and implantable devices, show similarly modest results; this necessitates a broader view of treatment as well as outcomes, such as those related to decreased suffering and improved functioning.

## Biopsychosocial Model

In contrast to the biomedical model, the biopsychosocial model (Engel, 1977) emphasizes the need to consider psychological and social factors along with biological factors and the interrelated nature these all have on health and illness. Thus, when a physiological abnormality is detected, the meaning to the patient and the impact on functioning must be understood within the context of the patient's coping resources, social relationships, and culture. The biopsychosocial model posits that all three of these levels of analysis are crucial to the understanding of the onset, course, and treatment of physical illness (Engel, 1980).

### Psychological Aspects

Some specific psychological issues in conditions of the musculoskeletal system include prolonged dependence on others; uncertainty about the ability to return to normal responsibilities and activities; restrictions due to braces or deformity; sense of powerlessness leading to anger, hostility, and later depression; dietary modifications; and pain deformity or alteration in body image that may affect sexual function (Falvo, 2005). Common emotional reactions to chronic pain include grief over the loss of a body part, bodily function, social and work roles, social status, or other perceived losses; fear and anxiety over the threats of loss of function, independence, and financial security; anger; depression; and denial (Moos & Holahan, 2007). It has been estimated that approximately 35% of patients with chronic pain also meet criteria for depression (Romano & Turner, 1985), compared with a 16% lifetime prevalence of depression in the general population (Kessler et al., 2003).

A number of cognitive, emotional, and behavioral factors also influence pain expression. For some individuals, chronic pain leads to cycles of false hope, frustration, and guilt. People suffering from this problem may be unable to work and begin to withdraw from friends, family, and social activities. They may also believe no one has endured the type of pain they are experiencing and become demoralized, depressed, and angry (Foley, 2003). Also, different styles of coping have been shown to have varied effects. For example, people who cope passively with their pain when it is at a high level of intensity may be more vulnerable to depression than those who cope through more active means (Brown, Nicassio, & Wallston, 1989).

Psychological processes and pain are bidirectional in nature, meaning that depression and anxiety, for instance, may be a result of experiencing pain but also play a role in differing experiences of pain. For example, in patients with rheumatoid arthritis, a history of previous depression was associated with increased difficulty coping and a greater experience of pain in response to stressors (Conner et al., 2006; Zautra, Fasman, Parish, & Davis, 2007). In fact, cognitive factors associated with depression in healthy populations also often present in patients with chronic pain, such as catastrophizing, passive coping, and cognitive distortions (Covic, Adamson, Spencer, & Howe, 2003; Edwards, Bingham, Bathon, & Haythornthwaite, 2006).

Research suggests that the strongest and most consistent psychosocial factor associated with pain and dysfunction in people with chronic pain is catastrophizing (Jensen, Moore, Bockow, Ehde, & Engel, 2011). Catastrophizing has been defined as the tendency to focus on pain and to negatively evaluate one's ability to deal with it (Keefe, Rumble, Scipio, Giordano, & Perri, 2004). Catastrophizing involves thoughts such as "I will never recover from this pain" or "This pain means there is something seriously wrong with me." Expression of these thoughts often leads to social responses that, while they are well-meaning in their intent (Sullivan et al., 2001), only serve to reinforce these negative thoughts and to exacerbate negative consequences (e.g., decreased activity, other maladaptive coping approaches to pain). Fortunately, catastrophizing is amenable to change.

## Social Aspects

Chronic pain does not occur in a vacuum, or to put it another way, there is seldom chronic pain behavior without an audience. The social milieu in which individuals find themselves can facilitate or discourage effective coping (Kosciulek, 2007). Coping with chronic pain occurs in broader social contexts, which include family, friends, neighbors, the community, employers, school, and healthcare service providers. Individuals have different pain thresholds, tolerance, and expression, and thus it may be confusing for friends or family members to comprehend what a person experiences. Also, due to differing opinions and experiences of pain, doctor-patient relationships are often strained. These negative consequences of chronic pain can significantly affect individual and family quality of life, tax one's coping resources, and place more costs and burdens on the healthcare system. For example, people who receive low or ineffective social support may be more likely to develop depression or suffer from adverse health consequences than those who receive high or effective support (Cohen, 1988; Cohen & Wills, 1985). The quality of the relationship and the way people learn to adapt to chronic illnesses and pain play an important role in helping individuals and families cope with, adapt to, and even survive these conditions (Atkins, Kaplan, & Toshima, 1991; Coyne et al., 2001; Lyons, Mickelson, Sullilvan, & Coyne, 1998; Manne, Alfieri, Taylor, & Dougherty, 1999).

A person's ability to adapt to chronic pain can be both positively and negatively affected by social influences. Research has long suggested that positive social support offers a buffer to many negative effects of chronic pain (Kerns, Rosenberg, & Otis, 2002; Lopez-Martinez, Esteve-Zarazaga, & Ramirez-Maestre, 2008). This has been demonstrated in regard to both emotional support as well as instrumental supporting (e.g., helping them get to appointments). As a specific example, social support was associated with less pain interference and increased mood in patients with chronic pain (Jensen et al., 2002). However, a significant person in one's family that reinforces pain behaviors can increase a patient's attention to pain as well as the reward for showing them, thus actually increasing suffering (Sanders, 1996).

To summarize, chronic pain can dramatically affect quality of life as it is a multidimensional concept and experience that encompasses physical, psychological, spiritual, and social functioning (Glajchen, 2001). Chronic pain affects social and family relationships, economic well-being, and recreational and vocational activities. Although all chronic conditions require some adjustments and alterations, the extent of the impact depends upon the nature of the condition, the individual's preinjury personality, the meaning of the condition to the individual, the individual's current life circumstances, and the degree of family and social support (Falvo, 2005). Reactions to chronic pain vary considerably as individuals have different tolerances to symptoms, functional limitations, and abilities to cope. Thus, maximally effective treatment accounts for all of these factors. Despite acknowledgments of psychological and social factors in chronic pain for centuries, it has only been during the past few decades that comprehensive frameworks for pain have emerged (Turk, 2001).

# Role of Concept: Biopsychosocial Approach to Pain Assessment

Having described a biopsychosocial approach, it is then important to use such concepts in a multifaceted approach to assessment wherein the *biological, psychological,* and *social/environmental* factors are evaluated. A biopsychosocial approach is an interdisciplinary approach, in which the assessments conducted by the patient's healthcare provider and psychologist or other mental health provider each contribute to the overall understanding of the patient's pain experience. The biological and psychosocial assessments are often conducted serially, but there are benefits to beginning psychosocial assessment earlier in the process—for example, to improve the patient's ability to cope with pain during the assessment period. The structure of pain assessment is based on the work of Jensen and Patterson (2008), and is described in further detail below.

## Assessment of Biological Factors

A biopsychosocial assessment of pain begins, just as a traditional pain assessment based on the medical model would, with a thorough evaluation by a physician or other healthcare provider, ideally with specialized training in the assessment and treatment of pain. Biological factors may include physiological or anatomical characteristics that may contribute to pain, such as injury at the pain site or plastic changes (e.g., responses to pain that become imprinted into the nervous system). The evaluation seeks to identify the nature of the pain—that is, whether the pain is neuropathic (caused by nerve damage) or nociceptive (resulting from signals from pain receptors) in nature.

The evaluation may include an examination and any number of diagnostic tests. Specific procedures and tests will vary widely based on the patient's presenting complaints and other medical conditions. While a detailed review of such evaluation is beyond the scope of this chapter, interested readers may see Loeser (2001) for more detail regarding the specific components of a medical evaluation of pain.

Clearly, if there is an identifiable reason that the patient is experiencing pain, it is good for it to be identified, and even more so if the underlying cause is correctable, as proper diagnosis can lead to proper treatment. For example, a pain assessment may reveal previously undiagnosed conditions, such as cancer, allowing for appropriate treatment and life planning. This may be particularly true in cases of acute pain, as this is expected to be temporary. The course of action may be to wait for a natural healing process to unfold while treating the patient's pain with medication and other treatments.

In contrast, the biological factors associated with chronic pain are frequently less clear. Often, the underlying cause of pain and appropriate treatments are not apparent. Even when the cause is identifiable, treatments frequently are meant to manage rather than eliminate pain, as is the case with pain associated with arthritis or multiple sclerosis. Nonetheless, a thorough assessment of biological factors is vital to the biopsychosocial assessment of chronic pain as patients with a biomedical focus often seek a medical explanation and cure for their pain. Ruling out biological causes of pain is an important step in increasing the patient's receptivity to other pain treatments.

## Assessment of Psychological Factors

The next step in the biopsychosocial assessment of pain is assessment of psychological and social factors by a psychologist or other mental health clinician with specialized training in the assessment and treatment of pain. In this assessment, the clinician seeks to understand the patient's experience of pain over time, including his or her experience of the onset, location(s) of pain, pain intensity, and changes in pain intensity throughout the day and over time. It is also important to assess the perceived effectiveness of any treatments attempted thus far and the perceived feasibility/utility of future treatment. Such an assessment is clearly useful to assist the clinician in better understanding the patient's perspective on his or her pain. It can also be an important step for patients, who are often concerned that they have been referred to a mental health provider because the pain is thought to be "in their head." The thorough assessment of the patient's experience of pain underscores that the clinician believes the patient's pain experience is a real and important concern. Assessment at this level is always linked toward treatment as well. For example, asking the patient to describe the variability in his or her pain, including the highest and lowest pain intensity, helps the patient to gain perspective that even chronic pain is variable and may lead to an initial treatment goal of increasing the amount of time in which the patient has lower intensity pain.

The clinician will also assess current psychological issues, including sleep problems, depression, anxiety, and stress, as these psychological issues may be increasing the patient's experience of pain. For example, chronic sleep problems may make it more difficult for the patient to learn new skills for coping with pain due to problems with energy, cognition, mood, and frustration tolerance. A patient who is anxious may tend to react fearfully to pain sensations and think of pain in catastrophic terms, and a patient who is depressed may focus excessively on times when pain was more difficult to manage while discounting times when they were able to do activity well with pain. In these cases, treatment would aim to address these maladaptive *pain cognitions* and to increase the patient's acceptance of pain while committing to engagement in potentially meaningful activity in spite of pain. Assessment of pain cognitions may also yield a better understanding of the patient's conceptualization of pain and potential receptivity to treatment options. For example, it is important to assess whether the patient has a predominantly biomedical conceptualization of his or her pain or an understanding of the more complex interplay among biopsychosocial factors. Some patients may, in fact, be so entrenched in the biomedical model of pain that they are described as having an *illness conviction*. Identifying such patients during the assessment process allows for delivery of education and may indicate that some treatment be delayed to allow patients time to work through the medical process and become more receptive to alternative explanations for their pain experience, or at least complementary strategies for pain management, as they await identification of an effective biomedical intervention.

The clinician will also assess how the patient copes with his or her pain, as well as the effectiveness of each of the coping strategies. The question of effectiveness is an important one as what may be effective in reducing the pain experience in the moment may not be the best long-term solution for managing pain and, in fact, may actually increase pain over time. The distinction has been made between adaptive coping strategies, which are usually active and promote better long-term adjustment to pain, and maladaptive coping strategies, which are usually passive and while effective in the moment may actually lead to worsening of the patient's pain experience over time (Boothby, Thorn, Stroud, & Jensen, 1999). Whether a strategy is adaptive or maladaptive depends on the type of pain being treated. Passive strategies, such as rest and limited use of the body part, may be initially beneficial and, therefore, recommended by a medical provider after an acute injury; however, prolonged use of rest and limited activity may lead to loss of muscle mass and range of motion over time, increasing functional disability and often pain itself. This underscores the importance of an active collaboration between the healthcare provider and behavioral health clinician in order to provide the patient with a clear and consistent message about behavioral strategies he or she can use to manage and improve his or her pain experience.

## Assessment of Social/Environmental Factors

In addition to psychological factors, the psychologist or other mental health clinician further assesses characteristics of the patient's social environment that affect his or her pain experience. The assessment will ideally include an interview with the patient's primary social support (e.g., spouse, parent, caregiver) in addition to an interview with the patient.

Social/environmental factors may have either a positive or negative effect on the patient's ability to cope with chronic pain. General positive social support has been shown to buffer the negative effects of pain and chronic illness (Kerns, Rosenberg, & Otis, 2002; Lopez-Martinez et al., 2008). While social supports provide many benefits, including a person to listen and to help the patient solve his or her problems, a patient's social supports appear to be particularly important in encouraging the person to continue with daily activities even when in pain. Given the importance of activity to mood, it is not surprising that research has found a positive link between social support and more positive mood among patients with chronic pain (Jensen et al., 2002).

Importantly, social support can also have a negative effect on the patient's pain experience—that is, social support can actually *increase* the patient's experience of pain over time. This occurs when the patient's pain behavior (e.g., grimacing) is followed by a consequence that either is positive or involves the removal of an unpleasant feeling or demand. For example, if every time a man with chronic pain cries out in pain, his wife gives him an enjoyable massage, he may actually be more likely to cry out—and have the subjective experience of pain—over time. Similarly, if a woman with chronic pain grimaces and holds her back when washing dishes, and her husband invariably takes over the task and asks her to sit down, the woman's pain experience may increase over time. In both cases, the intention of the spouse was to help the person with chronic pain, though, in fact, these helpful responses can be quite detrimental over time. In fact, neuroimaging studies show that over time, the very presence of the spouse may cause areas of the brain that process pain to show more activity in the person with chronic pain (Flor, 2003; Flor, Kerns, & Turk, 1987; Flor, Knost, & Birbaumer, 2002; Flor, Turk, & Rudy, 1989). In addition, social supports who are genuinely concerned about the patient's health can inadvertently undermine efforts to become more active, for example, by expressing worry or concern if the patient exercises or attempts to resume work or household activities (Schwartz, Jensen, & Romano, 2005). Thus, it is vital for the clinician to identify and target social factors that may be negatively affecting the patient's pain experience and to promote positive social support. Further details regarding carrying out such an assessment may be found in Jensen and Patterson (2008).

## Specifics for Faithful Application

Just as the biopsychosocial assessment of chronic pain is an interdisciplinary endeavor, the treatment of chronic pain is most effective when it integrates medical and psychological interventions as well as other treatments, including physical therapy and vocational counseling. Modifiable factors contributing to pain which were identified in the evaluation should be targeted. If psychological difficulties, such as depression, anxiety, or sleep disturbance have been identified, treatment should include application of appropriate treatments targeting these difficulties in addition to treatment for chronic pain. Psychological interventions for chronic pain are frequently multifaceted and may include education, cognitive behavioral strategies, activation and increasing activity, relaxation and imagery, hypnosis, and/or mindfulness. Each of these interventions is described in more detail below.

### Education

Educational approaches to chronic pain often involve carefully explaining the biopsychosocial approach outlined above to the patient. An important function of the assessment of the patient with chronic pain is to better understand his or her conceptualization of the pain problem. Frequently, such assessment reveals an underlying fear about the pain condition, in which the patient may be unduly concerned that the pain may be a signal of damage or an underlying problem that has yet to be revealed. Patients need to learn how their cognitions affect their pain and suffering as described below. Educational interventions can be delivered in multiple modalities, including through the use of booklets and other written materials, video, online and other mass media outlets, and group or individual didactics and counseling. The evidence for educational interventions is mixed, with some studies showing education based on the biopsychosocial model to be effective and others showing much more modest results. Educational treatments do appear to be most effective when they include individual counseling with a clinician knowledgeable about chronic pain management. However, educational treatments may be best applied as a complementary component to the other interventions detailed below (Dupeyron et al., 2011; Gross et al., 2012).

*Cognitive Behavioral Strategies*

As noted above, the way a patient thinks about pain may affect his or her experience of the pain and ability to cope. A patient who thinks, "I can't take this pain," may feel helpless to cope with the pain and exhausted, with little energy to allocate to other life activities. Cognitive behavioral therapy may be used to help the patient to examine these types of catastrophic thoughts objectively, paying attention to the function they serve (likely associated with lack of motivation and avoidance of activity). Patients are often asked to notice the natural variation in pain levels, offering the recognition and hope that even chronic pain does vary in intensity. In addition to addressing maladaptive (often catastrophic) thoughts, cognitive behavioral approaches also seek to promote more adaptive responses to pain, including increasing activity (see Activation and Increasing Activity below for more detail). Cognitive behavioral approaches have been shown to be an effective component of multidisciplinary treatment of chronic pain, with improvement in pain experience, pain behavior and activity level, cognitive coping and appraisal, and social functioning (Gatchel & Rollings, 2008; Morley, Eccleston, & Williams, 1999; van Tulder, Koes, & Bombardier, 2002).

*Activation and Increasing Activity*

The use of strategies for managing acute pain, such as rest and restriction of movement, when used to manage chronic pain can actually lead to loss of muscle tone and range of motion over time and, thus, more functional disability and pain. Responding to pain by limiting activity is particularly problematic as individuals often show the opposite behavior in the absence of pain—that is, when they do experience less pain they tend to engage in excessive activity. For example, a person may find that they have less pain one day and decide to clean the kitchen. Still feeling a low intensity of pain that day, they then decide to clean out the closets, mow the lawn, and do some grocery shopping. Understandably, the person then feels exhausted and with greater pain the next day and greatly limits activity again. This alternating pattern of overuse and inaction is particularly problematic because the level of activity in which the person engages tends to decrease over time as this pattern continues, even on their better days.

Behavioral interventions seek to target this maladaptive pattern of behavior by encouraging *pacing* of activity such that the person engages in a regular, moderate level of activity. One particularly useful method for paced increase of activity is the quota system; based on behavioral theory, this approach allows the person to slowly increase his or her level of activity based on preset and achievable goals in order to increase his or her endurance rather than remaining active to the point of pain and fatigue. Interventions targeting behavioral activation often aim to increase engagement in potentially pleasurable activities, as well as increasing physical activity. Activation and other interventions based on operant behavioral theory have been shown to be effective in the management of chronic pain, particularly in improving function and activity level (George & Zeppieri, 2009; Molton, Graham, Stoelb, & Jensen, 2007).

### Relaxation and Imagery

The experience of chronic pain is commonly associated with emotional stress as well as muscle tension. Because muscle tension itself can cause additional pain, these variables often build off of each other and progressively amplify in intensity. Relaxation and imagery strategies work to interrupt this cycle, bring about muscle relaxation rather than tension, and reduce associated emotional stress. Relaxation and imagery strategies, being largely generated by the patient, can improve his or her sense of control over pain (Gustavsson & von Koch, 2006). Relaxation has long been recognized as an effective treatment for the management of chronic pain in a variety of medical conditions ("Integration of Behavioral and Relaxation Approaches Into the Treatment of Chronic Pain and Insomnia," 1996). With deep relaxation, patients are often taught how to breathe properly and more slowly, as well as to focus on specific muscle groups progressively and allow tension release. Imagery, in turn, allows patient to engage in imagination and mental processes that facilitate pain reduction. For example, patients may be taught to imagine themselves lying in a cool mountain stream or to imagine their pain changing shape or color.

### Hypnosis

Hypnosis brings the element of suggestion to relaxation and imagery. When the patient is in a susceptible state of relaxation, suggestions are made about either managing pain directly or possibly addressing an array of possible areas that are associated with improved pain management (e.g., sleep, coping techniques, restructuring cognitions, increasing activity). When people are hypnotized, the critical/judgmental influences of active frontal lobe attention often seem to be replaced by a more passive, accepting state. Thus, patients seem to be able to accept suggestions for relief that would not seem tenable in a waking state. As described by Jensen (2009, 2010), patients can be trained in any number of hypnotic techniques that reduce pain directly (e.g., relaxation, changing sensations, amnesia for the duration of pain, positive future imagery of living more comfortably). Importantly, as described by Patterson (Jensen, 2010), hypnosis may be most effective when the emphasis of suggestions is on everything but the pain itself. Thus, the patient may be encouraged to try new and different approaches to life and pain management while under a hypnotic state. Such suggestions can integrate all of the other approaches to pain discussed in this section.

### Mindfulness

Mindfulness involves noticing one's experience in the moment without attaching judgment to that experience. Through mindfulness meditation, one is able to notice that his or her experience is constantly changing and, in fact, one cannot hold onto a single thought or feeling even if he or she tries. Similarly, the person with chronic pain can gain awareness that his or her pain sensations are constantly changing and fluctuating. Because mindfulness involves observation *without judgment,* this further allows the patient to notice his or her pain in a new way, without the negative emotional reaction to the pain that has often become all too automatic. Greater mindfulness has been shown to account for less depression, pain-related anxiety, and disability in persons with chronic pain (McCracken, Gauntlett-Gilbert, & Vowles, 2007), and brain mechanisms involved in mindfulness meditation-related pain relief have been identified (Zeidan, Grant, Brown, McHaffie, & Coghill, 2012).

Mindfulness-based interventions have gained recent interest, though the benefits of mindfulness for persons with chronic pain have been studied for over 30 years. Mindfulness-Based Stress Reduction (MBSR) developed by Kabat-Zinn has been shown to be effective in reducing present moment pain and inhibition of activity by pain and improving pain coping (Kabat-Zinn, 1982; Kabat-Zinn, Lipworth, & Burney, 1985). MBSR appears to be more effective in improving health-related quality of life in patients with certain pain conditions (e.g., arthritis) as compared to others (e.g., headache/migraine). Other mindfulness interventions, including those that integrate movement, have also shown a positive effect on pain and pain coping, though further research is warranted (Chiesa & Serretti, 2011; Patil, 2009).

### Acceptance and Commitment Therapy

In recent years, Acceptance and Commitment Therapy (ACT), a mindfulness-based treatment based on contemporary behavioral theory, has gained recognition as an effective intervention in the management of chronic pain (see Chapters 4, "Understanding and Enhancing Psychological Acceptance" and 7, "Chilling Out: Meditation, Relaxation, and Yoga"). ACT works to improve the psychological health and quality of life of persons with chronic pain by increasing the person's acceptance of his or her pain, mindfulness of his or her pain experience, and engagement in actions that are consistent with personal values even when pain is present. ACT has been shown to be effective in improving pain, depression, pain-related anxiety, disability, healthcare use, work status, physical performance, and social functioning (McCracken, Vowles, & Eccleston, 2005; Vowles & McCracken, 2008; Wetherell et al., 2011), and the improvements in physical and emotional functioning have been shown to be maintained for 3 years after treatment (Vowles, McCracken, & O'Brien, 2011). In a randomized controlled trial comparing ACT and CBT, both interventions had similar positive outcomes; however, participants who received ACT reported significantly higher levels of satisfaction as compared with those who received CBT (Wetherell et al., 2011).

## Multidisciplinary Pain Treatment

Outcomes dramatically improve when comprehensive pain programs which take a biopsychosocial approach are utilized (Gatchel & Okifuji, 2006). The critical elements of comprehensive pain programs include repeated, intensive monitoring of physical training progress to individualize treatment; psychosocial assessment; cognitive behavioral treatment; psychopharmacological interventions for detoxification and psychological management; interdisciplinary, coordinated teams; and ongoing assessment using standardized outcomes. Such comprehensive programs more than double rates of sustained employment, halve the rate of subsequent surgeries, substantially decrease subsequent healthcare utilization and greatly decrease use of opioid medication (as reviewed by Gatchel & Okifuji, 2006). Regrettably, in spite of clear evidence of effectiveness, such programs are not often covered by insurance and, as such, may be difficult to find.

## Prevention and Health Enhancement

Given that the experience of pain is unavoidable, it is important to consider ways to prevent acute pain from being chronic; it is also important to prevent related problems such as opioid dependence. As reviewed above, the manner by which chronic pain develops is multifactorial and often includes physiological changes which are difficult to prevent. The key to prevention of pain-related problems involves preventing the degree to which pain interferes with meaningful activity. This often involves pacing activity and preventing the formation of catastrophic beliefs by reinforcing maintenance of activity and realistic beliefs (e.g. "This pain is frustrating, but I can deal with it because it is important to spend quality time with my family"). Given the increasing recognition of the dangers of chronic opioid use, efforts are underway to prescribe these in a more systematic manner. For example, some large healthcare provider organizations now require care plans that include treatment goals for all patients prescribed opioids over 90 days. The purpose of this is to ensure that medication or therapeutic prescriptions directly relate to pain goals, and that these goals are frequently revisited in order to wean from medications as soon as feasible. Overall, the best prevention and treatment for pain involves maintaining engagement in meaningful activity; effective interventions target decreasing the amount pain interferes with this.

Despite what is often portrayed in the media, there are no quick fixes for chronic pain. Medications, supplements, braces, implants, and so on do not offer magic solutions to a chronic problem. That stated, activity-based interventions such as yoga, tai chi, or walking groups are supported by the research literature.

## Conclusions and Future Research

Chronic pain is a massive healthcare problem in the United States and worldwide, and it creates untold levels of suffering and substantial societal disruption and financial burden. Most chronic pain is difficult to manage simply and is a source of frustration for the patient and healthcare provider alike. It is not surprising that patients pursue a wide variety of complementary and alternative approaches for pain reduction, in spite of minimal evidence for their efficacy (Eisenberg et al., 1993). Further, patients often seek basic medical approaches for chronic pain, in spite of repeated evidence that they are often not useful for this problem and can even make it worse. What we now know is that most patients will do better if they try to *manage* their chronic pain rather than cure it by using a biopsychosocial approach. Chronic pain is a multifaceted problem involving changes in lifestyle and accepting gradual changes with discipline, rather than seeking dramatic reductions in symptoms. Biopsychosocial approaches offer maps for such lifestyle changes, but they are not easy and do not offer quick fixes.

The most important element of biopsychosocial approaches to chronic pain may be gently encouraging the patient to abandon quick fixes and cures and to engage in a number of approaches that require discipline and an open mind, but are well-supported in the literature. Education, increasing activity, modifying negative thoughts, changing coping activities, meditation, and hypnosis have all been demonstrated to enable people to live happier with chronic pain. Ironically, the most successful treatments for chronic pain often do not reduce the pain itself but rather enable people to coexist with it more happily.

Unfortunately, whether using medications or psychosocial treatment to target pain reduction itself, chronic pain tends to decrease about 30% in fewer than one half of those engaged in any given treatment (Turk et al., 2011). Fortunately, as reviewed above, there are many treatment options. Clinicians need to assess pain *and* outcomes that are meaningful to patients (e.g., depression, anxiety, engagement in meaningful activity) and if improvements are not evident, change treatment. Treatment response is individual, so no one approach will benefit all patients.

Researchers and clinicians need to investigate tailored treatment in order to identify what treatment is likely to be effective for which patients under what circumstances. Many of the failings of a strictly biomedical approach stem from conceptualizing the desired outcome as solely decreased pain. A large-scale study of nearly 1,000 people (Turk et al., 2008) with chronic pain identified 19 outcome domains of importance, 7 of which were rated as at least 8 out of 10 (10 = extremely important). These 7 outcomes were enjoyment of life, fatigue, emotional well-being, physical activities, sleep, weakness, and concentration difficulty; these outcomes are grossly underrepresented in pain research (Beale, Cella, & Williams, 2011) and are rarely targeted in medical treatment. There is no single pill that will improve all of these things. Researchers, clinicians, and patients would be well served to keep in mind that pain is a biopsychosocial phenomenon that requires biopsychosocial treatment.

# References

Andersson, H. I., Ejlertsson, G., Leden, I., & Schersten, B. (1999). Impact of chronic pain on health care seeking, self care, and medication. Results from a population-based Swedish study. *Journal of Epidemiology and Community Health, 53*(8), 503–509.

Arnow, B. A., Hunkeler, E. M., Blasey, C. M., Lee, J., Constantino, M., Fireman, B., . . . Hayward, C. (2006). Comorbid depression, chronic pain, and disability in primary care. *Psychosomatic Medicine, 68*(2), 262–268.

Atkins, C. J., Kaplan, R. M., & Toshima, M. T. (1991). Close relationships in the epidemiology of cardiovascular disease. In W. H. Jones & D. Perlman (Eds.), *Advances in personal relationships* (Vol. 3, pp. 207–231). London, UK: Jessica Kingsley.

Beale, M., Cella, M., & Williams, A. C. (2011). Comparing patients' and clinician-researchers' outcome choice for psychological treatment of chronic pain. *Pain, 152*(10), 2283–2286.

Boothby, J. L., Thorn, B. E., Stroud, M. W., & Jensen, M. P. (1999). Coping with pain. In R. J. Gatchel & D. C. Turk (Eds.), *Psychosocial Factors in Pain: Critical perspectives* (pp. 343–359). New York, NY: Guilford Press.

Breivik, H., Collett, B., Ventafridda, V., Cohen, R., & Gallacher, D. (2006). Survey of chronic pain in Europe: Prevalence, impact on daily life, and treatment. *European Journal of Pain, 10*(4), 287–333.

Brown, G. K., Nicassio, P. M., & Wallston, K. A. (1989). Pain coping strategies and depression in rheumatoid arthritis. *Journal of Consulting and Clinical Psychology, 57*(5), 652–657.

Carnes, D., Parsons, S., Ashby, D., Breen, A., Foster, N. E., Pincus, T., . . . Underwood, M. (2007). Chronic musculoskeletal pain rarely presents in a single body site: Results from a UK population study. *Rheumatology, 46*(7), 1168–1170.

Casey, C. Y., Greenberg, M. A., Nicassio, P. M., Harpin, R. E., & Hubbard, D. (2008). Transition from acute to chronic pain and disability: A model including cognitive, affective, and trauma factors. *Pain, 134*(1–2), 69–79.

Chan, C. W., & Peng, P. (2011). Failed back surgery syndrome. *Pain Medicine, 12*(4), 577–606.

Chiesa, A., & Serretti, A. (2011). Mindfulness-based interventions for chronic pain: A systematic review of the evidence. *Journal of Alternative and Complementary Medicine, 17*(1), 83–93.

Chou, R., Baisden, J., Carragee, E. J., Resnick, D. K., Shaffer, W. O., & Loeser, J. D. (2009). Surgery for low back pain: A review of the evidence for an American Pain Society Clinical Practice Guideline. *Spine 34*(10), 1094–1109.

Cohen, S. (1988). Psychosocial models of the role of social support in the etiology of physical disease. *Health Psychology, 7*(3), 269–297.

Cohen, S., & Wills, T. A. (1985). Stress, social support, and the buffering hypothesis. *Psychological Bulletin, 98*(2), 310–357.

Conner, T. S., Tennen, H., Zautra, A. J., Affleck, G., Armeli, S., & Fifield, J. (2006). Coping with rheumatoid arthritis pain in daily life: Within-person analyses reveal hidden vulnerability for the formerly depressed. *Pain, 15*(126), 198–209.

Covic, T., Adamson, B., Spencer, D., & Howe, G. (2003). A biopsychosocial model of pain and depression in rheumatoid arthritis: A 12-month longitudinal study. *Rheumatology, 42*(11), 1287–1294.

Coyne, J. C., Rohrbaugh, M. J., Shoham, V., Sonnega, J. S., Nicklas, J. M., & Cranford, J. A. (2001). Prognostic importance of marital quality for survival of congestive heart failure. *American Journal of Cardiology, 88*(5), 526–529.

Derry, S., Gill, D., Phillips, T., & Moore, R. A. (2012). Milnacipran for neuropathic pain and fibromyalgia in adults. *Cochrane Database of Systemic Reviews, 3*, CD008244.

Dupeyron, A., Ribinik, P., Gelis, A., Genty, M., Claus, D., Herisson, C., & Coudeyre, E. (2011). Education in the management of low back pain: Literature review and recall of key recommendations for practice. *Annals of Physical Rehabilitation Medicine, 54*(5), 319–335.

Edwards, R. R., Bingham, C. O., 3rd, Bathon, J., & Haythornthwaite, J. A. (2006). Catastrophizing and pain in arthritis, fibromyalgia, and other rheumatic diseases. *Arthritis and Rheumatism, 55*(2), 325–332.

Eisenberg, D. M., Kessler, R. C., Foster, C., Norlock, F. E., Calkins, D. R., & Delbanco, T. L. (1993). Unconventional medicine in the United States: Prevalence, costs, and patterns of use. *New England Journal of Medicine, 328*(4), 246–252.

Engel, G. L. (1977). The need for a new medical model: A challenge for biomedicine. *Science, 196*(4286), 129–136.

Engel, G. L. (1980). The clinical application of the biopsychosocial model. *American Journal of Psychiatry, 137*(5), 535–544.

Falvo, D. (2005). *Medical and psychological aspects of chronic illness and disability* (pp. 1–22). Boston, MA: Jones and Bartlett.

Flor, H. (2003). Cortical reorganisation and chronic pain: Implications for rehabilitation. *Journal of Rehabilitation Medicine* (41 Suppl), 66–72.

Flor, H., Kerns, R. D., & Turk, D. C. (1987). The role of spouse reinforcement, perceived pain, and activity levels of chronic pain patients. *Journal of Psychosomatic Research, 31*(2), 251–259.

Flor, H., Knost, B., & Birbaumer, N. (2002). The role of operant conditioning in chronic pain: An experimental investigation. *Pain, 95*(1–2), 111–118.

Flor, H., Turk, D. C., & Rudy, T. E. (1989). Relationship of pain impact and significant other reinforcement of pain behaviors: The mediating role of gender, marital status and marital satisfaction. *Pain, 38*(1), 45–50.

Foley, K. M. (2003). Opioids and chronic neuropathic pain. *New England Journal of Medicine, 348*(13), 1279–1281.

Gaskin, D. J., & Richard, P. (2011). The economic costs of pain in the United States. In Institute of Medicine (Ed.), *Relieving pain in America: A blueprint for transforming prevention, care, education, and research* (pp. 301–337). Washington, DC: National Academies.

Gatchel, R. J., & Okifuji, A. (2006). Evidence-based scientific data documenting the treatment and cost-effectiveness of comprehensive pain programs for chronic nonmalignant pain. *Journal of Pain, 7*(11), 779–793.

Gatchel, R. J., & Rollings, K. H. (2008). Evidence-informed management of chronic low back pain with cognitive behavioral therapy. *Spine Journal, 8*(1), 40–44.

George, S. Z., & Zeppieri, G. (2009). Physical therapy utilization of graded exposure for patients with low back pain. *Journal of Orthopaedic and Sports Physical Therapy, 39*(7), 496–505.

Glajchen, M. (2001). Chronic pain: Treatment barriers and strategies for clinical practice. *Journal of the American Board Family Practice, 14*(3), 211–218.

Gross, D. P., Deshpande, S., Werner, E. L., Reneman, M. F., Miciak, M. A., & Buchbinder, R. (2012). Fostering change in back pain beliefs and behaviors: When public education is not enough. *Spine Journal, 12*(11), 979–988.

Guereje, O., Von Korff, M., Simon, G. E., & Gater, R. (1998). Persistent pain and well-being: A World Health Organization study in primary care. *Journal of the American Medical Association, 280*(2), 147–151.

Gustavsson, C., & von Koch, L. (2006). Applied relaxation in the treatment of long-lasting neck pain: A randomized controlled pilot study. *Journal of Rehabilitation Medicine, 38*(2), 100–107.

Harstall, C., & Ospina, M. (2003). How prevalent is chronic pain? *Pain: Clinical Updates, 11*(2), 1–4.

Hoftun, G. B., Romundstad, P. R., & Rygg, M. (2013). Association of parental chronic pain with chronic pain in the adolescent and young adult: Family linkage data from the HUNT Study. *JAMA Pediatrics, 167*(1), 61–69.

IASP Newsletter. (1986). Classification of chronic pain. Descriptions of chronic pain syndromes and definitions of pain terms. *Pain Supplement, 3*, S1–226.

Integration of behavioral and relaxation approaches into the treatment of chronic pain and insomnia. NIH Technology Assessment Panel on Integration of Behavioral and Relaxation Approaches into the Treatment of Chronic Pain and Insomnia. (1996). *Journal of the American Medical Association, 276*(4), 313–318.

Jensen, M. P. (2009). Hypnosis for chronic pain management: A new hope. *Pain, 146*(3), 235–237.

Jensen, M. P. (2010). Measurement of pain. In S. M. Fishman, J. C. Ballantyne, & J. P. Rathmell (Eds.), *Bonica's management of pain* (4th ed., pp. 251–270). Media, PA: Williams & Wilkins.

Jensen, M. P., Ehde, D. M., Hoffman, A. J., Patterson, D. R., Czerniecki, J. M., & Robinson, L. R. (2002). Cognitions, coping and social environment predict adjustment to phantom limb pain. *Pain, 95*(1–2), 133–142.

Jensen, M. P., Moore, M. R., Bockow, T. B., Ehde, D. M., & Engel, J. M. (2011). Psychosocial factors and adjustment to chronic pain in persons with physical disabilities: A systematic review. *Archives of Physical Medicine and Rehabilitation, 92*(1), 146–160.

Jensen, M. P., & Patterson, D. R. (2008). Hypnosis and the relief of pain and pain disorders. In M. Nash & A. Barnier (Eds.), *The Oxford handbook of hypnosis* (pp. 503–533). New York, NY: Oxford University Press.

Johannes, C. B., Le, T. K., Zhou, X., Johnston, J. A., & Dworkin, R. H. (2010). The prevalence of chronic pain in United States adults: Results of an Internet-based survey. *Journal of Pain, 11*(11), 1230–1239.

Kaasboll, J., Lydersen, S., & Indredavik, M. S. (2012). Psychological symptoms in children of parents with chronic pain-the HUNT study. *Pain, 153*(5), 1054–1062.

Kabat-Zinn, J. (1982). An outpatient program in behavioral medicine for chronic pain patients based on the practice of mindfulness meditation: Theoretical considerations and preliminary results. *General Hospital Psychiatry, 4*(1), 33–47.

Kabat-Zinn, J., Lipworth, L., & Burney, R. (1985). The clinical use of mindfulness meditation for the self-regulation of chronic pain. *Journal of Behavioral Medicine, 8*(2), 163–190.

Keefe, F. J., Rumble, M. E., Scipio, C. D., Giordano, L. A., & Perri, L. M. (2004). Psychological aspects of persistent pain: Current state of the science. *Journal of Pain, 5*(4), 195–211.

Kerns, R. D., Rosenberg, R., & Otis, J. D. (2002). Self-appraised problem solving and pain-relevant social support as predictors of the experience of chronic pain. *Annals of Behavioral Medicine, 24*(2), 100–105.

Kessler, R. C., Berglund, P., Demler, O., Jin, R., Koretz, D., Merikangas, K. R.,... National Comorbidity Survey Replication. (2003). The epidemiology of major depressive disorder: Results from the National Comorbidity Survey Replication (NCS-R). *Journal of the American Medical Association, 289*(23), 3095–3105.

Kosciulek, J. F. (2007). The social context of coping. In E. Martz & H. Livneh (Eds.), *Coping with chronic illness and disability: Theoretical, empirical, and clinical aspects* (pp. 73–88). New York, NY: Springer.

Lipton, R. B., Bigal, M. E., Kolodner, K., Stewart, W. F., Liberman, J. N., & Steiner, T. J. (2003). The family impact of migraine: Population-based studies in the USA and UK. *Cephalalgia, 23*(6), 429–440.

Loeser, J. D. (2001). Evaluation of the pain patient. In J. D. Loeser (Ed.), *Bonica's management of pain* (3rd ed.). Philadelphia, PA: Lippincot, Williams, & Wilkins.

Lopez-Martinez, A. E., Esteve-Zarazaga, R., & Ramirez-Maestre, C. (2008). Perceived social support and coping responses are independent variables explaining pain adjustment among chronic pain patients. *Journal of Pain, 9*(4), 373–379.

Lyons, R., Mickelson, K., Sullilvan, M., & Coyne, J. (1998). Coping as a communal process. *Journal of Social and Personal Relationships, 5*(15), 579–605.

Manne, S. L., Alfieri, T., Taylor, K. L., & Dougherty, J. (1999). Spousal negative responses to cancer patients: The role of social restriction, spouse mood, and relationship satisfaction. *Journal of Consulting and Clinical Psychology, 67*(3), 352–361.

McCracken, L. M., Gauntlett-Gilbert, J., & Vowles, K. E. (2007). The role of mindfulness in a contextual cognitive-behavioral analysis of chronic pain-related suffering and disability. *Pain, 131*(1–2), 63–69.

McCracken, L. M., Vowles, K. E., & Eccleston, C. (2005). Acceptance-based treatment for persons with complex, long standing chronic pain: A preliminary analysis of treatment outcome in comparison to a waiting phase. *Behaviour Research and Therapy, 43*(10), 1335–1346.

Melnikova, I. (2010). Pain market. *Nature Reviews Drug Discovery, 9*(8), 589–590.

Molton, I. R., Graham, C., Stoelb, B. L., & Jensen, M. P. (2007). Current psychological approaches to the management of chronic pain. *Current Opinion in Anaesthesiology, 20*(5), 485–489.

Moos, R. H., & Holahan, C. J. (2007). Adaptive tasks and methods of coping with illness and disability. In E. Martz & H. Livneh (Eds.), *Coping with chronic illness and disability: Theoretical, empirical, and clinical aspects* (pp. 107–128). New York, NY: Springer.

Morley, S., Eccleston, C., & Williams, A. (1999). Systematic review and meta-analysis of randomized controlled trials of cognitive behaviour therapy and behaviour therapy for chronic pain in adults, excluding headache. *Pain, 80*(1–2), 1–13.

National Center for Health Statistics. (2011). *Health, United States, 2010: With special feature on death and dying.* Hyattsville, MD: Author.

Ospina, M., & Harstall, C. (2002). *Prevalence of chronic pain: An overview.* Edmonton, Canada: Alberta Heritage Foundation for Medical Research.

Patil, S. G. (2009). Effectiveness of mindfulness meditation (Vipassana) in the management of chronic low back pain. *Indian Journal of Anaesthesia, 53*(2), 158–163.

Pergolizzi, J. V., J.r., Raffa, R. B., & Taylor, R. J.r., (2014). Treating acute pain in light of the chronification of pain. *Pain Management Nursing, 15*(1), 380–390.

Portenoy, R. K., Ugarte, C., Fuller, I., & Haas, G. (2004). Population-based survey of pain in the United States: Differences among White, African American, and Hispanic subjects. *Journal of Pain, 5*(6), 317–328.

Reichling, D. B., & Levine, J. D. (2009). Critical role of nociceptor plasticity in chronic pain. *Trends Neurosciences, 32*(12), 611–618.

Romano, J. M., & Turner, J. A. (1985). Chronic pain and depression: Does the evidence support a relationship? *Psychological Bulletin, 97*(1), 18–34.

Sanders, S. H. (1996). Operant conditioning with chronic pain: Back to basics. In R. J. Gatchel & D. C. Turk (Eds.), *Psychological approaches to pain management: A practitioner's handbook* (pp. 112–130). New York, NY: Guilford Press.

Schwartz, L., Jensen, M. P., & Romano, J. M. (2005). The development and psychometric evaluation of an instrument to assess spouse responses to pain and well behavior in patients with chronic pain: The Spouse Response Inventory. *Journal of Pain, 6*(4), 243–252.

Simpson, K. H. (2004). Opioids for persistent non-cancer pain: Recommendations for clinical practice. *British Journal of Anaesthesia, 92*(3), 326–328.

Skinner, M., Wilson, H. D., & Turk, D. C. (2012). Cognitive-behavioral perspective and cognitive-behavioral therapy for people with chronic pain: Distinctions, outcomes, and innovations. *Journal of Cognitive Psychotherapy, 23*(2), 93–113.

Steglitz, J., Buscemi, J., & Ferguson, M. J. (2011). *The future of pain research, education, and treatment: A summary of the IOM report "Relieving pain in America: A blueprint for transforming prevention, care, education, and research."* Washington, DC: Institute of Medicine.

Sullivan, M. J., Thorn, B., Haythornthwaite, J. A., Keefe, F., Martin, M., Bradley, L. A., & Lefebvre, J. C. (2001). Theoretical perspectives on the relation between catastrophizing and pain. *Clinical Journal of Pain, 17*(1), 52–64.

Tsang, A., Von Korff, M., Lee, S., Alonso, J., Karam, E., Angermeyer, M. C., . . . Watanabe, M. (2008). Common chronic pain conditions in developed and developing countries: Gender and age differences and comorbidity with depression-anxiety disorders. *Journal of Pain, 9*(10), 883–891.

Turk, D. C. (2001). Combining somatic and psychosocial treatment for chronic pain patients: Perhaps 1 + 1 does = 3. *Clinical Journal of Pain, 17*(4), 281–283.

Turk, D. C. (2002). Clinical effectiveness and cost-effectiveness of treatments for patients with chronic pain. *Clinical Journal of Pain, 18*(6), 355–365.

Turk, D. C., Dworkin, R. H., Revicki, D., Harding, G., Burke, L. B., Cella, D., . . . Rappaport, B. A. (2008). Identifying important outcome domains for chronic pain clinical trials: An IMMPACT survey of people with pain. *Pain, 137*(2), 276–285.

Turk, D. C., & Okifuji, A. (2009). Pain terms and taxonomies of pain. In J. C. Fishmanm, J. C. Ballantyne, & J. P. Rathmell (Eds.), *Bonica's management of pain* (4th ed., pp. 13–23). New York, NY: Lippincott, Williams, & Wilkins.

Turk, D. C., Wilson, H. D., & Cahana, A. (2011). Treatment of chronic non-cancer pain. *Lancet, 377*(9784), 2226–2235.

van Tulder, M., Koes, B., & Bombardier, C. (2002). Low back pain. *Best Practice & Research Clinical Rheumatology, 16*(5), 761–775.

Vowles, K. E., & McCracken, L. M. (2008). Acceptance and values-based action in chronic pain: A study of treatment effectiveness and process. *Journal of Consulting and Clinical Psychology, 76*(3), 397–407.

Vowles, K. E., McCracken, L. M., & O'Brien, J. Z. (2011). Acceptance and values-based action in chronic pain: A three-year follow-up analysis of treatment effectiveness and process. *Behaviour Research and Therapy, 49*(11), 748–755.

Wetherell, J. L., Afari, N., Rutledge, T., Sorrell, J. T., Stoddard, J. A., Petkus, A. J., . . . Atkinson, J. H. (2011). A randomized, controlled trial of acceptance and commitment therapy and cognitive-behavioral therapy for chronic pain. *Pain, 152*(9), 2098–2107.

Zautra, A. J., Fasman, R., Parish, B. P., & Davis, M. C. (2007). Daily fatigue in women with osteoarthritis, rheumatoid arthritis, and fibromyalgia. *Pain, 128*(1–2), 128–135.

Zeidan, F., Grant, J. A., Brown, C. A., McHaffie, J. G., & Coghill, R. C. (2012). Mindfulness meditation-related pain relief: Evidence for unique brain mechanisms in the regulation of pain. *Neuroscience Letters, 520*(2), 165–173.

# 7

# Chilling Out

## Meditation, Relaxation, and Yoga

*Anne Malaktaris*

*Peter Lemons*

*Steven Jay Lynn*

*Liam Condon*

Binghamton University

Americans are overstressed. The Stress in America report published by the American Psychological Association (APA) states the problem plainly: "Americans are struggling to balance work and home life and make time to engage in healthy behaviors, with stress not only taking a toll on their personal physical health but also affecting the emotional and physical well-being of their families" (APA, 2010, p. 5). Three years later, an APA report, which included the findings of a survey of over 2,000 adults, revealed that Americans name job pressure, money, health, relationships, poor nutrition, media overload, and sleep deprivation as the top causes of stress. Even positive events, such as a wedding or a vacation, may evoke stress. A whopping 77% of respondents indicated that they regularly experience physical symptoms ostensibly caused by stress, including fatigue, headache, upset stomach, and muscle tension. Additionally, 73% of adults reported that they regularly experience stress-related psychological symptoms, including irritability or anger, nervousness, and lack of energy. Clearly, the repercussions of our active, stress-laden, and sometimes helter-skelter lives are very much with us.

Americans have increasingly turned to complementary and alternative health approaches, including meditation, relaxation, and yoga to increase physical relaxation and mental calmness, relieve stress, and promote psychological balance and general well-being. As we discuss in this chapter, these practices have been used to advantage for millennia in cultures around the world. Yet over the past several decades, medical, psychological, and neuroscientific research increasingly supports their efficacy and has begun to shine light on the processes mediating this efficacy. Nevertheless, we suggest that caution is warranted in drawing strong inferences regarding the effectiveness of these practices. In many cases, the assertions advanced for the benefits of these techniques outstrip an arguably inconclusive, yet steadily accumulating, body of research (see Sedlmeier et al., 2012).

## Overview and Definitions

Meditation has been practiced for health and healing for thousands of years. Although Buddhist, Christian, Islamic, Hindu, and Jewish traditions have integrated meditation into their spiritual practices, in recent years, meditation has made deep inroads into mainstream Western cultures and enjoyed wide application to prevent and treat psychological and physical maladies and to enhance quality of life (Grossman, Nieman, Schmidt, & Walach, 2004). In fact, meditation seems all the rage today. Famous people, including Oprah Winfrey, actor Hugh Jackman, singer Katy Perry, and governor of California Jerry Brown, vouch for its transformative power, and well-respected scientific journals do not shy away from publishing articles on meditation. As of December 2013, if you were to Google *meditation*, you would get more than 34 million hits and, with a little more digging, find apps to guide meditation, recorded music to promote a meditative state, and CDs to listen to while you walk or sit in meditative contemplation. Indeed, meditation has grown in popularity in the United States over a span as short as 5 years: In a 2007 national survey of 23,393 adults, 9.4% of respondents reported they had meditated in the past 12 months, compared with 7.6% in a similar survey conducted in 2002 (P. M. Barnes, Bloom, & Nahin, 2008). Respondents reported using meditation for a host of problems, including anxiety, pain, depression, stress, insomnia, and physical or emotional symptoms associated with chronic illnesses (e.g., heart disease, cancer).

Meditation encompasses a sizable corpus of practices and thereby eludes a consensus definition. Still, for our purposes, we will adopt Lama Surya Das's (1997) broad definition of meditation as "mental discipline, an effort to train the mind through the cultivation of mindful awareness and attention to the present moment" (p. 260). From a psychological vantage point, meditation represents a broad category of self-regulation practices that focus attention and awareness. Most types of meditation share four elements: a quiet environment, a specific posture, focused attention, and an open, non-judgmental attitude on the part of the practitioner.

In its most basic sense, mindfulness meditation involves focusing attention nonjudgmentally on moment-to-moment experience—whatever comes up in the flux of consciousness (see Chapter 4, "Understanding and Enhancing Psychological Acceptance"). Accordingly, individuals are often instructed simply to be attentive to/mindful of the ever-changing contents of consciousness. Alternately, the meditator may be taught to be mindful of the in-and-out flow of the breath or to alternate mindful attention from the breath to thoughts, feelings, and sensations, and vice versa. The Transcendental Meditation (V. A. Barnes & Orme-Johnson, 2012) technique, practiced for 15 to 20 minutes twice per day, is derived from Hindu traditions and uses a mantra (word, sound, or phrase repeated silently) to prevent or minimize distracting thoughts. Loving-kindness/compassion meditation refers to achieving a mental state of unselfish and unconditional kindness or compassion directed to all beings, usually going beyond compassion for the self to extend to wishes for the peace, health, and well-being of others, ranging from friends to adversaries, radiating to all sentient beings (Fredrickson, Cohn, Coffey, Pek, & Finkel, 2008). Qi gong is a discipline derived from traditional Chinese medicine that combines gentle physical movements, mental focus, and deep breathing (K. C. Tang, 1994). Finally, tai chi originated in traditional Chinese martial arts and is sometimes referred to as "moving meditation" (Jin, 1992). Tai chi practitioners move their bodies slowly, gently, and with awareness, while breathing deeply.

## Introduction: Relaxation and Yoga

From antiquity to the present time, people have used one or more relaxation techniques to contend with the storms and stresses of everyday life. A family of relaxation interventions, commonly used in clinical and research settings, include autogenic training (AT), progressive muscle relaxation (PMR), diaphragmatic breathing, and yoga. In a 2007 health survey of U.S. adults (P. M. Barnes et al., 2008), 12.7% of adults used deep-breathing exercises, 2.9% used progressive relaxation, and 2.2% used guided imagery for health purposes. The 2007 National Health Statistics Report on complementary and alternative medicine (CAM) stated that yoga was one of the most common CAM therapies used by adults in the United States, as it was practiced by 6.1% of the population (P. M. Barnes et al., 2008). Many respondents reported that they used books to learn these techniques, rather than consulting a professional provider, underscoring the ready availability of instructional materials regarding these practices.

The first relaxation practice we will discuss is AT. AT is a series of six standard 15-minute exercises, first described by the German psychiatrist Johannes Heinrich Schultz in 1932 (Rosa, 1976). The exercises are first taught and then self-administered on a daily or as-needed basis. They encourage participants, through the use of specific suggestions (e.g., "I am completely calm"), to alter the content of their thinking and visualization, relax their bodies by reducing muscle tension, and spread feelings of heaviness and warmth (e.g., "My hands are very warm . . . my arms are very warm") throughout their bodies (Brannon & Feist, 2009, p. 124). To accomplish this goal, participants often focus on physical sensations, such as their breathing or heartbeat.

PMR involves alternately tensing and relaxing muscles in a progressive manner, for example, starting with the head and finishing with the toes. In the early 1920s, Edmund Jacobson (1929) devised PMR and found that by tensing and relaxing 16 different muscle groups in the body, participants experienced extreme relaxation and stress symptom reduction (McCallie, Blum, & Hood, 2006). According to Manzoni, Pagnini, Castelnuovo, and Molinari (2008), PMR is one of the best-studied and most effective relaxation techniques and is commonly used in conjunction with other treatments (e.g., systematic desensitization for specific phobias).

Another widely used relaxation practice is yoga. The term *yoga* encompasses diverse traditions, represented in Buddhism, Hinduism, and Jainism, and styles that often have in common their use of breathing techniques, mental concentration, meditation, and a sequence of postures (Bussing, Ostermann, Ludtke, & Michalsen, 2012). The typical yoga session lasts 1 to 2 hours and is frequently combined with explicit relaxation instructions and visualizations or guided imagery to promote relaxation and well-being (Sarang & Telles, 2006).

## Promoting Psychological Health

In recent years, meditation and relaxation have emerged as promising adjunctive or stand-alone treatments for a variety of psychological maladies.

Their cost-effectiveness and lack of aversive effects make these interventions especially appealing and promising for disease prevention and health promotion.

## Mindfulness Meditation (MM)

MM is an integral feature of an expanding number of cognitive behavioral techniques, including Mindfulness-Based Stress Reduction (MBSR; Kabat-Zinn, 2003), Mindfulness-Based Cognitive Therapy (MBCT; Segal, Williams, & Teasdale, 2002), Dialectical Behavior Therapy (DBT; Linehan, 1993), Acceptance and Commitment Therapy (ACT; Hayes, Strosahl, & Wilson, 1999), and Integrative Behavioral Couples Therapy (IBCT; Christensen, Jacobson, & Babcock, 1995). Moreover, mindfulness can elicit positive emotions, promote response flexibility, decrease reactivity to thoughts and emotions, and minimize negative affect and rumination (Davis & Hayes, 2011).

Hofmann, Sawyer, Witt, and Oh (2010) conducted a meta-analysis of 39 studies of mindfulness-based therapies (mostly MBSR or MBCT) for a range of conditions, particularly anxiety and depression. Using Cohen's (1988) conventions for gauging effect sizes[1] (0.2 = small effect, 0.5 = medium effect, 0.8 = large effect), Hofmann et al. found medium effect sizes for pre- to posttreatment improvements in anxiety and mood symptoms for overall samples. In patients with both anxiety and mood disorders, mindfulness-based interventions were associated with even larger effects. Coelho, Canter, and Ernst (2007) reviewed four studies of MBCT for the prevention of relapse of major depression and concluded that evidence from randomized clinical trials suggests that MBCT adds benefit to treatment as usual in preventing relapse for individuals with recurrent (three or more) depressive episodes.

Clinicians have employed mindfulness and meditation, specifically, to treat anxiety (Roemer, Orsillo, & Salters-Pedneault, 2008), depression (Teasdale et al., 2000), chronic pain (Grossman, Tiefenthaler-Gilmer, Raysz, & Kesper, 2007), insomnia (Britton, Haynes, Fridel, & Bootzin, 2012), and substance abuse (Bowen et al., 2006), as well as to enhance overall health and quality of life (Grossman et al., 2004). For example, MBCT prevents relapse in depression on the order of 50% (Hofmann et al., 2010; Piet & Hougaard, 2011) and also produces substantial anxiety reductions in children and adults (Kim et al., 2010; Semple & Lee, 2011). In a meta-analysis of 163 studies of meditation, Sedlmeier et al. (2012) reported, on average, medium effect sizes for positive changes in emotionality, relationship problems, and attention.

In a randomized controlled trial (RCT), Jain et al. (2007) compared the efficacy of 1-month mindfulness meditation training with somatic relaxation training (combining autogenic training, progressive muscle relaxation, and diaphragmatic breathing) in treating students who reported distress. Brief training in mindfulness meditation or somatic relaxation reduced distress and increased positive mood states, compared with a waitlist control group. Mindfulness meditation appeared to be specific in its ability to reduce distracting and ruminative thoughts compared with relaxation alone. Moreover, Barrett et al. (2012) found that an 8-week mindfulnesss meditation training exerts a preventive effect on acute respiratory infections and reduces the days of illness associated with such infections, compared with an observational control condition.

## Loving-Kindness and Compassion Meditation

Researchers have recently begun to herald the healing and disease prevention potential of loving-kindness and compassion (e.g., meditating on compassion for all sentient beings) meditation. For example, Fredrickson et al. (2008) reported that following loving-kindness meditation, people experienced a wide range of salutary effects, including increases in positive emotions, mindfulness, social support, and decreased illness symptoms, compared with people who did not meditate, suggesting a possible preventive or ameliorative health role for loving-kindness meditation. Hofmann, Grossman, and Hinton (2011) reviewed studies of kindness/compassion-oriented meditation practices and concluded that they increase positive affect, decrease negative affect, reduce stress-induced subjective distress and immune response, and produce activation in brain regions associated with empathy and emotional processing.

## Autogenic Training (AT)

Schlamann, Naglatzki, de Greiff, Forsting, and Gizewski (2010) used functional magnetic resonance imaging (fMRI) during AT (i.e., imagine a heavy and warm right arm) to compare the hemodynamic activity of participants who had been practicing AT techniques for years with those who were AT-naïve. Experienced AT users exhibited greater activation in the left postcentral brain and prefrontal and insular areas compared with AT-naïve controls, reflecting differences in sensory and emotional processing (i.e. upregulation of cerebral activity associated with imagination and directed attention) in these participants. Furthermore, insular activity was positively correlated with the number of years of AT training, possibly as a result of an increase of emotional connection to sensory information. Interestingly, AT produced comparable levels of subjective relaxation across trained and naïve AT participants.

Stetter and Kupper's (2002) meta-analysis of 60 AT studies (35 RCTs) found medium-to-large effect sizes for pre-post comparisons and larger effect sizes still for RCTs. Positive effects in studies involving control of cognitions revealed beneficial outcomes (at least 3 studies) for coronary heart disease, somatoform pain disorder, sleep disorders, mild-to-moderate essential hypertension, and other medical conditions. Nevertheless, when compared with other treatments, AT generally showed no advantage or small negative effect sizes. More recent studies have also found support for the use of AT in clinical populations. For example, Yurdakul, Holttum, and Bowden (2009) found that participants using AT experienced a reduction in anxiety and panic attacks, and general improvements in sleep patterns, mood, and perceptions of well-being. Researchers have also shown that AT alleviates insomnia (Bowden, Lorenc, & Robinson, 2012) and have used AT in combination with other stress reduction techniques in treating posttraumatic stress disorder (PTSD; Staples, Abdel, Jamil, & Gordon, 2011). Additionally, an RCT that compared mindfulness meditation with general relaxation training heavily based on AT and a waitlist control found that both mindfulness and relaxation training significantly alleviated distress compared with the control group (Jain et al., 2007).

## Progressive Muscle Relaxation (PMR)

PMR has also been widely used to address psychological complaints, particularly in combination with other therapeutic techniques. For example, PMR has been combined with systematic desensitization for specific phobia and cognitive behavioral therapy (CBT) for social phobia, generalized anxiety disorder, and panic disorder (McCallie et al., 2006). PMR has also been used as a component in more encompassing therapies for the treatment of (a) PTSD in rape victims and (b) depression (McCallie et al., 2006). Moreover, in 1999 the American Academy of Sleep Medicine concluded that PMR was one of three effective nonpharmacological treatments for chronic insomnia (Morin et al., 1999) and produces treatment gains superior to a placebo (Morin et al., 2006). Finally, Vancampfort et al. (2011) found that PMR reduced state anxiety, psychological stress, and fatigue and increased well-being in an inpatient sample with schizophrenia as compared with schizophrenic patients randomly assigned to a resting control condition.

## Yoga

Forfylow (2011) reviewed studies spanning 2003 to 2010 on the effects of yoga on anxiety and depression. The author noted that although there seems to be consistent support for the efficacy of yoga-based practices in conjunction with therapy for these disorders, only half of the studies were RCTs, leaving room for doubt regarding the effectiveness of the interventions (Forfylow, 2011). Furthermore, Forfylow noted that a diverse array of practices fall under the *yoga* banner, and the many styles incorporated with psychotherapy across the studies she reviewed precluded the ability to pinpoint the types of yoga (ranging from gentle to more invigorating practices) that produced the best treatment outcomes (either in general or by disorder group). Moreover, none of the studies explored potential side-effects of treatment, even though the physical nature of certain types of yoga might be ill suited for some patients. In a recent study (using magnetic resonance spectroscopy; Streeter et al., 2010) of healthy subjects randomized into either a yoga group or a metabolically equivalent walking group, participants in the yoga group demonstrated greater decreases in mood and anxiety. Finally, in a review of RCTs based on CAM approaches for the treatment of insomnia, Sarris and Byrne (2011) reported that yoga and tai chi were useful in the treatment of chronic insomnia.

## Qi Gong

Chen, Comerford, Shinnick, and Ziedonis (2010) explored the benefits of adding integrative qi gong meditation (a blend of relaxation, guided imagery, breathing, inward attention, and mindfulness) to short-term residential treatment for substance abuse. Participants chose either qi gong meditation or Stress Management and Relaxation Training (SMART; Flannery, 1990), an established stress management program, as part of their treatment program. Both groups reported improvement in treatment outcome (e.g., anxiety, withdrawal symptoms). Moreover, the meditation group completed treatment at a higher rate and reported greater reduction in craving compared with the SMART group.

## Improving Physical Health and Well-Being

Several meta-analyses (see Baer, 2003; Hofmann et al., 2010) have provided support for mindfulness techniques in the treatment of a variety of problems and medical conditions, ranging from chronic pain to diabetes. Although a consensus has not yet emerged, largely due to limitations in the research base, we next review some of the most promising findings regarding the effectiveness of meditation and relaxation.

Davidson et al. (2003) conducted an RCT on the effects of mindfulness meditation training on brain and immune functions. Subjects participated in an 8-week training in mindfulness meditation (Kabat-Zinn et al., 1992). The researchers found an increase in antibody titers with influenza vaccination, a measure of immune response, in meditators compared with nonmeditating control subjects, suggesting that a short program in mindfulness mediation can exert demonstrable effects on immune function.

Grossman et al. (2004) conducted a comprehensive meta-analysis of 20 published and unpublished health-related studies that examined mindfulness-based stress reduction (MBSR) for a wide range of clinical populations (e.g., pain, cancer, heart disease, depression, anxiety) and stressed nonclinical groups. Overall, the studies showed similar, medium effect sizes (approximately 0.5), providing evidence that MBSR may ameliorate a broad range of clinical and nonclinical problems.

Noting the importance of separating the specific effects of meditation from nonspecific factors, especially placebo effects and demand characteristics, Zeidan, Johnson, Gordon, and Goolkasian (2010) determined that at least some effects of brief mindfulness training (3-day, 1-hour total) were the byproduct of active elements of the practice (notice flow of breath, passively acknowledge a thought and let it go by) and not demand characteristics. Specifically, participants in the active condition reported greater reductions in heart rate, depression, fatigue, negative mood, and confusion than participants who practiced sham mindfulness meditation (i.e., take deep breaths every 2–3 minutes as they sit in meditation) and a control condition in which they sat for 20 minutes each session and were allowed to speak to each other.

Researchers have found that qi gong, tai chi, PMR, and AT provide physical health benefits. In a review of the health benefits of qi gong and tai chi, Jahnke, Larkey, Rogers, Etnier, and Lin (2010) found that these methods were associated with positive effects on bone health, favorable cardiovascular and pulmonary outcomes (e.g., reduced blood pressure and heart rate), and improved strength and flexibility. These meditative movement techniques showed wide-ranging benefits, particularly for the elderly and for individuals with a chronically sedentary lifestyle. PMR has also been used with biofeedback to alleviate headache and hypertension (McCallie et al., 2006). Finally, AT appears to relieve chronic subjective dizziness, likely mediated by anxiety reduction (Goto, Tsutsumi, Kabeya, & Ogawa, 2012). Still, a problem in evaluating these methods, and yoga as well, is that they often are combined with other methods, making isolation of the specific practices and mechanisms problematic. For example, practices that fall under the rubric of yoga often include relaxation or meditation. Moreover, practices that rely on movement often do not include control conditions matched for metabolic activity (e.g., exercise), rendering the meaning of comparisons across conditions difficult, if not impossible, to interpret.

## Treating Pain

The treatment of chronic pain is another promising area for the application of relaxation and meditation techniques. For example, Vowles, McCracken, and Eccleston (2008) explored how acceptance influenced the relations between catastrophizing and patient functioning in individuals with chronic pain. Acceptance mediated the effects of catastrophic thinking on depression, anxiety, and avoidance (Vowles, et al., 2008). Accordingly, a focus on acceptance and psychological flexibility in treating chronic pain may be beneficial.

Zeidan, Gordon, Merchant, and Goolkasian (2010) investigated the effects of brief mindfulness meditation training on ratings of painful electrical stimulation. After a 3-day (20 minutes per day) mindfulness meditation intervention, participants' ratings of pain in response to electrical stimulation decreased between pre- and postmeditation ratings. Pain sensitivity likewise decreased after meditation training. The brief 3-day intervention was effective at reducing pain ratings and anxiety scores compared with baseline testing and other cognitive manipulations (i.e., math distraction and relaxation conditions).

Chapman and Bredin's (2011) review suggests that yoga may play a role in the prevention and treatment of chronic disease, exerting a positive influence on obesity, high blood pressure, high cholesterol, and chronic pain. In a recent meta-analysis of 16 clinical studies (Bussing et al., 2012), yoga-based interventions were found to reduce pain and pain-associated disability after collapsing across styles of yoga. According to Wren, Wright, Carson, and Keefe (2011), pre-1990 studies that investigated the effects of yoga on pain tended not to use controlled clinical trials. In their review of more recent controlled clinical trials, Wren et al. identified three studies that found reductions in chronic back pain using yoga and reported that (1) Iyengar yoga, which uses props such as belts, wooden implements, and ropes to help achieve postures, was more effective than an education control (K. A. Williams et al., 2009); (2) Viniyoga, an individualized yoga method, was more effective than aerobic exercise or education control (Sherman, Cherkin, Erro, Miglioretti, & Deyo, 2005); and (3) Hatha yoga, which focuses on developing mental and physical strength, reduced back and neck pain according to a survey of more than 2,000 U.S. adults (Saper, Eisenberg, Davis, Culpepper, & Phillips, 2004). Three additional RCTs found support for yoga-based interventions: John, Sharma, Sharma, and Kankane (2007) found that yoga was more effective than a psychoeducational control condition for alleviating migraine related distress; Sareen, Kumari, Gajebasia, and Gajebasia (2007) reported that yoga, in addition to treatment as usual (TAU), was more effective than TAU alone for improving quality of life for chronic pancreatitis patients; and Tekur, Singphow, Nagendra, and Raghuram (2008) determined that short-term intensive yoga was more effective than physical exercise in reducing lower back pain–related disability scores.

In contrast to these studies, a pilot RCT conducted by Galantino et al. (2004) to test a Hatha yoga protocol against a waitlist control group for chronic lower back pain did not obtain significant group differences. Wren et al. (2011) noted that the samples in the aforementioned RCTs were predominantly White, middle-aged women, generally of high socioeconomic status. Nevertheless, Saper et al. (2013) demonstrated that treatment gains following once- or twice-weekly yoga classes generalize to low-income minority adults with moderate to severe chronic low back pain.

# Reducing Stress

Recent research has provided support for the benefits of meditation practice. For example, Pace et al. (2009) explored the effects of meditation practices that foster compassion on immune, neuroendocrine, and behavioral responses to psychosocial stress. Healthy adult volunteers were randomized to 6 weeks of training in compassion meditation or a health discussion control group followed by exposure to a standardized laboratory stressor. Although group assignment had no effect on stress responses among meditators, increased meditation practice was correlated with reduced stress-induced immune and behavioral responses.

In another study (Mohan, Sharma, & Bijlani, 2011), healthy adult male student volunteers practiced 20 minutes of guided meditation either before or after exposure to a stress-inducing computer game. Control subjects waited quietly for an equivalent period of time. Psychological stress exposure was associated with an increase in physiological (e.g., galvanic skin response, heart rate, electromyography) and psychological (acute psychological stress questionnaire scores) markers of stress. However, meditation practiced before the stressful event was associated with relaxation, as indicated by decreases in physiological and acute psychological stress in response to the stressor.

# Conclusions From Review of Research Evidence

One major limitation of the research is that the heterogeneity of meditation practices and participants makes comparisons among studies and use of meta-analytic techniques difficult. Furthermore, given the dominance of cross-sectional studies, it is impossible to rule out preexisting differences in individuals who participate in meditation practice as an explanation for observed differences in brain structure and function. Moreover, the effects of relaxation and other variables (e.g., eyes closed, sitting quietly) have not been parceled out in many studies of meditation. Divergent results across studies may be due to differences in participants, type of meditation, and control conditions (Hölzel et al., 2011). As Sedlmeier et al. (2012) observed, methodological shortcomings have precluded both a comprehensive understanding of why and how meditation works and the ability to draw strong conclusions from the existing literature. We suggest that researchers conduct longitudinal RCTs, clearly operationalize procedures, assess theoretically relevant treatment mechanisms, and conduct studies pertinent to disease prevention.

With respect to research on Transcendental Meditation (TM), the findings have been somewhat mixed. Schneider, Walton, Salerno, and Nidich (2006) contend that RCTs pertinent to both primary and secondary prevention suggest that TM can play a role in cardiovascular disease prevention and health promotion, producing reductions in markers of cardiovascular disease including blood pressure and psychosocial stress. Nevertheless, although TM appears to play a preventive role in reducing alcohol use rates among male university students, it does not do so for female students (Haaga et al., 2011). Additionally, significant effects of TM have not been observed in the treatment of attention deficit hyperactivity disorder in children (Krisanaprakornkit, Ngamjarus, Witoonchart, & Piyavhatkul, 2010). Moreover, some of the findings may be biased given the affiliation of the researchers with the Transcendental Meditation organization (Canter & Ernst, 2004).

Despite these limitations, there exists at least tentative support for the benefits of the approaches we have reviewed, although few studies have examined the long-term effects of brief versus long-term practice. At least in the case of meditation, short-term practice has been demonstrated to be effective in several studies (e.g. Hölzel et al., 2011; Y. Tang et al., 2007; Wenk-Sormaz, 2005). Accordingly, meditation may benefit people who do not embark on long-term or intensive training and may emerge as a powerful and broadly applicable tool in the contemporary health care provider's arsenal. Still, long-term follow-ups are necessary to confirm this rosy conclusion and to document the role of interventions on disease prevention and health maintenance and promotion.

Like meditation, not all studies that evaluate PMR have yielded the same conclusions. One RCT evaluating PMR in the treatment of chronic neck pain found little effect (Viljanen et al., 2003), and high school students administered PMR did not report any change in trait anxiety following treatment (Rasid & Parish, 1998). Similarly, the effects of PMR on pediatric migraines were dubious in a 1995 meta-analysis (Herman, Kim, & Blanchard, 1995). Nevertheless, PMR is associated with health benefits across numerous studies that vary in methodological rigor.

## Roles of Meditation, Relaxation, and Yoga in the Healthcare Delivery System

Although meditation is increasingly being used as a stand-alone intervention or in conjunction with more traditional approaches, meditation remains a marginalized practice for many Westerners. A. Williams, Van Ness, Dixon, and McCorkle (2012) identified barriers to meditation practice in a survey of 150 family caregivers to adults with cancer visiting an outpatient chemotherapy center. Commonly cited barriers related to beliefs and misconceptions about meditation, such as "I can't sit still long enough to meditate," in which case individuals can be instructed to meditate while walking or lying down. Alternately, people who reject meditation because they associate it with religion can be assured that meditation is widely practiced in secular settings.

Himelstein (2011) contends that meditation-based programs can be rehabilitative for incarcerated populations. He reported that three meditation-based interventions have been used frequently in correctional populations—Transcendental Meditation, Mindfulness-Based Stress Reduction, and 10-day Vipassana (i.e., insight meditation) retreats—and concluded that benefits associated with meditation-based programs encompass increased psychological well-being and a decrease in substance use and recidivism.

Meditation, relaxation, and yoga have also been examined among healthcare providers themselves. A self-care program consisting of yoga, tai chi, meditation classes, and Reiki (a supposedly energy-based practice involving touch) healing sessions was designed for nurses at a university-based hospital (Raingruber & Robinson, 2007). Based on measures derived from self-care journals, the program provided benefits that include relaxing sensations, enhanced problem-solving ability, and increased ability to focus on patient needs. Goodman and Schorling (2012) conducted a pre-post study of healthcare providers in a university medical center. The intervention (2.5 hours a week for 8 weeks plus a 7-hour retreat) included training in four types of formal mindfulness/relaxation practices (body scan—a relaxation technique requiring practitioners to move their attention to different parts of the body—mindful movement, walking meditation, and sitting meditation) as well as discussion focusing on the application of mindfulness at work. Burnout decreased and well-being improved after treatment, although physical health scores did not change. Davis and Hayes (2011) reviewed the literature on the effects of mindfulness on therapists and therapist trainees and found that mindfulness training increased empathy, compassion, and counseling skills and decreased stress and anxiety.

Black, Milam, and Sussman (2009) observed that although the efficacy of meditation interventions has been examined among adult samples, the effects of meditation-based treatments among youth are less well established. Black and colleagues reviewed studies of the effects of sitting-meditative practices among youth (6 to 18 years) in school, clinic, and community settings. Meditation practices (mindfulness meditation, Transcendental Meditation, Mindfulness-Based Stress Reduction, and Mindfulness-Based Cognitive Therapy) yielded effect sizes that were slightly smaller than those obtained from adult samples. Referring to Cohen's (1988) guidelines, the researchers found small to medium effects for physiological outcomes and small to large effects for psychosocial/behavioral outcomes. The review implies that various meditation-based procedures are effective interventions in the treatment and possible prevention of physiological, psychosocial, and behavioral conditions among youth.

Eberth and Sedlmeier (2012) completed a comprehensive overview of the effects of mindfulness meditation on various psychological variables in non-clinical settings. The studies encompassed many variables, including attention, intelligence, self-attributed mindfulness, positive and negative emotions, emotion regulation, personality traits, self-concept, self-realization, stress, and well-being. Eberth and Sedlmeier found an effect size of $r = 0.27$ averaged across all studies and dependent variables, though the effects differed widely, thus suggesting that meditation practices may have a sizeable impact on physical and psychological health in nonclinical populations.

Along with meditation and mindfulness training, yoga-based interventions have been tested in a medical context. Pointing to the widespread contribution of stress to symptoms that warrant primary health care visits, researchers in Sweden (Kohn, Lundholm, Bryngelsson, Anderzen-Carlsson, & Westerdahl, 2013) conducted an RCT comparing a 12-week course of medical yoga therapy plus standard treatment with standard treatment alone in a primary care setting. Results revealed significant decreases in the stress level of patients and increases in their perceptions of overall health in the yoga group compared with the control group. Similarly, in a study of people ages

60 and up with dementia living in a long-term care facility, participants who received a 12-week yoga training experienced a reduction in depression and blood pressure and an increase in flexibility, muscle strength, and endurance compared with elders who simply maintained their regular daily activities (Fan & Chen, 2011). Clearly, yoga may play a role in the modern health-care environment.

## Specifics for Application

Clinicians and healthy individuals can select from a variety of approaches to foster relaxation, ranging from simply sitting still with eyes closed, to systematic and progressive relaxation of different muscle groups, to cue-controlled relaxation. We invite readers to implement these techniques amid the hustle and bustle of everyday life. For example, cue-controlled relaxation can be practiced on a daily basis. First pair a calm, relaxed state of mind and body with a cue, such as forming a circle with the thumb and forefinger, or thinking or saying a phrase such as "calm and at ease." Then use the cue to trigger a relaxation response on either a periodic basis, say, once every 1 or 2 hours, or in response to stressful situations or internal tension.

Breathing retraining or diaphragmatic breathing also can be practiced in either a relaxed or stressful environment. In this technique, engage in deep slow breathing (6 to 8 breaths per minute) from the diaphragm. The technique is widely used to counteract chronic anxiety associated with generalized anxiety disorder and the hyperventilation and autonomic nervous system arousal associated with panic disorder and posttraumatic stress disorder (Hazlett-Stevens & Craske, 2008). The ability to self-administer relaxation is a key advantage of this family of interventions (McCallie et al., 2006).

Like relaxation, enhanced mindfulness can be achieved after formal training or following brief instructions presented in many books or DVDs with scripts widely available on the Internet. In training mindfulness based on focusing on the breath, practitioners first get to know the ins and outs of the breath and pay attention to each inhalation and exhalation, perhaps counting breaths, from 1 to 10 as a way of promoting concentration, always bringing attention back to the breath when it wanders and resuming the 1 to 10 count. In mindfulness awareness meditation, practitioners acknowledge and label shifts of attention from the breath (e.g., thinking, feeling, remembering, judging) and allow the contents of consciousness to pass through awareness without judgment. As these examples illustrate, a fundamental element of mindfulness training is attention training. The same is true of loving-kindness meditative practices, which focus on achieving an expansive state or sense of compassion directed toward the self and others.

Mellinger and Lynn (2014) described attention-switching techniques to facilitate attention control, acceptance, and relaxation. These techniques can also short-circuit the tendency to ruminate about past or upcoming events. For example, participants are instructed to be aware of each body part, starting with the top of the head, paying nonjudgmental attention to what is experienced, and then releasing the attention from the designated part to refocus attention on the breath. The exercise may start as follows: "Experience the very top of your head . . . what do you notice . . . what are you aware of? What sensations, if any, can you feel? Whatever it is, whatever you experience, just notice, be aware . . . now release your attention gently from the top of your head and turn your awareness to your breath . . . perhaps you can be aware of the still point between inspiration and exhalation or the warmth or coolness of the breath . . . what is it you notice? And now, gently and easily, bring your attention to your forehead muscle and the area around your eyes . . . whatever you feel there, whatever you experience, let it be . . . no need to judge . . . just let it be." Participants continue in this manner until the entire body is scanned, from head to toes, always returning to the breath. Body scans can also facilitate relaxation, with the client scanning the body for tense spots and relaxing each in turn until the entire body is relaxed. Although relaxation and meditation approaches are often practiced while sitting, they can be implemented throughout the day while engaged in virtually any activity, thereby increasing the generalizability of gains.

MBSR is a specific application of mindfulness training that has been widely used and well researched. MBSR includes nonjudgmental awareness of bodily sensations and focused breathing to calm the mind. MBSR encourages individuals to have a sense of nonjudgmental awareness of bodily experiences and focuses attention on strengths and away from symptoms and eliminates judgment of sensations associated with symptoms. In a review, Praissman (2008) found that MBSR is effective for reducing the stress and anxiety that accompanies daily life and chronic illness. MBSR can also benefit healthcare providers (e.g., nurse practitioners) and enhance their interactions with patients. In Praissman's review, no reports of negative side effects from MBSR were documented. Praissman concluded that MBSR is safe and effective for patients and healthcare providers.

Relaxation and meditation/mindfulness techniques are often combined with other clinical interventions, as in the case of MBCT (Segal et al., 2002), introduced earlier. MBCT has demonstrated efficacy for preventing depressive relapse in patients with three or more depressive episodes (Coelho et al., 2007). MBCT consists of eight weekly, class-based sessions, which are two and a half hours in length, and one all-day practice between the sixth and seventh classes. Between sessions, participants develop their capacity for intentional, nonjudgmental awareness of the present moment through mindfulness practice. Formal practices may involve meditation, body scan/ relaxation, walking mindfully, and yoga. Informal practice encourages mindfulness during everyday distressing activities, or activities commonly performed on auto-pilot such as driving or showering.

MBCT principles and techniques taught in MBCT can also be applied on an individual basis. MBCT teaches patients to "disengage from dysphoria-activated depressogenic thinking" (Teasdale et al., 2000, p. 615). MBCT shifts the patient's *relation* to thoughts by teaching observation of thoughts and feelings from a "decentered" perspective, that is, as ephemeral mental events rather than meaningful reflections of the self or "facts" (Safran & Segal, 1990). Decentering prevents rumination from escalating transient dysphoric affect into persistent negative mood (Broderick, 2005). Patients practice a "being mode" of mind, observing their stream of consciousness without entanglement in distressing thoughts (Wenzlaff & Luxton, 2003).

Hofmann et al. (2011) have suggested that loving-kindness/compassion meditation may be combined to advantage with empirically supported treatments. Moreover, researchers (Ong, Shapiro, & Manber, 2008) have successfully integrated CBT and mindfulness meditation to treat insomnia. The combination of mindfulness meditation, relaxation, and yoga with empirically supported interventions will continue to be a fruitful area of inquiry, as will isolating the individual and interactive effects of component interventions in multifaceted treatments.

Before closing, we sound a note of caution given the widespread embrace of the approaches we have presented. Many of the studies in the literature are not RCTs, do not follow participants over time, do not control adequately for nonspecific effects, do not clearly define terms (e.g., mindfulness) and the procedures implemented, and do not contrast well-experienced practitioners with relative beginners. Still, the techniques we reviewed may be self-taught following initial instruction, are cost-effective, portable, and may be valuable adjunctive or stand-alone interventions for many psychological and medical conditions. Moreover, we suggest that meditation, relaxation, and yoga may play a role in disease prevention and health maintenance by reducing risk factors associated with acute (e.g., respiratory illness) and chronic diseases or conditions (e.g., recurrent major depression, hypertension) and in promoting healthy behaviors (e.g., reducing alcohol consumption). Given that relaxation, meditation, and yoga have few, if any, adverse side effects clearly attributable to their practice, they may be well worth implementing in psychotherapy and in everyday life.

# References

American Psychological Association. (2010). *Stress in America report*. Retrieved from http://www.apa.org/news/press/releases/stress/index.aspx

American Psychological Association. (2013). *Stress in America report*. Retrieved from http://www.apa.org/news/press/releases/stress/2012/full-report.pdf

Baer, R. A. (2003). Mindfulness training as a clinical intervention: A conceptual and empirical review. *Clinical Psychology: Science and Practice, 10,* 125–143.

Barnes, P. M., Bloom, B., & Nahin, R. L. (2008). Complementary and alternative medicine use among adults and children: United States, 2007. *National Health Statistics Reports, 12,* 1–24.

Barnes, V. A., & Orme-Johnson, D. W. (2012). Prevention and treatment of cardiovascular disease in adolescents and adults through the Transcendental Meditation Program: A research review update. *Current Hypertension Reviews, 8*(3), 227–242.

Barrett, B., Hayney, M. S., Muller, D., Rakel, D., Ward, A., Obasi, C. N., . . . Coe, C. L. (2012). Meditation or exercise for preventing acute respiratory infection: A randomized controlled trial. *Annals of Family Medicine, 10*(4), 337–346.

Black, D. S., Milam, J., & Sussman, S. (2009). Sitting-meditation interventions among youth: A review of treatment efficacy. *Pediatrics, 124*(3), 532–e541. doi:10.1542/peds.2008-3434

Bowden, A., Lorenc, A., & Robinson, N. (2012). Autogenic training as a behavioural approach to insomnia: A prospective cohort study. *Primary Health Care Research and Development, 13*(2), 175–185. Retrieved from http://proxy.binghamton.edu/login?url=http://search.proquest.com/docview/1011275035?accountid=14168

Bowen, S., Witkiewitz, K., Dillworth, T. M., Chawla, N., Simpson, T. L., Ostafin, B. D., . . . Marlatt, G. A. (2006). Mindfulness meditation and substance use in an incarcerated population. *Psychology of Addictive Behaviors, 20,* 343–347.

Brannon, L., & Feist, J. (2009). *Health psychology: An introduction to behavior and health* (7th ed.). Belmont, CA: Wadsworth.

Britton, W. B., Haynes, P. L., Fridel, K. W., & Bootzin, R. R. (2012). Mindfulness-based cognitive therapy improves polysomnographic and subjective sleep profiles in antidepressant users with sleep complaints. *Psychotherapy and Psychosomatics, 81,* 296–304.

Broderick, P. C. (2005). Mindfulness and coping with dysphoric mood: Contrasts with rumination and distraction. *Cognitive Therapy and Research, 29*(5), 501–510.

Bussing, A., Ostermann, T., Ludtke, R., & Michalsen, A. (2012). Effects of yoga interventions on pain and pain-associated disability: A meta-analysis. *Journal of Pain, 13*(1), 1–9. Retrieved from http://proxy.binghamton.edu/login?url=http://search.proquest.com/docview/927684831?accountid=14168

Canter, P. H., & Ernst, E. (2004). Insufficient evidence to conclude whether or not transcendental meditation decreases blood pressure: Results of a systematic review of randomized clinical trials. *Journal of Hypertension, 22*(11), 2049–2054.

Chapman, K. L., & Bredin, S. S. (2011). Why yoga? An introduction to philosophy, practice, and the role of yoga in health promotion and disease prevention. *Health & Fitness Journal of Canada, 3*(2), 13–21.

Chen, K. W., Comerford, A., Shinnick, P., & Ziedonis, D. M. (2010). Introducing qi gong meditation into residential addiction treatment: A pilot study where gender makes a difference. *Journal of Alternative and Complementary Medicine, 16*(8), 875–882. doi:10.1089/acm.2009.0443

Christensen, A., Jacobson, N. S., & Babcock, J. C. (1995). Integrative behavioral couple therapy. In N. S. Jacobson & A. S. Gurman (Eds.), *Clinical handbook of couples therapy* (pp. 31–64). New York, NY: Guilford Press.

Coelho, H. F., Canter, P. H., & Ernst, E. (2007). Mindfulness-based cognitive therapy: Evaluating current evidence and informing future research. *Journal of Consulting and Clinical Psychology, 75*(6), 1000–1005. doi:10.1037/0022–006X.75.6.1000

Cohen, J. (1988). *Statistical power analysis for the behavioral sciences* (2nd ed.). Hillsdale, NJ: Lawrence Erlbaum.

Das, L. S. (1997). *Awakening the Buddha within: Eight steps to enlightenment.* New York, NY: Broadway Books.

Davidson, R. J., Kabat-Zinn, J., Schumacher, J., Rosenkranz, M., Muller, D., Santorelli, S. F., & Sheridan, J. F. (2003). Alterations in brain and immune function produced by mindfulness meditation. *Psychosomatic Medicine, 65*(4), 564–570. doi:10.1097/01.PSY.0000077505.67574.E3

Davis, D. M., & Hayes, J. A. (2011). What are the benefits of mindfulness? A practice review of psychotherapy-related research. *Psychotherapy, 48*(2), 198–208. doi:10.1037/a0022062

Eberth, J., & Sedlmeier, P. (2012). The effects of mindfulness meditation: A meta-analysis. *Mindfulness, 3*(3), 174–189. doi:10.1007/s12671–012–0101-x

Fan, J. T., & Chen, K. M. (2011). Using silver yoga exercises to promote physical and mental health of elders with dementia in long-term care facilities. *International Psychogeriatrics, 23*(8), 1222–1230.

Flannery, R. B. (1990). *Becoming stress resistant through the project smart program.* New York, NY: Continuum.

Forfylow, A. L. (2011). Integrating yoga with psychotherapy: A complementary treatment for anxiety and depression. *Canadian Journal of Counseling and Psychotherapy, 45*(2), 132–150. Retrieved from http://proxy.binghamton.edu/login?url=http://search.proquest.com/docview/1023197989?accountid=14168

Fredrickson, B. L., Cohn, M. A., Coffey, K. A., Pek, J., & Finkel, S. M. (2008). Open hearts build lives: Positive emotions, induced through loving-kindness meditation, build consequential personal resources. *Journal of Personality and Social Psychology, 95*(5), 1045–1062.

Galantino, M. L., Bzdewka, T. M., Eissler-Russo, J. L., Holbrook, M. L., Mogck, E. P., Geigle, P., & Farrar, J. T. (2004). The impact of modified hatha yoga on chronic low back pain: A pilot study. *Alternative Therapies in Health & Medicine, 10*, 56–59.

Goodman, M. J., & Schorling, J. B. (2012). A mindfulness course decreases burnout and improves well-being among healthcare providers. *International Journal of Psychiatry in Medicine, 43*(2), 119–128. doi:10.2190/PM.43.2.b

Goto, F., Tsutsumi, T., Kabeya, M., & Ogawa, K. (2012). Outcomes of autogenic training for patients with chronic subjective dizziness. *Journal of Psychosomatic Research, 72*(5), 410–411. Retrieved from http://proxy.binghamton.edu/login?url=http://search.proquest.com/docview/1027508418?accountid=14168

Grossman, P., Niemann, L., Schmidt, S., & Walach, H. (2004). Mindfulness-based stress reduction and health benefits: A meta-analysis. *Journal of Psychosomatic Research, 57,* 35–43. doi:10.1016/S0022–3999(03)00573–7

Grossman, P., Tiefenthaler-Gilmer, U., Raysz, A., & Kesper, U. (2007). Mindfulness training as an intervention for fibromyalgia: Evidence of postintervention and 3-year follow-up benefits in well-being. *Psychotherapy and Psychosomatics, 76,* 226–233.

Haaga, D. A, Grosswald, S., Gaylord-King, C, Rainforth, M., Tanner, M., Travis, F., . . . Schneider, R. H. (2011). Effects of the transcendental meditation program on substance use among university students. *Cardiology Research and Practice, 2011,* 1–9. doi:10.4061/2011/537101.

Hayes, S. C., Strosahl, K. D., & Wilson, K. G. (1999). *Acceptance and commitment therapy: An experiential approach to behavior change.* New York, NY: Guilford Press.

Hazlett-Stevens, H., & Craske, M. G. (2008) Breathing retraining and diaphragmatic breathing techniques. In W. T. O'Donhue & J. F. Fisher (Eds.), *Cognitive behavior therapy: Applying empirically supported techniques in your practice* (pp. 68–74). Hoboken, NJ: John Wiley & Sons.

Hermann, C., Kim, M., & Blanchard, E. B. (1995). Behavioral and prophylactic pharmacological intervention studies of pediatric migraine: An exploratory meta-analysis. *Pain, 60*(3), 239–255.

Himelstein, S. (2011). Meditation research: The state of the art in correctional settings. *International Journal of Offender Therapy and Comparative Criminology, 55*(4), 646–661. doi:10.1177/0306624X10364485

Hofmann, S. G., Grossman, P., & Hinton, D. E. (2011). Loving-kindness and compassion meditation: Potential for psychological interventions. *Clinical Psychology Review, 31*(7), 1126–1132.

Hofmann, S. G., Sawyer, A. T., Witt, A. A., & Oh, D. (2010). The effect of mindfulness-based therapy on anxiety and depression: A meta-analytic review. *Journal of Consulting and Clinical Psychology, 78*(2), 169–183. doi:10.1037/a0018555

Hölzel, B. K., Carmody, J., Vangel, M., Congleton, C., Yerramsetti, S. M., Gard, T., & Lazar, S. W. (2011). Mindfulness practice leads to increases in regional brain gray matter density. *Psychiatry Research: Neuroimaging, 191*(1), 36–43.

Jacobson, E. (1929). *Progressive relaxation.* Chicago, IL: University of Chicago Press.

Jahnke, R., Larkey, L., Rogers, C., Etnier, J., & Lin, F. (2010). A comprehensive review of health benefits of qi gong and tai chi. *American Journal of Health Promotion, 24*(6), e1-e25.

Jain, S., Shapiro, S. L., Swanick, S., Roesch, S. C., Mills, P. J., Bell, I., & Schwartz, G. E. R. (2007). A randomized controlled trial of mindfulness meditation versus relaxation training: Effects on distress, positive states of mind, rumination, and distraction. *Annals of Behavioral Medicine, 33*(1), 11–21. doi:10.1207/s15324796abm3301_2

Jin, P. (1992). Efficacy of tai chi, brisk walking, meditation, and reading in reducing mental and emotional stress. *Journal of Psychosomatic Research, 36*(4), 361–370.

John P. J., Sharma N., Sharma C. M., & Kankane A. (2007). Effectiveness of yoga therapy in the treatment of migraine without aura: A randomized controlled trial. *Headache, 47,* 654–61.

Kabat-Zinn, J. (2003). Mindfulness-based interventions in context: Past, present, and future. *Clinical Psychology: Science & Practice, 10,* 144–156.

Kabat-Zinn, J., Massion, A. O., Kristeller, J., Peterson, L. G., Fletcher, K. E., Pbert, L., . . . Santorelli, S. F. (1992). Effectiveness of a meditation-based stress reduction program in the treatment of anxiety disorder. *American Journal of Psychiatry, 149*(7), 936–943.

Kim, B., Lee, S., Kim, Y. W., Choi, T. K., Yook, K., Suh, S. Y., & Yook, K. (2010). Effectiveness of a mindfulness-based cognitive therapy program as an adjunct to pharmacotherapy in patients with panic disorder. *Journal of Anxiety Disorders, 24*(6), 590–595. doi:10.1016/j.janxdis.2010.03.019

Kohn, M., Lundholm, U. P., Bryngelsson, I., Anderzen-Carlsson, A., & Westerdahl, E. (2013). Medical yoga for patients with stress-related symptoms and diagnoses in primary health care: A randomized controlled trial. *Evidence-Based Complementary and Alternative Medicine, 2013,* 1–8. doi:10.1155/2013/215348

Krisanaprakornkit, T., Ngamjarus, C., Witoonchart, C., & Piyavhatkul, N. (2010). Meditation therapies for attention-deficit/hyperactivity disorder (ADHD). *Cochrane Database of Systematic Reviews, 6.*

Linehan, M. M. (1993). *Cognitive–behavioral treatment of borderline personality disorder.* New York, NY: Guilford Press.

Manzoni, G. M., Pagnini, F., Castelnuovo, G., & Molinari, E. (2008). Relaxation training for anxiety: A ten-year systematic review with meta-analysis. *BMC Psychiatry, 8*(1), 41.

McCallie, M. S., Blum, C. M., & Hood, C. J. (2006). Progressive muscle relaxation. *Journal of Human Behavior in the Social Environment, 13*(3), 51–66. Retrieved from http://proxy.binghamton.edu/login?url=http://search.proquest.com/docvie w/621636949?accountid=14168

Mellinger, D., & Lynn, S. J. (2014). *Anxiety smarts: Cutting-edge strategies for overcoming everyday worry.* Unpublished manuscript.

Mohan, A., Sharma, R., & Bijlani, R. L. (2011). Effect of meditation on stress-induced changes in cognitive functions. *Journal of Alternative and Complementary Medicine, 17*(3), 207–212. doi:10.1089/acm.2010.0142

Morin, C. M., Bootzin, R. R., Buysse, D. J., Edinger, J. D., Espie, C. A., & Lichstein, K. L. (2006). Psychological and behavioral treatment of insomnia: Update of the recent evidence (1998–2004). *Sleep, 29*(11), 1398–1414.

Morin, C. M., Hauri, P. J., Espie, C. A., Spielman, A. J., Buysse, D. J., & Bootzin, R. R. (1999). Nonpharmacologic treatment of chronic insomnia. *Sleep, 22*(8), 1134–1156. Retrieved from http://ukpmc.ac.uk/abstract/MED/10617176

Ong, J. C, Shapiro, S. L., & Manber, R. (2008). Combining mindfulness meditation with cognitive-behavior therapy for insomnia: A treatment-development study. *Behaviour Therapy, 39,* 171–182.

Pace, T. W. W., Negi, L. T., Adame, D. D., Cole, S. P., Sivilli, T. I., Brown, T. D., . . . Raison, C. L. (2009). Effect of compassion meditation on neuroendocrine, innate immune and behavioral responses to psychosocial stress. *Psychoneuroendocrinology, 34*(1), 87–98. doi:10.1016/j.psyneuen.2008.08.011

Piet, J., & Hougaard, E. (2011). The effect of mindfulness-based cognitive therapy for prevention of relapse in recurrent major depressive disorder: A systematic review and meta-analysis. *Clinical Psychology Review, 31*(6), 1032–1040. doi:10.1016/j.cpr.2011.05.002

Praissman, S. (2008). Mindfulness-based stress reduction: A literature review and clinician's guide. *Journal of the American Academy of Nurse Practitioners, 20*(4), 212–216. doi:10.1111/j.1745–7599.2008.00306.x

Raingruber, B., & Robinson, C. (2007). The effectiveness of tai chi, yoga, meditation, and reiki healing sessions in promoting health and enhancing problem solving abilities of registered nurses. *Issues in Mental Health Nursing, 28*(10), 1141–1155. doi:10.1080/01612840701581255

Rasid, Z. M., & Parish, T. S. (1998). The effects of two types of relaxation training on students' level of anxiety. *Adolescence, 33*(129), 129–131.

Roemer, L., Orsillo, S. M., & Salters-Pedneault, K. (2008). Efficacy of an acceptance-based behavior therapy for generalized anxiety disorder: Evaluation in a randomized controlled trial. *Journal of Consulting and Clinical Psychology, 76,* 1083–1089.

Rosa, K. R. (1976). *Autogenic training.* London, UK: Victor Gollancz.

Safran, J. D., & Segal, Z. V. (1990). *Interpersonal process in cognitive therapy.* New York, NY: Basic Books.

Saper, R. B., Boah, A. R., Keosaian, J., Cerrada, C., Weinberg, J., & Sherman, K. J. (2013). Comparing once versus twice-weekly yoga classes for chronic low back pain in predominantly low income minorities: A randomized dosing trial. *Evidence-Based Complementary and Alternative Medicine, 2013,* 1–13.

Saper, R. B., Eisenberg, D. M., Davis, R. B., Culpepper, L., & Phillips, R. S. (2004). Prevalence and patterns of adult yoga use in the United States: Results of a national survey. *Alternative Therapies in Health Medicine, 10,* 44–49.

Sarang, P. S., & Telles, S. (2006). Oxygen consumption and respiration during and after two yoga relaxation techniques. *Applied Psychophysiology and Biofeedback, 31*(2), 143–153. doi:10.1007/s10484–006–9012–8

Sareen, S., Kumari, V., Gajebasia, K. S., & Gajebasia, N. K. (2007). Yoga: A tool for improving the quality of life in chronic pancreatitis. *World Journal of Gastroenterology, 13,* 391–397.

Sarris, J., & Byrne, G. J. (2011). A systematic review of insomnia and complementary medicine. *Sleep Medicine Reviews, 15*(2), 99–106.

Schlamann, M., Naglatzki, R., de Greiff, A., Forsting, M., & Gizewski, E. R. (2010). Autogenic training alters cerebral activation patterns in fMRI. *International Journal of Clinical and Experimental Hypnosis, 58*(4), 444–456.

Schneider, R. H., Walton, K. G., Salerno, J. W., & Nidich, S. I. (2006). Cardiovascular disease prevention and health promotion with the transcendental meditation program and Maharishi consciousness-based health care. *Ethnicity & Disease, 16*(3 Suppl 4), S4.

Sedlmeier, P., Eberth, J., Schwarz, M., Zimmermann, D., Haarig, F., Jaeger, S., & Kunze, S. (2012). The psychological effects of meditation: A meta-analysis. *Psychological Bulletin, 138*(6), 1139–1171.

Segal, Z. V., Williams, S., & Teasdale, J. (2002). *Mindfulness-based cognitive therapy for depression: A new approach to preventing relapse.* New York, NY: Guilford Press.

Semple, R. J., & Lee, J. (2011). *Mindfulness-based cognitive therapy for anxious children: A manual for treating childhood anxiety.* Oakland, CA: New Harbinger.

Sherman, K. J., Cherkin D. C., Erro J., Miglioretti, D. L., & Deyo, R. A. (2005). Comparing yoga, exercise, and a self-care book for chronic low back pain: A randomized, controlled trial. *Annals of Internal Medicine, 143,* 849–856.

Staples, J. K., Abdel, A., Jamil, A., & Gordon, J. S. (2011). Mind-body skills groups for posttraumatic stress disorder and depression symptoms in Palestinian children and adolescents in Gaza. *International Journal of Stress Management, 18*(3), 246–262. Retrieved from http://proxy.binghamton.edu/login?url=http://search.proquest.com/docview/873850965?accountid=14168

Stetter, F., & Kupper, S. (2002). Autogenic training: A meta-analysis of clinical outcome studies. *Applied Psychophysiology and Biofeedback, 27*(1), 45–98.

Streeter, C. C., Whitfield, T. H., Owen, L., Rein, T., Karri, S. K., Yakhkind, A., . . . Jensen, J. E. (2010). Effects of yoga versus walking on mood, anxiety, and brain GABA levels: A randomized controlled MRS study. *Journal of Alternative and Complementary Medicine, 16*(11), 1145–1152. Retrieved from http://proxy.binghamton.edu/login?url=http://search.proquest.com/docview/858914994?accountid=14168

Tang, K. C. (1994). Qigong therapy: Its effectiveness and regulation. *American Journal of Chinese Medicine, 22*(3–4), 235–242.

Tang, Y., Ma, Y., Wang, J., Feng, S., Yu, Q., Rothbart, M. K., . . . Posner, M. I. (2007). Short-term meditation training improves attention and self-regulation. *Proceedings of the National Academy of Sciences of the United States of America, 104,* 17152–17156.

Teasdale, J. D., Segal, Z. V., Williams, J. M., Ridgeway, V. A., Soulsby, J. M., & Lau, M. A. (2000). Prevention of relapse/recurrence in major depression by mindfulness-based cognitive therapy. *Journal of Consulting and Clinical Psychology, 68,* 615–623.

Tekur, P., Singphow, C., Nagendra, H. R., & Raghuram, N. (2008). Effect of short-term intensive yoga program on pain, functional disability and spinal flexibility in chronic low back pain: A randomized control study. *Journal of Alternative and Complementary Medicine, 14,* 637–644.

Vancampfort, D., De Hert, M., Knapen, J., Maurissen, K., Raepsaet, J., Deckx, S., . . . Probst, M. (2011). Effects of progressive muscle relaxation on state anxiety and subjective well-being in people with schizophrenia: A randomized controlled trial. *Clinical Rehabilitation, 25*(6), 567–575. Retrieved from http://proxy.binghamton.edu/login?url=http://search.proquest.com/docview/893269299?accountid=14168

Viljanen, M., Malmivaara, A., Uitti, J., Rinne, M., Palmroos, P., & Laippala, P. (2003). Effectiveness of dynamic muscle training, relaxation training, or ordinary activity for chronic neck pain: Randomized controlled trial. *British Medical Journal, 327*(7413), 475–485.

Vowles, K. E., McCracken, L. M., & Eccleston, C. (2008). Patient functioning and catastrophizing in chronic pain: The mediating effects of acceptance. *Health Psychology, 27*(2), S136-S143. doi:10.1037/0278–6133.27.2(Suppl.).S136

Wenk-Sormaz, H. (2005). Meditation can reduce habitual responding. *Alternative Therapies in Health and Medicine, 11*(2), 32–58.

Wenzlaff, R. M., & Luxton, D. D. (2003). The role of thought suppression in depressive rumination. *Cognitive Therapy and Research, 27*(3), 293–308.

Williams, A., Van Ness, P., Dixon, J., & McCorkle, R. (2012). Barriers to meditation by gender and age among cancer family caregivers. *Nursing Research, 61*(1), 22–27. doi:10.1097/NNR.0b013e3182337f4d

Williams, K. A., Abildso, C., Steinberg, L., Doyle, E. J., Epstein, B., Smith, D., . . . Cooper, L. (2009). Evaluation of the effectiveness and efficacy of Iyengar yoga therapy on chronic low back pain. *Spine, 34,* 2066–2076.

Wren, A. A., Wright, M. A., Carson, J. W., & Keefe, F. J. (2011). Yoga for persistent pain: New findings and directions for an ancient practice. *Pain, 152*(3), 477–480. Retrieved from http://proxy.binghamton.edu/login?url=http://search.proquest.com/docview/881003672?accountid=14168

Yurdakul, L., Holttum, S., & Bowden, A. (2009). Perceived changes associated with autogenic training for anxiety: A grounded theory study. *Psychology and Psychotherapy: Theory, Research and Practice, 82*(4), 403–419. Retrieved from http://proxy.binghamton.edu/login?url=http://search.proquest.com/docview/622128788?accountid=14168

Zeidan, F., Gordon, N. S., Merchant, J., & Goolkasian, P. (2010). The effects of brief mindfulness meditation training on experimentally induced pain. *Journal of Pain, 11*(3), 199–209. doi:10.1016/j.jpain.2009.07.015

Zeidan, F., Johnson, S. K., Gordon, N. S., & Goolkasian, P. (2010). Effects of brief and sham mindfulness meditation on mood and cardiovascular variables. *Journal of Alternative and Complementary Medicine, 16*(8), 867–873. doi:10.1089/acm.2009.0321

# Notes

1. All effect sizes reported in this chapter are Cohen's $d$, unless otherwise stated. Different ways of gauging effect sizes (e.g., $r$) based on variance explained have different metrics than Cohen's d.

# PART III

## Staying Healthy
## and Becoming Healthier

# 8

# Sleeping Well

*Richard R. Bootzin*

*Elaine Blank*

*Tucker Peck*

University of Arizona

Although we spend about one third of our lives asleep, there is much less research on sleep than on daytime activities. For example, in this book there is only one chapter on sleep, not one third of the chapters. Yet the quality of sleep affects a wide range of everyday activities, including daytime performance, memory, problem solving, sleepiness and fatigue, health, coping with stress, emotion regulation and the later development or protection from impulsivity, substance abuse, depression, and anxiety (e.g., Bootzin & Epstein, 2011). Sleeping well strengthens our capabilities whereas sleeping poorly saps our capabilities.

The importance of sleep has been long recognized. For example, Shakespeare's Macbeth said,

> *Me thought I heard a voice cry, Sleep no more!*
>
> *Macbeth does murder sleep,—the innocent sleep;*
>
> *Sleep that knits up the ravell'd sleave of care,*
>
> *The death of each day's life, sore labour's bath,*

*Balm of hurt minds, great nature's second course,*

*Chief nourisher in life's feast.* (Macbeth, Act II, Scene I)

In this chapter, we examine the many recommendations for how to sleep well and emphasize which among them have supporting evidence and which are myths. There are many tips, substances, and treatment programs for improving sleep. One category of suggestions, first described by Peter Hauri (1977) is called sleep hygiene.

# Sleep Hygiene: Myths and Facts

When we are sleeping well, most of us don't think about what factors contribute to a good night's sleep. However, as soon as sleep difficulties emerge, we naturally start looking for solutions. A common piece of advice, found in magazine articles, TV, the Internet, from doctors, and well-meaning friends, is to improve one's sleep hygiene. Sleep hygiene is defined as the control of behavioral and environmental factors that precede and may interfere with sleep. Although this broad definition can encompass nearly everything one might engage in or be around prior to sleep, the following factors are frequently discussed and are addressed in this section: sleep schedules, napping, physical exercise, alcohol, and caffeine and energy drink intake.

## Sleep Schedules

A consistent sleep schedule is often considered to be the best single thing one can do for one's sleep. In fact, in its section on sleep hygiene, the National Sleep Foundation states, "The most important sleep hygiene measure is to maintain a regular sleep and wake pattern seven days a week" (Thorpy, 2003, p. 1). Although this assertion seems intuitively correct, what does the research actually show? As it turns out, the research is mixed, with most of the evidence confirming the usefulness of a regular schedule but with some evidence showing that irregular sleep schedules may not be a problem for everyone.

A number of studies have found that regularizing one's sleep schedule has a positive effect on sleepiness and daytime functioning and, conversely, that going from a regular to an irregular sleep schedule has negative effects on these measures. For example, Manber, Bootzin, Acebo, and Carskadon (1996) found that when college students were assigned to go to bed and wake up within a predetermined one-hour window, they felt less sleepy and more alert during the day. These results held true even though participants in the control group to which they were compared got as much or more sleep every night but did not have to keep to a consistent wake-up schedule. Another study (Soehner, Kennedy, & Monk, 2011) examined sleep duration, timing, and quality in working adults aged 23 to 48. The authors found that more regular wake times, but not bed times, were associated with better overall sleep quality. Although this study did not examine participants' daytime functioning, we know from other studies (e.g., Cacioppo et al., 2002; Smith, Kozak, & Sullivan, 2012) that better sleep quality at night is associated with better mood and alertness during the day.

An important key for succeeding at having a consistent schedule is to keep technology out of the bedroom during the sleep period. This is of particular relevance for adolescents and young adults. Disruption due to television, computer games, Internet social networks, cell phones, and instant messaging does not allow for uninterrupted sound sleep. These disruptions increase daytime sleepiness (e.g., Van den Bulck, 2007).

Several studies have examined what happens when participants with a regular sleep schedule have to alter it. An early series of studies by Taub and Berger (1973) looked at the effects of shifting participants' sleep 2 to 4 hours forward or backward from their regular schedules. Under both circumstances, participants experienced greater levels of fatigue, worse mood, and worse performance on tests of attention and concentration. More recently, Wright, Bogan, and Wyatt (2013) reviewed a number of studies on shift work and found that people who went from having a regular sleep schedule to working shifts (and thus changing their sleep schedules) experienced more fatigue, poorer concentration, and lower moods compared with before the schedule changes. Taken together, these studies suggest that a regular sleep schedule, particularly a regular rise time, is beneficial for good functioning during the day.

In contrast, a few studies show that this may not always be the case. Bonnet and Alter (1982), in a small but intensive study (12 subjects had their sleep measured in the lab for 38 days!), found no differences in fatigue, mood, and performance on a variety of measures of attention between periods of regular and irregular sleep. The authors did find, however, that mood and performance showed a trend toward improvement following the period of regular sleep, implying that participants may have shown greater improvement if they stuck to a regular sleep schedule for longer. In summary, the evidence suggests that, generally, regularizing one's sleep schedule (particularly one's wake-up time) can be an effective tool for sleeping well.

## Napping

Generally people are advised not to take naps because naps can "disturb the normal pattern of sleep and wakefulness" (Thorpy, 2003, p. 1). It is important, however, to distinguish naps that are integrated into the daily schedule consistently, such as a siesta in Spain, from naps that occur irregularly depending on how sleepy the individual is. We know from a large number of studies (Edinger, Hoelscher, Marsh, Lipper, & Ionescu-Pioggia, 1992; Edinger & Sampson, 2003; Edinger, Wohlgemuth, Radtke, Marsh, & Quillian, 2001; Espie, Inglis, Tessier, & Harvey, 2001; Monk, Petrie, Hayes, & Kupfer, 1994; Monk, Reynolds, Buysse, DeGrazia, & Kupfer, 2003) that a regular daytime routine, even when naps are included, can be beneficial for nighttime sleep quality. Additionally, there is much evidence that naps can benefit alertness, performance, and mood, without interfering with nighttime sleep. However, the benefits of naps depend on when they are taken, for how long, how regularly, and if there had been sufficient sleep the night before.

Hayashi, Motoyoshi, and Hori (2005) found that both performance and alertness decreased after lunch when participants did not nap, and that naps improved both of these measures. Several other studies found that naps and caffeine combined were effective in combating midday sleepiness (Bonnet & Arand, 1994; Hayashi, Masuda, & Hori, 2003; Reyner & Horne, 1997). These studies recruited healthy individuals who were not sleep deprived, indicating that to benefit from naps one did not need to be sleep deprived. Several studies have compared naps with other alertness-promoting strategies, such as caffeine, bright light, and face washing. One study (Bonnet, Gomez, Wirth, & Arand, 1995) found that naps led to less sleepiness and more alertness, and that the effects of naps lasted longer than the effects of caffeine.

Along with evidence that naps can be beneficial, there is evidence that naps at particular times of day can be more beneficial than at other times, especially depending on how much sleep one has gotten the previous night. Broughton (1989) found that people are generally sleepier in the afternoon than at other times of the day, which makes naps more likely at this time. Older adults who wake up early and are sleepy in the evening are among those who would benefit from afternoon naps. Not surprisingly, naps taken in the afternoon tend to have better sleep quality (deeper sleep, less wakefulness during the nap, and shorter time to fall asleep) than naps taken later in the evening (Lavie & Weler, 1989). Similarly, there is evidence that naps taken at the wrong time—that is, outside of the afternoon sleepiness dip—can lead to more grogginess and a desire to return to sleep (Naitoh, 1981).

Several studies have examined the functional effects of naps taken at different times of day. A series of such studies (Hayashi & Hori, 1998; Hayashi, Ito, & Hori, 1999; Hayashi, Watanabe, & Hori, 1999) investigated the effects of a 20-minute nap on sleepiness and subjective and objective measures of performance. Naps were taken either midafternoon or before lunch.

Although participants felt less sleepy and thought they performed better after naps taken at either time, objective measures of performance revealed improvements only after the midafternoon naps. However, participants in another study (Dinges, Orne, Whitehouse, & Orne, 1987) showed greater improvements following earlier rather than later naps. The main difference was that the participants in the Dinges study were sleep deprived, whereas participants in the Hayashi studies were not. It appears that sleep-deprived individuals are more likely to benefit from earlier naps due to their extreme fatigue, whereas individuals who slept a normal amount the night before experience maximum benefits after a later nap.

If naps can have positive effects on alertness and daytime functioning, how long is an ideal nap? A series of studies (Brooks & Lack, 2006; Tietzel & Lack, 2001, 2002) has focused on this question. The studies looked at ultra-short naps of 30 and 90 seconds, short naps of 5 and 10 minutes (sometimes called power naps), and medium-length naps of 20 and 30 minutes. All of these nap lengths were compared with not taking a nap at all. Naps of 10, 20, and 30 minutes all revealed benefits in performance and alertness while decreasing fatigue, but naps of shorter lengths did not. Although benefits were immediately apparent following 10-minute naps, the 20- and 30-minute naps initially led to sleep inertia (a drive to continue to sleep) and only showed benefits 30 minutes or more after the nap. Additionally, the benefits of a 10-minute nap were greater than those following the longer naps. Thus, it appears that 10 minutes is the ideal length for a nap, as it leads to the greatest benefits and avoids the potential side effects of sleep inertia.

Of course, the final question about naps is whether they are harmful to one's nighttime sleep, as is commonly assumed. For healthy people, the answer appears to be *no*. Several studies of healthy younger and elderly adults (Buysse, Browman, Monk, & Reynolds, 1992; Pilcher, Michalowski, & Carrigan, 2001; Tamaki, Shirota, Tanaka, Hayashi, & Hori, 1999) have compared the nighttime sleep of people who nap with those who do not. These studies show that short naps (less than 20 minutes in duration) do not impact nighttime sleep. Hence, while long naps, especially when taken by people with insomnia, may have a negative impact on nighttime sleep, healthy adults can feel free to take a short nap in the afternoon.

## Physical Exercise

Another area of debate regarding sleep hygiene is physical exercise. Although exercise has been associated with better sleep quality (Ancoli-Israel, 2001), there are conflicting beliefs about when exercise should be undertaken and what type of exercise is best. Often strenuous exercise leads to worse sleep, whereas exercising regularly and being in good physical shape deepens and improves sleep (Hauri, 1977). In sleep hygiene recommendations, people are often told to exercise regularly, but not too close to bedtime. What does the research have to say?

The results appear somewhat contradictory. A review of a large number of studies (Kubitz, Landers, Petruzzello, & Han, 1996) found that morning exercise has positive effects on sleep quality the next night and found that evening exercise has the opposite effect. Conversely, other studies (O'Connor, Breus, & Youngstedt, 1998; Youngstedt, 2005) did not find any negative effects of prebedtime exercise on nighttime sleep. It should be remembered that there are large individual differences with regard to preference for time of day to exercise and many of those who exercise before going to bed report beneficial, not negative, effects on their sleep.

Two small studies have attempted to discover what factors contribute to the effect of exercise on sleep. Souissi and colleagues (2012) examined the effects of highly strenuous exercise performed at either 2:00 p.m. or 8:00 p.m. The exercise consisted of a warm-up period with jogging and stretching and then a series of increasingly intense sprints. Participants were encouraged to give their maximal effort throughout the session. The researchers found that participants who exercised at 8:00 p.m. (hence, close to bedtime) took longer to fall asleep and had more awakenings, although they also experienced deeper sleep than participants who exercised in the afternoon. In contrast, participants who exercised in the afternoon got more total sleep and had fewer awakenings. The results support the recommendation that strenuous exercise before bed can have negative effects on sleep, making it more disturbed and fragmented.

Another recent study (Flausino, Da Silva Prado, De Queiroz, Tufik, & Mello, 2012) examined the effects of less strenuous exercise performed in the evening. Participants exercised at various moderate levels of intensity for 30 to 60 minutes between 8:00 and 8:30 p.m. When compared with a pre-exercise baseline, exercise was associated with less fragmented sleep, less time spent awake, and deeper sleep. The participants were healthy adults, and none were athletes or exercised regularly prior to the study. Thus, although the evidence remains contradictory, it appears that whereas strenuous exercise before bed may have negative effects on sleep, moderate evening exercise, as well as moderate or strenuous morning or afternoon exercise, has positive effects.

## Alcohol

Alcohol is sometimes called the most frequently used over-the-counter (OTC) sleeping aid (Johnson, Roehrs, Roth, & Breslau, 1998). Many people report that drinking helps them fall asleep. However, general sleep hygiene recommendations discourage drinking alcohol close to bedtime for those trying to self-treat insomnia. Although scant research has attempted to determine an ideal evening cutoff time for drinking, the preponderance of evidence shows that drinking not only impairs driving but is harmful, rather than helpful, to sleep, especially during the second half of the night.

Alcohol can be sedating, and thus makes it easier to fall asleep in the evening (Papineau, Roehrs, Petrucelli, Rosenthal, & Roth, 1998). Additionally, alcohol has been associated with fewer awakenings and deeper sleep during the first half of the night, while elevated blood alcohol levels are still in the blood stream (Prinz, Roehrs, Vitaliano, Linnoila, & Weitzman, 1980; Stone, 1980; Williams, MacLean, & Cairns, 1983). In practical terms, this means that people sleep better for the first several hours after drinking alcohol. However, the story changes later in the night. The same studies found that people sleep less deeply and have more awakenings during the second half of the night, both as compared with the first half and as compared with their own baseline sleep without any alcohol. These findings suggest that people are more sensitive to arousing stimuli in their environment, such as lights or noises, during the second part of the night when they are withdrawing from alcohol. Indeed, Geoghegan, O'Donovan, and Lawlor (2012) found that people who drank alcohol in the evening slept less, awakened earlier, and were more tired the next day than when they had not consumed alcohol prior to bed. These effects were true for both high and low amounts of alcohol, and in fact were stronger for lower amounts, potentially as a result of more drinking being indicative of greater tolerance to alcohol. Thus, it would appear that alcohol before bed, even in relatively small amounts, disrupts sleep, even though the initial sedative effect of alcohol may lead individuals to believe that alcohol has improved their sleep.

## Caffeine and Energy Drinks

Caffeine is considered to be the most commonly used psychoactive substance in the world. Along with energy drinks that contain both caffeine and other additives, it is used to help consumers stay awake, decrease feelings of sleepiness and fatigue, and enhance alertness and mood. Although these positive effects have been demonstrated for caffeine in numerous studies, the data on energy drinks are much more mixed, and both caffeine and energy drinks may have detrimental effects on nighttime sleep.

When examining the effects of caffeine and other energy drinks on nighttime sleep, the data are relatively consistent. Calamaro, Mason, and Ratcliffe (2009) found adolescents who drink caffeine, especially in the late afternoon and evening, are more likely to have early morning awakenings and shorter sleep duration than those who do not. Similarly, Jay, Petrilli, Ferguson, Dawson, and Lamond (2006) found that the use of energy drinks was correlated with more disturbed sleep in adult workers. Caffeine use, however, has been shown to have beneficial effects on memory. In a study of older adults who had a tendency to be more alert in the morning than later in the day (Ryan, Hatfield, & Hofstetter, 2002), a 12-ounce cup of caffeinated or decaffeinated coffee was consumed 30 minutes before both an 8:00 a.m. and 4:00 p.m. memory testing session. Those who consumed decaffeinated coffee showed a decline in memory performance from the morning to the afternoon session. Those who consumed caffeine did not show a decline. Relatedly, a study of caffeine intake and morning/evening tendencies found a somewhat more mixed pattern (Nova, Hernandez, Ptolemy, & Zeitzer, 2012). Although people with morning preferences (larks) experienced more disturbed nighttime sleep when they had more coffee during the day and a higher amount of caffeine content during an evening saliva sample, those with evening preferences (owls) showed no increase in sleep disturbance. People classified as neither morning nor evening types had less sleep disturbance than the larks but more than the owls. Hence, although the general rule of not consuming caffeine too close to bedtime is probably true for most people, it appears to be somewhat less debilitating for those who have evening preferences.

Many people who seek better sleep have sought out solutions that promise to put them to sleep on the same night that they have sleep problems. These individuals often use over-the-counter substances and herbal preparations, both of which we discuss next.

# Over-the-Counter (OTC) Substances and Herbal Preparations

OTC substances and herbal preparations is a diverse category that includes antihistamines, melatonin, L-Tryptophan, Valerian root, St. John's Wort, chamomile tea, and many other substances. They can be obtained without prescriptions in the United States, and those that are dietary supplements are not regulated by the U.S. Food and Drug Administration (FDA).

Of the substances listed above, melatonin and antihistamines have supporting evidence for their effects on sleep but not without qualification. Melatonin is a hormone that comes from the pineal gland. Its release is suppressed by bright light. Melatonin is more of a timing substance, indicating when it is time to sleep, than it is a sleep aid. It has been used effectively for those with Delayed Sleep Phase Disorder; that is, with a sleep-wake circadian rhythm disorder in which sleep occurs later than desired. An individual with this problem has difficulty falling asleep until late at night, coupled with difficulty waking up in the morning. Although melatonin is generally safe to take, it lowers body temperature, which could prevent ovulation. Consequently, women of childbearing age who are trying to become pregnant are cautioned not to use it.

Antihistamines, particularly diphenhydramine (Benadryl), are frequently used as sleep aids. The American Academy of Sleep Medicine (2006) in a report on OTC sleep aids stated that "OTC sleep aids that contain antihistamine may provide modest, short-term benefits for adults with mild cases of insomnia. It is important to be aware, however, that the use of antihistamines may produce a variety of side effects" (p. 1). Antihistamines are FDA-approved but for only occasional or short-term use. Tolerance to the sleep effects develops quickly. After three nights, diphenhydramine was found to be no more effective than a placebo (Richardson et al., 2002). Side effects of antihistamines include morning sleepiness, dizziness, memory problems, and anticholinergic effects that can exacerbate heart problems (Neubauer & Flaherty, 2010). The side effects raise particular concern for older adults who are more at risk for balance problems, memory difficulties, and cardiac disorders.

The effectiveness of other OTC sleep aids is unknown. There are few scientific studies evaluating their success in improving sleep, and most of their support comes from case reports and endorsements from individuals who use them. Safety issues such as side effects can be severe when they are taken alone and are even more problematic when taken in combination with alcohol or other substances (Neubauer & Flaherty, 2010). In the United States, many individuals who seek better sleep get prescriptions for sleeping pills from their physicians; we discuss these medications next.

## Prescription Sleeping Pills

Americans filled over 60 million prescriptions for sleeping pills in 2012, an increase from 47 million in 2006 (Rabin, 2012) and approximately 25 million in 2000 (Saul, 2006). The most commonly prescribed sleeping pills, also called hypnotics, activate an inhibitory neurotransmitter, gamma amino butyric acid (GABA), which acts as a central nervous system depressant. These medications have multiple effects. Some benzodiazepines reduce anxiety (e.g., alprazolam, commonly prescribed as Xanax). Others reduce disturbed sleep (e.g., temazepam, commonly prescribed as Restoril). And still others reduce both anxiety and disturbed sleep (e.g., diazepam, commonly prescribed as Valium). A new generation of hypnotics, nonbenzodiazepine GABA agonists (often called the "z" medications for zolpidem, zaleplon, zopiclone, and eszopiclone), like benzodiazepines, selectively activate the GABA neurotransmitter. Zolpidem (commonly prescribed as Ambien) is the most frequently prescribed hypnotic for insomnia worldwide.

There is a substantial scientific literature on the efficacy and side effects of the GABA medications (e.g., Krystal, 2010; Roehrs & Roth, 2010). Tolerance develops to the benzodiazepines, often leading to patients taking higher doses to obtain the same effect on sleep. Withdrawing from benzodiazepines for either anxiety or sleep is difficult, as withdrawal produces anxiety and insomnia. Clinical guidelines for the treatment of insomnia (Schutte-Rodin, Broch, Buysse, Dorsey, & Sateia, 2008) recommend that the hypnotics should be limited to short-term use. In recent years, however, there have been multiple-year studies of the efficacy of z hypnotics and the FDA has approved them for long-term use.

Side effects are influenced by the dosage taken. To avoid side effects, hypnotics are prescribed at the lowest effective dose. Daytime impairment and sedation are affected by how long the hypnotic stays in the blood stream. This is referred to as the half-life of the medication and indicates when the amount of the medication in the blood stream has been reduced by half. Hypnotics with a half-life of more than 5 hours are likely to produce daytime sleepiness beyond the sleep period (Roehrs & Roth, 2010). Included among the newer nonbenzodiazepine hypnotics are melatonin agonists that affect the timing of sleep but do not produce the same feeling of sleepiness as do the GABA agonists (Zee & Reid, 2010).

Although the research literature on hypnotics is extensive, there are two important gaps in our knowledge (Krystal, 2010). First, hypnotics have not been evaluated for use with children even though physicians often prescribe them for this age group, and second, there is little evidence that quality of life and daytime functioning are improved along with sleep. Many individuals continue to sleep poorly or experience severe side effects when taking hypnotics. In searching for a sleeping pill that will be effective for patients, off-label medications are often prescribed because of their sedating properties. Included in this class are antidepressant, antipsychotic, and anticonvulsant medications. There are limited efficacy data on these medications for the treatment of disturbed sleep, and all have substantial side effects (McCall, 2010).

One alarming side effect for long-term use of sleeping pills is early death. In two large epidemiological studies, with over a million people per study, taking a sleeping pill every night was associated with early death, even after statistically controlling for 30 other possible causes of death that would be associated with sleeping pill use, such as insomnia and depression (Kripke, 2000).

These two large studies were performed on people mainly using an earlier generation of sleeping pills, so it is possible that newer medicines such as zolpidem (Ambien) would not produce the same side effects. However, a survey of 1,600 patients found that there was no difference in patient-reported side effects between the older medications and newer ones such as zolpidem (Siriwardena, Qureshi, Dyas, Middleton, & Orner, 2008). With respect to earlier mortality, a recent study found that taking even 18 sleeping pills a year was associated with an increased risk of death over the 2.5-year period during which the subjects were followed and that sleeping pills were also associated with higher rates of getting cancer (Kripke, Langer, & Kline, 2012).

Why might sleeping pills lead to earlier mortality? One possibility is that many individuals who take sleeping pills have comorbid diseases such as cancer, sleep apnea, and other respiratory problems along with poor sleep. Sleep apnea has been found to lead to increased risk for heart attacks and other cardiac problems. Because sleeping pills are central nervous system depressants, they make respiratory problems worse.

Second, as central nervous system depressants, sleeping pills lead to slower reaction times. Thus, individuals taking sleeping pills are more likely to be in car accidents (Gujna, 2013). In addition, hypnotics impair a person's balance, which can lead to falls, particularly in older individuals (Mets, Volkerts, Olivier, & Verster, 2010). A higher percentage of older than younger individuals report problems with sleep and use sleeping pills.

Third, one side effect of hypnotics, dissociative behavior, is so important that the FDA accords it special emphasis and lists it as a warning for hypnotics, including for the new generation of z medications. In some dissociative reactions, the person engages in complex behavior but has no memory of doing so. Thus, the person is not cognitively alert even though it appears that she or he is awake. Both personal and industrial accidents have been identified as due to dissociative behavior from taking hypnotics.

Although there are many reasons for why sleeping pills might lead to early mortality, these studies were not randomly controlled trials that compared sleeping pills with placebos. Thus, what can be concluded, so far, is that there is an association between sleeping pills and early mortality, not that sleeping pills conclusively cause early mortality.

Despite the popularity of hypnotics even with their numerous known risk factors, it is not clear that they are particularly effective. A recent study examined all the placebo-controlled trials of sleeping pills that had been submitted to the FDA—13 studies containing 65 comparisons between a number of different sleeping pills and placebos—and found that people taking sleeping pills do not fall asleep much faster nor sleep much more than those taking placebo pills (Huedo-Medina, Kirsch, Middlemass, Klonizakis, & Siriwardena, 2012). Some sleep researchers have concluded that the major effect of hypnotics, stemming from their impact on memory, is their influence on the patient's perception of sleep, not the actual amount of sleep obtained (Mendelson, 1995).

Because pharmacology does not yet provide the best answer for treating insomnia, it is useful to examine the status of psychological treatments. We examine these interventions next.

## Cognitive Behavioral Treatment for Insomnia (CBT-I)

In comparison to sleeping pills, a psychological multicomponent treatment, CBT-I, has been shown to produce results that are equivalent to those from medication after treatment. Additionally, CBT-I has an advantage over medication during follow-up, as improvement in sleep is maintained for as long as 2 years without additional treatment (National Institutes of Health, 2005). The component treatments of CBT-I are therapies that have been found to be effective as stand-alone treatments and typically include Stimulus Control Therapy, Sleep Restriction Therapy, and Sleep Hygiene/Education (e.g., Perlis, Jungquist, Smith, & Posner, 2005). Cognitive Therapy and Relaxation Training/Meditation are also employed with some patients.

## Stimulus Control Therapy (SCT)

Proposed by Bootzin (1972, 1977), SCT is based on learning principles with the goal of reestablishing the bed and bedroom as powerful cues for sleep. For the person with insomnia, the bed and bedroom often become associated with behaviors that are incompatible with sleep, such as reviewing the day's events, worrying, watching TV, reading, and becoming anxious and frustrated from trying to fall asleep or fall back to sleep. The aims of SCT are to strengthen the bed and bedroom as conditioned cues for sleep, to weaken them as cues for behaviors that are incompatible with sleep, and to develop a consistent sleep-wake pattern.

To meet those aims, the stimulus control instructions are as follows (Bootzin 1972, 1977):

1. Lie down to go to sleep only when you are sleepy.

2. Do not use your bed for anything except sleep; that is, do not read, watch television, eat, or worry in bed. Sexual activity is the only exception to this rule. On such occasions, the instructions are to be followed afterward, when you intend to go to sleep.

3. If you find yourself unable to fall asleep, get up and go into another room. Stay up as long as you wish and then return to the bedroom to sleep. Although we do not want you to watch the clock, we want you to get out of bed if you do not fall asleep immediately. Remember, the goal is to associate your bed with falling asleep quickly! If you are in bed more than about 10 minutes without falling asleep and have not gotten up, you are not following this instruction.

4. If you still cannot fall asleep, repeat Step 3. Do this as often as is necessary throughout the night.

5. Set your alarm, and get up at the same time every morning irrespective of how much sleep you got during the night. This will help your body acquire a consistent sleep rhythm.

6. Do not nap during the day.

Reserving the bed for sleep and sex helps the insomniac to establish new sleep habits. Getting out of bed and leaving the bedroom when unable to fall asleep decreases anxiety, maladaptive sleep-related cognitions, and arousal (Morin & Espie, 2003). It is also likely to increase the patient's need for sleep, making it easier to fall asleep or fall back to sleep when returning to bed (Bootzin & Epstein, 2011). It may appear that instruction Step 6 about not napping during the day is contradicted by the earlier discussion of the benefits of short naps. The instruction about napping in SCT is included to facilitate the therapy. Waking up at the same time every morning coupled with not napping during the day helps establish a consistent sleep rhythm and uses whatever sleep loss there was on the previous night to make it more likely that the patient will fall asleep faster on the next night.

Detailed rationales for each of the stimulus control instructions are provided to patients (Bootzin, Smith, Franzen, & Shapiro, 2010). Meta-analyses and systematic reviews (e.g., Morin, Colecchi, Stone, & Sood, 1999; Morin et al., 2006) indicate that SCT is one of the most effective, if not the most effective, single-component intervention for insomnia.

## Sleep Restriction Therapy (SRT)

SRT is a nonpharmacologial treatment for insomnia developed by Spielman, Saskin, and Thorpy (1987). The rationale for SRT is that individuals with insomnia often spend too much time in bed attempting to sleep, which leads to increased wakefulness, fragmented sleep, and variability in the timing of sleep and wake (Bootzin & Epstein, 2011). The patient keeps a daily sleep diary that records how much time is spent in bed and the total amount of sleep he or she achieved each night. The patient is then prescribed a sleep period that matches the average nightly amount of sleep obtained, not the average time spent in bed. To prevent severe sleep deprivation, the prescribed sleep period is never less than 5 hours. The aims of SRT are reducing time in bed awake and the establishment of a consistent sleep-wake schedule. As the proportion of time in bed asleep increases over time, the patient's sleep window is gradually expanded to allow the patient to get more sleep without reverting to the old pattern of spending too much time in bed without sleeping. Additional details on the use of SRT are provided by Spielman, Yang, and Glovinsky (2010). SRT has been used as a single treatment as well as included in multicomponent interventions.

SCT and SRT have been directly compared along with combined treatment (Epstein, Sidani, Bootzin, & Belyea, 2012). All three treatments were found to be equally effective. The combined treatment was no more effective than either SCT or SRT alone.

## Stress Reduction: Relaxation and Meditation

An early and widely used treatment for insomnia is the use of relaxation training to reduce the physiological arousal that may be preventing good sleep. Many assume that having a stressful life is a major contributor to insomnia, but research suggests that the relationship between stress and sleep is more complicated. In one study, people with good and bad sleep reported about the same number of daily stressful events in their life, but people with poor sleep felt more of an impact from these events than people who slept well (Morin, Rodriguez, & Ivers, 2003). This same study found that the ability to reduce one's state of mental arousal before falling asleep helps individuals sleep, even for those who react strongly to stressful events. Consequently, to sleep better, it would be helpful to decrease arousal before trying to fall asleep and also to find a way to modify interpretations of the stressful events of the day. There is strong evidence that different exercises in relaxation or meditation develop the ability to do just this.

Harvard psychiatrist Herbert Benson and Miriam Klipper (1976) described a process called the relaxation response, which is the opposite of the stress response. When people engage in a practice that brings on the relaxation response, they reduce their oxygen consumption, blood pressure, and heart rate; their brain waves change; they feel calmer; and changes in gene expression may even occur (Dusek et al., 2008). These alterations are likely to occur during a number of different practices, such as tai chi, qi gong, yoga, certain types of prayer, and a variety of forms of meditation

(Esch, Fricchione, & Stefano, 2003; see also Chapter 7, "Chilling Out: Meditation, Relaxation, and Yoga"). Not only do individuals become more relaxed, there is research evidence that relaxation, meditation, tai chi, acupressure, and yoga all help decrease insomnia (Nicassio & Bootzin, 1974; Ong, Shapiro, & Manber, 2008; Sarris & Byrne, 2011).

One method for relaxing the body and consequently the mind is progressive muscle relaxation (PMR; Jacobson, 1938; see Chapter 7, "Chilling Out: Meditation, Relaxation, and Yoga"). The basic premise of PMR is to learn to relax muscles to minimize the amount of muscle tension experienced. It involves moving attention throughout the body, tensing a body part to notice what it feels like when tense, relaxing it, and then moving to another part of the body. In general, PMR has been shown to lead to a state of relaxation in both the body and the mind, and that this relaxation leads to alleviating insomnia (McCallie, Blum, & Hood, 2006). A number of studies have found that PMR works above and beyond the mere expectation of improvement associated with an attention-placebo treatment (Morin et al., 2006). A common placebo treatment used for this purpose has participants imagine bedtime events such as brushing teeth alternated with neutral scenes but without any relaxation training (e.g., Lichstein, Riedel, Wilson, Lester, & Aguillard, 2001). Participants are told that this constitutes a treatment that has been found to reduce insomnia in many individuals.

Although research shows that PMR is superior to placebo, what we know so far about how PMR compares with other treatments for insomnia remains inconclusive. For example, one study found that PMR was just as effective at reducing the amount of time people spent awake in bed as SCT (Pallensen et al., 2003). Another study found that PMR was more effective than CBT-I on certain measures of insomnia, but CBT-I was better on other measures (Rybarczyk, Lopez, Benson, Alsten, & Stepanski, 2002). Still another study found that the improvement of sleep following PMR was relatively small overall compared with the effects of CBT-I (Edinger et al., 2001). This rather contradictory state of the evidence would appear to indicate that PMR works well for some individuals, but that its effects are fairly small for others.

Although decreasing one's stress level is helpful in improving sleep, it may be more important to change one's relationship to unpleasant external and mental events given that it is often difficult to control the number of stressful events that occur in life. Mindfulness meditation (MM) is a practice that involves cultivating "the awareness that emerges through paying attention on purpose, in the present moment, and nonjudgmentally to the unfolding of experience moment by moment" (Kabat-Zinn, 2003, p. 145). This practice, therefore, seems ideally suited to developing what's called *equanimity*, the ability to remain in a state of mental peace regardless of whether things in one's life are going well or poorly (Salzberg, 2002). Using mindfulness, people with insomnia are instructed to notice their mental talk and let it go, without trying to change it. This helps stop the process of attempting to suppress arousal and mental talk, which often worsens people's anxiety.

Although there is evidence for the effectiveness of MM for insomnia, scientific research on this question is still in its infancy. One study, however, found that an 8-week meditation course both improved self-reported sleep quality and decreased the amount of cortisol, a stress hormone, produced in the morning (Brand, Holsboer-Tachsler, Nranjo, & Schmidt, 2012). A number of studies have used mindfulness to help people suffering from insomnia and a comorbid disorder. They have revealed that mindfulness improves insomnia for people suffering from cancer (Carlson & Garland, 2005), recipients of organ transplants (Gross et al., 2004), people taking medication for depression (Britton, Haynes, Fridel, & Bootzin, 2012), and psychiatric outpatients (Ree & Craigie, 2007) among others. Some studies have successfully integrated MM with existing therapies for insomnia (e.g. Ong et al., 2008).

No studies have shown that MM is superior to relaxation or other types of meditation. The reason might be that mindfulness is historically a skill that is developed over the course of many months or years, whereas relaxation can be learned more quickly. However, although more research is necessary to determine how mindfulness affects sleep, or which treatments may be better or worse than mindfulness for different people in different situations, the literature is clear that mindfulness is likely to help improve people's reports of their sleep quality. Perhaps most promisingly, a recent study found that those who learned mindfulness improved their sleep as much as those who took the sleeping pill eszopiclone (Lunesta), both after 8 weeks of treatment and at 5-month follow-up (Gross et al., 2011).

## Case Study

In the following case study, we describe the treatment of a woman (L.) with insomnia. L.'s case is complicated by her use of sleeping pills, the presence of comorbid psychological disorders, and experiencing a life crisis during therapy. Many of the suggestions and treatments described throughout the chapter were used during therapy with her.

At the time she sought treatment, L. was a married 27-year-old woman who complained of severe problems in both initiating and maintaining sleep (Bootzin, 1985). She reported that it often took her more than 2 hours to fall asleep, that her sleep was restless, and that she had frequent awakenings accompanied by long periods of wakefulness. On the days following a poor night's sleep, L. felt fatigued, irritable, and incapable of meeting the ordinary demands of everyday life. To cope with her insomnia, she had been taking Valium (diazepam, a benzodiazepine) nightly. Even though the medication was no longer effective in providing good-quality sleep, L. remained convinced that she needed the Valium or her sleep would be even worse.

L. and her husband had a 2-year-old daughter. L. reported that up until the birth of her daughter, she had no sleep problems. But during the first few months following her daughter's birth, L. was hypervigilant at night and slept poorly. Her insomnia persisted even after her daughter matured and no longer required attention at night. After 1 year of insomnia, L. went to a sleep disorders center for evaluation and underwent two overnight sleep studies. On the first night, L. could sleep only 2 hours, but on the second night, she slept 6 hours. This poor initial night in the lab is called a "first-night effect" and is frequently related to anxiety about being watched and assessed in an unfamiliar environment.

The staff of the sleep disorder center concluded that aspects of L.'s sleep were consistent with someone who was depressed, and they recommended that she make an appointment with a psychiatrist. Although aspects of her sleep were consistent with depression, other aspects were consistent with insomnia caused by worry and anxiety. L. sought out a psychiatrist and the psychiatrist concluded that L. was not depressed and prescribed diazepam (Valium) for her anxiety and sleep disturbance.

A year later, L. sought out nonpharmacological treatment because she became pregnant. Her gynecologist insisted that she stop taking Valium, which she did. However, L. experienced considerable distress during withdrawal and her insomnia persisted. During her first session, L. was interviewed about the history of her sleep problems and completed additional questionnaires. She scored as having moderate depression, but below clinical levels, and as being highly anxious.

L. was given daily sleep diaries to fill out at home. Sleep diaries are a critical assessment tool for the treatment of insomnia. By filling out daily sleep diaries, those with insomnia often learn that their sleep problems are not as frequent as they thought. That was exactly what happened in L.'s case. When she returned for her next session with 2 weeks of sleep diaries, on only 2 of the 14 nights had L. awakened exhausted in the morning, and on only 1 night did she get less than 4 hours of sleep. Although L.'s problem was not as severe as she anticipated, she did not consider her problem solved. Consequently, treatment was begun with sleep hygiene and education.

Sadly, following that session, L. had a miscarriage. She experienced considerable grief and distress. L.'s insomnia continued, and she resumed taking Valium on occasion. L. returned to treatment determined to free herself from Valium because she planned to get pregnant again.

After returning for treatment, L. was seen for seven sessions over a 15-week period. The first two sessions focused on her thoughts and feelings about her miscarriage. Although her grief and general distress diminished during this time, her insomnia worsened. L. had become increasingly distressed about a winter vacation she, her husband, and their daughter were going to take to visit her husband's parents. The week before they were to leave, L. averaged more than 2 and a half hours to fall asleep and averaged only 5 hours of sleep a night. L. was worried that if she did not sleep well when visiting her in-laws, she would be fatigued and irritable but yet would need to participate in family activities. She was also concerned that she would not be able continue using stimulus control instructions that she had just started, because getting out of bed and being awake would likely disrupt the sleep of others.

The session just before departure focused on ways of coping while at her in-laws' house. L. had learned relaxation training, and it was suggested that she use relaxation during the day as a means of restoring energy. She was also reminded that the energy one has when engaging in activities is not dependent only on how much sleep was obtained the night before. For example, engaging in interesting activities produces energy. Further, there is a circadian rhythm to wakefulness. Even after a night of complete sleep deprivation, individuals are more alert during the morning and less so at times when they would ordinarily be sleeping.

L. returned from her vacation 3 weeks later refreshed and enthusiastic about continuing her insomnia treatment. She had only sporadic nights of insomnia and found that she could cope with them. She followed the stimulus control instructions without difficulty and used relaxation on occasions when she became fatigued during the day.

The next three sessions were spent reviewing and consolidating gains. Increasingly, the focus of the sessions shifted from problems with sleep to more general concerns of stress management. At the end of therapy, L. averaged about 45 minutes to fall asleep and 7 hours of total sleep a night, compared with more than 2 hours to fall asleep and 6 hours of total sleep at the beginning of therapy. L. still had a poor night's sleep about once a week but was capable of coping with it without taking a sleeping pill.

Four months later, L. called for another appointment. She reported that she was pregnant again and had begun to have some difficulty sleeping. She was seen for two booster sessions that included a review of the procedures she had used successfully before and a discussion of her concerns about another miscarriage. Once the point in her pregnancy passed when she previously had a miscarriage, L. was able to reestablish having good sleep and remained free of the need for sleeping pills.

As seen throughout this chapter, sleep affects many areas of functioning as well as being affected by them. Sleep is affected by what happens during the day, not just what happens when trying to sleep. Daytime problems such as depression, anxiety, posttraumatic stress disorder (PTSD), and substance abuse are risk factors for insomnia. Interestingly, the causal arrows go in both directions; thus, insomnia is a risk factor for the development and worsening of depression, anxiety, PTSD, and substance abuse. In this regard, there is evidence that insomnia and depression both improve along with broader outcomes such as coping with stress, happiness, and increased energy when treating the insomnia with CBT-I in patients having comorbid insomnia and depression (Manber et al., 2011).

In this case study, there was a strong interdependence between L.'s method of coping with stress, the emotional turmoil of her miscarriage, her initial dependence on sleeping pills, and the treatment of her insomnia. L. was resilient in responding to the emotional stresses in her life and cooperative and adherent with the treatment. These characteristics of L. were important contributors to the treatment's success.

## Future Directions

Although much has been learned about how to sleep well, there is still much that we do not know. Likely future directions in research include (1) the extent to which treatments and recommendations for those with disturbed sleep can also prevent the development of sleep problems; (2) whether sleep and its disorders differ across the life span or with different ethnic and cultural populations; (3) identifying the extent to which sleep affects risk and resilience in dealing with stress; (4) treating comorbid problems of insomnia and depression, anxiety, pain, or substance abuse; (5) whether treatments can be individualized so that there will be a more effective match between treatments and the resources and characteristics of those with insomnia; (6) the use of technology (ambulatory sleep psychophysiology equipment, the Internet, phone apps) for both the assessment and treatment of sleep quality; and (7) dissemination of treatments for sleep to primary care service providers in community settings. There are strong beginnings of research in all of these areas, and the next decade promises to be an exciting time for sleep research.

# References

American Academy of Sleep Medicine (2006). *AASM position statement: Treating insomnia with over-the-counter sleep aids.* Retrieved from http://www.aasmnet .org/articles.aspx?id=253

Ancoli-Israel, S. (2001). "Sleep is not tangible" or what the Hebrew tradition has to say about sleep. *Psychosomatic Medicine, 63,* 778–787.

Benson, H., & Klipper, H. Z. (1976). *The relaxation response.* New York, NY: HarperCollins.

Bonnet, M., & Alter, J. (1982). Effects of irregular versus regular sleep schedules on performance, mood and body temperature. *Biological Psychology, 14,* 287–96. doi:10.1016/0301-0511(82)90009-6

Bonnet, M. H., & Arand, D. L. (1994). The use of prophylactic naps and caffeine to maintain performance during a continuous operation. *Ergonomics, 37,* 1009–1020. doi:10.1080/00140139408963714

Bonnet, M. H., Gomez, S., Wirth, O., & Arand, D. L. (1995). The use of caffeine versus prophylactic naps in sustained performance. *Sleep, 18,* 97–104.

Bootzin, R. R. (1972). *A stimulus control treatment for insomnia.* Proceedings of the 80th Annual American Psychological Association Convention, 395–396.

Bootzin, R. R. (1977). Effects of self-control procedures for insomnia. In R. Stuart (Ed.), *Behavioral self-management: Strategies and outcomes.* New York, NY: Brunner/Mazel.

Bootzin, R. R. (1985). Insomnia. In M. Hersen & C. G. Last (Eds.), *Behavior therapy casebook.* New York, NY: Springer.

Bootzin, R. R., & Epstein, D. R. (2011). Understanding and treating insomnia. *Annual Review of Clinical Psychology, 11,* 435–458. doi:10.1146/annurev .clinpsy.3.022806.091516

Bootzin, R. R., Smith, L. J., Franzen, P. L., & Shapiro, S. L. (2010). Stimulus control therapy. In M. J. Sateia & D. J. Buysse (Eds.), *Insomnia: Diagnosis and treatment* (pp. 268–276). Informa Healthcare. doi:10.3109/9781420080803.024

Brand, S., Holsboer-Tachsler, E., Nranjo, J. R., & Schmidt, S. (2012). Influence of mindfulness practice on cortisol and sleep in long-term and short-term meditators. *Neuropsychobiology, 65,* 109–118. doi:10.1159/000330362

Britton, W. B., Haynes, P. L., Fridel, K. W., & Bootzin, R. R. (2012). Mindfulness-based cognitive therapy improves polysomnographic and subjective sleep profiles in antidepressant users with sleep complaints. *Psychotherapy and Psychosomatics, 81,* 296–304. doi:10.1159/000332755

Brooks, A. J., & Lack, L. C. (2006). A brief afternoon nap following nocturnal sleep restriction: Which nap duration is most recuperative? *Sleep, 29,* 831–840.

Broughton, R. J. (1989), Chronobiological aspects and models of sleep and napping. In D. F. Dinges & R. J. Broughton (Eds.), *Sleep and alertness: Chronobiological, behavioural, and medical aspects of napping* (pp. 71–98). New York, NY: Raven Press.

Buysse, D. J., Browman, K. E., Monk, T. H., & Reynolds, C. F. (1992). Napping and 24-hour sleep/wake patterns in healthy elderly and young adults. *Journal of the American Geriatrics Society, 40*(8), 779–786.

Cacioppo, J. T., Hawkley, L. C., Berntson, G. G., Ernst, J. M., Gibbs, A. C., Stickgold, R., & Hobson, J. A. (2002). Do lonely days invade the nights? Potential social modulation of sleep efficiency. *Psychological Science, 13,* 384–387. doi:10.1111/j.0956–7976.2002.00469.x

Calamaro, C. J., Mason, T. B., & Ratcliffe, S. J. (2009). Adolescents living the 24/7 lifestyle: Effects of caffeine and technology on sleep duration and daytime functioning. *Pediatrics, 123*(6), 1005–1010. doi:10.1542/peds.2008–3641

Carlson, L. E., & Garland, S. N. (2005). Impact of mindfulness-based stress reduction (MBSR) on sleep, mood, stress and fatigue symptoms in cancer outpatients. *International Journal of Behavioral Medicine, 12*(4), 278–285. doi:10.1207/s15327558ijbm1204_9

Dinges, D. F., Orne, M. T., Whitehouse, W. G., & Orne, E. C. (1987). Temporal placement of a nap for alertness: Contributions of circadian phase and prior wakefulness. *Sleep, 10,* 313–329.

Dusek, J.A., Otu, H. H., Wohlhueter, A. L., Bhasin, M., Zerbini, L. F., et al. (2008). Genomic counter-stress changes induced by the relaxation response. *PLoS One, 1*(7), 1–8. doi:10.1371/journal.pone.0002576

Edinger, J. D., Hoelscher, T. J., Marsh, G. R., Lipper, S., & Ionescu-Pioggia, M. (1992). A cognitive behavioral therapy for sleep-maintenance insomnia in older adults. *Psychological Aging, 7,* 282–289. doi:10.1037/0882–7974.7.2.282

Edinger, J. D., & Sampson, W. S. (2003). A primary care "friendly" cognitive behavioral insomnia therapy. *Sleep, 26,* 177–182.

Edinger, J. D., Wohlgemuth, W. K., Radtke, R. A., Marsh, G. R., & Quillian, R. E. (2001). Cognitive behavioral therapy for treatment of chronic primary insomnia: A randomized controlled trial. *Journal of the American Medical Association, 285,* 1856–1864. doi:10.1001/jama.285.14.1856.

Epstein, D. R, Sidani, S., Bootzin, R. R., & Belyea, M. J. (2012). Dismantling multicomponent behavioral treatment for insomnia in older adults: A randomized controlled trial. *Sleep, 35,* 797–805. doi:10.5665/sleep.1878.

Esch, T., Fricchione, G. L., & Stefano, G. B. (2003). The therapeutic use of the relaxation response in stress-related diseases. *Medical Science Monitor, 9*(2), 23–34.

Espie, C. A., Inglis, S. J., Tessier, S., & Harvey, L. (2001). The clinical effectiveness of cognitive behavior therapy for chronic insomnia: Implementation and evaluation of a sleep clinic in general medical practice. *Behaviour Research and Therapy, 39,* 45–60. doi:10.1016/S0005–7967(99)00157–6.

Flausino, N., Da Silva Prado, J., De Queiroz, S., Tufik, S., & De Mello, M. (2012). Physical exercise performed before bedtime improves the sleep pattern of healthy young good sleepers. *Psychophysiology, 49*(2), 186–192. doi:10.1111/j.1469–8986.2011.01300.x

Geoghegan, P., O'Donovan, M. T., & Lawlor, B. A. (2012). Investigation of the effects of alcohol on sleep using actigraphy. *Alcohol and Alcoholism, 48*(1), 126–127. doi:10.1093/alcalc/ags131.

Gross, C. R., Kreitzer, M. J., Reilly-Spong, M., Wall, M., Winbush, N. Y., Patterson, R., . . . Cramer-Bornemann, M. (2011). Mindfulness-based stress reduction versus pharmacotherapy for chronic primary insomnia: A randomized controlled clinical trial. *Explore, 7*(2), 76–87. doi:10.1016/j.explore.2010.12.003

Gross, C. R., Kreitzer, M. J., Russas, V., Treesak, C., Frazier, P. A., & Hertz, M. I. (2004). Mindfulness meditation to reduce symptoms after organ transplant: A pilot study. *Advances, 20*(2), 20–29.

Gujna, N. (2013). In the zzz zone: The effects of z-drugs on human performance and driving. *Journal of Medical Toxicology, 9*(2), 163–171. doi:10.1007/s13181-013-0294-y

Hauri, P. (1977). *The sleep disorders.* Kalamazoo, MI: Upjohn.

Hayashi, M., & Hori, T. (1998). The effects of a 20-min nap before postlunch dip. *Psychiatry Clinical Neuroscience, 52,* 203–204. doi:10.1111/j.1440-1819.1998.tb01031.x

Hayashi, M., Ito, S., & Hori, T. (1999). The effects of a 20-min nap at noon on sleepiness, performance and EEG activity. *International Journal of Psychophysiology, 32,* 173–180. doi:10.1016/S0167-8760(99)00009-4

Hayashi, M., Masuda, A., & Hori, T. (2003). The alerting effects of caffeine, bright light and face washing after a short daytime nap. *Clinical Neurophysiology, 114,* 2268–2278. doi:10.1016/S1388-2457(03)00255-4

Hayashi, M., Motoyoshi, N., & Hori, T. (2005) Recuperative power of a short daytime nap with or without Stage 2 sleep. *Sleep, 28,* 829–836.

Hayashi, M., Watanabe, M., & Hori, T. (1999). The effects of a 20 min nap in the mid-afternoon on mood, performance and EEG activity. *Clinical Neurophysiology, 110,* 272–279. doi:10.1016/S1388-2457(98)00003-0

Huedo-Medina, T. B., Kirsch, I., Middlemass, J., Klonizakis, M., & Siriwardena, A. N. (2012). Effectiveness of non-benzodiazepine hypnotics in treatment of adult insomnia: Meta-analysis of data submitted to the Food and Drug Administration. *British Medical Journal, 345*(8343). doi:10.1136/bmj.e8343

Jacobson, E. (1938). *Progressive relaxation.* Chicago, IL: University of Chicago Press.

Jay, S. M, Petrilli, R. M., Ferguson, S. A., Dawson, D., & Lamond, N. (2006). The suitability of a caffeinated energy drink for night-shift workers. *Physiology and Behavior, 87*(5), 925–931. doi:10.1016/j.physbeh.2006.02.012

Johnson, E. O., Roehrs, T., Roth, T., & Breslau, N. (1998). Epidemiology of medication as aids to alertness in early adulthood. *Sleep, 22*(4), 485–488.

Kabat-Zinn, J. (2003). Mindfulness-based interventions in context: Past, present, and future. *Clinical Psychology: Science and Practice, 10*(2), 144–156.

Kripke, D. F. (2000). Chronic hypnotic use: Deadly risks, doubtful benefit. *Sleep Medicine Reviews, 4*(1), 5–20. doi:10.1053/smrv.1999.0076

Kripke, D. F., Langer, R. D., & Kline, L. E. (2012). Hypnotics' association with mortality or cancer: A matched cohort study. *British Medical Journal, 2,* e000850. doi:10.1136/bmjopen-2012–000850

Krystal, A. D. (2010). Benzodiazepine receptor agonists: Indications, efficacy, and outcome. In M. J. Sateia & D. J. Buysse (Eds.), *Insomnia: Diagnosis and treatment* (pp 375–386). Informa Healthcare. doi:10.3109/97814200 80803.032

Kubitz, K. A., Landers, D. M., Petruzzello, S. J., & Han, M. (1996). The effects of acute and chronic exercise on sleep. A meta-analytic review. *Sports Medicine, 21,* 277–291. doi:10.2165/00007256–199621040–00004

Lavie, P., & Weler, B. (1989). Timing of naps: Effects on post-nap sleepiness levels. *Electroencephalography and Clinical Neurophysiology, 72,* 218–224. doi:10.1016/0013–4694(89)90246–0

Lichstein, K. L., Riedel, B. W., Wilson, N. M., Lester, K. W., & Aguillard, R. N. (2001) Relaxation and sleep compression for late-life insomnia: A placebo controlled trial. *Journal of Consulting and Clinical Psychology, 69,* 227–239. doi:10.1037/0022–006X.69.2.227

Manber, R., Bernert, R. A., Suh, S., Nowakowski, S., Siebern, A. T., & Ong, J. C. (2011). CBT for insomnia in patients with high and low depressive symptom severity: Adherence and clinical outcomes. *Journal of Clinical Sleep Medicine, 7*(6), 645–652. doi:10.5664/jcsm.1472

Manber, R., Bootzin, R. R., Acebo, C., & Carskadon, M. A. (1996). The effects of regularizing sleep-wake schedules on daytime sleepiness. *Sleep, 19*(5), 432–441.

McCall, W. V. (2010). Off-label use of prescription medications for insomnia: Sedating antidepressants, antipsychotics, anxiolytics, and anticonvulsants. In M. J. Sateia & D. J. Buysse (Eds.), *Insomnia: Diagnosis and treatment* (pp. 397–409). Informa Healthcare. doi:10.3109/9781420080803.034

McCallie, M. S., Blum, C. M., & Hood, C. J. (2006). Progressive muscle relaxation. *Journal of Human Behavior in the Social Environment, 13*(3), 51–66. doi:10.1300/J137v13n03_04

Mendelson, W. B. (1995). Effects of flurazepam and zolpidem on the perception of sleep in normal volunteers. *Sleep, 18,* 88–91.

Mets, M. A., Volkerts, E. R., Olivier, B., & Verster, J. C. (2010). Effect of hypnotic drugs on body balance and standing steadiness. *Sleep Medicine Reviews, 14*(4), 259–267. doi:10.1016/j.smrv.2009.10.008

Monk, T. H., Petrie, S. R., Hayes, A. J., & Kupfer, D. J. (1994). Regularity of daily life in relation to personality, age, gender, sleep quality and circadian rhythms. *Journal of Sleep Research, 3,* 196–205.

Monk, T. H., Reynolds, C. F., Buysse, D. J., DeGrazia, J. M., & Kupfer, D. J. (2003). The relationship between lifestyle regularity and subjective sleep quality. *Chronobiology International, 20,* 97–107. doi:10.1081/CBI-120017812

Morin, C. M., Bootzin, R. R., Buysse, D. J., Edinger, J. D., Espie, C. A., & Lichstein, K.L. (2006). Psychological and behavioral treatment of insomnia: Update of the recent evidence (1998–2004). *Sleep, 29*(11), 1398–1414.

Morin, C. M., Colecchi, C., Stone, J., & Sood, R. (1999). Behavioral and pharmacological therapies for late-life insomnia: A randomized controlled trial. *Journal of the American Medical Association, 281*(11), 991–999. doi:10.1001/jama.281.11.991

Morin, C. M., & Espie, C. A. (2003). *Insomnia: A clinical guide to assessment and treatment.* New York, NY: Springer.

Morin, C. M., Rodriguez, S., & Ivers, H. (2003). Role of stress, arousal, and coping skills in primary insomnia. *Psychosomatic Medicine, 65*(2), 259–267. doi:10.1097/01.PSY.0000030391.09558.A3

Naitoh, P. (1981). Circadian cycles and restorative power of naps. In L. C. Johnson, D. I. Tepas, W. P. Colquhoun, & M. J. Colligan (Eds.), *Biological rhythms, sleep and shift work* (pp. 553–580). New York, NY: SP Medical and Scientific Books.

National Institutes of Health. (2005). National Institutes of Health State of the Science Conference statement on manifestations and management of chronic insomnia in adults. *Sleep, 28*(9), 1049–1057.

Neubauer, D. N., & Flaherty, K. N. (2010). Nonprescription pharmacotherapies: Alcohol, over-the-counter, and complementary and alternative medicines. In M. J. Sateia & D., J. Buysse (Eds.), *Insomnia: Diagnosis and treatment* (pp. 417–426). Informa Healthcare. doi:10.3109/9781420080803.036

Nicassio, P., & Bootzin, R. R. (1974). A comparison of progressive relaxation and autogenic training as treatments for insomnia. *Journal of Abnormal Psychology, 83,* 253–260. doi:10.1037/h0036729

Nova, P., Hernandez, B., Ptolemy, A. S., & Zeitzer, J. M. (2012). Modeling caffeine concentrations with the Stanford Caffeine Questionnaire: Preliminary evidence for an interaction of chronotype with the effects of caffeine on sleep. *Sleep Medicine, 13,* 362–367. doi:10.1016/j.sleep.2011.11.011

O'Connor, P. J., Breus, M. J., & Youngstedt, S. D. (1998). Exercise-induced increase in core temperature does not disrupt a behavioral measure of sleep. *Physiology & Behavior, 64,* 213–217. doi:10.1016/S0031-9384(98)00049-3

Ong, J. C, Shapiro, S. L., & Manber, R. (2008). Combining mindfulness meditation with cognitive-behavior therapy for insomnia: A treatment-development study. *Behaviour Therapy, 39,* 171–182. doi:10.1016/j.beth.2007.07.002

Pallensen, S., Nordhus, I. H., Kvale, G., Nielsen, G. H., Havik, O. E., Johnsen, B. H., & Skjotskift, S. (2003). Behavioral treatment of insomnia in older adults: An open clinical trial comparing two interventions. *Behaviour Research and Therapy, 41,* 31–48.

Papineau, K. L., Roehrs, T. A., Petrucelli, N., Rosenthal, L. D., & Roth, T. (1998). Electrophysiological assessment (The Multiple Sleep Latency Test) of the biphasic effects of ethanol in humans. *Alcoholism: Clinical and Experimental Research, 22*(1), 231–235.

Perlis, M. L., Jungquist, C., Smith, M. T., & Posner, D. (2005). *Cognitive behavioral treatment of insomnia*. New York, NY: Springer.

Pilcher J. J., Michalowski K. R., & Carrigan R. D. (2001). The prevalence of daytime napping and its relationship to nighttime sleep. *Behavioral Medicine, 27,* 71–76.

Prinz, P. N., Roehrs, T. A., Vitaliano, P. P., Linnoila, M., & Weitzman, E. D. (1980). Effect of alcohol on sleep and nighttime plasma growth hormone and cortisol concentrations. *Journal of Clinical Endocrinology & Metabolism, 51*(4), 759–764. doi:10.1080/08964280109595773

Rabin, R. C. (2012, March 12). New worries about sleeping pills. *New York Times.* Retrieved from http://well.blogs.nytimes.com/2012/03/12/new-worries-about-sleeping-pills/

Ree, M. J., & Craigie, M. A. (2007). Outcomes following mindfulness-based cognitive therapy in a heterogeneous sample of adult outpatients. *Behaviour Change, 24*(2), 70–86. doi:10.1375/bech.24.2.70

Reyner, L. A., & Horne, J. A. (1997). Suppression of sleepiness in drivers: Combination of caffeine with a short nap. *Psychophysiology, 34,* 721–725. doi:10.1111/j.1469–8986.1997.tb02148.x

Richardson, G. S., Roehrs, T. A., Rosenthal, L., et al. (2002). Tolerance to daytime sedative effects of H1 antihistamines. *Journal of Clinical Psychopharmacology, 22,* 511–515. doi:10.1097/00004714–200210000–00012

Roehrs, T., & Roth, T. (2010). Benzodiazepine receptor agonist safety. In M. J. Sateia & D. J. Buysse (Eds.), *Insomnia: Diagnosis and treatment* (pp. 387–296). Informa Healthcare. doi:10.3109/9781420080803.033

Ryan, L., Hatfield, C., & Hofstetter, M. (2002). Caffeine reduces time-of-day effects on memory performance in older adults. *Psychological Science, 13,* 68–71. doi:10.1111/1467–9280.00412

Rybarczyk, B., Lopez, M., Benson, R., Alsten, C., & Stepanski, E. (2002). Efficacy of two behavioral treatment programs for comorbid geriatric insomnia. *Psychology and Aging, 17,* 288–98. doi:10.1037/0882–7974.17.2.288

Salzberg, S. (2002). *Lovingkindness: The revolutionary art of happiness*. Boston, MA: Shambhala.

Sarris, J., & Byrne, G. J. (2011). A systematic review of insomnia and complementary medicine. *Sleep Medicine Reviews, 15*(2), 99–106.

Saul, S. (2006, February 7.) Record sales of sleeping pills are causing worries. *New York Times.* Retrieved from http://webzoom.freewebs.com/killerpillre search/recordsalesofsleepingpills.pdf

Schutte-Rodin, S., Broch, L., Buysse, D., Dorsey, C., & Sateia, M. (2008). Clinical guideline for the evaluation and management of chronic insomnia in adults. *Journal of Clinical Sleep Medicine, 4*(5), 487–504.

Siriwardena, N. A., Qureshi, M. Z., Dyas, J. V., Middleton, H., & Orner, R. (2008). Magic bullets for insomnia? Patients' use and experiences of newer (Z drugs) versus older (benzodiazepine) hypnotics for sleep problems in primary care.

*British Journal of General Practice, 58*(551), 417–422. doi:10.3399/bjgp08X299290

Smith, S., Kozak, N., & Sullivan, K. (2012). An investigation of the relationship between subjective sleep quality, loneliness and mood in an Australian sample: Can daily routine explain the links? *International Journal of Social Psychiatry, 58*(2), 166–171. doi:10.1177/0020764010387551

Soehner, A. M., Kennedy, K. S., & Monk, T. H. (2011). Circadian preference and sleep-wake regularity: Associations with self-report sleep parameters in daytime-working adults. *Chronobiology International, 28*(9), 802–809. doi:10.3109/07420528.2011.613137

Souissi, M., Chtourou, H., Zrane, A., Ben Cheikh, R., Dogui, M., Tabka, Z., & Souissi, N. (2012). Effect of time-of-day of aerobic maximal exercise on the sleep quality of trained subjects. *Biological Rhythm Research, 43*(3), 323–330. doi:10.1080/09291016.2011.589159.

Spielman, A. J., Saskin, P., & Thorpy, M. J. (1987). Treatment of chronic insomnia by restriction of time in bed. *Sleep, 10,* 45–56.

Spielman, A. J., Yang, C. M., & Glovinsky, P. B. (2010). Insomnia: Sleep restriction therapy. In M. J. Sateia & D. J. Buysse (Eds.), *Insomnia: Diagnosis and treatment* (pp. 387–396). Informa Healthcare. doi:10.3109/97814200 80803.025

Stone, B. M. (1980). Sleep and low doses of alcohol. *Electroencephography and Clinical Neurophysiology, 48,* 706–709. doi:10.1016/0013–4694(80)90427-7

Tamaki, M., Shirota, A. I., Tanaka, H., Hayashi, M., & Hori, T. (1999). Effects of a daytime nap in the aged. *Psychiatry and Clinical Neurosciences, 53,* 273–275. doi:10.1046/j.1440–1819.1999.00548.x

Taub, J., & Berger, R. (1973). Performance and mood following variations in the length and timing of sleep. *Psychobiology, 10,* 559–70.

Thorpy, M. (2003). Sleep hygiene. Retrieved from http://www.sleepfoundation.org/article/ask-the-expert/sleep-hygiene

Tietzel, A. J., & Lack, L. C. (2001). The short-term benefits of brief and long naps following nocturnal sleep restriction. *Sleep, 24,* 293–300.

Tietzel, A. J., & Lack, L. C. (2002). The recuperative value of brief and ultrabrief naps on alertness and cognitive performance. *Journal of Sleep Research, 11,* 213–218. doi:10.1046/j.1365–2869.2002.00299.x

Van den Bulck, J. (2007). Adolescent use of mobile phones for calling and for sending text messages after lights out: Results from a prospective cohort study with a one-year follow-up. *Sleep, 30,* 1220–23.

Williams, D. L., MacLean, A. W., & Cairns, J. (1983) Dose-response effects of ethanol on the sleep of young women. *Journal of Alcohol Studies, 44,* 515–23.

Wright, K. R., Bogan, R. K., & Wyatt, J. K. (2013). Shift work and the assessment and management of shift work disorder (SWD). *Sleep Medicine Reviews, 17*(1), 41–54. doi:10.1016/j.smrv.2012.02.002

Youngstedt, S. D. (2005). Effects of exercise on sleep. *Clinics in Sports Medicine, 24,* 355–365. doi:10.1016/j.csm.2004.12.003

Zee, P. C., & Reid, K. J. (2010). Melatonin in sleep-wake regulation. In M. J. Sateia & D. J. Buysse (Eds.), *Insomnia: Diagnosis and treatment* (pp. 410–416). Informa Healthcare. doi:10.3109/9781420080803.035

# 9

# Science Weighs in on Obesity

*Adria Pearson*
University of Colorado, Denver
School of Medicine

*Linda W. Craighead*
Emory University

M any people trying to lose weight scan the covers of magazines at the grocery checkout counter, hoping for a new diet discovery. Like many of you, we don't believe there will ever be a secret ingredient, a specific diet, or a pill that will solve the world's weight woes. Reading articles in the media from a scientist's perspective will help you focus on the facts not the hype. In this chapter, we offer some insight into the science behind dieting and weight loss and describe some helpful strategies to try amid the onslaught of promises for a quick fix.

We are familiar with the latest fad diets, the latest supplement being pushed, and the newest diet guru's pronouncement. As clinical scientists and psychologists providing mental health services, we need to know what people are hearing on TV, from their friends and their hairdressers. We scrutinize each claim that emerges for potential scientific backing. Usually the claim or article reflects just one expert's diet or weight loss plan with stories and testimonials from satisfied customers. Those who have been successful with a particular plan often become spokespeople. Individual stories can be inspiring and encourage people in positive directions, but they can also be misleading if taken as scientific evidence. Too-good-to-be-true media reports often sound scientific, but what they report typically fails to reflect sound science methodology. We call that *pseudoscience*. If the story actually provides a reference to a scientific study, we read the methods section to see what was actually done. The conclusions may go far beyond what was actually demonstrated. The most common problem in weight loss reports is that the results are not representative, that is, only the most successful cases are showcased or the number of cases is small and participants were specially selected, not randomly assigned so the results can be biased. Remember the small note on many ads, "results may not represent the typical response." Individual successes and endorsements are just not science. The program being promoted may not be compared with other options that might work equally well and take less time or money, or that might be simpler to follow or have fewer potential adverse effects (always an issue with medication and surgery). There may be no follow-up to see how people fare months or years later (do they keep they weight off or regain it). Finally, the results are often not replicated, meaning the results aren't repeated with larger groups, with different types of people, or by independent investigators (people who didn't develop the product or plan and don't have a vested interest in showing it is effective). Consider these limitations the next time you are tempted to sign up for a new program, buy a product that you see on television, or buy a new diet book. Scientists know there is no magic solution for obesity, but they have learned a great deal about the all-too-common struggle to attain or stay a healthy weight.

In this chapter, we present what is known about obesity from scientific study and what we know about weight management as clinical-scientist psychologists. We hope this joint perspective will help you make sense of your day-to-day experiences with eating and dieting, losing weight, or perhaps not losing weight. In turn, we hope this information transforms how you feel about your body and about yourself, because the real goal is to improve your health and happiness, not reach a number on a scale.

## What Does Current Science Tell Us About Obesity?

The National Institutes of Health put together a "Blue Ribbon" committee to ask this question and their recent report (Casazza et al., 2013) provides a summary designed to help the public and policy makers identify the facts about obesity that science actually upholds and the beliefs about obesity that are just clinical lore. The hope is that any regulations, policies, or programs the government chooses to support will be based more on facts and less on opinions, prejudices, and personal experiences. But it turns out that solid evidence is not available for much of what many have presumed to be true. For example, evidence shows breast-feeding does not prevent childhood obesity though it has many other health benefits. We don't actually know if skipping breakfast or snacking promotes obesity, but we presume it does. Increasing consumption of fruits and vegetables does reduce weight but only if the person reduces consumption of other foods sufficiently to create a net calorie deficit. The following conclusions about obesity were deemed to be scientifically supported.

Genetics play a large role in determining how vulnerable a given individual is to becoming overweight, but "heritability is not destiny" (Casazza et al., 2013, p. 448). Some people are fairly protected from obesity by their physiological makeup whereas others easily become overweight in a food-rich environment unless they exercise self-control regarding food and stay active. Thus, intervention to make one immune to food temptation is needed, but so far success in achieving that goal has been modest. Since the social context is a major part of the problem, interventions such as medication and surgery are unlikely to ever provide a simple solution to the complex problem of obesity.

Lifestyle interventions which encourage eating healthier and lower calorie foods and reducing portions of high-calorie foods as well as increasing activity of all sorts are the treatments of choice. Those demonstrating the most enduring success fall into a broad overarching category of treatment called behavioral weight loss (BWL) or cognitive behavioral therapy (CBT). BWL and traditional CBT programs emphasize change-based strategies, such as challenging thoughts as maladaptive and prompting and reinforcing behavior change directly. The more successful programs are generally the longer ones and those that provide accountability and social support. While these approaches are the most effective we have (Butryn, Webb, & Wadden, 2011; Michael, Belendink, Kuchera, & Rofey, 2013), even when they are used, weight loss is modest. On average, 10% of body weight is lost, which is often enough to improve comorbid health problems like hypertension and diabetes but not usually enough to normalize weight (or meet the individual's expectations). Maintenance of weight loss is highly variable and most of the regain occurs within the first 6 months after treatment. CBT approaches are currently being expanded to include mindfulness and motivation enhancement strategies described in this chapter, but demonstrating the added value of these strategies within a multicomponent intervention that is already fairly effective will be a challenge.

Simply going on a diet may or may not lead to weight loss. However, if caloric intake is decreased significantly, ultimately weight loss will occur—regardless of how that decrease is achieved. For example, eating (rather than skipping) breakfast is a dietary strategy generally known to be helpful. This is because people who eat breakfast are typically less likely to get too hungry and overeat at subsequent meals so their overall intake is decreased. Notably, increasing exercise without lowering caloric intake is *not* typically adequate to promote significant weight loss. Some people feel hungrier and eat more or feel justified in eating more since they exercised, so their overall energy balance remains about the same. But an active lifestyle is the best way to *prevent* obesity, and maintaining a consistent high level of exercise has repeatedly been shown to be the single most effective strategy to maintain one's weight after a period of weight loss. Unfortunately, people overestimate the effects of small changes. One popular belief is that any increase (or decrease) of 3,500 kcal will lead to an increase (or decrease) of 1 pound. However, this so-called *fact* was demonstrated in short-term studies of men who had been put on an 800 kcal per day diet and overestimates the cumulative effect of small changes in intake or activity. The rule would suggest that a person increasing calories burned by 100 calories a day (walking a mile) or cutting out a 100 calorie snack would lose 50 pounds over 5 years. However, due to changes in body composition (fewer calories needed as one loses weight), the total weight loss during that time would be only 10 pounds. Substantial lifestyle changes are needed for meaningful weight loss. Real-life stories of individuals who have lost a significant amount of weight are instructive in this regard. Those who maintain their healthy weight describe a substantial makeover of their life, leisure activities, and relationships, sometimes even to the point of changing jobs or careers to help maintain their changes.

Exercise has significant positive effects whether or not you lose any weight. Ratey (2008) reviews the evidence and comes to the startling conclusion that exercise is not only the single best thing you can do for your health but it is also the best thing you can do for your brain (improves mood, memory, and ability to learn). Exercise is often labeled a "positive addiction." However, it must be noted that some individuals become obsessive and experience negative effects. The signs of obsessive exercise are (1) exercising even when injuries dictate rest, (2) not being able to skip days or scheduled workouts without guilt or distress, (3) allowing exercise to crowd out other valued activities, and (4) exercising in a compensatory manner such as after binge eating.

Preventing the development of obesity is much easier than waiting to treat obesity. Changing behavior enough to prevent weight gain is much more feasible and less aversive, and one feels successful right away. Losing weight is inherently confusing and frustrating because weight varies for so many reasons, and it takes so long to see meaningful results. Once established, obesity is best treated as a chronic health condition that requires significant sustained personal effort to manage effectively and may well require ongoing medical/supportive intervention to maintain optimal health.

Regardless of what science has to say about obesity, the ultimate goal for any individual is health with happiness, not weight or fitness! Lower weight and higher fitness are *means to an end*. It turns out that efforts to lose weight or become fit are more successful when individuals keep the ultimate goal in mind, as these efforts can lead to misery, injury, eating disorders, or problems with life (work and relationships) when individuals fail to stay focused on what is truly important to them.

## What Does Current Science Tell Us About Overeating?

The primary goal of this chapter is to help readers understand the most common paradox of dieting. Why is it so hard to stop overeating when individuals feel so highly motivated to do so? Why do individuals find themselves overeating often, even though time and time again they end up saying, "I wish I hadn't eaten that!" Why don't they learn to eat less? They end up confused and frustrated by their own choices. They may give up or try ever more desperate measures. They may lose and regain weight frequently (described as yo-yo dieting). At one point, scientists thought that weight cycling up and down might be even less healthy than remaining overweight. There is little evidence to support that conclusion, but yo-yo dieting certainly contributes to misery rather than promoting happiness. What has become increasingly clear to clinical scientists is: If you are not very aware of your internal responses (appetite and emotions), you will often eat when you aren't even hungry and often eat more than you need to feel full. Moreover, when you tune out after you overeat, you fail to learn the lessons you need to learn. You will continue to make similar choices in the future. We encourage you to try the mindful eating strategies described in this chapter, and we believe these strategies will help you feel better about what and how much you eat much more of the time.

Let's take a brief look at how overeating became a significant problem for humans. You don't see pictures of overweight cavemen on the walls of early caverns. Obviously, cavemen were very physically active so being more active is the no-brainer part of the weight management equation. But what did they eat? Cavemen ate what is now called the Paleo diet. It isn't too surprising that many experts suggest that some type of *Paleo* approach to choosing food is likely to be the healthiest and also help us keep our weight reasonable (see Cordain, 2011). Notably, the problem of obesity has skyrocketed in the past 50 years, but our bodies do not evolve so quickly that physical changes could account for the current obesity epidemic. Our basic physiology is pretty much the same as the caveman. Current science does back up the proposition that you are more likely to maintain a healthy weight if you eat more like a caveman (debate continues about the actual amount and type of protein that cavemen ate and what would be optimal now). Regardless, the take-home message from the Paleo solution is to eat fewer processed foods high in fat and sugar, which unfortunately excludes much of what is most easily available in the current food environment. *U.S. News & World Report* ("Best Diets," 2013) posted a list of the most highly rated diets. The details vary, but all are fairly congruent with the Paleo solution. Asking, "Would a caveman be eating this?" is a good way to decide what types of food to eat today. However, our guess is that this is not news to anyone. In short, science suggests that people should

- eat mostly unprocessed foods;
- eat lean types of protein and watch serving sizes (dairy is particularly useful in antihypertensive diets);
- eat berries, nuts, and other vegetables (particularly those originally foraged);
- eat whole grains (particularly grains other than hybrid wheat);
- drink water (certainly not regular soda or high-calorie beverages); and
- limit artificial sweeteners (which do save calories but may maintain individuals' preference for high sweetness and may send signals that confuse natural satiety signals).

Why doesn't the Paleo approach solve today's weight problems? While our bodies have not changed much, the environment has. The current food-rich low-activity environment (some call it *toxic*) is the reason rates of obesity are skyrocketing in the United States and why obesity increases in every country as the country industrializes. Paleo foods are still available today, but access to food is no longer limited by scarcity, seasonal availability, difficulty storing food, or high cost. Choosing to eat Paleo foods is far more difficult when you are continuously exposed to the temptations of *bliss* foods (today's processed foods engineered to appeal to our natural preferences for high sugar and high fat). Living the Paleo way in the current world is just not easy. Thus, we need guidelines geared to today's food environment.

An approach called Volumetrics (Rolls, 2005) provides a science-based guideline for food choices that is a bit easier to follow and generally more satisfying: eat lower density foods, meaning high volume relative to calories, for example, stews and vegetables. This approach is compatible with the Paleo solution (which is mostly lower density foods), and it discourages bliss foods (which are high density). It is more helpful in today's world because it focuses attention squarely on the scientific fact that reducing total calories ingested is largely what determines weight loss (regardless of how that is accomplished). This approach outlines a way to reduce calories by altering the type and preparation of foods rather than simply eating less of the foods you are currently eating. This approach capitalizes on the fact that the stomach sensations provided by higher volumes tend to feel more satisfying. Higher volume may also feel less depriving (psychologically) because you consume a larger amount of food and likely take longer to eat it. Many people do find choosing low-density foods a less effortful way to reduce calories, but this is not a panacea. You still have to manage the initial temptation of tasty foods and actually make those choices. If you are not aware of your fullness cues, you can easily override those cues and eat too many calories even when eating low-density foods. If you feel deprived of your high-density favorites, you may start eating even larger amounts of low-density foods in an effort to compensate for not eating what you want, or you may periodically overeat high-density foods for a splurge. Both these responses undermine the Volumetrics strategy. The psychological strategies we discuss later can help provide the motivation and awareness you need to use the Volumetrics strategy effectively.

The problem of today's highly tasty food brings us to another current controversy about obesity. Some experts suggest that obesity might be better understood within an addiction model. Within that model, some foods, especially high-sugar foods, are viewed as not so different from other substances of abuse in that they have such highly rewarding effects in the brain that they are believed to promote an addiction-like process that can include the development of cravings and tolerance (an increasing need for more of a substance to get a similar effect; Ziauddeen, Farooqi, & Fletcher, 2012). This controversy will be hotly debated over the next decade (see Brownell & Gold, 2012; Wilson, 2010, for both sides of the argument). It may turn out that some individuals are more sensitive to the rewarding effects of food than others. From our point of view, the salient fact is that the bliss foods that are hypothesized to have addiction-like qualities are all highly processed, high-density foods that healthy diets all discourage.

Whether or not any foods are biologically addictive, food can function as a psychological addiction. Food is self-comforting, that is, a way to cope with unpleasant thoughts and feelings in the same way that other substances are used to soothe negative feelings or provide pleasure. But, unlike substances with higher abuse potential, bliss foods are legal, and the pursuit of them rarely hurts anyone else directly or promotes crime. Most importantly, one must eat; so abstinence (the most effective way that other addictions are treated) is not an option. Moderation training (called harm reduction in the addiction field) is the only option. Some diet gurus do encourage eliminating most or all sugar and white flour. Some programs promote very low-fat diets believing that our innate preference for high-fat food is at least as much of a problem as our preference for high-sugar foods. However, the current consensus among behavioral psychologists is that having forbidden foods of any sort promotes a rigid and obsessional eating style that can be psychologically and socially as maladaptive as overindulgence. Currently, there is no scientific evidence to support the exclusion of any specific foods or food groups, and there is much evidence to support the gradual shaping of preferences for low-density foods and learning to eat what you want in moderation.

In summary, since the current, abundant food environment makes it a challenge to choose healthier (Paleo-like, low-density) foods consistently, and the easily available bliss foods may even have addictive qualities, more attention to the psychology of overeating is needed. We can't rely on nutrition or health information to provide sufficient motivation for us to make healthy choices consistently. We must understand the psychological principles underlying our motivational processes. We need strategies to manage emotional eating, which includes the drive to obtain positive effects from food (that we will call *desire*—cravings, strong preferences for high-calorie foods), as well as the drive to soothe negative feelings or relieve boredom with food (eating when not hungry). We also need to confront the body dissatisfaction that makes us so desperate to be thin (or at least lose weight) that we tune out and therefore fail to learn from our own repeated negative experiences with overeating.

## What Is the Role of Emotional Eating in Obesity?

Recently, the media has been more prominently suggesting that overeating is tied to negative emotional states. This is a very positive step since it acknowledges the psychological aspects of overeating that we believe are more important for most individuals. The term *emotional overeating* has been popularized, as shown in such clips as an unhappy woman eating ice cream alone from the carton or a despairing man watching TV on the couch with some chips and beer. Most people can relate to these images. Who hasn't taken comfort in an ice cream sundae or a delicious burger after a difficult day? Paradoxically, the media also pushes exercise and diet programs with spokespeople happily chirping their successes with weight loss and (unbelievably) fast results. Thus, the media sends a frustrating message for consumers, implying it is easy to succeed quickly, yet providing few concrete solutions (other than taking medication) about how to respond differently to the negative emotions that have been shown to perpetuate the overeating. Failure to manage one's eating further perpetuates body dissatisfaction and feelings of helplessness. This is a set-up, which elicits hope for a quick solution to overeating, inactivity, and the resultant weight gain in the face of common human emotional suffering.

The flaw in the media's messages is the suggestion that there is a quick and easy solution to the underlying emotional suffering that is the anteced-ent to much overeating. This is oversimplified. People overeat for many reasons in addition to eating to reduce emotional discomfort: food avail-ability, learned culture-based traditions and taste preferences, lack of resources to obtain healthy options, needing quick options for meals, and lack of knowledge about healthy dietary choices. Likely, a number of these factors are involved in any one scenario of individual dietary problems. However, evidence does suggest that emotional eating may be the most dif-ficult of these challenges to overcome. Oprah described making her peace with food in the following way, "I quit depriving myself and stopped using food as a pacifier. . . . it is a daily effort to stay connected and centered and not use food as a drug . . . as I have for years" (Winfrey, 2010). Clinical sci-entists are now studying the following ways of thinking about thinking, which we hope will challenge you to think differently about your own fail-ures to cope effectively with urges to eat.

## Experiential Avoidance (EA)

EA is a term that refers to the tendency to reduce one's experience of aversive thoughts and feelings by avoiding triggers that elicit those experi-ences and by suppressing awareness of the whole process of doing so (e.g., procrastination; Hayes, Wilson, Gifford, Follette, & Strosahl, 1996). EA plays a central role in a version of behavior therapy called Acceptance and Commitment Therapy (ACT; Hayes, Strosahl, & Wilson, 2012). ACT is showing promise as an alternative approach to overeating and weight loss (Lillis, Hayes, Bunting, & Masuda, 2009; Forman, Butryn, Hoffman, & Herbert, 2009; Tapper et al., 2009), body dissatisfaction (Pearson, Follette, & Hayes, 2012) and eating disorders (Berman, Boutelle, & Crow, 2009; Heffner, Sperry, Eifert, & Detweiler, 2002; Juarascio, Forman, & Herbert, 2010).

Experiential avoidance is importantly related to the concept of emotional eating in that eating is one way in which a person may try to suppress, reduce, or otherwise avoid a difficult emotional or physical state or even to suppress unwanted thoughts. The premise of ACT is that human *suffering* results from these behavioral attempts to move away from (i.e., avoid the experience of) difficult human emotions, such as anxiety, sadness, loss, loneliness, or emptiness, as well as attempts to avoid aversive physical sensations such as hunger and pain. Understandably, most people do not want to experience aversive emotions. However, some people are even less willing than others to tolerate even temporary distress that they experience in a given moment so they distract themselves in a variety of ways in order not to be so aware of those uncomfortable feelings. Some of those distracting activities are helpful (including calling a friend and moderate exercise), but many of those distractions are very short-lived. Notably, some have significant long-term negative consequences, such as the overeating that leads to weight gain. Even more important is that people learn to over-rely on this strategy of tuning out feelings and thoughts. In so doing, they reduce their awareness of what they are experiencing and consequently impair their ability to inhibit self-destructive choices or to problem-solve a more effective response. Most of us want a panacea to remove uncomfortable states and bring us into a joyful, or least a more neutral, place. Furthermore, we want that panacea quickly. It turns out that getting what you want in the short run is often a more powerful force than avoiding negative consequences later, even if those consequences are substantially worse. Relatedly, not only do we want things and to control other people's behavior, we also want to control how we feel and what thoughts we have. Tuning out (also called numbing) is one way we can avoid uncomfortable feelings we don't want to be having, and eating is a common way to do that.

Aligned with our very strong urge to move away from difficult emotions is an incredibly ever-active mind (often called the *monkey mind*), sending us thoughts about what people should do, how they should act, and how they should be in their lives. Attachment to these thoughts (beliefs that the thoughts are true rather than mere personal momentary experiences that may or may not reflect objective reality) is called *cognitive fusion*. For example, Weiner (2005) challenged the thought "I feel fat" by noting that "fat is not a feeling" and encouraging people to refocus on feelings (e.g., feeling lonely). Much of this internal dialogue has been learned from sociocultural exposures such an individual's family of origin, teachers, and peers and ever more so in this day, media exposure. Experiential avoidance is one way individuals attempt to get rid of the negative thoughts that come up, those that we might label as self-critical and unhelpful. You may distract yourself for a while by focusing your attention elsewhere, but the thoughts are still in your memory banks and they are *hot* thoughts, that is, they have unresolved emotions associated with them. When you aren't actively suppressing those thoughts, they are likely to pop up again as your attention shifts over the course of a day. The thought "I can't work out, I'm too busy" might later be supplanted by thoughts such as "I can't work out, I'm too tired" or "I can't work out, because I feel uncomfortable in a gym"; the possibilities of various manifestations of this ongoing verbal dialogue are endless. Meanwhile, these thoughts are interfering with your goal of getting to the gym. Just as difficult feelings can interfere with choosing healthy action, so can critical or unwanted thoughts.

The irony of the desire to press away, avoid, or otherwise ignore one's unwanted thoughts and difficult feelings is that this process has been shown to promote an even stronger cognitive, emotional, and behavioral response (Beevers, Wenzlaff, Hayes, & Scott, 1999; Wenzlaff & Wegner, 2000). Recently, this phenomenon was shown to apply to food cravings (Hooper, Sandoz, Ashton, Clarke, & McHugh, 2012). In this study, participants ate more chocolate following trials using thought suppression compared with trials using a defusion technique to deal with thoughts about chocolate cake.

## Defusion

Defusion is a technique described in ACT where one accepts rather than pushes away or suppresses thoughts (Luoma, Hayes, & Walser, 2007). Try it yourself: As you are reading this, no matter what, try not to think of an ice cream cone. The harder you try to suppress the thought, the more likely an image of ice cream will enter your mind. The same example can be applied to anger, anxiety, or nearly any emotion that in the moment, one wishes to avoid feeling (or at least expressing). The process of suppressing awareness of thoughts and feelings is called experiential avoidance (Hayes et al., 1996). The process of suppressing thoughts has been shown to be quite difficult for humans and actually causes the thought to increase in frequency (Wegner, Schneider, Carter, & White, 1987).

It isn't difficult to see how the principles of experiential avoidance and cognitive fusion apply to overeating. Tasty food is an easily available, legal way to feel better quickly so the idea of having some is likely to come into your mind often. The desire to decrease stress, loneliness, sadness, or the like pushes the intensity of a craving higher. Thoughts about food may intensify, and you may give in to the craving. Three problematic eating scenarios could evolve. One, you give into the desire to self-soothe with food because it initially works; you know that it has worked in the past. You rationalize this with thoughts like "I deserve it, I've had a bad day" and perhaps you don't feel too bad at the time. Two, the self-critical thoughts win; you don't give in to the craving, but your behavior around food becomes rigid and self-punishing at times. In the extreme, you establish very strict rules about "good foods" and "bad foods" that set you up for disordered eating. The third scenario is that you give in to the desire to suppress difficult emotions; you eat the craved food but are then filled with guilt, shame, and self-critical verbal dialogue (e.g., "I'm a bad person; I have no self-control; I am hopeless when it comes to food").

If you are sufficiently driven to get rid of the guilt, shame, and self-critical talk, compensatory behaviors may emerge to reduce the aversive sensations of fullness and associated fear of weight gain. Compensatory behaviors may initially be subtle and not terribly self-destructive, such as eating less or eating healthy the next day, but such behavior sometimes becomes more problematic, such as overexercising, using laxatives or other dietary pills, or purging. Any of these three scenarios can lead to eating problems. If scenario one (overeating) is repeated, the result can be obesity. If scenario two becomes well established, the result can be excessive food focus, anorexia nervosa, or the female athlete triad (i.e., low body weight, amenorrhea, and brittle bones). If scenario three is carried to its extreme, bulimia can emerge.

If you can reduce the guilt and shame associated with overeating, you will be more likely to remember the aversive consequences of past overeating that can motivate you to make healthier choices next time. Science tells us that positive reinforcement works even better than avoiding negative feelings (negative reinforcement), so the ideal strategy is to focus on the positive feelings and thoughts you have when you do make healthy choices so those positive memories provide incentives for future positive choices. It can be helpful to remember aversive sensations or feelings after overeating because those memories help provide incentives to avoid negative feelings in the future. But it is important to reduce your self-critical judgments as those just push you to tune out the whole experience and you don't learn from it.

Thoughts feel powerful. How can you reduce those self-critical thoughts? As noted earlier, attempting to just stop thinking them rarely works. However, psychological science has shed some light on ways to cope with such thoughts, ways to get distance, to decrease the power of thoughts to dictate your behavior (i.e., defusion). One strategy is to pretend your thoughts are like words on a printed piece of paper from the computer. After all, in certain ways, the mind is a bit like a computer, storing information, some of which may be incorrect and not helpful. Imagine your thoughts on a piece of paper; then imagine moving that piece of paper a little bit away from you. Instead of the thoughts being in your mind, they are now in front of you, maybe an inch, or some days perhaps even further. With time, you may realize they are far enough away that you can barely read the paper. As you move the thoughts further away, you feel freer to make different choices in your behavior. The key is that you learn, "Don't believe everything you think." Thoughts and feelings are just phenomena you experience; some may reflect reality, but clearly some do not. There is a choice point when you hear those harsh, distorted critical thoughts. When you start noticing your thoughts as just thoughts instead of facts, you can choose to respond to them, or you may choose to notice them and make alternative responses, choices that move you toward a more meaningful goal in your life.

## The Pressure to Be Thin Among Plenty

The widespread acceptance of the *thin ideal*, at least in more Westernized countries, makes health and weight issues even more complicated than they need to be. Underlying many manifestations of problematic eating is body image dissatisfaction. Anxiety about appearance makes it difficult to accept oneself in the present moment, increasing experiential avoidance, which then makes it difficult to respond in a constructive way when difficulties are encountered. When dissatisfaction is high, it is very hard to accept occasional overeating without the escalation of negative judgments, distress, and compensatory dieting that perpetuates problematic eating.

As noted earlier, along with the struggle of emotions; cravings; and thoughts about food, exercise, and weight, there is currently what might easily be termed an epidemic of body image dissatisfaction among both women and men. CBT interventions rely heavily on challenging an individual's negative body thoughts (called cognitive restructuring), but such interventions have had limited success, probably because being thin is highly reinforced in the current culture. In an initial clinical trial, a brief ACT intervention was shown to reduce body image dissatisfaction (Pearson, Follette, & Hayes, 2012). The Pearson et al. (2010) self-help manual describes this alternative approach to body dissatisfaction: the underlying emotions and thoughts that humans tend to experientially avoid are the target, not the accuracy or reasonableness of one's thoughts about one's body. The theory behind this intervention is that one's body (shape, size, and weight) is perceived as being somewhat more controllable or changeable than other, more difficult to address concerns such as interpersonal relationships, losses, and unwanted thoughts and feelings which actually need to be addressed.

Society bombards all of us with intense messages about one's capacity to fix one's exterior through diet, cosmetic surgery, and other external enhancements; this message reinforces our all-too-human tendency to fixate on what we think we can change. We are left with the perfect storm for suffering: our innate tendency to use food to soothe unpleasant emotions paired with judgmental thoughts about needing to eat right and the near impossibility of achieving the thin ideal so unabashedly promoted through the media. Efforts devoted to changing our exterior could be better directed toward changing other aspects of our self that may be difficult to change but are more likely to actually increase our happiness.

Consider the following: Thinness does not guarantee happiness or success. Many people do feel more satisfied with their appearance and report more self-confidence or higher self-esteem when they lose weight, and most do report increased negative feelings when they gain weight (particularly if they regain weight they just lost). However, research on happiness tells us that people's overall level of happiness in life is remarkably stable and not likely to be substantially altered by a few pounds up or down. Interestingly, body dissatisfaction has been shown to stay fairly consistent over one's lifetime (Bennett & Stevens, 1996; Tiggemann & Lynch, 2001). Individuals in the normal weight range who are dissatisfied tend to remain dissatisfied despite some fluctuations in weight, often becoming very focused on shape (e.g., wide hips, short legs, no waist) rather than weight per se. Individuals who are dissatisfied because they are overweight are rarely satisfied with whatever loss they are able to achieve. The intense beliefs some people develop that everything would be fine if only they could lose weight are illusory; some label such thinking as "magical thinking." Obsessional devotion to achieving weight loss can lead to greater unhappiness if an individual allows weight goals to take priority over other important life goals.

A person can be happy, healthy, confident, and competent no matter what they weigh; it's all about one's attitude. This is the main message of the *Health at Every Size* movement (see Bacon, 2008). This group seeks to inform the public about the science related to health and weight, particularly correcting misinformation suggesting that thinness is more important to health than being fit. This organization provides support for the positive message that individuals need to prioritize their health through increasing fitness rather than weight loss, and that we all need to fight the stigma associated with beliefs that being overweight is not acceptable or reflects a lack of effort.

Overvaluing appearance (which includes more than weight, but weight is the part for which we feel most responsible) is at the heart of eating-related unhappiness, which can include engaging in self-diminishing behaviors such as purging, overexercising, misuse of substances to lose weight or build muscles, and damage to social relationships due to avoidance behaviors and preoccupation with weight and shape. For that reason, we can't talk about obesity and happiness without talking about personal values.

# Unhealthy Consumption: As Easy as Pie

Satisfying an urge or craving works in the short term. Think of the last time you indulged in a favorite treat; you initially felt better. This situation is quite simply an example of the clearly established power of immediate gratification over long-term negative consequences, which means that you are set up to repeat the behavior even when you have some awareness of what you are doing. This is why you find yourself repeatedly saying, "I wish I hadn't eaten that," but turning around and indulging again the next time. The phenomenon of experiential avoidance ensures that the more you try to mask a craving, avoid the craving, or dampen the thoughts and emotions associated with the craving, the less successful you will be. This process is akin to holding a bone in front of a dog and telling him, "I know you want it, but you can't have it." The more you show the dog the bone, the more he will want it, the stronger the craving will become, and the more agitated he will become. However, unlike dogs, humans have the complexity of higher learning and language to remember the past and to think about the future. The dog is spared much of our uniquely human misery. Dogs live in the present moment, humans less so. Humans tend to ruminate, that is, hold on to memories, both emotional and cognitive, for very long periods of time as well as expectations about future events, whether those are anticipated pleasures or dangers. So, whereas you might initially be successful in driving past your favorite pizza place on your way home from work, not giving in to your craving, your mind can easily reproduce thoughts about the food repetitively, any visible reminder of it. That thought may haunt you the rest of the evening (or even without the rest of the week) until you finally give in and satisfy your craving.

# Taking It Off: Not So Easy; Keeping It Off: Even Harder

Every diet or program promoted for weight loss has worked well for someone. No diet or program has been successful for everyone who has tried it. But even for those who lose weight, the challenge remains sustaining motivation, managing feelings of deprivation and other negative emotions, and coping with eating-focused social events, stress, and a fast-paced lifestyle. One has to continue the changes that have been made or the weight creeps back on. A survey by Consumer Reports ("New Diet Winners," 2007) indicated that only 25% of individuals who reported ever attempting weight loss had achieved and maintained a loss of at least 10% of body weight for at least a year. If the underlying behavioral patterns and emotional motivations are not addressed, a cycle of weight loss–weight gain will likely persist. Typically, successful dieters have made several attempts before they find an approach that works well for them, and even then they are vulnerable to periods of regain when life stressors take priority over vigilant weight management. The NIH expert panel mentioned earlier (Casazza et al., 2013) listed only four conclusions about interventions for weight loss that they deemed clearly supported by current research.

1. Successful programs for overweight children need to involve the parents and the home setting (school-based physical education or after-school programs are helpful but not adequate by themselves—not sufficiently intense or frequent). Most overweight children have one or more parents who are or have been overweight. This is related in part to genetic factors and in part to behavioral factors. It is not surprising that in order to effectively help children lose weight, the home eating environment must change (Okie, 2005).

2. Provision of meals and use of various meal-replacement products does promote greater initial weight loss, and the use of such products does not appear to compromise one's ability to maintain weight loss, as was initially feared. This report does not comment specifically on the effectiveness of immersion approaches, where adults (or children) live in a therapeutic environment for moderate to extended periods of time to learn new habits in the relative absence of temptation. However, clinical reports support the conclusion that immersion is the most effective way to lose weight in the shortest period of time. However, the approach is not practical due to cost, interference with life responsibilities, and the slow rate of weight loss even under ideal circumstances. In practice, many immersion programs provide significant aftercare contact and often encourage brief return visits to address weight regain and help people get back on track.

The television show *The Biggest Loser* is an extreme example of an immersion intervention embedded within the context of a motivational game show. Recently, the show even took on the challenge of childhood obesity, showcasing three children. This show illustrates both the potential for success and the effort needed to achieve significant weight loss. Even in this ideal environment, the show displays to all the underlying emotional suffering among contestants. There is little doubt about the degree of motivation being on the show provides while the contestants are participating. But how can one adapt this approach to real, daily life off *The Biggest Loser* ranch? This has proven much more difficult, even for those who have been highly successful while at the ranch.

3. While psychosocial interventions are the first-line treatment, for those who fail in such efforts, medication is an option to consider. Some pharmaceutical agents (medications) help some individuals lose meaningful but modest amounts of weight, but losses are typically only maintained as long as the medication is continued. Interestingly, in light of the addiction model debate described earlier, the most promising recent report (Wadden et al., 2011) demonstrated that a combination of medications used in addiction treatment and to reduce smoking was able to modestly enhance the results of a lifestyle intervention.

4. Invasive approaches such as bariatric surgery essentially guarantee initial weight loss but carry significant risk of complications either initially or down the road. Thus, they are reserved for those who have clearly failed to achieve adequate loss through lifestyle change. For these folks, the health benefits can be lifesaving and may outweigh the risks. Unfortunately, many individuals regain half to all of the weight they lose, illustrating that the underlying emotional and lifestyle issues must be successfully addressed to maintain weight loss regardless of how it is achieved.

## Illustration: Enhance Healthy Eating Through Mindfulness Practices

The term *mindfulness* is rooted in the ancient spiritual practice of meditation; however, its current use in psychology is that of a tool for increasing awareness. Mindfulness practices have long been used to promote general well-being and have been integrated more recently into interventions for psychological disorders. When mindfulness is applied specifically to eating (e.g., the term *mindful eating*), it refers to paying attention to the full body experience of eating (e.g., stomach sensations) rather than focusing more exclusively on the taste of food. Traditional practices of mindful eating also emphasize awareness of and gratitude for all the people and processes that go into making the food available to you. Two books written for the layperson describing the applications for eating are *Mindful Eating* by Bays (2009) and *Savor* by Hanh and Cheung (2010).

Many communities offer low-cost classes in mindfulness/meditation (for example, Mindfulness-Based Stress Reduction; MBSR). Mindfulness is also often part of yoga classes, where one lies in *savassana* (a resting pose) and is instructed to notice thoughts and redirect attention to one's breath or some other aspect of being present in the room (not being off in your head thinking about something in the past or something about the future). The process of noticing thoughts, feelings, and other sensations without reacting and while letting go of judgments is the practice of mindfulness. This is not an easy practice, and by all means, it needs to be approached as a practice, meaning that there is no goal, no perfect practice of mindfulness for which one needs to be striving. In fact, striving would be counterproductive to the practice; it is all about just being in the present moment, observing and describing non-judgmentally. The theory behind mindfulness is that human beings are verbal creatures who automatically evaluate (think), feel, and react to their environments and experiences. It is judgmental (emotional) reactions to thoughts that can sometimes cause problems and a narrowing of behavioral choices (e.g., repetitive behaviors like overeating). Essentially, mindfulness strives to provide one with a choice point, a split-second pause in which to consider one's internal response before acting on it rather than reacting automatically. Practicing mindfulness is a tool to facilitate acceptance versus avoidance as well as a tool to facilitate gaining distance from thoughts (defusion).

For example, if one was more aware of the internal sensations of hunger (that is, more mindful of hunger), one could choose to respond to that sensation by eating (or by not eating); being mindful of the absence of hunger in the presence of appealing food, one could choose from a variety of options including consciously eating although not hungry, talking to a friend, or leaving the room. Similarly, by being more aware of the experience of craving (that is, more mindful of desire), one could choose to respond by eating or by not eating (choosing to tolerate the discomfort of unfulfilled desire). As such, mindfulness provides a means of choosing more wisely and a tool for tolerating distress without necessarily acting on it.

Let's walk through an example of using mindfulness to make healthier food choices and tolerating versus avoiding distress. Imagine that you are faced with multiple high-calorie food options at a work party. Using mindfulness, you become more aware of your situation—you are very hungry and there are many tempting foods. At this point, you have a choice. You can choose with awareness a lower calorie option (i.e., the vegetable tray and some cheese), versus the option to which you are automatically drawn. This may be a little bit uncomfortable, because you may really want the fried or sweet foods you see. Let's add, for example, that you are also a bit uncomfortable at the party because it is at your boss's house. You are anxious about your job performance, and you are worried about interacting socially in front of your boss. If you are being mindful, you are aware of your anxiety as well as your hunger. Anxiety and hunger and food available are a recipe for overeating because you are motivated to avoid or lessen your discomfort, both emotionally and physically. Mindfulness can be a means of tolerating this distress without resorting to food.

One exercise that is common in mindfulness practice is to focus on your breath. Since you always carry your breath with you, the instruction is to remember to slow your breath and bring your attention to it for a few minutes (one practice is called the Three-Minute Breathing Space); this can lessen physiological anxiety cues (e.g., racing heart, sweaty palms, shallow breathing). Just as you can bring attention to the breath, you can also choose to bring attention to anything in the room or at the party that is soothing. Maybe you have a good friend who also is a colleague. Grabbing some veggies and cheese, you can choose to walk over to this person and engage her in a conversation. During that conversation, you can be mindful of what the person is saying, what you appreciate about her as a friend, or any other positive attribute about your relationship. Drawing your attention toward these other positive and meaningful aspects of your experience can be very helpful in moving through distress versus having to avoid or reduce your distress by eating. On the other hand, if you remain focused on (cognitively fused to) just your thoughts about wanting the tasty food, you will be more likely to go back to the food to stop those aversive, perseverative thoughts about wanting but not allowing yourself the food.

## Enhance Motivation for Healthy Eating Through Focus on Values

Within a cognitive behavioral model, motivation is created through three processes: positive reinforcement, negative reinforcement, and punishment. These motivating processes involve internal and external sources of pleasure or aversion. Setting up a self-reward system, such as "if I lose 10 pounds I will buy myself a piece of jewelry" is common. In cognitive behavioral terms, this would be termed positive reinforcement. Positive reinforcement occurs when something pleasant is provided contingent upon a behavior, and it increases the probability that you will do that behavior again. Of note, the external reward just described is based on the outcome (e.g., weight loss) but it is more effective to make the reward for the specific behaviors that lead to the desired outcome (making lower calorie food choices or going to the gym). Importantly, rewards do not need to be large (e.g., a trip to Paris when you reach goal weight) to be effective. In fact, small rewards provided more frequently work better, especially when you are first trying to establish a new behavior (e.g., downloading a tune every time you make it to the gym, getting a manicure if you meet your goal of no more than 3 desserts in a week). Rewards typically work better if someone else is providing them (your significant other gives you a massage or your company provides incentives for participation in Weight Watchers) since you can't cheat, but don't underestimate the power of self-provided rewards. If you experiment, you may be surprised to find how much allowing yourself small (nonfood) indulgences can help you remain positive (i.e., stay motivated) about the daily effort you need to put into making healthy food choices.

The feeling of pride when you successfully lose weight is an example of internal positive reinforcement. Deliberate positive self-talk is an excellent way to motivate yourself to keep on doing the exercise or making the healthier food choices. Unfortunately, most people aren't very good at positive self-talk. You are much more likely to attempt to motivate yourself with negative self-talk, that is, calling yourself names ("I'm a fat pig" when trying on clothing) or harshly criticizing yourself when you overeat or can't get to the gym. The feelings of shame or guilt elicited are self-punishment. Similarly, other people typically believe they can motivate you to lose weight by social punishment (their criticism). Consider these examples: A well-meaning physician, seeing a patient gained 20 pounds, states critically, "If you don't lose 25 pounds, you're setting yourself up for diabetes." A man returning to the kitchen for seconds at dinner is scolded by his wife, "That's not going to help you lose weight!" A teenager shopping with her overweight sister says sarcastically, "There's not going to be anything in that store to fit you!" In these scenarios, individuals may be initially motivated to change by the shame or fear, but unfortunately, the effects of such punishment rarely last. They just make people feel worse about themselves, and in so doing, may even increase emotional eating as people try to manage their distressing feelings.

Behavioral science (see Pryor, 1999) explains why punishment is generally ineffective (it doesn't teach new behaviors, and you try to avoid the punisher). The problem is most obvious in overweight children; when parents limit access to treats too severely, their children learn to sneak food, not make better choices. Punishment by others doesn't work well because it creates negative feelings (e.g., anger), which interferes with learning more adaptive behaviors. Most importantly, when you attempt to punish yourself (with criticism) you increase motivation to tune out; you try to avoid your own thoughts and feelings, resulting in the experiential avoidance discussed earlier. Avoiding distressing feelings is a setup for mindless eating.

The third motivational process is negative reinforcement, which can be a productive type of motivation, but it can be tricky. Negative reinforcement occurs when an unpleasant consequence is terminated. Examples of negative reinforcement that encourage weight-controlling behaviors are reduced difficulty breathing while walking when you lose weight, reduced clothing discomfort with weight loss, and reduced anxiety about eating in front of others when you lose weight. In addition, your own self-critical thoughts may diminish, and others may reduce their nagging.

A caution in this regard is that avoidance is often increased by negative reinforcement. When we avoid uncomfortable emotions, for example, anxiety is initially reduced. However, as noted, anxiety ultimately becomes stronger with avoidance strategies because one starts avoiding more and more. If you worry about your weight, you may develop an intense belief that you must keep worrying about your weight in order to successfully lose weight or keep off weight you have lost. Worry itself can become an avoidance strategy. Initially, when you worry you feel better because you think you are doing something constructive about your weight. The process of negative reinforcement ensures that you will continue to worry, and you may worry more. However, the increased worry backfires; it creates additional negative feelings that lead to emotional eating or experiential avoidance, which is a setup for mindless eating and weight gain (which will make you worry even more, and the cycle escalates). This is the reason that accepting your current weight works much better than excessive worry about it. Acceptance increases your ability to problem-solve and take action whereas worry increases avoidance, interfering with adaptive choices.

Interestingly, before you try to set up systems of positive or negative reinforcement to help you manage your weight, it is important to first find out what is meaningful about weight loss for you as an individual. Just as people overeat for different reasons, individuals lose weight for different reasons. Although better health is a universal benefit of weight loss when someone is overweight, it isn't always an individual's primary motivation. Attention to other, especially specific, aspects of your life may be more motivating. Family is an example. For example, Jim, who is 70 pounds overweight, can no longer play baseball with his son. He also worries that he won't live long enough to see his grandkids. Career endeavors can be another valued area of life providing motivation for weight loss. Sandy is a chef at a restaurant but recently has been unable to stand for the necessary period of time because of a 60-pound rapid weight gain after the death of her mother. The weight has resulted in pressure on her lower back, creating chronic pain. She has considered working part time but cannot afford it. Weight loss in her case could be motivated by the pleasure she has working and the financial burden that is created by having to cut her hours. Her health is a meaningful factor but for some specific reasons unique to her. Each person has meaningful areas of life that could be positively impacted. The key is to find what these are for you and to make them very salient. It is important to spell out all the reasons you really want to lose weight rather than leave it as a general thought that weight loss is good and you will feel better. This process is called *values clarification,* and it is an important component of ACT. Terms such as goal setting or creating meaningful goals may be used in other approaches.

To get started on finding meaningful reasons to stay motivated, it's good to first take a look at what areas of life matter to you. Make a list of short- and long-term goals that are meaningful. Next, it's helpful to look at barriers to those goals: Do they relate to your weight? It may be that the barriers do not directly relate to your weight. As we mentioned, overeating may serve a role in helping you avoid uncomfortable emotions. There may be areas of your life that are difficult to change, emotionally difficult to face. Overeating may have served the role of helping you forget about those things. If you stop overeating, it's quite likely that you may face directly the emotions or challenging areas of your life. They may become more uncomfortable and more present for you. What is this telling you? It's showing you that those areas of life in which you experience emotional pain are those you also value. The overeating may have been a way to move away from those topics.

In fact, overeating and stopping overeating are intertwined with one's life. Keeping your true goals in mind helps you stay focused on the strategies that are actually working for you and encourages you to modify or give up strategies that aren't working even though you wish they would.

## Pitfalls Associated With Dieting: What to Avoid

1. Stay away from short-term diet solutions: This may include anything from a very strict short-term diet plan to pills, beverages, or other supplements that claim fast weight loss.

2. Ask yourself this question when considering a dietary plan: "Could I eat like this until I am 85 years old?" If the answer is no, it's not going to work long term.

3. Does the dietary or exercise plan fit into your existing lifestyle without major financial burden? If you cannot maintain the program financially, it isn't going to be a long-term solution.

4. Do you understand why you want to lose weight? Find a way to keep your real goals salient, that is, "in your face." Vague goals like "I'll have higher self-esteem" are not as effective as concrete, specific goals such as "I will be able to play tennis with my son."

5. Build in positive reinforcement for changing eating behaviors, but avoid using food as a reward for changing behavior or for weight loss, for example, saying you will go out to eat after you have lost five pounds. Some diets even allow a cheat day where you can eat whatever you want, but such

practices use unhealthy foods as a reward for healthy eating and this is not the best long-term strategy. It works better to make treat foods a predictable part of your eating to prevent feelings of deprivation and to reduce the exaggerated belief that some foods are just so irresistible that you have to have them whenever they are available. Tasty food is to be enjoyed, but when any food is overvalued it can be a problem (just as when appearance is overvalued).

## First Steps: Getting Started

1. Find social support and be accountable to someone whether it is a friend, a self-help group, a counselor, or a group program. We know through research that social accountability promotes and maintains behavior change.

2. Start with specific small goals for weight loss and exercise so you can achieve them. This will serve as positive reinforcement for continued progress.

3. Consult with your physician about any health issues or possible limitations regarding exercise. Consider consultation with a nutritionist if you need recipes or do not already know a good bit about recommended daily allowances of food groups, calories, and vitamins.

4. Find an exercise or exercises you enjoy. If you don't like to run, don't pick running to lose weight. It will be aversive and ultimately will not be maintained.

As we've suggested throughout this chapter, mindfulness, acceptance of emotions, distancing from thoughts, and clarifying meaningful goals for weight loss are important tools for emotional wellness and weight management. Self-help books can be a useful start. You can use the self-help manual for ACT described earlier to address the experiential avoidance that can sabotage weight loss efforts. ACT prioritizes acceptance of uncomfortable experiences while making one's life goals very salient to increase motivation to move toward those goals (i.e. helping you do what you know needs to be done but you don't feel like doing). You also can use the self-help manual for Appetite Awareness Training (AAT; Craighead, 2006) to learn to eat more mindfully. AAT is similar to the popular notion of intuitive eating; the goal is to eat when you are hungry and stop when you are full. But AAT provides a very structured approach to help you develop awareness of psychological versus biological hunger, to choose foods with full awareness of how you are likely to feel after eating, and to stay tuned into your feelings after eating so you can learn from your own experiences with eating moderately versus overeating. See Table 1 for a flow chart showing how AAT helps you cope with urges to eat. If you find these skills difficult to do on your own, find a

## Table 9.1    HELP! I Want to Eat!

There are many reasons why you might want to eat: hunger, regularly scheduled mealtimes, food is available, or emotions (which include boredom and procrastination). The trick is to figure out why you want to eat and then to make a Conscious Decision (CD) about whether or not eating is the best option at this time. Go through the following steps the next time you have an urge to eat.

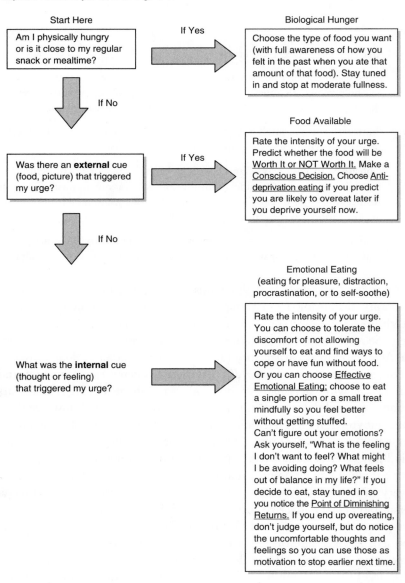

Start Here

Am I physically hungry or is it close to my regular snack or mealtime?

If Yes

Biological Hunger

Choose the type of food you want (with full awareness of how you felt in the past when you ate that amount of that food). Stay tuned in and stop at moderate fullness.

If No

Was there an **external** cue (food, picture) that triggered my urge?

If Yes

Food Available

Rate the intensity of your urge. Predict whether the food will be Worth It or NOT Worth It. Make a Conscious Decision. Choose Anti-deprivation eating if you predict you are likely to overeat later if you deprive yourself now.

If No

Emotional Eating
(eating for pleasure, distraction, procrastination, or to self-soothe)

What was the **internal** cue (thought or feeling) that triggered my urge?

Rate the intensity of your urge. You can choose to tolerate the discomfort of not allowing yourself to eat and find ways to cope or have fun without food. Or you can choose Effective Emotional Eating; choose to eat a single portion or a small treat mindfully so you feel better without getting stuffed.
Can't figure out your emotions? Ask yourself, "What is the feeling I don't want to feel? What might I be avoiding doing? What feels out of balance in my life?" If you decide to eat, stay tuned in so you notice the Point of Diminishing Returns. If you end up overeating, don't judge yourself, but do notice the uncomfortable thoughts and feelings so you can use those as motivation to stop earlier next time.

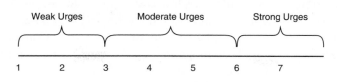

|  | Weak Urges | Moderate Urges | Strong Urges |
|---|---|---|---|

| 1 | 2 | 3 | 4 | 5 | 6 | 7 |

- Try distraction
- Get rid of tempting food
- Leave the environment

- Try distraction
- "Urge Surf"

- Don't fight with it!
- Acknowledge it. Make a Conscious Decision.
- Eat mindfully. Enjoy!
- Notice the Point of Diminishing Returns.

**AAT Skills**

- Conscious Decision (CD): Just like it sounds…make a conscious decision to eat instead of eating mindlessly. With this skill, you practice making the choice to eat. CDs bring back your sense of control.
- Anti-Deprivation Eating (ADE): You make a conscious decision to enjoy a particular food, even though you aren't *that* hungry. You allow yourself a satisfying amount of the food you are wanting…so you won't feel deprived and end up overeating later on. ADE is NOT an excuse to get stuffed! In fact, the purpose of ADE is to keep you from setting yourself up to overindulge in the future!
- Effective Emotional Eating  (EEE): All people eat for emotional reasons at times; this is part of "normal" eating. As long as you actually do feel better after a treat, you have been effective. Anytime you end up feeling worse after you eat (wishing you hadn't eaten something), then it wasn't effective. Staying aware will allow you to learn from yourself that whenever a treat doesn't work, eating more makes you feel worse. You are not your practicing EEE when you use emotions as an excuse to get stuffed or when your eating has a "What the Heck" quality to it. When you say "I don't care," you are tuning out your feelings (You do care!).
- Point of Diminishing Returns: Stay tuned in as you eat so you notice when the food no longer tastes as good or you don't feel good. When you reach that point, food is no longer working well for you. Use that awareness to stop, then leave the situation or change to a non-food strategy if you are trying to cope with emotions.
- Urge Surf: Do not distract yourself or push away the urge or desire to eat. Use mindfulness (the knowledge that all thoughts and feelings are impermanent and the urge will subside on its own if you do not give in to it). Your job is to ride out the urge, just as a surfer stays on a board and rides the crest of the wave until it dissipates. Thoughts (just like waves) are replaced by other thoughts them. unless you are actively holding on to them.

Reproduced with permission of Linda W. Craighead.

group program or consult with a therapist who is trained in CBT as well as mindfulness approaches who can guide and support your efforts.

## Summary

Weight loss is a difficult endeavor. Overeating is a challenging behavior to change because it is immediately rewarding. Our society is set up for people to overeat, to become and remain overweight, and to be miserable about their eating due to high food availability, low cost of many foods, the high socio-cultural value of food, and the thin ideal. If you are faced with needing to lose weight, you are among the majority of the American public. Commercials for quick fixes to obesity are hard to ignore because most people want hope for fast change. However, as we have described, the complexity of humans and food is substantial, and obesity defies a simple solution such as just eating less or taking a pill. After all, if you could just stop eating, you would have done so long ago. Losing weight is a lifestyle change that involves both activities and alternative ways to manage emotions, and those must be maintained if the benefits are to last. We hope we have offered some information based on clinical science that (1) explains why the process is so often difficult and (2) offers suggestions about how to get started if you are ready to take on the challenge of getting and staying healthier and happier for the rest of your life.

# References

Bacon, L. (2008). *Health at every size: The surprising truth about your weight.* Dallas, TX: BenBella Books.

Bays, J. C (2009). *Mindful eating.* Boston, MA: Shambhala.

Beevers, C. G., Wenzlaff, R. M., Hayes, A. M., & Scott, W. D. (1999). Depression and the ironic effects of thoughts suppression: Therapeutic strategies for improving mental control. *Clinical Psychology: Science and Practice, 6,* 133–148.

Bennett, K., & Stevens, R. (1996). Weight anxiety in older women. *European Eating Disorders Review, 4*(1), 32–29.

Berman, M. I., Boutelle, K. N., & Crow, S. J. (2009). An open trial of acceptance and commitment therapy for previously treated unremitted patients with anorexia nervosa. *European Eating Disorders Review, 17*(6), 426–434.

Best diets. (2013). *U.S. News and World Report.*

Brownell, K. D., & Gold, M. S. (2012). *Food and addiction: A comprehensive handbook.* New York, NY: Oxford University Press.

Butryn, M. L., Webb, V., & Wadden, T. A (2011). Behavioral treatment of obesity. *Psychiatry Clinics of North America, 34,* 841–859.

Casazza, K., Fontaine, K. R., Astrup, A, Birch, L. L., Brown, A. W., Brown, . . . Allison, D. B. (2013). Myths, presumptions, and facts about obesity. *New England Journal of Medicine, 368,* 446–454.

Cordain, L. (2011). *The Paleo diet* (Rev. ed.). Hoboken, NJ: John Wiley & Sons.

Craighead, L. W. (2006). *The appetite awareness workbook: How to listen to your body and overcome bingeing, overeating, and obsession with food.* Oakland, CA: New Harbinger.

Forman, E. M., Butryn, M., Hoffman, K. L., & Herbert, J. D. (2009). An open trial of acceptance-based behavioral treatment for weight loss. *Cognitive and Behavioral Practice, 16,* 223–235.

Hanh, T. N., & Cheung, L. (2010). *Savor: Mindful eating, mindful Life*. New York, NY: Harper One.

Hayes, S. C., Strosahl, K. D., & Wilson, K. G. (2012). *Acceptance and commitment therapy: The process and practice of mindful change* (2nd ed.). New York, NY: Guilford Press.

Hayes, S. C., Wilson, K. G., Gifford, E. V., Follette, V. M., & Strosahl, K. D. (1996). Experiential avoidance and behavioral disorders: A functional dimensional approach to diagnosis and treatment. *Journal of Consulting and Clinical Psychology, 64*, 1152–1168.

Heffner, M., Sperry, J., Eifert, G. H., & Detweiler, M. (2002). Acceptance and commitment therapy in the treatment of an adolescent female with anorexia nervosa: A case example. *Journal of Cognitive and Behavioral Practice, 9*, 232–236.

Hooper, N., Sandoz, E. K., Ashton, J., Clarke, A., & McHugh, L. (2012). Comparing thought suppression and acceptance as coping techniques for food cravings. *Eating Behavior, 13*, 62–64.

Juarascio, A. S., Forman, E. M., & Herbert, J. D. (2010). Acceptance and commitment therapy versus cognitive therapy for the treatment of comorbid eating pathology. *Behavior Modification, 34*(2), 175–190.

Lillis J., Hayes, S. C., Bunting K., & Masuda, A. (2009). Teaching acceptance and mindfulness to Improve the lives of the obese: A preliminary test of a theoretical model. *Annals of Behavioral Medicine, 37*(1), 58–69.

Luoma, J. B., Hayes, S. C., & Walser, R. D. (2007). *Learning ACT: An acceptance and commitment therapy manual for therapists*. Oakland, CA: New Harbinger.

Michael, J. C., Belendink, K.A., Kuchera, A. M., & Rofey, D. L. (2013). Cognitive behavioral therapy for weight management. *The Behavior Therapist*, 28–38.

New diet winners. (2007, June). *Consumer Reports*, pp. 12–17.

Okie, S. (2005). *Fed up! Winning the war against childhood obesity*. Washington, DC: Joseph Henry Press.

Pearson, A. N., Follette, V. M., & Hayes, S. C. (2012). A pilot study of acceptance and commitment therapy as a workshop intervention for body image dissatisfaction and disordered eating attitudes. *Cognitive and Behavioral Practice, 19*, 181–197.

Pearson, A. N., Heffner, H., & Follette, V. M. (2010). *Acceptance and commitment therapy for body image dissatisfaction: A practitioner's guide to using mindfulness, acceptance and values-based behavior change strategies*. Oakland, CA: New Harbinger.

Pryor, K. (1999). *Don't shoot the dog: The new art of training*. New York, NY: Bantam.

Ratey, J. J. (2008). *Spark: The revolutionary new science of exercise and the brain*. New York, NY: Little, Brown.

Rolls, B. J. (2005). *The Volumetrics eating plan*. New York, NY: HarperCollins.

Tapper, K., Shaw, C., Ilsley, J., Hill, A. J., Bond, F. W., & Moore, L. (2009). Exploratory randomized controlled trial of a mindfulness-based weight loss intervention for women. *Appetite, 52*(2), 396–404.

Tiggemann, M., & Lynch, J. E. (2001). Body image across the life span in adult women: The role of self-objectification. *Developmental Psychology, 37,* 243–253.

Wadden, T. A., Foreyt, J. P., Foster, G. D., Hill, J. O., Klein, S., O'Neil, P. M., & Dunayevich, E. (2011). Weight loss with naltrexone buproprion combination therapy as an adjunct to behavior modification: The COR_BMOD trial. *Obesity, 19,* 110–12

Wegner, D. M., Schneider, D. J., Carter S. R., & White, T. L. (1987). Paradoxical effects of thought suppression. *Journal of Personality and Social Psychology, 53*(1), 5–13.

Weiner, J. (2005). *Life doesn't begin 5 pounds from now.* New York, NY: Simon & Schuster.

Wenzlaff, R. M., & Wegner, D. M. (2000). Thought suppression. *Annual Review of Psychology, 51,* 59–91.

Wilson, G. T. (2010). Eating disorders, obesity and addiction. *European Eating Disorders Review, 18,*341–351.

Winfrey, O. (2010, July). What I know for sure. O, p. 160.

Ziauddeen, H, Farooqi, I. S., & Fletcher, P. C. (2012). Obesity and the brain: How convincing is the addiction model? *Nature Reviews Neuroscience, 13,* 279–286.

# 10

# Exercise

## A Path to Physical and Psychological Well-Being

*Reed Maxwell*

*Steven Jay Lynn*

Binghamton University

*It is exercise alone that supports the spirits, and keeps the mind in vigor.*

Marcus Tullius Cicero

*If it weren't for the fact that the TV set and the refrigerator are so far apart, some of us wouldn't get any exercise at all.*

Joey Adams

From the Greek *palaestra* to Pilates, from tai chi to Tae Bo, exercise and physical fitness have been entwined with conceptualizations of well-being from antiquity to the present day. The many and varied health benefits of exercise strike us as almost self-evident truths in the early 21st century. Yet the idea of exercise as the royal road to a better life was neither highly popularized nor systematically studied in the United States until only about

223

60 years ago (Brannon & Feist, 2009). Since researchers' pioneering studies made a splash in the scientific community, and champions of fitness like Jim Fixx disseminated them to a general audience with evangelical zeal (Brannon & Feist, 2009), recognition of the benefits of exercise has blossomed in the public eye. Today, psychologists and other helping professionals sing the praises of regular exercise's preventative and ameliorative consequences. Hard-nosed scientists have documented dozens upon dozens of preventive or therapeutic applications of exercise over the years, including mitigating deleterious coronary effects of Type A behavior (Jasnoski, Cordray, Houston, & Osness, 1987), discomforts during adolescent pregnancy (Koniak-Griffin, 1994), and social anxiety disorder (social phobia; Jazaieri, Goldin, Werner, Ziv, & Gross, 2012), with positive findings lending force to the claims of proponents of exercise.

As the media and scientific opinion have zeroed in on the promise of exercise to foster general well-being, Americans have turned in increasingly large numbers to one form or another of exercise to prevent disease, promote health, and calm the mind. This is surely a positive development, as our increasingly sedentary and unhealthy lifestyles—fed by junk food, desk jobs, and mind- and body-numbing entertainment options—have compelled some researchers to dub obesity "the disease of the 21st century" (Rössner, 2002). Public health trends in developing countries underline this clam. Indeed, it may be said that with more wealth comes poorer health, marked by increased obesity and its related health problems (Prentice, 2006).

Although there is much room for improvement, in 2011, about half of American adults (48.4%) met the Centers for Disease Control and Prevention's (CDC's) Physical Activity Guidelines for aerobic physical activities (i.e., moderate intensity exercise, such as brisk walking for 2 hours and 30 minutes a week); about one quarter (24%) met guidelines for strength training (i.e., 2 or more days a week exercising all major muscle groups); and about one fifth (20.6%) met guidelines for both types of exercise (CDC, 2010). Nearly a third (29%) of American adolescents (e.g., high school students) participate in at least 60 minutes of physical activity each day of the week. Nationally, exercise frequency correlates positively with level of education (i.e., high school, college, postgraduate) and negatively with age (CDC, 2007).

# A Taxonomy of Exercise

What are people doing when they exercise? Not necessarily the same thing. Exercise can be categorized into the following five types that do not always produce the same results. Isometric exercise is performed when muscles contract without limb movement (e.g., pressing the hands tightly together). Isotonic exercise is performed when muscles contract and joints move (e.g., weightlifting). Isokinetic exercise is performed when muscles contract and limbs move such that exertion is required to both extend and return them to their original position (this requires special equipment and often occurs in a rehabilitative setting; Brannon & Feist, 2009). Anaerobic exercise requires intense, brief surges of energy but no increase in oxygen use (e.g., swinging a bat to hit a fastball). Finally, aerobic exercise requires dramatically increased oxygen use over an extended duration, as in long-distance running. The preponderance of exercise studies have examined the effects of aerobic exercise on physical and psychological well-being. Although we initially review a number of findings pertinent to nonaerobic exercise research, the lion's share of our discussion focuses on aerobic exercise.

## Anaerobic Exercise

Córdova, Silva, Moraes, Simões, and Nóbrega (2009) examined the effects of acute (i.e., single-session) anaerobic exercise of differing intensities (e.g., stationary bicycling with incrementally increased resistance loadings) on measures of executive functioning in active elderly female participants. Compared with nonexercising controls, the authors observed more positive outcomes in measures of planning, alertness, cognitive flexibility, and verbal fluency among subjects completing the anaerobic task. The authors noted that aerobic research does not confirm their tentative conclusion that acute anaerobic exercise produces immediate cognitive improvements. In fact, Córdova et al.'s findings are inconsistent with previous research (Kramer et al., 1999) documenting improvements (relative to nonexercising controls) in executive functioning among elderly individuals who participate in acute *aerobic* exercise but not anaerobic exercise. Researchers examining other cognitive measures (e.g., memory; Blumenthal & Madden, 1988) have likewise failed to find performance boosts in response to anaerobic exercise such as strength training (however, see Winter et al., 2007).

## Isotonic, Isometric, and Isokinetic Exercise

Few studies of isometric, isotonic, and isokinetic exercise can be gleaned from the psychological literature, although a slim body of research exists. For example, Ussher, Taylor, and Faulkner (2012) compared the effects of mindful body scanning, isometric exercise (e.g., fist clenching, jaw clenching, pressing the hands together), and listening to an audiobook in terms of reducing desire to smoke and withdrawal symptoms among temporarily abstinent smokers. The investigators observed significant reductions in both desire to smoke and withdrawal symptoms in body scanning and isometric exercise conditions compared with control conditions. Koltyn, Trine, Stegner, and Tobar (2001) examined the effects of an isometric handgrip exercise on blood pressure and pain perception. Participants squeezed a hand dynamometer with the right hand as hard as possible during the first session and then squeezed between 40% and 50% of maximum strength in the second session. Both maximal and submaximal isometric exercises were associated with increased pain thresholds in women immediately after exercise. This effect was less consistent in men and was apparent only after maximal exercise. Because women also evidenced increased systolic blood pressure, changes in blood pressure may have mediated pain sensitivity, although distraction provided by exercise-related arousal may be another operative mechanism. Whatever the mechanism, the overall outcomes are consistent with previous findings of an analgesic effect of isometric exercise on pain (Kosek & Ekholm, 1995; Paalasmaa, Kemppainen, & Pertovaara, 1991).

With regard to isokinetic exercise, Bilicp et al. (2001) found differences between participants with major depressive disorder (MDD) and healthy control participants on measures of isokinetic muscle function. Individuals with MDD presented with lower isokinetic muscle performance (as measured by dynamometer) than did nondepressed participants. After a 3-month treatment period with selective serotonin reuptake inhibitors (SSRIs), isokinetic muscle performance of depressed participants increased significantly. The authors suggested that isokinetic exercise may ameliorate depressive symptoms, although this hypothesis remains untested. Finally, although scant psychological research has incorporated isotonic exercises, two dissertations involving randomized controlled trials (RCTs) reported an ameliorative effect of isotonic exercise (e.g., weight machines) on aggressive behaviors among male prisoners (Wagner, 1997) and on depression among older adults who participated in a 10-week isotonic resistance training program (Collier, 1998). Clearly, different types of exercise—apart from aerobic exercise we consider next—are understudied and warrant further scrutiny before strong inferences regarding whether, for whom, and how they are effective are warranted.

## Aerobic Exercise

A comprehensive review of aerobic exercise would require an entire volume. In keeping with other reviews (e.g., Penedo & Dahn, 2005), from this point forward, we will review a swath of studies of aerobic exercise across three domains: physical well-being, general psychological health and well-being, and specific mental disorders.

## Aerobic Exercise Does a Brain and Body Good

### Heart Disease

What does the literature say about the effects of aerobic exercise on physical health and well-being? Heart disease is one of the leading causes of death throughout the world (Ferrari et al., 2013). In fact, a sedentary lifestyle ranks among the top five risk factors for coronary disease (Franklin, Brinks, & Friedman, 2013). Studies that examine the effects of exercise on heart health are plentiful. In one highly cited study, using a sample of more than 70,000 women, Manson et al. (1999) found that both vigorous aerobic exercise and walking were associated with a 30% to 40% lower risk of cardiovascular events over an 8-year period compared with the risk of women in the lowest quartile of energy expenditure. Still, the authors noted that more active women had more favorable risk profiles, and that the study population (registered nurses) was not representative of the general population. Whelton, Chin, Xin, and He (2002) reported that regular aerobic exercise reduces blood pressure—a key risk factor for coronary disease—in both normotensive and hypertensive individuals (see also Hamer, Taylor, & Steptoe's, 2006, meta-analysis). According to Myers's (2003) review, regular aerobic exercise also protects individuals from heart disease by reducing body weight, blood pressure, and "bad" cholesterol (LDL) and increasing insulin sensitivity and "good" cholesterol (HDL). Finally, among patients with existing coronary heart disease, neither moderate- nor high-intensity aerobic exercise is associated with increased risk of cardiovascular events, such as a heart attack (Rognmo et al., 2012). So not only does regular aerobic exercise help the heart, but it may never be too late for a heart to be helped.

### Neurodegenerative Diseases

As the youngest of the baby boomers turn 50 in 2014 ("The Graying of America: Youngest Boomers Turn 50 This Year," 2014), the number of Americans over age 65 is poised to surge from 40 million today to over 70 million by 2030. It is a safe bet that age-related neurodegenerative diseases will become an increasingly vexing public health issue for years to come. Regular aerobic exercise has emerged as a potential ally in the prevention of these devastating diseases. Aarsland, Sardahaee, Anderssen, Ballard, and the Alzheimer's Society Systematic Review Group's (2010) systematic review and meta-analysis of longitudinal studies reported a significant reduced risk for vascular dementia in more physically active people compared with their more sedentary peers.

Randomized controlled longitudinal research also supports the benefits of aerobic exercise on risk for vascular dementia. For example, Aarsland et al. (2010) cite a study (Lautenschlager et al., 2008) in which elderly individuals with symptoms of cognitive decline were randomly assigned to either a 24-week program of home-based moderate-intensity exercise (e.g., three 50-minute sessions of walking per week) or an education and usual care group. Lautenschlager and colleagues (2008) reported that a year after the intervention, differences in cognitive outcome measures favored the exercisers. Rockwood and Middleton (2007) were persuaded by the available evidence to conclude that observational studies since 1995 have provided replicable and robust evidence that physical activity, namely aerobic exercise, reduces the risk of cognitive decline and dementia (e.g., vascular dementia, Alzheimer's disease). Additionally, studies suggest that regular exercise (e.g., at least 30 minutes of walking three times per week) in early adulthood (e.g., age 25) may positively impact cognitive functioning in later life, although additional longitudinal studies are necessary to firm up this claim. We now turn to the more general effects of exercise on cognition.

## From Dumbbells to Smartbells

To what extent can aerobic exercise preserve and enhance cognitive functioning in the general population? If you are quicker on your feet, are you better at thinking on your feet? Two lines of research bear on this question, namely (a) studies of exercise's immediate effects on specific cognitive measures (e.g., attention, memory) during and after a single workout and (b) comparative and longitudinal studies of regular exercisers' and more sedentary people's cognitive abilities. The latter line of research has been the main focus of popular interest, but the former warrants mention, as it is particularly crucial to prevention.

When we consider the real-time effects of aerobic exercise on cognition, different theoretical perspectives predict different outcomes. Although some theories predict enhanced cognition after or during exercise due to its rousing of the brain and body (e.g., Audiffren, 2009), other theories predict impairment as fatigue sets in (e.g., McMorris & Graydon, 2000). Lambourne and Tomporowski (2010) surveyed recent studies and analyzed the magnitude and directions of their effects. The authors analyzed dual-task (i.e., a cognitive task is performed while exercising) and single-task (i.e., a task is performed after exercising) studies separately. A meta-analysis of 109 single-task effects yielded a statistically significant and small effect size, indicating a slight boost in cognitive performance immediately after exercise. Studies using memory tasks and exercise bike workouts more frequently reported larger effect sizes; that is, the less (cognitively) demanding exercise was more often associated with gains that were more frequently evident for measures of memory.

In contrast, a meta-analysis of 126 dual-task effects overall yielded a significant and small *deleterious* effect on perceptual tasks (e.g., line matching and processing speed tasks). Nevertheless, some differences among studies are worthy of mention. For unknown reasons, those that employed tread-mills more often returned nonsignificant or even detrimental effects, whereas those using exercise bikes yielded positive effects; however, the authors observed that some studies using treadmills required participants to exert more anaerobic energy as exercise demand increased, which may have confounded results. Additionally, tasks administered during the first 20 minutes of exercise coincided with performance losses, whereas tasks administered later were associated with gains. Moreover, performance decreased in exercises that demanded more concentrated effort (e.g., actively maintaining one's balance on a treadmill).

A single aerobic workout may also affect attentional processes. Huertas, Zahonero, Sanabria, and Lupiáñez (2011) observed real-time differences in measures of reaction time and alerting responses (i.e., preparations for fast reactions measured by norepinephrine system changes) among highly experienced cyclists randomly assigned to intense aerobic exercise, moderate exercise, or resting control conditions. The authors observed enhanced reaction time and more rapid alerting response among subjects assigned to both high- and moderate-intensity stationary bicycling exercise conditions relative to controls and tentatively concluded that exercise sensitized alerting response so that subjects responded as would be expected in the presence of a salient stimulus. The authors noted that additional research with different populations is required to infer broader generalizability of the effects of exercise on attention.

Although Huertas et al. (2011) found no effect of acute (i.e., single-session, aerobic) exercise on real-time measures of executive attentional control, other researchers have reported contrasting results. For example, Pesce, Tessitore, Casella, Pirritano, and Capranica (2007) reported significant differences in attention switching speed from local to global stimulus features among expert soccer players assigned to either an acute aerobic exercise condition (i.e., stationary bicycling) or a nonexercise resting condition. The authors observed enhanced performance among subjects in the exercise condition and concluded that their results support a hypothesized relation between exercise-induced arousal and attentional resource allocation. Other studies suggest augmentative effects of acute aerobic exercise on visual attention, including (a) orienting toward peripheral stimuli and focusing on foveal stimuli (Cereatti, Casella, Manganelli, & Pesce, 2009); (b) deployment of spatial attention (Sanabria et al., 2011); and (c) visual search and detection (Aks, 1998). Recent work also suggests that moderate acute aerobic exercise, such as stationary bicycling, may bias attention away from unpleasant stimuli and toward pleasant stimuli (Tian & Smith, 2011), a finding with implications for treating anxiety and depression. However, other research reports contradictory findings; namely, Shields, Larson, Swartz, and Smith (2011) reported enhanced efficiency of visual detection of both threatening and nonthreatening visual targets after moderate and intense stationary bicycling.

In sum, a survey of the literature implies that aerobic exercise exerts mostly beneficial effects on real-time cognitive and attentional processes, although the reasons for contradictory findings remain unexplained. One may question whether the salutatory effects of exercise on cognitive abilities result from arousal alone, with or without exercise. Hopkins, Davis, Vantieghem, Whalen, and Bucci (2012) compared the effects of acute exercise (i.e., a single session of walking or running for 30 minutes immediately before testing) on visual recognition memory either preceded by a 4-week exercise regimen (i.e., walking or running for 30 minutes per day for 4 days per week) or not preceded by regular exercise. The investigators reported that immediate effects of the exercise session on the memory test were greatest for those who exercised regularly for at least 4 days per week for 4 weeks preceding the session. Additionally, the researchers correlated a particular genetic allelic configuration with greater cognitive effects. Accordingly, the effects of exercise may be particularly salient for individuals with certain genotypes, a speculation that requires additional research to evaluate.

Most regular exercisers are in it for the long haul. Inspired by promising news reports (e.g., Reynolds, 2012), for example, many individuals exercise to achieve cognitive benefits over the next 30 years, rather than the next 30 minutes. After all, if arms, abs, and glutes can be kept strong and youthful in middle and older adulthood, why not (frontal) lobes? Indeed, higher order cognitive processes pursuant to planning, attention (sustained and selective), volitional inhibition, working memory, and mental flexibility, which are frequently subsumed under the rubric *executive functioning* (Chan, Shum, Toulopoulou, & Chen, 2008), gradually deteriorate over the course of normal aging (e.g., Tomporowski, Lambourne, & Okumura, 2011).

Guiney and Machado (2013) reviewed executive functioning components "shown to improve with regular aerobic exercise in healthy populations" (p. 73). Departing from previous reviews, they (a) considered only studies that examined effects for nonclinical samples (i.e., cognitively unimpaired ordinary Joes) and (b) identified an exercise-related variable linked to each type of executive function (e.g., attention). The authors identified task switching, selective attention/inhibitory control, and working memory as the three most frequently tested components of executive functioning. Task switching requires that participants alternate and modify responses according to rules for different situations (e.g., press a button once when given letters, pull a level twice when given numbers), selective attention/inhibitory control tasks require that participants inhibit motoric responses to or disengage attention from irrelevant stimuli, and working memory tasks require real-time maintenance and update of task-relevant information.

Effective task switching exacts a cognitive toll evident in slowed reaction times between rule-switch and rule-nonswitch trials. Guiney and Machado (2013) reported that most studies have shown diminished switching costs, particularly among older regular aerobic exercisers, compared with their more sedentary peers (effects have been less pronounced for younger adults, but favorable preliminary evidence exists). The authors surveyed similar findings for selective attention and inhibitory control tasks (e.g., Stroop tasks, flanker tasks). Again, regular aerobic exercise coincided with performance gains among older participants; however, minimal gains were evident for children or young adults. For working memory tasks, the review reported that regular exercise can augment memory capacity in both children and older adults. Additionally, in a review examining the effects of exercise on measures of executive functioning in children (operationalized as processes required to select, organize, and initiate goal-directed actions), Tomporowski, Davis, Miller, and Naglieri (2008) concluded that exercise facilitates children's executive functioning in a manner similar to that observed among adults and noted that exercise may well be included among interventions that enhance children's cognitive development.

Regular aerobic exercise may also boost attention. Hawkins, Kramer, and Capaldi (1992) compared outcomes for measures of attentional flexibility and time-sharing (i.e., a measure requiring participants to respond simultaneously to two stimuli in differing modalities) between a randomly assigned group of elderly adults who completed a 10-week aquatics aerobic exercise training course and a control group of nonexercisers. Elderly exercisers outperformed sedentary controls on both measures. A meta-analysis of RCTs by Smith et al. (2010) revealed that aerobic exercise training is associated with modest boosts in attention, executive functioning, processing speed, and memory; however, the effects of exercise on working memory are less consistent. Masley, Roetzheim, and Gualtieri (2009) also reported significant increases in cognitive flexibility among adult subjects randomly assigned to a 10-week aerobic exercising training program consisting of walking or running on a treadmill 30 minutes per day for 5 days per week compared with controls asked to "continue their current activity level and dietary intake for 10 weeks" (p. 187).

Many studies have found that regular aerobic exercise can slow or deter memory deterioration in older adults. Indeed, a growing body of psychophysiological research using both human (see Erickson et al., 2011, for a review; Erickson, Miller, & Roecklein, 2012) and nonhuman (see van Praag, 2008, for a review) subjects has consistently found evidence for neurogenesis and protective effects against degeneration in the hippocampus among exercising participants. In humans, the protective effects of regular aerobic exercise extend into old age and buffer against the deleterious effects of life stressors (Head et al., 2012).

To be clear, the positive effects of aerobic exercise on cognitive functioning reported to date have been chiefly protective or preservative. Regular aerobic exercise does not transform our workaday brains into supernormal powerhouses, but it may help to keep our existing faculties in shape over the long run, especially as we enter middle and later adulthood.

In sum, much research implies that regular aerobic exercise can improve or slow cognitive decline as we age. Yet support for the beneficial consequences of exercise is not unanimous. For example, Geda et al. (2010) reported no significant predictive effect of light and vigorous regular aerobic exercise frequency for mild cognitive impairment among older adults. Snowden et al.'s (2011) review likewise reported that insufficient evidence exists to support claims of prevention or improvement with respect to cognitive decline in community-dwelling older adults. Still, Colcombe et al. (2006) observed increases in brain volume in regions associated with age-related cognitive decline among randomly assigned older adults after completing aerobic exercise training, whereas similar increases were not observed among control subjects in a stretching/toning exercise control group. Additional controlled randomized trials (e.g., flexibility exercise; Dunn, Trivedi, Kampert, Clark, & Chambliss, 2005) using consensus-based operationalizations of exercise and a common battery of measures may help to resolve some of the discrepancies across studies. We now shift our focus to the relations among exercise, mood, and mental health.

# A Psychological "Buff"er?

## Mood

People with diverse characteristics have enjoyed short- and long-term improvements in mood and well-being. Based on their meta-analysis, Arent and Landers (2000) concluded that regular aerobic exercise is associated with improved mood in elderly adults. Researchers have also reported reductions in negative affect and impaired concentration after regular exercise among menstruating women (Aganoff & Boyle, 1994). Indeed, regular exercise may protect against mood deterioration among premenstrual and menstrual women (Choi & Salmon, 1995). Nevertheless, most studies of exercise and PMS are lacking in methodological rigor (e.g., assessors not blinded to conditions; allocation concealment inadequate; no intent-to-treat analysis); thus, further research is needed to confirm these promising findings (Daley, 2009). Rojas Vega et al. (2011) observed increases in mood-regulating neurotrophic factors among pregnant and postpartum women after acute stationary bicycling exercise and suggested that exercise may be a beneficial lifestyle factor with therapeutic/public health implications. For example, exercise may facilitate healthier eating and weight loss among previously sedentary obese individuals, mediated by enhanced mood, self-efficacy, physical self-concept, and body satisfaction (Annesi & Marti, 2011). Among individuals with multiple sclerosis, exercise appears to reduce depression, anger, and fatigue, and to improve ambulation, mobility, body-care (Petajan et al., 1996), vigor, and sexual functioning (Sutherland & Andersen, 2001).

Aerobic exercise may exert protective effects against stressors and inductions of negative mood in the laboratory. Among adolescents, Gerber et al. (2012) observed significantly elevated scores of mental toughness among physically active subjects in the face of stress-related anxiety, compared with their sedentary counterparts. Mata et al. (2012) randomly assigned recovered-once depressed and control participants with no history of depression to either a 15-minute acute aerobic exercise condition (stationary bicycle riding) or a nonexercise control condition, followed by viewing a sad film clip. Both recovered-depressed and control participants assigned to the exercising condition reported less negative emotion in response to the film than did participants assigned to the nonexercising condition.

Individual differences may moderate mood-related responses to aerobic exercise. For example, researchers have found a positive relation between enjoyment of exercise and increased positive affect—participants who reported that they enjoyed exercising were more likely to experience increases in positive affect after acute exercise than those who did not (Raedeke, 2007).

In a meta-analysis of the effects of acute aerobic exercise on self-reported positive-activated affect (PAA; e.g., subjective energy and enthusiasm), Reed and Ones (2006) reported an overall significant effect of aerobic exercise on PAA, with increased PAA for durations up to 35 minutes after the cessation of exercise. The authors ascertained a dose-response relation between low- and moderate-intensity exercise (i.e., a 30-minute maximum duration) and PAA elevations and suggested that exercise-induced affective change may be best understood as a function of intensity and duration. After a meta-analysis of studies examining effects of regular exercise on positive-activated affect, Reed and Buck (2009) concluded that regular exercise is associated with moderate increases in self-reported PAA. Notably, this effect appears to be moderated by study quality (i.e., controlling for selection bias and demand characteristics), with larger effects associated with higher quality studies. Research regarding how exercise produces mood improvement (e.g., distraction from negative thoughts, changes in arousal) is lacking and would contribute to knowledge in this area of exercise science.

# Maybe You Actually Can Run Away From Your Problems?

## Depression

In contrast, a sizable body of research has focused on the effects of aerobic exercise on depressive symptoms. A number of reviews are available (Callaghan, 2004; Craft & Landers, 1998; Daley, 2008; North, McCullagh, & Tran, 1990; Penedo & Dahn, 2005; Ströhle, 2009), and the findings have been incorporated into popular "drug-free" interventions, such as the *The Depression Cure* (Ilardi, 2010), in which regular exercise is recommended along with other lifestyle changes (e.g., improved sleep hygiene, social connectedness) to contend with depression. In an early meta-analysis of the effects of exercise on depressive symptoms, North et al. (1990) reported significant effects of exercise across studies for nonclinical populations and even greater effects for clinical populations.

To determine if "prescribing exercise" for depression is useful in real treatment settings, Krogh, Nordentoft, Sterne, and Lawlor (2011) analyzed the effect sizes of available RCTs that compared exercise interventions with no exercise control conditions using clinical patients or volunteers diagnosed with depression according to a formal diagnostic system. This analysis superseded previous reviews with more liberal inclusion criteria (e.g., studies using samples based on cutoff scores on self-report measures). In a more inclusive analysis of 13 trials that employed both actual clinical patients or formally diagnosed volunteers, the researchers observed a small significant effect of exercise on depression. For the more stringent analysis, restricted to samples of only present clinic patients, four trials yielded a similar small effect size. Noting that sources of study heterogeneity (study quality, intervention duration, and so forth) were similar across both analyses, the authors examined how those sources impacted effect size differences across all 13 studies. Only length of treatment accounted for differences in effects among studies. That is, lengthier treatments (e.g., more than 10 weeks) produced smaller, indeed often null, effects, whereas shorter interventions (e.g., 4 weeks) produced larger effects, although the reason for this discrepancy is not clear. Additionally, no long-term, postintervention advantages for exercise were evident. The authors concluded that "prescribing" an exercise regimen may stimulate a fleeting antidepressant effect with no worthwhile postregimen gain.

But what if aerobic exercise is paired with an empirically supported treatment for depression? Silveira, Moraes, Oliveira, Laks, and Deslandes's (2013) more recent meta-analysis qualified Krogh and colleagues' (2011) pessimistic conclusions. Whereas the latter authors examined RCTs that treated clinical depression with exercise alone, the former included RCTs that added pharmacotherapy. Moreover, Silviera et al. considered aerobic and anaerobic (i.e., strength training) interventions in a separate meta-analysis for each in addition to an aggregate analysis. Between the two exercise types, only the pooled effect size of aerobic interventions attained statistical significance. Yet when combined with treatment, a moderate pooled effect revealed that the scores of depressed exercisers across studies were 0.62 standard deviations lower than the scores of patients assigned to a control group. Moreover, exercise enhanced the probability of treatment response by 49%. Notably, both age and symptom severity moderated the effect: Mildly depressed patients reaped greater benefits from exercise than more moderately depressed patients, and older patients (i.e., those over 60) profited more than did younger ones.

Because the researchers did not differentiate the effects of adjuvant, secondary interventions from the effects of exercise alone, their findings may not contest the central conclusion of the Krogh et al. (2011) analysis—that exercise alone cannot be recommended for major depression. Indeed, the best controlled research since the middle of the 20th century indicates that exercise by itself may be of minimal use in treating full-blown clinical depression, but it may be a useful adjunct to current empirically supported treatments. Studies that parse out the effects of exercise from other interventions are essential to arrive at firmer conclusions regarding the specific role of exercise in alleviating clinical depression.

Daley (2008) produced a "review of reviews" and noted two hypothesized mechanisms of action for therapeutic effects of aerobic exercise on depression: biochemical-physiological and psychological explanations. The endorphin hypothesis suggests that exercise triggers endogenous opiates that facilitate positive feelings and enhanced well-being. Although several studies support this hypothesis, Daley noted that it is unclear whether increases in endorphins result from exercise or from the alleviation of depression itself. The monoamine hypothesis (see Chaouloff, 1989) suggests that exercise increases the availability of neurotransmitters (e.g., serotonin) associated with reductions in depressive symptoms. Daley noted sparse preliminary support for this hypothesis in studies of animal models (e.g., Dunn, Reigle, Youngstedt, Armstrong, & Dishman, 1996), yet questions about causality pertain here as well. Daley suggested that distraction and enhanced self-efficacy are two possible psychological mechanisms of action. According to the distraction hypothesis, exercise distracts from depressive feelings and thoughts (Gleser & Mendelberg, 1990), whereas the self-efficacy hypothesis suggests that exercise promotes feelings of empowerment and accomplishment and thereby constitutes a form of behavioral activation by increasing the exerciser's repertoire of positively reinforcing activities (Brosse, Sheets, Lett, & Blumenthal, 2002). As suggested earlier, the available evidence does not permit definitive conclusions regarding mechanisms of action that mediate the positive effects of exercise.

## Anxiety

Reviews of the literature strongly implicate anxiolytic effects of aerobic exercise for healthy, nonclinical participants (Ströhle, 2009), as well as clinical subjects, with notable exceptions. For example, exercise may trigger panic attacks or increased anxiety among subjects with panic disorder (Broocks et al., 1998; however, see Broman-Fulks, Berman, Rabian, & Webster, 2004; Broman-Fulks & Storey, 2008; Esquivel, Schruers, Kuipers, & Griez, 2002; Ströhle et al., 2005). Still, among individuals with general anxiety disorder, aerobic exercise training may be as effective as cognitive behavioral therapy for symptom reduction (McEntee & Halgin, 1999). Exercise training may also benefit individuals with posttraumatic stress disorder (PTSD: Manger & Motta, 2005); these effects extend across age cohorts as researchers have reported salutary effects of aerobic exercise interventions for childhood and adolescent PTSD, as well as for childhood anxiety and depression (Diaz & Motta, 2007; Motta, McWilliams, Schwartz, & Cavera, 2012; Newman & Motta, 2007).

Studies examining effects of aerobic exercise for obsessive-compulsive disorder (OCD) have also produced encouraging results. Brown et al. (2007) conducted a study in which treatment-resistant subjects participated in a 12-week moderate intensity exercise intervention using some mix of treadmills, elliptical machines, and recumbent bicycles. Compared with baseline, measures of symptom severity were significantly diminished and outcomes persisted for 6 months. Lancer, Motta, and Lancer (2007) reported reductions in symptoms from severe to moderate among subjects with OCD. In their study, 11 participants with treatment-resistant OCD completed a 6-week exercise program of 30-minute aerobic walking sessions three times per week. After the protocol, participants' self-reported obsessions and compulsions decreased significantly and remained reduced after 1 month. Moreover, participants with severe symptoms at baseline reported only moderate symptoms after the intervention. Abrantes et al. (2009) observed similar effects with reported reductions in depressive symptoms, anxiety, and obsessive-compulsive symptoms following a 12-week moderate-intensity aerobic exercise intervention, using the protocol devised by Brown et al. (2007). Reductions in negative mood, anxiety, and self-reported obsessions and compulsions were evident immediately after exercise sessions, and symptoms decreased steadily over the life of the protocol. Although exercise holds promise for reducing OCD symptoms, RCTs are a research priority; further studies may also elucidate treatment mechanisms and whether they are specific for OCD or a nonspecific effect of anxiety reduction on OCD symptoms. Abrantes et al. suggest that exercise's mood-enhancing effects may explain its ameliorative effect on OCD symptoms in light of their well-documented inverse relation to negative mood; alternatively, the authors posit that exercise may shore up deficits in executive functioning related to the disorder.

Wipfli, Rethorst, and Landers (2008) conducted a meta-analysis of RCTs examining the effects of aerobic exercise on clinically significant anxiety symptoms (e.g., panic attacks) as measured by self-report questionnaires. The authors concluded that anxiety was reduced among exercisers compared with individuals who participated in other interventions (e.g., light therapy, relaxation/meditation, CBT, pharmacotherapy). The authors concluded that exercise alone may produce anxiolytic effects on a par with traditional anxiety treatments, including psychotherapy and pharmacotherapy. However, a more recent meta-analysis (Bartley, Hay, & Bloch, 2013) of RCT effect sizes concluded that exercise can presently not be considered an efficacious treatment for anxiety disorders, such as generalized anxiety disorder, social anxiety disorder, and panic disorder. The decidedly mixed findings reported to date imply that the verdict is still out with respect to the effects of exercise on anxiety disorders. Because symptoms of arousal, which often accompany anxiety, may increase with exercise, it is not surprising that absent psychotherapy or intervention to contextualize physiological changes that occur following exercise, some anxiety disorders may not respond favorably to an exercise regimen.

## Drug and Alcohol Use

Researchers have examined the effects of aerobic exercise on problematic drug and alcohol use. Williams et al. (2011) examined the effects of moderate-intensity exercise (i.e., three sessions per week brisk walking for 50-minutes/session) as an adjunct to standard smoking cessation treatments for women. The investigators implemented an 8-week smoking cessation program for previously sedentary healthy smokers with and without an additional 150-minute-per-week aerobic exercise component. Added exercise enhanced short-term smoking cessation compliance among randomly assigned exercising women compared with controls who watched educational health and wellness films with no smoking cessation–related content. Schneider, Spring, and Pagoto (2007) reported that exercise may reduce negative affect during smoking cessation among women with smoking-specific weight concerns. Elibero, Van Rensburg, and Drobes (2011) compared the effects of aerobic exercise (i.e., brisk walking on a treadmill) and hatha yoga on cravings to smoke among daily smokers, with a nonactive control condition. Both hatha yoga and aerobic exercise increased positive affect, reduced cravings, and decreased negative affect. The authors reported that craving in response to smoking cues was specifically reduced among subjects in the aerobic exercise condition. Taylor, Ussher, and Faulkner (2007) reviewed studies examining short-term effects of exercise on smoking cessation and recommended small doses of exercise for cravings and withdrawal. Other researchers have reported mixed results. A review (Ussher et al., 2012) of long-term effects of exercise as a primary or supplementary intervention for smoking cessation suggests methodological problems (e.g., inadequate detail describing randomization methods, differing measures of abstinence across studies, differences in exercise regimen adherence) render findings ambiguous. Nevertheless, researchers have reported overall modest success, including evidence that exercise aids in maintaining smoking cessation. Roberts, Maddison, Simpson, Bullen, and Prapavessis's (2012) more recent meta-analysis reaffirmed the usefulness of exercise for cravings and withdrawal, although optimal exercise intensity for craving reductions remains a question for future study.

Although researchers have assessed the effects of aerobic exercise on alcohol recovery, existing research is sparse. Brown et al. (2010) reported only two studies (Murphy, Pagano, & Marlatt, 1986; Sinyor, Brown, Rostant, & Seraganian, 1982) prior to their research on exercise as an intervention for excessive alcohol use. The investigators assigned sedentary adult alcoholic subjects to a 12-week individually tailored moderate-intensity aerobic exercise program. Subjects reported reductions in drinks per day and increases in percentage of days abstinent. Although these data imply that exercise may be an effective intervention, additional RCTs and placebo-controlled trials are required to arrive at more definitive conclusions.

Exercise may be a useful intervention for abuses of other substances as well. Brown et al. (2010) noted a dearth of research examining the effects of exercise on drug dependence and conducted a study in which outpatient drug-dependent adult subjects participated in a 12-week moderate-intensity aerobic exercise (i.e., treadmill jogging and stationary bicycling) program. The researchers reported significant increases in percentage of days of drug and alcohol abstinence, compared with baseline, at the end of treatment and at 3-month follow-up. Additionally, subjects who attended at least 75% of the exercise sessions had significantly better substance use outcomes than nonattendees. Finally, Buchowski et al. (2011) reported significant decreases in cannabis cravings in response to aerobic exercise. Overall, studies of the beneficial effects of aerobic exercise on problematic alcohol and drug use are promising.

## Schizophrenia

Only a few studies have examined the effects of aerobic exercise on schizophrenia. Studies often report reductions of anxiety, depression, and psychosis and increases in social interactions after exercise training among inpatients and outpatients with schizophrenia (Beebe et al., 2005). Beebe et al. (2005) implemented a 16-week aerobic exercise program among individuals with schizophrenia and examined changes in physical fitness and psychiatric symptoms afterward. Compared with no exercise, aerobic exercise increased aerobic fitness, lowered body mass indexes, and reduced psychiatric symptoms (see also Biddle, 1999). Vancampfort et al. (2011) found that compared with no intervention, patients with schizophrenia randomly assigned to either acute aerobic exercise or yoga sessions experienced reductions in state anxiety and psychological stress and improved subjective well-being. Gorczynski and Faulkner (2010) conducted a meta-analysis of RCTs of the effects of exercise on schizophrenia and schizophrenia-like illnesses. After excluding studies that did not meet inclusion criteria, the authors noted that three remaining studies reported beneficial physical and mental health changes. However, they contended that larger RCTs are required to warrant more definitive conclusions. Additionally, research suggests that exercise interventions for individuals with schizophrenia can be implemented effectively in group settings (Marzolini, Jensen, & Melville, 2009). In sum, the available evidence implies that exercise can play a role as an adjunctive intervention for schizophrenia and schizophrenia-like illnesses.

In light of so much favorable research, it is tempting to stamp aerobic exercise as a formidable tool for treating psychological problems of any kind. Nevertheless, this perspective does not consider the fact that excessive exercise is a symptom of some disorders (e.g., eating disorders, body dysmorphic disorder) and can lead to serious physical and psychological health complications. Moreover, given that a comprehensive review is beyond the scope of this chapter, we did not discuss a number of major disorders, including bipolar disorder, eating disorders, and personality disorders. Still, we can reasonably conclude that properly executed exercise of moderate intensity is a safe and often helpful adjunctive intervention for many psychological disorders among physically healthy adults.

## Concluding Remarks

Our review implies that exercise, and aerobic exercise in particular, "does a body and brain good." People across the age spectrum can incorporate aerobic exercise into their daily and weekly activities and reap benefits in physical, cognitive, and emotional well-being. Although the findings in most areas are not uniformly positive, we identified no deleterious consequences of a well-planned and executed exercise program. Across the studies we reviewed, participants who exercised regularly typically engaged in at least 30 minutes of moderate-intensity exercise per day for at least 3 days per week, and types of exercise ranged from walking, to jogging, to bicycling on a stationary bike. Importantly, exercise need not be complicated, time consuming, or particularly intense to confer benefits. According to recommendations put forth by the American College of Sports Medicine and the American Heart Association (Haskell et al., 2007), healthy adults aged 18 to 65 should partake in at least (a) 30 minutes of moderate intensity endurance exercise (e.g., walking briskly) 5 times a week, (b) vigorous intensity aerobic activity (e.g., jogging) for a minimum of 20 minutes three times a week, or (c) a combination of moderate and vigorous exercise. Readers would do well to embark on an exercise regimen that follows these guidelines. Additionally, clinicians ought to assess past and present exercise habits, and, when appropriate, educate clients about the many benefits of regular exercise. Finally, unless contraindicated by psychopathology, aerobic exercise adapted to the client's lifestyle may be prescribed alongside treatment as usual.

Research-wise, much remains to be done. We invite researchers to examine genetic factors and other individual differences (e.g., age, socioeconomic background, health status, attitudes toward exercise) in moderating or mediating the effects of exercise. Moreover, researchers would do well to investigate epigenetic changes (i.e., changes in genes activated or inactivated) resulting from regular exercise. More direct comparisons of different types of exercise of varying intensity are also a priority. We further suggest that researchers (a) randomize participants and conduct longitudinal studies; (b) include attention and placebo control groups (e.g., flexibility exercise; Dunn et al., 2005) to evaluate nonspecific factors; (c) control for arousal; (d) develop consensus operationalizations of exercise intensity and frequency; (e) monitor adherence to protocols and compare self-report with objective measures; and (f) develop standardized measures of physical and psychological variables. The research on exercise, combined with the many unanswered questions regarding how exercise exercises its salutary effects, implies that exercise science most certainly has a healthy future.

# References

Aarsland, D., Sardahaee, F. S., Anderssen, S., Ballard, C., & the Alzheimer's Society Systematic Review Group. (2010). Is physical activity a potential preventive factor for vascular dementia? A systematic review. *Aging & Mental Health, 14,* 386–395.

Abrantes, A. M., Strong, D. R., Cohn, A., Cameron, A. Y., Greenberg, B. D., Mancebo, M. C., & Brown, R. A. (2009). Acute changes in obsessions and compulsions following moderate-intensity aerobic exercise among patients with obsessive-compulsive disorder. *Journal of Anxiety Disorders, 23,* 923–927.

Aganoff, J. A., & Boyle, G. J. (1994). Aerobic exercise, mood states and menstrual cycle symptoms. *Journal of Psychosomatic Research, 38,* 183–192.

Aks, D. J. (1998). Influence of exercise on visual search: Implications for mediating cognitive mechanisms. *Perceptual and Motor Skills, 87,* 771–783.

Annesi, J. J., & Marti, C. N. (2011). Path analysis of exercise treatment-induced changes in psychological factors leading to weight loss. *Psychology & Health, 26,* 1081–1098.

Arent, S., & Landers, M. (2000). The effects of exercise on mood in older adults: A meta analytic. *Journal of Ageing and Physical Activity, 8,* 407–430.

Audiffren, M. (2009). Acute exercise and psychological functions: A cognitive-energetic approach. In T. McMorris, P. D. Tomporowski, & M. Audiffren (Eds.), *Exercise and cognitive function* (pp. 1–39). Chichester, UK: John Wiley & Sons doi: 10.1002/9780470740668.fmatter

Bartley, C. A., Hay, M., & Bloch, M. H. (2013). Meta-analysis: Aerobic exercise for the treatment of anxiety disorders. *Progress in Neuro-Psychopharmacology and Biological Sychiatry, 45,* 34–39.

Beebe, L. H., Tian, L., Morris, N., Goodwin, A., Allen, S. S., & Kuldau, J. (2005). Effects of exercise on mental and physical health parameters of persons with schizophrenia. *Issues in Mental Health Nursing, 26,* 661–676.

Biddle, G. F. S. (1999). Exercise as an adjunct treatment for schizophrenia: A review of the literature. *Journal of Mental Health, 8,* 441–457.

Bilicp, M., Koroglu, M. A., Cakirbay, H., Guler, M., Tosun, M., Aydin, T., & Tan, U. (2001). Isokinetic muscle performance in major depressive disorder: Alterations by antidepressant therapy. *International Journal of Neuroscience, 109,* 149–164.

Blumenthal, J. A., & Madden, D. J. (1988). Effects of aerobic exercise training, age, and physical fitness on memory-search performance. *Psychology and Aging, 3,* 280–285.

Brannon, L., & Feist, J. (2009). *Health psychology: An introduction to behavior and health* (7th ed.). Boston, MA: Cengage Learning.

Broman-Fulks, J. J., Berman, M. E., Rabian, B. A., & Webster, M. J. (2004). Effects of aerobic exercise on anxiety sensitivity. *Behaviour Research and Therapy, 42,* 125–136.

Broman-Fulks, J. J., & Storey, K. M. (2008). Evaluation of a brief aerobic exercise intervention for high anxiety sensitivity. *Anxiety, Stress, & Coping, 21,* 117–128.

Broocks, A., Bandelow, B., Pekrun, G., George, A., Meyer, T., Bartmann, U., . . . Rüther, E. (1998). Comparison of aerobic exercise, clomipramine, and placebo in the treatment of panic disorder. *American Journal of Psychiatry, 155,* 603–609.

Brosse, A. L., Sheets, E. S., Lett, H. S., & Blumenthal, J. A. (2002). Exercise and the treatment of clinical depression in adults. *Sports Medicine, 32,* 741–760.

Brown, R. A., Abrantes, A. M., Read, J. P., Marcus, B. H., Jakicic, J., Strong, D. R., . . . Gordon, A. A. (2010). A pilot study of aerobic exercise as an adjunctive treatment for drug dependence. *Mental Health and Physical Activity, 3*(1), 27–34.

Brown, R. A., Abrantes, A. M., Strong, D. R., Mancebo, M. C., Menard, J., Rasmussen, S. A., & Greenberg, B. D. (2007). A pilot study of moderate-intensity aerobic exercise for obsessive compulsive disorder. *Journal of Nervous and Mental Disease, 195,* 514–520.

Buchowski, M. S., Meade, N. N., Charboneau, E., Park, S., Dietrich, M. S., Cowan, R. L., & Martin, P. R. (2011). Aerobic exercise training reduces cannabis craving and use in non-treatment seeking cannabis-dependent adults. *PLOS ONE, 6*(3), e17465. doi:10.1371/journal.pone.0017465

Callaghan, P. (2004). Exercise: A neglected intervention in mental health care? *Journal of Psychiatric and Mental Health Nursing, 11,* 476–483.

Centers for Disease Control and Prevention. (2007). *Faststats.* Retrieved from http://www.cdc.gov/nchs/fastats/exercise.htm

Centers for Disease Control and Prevention. (2010). *2001–2008 State physical activity comparisons by demographic group.* Retrieved from http://www.cdc.gov/nccdphp/dnpa/physical/stats/

Cereatti, L., Casella, R., Manganelli, M., & Pesce, C. (2009). Visual attention in adolescents: Facilitating effects of sport expertise and acute physical exercise. *Psychology of Sport and Exercise, 10,* 136–145.

Chan, R. C., Shum, D., Toulopoulou, T., & Chen, E. Y. (2008). Assessment of executive functions: Review of instruments and identification of critical issues. *Archives of Clinical Neuropsychology, 23,* 201–216.

Chaouloff, F. (1989). Physical exercise and brain monoamines: A review. *Acta Physiologica Scandinavica, 137*, 1–13.

Choi, P. Y., & Salmon, P. (1995). Symptom changes across the menstrual cycle in competitive sportswomen, exercisers and sedentary women. *British Journal of Clinical Psychology, 34*, 447–460.

Colcombe, S. J., Erickson, K. I., Scalf, P. E., Kim, J. S., Prakash, R., McAuley, E., . . . Kramer, A. F. (2006). Aerobic exercise training increases brain volume in aging humans. *Journals of Gerontology Series A: Biological Sciences and Medical Sciences, 61*, 1166–1170.

Collier, C. D. (1998). Isotonic resistance training related to functional fitness, physical self-efficacy, and depression in adults ages 65–85. *Dissertation Abstracts International Section A: Humanities and Social Sciences, 59*, 2A.

Córdova, C., Silva, V. C., Moraes, C. F., Simões, H. G., & Nóbrega, O. T. (2009). Acute exercise performed close to the anaerobic threshold improves cognitive performance in elderly females. *Brazilian Journal of Medical and Biological Research, 42*, 458–464.

Craft, L. L., & Landers, D. M. (1998). The effect of exercise on clinical depression and depression resulting from mental illness: A meta-analysis. *Journal of Sport & Exercise Psychology, 20*, 339–357.

Daley, A. (2008). Exercise and depression: A review of reviews. *Journal of Clinical Psychology in Medical Settings, 15*, 140–147.

Daley, A. (2009). Exercise and premenstrual symptomatology: A comprehensive review. *Journal of Women's Health, 18*, 895–899.

Diaz, A. B., & Motta, R. (2007). The effects of an aerobic exercise program on post-traumatic stress disorder symptom severity in adolescents. *International Journal of Emergency Mental Health, 10*, 49–59.

Dunn, A. L., Reigle, T. G., Youngstedt, S. D., Armstrong, R. B., & Dishman, R. K. (1996). Brain norepinephrine and metabolites after treadmill training and wheel running in rats. *Medicine & Science in Sports & Exercise, 28*, 204–209.

Dunn, A. L., Trivedi, M. H., Kampert, J. B., Clark, C. G., & Chambliss, H. O. (2005). Exercise treatment for depression: Efficacy and dose response. *American Journal of Preventive Medicine, 28*, 1–8.

Elibero, A., Van Rensburg, K. J., & Drobes, D. J. (2011). Acute effects of aerobic exercise and hatha yoga on craving to smoke. *Nicotine & Tobacco Research, 13*, 1140–1148.

Erickson, K. I., Miller, D. L., & Roecklein, K. A. (2012). The aging hippocampus interactions between exercise, depression, and BDNF. *The Neuroscientist, 18*, 82–97.

Erickson, K. I., Voss, M. W., Prakash, R. S., Basak, C., Szabo, A., Chaddock, L., . . . Kramer, A. F. (2011). Exercise training increases size of hippocampus and improves memory. *Proceedings of the National Academy of Sciences, 108*, 3017–3022.

Esquivel, G., Schruers, K., Kuipers, H., & Griez, E. (2002). The effects of acute exercise and high lactate levels on 35% $CO_2$ challenge in healthy volunteers. *Acta Psychiatrica Scandinavica, 106*, 394–397.

Ferrari, A. J., Charlson, F. J., Norman, R. E., Patten, S. B., Freedman, G., Murray, C. J., . . . Whiteford, H. V. (2013). Burden of depressive disorders by country, sex, age, and year: Findings from the global burden of disease study 2010. *PLOS Medicine, 10*(11). Retrieved from https://owl.english.purdue.edu/owl/resource/560/10/

Franklin, B. A., Brinks, J., & Friedman, H. (2013, November 27). *Foundational factors for cardiovascular disease: Behavior change as a first-line preventive strategy.* Retrieved from http://my.americanheart.org/professional/ScienceNews/Foundational-Factors-for-Cardiovascular-Disease-Behavior-Change-as-a-First-Line_UCM_457215_Article.jsp

Geda, Y. E., Roberts, R. O., Knopman, D. S., Christianson, T. J., Pankratz, V. S., Ivnik, R. J., . . . Rocca, W. A. (2010). Physical exercise, aging, and mild cognitive impairment: A population-based study. *Archives of Neurology, 67,* 80–86. doi: 10.1001/archneur01.2009.297

Gerber, M., Kalak, N., Lemola, S., Clough, P. J., Pühse, U., Elliot, C., . . . Brand, S. (2012). Adolescents' exercise and physical activity are associated with mental toughness. *Mental Health and Physical Activity, 5,* 35–42.

Gleser, J., & Mendelberg, H. (1990). Exercise and sport in mental health: A review of the literature. *Israel Journal of Psychiatry and Related Sciences, 27,* 99–112.

Gorczynski, P., & Faulkner, G. (2010). Exercise therapy for schizophrenia. *Cochrane Database Systematic Reviews, 2010*(5). doi:10.1002/14651858.CD004412.pub2

The graying of America: Youngest boomers turn 50 this year. (2014, January 2). *Wall Street Journal.* Retrieved from http://blogs.wsj.com/economics/2014/01/02/the-graying-of-america-youngest-boomers-turn-50-this-year/

Guiney, H., & Machado, L. (2013). Benefits of regular aerobic exercise for executive functioning in healthy populations. *Psychonomic Bulletin & Review, 20,* 73–86.

Hamer, M., Taylor, A., & Steptoe, A. (2006). The effect of acute aerobic exercise on stress related blood pressure responses: A systematic review and meta-analysis. *Biological Psychiatry, 71,* 183–190.

Haskell, W. L., Lee, I., Pate, R. R., Powell, K. E., Blair, S. N., Franklin, B. A., . . . Bauman, A. (2007). Physical activity and public health: Updated recommendation for adults from the American College of Sports Medicine and the American Heart Association. *Medicine and Science in Sports and Exercise, 39,* 1423–1434.

Hawkins, H. L., Kramer, A. F., & Capaldi, D. (1992). Aging, exercise, and attention. *Psychology and Aging, 7,* 643–653.

Head, D., Bugg, J. M., Goate, A. M., Fagan, A. M., Mintun, M. A., Benzinger, T., . . . Morris, J. C. (2012). Exercise engagement as a moderator of the effects of APOE genotype on amyloid deposition. *Archives of Neurology, 69,* 636–643. doi:10.1001/archneur01.2011.845.

Hopkins, M. E., Davis, F. C., Vantieghem, M. R., Whalen, P. J., & Bucci, D. J. (2012). Differential effects of acute and regular physical exercise on cognition and affect. *Neuroscience, 215,* 59–68.

Huertas, F., Zahonero, J., Sanabria, D., & Lupiáñez, J. (2011). Functioning of the attentional networks at rest vs. during acute bouts of aerobic exercise. *Journal of Sport & Exercise Psychology, 33,* 649–655.

Ilardi, S. S. (2010). *The depression cure: The 6-step program to beat depression without drugs.* Cambridge, MA: Da Capo Lifelong Books.

Jasnoski, M. L., Cordray, D. S., Houston, B. K., & Osness, W. H. (1987). Modification of Type A behavior through aerobic exercise. *Motivation and Emotion, 11,* 1–17.

Jazaieri, H., Goldin, P. R., Werner, K., Ziv, M., & Gross, J. J. (2012). A randomized trial of MBSR versus aerobic exercise for social anxiety disorder. *Journal of Clinical Psychology, 68,* 715–731.

Koltyn, K. F., Trine, M. R., Stegner, A. J., & Tobar, D. A. (2001). Effect of isometric exercise on pain perception and blood pressure in men and women. *Medicine and Science in Sports and Exercise, 33,* 282–290.

Koniak-Griffin, D. (1994). Aerobic exercise, psychological well-being, and physical discomforts during adolescent pregnancy. *Research in Nursing & Health, 17,* 253–263.

Kosek, E., & Ekholm, J. (1995). Modulation of pressure pain thresholds during and following isometric contraction. *Pain, 61,* 481–486.

Kramer, A. F., Hahn, S., Cohen, N. J., Banich, M. T., McAuley, E., Harrison, C. R., . . . Colcombe, A. (1999). Ageing, fitness and neurocognitive function. *Nature, 400,* 418–419.

Krogh, J., Nordentoft, M., Sterne, J. A., & Lawlor, D. A. (2011). The effect of exercise in clinically depressed adults: Systematic review and meta-analysis of randomized controlled trials. *Journal of Clinical Psychiatry, 72,* 529–538.

Lambourne, K., & Tomporowski, P. (2010). The effect of exercise-induced arousal on cognitive task performance: A meta-regression analysis. *Brain Research, 1341,* 12–24.

Lancer, R., Motta, R., & Lancer, D. (2007). The effect of aerobic exercise on obsessive-compulsive disorder, anxiety, and depression: A preliminary investigation. *The Behavior Therapist, 30,* 57–62.

Lautenschlager, N. T., Cox, K. L., Flicker, L., Foster, J. K., van Bockxmeer, F. M., Xiao, J., . . . Almeida, O. P. (2008). Effect of physical activity on cognitive function in older adults at risk for Alzheimer disease. *Journal of the American Medical Association, 300,* 1027–1037.

Manger, T. A., & Motta, R. W. (2005). The impact of an exercise program on posttraumatic stress disorder, anxiety, and depression. *International Journal of Emergency Mental Health, 7,* 49–57.

Manson, J. E., Hu, F. B., Rich-Edwards, J. W., Colditz, G. A., Stampfer, M. J., Willett, W. C., . . . Hennekens, C. H. (1999). A prospective study of walking as a compared with vigorous exercise in the prevention of coronary heart disease in women. *New England Journal of Medicine, 341,* 650–658. doi:10.1056/NEJM199908263410904

Marzolini, S., Jensen, B., & Melville, P. (2009). Feasibility and effects of a group-based resistance and aerobic exercise program for individuals with severe schizophrenia: A multidisciplinary approach. *Mental Health and Physical Activity, 2,* 29–36.

Masley, S., Roetzheim, R., & Gualtieri, T. (2009). Aerobic exercise enhances cognitive flexibility. *Journal of Clinical Psychology in Medical Settings, 16,* 186–193.

Mata, J., Thompson, R. J., Jaeggi, S. M., Buschkuehl, M., Jonides, J., & Gotlib, I. H. (2012). Walk on the bright side: Physical activity and affect in major depressive disorder. *Journal of Abnormal Psychology, 121,* 297–308.

McEntee, D. J., & Halgin, R. P. (1999). Cognitive group therapy and aerobic exercise in the treatment of anxiety. *Journal of College Student Psychotherapy, 13,* 37–55.

McMorris, T., & Graydon, J. (2000). The effect of incremental exercise on cognitive performance. *International Journal of Sport Psychology, 31,* 66–81.

Motta, R. W., McWilliams, M. E., Schwartz, J. T., & Cavera, R. S. (2012). The role of exercise in reducing childhood and adolescent PTSD, anxiety, and depression. *Journal of Applied School Psychology, 28,* 224–238.

Murphy, T. J., Pagano, R. R., & Marlatt, G. A. (1986). Lifestyle modification with heavy alcohol drinkers: Effects of aerobic exercise and meditation. *Addictive Behaviors, 11,* 175–186.

Myers, J. (2003). Exercise and cardiovascular health. *Circulation, 107,* e2–e5. doi: 10.1161/01.CIR.0000048890.59383.8D

Newman, C. L., & Motta, R. W. (2007). The effects of aerobic exercise on childhood PTSD, anxiety, and depression. *International Journal of Emergency Mental Health, 9,* 133–158.

North, T. C., McCullagh, P., & Tran, Z. V. (1990). Effect of exercise on depression. *Exercise and Sport Sciences Reviews, 18,* 379–416.

Paalasmaa, P., Kemppainen, P., & Pertovaara, A. (1991). Modulation of skin sensitivity by dynamic and isometric exercises in man. *European Journal of Applied Physiology, 62,* 279–285.

Penedo, F. J., & Dahn, J. R. (2005). Exercise and well-being: A review of mental and physical benefits associated with physical activity. *Current Opinion in Psychiatry, 18,* 189–193.

Pesce, C., Tessitore, A., Casella, R., Pirritano, M., & Capranica, L. (2007). Focusing of visual attention at rest and during physical exercise in soccer players. *Journal of Sports Sciences, 25,* 1259–1270.

Petajan, J. H., Gappmaier, E., White, A. T., Spencer, M. K., Mino, L., & Hicks, R. W. (1996). Impact of aerobic training on fitness and quality of life in multiple sclerosis. *Annals of Neurology, 39,* 432–441.

Prentice, A. M. (2006). The emerging epidemic of obesity in developing countries. *International Journal of Epidemiology, 35,* 93–99.

Raedeke, T. D. (2007). The relationship between enjoyment and affective responses to exercise. *Journal of Applied Sport Psychology, 19,* 105–115

Reed, J., & Buck, S. (2009). The effect of regular aerobic exercise on positive-activated affect: A meta-analysis. *Psychology of Sport and Exercise, 10,* 581–594.

Reed, J., & Ones, D. S. (2006). The effect of acute aerobic exercise on positive activated affect: A meta-analysis. *Psychology of Sport and Exercise, 7,* 477–514.

Reynolds, G. (2012, April 18). How exercise could lead to a better brain. *New York Times*. Retrieved from http://www.nytimes.com/2012/04/22/magazine/how-exercise-could-lead-to-a-better-brain.html?pagewanted=all&_r=0

Roberts, V., Maddison, R., Simpson, C., Bullen, C., & Prapavessis, H. (2012). The acute effects of exercise on cigarette cravings, withdrawal symptoms, affect, and smoking behaviour: Systematic review update and meta-analysis. *Psychopharmacology, 222*, 1–15.

Rockwood, K., & Middleton, L. (2007). Physical activity and the maintenance of cognitive function. *Alzheimer's & Dementia, 3*, S38–S44.

Rognmo, Ø., Moholdt, T., Bakken, H., Hole, T., Mølstad, P., Erling, N., . . . Wisløff, U. (2012). Cardiovascular risk of high- versus moderate-intensity aerobic exercise in coronary heart disease patients. *Circulation, 126*, 1436–1440. doi:10.1161/CIRCULATIONAHA.112.123117

Rojas Vega, S., Kleinert, J., Sulprizio, M., Hollmann, W., Bloch, W., & Strüder, H. K. (2011). Responses of serum neurotrophic factors to exercise in pregnant and postpartum women. *Psychoneuroendocrinology, 36*, 220–227.

Rössner, S. (2002). Obesity: The disease of the twenty-first century. *International Journal of Obesity and Related Metabolic Disorders: 26*, S2–4.

Sanabria, D., Morales, E., Luque, A., Gálvez, G., Huertas, F., & Lupiañez, J. (2011). Effects of acute aerobic exercise on exogenous spatial attention. *Psychology of Sport and Exercise, 12*, 570–574.

Schneider, K. L., Spring, B., & Pagoto, S. L. (2007). Affective benefits of exercise while quitting smoking: Influence of smoking-specific weight concern. *Psychology of Addictive Behaviors, 21*, 255–260.

Shields, M. R., Larson, C. L., Swartz, A. M., & Smith, J. C. (2011). Visual threat detection during moderate- and high-intensity exercise. *Emotion, 11*, 572–581.

Silveira, H., Moraes, H., Oliveira, N., Laks, J., & Deslandes, A. (2013). Physical exercise and clinically depressed patients: A systematic review and meta-analysis. *Neuropsychobiology, 67*, 61–68.

Sinyor, D., Brown, T., Rostant, L., & Seraganian, P. (1982). The role of a physical fitness program in the treatment of alcoholism. *Journal of Studies on Alcohol and Drugs, 43*, 80–385.

Smith, P. J., Blumenthal, J. A., Hoffman, B. M., Cooper, H., Strauman, T. A., Welsh-Bohmer, K., . . . Sherwood, A. (2010). Aerobic exercise and neurocognitive performance: A meta-analytic review of randomized controlled trials. *Psychosomatic Medicine, 72*, 239–252.

Snowden, M., Steinman, L., Mochan, K., Grodstein, F., Prohaska, T. R., Thurman, D. J., . . . Anderson, L. A. (2011). Effect of exercise on cognitive performance in community-dwelling older adults: Review of intervention trials and recommendations for public health practice and research. *Journal of the American Geriatrics Society, 59*, 704–716.

Steinberg, H., Sykes, E. A., Moss, T., Lowery, S., LeBoutillier, N., & Dewey, A. (1997). Exercise enhances creativity independently of mood. *British Journal of Sports Medicine, 31*, 240–245.

Ströhle, A. (2009). Physical activity, exercise, depression and anxiety disorders. *Journal of Neural Transmission, 116,* 777–784.

Ströhle, A., Feller, C., Onken, M., Godemann, F., Heinz, A., & Dimeo, F. (2005). The acute antipanic activity of aerobic exercise. *American Journal of Psychiatry, 162,* 2376–2378.

Sutherland, G., & Andersen, M. B. (2001). Exercise and multiple sclerosis: Physiological, psychological, and quality of life issues. *Journal of Sports Medicine and Physical Fitness, 41,* 421–432.

Taylor, A. H., Ussher, M. H., & Faulkner, G. (2007). The acute effects of exercise on cigarette cravings, withdrawal symptoms, affect and smoking behaviour: A systematic review. *Addiction, 102,* 534–543.

Tian, Q., & Smith, J. C. (2011). Attentional bias to emotional stimuli is altered during moderate- but not high-intensity exercise. *Emotion, 11,* 1415–1424.

Tomporowski, P. D., Davis, C. L., Miller, P. H., & Naglieri, J. A. (2008). Exercise and children's intelligence, cognition, and academic achievement. *Educational Psychology Review, 20,* 111–131.

Tomporowski, P. D., Lambourne, K., & Okumura, M. S. (2011). Physical activity interventions and children's mental function: An introduction and overview. *Preventive Medicine, 52,* S3-S9.

Ussher, M. H., Taylor, A., & Faulkner, G. (2012). Exercise interventions for smoking cessation. *Cochrane Database of Systematic Reviews, 2012*(1), doi:10.1002/14651858.CD002295.pub4

van Praag, H. (2008). Neurogenesis and exercise: Past and future directions. *Neuromolecular Medicine, 10,* 128–140.

Vancampfort, D., Probst, M., Sweers, K., Maurissen, K., Knapen, J., & De Hert, M. (2011). Relationships between obesity, functional exercise capacity, physical activity participation and physical self-perception in people with schizophrenia. *Acta Psychiatrica Scandinavica, 123,* 423–430.

Wagner, M. C. (1997). The effects of isotonic resistance exercise on aggression variables in adult male inmates in the Texas Department of Criminal Justice. *Dissertation Abstracts International Section A: Humanities and Social Sciences, 57,* 8A.

Whelton, S. P., Chin, A., Xin, X., & He, J. (2002). Effect of aerobic exercise on blood pressure: A meta-analysis of randomized, controlled trials. *Annals of Internal Medicine, 136,* 493–503.

Williams, D. M., Dunsiger, S., Whiteley, J. A., Ussher, M. H., Ciccolo, J. T., & Jennings, E. G. (2011). Acute effects of moderate intensity aerobic exercise on affective withdrawal symptoms and cravings among women smokers. *Addictive Behaviors, 36,* 894–897.

Winter, B., Breitenstein, C., Mooren, F.C., Voelker, K., Fobker, M., Lechtermann, A., . . . Knecht, S. (2007). High impact running improves learning. *Neurobiology of Learning and Memory, 87,* 597–609.

Wipfli, B. M., Rethorst, C. D., & Landers, D. M. (2008). The anxiolytic effects of exercise: A meta-analysis of randomized trials and dose–response analysis. *Journal of Sport & Exercise Psychology, 30,* 392.

# PART IV

## Happiness and Spirituality

# 11

# What Psychological Science Knows About Achieving Happiness

*S. Katherine Nelson*
University of California, Riverside

*Jaime L. Kurtz*
James Madison University

*Sonja Lyubomirsky*
University of California, Riverside

Entrenched in both ancient and modern cultural tradition, the pursuit of happiness is a popular preoccupation around the world (Diener, 2000). Despite the centrality of this goal, the path to happiness is anything but obvious, in part because people are notoriously inaccurate at knowing what will make them lastingly happy (Wilson & Gilbert, 2005). This lapse in self-knowledge can lead to poor choices, both in the short term and in the long term. After years spent saving for a larger house, trying to achieve a promotion, or finally being able to retire and move to the beach, individuals may be frustrated and baffled to discover that lasting happiness still manages to elude them. To demystify the determinants of happiness, people seek insight and advice from a vast range of sources, which—unfortunately—vary tremendously in credibility.

For example, people often turn to the self-help literature, which has capitalized on readers' deep-seated desire for happiness. Amazon.com currently boasts more than 6,000 titles in the categories "happiness" and "self-help," and many of these achieve best-seller status. Unfortunately, the vast majority of self-help books are not based on empirical evidence, and the casual reader can easily be taken in and ultimately frustrated by their quick-and-easy paths to lasting happiness.

Fortunately, with the emergence of positive psychology (Seligman & Csikszentmihalyi, 2000), the scientific study of happiness desperately missing from self-improvement manuals has become a priority. Numerous investigations have provided empirical evidence for what does—as well as what does not—promote well-being.

## What Is Happiness?

Before describing what psychological scientists have learned about the keys to happiness, it is important to unpack exactly what we mean by the term and how it is empirically investigated. Researchers have been theorizing about the causes, correlates, and consequences of happiness for more than three decades (Diener, 1984; Diener, Suh, Lucas, & Smith, 1999; Ryan & Deci, 2001; Ryff, 1989). According to the most frequently used definition, happiness (also known as subjective well-being) comprises both an affective component (i.e., the experience of relatively frequent positive and relatively infrequent negative emotions) and a cognitive component (i.e., relatively high life satisfaction or a positive overall evaluation of one's life; Diener, 1984; Diener et al., 1999). Throughout this chapter, we use the terms *happiness* and *subjective well-being* interchangeably.

## How Do Psychological Scientists Study Happiness?

A great deal of research has contributed to the scientific understanding of the paths to achieving happiness. Three general approaches to studying happiness involve (1) need and goal satisfaction theories, (2) genetic and personality predisposition theories, and (3) process or activity theories (see Diener, Oishi, & Lucas, 2009, for a review). Need satisfaction and goal theories posit that pursuing appropriate goals and satisfying fundamental human needs will result in happiness. For example, self-determination theory holds that human beings have basic needs for autonomy, competence, and relatedness (Deci & Ryan, 2000), and the fulfillment of these needs is associated with greater well-being (Sheldon et al., 2010). A second approach involves studying how people's genes and personality traits relate to their happiness levels. For example, studies have found that well-being has a strong genetic component (Lykken & Tellegen, 1996), is closely linked to the personality traits of extraversion and neuroticism (Diener & Lucas, 1999), and is relatively stable over time (Diener, Sandvik, Seidlitz, & Diener, 1993). Finally, process and activity theories, which motivate the research at the heart of this chapter, emphasize the potential to improve well-being by engaging in effortful activities (e.g., Lyubomirsky & Layous, 2013; Lyubomirsky, Sheldon, & Schkade, 2005; Seligman, Steen, Park, & Peterson, 2005).

Although much work on well-being is correlational (e.g., comparing the average happiness of different types of individuals), we will primarily focus on the results of experimental research—specifically, positive activity interventions. These studies are primarily longitudinal in nature, examining the effectiveness of an intervention over the course of several weeks or months. Participants are typically randomly assigned to complete either an activity believed to promote happiness or a control (neutral) activity. Then, the participants' well-being is tracked regularly and systematically over time. Such studies, a specific type of randomized controlled trial, are considered the gold standard in experimental approach, as they represent the only design that allows researchers to determine causality.

As discussed above, participants in randomized controlled trials are assigned to either a treatment group (e.g., to express gratitude each week) or to a control group (e.g., to list what they did each week). Because this design increases the likelihood that any potentially relevant individual differences at the beginning of the experiment (e.g., the possibility that people in one group may be more motivated or less happy to begin with) will be equivalent across the treatment and control groups, it increases the likelihood that any differences between groups by the end of the experiment can be attributed to the manipulation—in our case, the delivery of a positive activity intervention (e.g., the expression of gratitude). Randomized controlled trials are critical to understanding how people can reach greater levels of happiness. Just as the effectiveness of medical treatments must be established prior to their dissemination, potential positive activities require experimental empirical support before psychologists can confidently recommend to happiness seekers which strategies reliably boost happiness.

# Review of Research on Well-Being

## Is It Possible to Become Happier?

Some research suggests that people cannot become sustainably happier because happiness levels are, in part, due to genetic factors (Lykken & Tellegen, 1996; Nes, Roysamb, Tambs, Harris, & Reichborn-Kjennerud, 2006), personality influences (Diener & Lucas, 1999; McCrae & Costa, 1990), and human beings' tendency to adapt to any positive life changes (Frederick & Loewenstein, 1999; Lyubomirsky, 2011). Despite these sources of pessimism, other work provides evidence that happiness can indeed be enhanced and sustained. For example, research indicates that happiness is not always constant across a person's lifetime (Fujita & Diener, 2005), and personality traits correlated with happiness, such as neuroticism, can change in adulthood (R. Helson, Jones, & Kwan, 2002; Roberts, Walton, & Viechtbauer, 2006). In addition, studies suggest that well-being can be improved via lifestyle changes, such as implementing a new exercise routine or improving one's nutrition (Walsh, 2011), and by engaging in positive activities, such as performing acts of kindness, becoming more grateful, or practicing optimism (see Sin & Lyubomirsky, 2009, for a meta-analytic review, or "study of studies").

To reconcile and integrate the sometimes conflicting findings regarding the determinants of happiness, Lyubomirsky, Sheldon, et al. (2005) developed the sustainable happiness model. They argue that, although more than half of individual differences in happiness are due to people's genetics, personalities, and life circumstances—all factors that are relatively immutable—intentional activities likely account for a large portion of individual differences in happiness. That is, how people think (e.g., whether they think optimistically or gratefully) and what they do (e.g., whether they practice forgiveness or do kind acts for others) in their daily lives can play a large role in how happy they are. In sum, the sustainable happiness model suggests that people can exercise a substantial amount of control over their well-being (Lyubomirsky, 2008).

# Empirically Supported Ways to Become Happier

Early research attempting to understand how people can improve their happiness levels relied on comparing happy people to their less happy peers. Such cross-sectional, or correlational, studies found that happy people are relatively more likely to express gratitude for the good things in their lives (McCullough, Emmons, & Tsang, 2002), to act more generously toward others (Krueger, Hicks, & McGue, 2001; Lucas, 2001), and to think more optimistically about their futures (Lucas, Diener, & Suh, 1996; Lyubomirsky, Tkach, & DiMatteo, 2006). In general, happy people were found to construe information in more positive ways than their less happy peers (see Lyubomirsky, 2001, for a review). In sum, it appears that happy and unhappy people think about and approach their environments differently.

These studies provide some insight into the cognitions (e.g., thinking about the world optimistically) and behaviors (e.g., performing kind acts) that might improve happiness. However, because they are correlational, the direction and source of causality cannot be determined. For example, if happy people report being more optimistic, does this mean that optimism causes happiness, that happiness causes optimism, or a third variable (e.g., a nurturing parent) causes both?

To address the problems inherent in correlational designs, scientists have increasingly relied on experimental research—the randomized controlled studies described above—to pinpoint the determinants of happiness. For example, after first identifying some of the differences in cognition and action between happy and unhappy people, researchers then began to randomly assign participants to engage in these patterns of thought and behavior to establish their causal role in improving happiness. A number of such activities have now been identified as effective ways for people to increase their happiness. These include counting one's blessings (Chancellor, Layous, & Lyubomirsky, 2013; Emmons & McCullough, 2003; Froh, Sefick, & Emmons, 2008; Lyubomirsky, Sheldon, et al., 2005; Seligman et al., 2005), writing letters of gratitude (Boehm, Lyubomirsky, & Sheldon, 2011a; Layous, Lee, Choi, & Lyubomirsky, 2013; Lyubomirsky, Dickerhoof, Boehm, & Sheldon, 2011; Seligman et al., 2005), practicing optimistic thinking (Boehm et al., 2011a; King, 2001; Layous, Nelson, & Lyubomirsky, 2013; Lyubomirsky et al., 2011; Sheldon & Lyubomirsky, 2006), doing acts of kindness (Dunn, Aknin, & Norton, 2008; Layous, Nelson, Oberle, Schonert-Reichl, & Lyubomirsky, 2012; Nelson et al., 2012; Sheldon, Boehm, & Lyubomirsky, 2012, Study 2), affirming one's most important values (Nelson, Fuller, Choi, & Lyubomirsky, 2012), using one's signature strengths in new ways (Seligman et al., 2005), practicing self-compassion (Neff, Kirkpatrick, & Rude, 2007), and meditating on loving feelings toward oneself and others (Fredrickson, Cohn, Coffey, Pek, & Finkel, 2008).

# How and Why Do Positive Activities Improve Happiness?

An important goal of advancing psychological science regarding the pursuit of happiness is not only to understand *what* makes people happier but also to understand the mediating factors that lead to greater happiness—in other words, *how* and *why* positive activities (the intentional actions that people take to become happier) make people happier. This approach is akin to medical researchers attempting to discover the active ingredients in effective medications and treatments. For example, at one time, scurvy (a disease caused by Vitamin C deficiency) was prevalent among sailors who were unable to carry perishable fruits and vegetables on long voyages. Sailors soon learned that eating citrus fruits cured the disease, yet many years passed before they grasped that the Vitamin C that is abundant in such fruits explained the cure. Similarly, happiness researchers are currently exploring the possible mechanisms or active ingredients that explain the effectiveness of positive activities to enhance happiness.

The positive activity model (Lyubomirsky & Layous, 2013) was developed to better understand the mediating variables that explain how and why positive activities work to improve happiness. The model proposes that positive activities give rise to greater positive emotions, positive thoughts, positive behaviors, and satisfaction of basic needs, which, in turn, foster happiness. In other words, just as improved levels of Vitamin C explained how and why eating citrus fruit led to the reduction of scurvy, the model posits that more positive emotions, positive thoughts, positive behaviors, and need satisfaction explain how and why performing positive activities leads to greater happiness.

If a presumed positive activity—whether it involves practicing optimism, meditation, gratitude, or kindness—fails to boost positive emotions, positive thoughts, positive behaviors, and satisfaction of basic needs, the individual's attempt at becoming happier will be futile. For example, a high school graduate who diligently writes thank-you notes to friends and family who supported her and bestowed gifts because her parents have instructed her to do so would not become happier if she did not actually feel more grateful. Thus, it is possible to perform a positive activity (e.g., writing gratitude letters) but not experience greater positive emotions and so forth, and, as a result, fail to achieve more happiness. Along the same line, when people engage in activities that fit better with their personalities and interests, they show larger well-being gains (Dickerhoof, 2007).

Several studies have shown preliminary support for the positive activity model. Providing evidence for the mediating role of positive emotions, one study found that participants who practice gratitude or optimism become happier over time, and that this effect is mediated by their ability to derive positive emotions from their daily experiences and to find those experiences satisfying (Lyubomirsky & Dickerhoof, 2010). In another study, participants who received social support for performing acts of kindness became happier over a 9-week period, and this effect was mediated by their enjoyment of the kindness activity (Della Porta, 2013).

Studies also suggest that positive activities improve well-being because they foster the satisfaction of three basic human needs (Deci & Ryan, 2000): autonomy (feeling in control of one's environment), relatedness (feeling close and connected to others), and competence (feeling effective and skilled). For example, in one experiment, expressing gratitude and optimism increased the need for satisfying feelings of autonomy and relatedness (but not competence), which, in turn, led to increased well-being (Boehm, Lyubomirsky, & Sheldon, 2011b). Similarly, another study found that students who were prompted to set and pursue goals to enhance their autonomy or relatedness increased in well-being over a 6-month period, compared to students who were prompted to change something about their life circumstances (Sheldon et al., 2010).

In sum, several studies have provided preliminary empirical support for the mediating variables of the positive activity model. In particular, these studies suggest that one reason people become happier when they partake of happiness-enhancing strategies is that those strategies increase their levels of positive emotions as well as their need satisfying feelings of autonomy and relatedness. More work is needed to investigate other mediators proposed by the model—specifically, positive thoughts (e.g., "I'm loved") and positive behaviors (e.g., healthy eating, higher work productivity). Furthermore, researchers do not yet fully understand the causal role of the mediating factors that lead to improved well-being. Just as randomized controlled trials are essential to understand the causal effect of a positive activity, they are also needed to understand the causal role of mediating variables (Rosenthal & Rosnow, 2008). To establish that the mediating variables (e.g., positive emotions, feelings of relatedness) bring about greater happiness, future investigators should compare the happiness levels of participants who have been prompted to experience higher levels of such variables with those who have been instructed to engage in a neutral activity.

# How Can Positive Activities Be More Effective?

Scientists have demonstrated how and why positive activities improve well-being and identified specific ways that people can perform positive activities to enhance their effectiveness. Specifically, this research suggests that the most efficacious positive activity will be performed by an individual who is motivated to fully engage in the activity (Lyubomirsky et al., 2011) and performs it with variety (Sheldon et al., 2012; Lyubomirsky, Sheldon, et al., 2005) and appropriate timing (Lyubomirsky, Sheldon, et al., 2005).

## Motivation and Effort

Researchers have shown that people who are motivated to become happier and summon effort toward achieving that goal will reap relatively more benefits from positive activities. In one investigation, students elected to participate in either a study described as a "happiness activity" (and were presumably motivated to become happier) or in a study described as "cognitive exercises" (and were presumably relatively unmotivated to become happier; Lyubomirsky et al., 2011). Students who were motivated to pursue happiness showed greater gains in well-being after engaging in positive activities (in this case, expressing gratitude or optimism) than after engaging in control activities. In addition, as students mustered more effort in participating in the optimism and gratitude activities (judged by independent raters), they showed greater increases in well-being. Notably, however, motivation in this study was inferred from individuals' choices to participate in one of two groups (rather than being determined by random assignment), which limits the causal conclusions that can be made.

## Variety

Practicing a positive activity with variety leads to greater happiness gains than practicing the activity in the exact same way each time. Instilling variety into a positive activity (e.g., doing acts of kindness) allows that activity to remain fresh, interesting, and rewarding (Berlyne, 1970; Pronin & Jacobs, 2008; Rolls, Rolls, Rowe, & Sweeney, 1981) and decreases the chances that it becomes dull and boring, such that the individual adapts to it (Frederick & Loewenstein, 1999; see also H. Helson, 1964; Parducci, 1995). Two recent investigations have demonstrated the role of variety in enhancing well-being (Sheldon et al., 2012). In the first study, people who reported making a life change (e.g., joining a sorority) that enhanced the variety in their day-to-day lives (e.g., preparing for new events, interacting with new people) showed relatively bigger boosts in positive emotions. In a second study, participants who were instructed to vary their kind acts over the course of a 10-week acts-of-kindness intervention reported increases in well-being, whereas participants who were prompted to perform the same acts each week actually became less happy (Sheldon et al., 2012). These findings suggest that individuals can enhance their happiness by varying strategies and positive activities—in sequence or concurrently—that promote happiness. Indeed, research with large and diverse samples shows that happiness seekers typically practice up to eight strategies (e.g., doing kind acts, expressing gratitude) during a given period of time (e.g., within a week or month) to improve their happiness (Parks, Della Porta, Pierce, Zilca, & Lyubomirsky, 2012).

## Timing

Multiple studies have demonstrated the importance of practicing positive activities with appropriate timing. One experiment manipulated timing by instructing participants to count their blessings either three times per week or once per week (Lyubomirsky, Sheldon, et al., 2005). Interestingly, participants who counted their blessings once a week showed significantly larger increases in happiness than those who performed a neutral activity, but this difference was not observed among participants who counted their blessings three times a week. Participants who counted their blessings weekly may have found the practice more fresh, meaningful, and rewarding, whereas those who counted their blessings three times a week may have found the activity boring or had difficulty generating things for which to be grateful.

In another investigation, students were asked to perform five acts of kindness all in one day (e.g., all on Thursday) or throughout the week (Lyubomirsky, Sheldon, et al., 2005). Those who performed all five acts of kindness in one day showed happiness gains over the course of the study, but those who spread their kind acts across the week did not show such gains. Carrying out multiple acts of kindness during a single day may have produced relatively larger and more salient bursts of positive emotions than dispersing such acts. Although learning theory posits that distributing practices is most effective (Cepeda, Pashler, Vul, Wixted, & Rohrer, 2006), emotion researchers have found that experiencing more positive emotions than negative emotions is optimal for human flourishing (Fredrickson, 2013; Fredrickson & Losada, 2005), and performing multiple kind acts in a given day likely increases the ratio of positive to negative emotions. Furthermore, such bursts may have precipitated upward spirals—for example, feeling appreciated or proud on Thursday may have enhanced a person's creativity or a close relationship on the same day, which may have resulted in even more positive emotions on Friday, and so on (cf. Fredrickson & Joiner, 2002). Because this finding has not yet been replicated, however, future studies are needed to illuminate the mechanisms involved.

## Person-Activity Fit

Some people may benefit more or less from practicing various positive activities than others. Accordingly, the extent to which an activity matches a person's personality, resources, goals, values, and preferences is an important factor that impacts the success of any activity. For example, extraverts may benefit relatively more from a social activity (e.g., doing kind acts), whereas introverts may benefit relatively more from a reflective activity (e.g., visualizing their best possible selves). We term this concept *person-activity fit* (Lyubomirsky, 2008; Lyubomirsky, Sheldon, et al., 2005), with greater fit predicting greater benefit from the activity (Sin, Della Porta, & Lyubomirsky, 2011).

In one test of person-activity fit, participants were assigned to engage in a positive activity based on their previously reported activity preferences or based on random selection. Participants who were matched to an activity based on their preferences (and presumably experienced greater fit with the activity) reported greater boosts in well-being than those who were randomly assigned to an activity (Schueller, 2011). Similarly, another study found that performing a happiness-increasing activity that fit students' personalities and interests (i.e., they enjoyed it and it felt natural to them) led to greater gains in well-being relative to practicing a poor-fitting happiness activity or a control activity (Dickerhoof, 2007). These findings support the hypothesis that person-activity fit moderates—or influences—activity effectiveness.

## Summary

In sum, multiple studies have evaluated the most effective ways to perform positive activities so that people can profit the most from such activities, garnering the most impressive and most lasting benefits. To date, scientists have identified important empirically supported variables related to enhancing happiness that include practicing the activity with motivation and effort, with the appropriate timing and variety, and choosing an activity that fits one's personality and goals. For more detailed discussions of these and other factors, see Layous and Lyubomirsky (2014) and Nelson and Lyubomirsky (2014).

## Evaluating Popular Claims About Becoming Happier

Because happiness is a popular topic and near-universal goal, and because the secret to a happy life may *seem* obvious or easy, many popular claims exist about ways that people can become happier. Three such claims, which we evaluate below, include the idea that money can buy happiness, that following self-help recommendations will improve happiness, and that more happiness is always better.

## Hedonic Adaptation and Its Implications for "Buying" Happiness

When considering what it might take to make them happier, most people put "more money" at the top of their lists. Although money and happiness are indeed related, the correlation is not particularly strong (for a review, see Diener & Biswas-Diener, 2002). Moreover, because almost all investigations of the link between money and happiness are correlational, one cannot assume that money (versus some other related factor) causes greater happiness. In fact, some research indicates the opposite—happier people are more likely to earn more money (see Lyubomirsky, King, & Diener, 2005, for a meta-analytic review).

One reason for the relatively low correlation between money and happiness is that over time people begin to take their income level and standard of living for granted (Lyubomirsky, 2011). Research suggests that life's joys and sorrows abate with time—a phenomenon known as hedonic adaptation. Specifically, hedonic adaptation is the process by which the emotional effects of a stimulus, like the size of one's bank account, attenuate over time (Frederick & Loewenstein, 1999; Wilson & Gilbert, 2008). Many studies have demonstrated that people inevitably adapt to positive and negative events, such as marriage, birth of a child, promotion, divorce, widowhood, and winning the lottery (Boswell, Boudreau, & Tichy, 2005; Brickman, Coates, & Janoff-Bulman, 1978; Lucas, 2007). Indeed, hedonic adaptation poses a specific challenge to achieving lasting happiness because people may even adapt to their attempts to becoming happier (see Jacobs Bao & Lyubomirsky, in press, for a review).

The notion of hedonic adaptation can be invoked to explain the association between money and happiness. Research suggests that even if people experience a boost in happiness after a promotion and raise, they will quickly adapt to their new income, as they begin to compare themselves to better-heeled colleagues and will begin to desire an even larger salary. The best way to derive happiness from money, then, may be to spend it on things that are resistant to adaptation. For example, spending discretionary income on other people has been shown to provide lasting mood increases, presumably because this sort of spending strengthens interpersonal relationships and sets into motion upward spirals of gratitude (Algoe, Haidt, & Gable, 2008; Dunn et al., 2008). Also, research suggests that spending money on life experiences rather than material possessions provides more long-lasting happiness (Van Boven & Gilovich, 2003). Even the most state-of-the-art home entertainment system will quickly become a dusty background fixture in one's living room. However, memories of seeing one's favorite band or reminiscences of a travel adventure are relatively more enduring. Moreover, whereas the home entertainment system can only depreciate with time, positive memories are prone to a rosy view in which they actually get better over time (Mitchell, Thompson, Peterson, & Cronk, 1997). In short, although receiving a hike in one's paycheck does not guarantee a corresponding hike in happiness, money can promote happiness if that money is spent wisely (see Dunn, Gilbert, & Wilson, 2011, for a review).

## The Self-Help Literature

The popularity and availability of self-help books render them a common approach that people use to improve their happiness (Bergsma, 2008). As mentioned previously, however, many self-help books are not backed by scientific evidence and do not undergo the type of peer review required by academic journals. Accordingly, an incredibly wide variety of books are available that claim to have uncovered the key to a happy life. For example, a popular self-help book, *The Secret* (Byrne, 2006), contends that the world operates by a law of attraction and that, by this law, people's thoughts attract specific outcomes—including health, wealth, and happiness. Accordingly, people can attract happiness by simply wishing it. To the contrary, research suggests that people should actively engage in behaviors (e.g., performing kind acts, writing gratitude letters to close others) to change their lives for the better and thereby become happier (Lyubomirsky, 2008). This is just one example of many of why consumers of self-help should be particularly cautious when evaluating self-help books and choosing empirically validated recommendations.

## Potential Costs of Actively Pursuing Happiness

One concern with the self-help literature is that it can send the message that happiness is always good and that people should attempt to max out on happiness. This notion has recently been called into question, with the suggestion that the pursuit and attainment of happiness may have caveats or downsides. For example, recent work indicates that people who value happiness too much experience less happiness in response to a positive experience (Mauss, Tamir, Anderson, & Savino, 2011) and are more likely to suffer from depression (Ford, Shallcross, Mauss, Floerke, & Gruber, 2012). Other research has indicated that too much happiness may be detrimental in certain problem-solving situations (e.g., when calculating one's taxes) and social contexts (e.g., when comforting a grieving friend; see Gruber, Mauss, & Tamir, 2011, for a review).

Although, at first glance, these findings appear to challenge some of the research cited in this chapter, we believe that the two perspectives are not incongruent. First, we do not suggest that people should pursue happiness via positive activities without end, or that they should attempt to eliminate negative emotions altogether. Indeed, recent studies reveal that the optimal level of happiness is an "8 out of 10" (rather than a "10 out of 10"; Oishi, Diener, & Lucas, 2007), and that experiencing frequent mild positive emotions along with occasional negative emotions is the most adaptive combination (Diener & Oishi, 2011).

Second, our work suggests that if people focus on being more grateful, optimistic, and kind (rather than focusing on the end state and continually asking themselves if they're "happy yet"), then they can become lastingly happier. This is a notably different approach from being preoccupied with happiness as an end in itself, which may be problematic (Schooler & Mauss, 2010). Certainly, constantly monitoring and trying to control one's happiness levels while engaging in a rewarding activity or helping others is likely to be counterproductive.

## Mental Health: The Positive Psychological Perspective

Positive psychological science is a relatively new development within psychology. In the 20th century, researchers focused almost exclusively on understanding and alleviating mental illness, rather than focusing on what makes life worth living (Seligman & Csikszentmihalyi, 2000). Along with the birth of positive psychology came a renewed focus (at least in the psychological literature) on what it means to be mentally healthy.

Because past work focused primarily on alleviating mental health conditions, psychological wellness came to be defined by an absence of disease. Positive psychological research, however, has taken the concept of wellness one step further, capitalizing on the observation that people do not just want to be "not depressed" but to be happy. Accordingly, positive activities aim to help people achieve happiness, rather than simply alleviating such conditions as depression, anxiety, and addiction.

One common lay belief is that the pursuit of happiness is a luxury—a pastime reserved for those who have attained a certain level of material comfort and physical well-being. Both Maslow's (1943) influential hierarchy of needs and an updated hierarchy informed by contemporary evolutionary perspectives (Kenrick, Griskevicius, Neuberg, & Schaller, 2010) formalize this notion, positing that the pursuit of higher psychological needs (esteem, love) will be more successful only when lower level needs, such as self-protection and satiety, are met. A logical extension is that happiness-increasing activities may not be effective for those who are depressed or physically unwell. However, research suggests otherwise. Indeed, happiness interventions have proven effective (and sometimes even relatively more effective) for those with chronic illness (Emmons & McCullough, 2003) and with mild-to-moderate depression (Seligman et al., 2005; Seligman, Rashid, & Parks, 2006). In fact, evidence even shows that optimism and positive affect can aid in healing and recovery from physical ailments (see Cohen & Pressman, 2006; Kiecolt-Glaser, McGuire, Robles, & Glaser, 2002, for reviews).

## Case Study

To illustrate how happiness-increasing practices should (and should not) be implemented in everyday life, consider Michelle, a hypothetical 38-year-old educated single woman who works as an office manager. Michelle has a comfortable life. She is not wealthy but has no debt and is able to afford to go out to occasional dinners with friends, pay for a gym membership, and take annual vacations. Her social life is reasonably full and she is healthy and fit.

Despite the objective goodness of her life, Michelle feels she is not as happy as she could be. As she reflects, she realizes that she is "in a rut" and has begun to take the positive things around her for granted. She confides in her friends and receives a wealth of well-meaning advice based on their personal experiences ("You should get a pet!" "Get rid of your TV!" "Go back to school!"). Overwhelmed, she goes to her local bookstore and browses the self-help aisle, searching for a more universal answer to the secret of happiness. She picks up one title, which promises surefire and easy techniques to increase happiness. The book is straightforward, and the author seems reputable, so she purchases it and reads it quickly and excitedly. She begins to put the recommended strategies into practice the very next day, feeling inspired and eager for transformation. To her delight, Michelle obtains an immediate boost to her general mood, yet, over a few weeks, the "thrill is gone." She realizes that she doesn't feel much different from before she started, her enthusiasm wanes, and she becomes increasingly frustrated ("I read the book; I'm following the advice. Why am I not happier?"). Eventually, she gives up completely.

In discussing her experience with friends, Michelle likens it to a time she tried a fad diet. She began it with gusto, saw an immediate small benefit, but the diet became onerous and she stopped seeing results after a few weeks. So she gave up, gained the weight back, and felt like a failure. In the same way that her weight seemed stuck at a particular number, she concludes that maybe her happiness is similarly static. "Maybe I'm just not meant to be any happier," she remarks. "Happiness is something you either have or you don't."

Our research could offer Michelle some guidance on how to increase her happiness using potentially much more successful strategies. First, rather than seeking a one-size-fits-all approach to increasing happiness, she should take inventory of her personality and interests. Is she an introvert? If so, she might prefer to engage in a relatively more reflective happiness-increasing activity, such as keeping a gratitude journal. Is she active and outdoorsy? If so, she may enjoy volunteering to help maintain a local nature trail.

After she has identified an activity or two that may fit her well, she needs to consider the important question of exactly how she will enact the activities. Of course, in the same way that working out at the gym only once or twice will not lead to lasting health benefits, writing in a gratitude journal or volunteering is only likely to be beneficial if it is made habitual. However, due to hedonic adaptation, the danger of making something a habit is that it can become less fresh and rewarding over time. Therefore, Michelle should be discouraged from doing the same activity every day, in the exact same way. Instead, if she opts for a gratitude journal, she might decide to write in it only once or twice per week. She might also vary the topic she focuses on. One day she can write about her family, the next about her health, the next about her neighborhood, and so forth. If she chooses to volunteer on a nature trail, she may choose to do it only on the weekends, sometimes alone, sometimes in a group of like-minded peers. She may ask to work on different parts of the trail or to take on different tasks, to keep the experience novel and interesting.

Finally, Michelle seems to be very consciously and systematically monitoring her happiness levels, in the same way that a careful dieter monitors her weight. Such calculated monitoring is known to be counterproductive. Although this may be easier said than done, if Michelle could reframe her positive activities not as happiness-ensurers but as practices that may be rewarding in and of themselves, she may be more likely to experience happiness as a by-product.

Note that the two activities we suggested for Michelle are quite simple cognitive and behavioral changes. We are not suggesting that Michelle change jobs, move to the seashore, or find Mr. Right in order to achieve happiness. Instead, simply reframing the way that Michelle thinks about and engages in her everyday life is likely to ultimately be beneficial.

## Concluding Remarks

In a relatively short time, psychological science has made great strides in understanding how people can achieve happiness. Using some of the most effective methodologies available, researchers have found that happiness can be attained via simple, cost-effective, nonstigmatizing, self-directed activities, such as writing gratitude letters or keeping an optimism diary. Although research on happiness has come a long way in the last 2 decades, much more work remains. Future studies should continue to investigate how and why particular positive activities work to increase happiness and should continue to implement randomized controlled trials to understand the causal role of potential mechanisms or factors.

Unfortunately, limited self-knowledge and unwise decision making (e.g., Wilson & Gilbert, 2005), combined with the well-meaning but often misguided claims from the self-help industry, can make the goal of lasting happiness seem frustratingly unattainable. Even for those positive strategies that seem intuitive, such as expressing gratitude, when and how to best enact such strategies is far from obvious. Our research has generated compelling evidence that when implemented correctly, happiness-increasing activities are quite effective at promoting positive and lasting changes. Science shows that happiness is indeed within each person's reach.

## References

Algoe, S. B., Haidt, J., & Gable, S. L. (2008). Beyond reciprocity: Gratitude and relationships in everyday life. *Emotion, 8*, 425–429.

Bergsma, A. (2008). Do self-help books help? *Journal of Happiness Studies, 9*, 341–360.

Berlyne, D. E. (1970). Novelty, complexity, and hedonic value. *Perception & Psychophysics, 8*, 279–286.

Boehm, J. K., Lyubomirsky, S., & Sheldon, K. M. (2011a). A longitudinal experimental study comparing the effectiveness of happiness-enhancing strategies in Anglo Americans and Asian Americans. *Cognition & Emotion, 25*, 1263–1272.

Boehm, J. K., Lyubomirsky, S., & Sheldon, K. M. (2011b). [The role of need satisfying emotions in a positive activity intervention]. Unpublished raw data.

Boswell, W. R., Boudreau, J. W., & Tichy, J. (2005). The relationship between employee job change and job satisfaction: The honeymoon-hangover effect. *Journal of Applied Psychology, 90*, 882–892.

Brickman, P., Coates, D., & Janoff-Bulman, R. (1978). Lottery winners and accident victims: Is happiness relative? *Journal of Personality and Social Psychology, 36,* 917–927.

Byrne, R. (2006). *The secret.* New York, NY: Atria Books.

Cepeda, N. J., Pashler, H., Vul, E., Wixted, J. T., & Rohrer, D. (2006). Distributed practice in verbal recall tasks: A review and quantitative synthesis. *Psychological Bulletin, 132,* 354–380.

Chancellor, J., Layous, K., & Lyubomirsky, S. (2013). *Recalling positive events at work makes employees feel happier, move more, and talk less: A 6-week randomized controlled intervention at a Japanese workplace.* Manuscript under review.

Cohen, S., & Pressman, S. D. (2006). Positive affect and health. *Current Directions in Psychological Science, 15,* 122–125

Deci, E. L., & Ryan, R. M. (2000). The "what" and "why" of goal pursuits: Human needs and the self-determination of behavior. *Psychological Inquiry, 11,* 227–268.

Della Porta, M. D. (2013). Enhancing the effects of happiness-boosting activities: The role of autonomy support in an experimental longitudinal intervention. *Dissertation Abstracts International: Section B. Sciences and Engineering, 73.*

Dickerhoof, R. (2007). Expressing optimism and gratitude: A longitudinal investigation of cognitive strategies to increase well-being. *Dissertation Abstracts International: Section B. Sciences and Engineering, 68,* 4174.

Diener, E. (1984). Subjective well-being. *Psychological Bulletin, 95,* 542–575.

Diener, E. (2000). Subjective well-being: The science of happiness and a proposal for a national index. *American Psychologist, 55,* 34–43.

Diener, E., & Biswas-Diener, R. (2002). Will money increase subjective well-being? A literature review and guide to needed research. *Social Indicators Research, 57,* 119–169.

Diener, E., & Lucas, R. E. (1999). Personality and subjective well-being. In D. Kahneman, E., Diener, & N. Schwarz (Eds.), *Well-being: The foundations of hedonic psychology* (pp. 213–229). New York, NY: Russell Sage.

Diener, E., & Oishi, S. (2011). *An evolutionary paradox? If happy people have better health, longevity, fecundity, and healthier children, why aren't we all happy?* Unpublished manuscript, Department of Psychology, University of Illinois, Champaign, IL.

Diener, E., Oishi, S., & Lucas, R. E. (2009). Subjective well-being: The science of happiness and life satisfaction. In C. R. Snyder & S. J. Lopez (Eds.), *Handbook of positive psychology* (2nd ed., pp. 62–73). New York, NY: Oxford University Press.

Diener, E., Sandvik, E., Seidlitz, L., & Diener, M. (1993). The relationship between income and subjective well-being: Relative or absolute? *Social Indicators Research, 28,* 195–223.

Diener, E., Suh, E. M., Lucas, R. E., & Smith, H. L. (1999). Subjective well-being: Three decades of progress. *Psychological Bulletin, 125,* 276–302.

Dunn, E. W., Aknin, L. B., & Norton, M. I. (2008). Spending money on others promotes happiness. *Science, 319,* 1687–1688.

Dunn, E. W., Gilbert, D. T., & Wilson, T. D. (2011). If money doesn't make you happy, then you probably aren't spending it right. *Journal of Consumer Psychology, 21,* 115–125.

Emmons, R. A., & McCullough, M. E. (2003). Counting blessings versus burdens: An experimental investigation of gratitude and subjective well-being in daily life. *Journal of Personality and Social Psychology, 84,* 377–389.

Ford, B. Q., Shallcross, A. J., Mauss, I. B., Floerke, V. A., & Gruber, J. (2012). *If you seek it, it won't come: Valuing happiness is associated with symptoms and diagnosis of depression.* Manuscript submitted for publication.

Frederick, S., & Loewenstein, G. (1999). Hedonic adaptation. In D. Kahneman, E. Diener, & N. Schwarz (Eds.), *Well-being: The foundations of hedonic psychology* (pp. 302–329). New York, NY: Russell Sage.

Fredrickson, B. L. (2013). Updated thinking on positivity ratios. *American Psychologist, 68,* 814–822.

Fredrickson, B. L., Cohn, M. A., Coffey, K. A., Pek, J., & Finkel, S. M. (2008). Open hearts build lives: Positive emotions, induced through loving-kindness meditation, build consequential personal resources. *Journal of Personality and Social Psychology, 95,* 1045–1062.

Fredrickson, B. L., & Joiner, T. (2002). Positive emotions trigger upward spirals toward emotional well-being. *Psychological Science, 13,* 172–175.

Fredrickson, B. L., & Losada, M. F. (2005). Positive affect and the complex dynamics of human flourishing. *American Psychologist, 60,* 678–686.

Froh, J. J., Sefick, W. J., & Emmons, R. A. (2008). Counting blessings in early adolescents: An experimental study of gratitude and subjective well-being. *Journal of School Psychology, 46,* 213–233.

Fujita, F., & Diener, E. (2005). Life satisfaction set point: Stability and change. *Journal of Personality and Social Psychology, 88,* 158–164.

Gruber, J., Mauss, I. B., & Tamir, M. (2011). A dark side of happiness? How, when, and why happiness is not always good. *Perspectives on Psychological Science, 6,* 222–233.

Helson, H. (1964). Current trends and issues in adaptation-level theory. *American Psychologist, 19,* 26–38.

Helson, R., Jones, C., & Kwan, V. S. Y. (2002). Personality can change over 40 years of adulthood: Hierarchical linear modeling analyses of two longitudinal samples. *Journal of Personality and Social Psychology, 83,* 752–766.

Jacobs Bao, K., & Lyubomirsky, S. (in press). Making happiness last. In A. Parks (Ed.), *The handbook of positive interventions.* New York, NY: Wiley-Interscience.

Kenrick, D.T., Griskevicius, V., Neuberg, S.L., & Schaller, M. (2010). Renovating the pyramid of needs: Contemporary extensions built upon ancient foundations. *Perspectives on Psychological Science, 5,* 292–314.

Kiecolt-Glaser, J. K., McGuire L., Robles T., & Glaser R. (2002). Emotions, morbidity, and mortality: New perspectives from psychoneuroimmunology. *Annual Review of Psychology, 53,* 83–107.

King, L. A. (2001). The health benefits of writing about life goals. *Personality and Social Psychology Bulletin, 27,* 798–807.

Krueger, R. F., Hicks, B. M., & McGue, M. (2001). Altruism and antisocial behavior: Independent tendencies, unique personality correlates, distinct etiologies. *Psychological Science, 12,* 397–402.

Layous, K., Lee, H. C., Choi, I., & Lyubomirsky, S. (2013). Culture matters when designing a successful happiness-increasing activity: A comparison of the United States and South Korea. *Journal of Cross-Cultural Psychology, 44,* 1294–1303.

Layous, K., & Lyubomirsky, S. (2014). The how, why, what, when, and who of happiness: Mechanisms underlying the success of positive activity interventions. In J. Gruber & J. Moskowitz (Eds.), *Positive emotion: Integrating the light and dark sides* (pp. 473–495). Oxford, UK: Oxford University Press.

Layous, K., Nelson, S. K., & Lyubomirsky, S. (2013). What is the optimal way to deliver a positive activity intervention? The case of writing about one's best possible selves. *Journal of Happiness Studies, 14,* 635–654.

Layous, K., Nelson, S. K., Oberle, E., Schonert-Reichl, K. A., & Lyubomirsky, S. (2012). Kindness counts: Prompting prosocial behavior in preadolescents boosts peer acceptance and well-being. *PLOS ONE, 7,* e51380.

Lucas, R. E. (2001). Pleasant affect and sociability: Toward a comprehensive model of extraverted feelings and behaviors. *Dissertation Abstracts International, 61* (10-B), 5610. (UMI No. AAI9990068).

Lucas, R. E. (2007). Adaptation and the set-point model of subjective well-being: Does happiness change after major life events? *Current Directions in Psychological Science, 16,* 75–79.

Lucas, R. E., Diener, E., & Suh, E. M. (1996). Discriminant validity of well-being measures. *Journal of Personality and Social Psychology, 71,* 616–628.

Lykken, D., & Tellegen, A. (1996). Happiness is a stochastic phenomenon. *Psychological Science, 7,* 186–189.

Lyubomirsky, S. (2001). Why are some people happier than others? The role of cognitive and motivational processes in well-being. *American Psychologist, 56,* 239–249.

Lyubomirsky, S. (2008). *The how of happiness: A scientific approach to getting the life you want.* New York, NY: Penguin Press.

Lyubomirsky, S. (2011). Hedonic adaptation to positive and negative experiences. In S. Folkman (Ed.), *Oxford handbook of stress, health, and coping* (pp. 200–224). New York, NY: Oxford University Press.

Lyubomirsky, S., & Dickerhoof, R. (2010). A construal approach to increasing happiness. In J. Tangney & J. E. Maddux (Eds.), *Social psychological foundations of clinical psychology* (pp. 229–244). New York, NY: Guilford Press.

Lyubomirsky, S., Dickerhoof, R., Boehm, J. K., & Sheldon, K. M. (2011). Becoming happier takes both a will and a proper way: An experimental longitudinal intervention to boost well-being. *Emotion, 11,* 391–402.

Lyubomirsky, S., King, L. A., & Diener, E. (2005). The benefits of frequent positive affect: Does happiness lead to success? *Psychological Bulletin, 131,* 803–855.

Lyubomirsky, S., & Layous, K. (2013). How do simple positive activities increase well-being? *Current Directions in Psychological Science, 22,* 57–62.

Lyubomirsky, S., Sheldon, K. M., & Schkade, D. (2005). Pursuing happiness: The architecture of sustainable change. *Review of General Psychology, 9,* 111–131.

Lyubomirsky, S., Tkach, C., & DiMatteo, M. R. (2006). What are the differences between happiness and self-esteem? *Social Indicators Research, 78,* 363–404.

Maslow, A. H. (1943). A theory of human motivation. *Psychological Review, 50,* 370–396.

Mauss, I. B., Tamir, M., Anderson, C. L., & Savino, N. S. (2011). Can seeking happiness make people unhappy? Paradoxical effects of valuing happiness. *Emotion, 11,* 807–815.

Mitchell, T. R., Thompson, L., Peterson, E., & Cronk, R. (1997). Temporal adjustment of the evaluation of events: The "rosy view." *Journal of Experimental Social Psychology, 33,* 421–448.

McCrae, R. R., & Costa, P. T. (1990). *Personality in adulthood.* New York, NY: Guilford Press.

McCullough, M. E., Emmons, R. A., & Tsang, J.-A. (2002). The grateful disposition: A conceptual and empirical topography. *Journal of Personality and Social Psychology, 82,* 112–127.

Neff, K. D., Kirkpatrick, K. L., & Rude, S. S. (2007). Self-compassion and adaptive psychological functioning. *Journal of Research in Personality, 41,* 139–154.

Nelson, S. K., Della Porta, M. D., Jacobs Bao, K., Lee, H. C., Choi, I., & Lyubomirsky, S. (2012). *"It's up to you": Experimentally manipulated autonomy support for prosocial behavior improves well-being in two cultures over six weeks.* Manuscript submitted for publication.

Nelson, S. K., Fuller, J. A. K., Choi, I., & Lyubomirsky, S. (2012). Beyond self-protection: Self-affirmation benefits hedonic and eudaimonic well-bieng. *Personality and Social Psychology Bulletin.*

Nelson, S. K., & Lyubomirsky, S. (2014). Finding happiness: Tailoring positive activities for optimal well-being benefits. In M. Tugade, M. Shiota, & L. Kirby (Eds.), *Handbook of positive emotions* (pp. 275–293). New York, NY: Guilford Press.

Nes, R. B., Roysamb, E., Tambs, K., Harris, J. R., & Reichborn-Kjennerud, T. (2006). Subjective well-being: Genetic and environmental contributions to stability and change. *Psychological Medicine, 36,* 1033–1042.

Oishi, S., Diener, E., & Lucas, R. E. (2007). The optimum level of well-being: Can people be too happy? *Perspectives on Psychological Science, 2,* 346–360.

Parducci, A. (1995). *Happiness, pleasure, and judgment: The contextual theory and its applications.* Mahwah, NJ: Lawrence Erlbaum.

Parks, A. C., Della Porta, M. D., Pierce, R. S., Zilca, R., & Lyubomirsky, S. (2012). Pursuing happiness in everyday life: The characteristics and behaviors of online happiness seekers. *Emotion, 12,* 1222–1234.

Pronin, E., & Jacobs, E. (2008). Thought speed, mood, and the experience of mental motion. *Perspectives on Psychological Science, 3,* 461–485.

Roberts, B. W., Walton, K. E., & Viechtbauer, W. (2006). Patterns of mean-level change in personality traits across the life course: A meta-analysis of longitudinal studies. *Psychological Bulletin, 132,* 1–25.

Rolls, B. J., Rolls, E. T., Rowe, E. A., & Sweeney, K. (1981). Sensory specific satiety in man. *Physiology & Behavior, 27,* 137–142.

Rosenthal, R., & Rosnow, R. L. (2008). *Essentials of behavioral research* (3rd ed.). Boston, MA: McGraw-Hill.

Ryan, R. M., & Deci, E. L. (2001). On happiness and human potentials: A review of research on hedonic and eudaimonic well-being. *Annual Review of Psychology, 52,* 141–166.

Ryff, C. D. (1989). Happiness is everything, or is it? Explorations on the meaning of psychological well-being. *Journal of Personality and Social Psychology, 57,* 1069–1081.

Schooler, J. W., & Mauss, I. B. (2010). To be happy and to know it: The experience and meta-awareness of pleasure. In M. L. Kringelbach & K. C. Berridge (Eds.), *Pleasures of the brain* (pp. 244–254). Oxford, UK: Oxford University Press.

Schueller, S. M. (2011). To each his own well-being boosting intervention: Using preference to guide selection. *Journal of Positive Psychology, 6,* 300–313.

Seligman, M. E. P., & Csikszentmihalyi, M. (2000). Positive psychology: An introduction. *American Psychologist, 55,* 5–14.

Seligman, M. E. P., Rashid, T., & Parks, A. C. (2006). Positive psychotherapy. *American Psychologist, 61,* 774–788.

Seligman, M. E. P., Steen, T. A., Park, N., & Peterson, C. (2005). Positive psychology progress: Empirical validation of interventions. *American Psychologist, 60,* 410–421.

Sheldon, K. M., Abad, N., Ferguson, Y., Gunz, A., Houser-Marko, L., Nichols, C. P., & Lyubomirsky, S. (2010). Persistent pursuit of need satisfying goals leads to increased happiness: A 6-month experimental longitudinal study. *Motivation & Emotion, 34,* 39–48.

Sheldon, K. M., Boehm, J. K., & Lyubomirsky, S. (2012). Variety is the spice of happiness: The hedonic adaptation prevention (HAP) model. In I. Boniwell & S. David (Eds.), *Oxford handbook of happiness* (pp. 901–914). Oxford, UK: Oxford University Press.

Sheldon, K. M., & Lyubomirsky, S. (2006). How to increase and sustain positive emotion: The effects of expressing gratitude and visualizing best possible selves. *Journal of Positive Psychology, 1,* 73–82.

Sin, N. L., Della Porta, M. D., & Lyubomirsky, S. (2011). Tailoring positive psychology interventions to treat depressed individuals. In S. I. Donaldson, M. Csikszentmihalyi, & J. Nakamura (Eds.), *Applied positive psychology: Improving everyday life, health, schools, work, and society* (pp. 79–96). New York, NY: Routledge.

Sin, N. L., & Lyubomirsky, S. (2009). Enhancing well-being and alleviating depressive symptoms with positive psychology interventions: A practice-friendly meta-analysis. *Journal of Clinical Psychology: In Session, 65,* 467–487.

Van Boven, L., & Gilovich, T. (2003). To do or to have? That is the question. *Journal of Personality and Social Psychology, 85*, 1193–1202.

Walsh, R. (2011). Lifestyle and mental health. *American Psychologist, 66*, 579–592.

Wilson, T. D., & Gilbert, D. T. (2005). Affective forecasting: Knowing what to want. *Current Directions in Psychological Science, 14*, 131–134.

Wilson, T. D., & Gilbert, D. T. (2008). Explaining away: A model of affective adaptation. *Perspectives on Psychological Science, 3*, 370–386.

# 12

# Integrating Religion and Spirituality Into Treatment

## Research and Practice

*Emily A. Padgett*

*Katherine G. Kusner*

*Kenneth I. Pargament*
Bowling Green State University

Although healthcare professionals and social scientists have long kept their distance from the realm of religion and spirituality, the past 50 years has witnessed a surge of research on the role of religion and spirituality in a number of areas of human life, such as health, well-being, relationships, and coping with life stressors (Koenig, King, & Carson, 2012; Pargament, 1997). Overall, the literature indicates that religion and spirituality can significantly relate to mental and physical health, and some research suggests that many people would like their healthcare providers to address spirituality in their journey to achieve better health. Medical patients commonly express a desire that their physicians inquire about religious and spiritual beliefs as well as pray for them during routine visits (MacLean et al., 2003). Similarly, many psychotherapy clients express a desire to discuss such topics in therapy (Rose, Westefeld, & Ansley, 2001) and would like their therapists to pray audibly for them (Weld & Erikson, 2007). Furthermore, multiple studies highlight the utility of integrating spirituality into medical and psychological interventions to improve overall well-being (Hook et al., 2010; Pargament, 2007).

Our goal in this chapter is to describe current efforts to integrate religion and spirituality more effectively into physical and mental healthcare. We begin by considering the meaning of religion and spirituality. We then provide a brief review of research linking religion and spirituality to healthy functioning. This is followed by an overview of what we believe to be exciting efforts to bring religion and spirituality into programs to enhance health and well-being, and we describe one such program in detail. This chapter concludes with research and practice recommendations to foster a spiritually integrated approach in advancing health and well-being.

## The Meaning of Religion and Spirituality

The terms *religion* and *spirituality* can evoke countless cognitions, emotions, and reactions. For some, they bring to mind a grandmother praying with her rosary, sharing a sacred moment with a child in the quiet of the woods, or attending synagogue. Others may think of protestors marching to advocate for their prolife sentiments or clergy sexual abuse scandals. When someone dares to broach such topics at family or social gatherings, reactions may be positive or negative, flexible or rigid, angry or apathetic. This is likely due to the concepts of religion and spirituality meaning different things to different people.

Indeed, scholars of the psychology of religion and spirituality have struggled to define these concepts, and the meanings of religion and spirituality have changed in important ways in the past 40 years (Pargament, 2007). William James (1985), considered the founding father of the field, defined religion as "the feelings, acts, and experiences of individual men in their solitude, as far as they apprehend themselves to stand in relation to whatever they may consider the divine" (p. 32). Religion has traditionally been viewed as a broad construct including individual beliefs, thoughts, and feelings and outward behaviors that could be both helpful and harmful, but current trends in society have altered this perspective. Nowadays, however, religion is increasingly viewed as "static, institutional, objective, and belief-based" and essentially, "bad"; conversely, spirituality is seen as "functional, dynamic, personal, subjective, and experience-based" and essentially, "good" (Zinnbauer & Pargament, 2005, p. 24). This trend toward the polarization of religion and spirituality has serious social, intellectual, and academic implications (for discussion see Pargament, 1999; Zinnbauer & Pargament, 2005). It is important to note, though, that most people in the United States (74%) identify as both religious *and* spiritual, suggesting that the general population sees these concepts as broadly overlapping (Zinnbauer et al., 1997).

Though challenging, it is necessary to draw some boundaries around the concepts of spirituality and religion by providing working definitions. We define spirituality as "a search for the sacred" (Pargament, 1999, p. 12) and define religion as "the search for significance that occurs within the context of established institutions that are designed to facilitate spirituality" (Pargament, Mahoney, Exline, Jones, & Shafranske, in press). Embedded in the term *search* is the idea that spirituality is a process or a journey. Spiritual journeys are dynamic and fluid as opposed to fixed and frozen in time; they involve a process of discovering, maintaining, and transforming one's relationship to the sacred. The search begins with the discovery of the sacred through revelation, intuition, or socialization. Once discovered, the search continues as people try to maintain and sustain their relationship with the sacred. However, when personal or environmental changes push individuals beyond their ability to preserve and protect their understanding of the sacred, a transformation may occur. Transformations may involve a temporary or permanent disengagement from the sacred or a change in how the sacred is understood or experienced. Once this transformation unfolds, the individual's search returns to the process of sustaining this now-changed relationship to the sacred, and the journey continues.

Spirituality is set apart from other human processes in that the ultimate destination of the spiritual journey centers on the human need for a connection to something larger than the self—something sacred. The term *sacred* encompasses traditional notions of God, divinity, and higher powers but also other aspects of life that are imbued with divine qualities through an association with, or representation of, the sacred (Pargament & Mahoney, 2005). Through this process of *sanctification*, people can perceive God's direct involvement in their relationships, possessions, or experiences and can also imbue the same aspects of life with sacred qualities such as transcendence, ultimacy, and boundlessness (Pargament & Mahoney, 2005).

The search for the sacred can unfold within or outside of traditional religious contexts. Many begin their spiritual journey by taking age-old paths of established religious institutions and through engagement with organized religious communities. Indeed, religious institutions are designed first and foremost to facilitate the individual's search for the sacred. Many other individuals, however, create new trails, stepping into areas distinct from traditional religious life. For example, some may practice meditation as a spiritual exercise without following Buddhism, or may have dietary restrictions that are similar to some religions, but are followed due to sacred beliefs about the humane treatment of animals or about living a healthy life.

Spirituality is a rich and complex process. People understand the sacred in many different ways. Similarly, they can take many different pathways—composed of diverse beliefs, practices, emotions, and relationships—in their search for the sacred. It follows that spirituality is not necessarily good or bad in and of itself. It is, instead, multivalenced. Some find solace and comfort in their spirituality when faced with the death of a loved one that facilitates peace and healing; others may resent or blame God and in turn experience psychological distress and negative feelings. People can imbue destructive ends (e.g., violence, child abuse) with sacred qualities or take destructive pathways (e.g., drugs, alcohol) in the pursuit of sacred destinations. Whether spirituality is good or not depends on the kind of spirituality we are talking about. In sum, spirituality involves a potentially dynamic, fluid, multidimensional, multivalent, lifelong journey of discovering, conserving, and transforming one's relationship to the sacred. As mentioned previously, most people see themselves as both religious and spiritual; henceforth, we shall refer to both religion and spirituality as R/S to conserve space.

# Research on Religion, Spirituality, Health, and Well-Being

## The Positive Side

The question of whether R/S is good or not can also include the question of whether R/S is good *for* us or not. In recent years, links between spirituality, religion, health, and well-being have been demonstrated through a large body of empirical research. In their extensive review of this literature, Koenig and colleagues (2012) found that aspects of religion and spirituality related to the following nonexhaustive list: (1) greater well-being, happiness, and life satisfaction; (2) lower rates of depression and suicide; (3) less anxiety; (4) lower use and abuse of alcohol and drugs; (5) lower risk of delinquent behavior and crime; (6) greater marital stability; (7) more adaptive personality traits (e.g. altruism, optimism); (8) greater senses of self-esteem, optimism, hope, and purpose or meaning in life; (9) lower rates of cardiac difficulties (albeit a weak relationship); (10) lower blood pressure; (11) indicators of a healthy immune system; (12) improved cancer prognosis and prevention of cancer development; (13) greater longevity; (14) enhanced coping with physical disability and chronic pain; and (15) decision making related to better health, such as frequent exercise, eating healthy, and less risky sexual practices.

Although research points to significant ties between R/S and health and well-being, the literature is limited in some key respects. First, much of the research has used a cross-sectional design, limiting the understanding of causality. However, there is an accumulating body of experimental and longitudinal research that does point to benefits of certain forms of R/S. Additionally, much of the published research has depended on global, rudimentary measures of R/S consisting of only a few items, such as frequency of service attendance, frequency of prayer, or religious affiliation. While such measures may seem to be a valid way to capture R/S, such indices do not reveal how and to what level of depth individuals actually use spirituality in their lives. As R/S are complex and multifaceted constructs, researchers must move beyond global measures to identify the specific ways in which R/S play a role in well-being.

In this direction, several promising lines of research have provided an in-depth look into the workings of R/S within the lives of people (Pargament, 2002). Building on the work of Gordon Allport (Allport & Ross, 1967), studies have shown that an intrinsic religiousness, motivated by a desire to "live out" one's faith, is associated with better mental health outcomes and less prejudice compared with an extrinsic religious orientation, motivated by the desire for personal or social gain (see Donahue, 1985). Additionally, a spirituality that is personally chosen and valued is related to lower levels of anxiety, depression, and social dysfunction and higher levels of self-esteem, whereas a spirituality founded on social pressure, guilt, or fear of social rejection is related to more emotional distress and lower self-esteem (Ryan, Rigby, & King, 1993).

The potential role of R/S in positive well-being can also be understood by examining how people use their spirituality to cope when faced with difficult decisions and traumatic circumstances: R/S appears to be especially valuable in situations that push people to the limits of their resources (Pargament, 2002). Pargament (1997, 2011) identified a variety of positive forms of religious and spiritual coping, including seeking spiritual support from others, accessing God as a loving and caring figure, working collaboratively as a team with God to handle difficulties, reframing one's situation in a spiritually benevolent light (e.g., God is trying to teach me something through this experience), engaging in forgiveness, and seeking spiritual direction from God or spiritual leaders.

Studies of participants dealing with a range of significant life stressors, including combat veterans, widows, and abused spouses, reveal that a majority found religion to be helpful when coping with their difficulties (Pargament, 1997). Further, meta-analytic results indicate that positive religious coping is significantly tied to more optimism, happiness, quality of life, and self-esteem while adjusting to stress (Ano & Vasconcelles, 2005). Additionally, positive religious coping was predictive of better clinical and functional status in a 3-year study of individuals living with schizophrenia and schizoaffective disorder (Mohr et al., 2010) and predicted more post-traumatic growth 1 year postdivorce among adult divorcees (Krumrei, Mahoney, & Pargament, 2011).

The use of positive religious coping may also be helpful while experiencing health concerns, as it has been found to relate to better psychological well-being for individuals coping with medical difficulties such as breast cancer (Gall, 2000) and arthritis (Abraído-Lanza, Vásquez, & Echeverría, 2004). Furthermore, longitudinal designs indicate that positive religious coping predicts better postoperative functioning after cardiac surgery (Ai, Peterson, Bolling, & Rodgers, 2006); increased 5-year survival rates for those with HIV (Ironson & Kremer, 2009); and increases in mental health, stress-related growth, and cognitive functioning among medically ill older adults (Pargament, Koenig, Tarakeshwar, & Hahn, 2004).

The tendency to sanctify aspects of life, or to see life through a sacred lens, has also been associated with health and well-being. One important area of well-being for working adults is their employment, and there is evidence that people who view their job as sacred (i.e., a vocation) experience higher job satisfaction, more commitment to their organization, and lower intention of quitting their job (Walker, Jones, Wuensch, Aziz, & Cope, 2008). Similarly, mothers who sanctify their jobs experience less role conflict between their work and parenting roles (Hall, Oates, Anderson, & Willingham, 2012). With respect to physical health, individuals who perceive their bodies as sacred report greater body satisfaction, engagement in more health-protective behaviors, and more disapproval of illicit drug use (Mahoney et al., 2005).

Sanctification also appears to play a role in sex, marriage, and parenting. A sample of married individuals who sanctified sex had greater sexual intimacy, marital satisfaction, and spiritual intimacy (Hernandez, Mahoney, & Pargament, 2011). Perceiving one's marriage as sanctified is related to greater marital satisfaction, more collaborative communication, and less negative communication behaviors (Mahoney et al., 1999), more marital commitment, and more displays of positive emotions and bonding (Ellison, Henderson, Glenn, & Harkrider, 2011). Married parents who sanctify their roles as parents show more consistent parenting, less verbal hostility toward their children (A. Murray-Swank, Mahoney, & Pargament, 2006), and more positive parenting strategies (e.g., praise, induction; Volling, Mahoney, & Rauer, 2009).

## The Darker Side

Despite the large body of evidence that R/S can relate positively to well-being, empirical studies also suggest that there is a darker side to R/S. One indicator of possible trouble involves negative religious coping, more specifically the construct of religious and spiritual struggles. Major life crises not only affect individuals psychologically, socially, and physically, but can also potentially interact with peoples' spiritual lives. These events can elicit R/S struggles—tensions and conflicts about spiritual matters (Exline, in press). Pargament, Murray-Swank, Magyar, and Ano (2005) have identified and describe three types of R/S struggles: divine (e.g., feeling angry at, abandoned, or punished by God), intrapersonal (e.g., conflicts between one's higher and lower self or doubting one's beliefs), or interpersonal (e.g., spiritual tensions with family, friends, or one's religious community).

Cross-sectional and longitudinal research has shown a consistent association between measures of R/S struggle and negative psychological adjustment, including depression, paranoia, bodily symptoms, anxiety, substance abuse, serious mental illness, and posttraumatic stress (see Exline, in press). For example, in a study of adolescents diagnosed with depression, loss of faith predicted less improvement in self-reported depression symptoms over 6 months (Dew et al., 2010). Spiritual struggle has also been linked to interpersonal difficulties, including childhood sexual abuse, caregiving, grief, and divorce (Exline, in press). One such example is that viewing one's divorce as a sacred loss or desecration predicted more depressive symptoms and dysfunctional conflict tactics with the ex-partner a year later (Krumrei et al., 2011). R/S struggle also has significant ties to poorer health status of patients dealing with cardiovascular disease, cancer, chronic pain, HIV/AIDS, diabetes, lung disease, and end-of-life issues (Exline, in press). For instance, longitudinal research among medically ill older adults showed that spiritual struggle not only predicted declines in mental and physical health (Pargament, Koenig, Tarakeshwar, & Hahn, 2004), but also predicted mortality (Pargament, Koenig, Tarakeshwar, & Hahn, 2001).

It is interesting to note that, although R/S struggles have been robustly tied to harmful outcomes, a few studies indicate that R/S struggle results in spiritual and posttraumatic growth. For example, researchers have related R/S struggle to stress-related growth in individuals who view their romantic relationships as being a sacred loss and desecration (Magyar, Pargament, & Mahoney, 2000), and individuals closely impacted by the Oklahoma City bombing experienced both stress-related and spiritual growth (Pargament,

Smith, Koenig, & Perez, 1998). Additionally, in the previously mentioned longitudinal study of older adults with medical difficulties, although spiritual struggle predicted declines in physical and mental health, it also related to greater spiritual growth (Pargament, Koenig, Tarakeshwar, & Hahn, 2004). The current findings are consistent with clinical views that struggles can be a source of growth and positive transformation. Similarly, the sacred literatures from all over the world contain powerful stories of religious exemplars who encountered R/S struggles as a vital part of their spiritual journeys (Pargament, 1997). Thus, it appears that R/S struggle is essentially a fork in the road, with one path leading to despair, pain, and psychospiritual decline, and the other path resulting in positive development, growth, and potential transformation (Pargament, 2006).

Theorists and researchers have proposed a number of psychological and social mechanisms that might explain the links between religion, spirituality, health, and well-being, albeit many of them are reductionistic and overly simplified in nature. For example, Freud (1927/1961) saw religion as a way to manage anxiety; others assert that beliefs in God represent a way to achieve a secure relational attachment (Kirkpatrick, 2004). Some propose that spiritual experience is simply a product of brain structures (Persinger, 1983) and neurochemical processes (Griffiths, Richards, McCann, & Jesse, 2006), whereas others see R/S as a form of social cohesiveness and control (Durkheim, 1951) and as a way of binding people together into communities through shared morality (Graham & Haidt, 2010).

Whereas each of these explanations may help to account for the ties between R/S and health, R/S may not be fully reducible to psychological and social mechanisms. Instead, R/S may offer something special to health and well-being. The search for the sacred may rest on a distinctive human yearning and bring distinctive ingredients to the most fundamental challenges of living. Perhaps most importantly, with their focus on the sacred, R/S offer unique ways of helping people come to terms with human limitations, finitude, and frailty (Pargament, in press). That is the distinctive function of R/S, and it is worth researching and understanding in its own right. The remainder of this chapter discusses specific ways to help people integrate the sacred more fully into their lives.

## The Roles of Religion and Spirituality in Healthcare

To integrate R/S into healthcare, the provider must be equipped with several key skills. Because spirituality is a highly personal topic, providers must create an atmosphere of safety and acceptance if they are to be invited into the R/S worlds of their clients. Toward this end, providers must demonstrate spiritual self-awareness, sensitivity to and respect of others' spiritual perspectives, and knowledge about R/S. First, it is important to recognize that providers, like their clients, may have a spiritual dimension to their lives that affects their worldview and understanding of health problems; thus, it is vital that they have spiritual self-awareness. Given the power differential inherent in the relationship between providers and clients, providers without self-awareness may inadvertently exert inappropriate influence on their clients (e.g., subtly or overtly manipulate the client with their own spiritual viewpoints). Second, providers should strive to convey openness, tolerance, and sensitivity toward their clients' perspectives. This does not mean having to affirm or hold to clients' beliefs; rather, this means respecting the clients' right to choose their spiritual path and most deeply held values (Pargament, 2007). Third, providers should strive to gain basic fundamental knowledge and understanding of traditional and nontraditional spiritualities and religions, especially those that are popular in or specific to the geographic region in which they practice. Most importantly, providers should know how to assess and address the spiritual dimension of clients' lives.

## Spiritual Assessment

Although most clients do not schedule medical or psychological appointments due to overtly R/S problems, R/S in healthcare contexts should still be discussed with clients since their R/S may be woven into their understanding of, and means of coping with, difficulties. Talking with clients about R/S is both a learned skill and a conversational art. The process of understanding a client's R/S begins with an initial assessment. Just as providers assess clients' medical and family history, social and adaptive functioning, cognitions, behaviors, and emotions during initial appointments, providers should conduct an initial assessment of R/S. Often this includes a few basic questions, such as "Do you see yourself as a spiritual or religious person? If so, in what way?" and "Are you affiliated with a religious or spiritual denomination or community? If so, which one?" (Pargament, 2007, p. 211). Following these questions, providers should inquire about the possible role R/S plays in the clients' problems and means of coping. Through this first dialogue, clients' responses will provide a glimpse into the R/S dimension of their lives and open the door for future assessment.

### Implicit Spiritual Assessment

Further assessment includes both implicit and explicit conversations about the sacred (Pargament, 2007). Implicit spiritual assessments have two critical components. First, they involve asking questions that allude to a deeper and richer dimension of life that draw on psychospiritual language to elicit spiritual exploration. When queried about where they find peace and solace, what they put their faith and hope in, and their deepest moments of despair, often clients respond with their own spiritual language. The second component in implicit R/S assessments involves the provider's keen awareness of the subtle ways clients may communicate about their R/S. Clients may end up discussing R/S without direction from the provider, spontaneously using spiritual or psychospiritual language (e.g., "This peace came over me," "It was the deepest despair"), describing spiritual emotions (e.g., awe, wonder, profound sorrow), or explaining spiritual-like experiences, beliefs, or practices (e.g., "I felt transformed, made new," "I finally forgave him and let it go"). Perceptive providers may recognize these disclosures as opportunities to help clients identify and elaborate on their R/S. Such implicit spiritual assessments sometimes provide opportunities for clients to explore and express their deeper selves. However, assessment does not end here.

### Explicit Spiritual Assessment

In explicit spiritual assessment, the provider broaches R/S topics more directly. There are three goals in this process. First, the provider attempts to identify where clients are in their spiritual journey. Have they recently discovered the sacred? Are they in the midst of an R/S struggle? Or are they on the verge of transforming their understanding of the sacred? Second, the provider seeks to understand the integration and development of the client's R/S. The provider may ask questions to elicit the client's "vision of the sacred; the place of the sacred in the client's strivings; the breadth, depth, and flexibility of the client's pathways; and the fit between the client's pathways with his or her destinations, problem, and social context" (Pargament, 2007, p. 223). However, questions are not the only means to this information, and the provider should remain attentive to the client's nonverbal and emotional reactions to R/S material. Providers may consider implementing R/S assessment measures in their practice, as a promising set of such tools for use in healthcare settings is now emerging (see Aten, O'Grady, & Worthington, 2012, for examples). Finally, the provider should evaluate the quality and effectiveness of the client's R/S for the degree to which his or her spirituality leads to "valuable outcomes" (Pargament, 2007, p. 224). In what ways has the client's R/S changed his or her life for the better? What about for the worse? How has the client's R/S been a source of pleasure? What about pain and struggle? Questions such as these can help orient and guide the clinician's evaluative thinking process. The provider should be attentive to potential constructive and destructive spiritual means or ends in the client's life.

## Integrating Spirituality Into Treatment

Initial and ongoing spiritual assessment that results in a deep and rich understanding of a client's R/S can provide a strong foundation for integrating spirituality into treatments. There are two main ways that spirituality tends to be addressed within the context of healing professions. First, healthcare providers may help clients draw on spiritual resources to cope more effectively with physical or psychological disorders, and second, providers may help clients anticipate, address, and resolve spiritual problems, such as R/S struggles. Promising results have emerged from innovative research-based psychospiritual interventions designed to help clients access and strengthen their spiritual resources and address R/S struggle. Meta-analytic studies and scholarly reviews show that spiritually integrated treatments are as effective as secular treatments and more effective in terms of R/S outcomes (McCullough, 1999; Smith, Bartz, & Richards, 2007); further, many clients prefer spiritually integrated counseling (Stanley et al., 2011). Although spiritually integrated interventions are in early stages of development and research, many of these innovative programs show great potential. We now turn to further discussion about these interventions that span a range of psychological and medical problems (e.g., eating disorders, heroin addiction), treatment modalities (e.g., individual, group, couples), clients (e.g., African American, women), and spiritual resources (e.g., prayer, meditation, spiritual beliefs). We conclude this section with an in-depth overview of one spiritually integrated program designed to help individuals with HIV explore spiritual issues related to their medical condition as well as access spiritual resources to cope with the associated R/S struggles.

### Spiritual Renewal

Richards, Hardman, and Berrett (2000) created "Spiritual Renewal: A Journey of Faith and Healing," a manualized 10-session theistic-centered approach to treating females with eating disorders, one of the most challenging medical and psychological disorders, with the goals of spiritual growth and living more harmonious lives. This focused intervention includes sessions on identifying and addressing deep issues such as the spiritual purpose the eating disorder replaces, exploring a guiding life vision, and creating a plan and commitment to realizing clients' vision. Additionally, clients explore and practice psychospiritual concepts and exercises involving understanding their divine worth, creating a balanced life, forgiveness of self and others, gratitude, and spiritual responsibility for the behaviors within their control. A controlled randomized research study provided preliminary evidence that the Spiritual Renewal intervention may be as or more effective in treating eating disorders than a cognitive-based intervention or emotional support group (Richards, Berrett, Hardman, & Eggett, 2006).

### Spiritual Self-Schema Therapy

Avants and Margolin (2003), in an effort to help treatment-resistant heroin addicts, created the "Spiritual Self-Schema Therapy" (3S) program. This 8-week group program helps clients understand how their "addict self," the part of them driven by cravings and avoidance, does not represent their authentic self. Instead, it teaches that they have a true, authentic "spiritual self" that can be identified and reinforced as a replacement for the "addict self." To this end, the program uses meditation, prayers, Buddhist teachings, spiritual reframing, and discussions about spiritual beliefs and virtues. In a sample of 29 cocaine- and opiate-dependent treatment-resistant clients, program completion was related to a significant decrease in illicit drug use and increases in spiritual coping, religious service attendance, and private religious and spiritual experiences (Avants, Beitel, & Margolin, 2005).

### Spiritually Integrated Couples Treatment

Research on spiritually integrated treatments has expanded beyond serious mental and physical health issues and has begun addressing the spiritual dimension in interventions focused on family relationships. For example, "Prayer-Focused PREP," a spiritual version of one popular secular marital program, PREP (Prevention and Relationship Enhancement Program), incorporates prayer to help reduce marital distress and improve marital functioning in African American marriages (Beach et al., 2011). In addition to focusing on building communication, problem-solving, and listening skills, praying for one's partner is emphasized throughout the program. Prayer-Focused PREP provides spouses with illustrative prayers and also encourages spouses to create their own prayers focused on selfless love for their partner. A randomized treatment-outcome study found that African American wives, but not husbands, in the Prayer-Focused PREP group experienced more improvements in relationship satisfaction than those in the culturally sensitive version of PREP group or those in the control group that received no training.

*Addressing Spiritual Struggles*

As mentioned previously, the second significant way that healthcare providers incorporate spirituality into treatment involves helping clients anticipate, address, and resolve R/S struggles. Arising from challenging life events, R/S struggles may represent a fork in the road for people, leading either to growth or to psychological distress (Exline & Rose, 2005; Pargament et al., 2005). A few promising psychospiritual intervention programs have emerged within the past decade to help clients move toward psychological and spiritual growth, rather than distress, when faced with spiritual struggles.

**Solace for the Soul.** Nichole Murray-Swank's (2003) "Solace for the Soul: A Journey Toward Wholeness" is an eight-session psychospiritual intervention aimed at helping female sexual abuse survivors address and resolve spiritual struggles. This intervention employs diverse spiritual methods including prayers to enhance spiritual connection, spiritual reframing, meditation and focused breathing, spiritual visualization (e.g., God's love is a waterfall within), two-way journaling to God to express emotions, and spiritual rituals to reduce feelings of shame and self-loathing. Solace for the Soul demonstrated potential as an effective intervention through an N of 1 time-series design with two participants; both women evidenced significant positive changes in their self-reported religious coping, spiritual well-being, and positive images of God (N. Murray-Swank & Pargament, 2005).

**Winding Road.** Researchers more recently designed "Winding Road" to address the R/S struggles of college students (Oemig Dworsky et al., in press). This 9-week group intervention is inclusive of a variety of spiritualities; it is not affiliated with a particular religion. Goals of the intervention include helping students accept their spiritual questions, doubts, and conflicts; identify and explore their spiritual struggles; broaden and deepen their spirituality; and increase their flexibility in addressing their struggles. Using the metaphor of "a winding road," the program views R/S struggles as a natural part of one's spiritual journey that can be openly explored and considered. Sessions include sharing spiritual autobiographies, creating spiritual genograms, discussing one's current and future spiritual self, forgiveness, spiritual acceptance, and meaning making. The sessions implement resources such as meditation, visualization, and ritual exercises. Results from a small open-trial study suggest that the process of addressing R/S struggles is psychologically and spiritually helpful for students (Oemig Dworsky et al., in press).

## Case Study: "Lighting the Way"

We now turn to a description of one spiritually focused intervention to exemplify how spiritual struggle can be addressed in the mental and physical health treatment of those facing a difficult medical diagnosis. "Lighting the Way: A Spiritual Journey to Wholeness" is an eight-session group intervention originally inspired by interviews with African American urban women with human immunodeficiency virus (HIV; Pargament, McCarthy, et al., 2004). Both African Americans and women are subgroups of HIV sufferers who tend to use and rely on spirituality in their day-to-day life (Mattis & Grayman-Simpson, in press). We first briefly describe each of the sessions (for more thorough descriptions, please see Pargament, McCarthy, et al., 2004) and then review empirical results from a slightly modified version of the program.

Session 1: Introduction. The program uses the metaphor of a journey to describe the pathway toward healing and wholeness. In this first session, the participants discuss the barriers that have impeded them from reaching the destination of healing physically, emotionally, and spiritually. They also discuss potential spiritual resources they could use to travel the pathway toward wholeness and healing more effectively (e.g., prayer, rituals). Participants are also provided with a short description of each session. This session ends with a prewritten group prayer and candle lighting ceremony, which is used in each of the following sessions.

Session 2: Body and Spirit. Clearly, HIV takes a toll on the body. This session asks participants to draw a picture of how they view their bodies and their souls. They then compare the two to demonstrate that body and soul, while connected, are separate, and HIV leaves the soul intact. Participants also discuss forms of unhealthy coping they have used to try to feed and sustain their soul (e.g., substance abuse, unhealthy relationships) as well as new and healthy ways they can nourish their spiritual selves (e.g., self-care, meditation, intimate relationships).

Session 3: Control and Surrender. It is likely that a diagnosis of HIV may leave patients feeling as if they no longer have control of their own lives. This session helps participants identify which aspects of their life are in and out of their personal control. For example, aspects within one's control could be proper diet, taking medication, and being intentional with one's time, while aspects outside of personal control could be how one's body reacts to treatment or how other people respond to their diagnosis of HIV. This session does not encourage participants to be passive about uncontrollable areas of their life but rather to actively relinquish control in such areas so they can focus their energy on spheres of their life they can actually influence. The session ends with a guided imagery exercise that encourages participants to actively surrender things beyond their control to a higher power.

**Session 4: Letting Go of Anger.** The diagnosis of an illness such as HIV may lead to anger at God and questions such as "Why me?" The first goal of the session is to encourage participants to discuss and let go of their anger instead of holding on to it tightly. Second, participants identify whether their anger is directed toward appropriate targets. Third, the session normalizes and validates the anger they may feel toward God as well as affording them a safe space to discuss and experience such feelings. The session ends with an exercise designed to help participants rely on their relationship with a higher power to relinquish their anger.

**Session 5: Shame and Guilt.** This session focuses on the shame participants may experience regarding the choices they have made in life, which may or may not have played a role in the contraction of HIV, as well as guilt regarding how their diagnosis has impacted others. Facilitators normalize shame and guilt and support participants in sharing how shame and guilt influence their journey toward healing. Participants are encouraged to seek forgiveness from a higher power and to extend forgiveness to themselves. Participants then engage in an exercise in which they write a letter to God about their feelings of shame and guilt and then await the higher power's response. The session ends with a guided imagery exercise in which participants imagine that they are removing shame and guilt as they approach and step into a healing lake.

**Session 6: Isolation and Intimacy.** The stigma attached to HIV can lead to feelings of disconnectedness from family, friends, and society. This session normalizes the experience and feeling of isolation, but it also normalizes the basic human need for intimacy and closeness. Participants hear stories of other individuals who have been successful at reaching out and finding intimacy from others, and they identify specific people who can provide spiritual and interpersonal support and intimacy. At the end, participants use string from a ball of yarn to connect to each other, symbolizing the ties they have created with one another.

**Session 7: Hopes and Dreams.** This session facilitates a discussion about the sacred hopes and dreams participants may feel they have lost due to their diagnosis, such as not being able to pursue certain careers or dying before they get to see their children grow up. Participants discuss the dreams they feel are attainable and unattainable and how they might achieve the sacred hopes and dreams still within their reach so they can experience meaning and purpose in their lives. They hear the story of how one quadriplegic found meaning in her life and are then encouraged to seek out their higher power to find and create their own meaning and purpose.

**Session 8: A Review of the Journey.** The eighth and final session reviews each of the sessions on the journey toward healing and wholeness. Additionally, group members are provided with a kit containing symbols of their journey. The kit includes items such as a compass symbolizing direction during their journey, a rock reminding them of how anger can become a burden, and a piece of yarn symbolizing the intimate connections they have made with each other and their higher power. The session ends with a poem/prayer about self-growth.

### Empirical Support

One of the original developers of Lighting the Way implemented and studied the program at the Department of Epidemiology and Public Health at Yale University. A slightly modified version of the program was used with three separate groups of women ($n = 5$), heterosexual men ($n = 4$), and gay men ($n = 5$) all with HIV-positive diagnoses (Tarakeshwar, Pearce, & Sikemma, 2005). Over the course of the program, participants reported lower levels of depression and negative spiritual coping, higher self-rated religiosity, and use of more forms of positive spiritual coping.

According to qualitative interviews following the program, many participants appreciated the unique nature of Lighting the Way and its distinctive focus on spirituality and HIV. Although many were unsure of what to expect at the outset of the program, participants felt that the program was open to any sort of spirituality. The participants believed that the program allowed them to reengage with their previously disconnected spiritual selves. More critically, however, participants would have preferred more sessions. While all participants were satisfied with the topics discussed in the program, women desired more focus on self-esteem issues, and men asked for more help in building more specific skills to cope with their daily stressors. Although this program is in the very early stages of establishing its efficacy and needs to be replicated and evaluated through a larger sample size, long-term follow-up, and randomized control, Lighting the Way is a fine example of spiritually integrated treatment, and it appears to be a promising program for HIV-positive adults.

# Future Directions

## Research

Although research in this domain is still relatively young, it suggests that R/S adds a vital ingredient to our efforts to maintain and enhance health and well-being. However, additional studies are needed to more fully understand for whom, when, and how R/S can be best integrated into healthcare to produce long-standing health benefits. There are three directions for future research that we believe will be particularly useful. First, while there is empirical evidence that there are positive gains from spiritually integrated treatments, much more research is necessary to determine the efficacy of such treatments, such as replication, random assignment, larger sample sizes, and comparison to control groups or secular treatment. Additionally, while we are proponents of the integration of R/S in healthcare, we recognize that there are other potential mediating and moderating factors that may be responsible for positive outcomes, and it is important to identify such factors to understand the true agent of change. Some possible variables to consider may be social support from a spiritual community, importance or salience of R/S in one's life, engagement in treatment, the use of secular coping resources, and quasispiritual constructs (e.g., forgiveness, gratitude, mindfulness) that are often studied in the field of positive psychology.

Second, most R/S research has been conducted in the United States with Christians, so future research should focus on the effects of R/S among diverse groups of people. For example, more knowledge is needed about those who practice nontheistic and Eastern world religions, as well as the effectiveness of spiritually integrated treatments for individuals who identify as spiritual but not religious. Creating, implementing, and testing less traditionally defined programs for such individuals would be helpful. Likewise, understanding whether and how R/S operates for marginalized and minority groups is an important aspect of multicultural sensitivity and may help facilitate the effective incorporation of R/S into healthcare for such populations. For example, research indicates that R/S may be more salient and important to African Americans (e.g., Ferraro & Koch, 1994), Hispanics (e.g., Herrera, Lee, Nanyonjo, Laufman, & Torres-Vigil, 2009), and the elderly (e.g., Neighbors, Jackson, Bowman, & Gurin, 1983). As there is no single formula for integrating R/S into healthcare, research is sorely needed to foster nuanced and effective spiritually integrated programs that meet the needs of such diverse groups.

Third, future studies should continue to expand beyond programs and therapies for the individual to spiritually integrated programs for families, organizations, and communities. Unfortunately, very little treatment-outcome research on the efficacy of integrating spirituality into couples and family therapy has yet to be conducted. However, researchers and practitioners alike have begun to recognize the important role of spirituality in family life. Mahoney (2010) offers a relational spirituality framework that helps put into context the last decade of faith and family research and seeks to stimulate future in-depth research in the area. Treatment that addresses the spiritual dimension of family problems and draws on spiritual resources may offer a unique, helpful, and welcomed approach to couples and family therapy. This work may also facilitate change for organizations and communities.

## Training and Practice

As noted previously, few healthcare professionals receive training and education in how to assess and address the spiritual dimension of healthcare. As a result, they may view spiritual concerns or beliefs as pathological or unhealthy, or feel ill equipped to identify and address the spiritual dimension of problems. Both formal and informal training is essential to provide clinicians with the necessary skills to integrate spirituality into healthcare. Formal training may include (1) a graduate seminar in the psychology of religion and spirituality to provide a deep and rich understanding of classic and contemporary theory and research; (2) a course in comparative religion to supply students with a foundational understanding of diverse world religions; (3) a course in spiritually integrated psychotherapy; (4) formal integration of spiritual topics and issues into graduate courses such as psychopathology, diversity, assessment, and supervision; (5) providing spiritually sensitive supervision; and (6) offering continuing education programming on spiritual topics and issues (Pargament, 2007, p. 334).

The effective integration of R/S into healthcare calls for more than formal coursework and intellectual exercises; one must cultivate an integrated perspective on R/S. This cannot be explicitly taught in the classroom but rather is developed in conjunction with informal personal experiences with R/S. Specifically, we are talking about informal experiences with traditional and nontraditional forms of spirituality that lead to greater spiritual self-awareness, increased appreciation for diverse spiritualities, and a genuine interest in the role of R/S in people's lives. Informal training may include attending different religious services (e.g., a service at a synagogue, mosque, or temple) or participating in different spiritual activities (e.g., yoga, silent retreats, meditation). Informal training may also involve spiritual self-exploration and exercises such as writing a spiritual autobiography, guided by questions that parallel those asked of clients: "What do I hold sacred? How did I discover the sacred? What have I tried to develop and sustain myself spiritually over the years? Where do I currently stand in the search for the sacred?" (for full set of questions see Pargament, 2007, p. 336). Together, these formal and informal training components can help advance the skills needed to integrate spirituality into healthcare treatment.

## Conclusion

Spiritual functioning, like physical, psychological, social, and emotional functioning, is an integral part of health and well-being and should be addressed and acknowledged by helping professionals. The scientific study of the interface of R/S with health and well-being has resulted in several well established positive links between the two domains as well as a smaller but noteworthy number of negative associations. Drawing on this body of empirical research, a set of guidelines for integrating spirituality into health-care assessment and treatment and several spiritually integrated programs to address psychological, medical, and spiritual problems has been developed (Pargament, 2007). Promising results have emerged from studies examining the efficacy of integrating spirituality into treatment in healthcare settings. In future years, we are likely to see additional developments in this important area of research and practice.

## References

Abraído-Lanza, A. F., Vásquez, E., & Echeverría, S. E. (2004). En las manos de dios [in god's hands]: Religious and other forms of coping among Latinos with arthritis. *Journal of Consulting & Clinical Psychology, 72*(1), 91–102. doi: 10.1037/0022–006X.72.1.91

Ai, A. L., Peterson, C., Bolling, S. F., & Rodgers, W. (2006). Depression, faith-based coping, and short-term postoperative global functioning in adult and older patients undergoing cardiac surgery. *Journal of Psychosomatic Research, 60*(1), 21–28. doi:10.1016/j.jpsychores.2005.06.082

Allport, G. W., & Ross, J. M. (1967). Personal religious orientation and prejudice. *Journal of Personality and Social Psychology, 5*(4), 432–443. doi:10.1037/0022–3514.5.4.432

Ano, G. G., & Vasconcelles, E. B. (2005). Religious coping and psychological adjustment to stress: A meta-analysis. *Journal of Clinical Psychology, 61*(4), 461–480. doi:10.1002/jclp.20049

Aten, J. D., O'Grady, K., & Worthington, E. L. (Eds.). (2012). *The psychology of religion and spirituality for clinicians: Using research in your practice*. New York, NY: Routledge.

Avants, S. K., Beitel, M., & Margolin, A. (2005). Making the shift from "addict self" to "spiritual self": Results from a stage I study of spiritual self-schema (3-S) therapy for the treatment of addiction and HIV risk behavior. *Mental Health, Religion & Culture, 8*(3), 167–177. doi:10.1080/13694670500138924

Avants, S. K., & Margolin, A. (2003). *The Spiritual Self-Schema (3-S) Development Program.* Retrieved from http://www.3-s.us/3-S_manuals/3S_general.doc.

Beach, S. R. H., Hurt, T. R., Fincham, F. D., Franklin, K. J., McNair, L. M., & Stanley, S. M. (2011). Enhancing marital enrichment through spirituality: Efficacy data for prayer focused relationship enhancement. *Psychology of Religion and Spirituality, 3*(3), 201–216. doi:10.1037/a0022207

Dew, R. E., Daniel, S. S., Goldston, D. B., McCall, W. V., Kuchibhatla, M., Schleifer, C., . . . Koenig, H. G. (2010). A prospective study of religion/spirituality and depressive symptoms among adolescent psychiatric patients. *Journal of Affective Disorders, 120*(1–3), 149–157. doi:10.1016/j.jad.2009.04.029

Donahue, M. J. (1985). Intrinsic and extrinsic religiousness: The empirical research. *Journal for the Scientific Study of Religion, 24*(4), 418–423. doi:10.2307/1385995

Durkheim, E. (1951). *Suicide: A study in sociology* (J. A. Spaulding & G. Simpson, Trans.). New York, NY: Free Press.

Ellison, C. G., Henderson, A. K., Glenn, N. D., & Harkrider, K. E. (2011). Sanctification, stress, and marital quality. *Family Relations, 60*(4), 404–420. doi:10.1 111/j.1741–3729.2011.00658.x

Exline, J. (in press). Religious and spiritual struggles. In K. I. Pargament, J. Exline, & J. Jones (Eds.), *APA handbook of psychology, religion, and spirituality* (Vol. 1). Washington, DC: APA Press.

Exline, J. J., & Rose, E. (2005). Religious and spiritual struggles. In R. F. Paloutzian, & C. L. Park (Eds.), *Handbook of the psychology of religion and spirituality* (pp. 315–330). New York, NY: Guilford Press.

Ferraro, K. F., & Koch, J. R. (1994). Religion and health among black and white adults: Examining social support and consolation. *Journal for the Scientific Study of Religion, 33*(4), 362. doi:10.2307/1386495

Freud, S. (1961). *The future of an illusion.* New York, NY: Norton. (Original work published 1927)

Gall, T. L. (2000). Integrating religious resources within a general model of stress and coping: Long-term adjustment to breast cancer. *Journal of Religion & Health, 39*(2), 167. Retrieved from http://www.springer.com/public+health/journal/10943

Graham, J., & Haidt, J. (2010). Beyond beliefs: Religions bind individuals into moral communities. *Personality & Social Psychology Review, 14*(1), 140–150. doi:10.1177/1088868309353415

Griffiths, R., Richards, W., McCann, U., & Jesse, R. (2006). Psilocybin can occasion mystical-type experiences having substantial and sustained personal meaning and spiritual significance. *Psychopharmacology, 187*(3), 268–283. doi:10.1007/s00213–006–0457–5

Hall, E. M. L., Oates, K. L. M., Anderson, T. L., & Willingham, M. W. (2012). Calling and conflict: The sanctification of work in working mothers. *Psychology of Religion and Spirituality, 4*(1), 71–83. doi:10.1037/a0023191

Hernandez, K. M., Mahoney, A., & Pargament, K. I. (2011). Sanctification of sexuality: Implications for newlyweds' marital and sexual quality. *Journal of Family Psychology, 25*(5), 775–780. doi:10.1037/a0025103

Herrera, A. P., Lee, J. W., Nanyonjo, R. D., Laufman, L. E., & Torres-Vigil, I. (2009). Religious coping and caregiver well-being in Mexican-American families. *Aging & Mental Health, 13*(1), 84–91. doi:10.1080/13607860802154507

Hook, J. N., Worthington, E. L., Jr., Davis, D. E., Gartner, A. L., Jennings, D. J., II., & Hook, J. P. (2010). Empirically supported religious and spiritual therapies. *Journal of Clinical Psychology, 66*, 46–72.

Ironson, G., & Kremer, H. (2009). Spiritual transformation, psychological well-being, health, and survival in people with HIV. *International Journal of Psychiatry in Medicine, 39*(3). 263–281. doi:10.2190/PM.39.3.d

James, W. (1985). *The varieties of religious experience* (Vol. 13). Cambridge, MA: Harvard University Press.

Kirkpatrick, L. A. (2004). *Attachment, evolution, and the psychology of religion.* New York, NY: Guilford Press.

Koenig, H. G., King, D. E., & Carson, V. B. (2012). *Handbook of religion and health* (2nd ed.). New York, NY: Oxford University Press.

Krumrei, E. J., Mahoney, A., & Pargament, K. I. (2011). Spiritual stress and coping model of divorce: A longitudinal study. *Journal of Family Psychology, 25*(6), 973–985. doi:10.1037/a0025879

MacLean, C. D., Susi, B., Phifer, N., Schultz, L., Bynum, D., Franco, M., . . . Cykert, S. (2003). Patient preference for physician discussion and practice of spirituality. *Journal of General Internal Medicine, 18*(1), 38–43. doi:10.10 46/j.1525–1497.2003.20403.x

Magyar, G. M., Pargament, K. I., & Mahoney, A. (2000, August). Violating the sacred: A study of desecration among college students. *Proceedings of the annual meeting of the American Psychological Association.* Washington, DC: American Psychological Association.

Mahoney, A. (2010). Religion in families, 1999–2009: A relational spirituality framework. *Journal of Marriage & Family, 72*(4), 805–827. doi:10.1111/j.1741–3737.2010.00732.x

Mahoney, A., Carels, R. A., Pargament, K. I., Waccholtz, A. L., Kaplar, L. E., & Frutchey, R. M. (2005). The sanctification of the body and behavioral health patterns of college students. *International Journal for the Psychology of Religion, 15*(3), 221–238. doi:10.1207/s15327582ijpr1503_3

Mahoney, A., Pargament, K. I., Jewell, T., Swank, A. B., Scott, E., Emery, E., & Rye, M. (1999). Marriage and the spiritual realm: The role of proximal and distal religious constructs in marital functioning. *Journal of Family Psychology, 13*(3), 321–338. doi:10.1037/0893–3200.13.3.321

Mattis, J. S., & Grayman-Simpson, N. A. (in press). Faith and the sacred in African American life. In K. Pargament, J. Exline, & J. Jones (Eds.), *APA handbook of psychology, religion, and spirituality* (Vol. 1). Washington, DC: APA Press.

McCullough, M. E. (1999). Research on religion-accommodative counseling: Review and meta-analysis. *Journal of Counseling Psychology, 46*(1), 92. doi:10.1037//002 2–0167.46.1.92

Mohr, S., Borras, L., Rieben, I., Betrisey, C., Gillieron, C., Brandt, P., . . . Huguelet, P. (2010). Evolution of spirituality and religiousness in chronic schizophrenia or schizo-affective disorders: A 3-year follow-up study. *Social Psychiatry & Psychiatric Epidemiology, 45*(11), 1095–1103. doi:10.1007/s00127–009–0151–0

Murray-Swank, A., Mahoney, A., & Pargament, K. I. (2006). Sanctification of parenting: Links to corporal punishment and parental warmth among biblically conservative and liberal mothers. *International Journal for the Psychology of Religion, 16*, 271–287. doi:10.1207/s15327582ijpr1604_3

Murray-Swank, N. A. (2003). *Solace for the soul: An evaluation of a psycho-spiritual intervention for female survivors of sexual abuse.* Unpublished doctoral dissertation, Bowling Green State University, Bowling Green, OH.

Murray-Swank, N., & Pargament, K. I. (2005). God, where are you? Evaluating a spiritually-integrated intervention for sexual abuse. *Mental Health, Religion & Culture, 8*(3), 191–203. doi:10.1080/13694670500138866

Neighbors, H. W., Jackson, J. S., Bowman, P. J., & Gurin, G. (1983). Stress, coping, and Black mental health: Preliminary findings from a national study. *Journal of Prevention in Human Service, 2*(3), 5–29. doi:10.1300/J293v02n03_02

Oemig Dworsky, C. K., Pargament, K. I., Gibbel, M. R., Krumrei, E. J., Faigin, C. A., Haugen, M. R. G., . . . Warner, H. L. (in press). Winding road: Preliminary support for a spiritually integrated intervention addressing college students' spiritual struggles. *Research in the Social Scientific Study of Religion. Psychosomatic Medicine, 57.*

Pargament, K. I. (1997). *The psychology of religion and coping: Theory, research, practice.* New York, NY: Guilford Press.

Pargament, K. I. (1999). The psychology of religion and spirituality? Yes and no. *International Journal for the Psychology of Religion, 9*(1), 3. doi:10.1207/ s15327582ijpr0901_2

Pargament, K. I. (2002). The bitter and the sweet: An evaluation of the costs and benefits of religiousness. *Psychological Inquiry, 13*(3), 168–181. doi:10.1207/ S15327965PLI1303_02

Pargament, K. I. (2006). Spiritual struggle. *Human Development, 27*(3), 5–13.

Pargament, K. I. (2007). *Spiritually integrated psychotherapy: Understanding and addressing the sacred.* New York, NY: Guilford Press.

Pargament, K. I. (2011). Religion and coping: The current state of knowledge. In S. Folkman (Ed.), *The Oxford handbook of stress, health, and coping* (pp. 269–288). New York, NY: Oxford University Press.

Pargament, K. I. (in press). Searching for the sacred: Toward a nonreductionistic theory of spirituality. In K. Pargament, A. Mahoney, & E. Shafranske (Eds.), *APA handbook of psychology, religion, and spirituality* (Vol. 2). Washington, DC: APA Press.

Pargament, K. I., Koenig, H. G., Tarakeshwar, N., & Hahn, J. (2001). Religious struggle as a predictor of mortality among medically ill elderly patients. *Archives of Internal Medicine, 161*(15), 1881. doi:10.1001/archinte.161.15.1881

Pargament, K. I., Koenig, H. G., Tarakeshwar, N., & Hahn, J. (2004). Religious coping methods as predictors of psychological, physical and spiritual outcomes among medically ill elderly patients: A two-year longitudinal study. *Journal of Health Psychology, 9*(6), 713–730. doi:10.1177/1359105304045366

Pargament, K. I., & Mahoney, A. (2005). Theory: "Sacred matters: Sanctification as a vital topic for the psychology of religion." *International Journal for the Psychology of Religion, 15*(3), 179–198. doi:10.1207/s15327582ijpr1503_1

Pargament, K. I., Mahoney, A., Exline, J., Jones, J., & Shafranske, E. (in press). Envisioning an integrative paradigm for the psychology of religion and spirituality: An introduction to the APA handbook of psychology, religion and spirituality. In K. I. Pargament, J. Exline, & J. Jones (Eds), *APA handbook of psychology, religion, and spirituality,* (Vol. 1). Washington, DC: APA Press.

Pargament, K. I., McCarthy, S., Shah, P., Ano, G., Tarakeshwar, N., Wachholtz, A., . . . Duggan, J. (2004). Religion and HIV: A review of the literature and clinical implications. *Southern Medical Journal, 97*(12), 1201–1209. doi:10.1097/01.SMJ.0000146508.14898.E2

Pargament, K. I., Murray-Swank, N., Magyar, G. M., & Ano, G. G. (2005). Spiritual struggle: A phenomenon of interest to psychology and religion. In W. R. Miller & H. D. Delaney (Eds.), *Judeo-christian perspectives on psychology: Human nature, motivation, and change* (pp. 245–268). Washington, DC: American Psychological Association. doi:10.1037/10859–013

Pargament, K. I., Smith, B. W., Koenig, H. G., & Perez, L. (1998). Patterns of positive and negative religious coping with major life stressors. *Journal for the Scientific Study of Religion, 37*(4), 710–724. doi:10.2307/1388152

Persinger, M. A. (1983). Religious and mystical experiences as artifacts of temporal lobe function: A general hypothesis. *Perceptual and Motor Skills, 57*(3f), 1255–1262. doi:10.2466/pms.1983.57.3f.1255

Richards, P. S., Berrett, M. E., Hardman, R. K., & Eggett, D. L. (2006). Comparative efficacy of spirituality, cognitive, and emotional support groups for treating eating disorder inpatients. *Eating Disorders: The Journal of Treatment & Prevention, 14*(5), 401–415. doi:10.1080/10640260600952548

Richards, P. S., Hardman, R. K., & Berrett, M. E. (2000). *Spiritual renewal: A journey of healing and growth.* Orem, UT: Center for Change.

Rose, E. M., Westefeld, J. S., & Ansley, T. N. (2001). Spiritual issues in counseling: Clients' beliefs and preferences. *Journal of Counseling Psychology, 48*(1), 61. doi:10.1037//0022–0167.48.1.61

Ryan, R. M., Rigby, S., & King, K. (1993). Two types of religious internalization and their relations to religious orientations and mental health. *Journal of Personality & Social Psychology, 65*(3), 586–596. doi:10.1037//0022–3514.65.3.586

Smith, T. B., Bartz, J., & Richards, P. S. (2007). Outcomes of religious and spiritual adaptations to psychotherapy: A meta-analytic review. *Psychotherapy Research, 17*(6), 643–655. doi:10.1080/10503300701250347

Stanley, M. A., Bush, A. L., Camp, M. E., Jameson, J. P., Phillips, L. L., Barber, C. R., . . . Cully, J. A. (2011). Older adults' preferences for religion/spirituality in treatment for anxiety and depression. *Aging & Mental Health, 15*(3), 334–343. doi: 10.1080/13607863.2010.519326

Tarakeshwar, N., Pearce, M. J., & Sikkema, K. J. (2005). Development and implementation of a spiritual coping group intervention for adults living with HIV/AIDS: A pilot study. *Mental Health, Religion & Culture, 8*(3), 179–190. doi: 10.1080/13694670500138908

Volling, B. L., Mahoney, A., & Rauer, A. J. (2009). Sanctification of parenting, moral socialization, and young children's conscience development. *Psychology of Religion and Spirituality, 1,* 53–68. doi:10.1037/a0014958

Walker, A. G., Jones, M. N., Wuensch, K. L., Aziz, S., & Cope, J. G. (2008). Sanctifying work: Effects on satisfaction, commitment, and intent to leave. *International Journal for the Psychology of Religion, 18*(2), 132–145. doi:10.1080/105086 10701879480

Weld, C., & Eriksen, K. (2007). Christian clients' preferences regarding prayer as a counseling intervention. *Journal of Psychology & Theology, 35*(4), 328–341. Retrieved from http://journals.biola.edu/jpt/

Zinnbauer, B. J., & Pargament, K. I. (2005). Religiousness and spirituality. In R. F. Paloutzian, & C. L. Park (Eds.), *Handbook of the psychology of religion and spirituality* (pp. 21–42). New York, NY: Guilford Press.

Zinnbauer, B. J., Pargament, K. I., Cole, B., Rye, M. S., Butter, E. M., Belavich, T. G., . . . Kadar, J. L. (1997). Religion and spirituality: Unfuzzying the fuzzy. *Journal for the Scientific Study of Religion, 36*(4), 549–564. doi:10 .2307/1387689

# 13

# Building Wisdom and Character

*Robert J. Sternberg*
Cornell University

I n 2008, the world entered into a recession unequaled since the Great Depression of 1929. Even years later, the recession continues in many countries. While it is technically over in other countries, many of those countries continue to suffer high unemployment, depressed housing markets, and generalized economic hardship. Many people, including economists, once thought that such a recession was no longer even possible. What made the recession particularly odd is that it came after, not before, investment banking started attracting the best and the brightest among the graduates of the top universities in the world. Bankers created dizzyingly complex mathematical formulas that brought them enormous profits and that seemed to have no downside. The top investment banks, at least in the United States, only recruited employees from the top universities in the country. In this way, they hoped to ensure the growth, and at the same time the security, of the world's financial system. How could such smart people have created so much misery for so many people? Even more curiously, how could these smart people have then tried to profit from the misery they created? How can smart people be so stupid? (See Sternberg, 2002, for a book on this topic.)

The idea that smart people can be stupid is echoed throughout the psychological literature. For example, Stanovich (2009) has argued that rational thought is a construct largely distinct from the intelligence measured by conventional standardized tests of intelligence. He has even introduced a concept of *dysrationalia* to characterize the idea that, just as intelligent people can have a reading or mathematical disability, so can they have a disability of rational thought. Hyman (1989) and Shermer (2002) have explored why intelligent people can believe in magical, supernatural, or other phenomena that defy rational explanations of empirical phenomena. Both conclude that being smart actually can be disadvantageous because it can allow a person to construct a rather complexly reasoned interpretation of events that just happens not to be veridical.

In a related fashion, I argue in this chapter that smart people can be so stupid, or to be exact, foolish, because many of them are unwise or lack character and hence ethical reasoning and behavior. Having intelligence is not tantamount to being wise or ethical. The world will be a better place when parents and teachers place more emphasis upon the acquisition of wisdom and the promotion of ethical thinking and action and not just upon the accumulation of knowledge and the production of smart graduates. I first discuss wisdom and then discuss character as manifested in ethical reasoning and behavior.

# Wisdom

I define wisdom as the use of one's skills and knowledge, as mediated by positive ethical values, toward the achievement of a common good through a balance among (a) intrapersonal, (b) interpersonal, and (c) extrapersonal interests, over the (a) short and (b) long terms (Sternberg, 2004; Sternberg, Reznitskaya, & Jarvin, 2007). (For other views of wisdom, see Sternberg & Jordan, 2005.) Positive ethical values are defined here as basic core beliefs and reasoning that help lead one to do what one considers to be the right thing to do in benefit of the common good.

These definitions draw heavily on the idea of *balance:* the balance among multiple interests, immediate and lasting consequences, and environmental responses. What are these different interests and responses? *Intrapersonal interests* affect only the individual. They have to do with one's own sense of identity and may include such things as the desire for self-actualization, popularity, prestige, power, prosperity, or pleasure. *Interpersonal interests* involve other people. They relate not only to one's sense of self but also to desirable relationships with others. *Extrapersonal interests* are those that affect a wider organization, community, country, or environment. In addition to multiple interests, the consequences of each decision are assessed in order to balance short- and long-term objectives.

Importantly, the balance in wisdom does not mean that each interest, consequence, or response is weighted equally. The relative weightings are determined by the extent to which a particular alternative contributes to the achievement of a common good.

Choosing the right balance depends on one's system of ethical values. In fact, *positive ethical values* can, or at least should, lie at the core of wise decision making, and not only in the balance theory described here. According to Csikszentmihalyi and Rathunde (1990, p. 32), "wisdom becomes the best guide for what is the *summum bonum*, or 'supreme good'" (see also Csikszentmihalyi & Nakamura, 2005). Pascual-Leone (1990) also considers "moral feelings and ethical evaluations (right-wrong or bad-good judgments) of motives and possible acts (e.g., morality)" as an important component of wisdom (p. 267; see Sternberg & Stemler, 2004). In this theory, positive ethical values not only establish what constitutes the common good, they also influence the relative weightings of the various interests, conflicting consequences, and alternative responses to environment.

The central place of positive ethical values in wisdom brings up the question of who determines what the right positive ethical values are. We know that people's ethical values differ in different cultures and at different points in history. In fact, our own democratic values dictate that we respect others' differences in deciding what is right or wrong. But certain ethical values seem to transcend cultures and the world's great ethical systems, such as honesty, reciprocity, fairness, and justice. The development and promotion of ethical reasoning are discussed later in this chapter.

When faced with a problem, wise individuals rely on their ethical values and knowledge to help them find a solution that balances conflicting intrapersonal, interpersonal, and extrapersonal interests over short and long terms. This conceptual model of wisdom, however, is not merely an esoteric intellectual exercise. Rather, it is oriented toward *action*. Applying relevant ethical values and knowledge, together with considering multiple interests and consequences, must lead to choosing a particular behavior (Sternberg, Jarvin, & Reznitskaya, 2008; Sternberg et al., 2007). Although this balance theory of wisdom cannot determine a wise answer to any problem, it can help to assess how well a particular solution meets the theory specifications in a given context.

## Measuring Wisdom

My colleagues and I have engaged in two projects that have involved measurement of wisdom: Kaleidoscope (see Sternberg, 2010; Sternberg, Bonney, Goabora, & Merrifield, 2012) and a current project, Panorama.

Kaleidoscope was a project initiated at Tufts University in 2006 for use in undergraduate admissions. It was based on my WICS (*w*isdom, *i*ntelligence, *c*reativity, *s*ynthesized) theory of leadership (Sternberg, 2003, 2007), according to which successful leaders possess the creative skills to formulate a vision, the analytical skills to ascertain the value of that vision, the practical skills to implement the vision and persuade others of its value, and the wisdom-based skills to ensure that the vision helps to attain a common good. Roughly a dozen supplemental questions were placed on the Tufts undergraduate application each year starting in 2006, and applicants optionally could answer one of them. About two thirds of applicants did so. An example of a wisdom-based question is "A high-school curriculum does not always afford much intellectual freedom. Describe one of your unsatisfied intellectual passions. How might you apply this interest to serve the common good and make a difference in society?"

Questions for each of creative, analytical, practical, and wisdom-based thinking were analyzed jointly rather than separately. On the whole, the results showed (a) significantly increased prediction of college grade point average over SATs and high school GPAs, (b) significantly increased prediction as well of extracurricular and leadership activities, (c) reduction in ethnic-group differences as a function of test scores, and (d) increased satisfaction on the part of applicants with the admissions process.

At Oklahoma State University, we have introduced a program called Panorama that is similar to the Kaleidoscope program at Tufts, although geared to a different applicant population. This program was initiated in July 2012 so there are not as yet any data at the time this chapter is being written. Examples in the ethics/wisdom category are:

1. "After submitting a class project, you realize one of your partners committed plagiarism. Your teacher previously announced that if he or she learned that cheating had occurred, all members of the work group would receive an F grade. How would you handle the situation and what would be your ideal outcome?"

2. "Robert Frost is often credited with saying, 'Don't ever take a fence down until you know why it was put up.' To what do you think Frost was referring? Do you agree or disagree with his statement? Why?"

We plan to analyze the data in late 2013 once we have sufficient responses in order to be able to draw inferences with confidence.

## Teaching for Wisdom

Teaching for wisdom not only enhances students' thinking skills; it also helps educators to develop more integrated curriculum units. Integrated units are beneficial because they help students see the bigger picture and understand how literature is related to history, how science and scientific discoveries and facts are embedded in a specific time and place (history), how social science and social policy relates to history and geography, how economics are influenced by philosophical and political beliefs as well as by climate and geography, or how foreign language is inseparable from culture. Even within disciplines, far more integration is needed for students to acquire a complete and complex understanding of a topic.

Why should schools include instruction in wise-thinking skills in their curriculum? Consider four reasons.

First, knowledge is insufficient for wisdom and certainly does not guarantee satisfaction or happiness. Wisdom seems a better vehicle to the attainment of these goals. Second, wisdom provides a mindful and considered way to enter thoughtful and deliberative values into important judgments. One cannot be wise and at the same time impulsive or mindless in one's judgments. Third, wisdom represents an avenue to creating a better, more harmonious world. Dictators such as Adolph Hitler and Joseph Stalin may have been knowledgeable and may even have been good critical thinkers, at least with regard to the maintenance of their own power. Given the definition of wisdom, however, it would be hard to argue they were wise. Fourth and finally, students—who later will become parents and leaders—are always part of a greater community and hence will benefit from learning to judge rightly, soundly, or justly on behalf of their community.

We especially should teach for wisdom because smart people are especially susceptible to foolishness, that is, lack of wisdom. They are especially susceptible to foolishness precisely because they think they are immune from it (Sternberg, 2005). Foolish behavior, I suggest, is due largely, although certainly not exclusively, to six fallacies in thinking. These fallacies resemble those we might associate with adolescent thinking, because they are the kind of thinking often seen in adolescents (Sternberg, 2005).

1. *The unrealistic optimism fallacy.* This fallacy occurs when one believes one is so smart or powerful that it is pointless to worry about the outcomes, and especially the long-term ones, of what one does because everything will come out all right in the end—there is nothing to worry about, given one's brains or power. If one simply acts, the outcome will be fine. Bill Clinton tended to repeat sexual behavior that, first as governor and then as president, was likely to come to a bad end. He seemed not to worry about it.

2. *The egocentrism fallacy.* This fallacy arises when one comes to think that one's own interests are the only ones that are important. One starts to

ignore one's responsibilities to other people or to institutions. Sometimes, people in positions of responsibility may start off with good intentions but then become corrupted by the power they wield and their seeming unaccountability to others for it. John Edwards, for example, seemed to let egocentrism get the better of him when he ran for president at the same time he was having an extramarital affair from which he fathered a child out of wedlock. Newt Gingrich's 2011 primary campaign was so centered around himself and his ideas that eventually it imploded.

3. *The omniscience fallacy.* This fallacy results from having available at one's disposal essentially any knowledge one might want that is, in fact, knowable. With a phone call, a powerful leader can have almost any kind of knowledge made available to him or her. At the same time, people look up to the powerful leader as extremely knowledgeable or even close to all knowing. The powerful leader may then come to believe that he or she really is all knowing. So may his or her staff.

4. *The omnipotence fallacy.* This fallacy results from the extreme power one wields, or believes one wields. The result is overextension, and often, abuse of power. Sometimes, leaders create internal or external enemies in order to demand more power for themselves to deal with the supposed enemies. In Zimbabwe, Robert Mugabe has turned one group against another, with the apparent goal of greatly expanding and maintaining his own power.

5. *The invulnerability fallacy.* This fallacy derives from the presence of the illusion of complete protection, such as might be provided by a large staff. People and especially leaders may seem to have many friends ready to protect them at a moment's notice. The leaders may shield themselves from individuals who are anything less than sycophantic.

6. *The ethical-disengagement fallacy.* This fallacy occurs when one starts to believe that ethics are important for other people but not for oneself (see also Bandura, 1999). Many leaders of countries and corporations alike have seemed to think themselves exempt from the ethical standards to which they hold others. Kim Jong Il and his successor, Kim Jong Un, of North Korea come to mind.

What kinds of evidence suggest that smart people are particularly susceptible to foolishness? The best examples are case studies: Eliot Spitzer, who prosecuted prostitution crimes and then got caught up in one; Bill Clinton, who was a lawyer but most likely perjured himself in his testimony regarding

Monica Lewinsky; Newt Gingrich, who argued for the importance of morality but did not show it in his relationships with his previous wives; Jimmy Swaggart, who preached morality while seeing prostitutes; Bernard Madoff, who arranged very clever ways to steal people's money; and so forth. Each of these individuals, and countless others like them, tried to leverage their intelligence to argue for the importance of ethics while themselves failing to follow the ethical code they preached.

Western education in the past couple of centuries has typically focused on imparting content knowledge and developing cognitive skills in students. Schools promote intelligent—but not necessarily wise—students. These students may have admirable records in their schools and yet make poor judgments in their own lives and in the lives of others. An important goal of educators, I believe, is to help prepare students to lead happy, satisfying, and productive lives. An increasing number of both researchers and policy makers share this belief that schools must foster both the cognitive and the moral development of their students (Reznitskaya & Sternberg, 2004). Leading a successful life inevitably involves the ability to solve difficult and uncertain everyday life problems. The problems people are exposed to vary depending on their environment and the responsibilities they carry, but all people will at one point or another be exposed to situations in which they have to rely on wisdom to make the right decision. We therefore believe that school *should* help enhance these wise thinking skills in students. How can teachers help their students develop all the explicit and implicit insights requisite for the display of wisdom?

The goal of teaching for wisdom can be achieved by providing students with educational contexts where students can formulate their own understanding of what constitutes wise thinking. In other words, teaching for wisdom is not accomplished through a didactic method of imparting information about wisdom and subsequently assessing students with multiple-choice questions. Instead, students need to actively experience various cognitive and affective processes that underlie wise decision making. In other words, teachers can provide scaffolding for the development of wisdom and case studies to help students develop wisdom, but a teacher cannot teach particular courses of actions, or give students a list of do's and don'ts, regardless of circumstances.

What are the processes underlying wise thinking that students have to acquire, and how can they be introduced into the classroom? Sternberg (2001) outlined 16 pedagogical principles and 6 procedures derived from the theory of wisdom, described in Figures 13.1 and 13.2. The fundamental idea behind all these educational guidelines is that the instructor teaches children not *what* to think but, rather, *how* to think.

Figure 13.1   Principles of Teaching for Wisdom

| Principles 1–8 | | Principles 9–16 | |
|---|---|---|---|
| 1. | Explore with students the notion that conventional abilities and achievements are not enough for a satisfying life. Many people become trapped in their lives and, despite feeling conventionally successful, feel that their lives lack fulfillment. Fulfillment is not an alternative to success, but rather, is an aspect of it that, for most people, goes beyond money, promotions, large houses, and so forth. | 9. | Wise judgments are dependent in part on selecting among adaptation to, shaping of, and selection of environmental responses. |
| 2. | Demonstrate how wisdom is critical for a satisfying life. In the long run, wise decisions benefit people in ways that foolish decisions never do. | 10. | Encourage students to form, critique, and integrate their own ethical values in their thinking. |
| 3. | Teach students the usefulness of interdependence—a rising tide raises all ships; a falling tide can sink them. | 11. | Encourage students to think dialectically, realizing that both questions and their answers evolve over time, and that the answer to an important life question can differ at different times in one's life (such as whether to go to college). |
| 4. | Role model wisdom because what you do is more important than what you say. Wisdom is action-dependent and wise actions need to be demonstrated. | 12. | Show students the importance of dialogical thinking, whereby they understand interests and ideas from multiple points of view. |
| 5. | Have students read about wise judgments and decision making so that students understand that such means of judging and decision making exist. | 13. | Teach students to search for and then try to reach the common good—a good where everyone wins and not only those with whom one identifies. |
| 6. | Help students to learn to recognize their own interests, those of other people, and those of institutions. | 14. | Encourage and reward wisdom. |
| 7. | Help students learn to balance their own interests, those of other people, and those of institutions. | 15. | Teach students to monitor events in their lives and their own thought processes about these events. One way to learn to recognize others' interests is to begin to identify your own. |
| 8. | Teach students that the means by which the end is obtained matters, not just the end. | 16. | Help students understand the importance of inoculating oneself against the pressures of unbalanced self-interest and small-group interest. |

*Source:* Why Schools Should Teach for Wisdom: The Balance Theory of Wisdom in Educational Settings, Robert J. Sternberg, *Educational Psychologist*, 36 (4), pp. 227-45 c 2001, Taylor and Francis. Reprinted by permission of the publisher (Taylor & Francis Ltd, http://www.tandf.co.uk/journals).

## Figure 13.2 Procedures of Teaching for Wisdom

| | Procedures |
|---|---|
| 1 | Encourage students to read classic works of literature and philosophy to learn and reflect on the wisdom of the sages. |
| 2 | Engage students in class discussions, projects, and essays that encourage them to discuss the lessons they have learned from these works and how they can be applied to their own lives and the lives of others. A particular emphasis should be placed on dialogical (see Principle 12) and dialectical (see Principle 11) thinking. |
| 3 | Encourage students to study not only truth but also ethical values, as developed during their reflective thinking. |
| 4 | Place an increased emphasis on critical, creative, and practical thinking in the service of good ends that benefit the common good. |
| 5 | Encourage students to think about how almost *any* topic they study might be used for better or for worse ends, and about how important that final end is. |
| 6 | Remember that a teacher is a role model! To role model wisdom, the teacher should adopt a Socratic approach to teaching and invite students to play a more active role in constructing learning—from their own point of view and from that of others. |

*Source:* Why Schools Should Teach for Wisdom: The Balance Theory of Wisdom in Educational Settings, Robert J. Sternberg. *Educational Psychologist*, 36 (4), pp. 227-45 c 2001, Taylor and Francis. Reprinted by permission of the publisher (Taylor & Francis Ltd, http://www.tandf.co.uk/journals).

Let us review the six procedures for teaching for wisdom presented in Figure 13.2 in more detail.

## Procedure 1: Reflection

Whenever possible, encourage students to engage in *reflective thinking*, to reflect on their own functioning to increase their metacognition (Flavell, 1987), that is, their awareness of their cognitions, emotions, and beliefs. The process of making a wise decision is strategic and goal oriented and therefore requires an ongoing monitoring of selected strategies, as well as an ability to modify less successful strategies to better fit the situational demands. Teachers can help students to practice reflective thinking by designing instructional activities that allow students to explore and shape their own ethical values. Also, students can be explicitly instructed in useful metacognitive strategies such as self-questioning or the use of self-monitoring checklists.

## Procedure 2: Project-Based Learning

Engage students in class discussions, projects, and essays that encourage them to discuss the lessons they have learned from the literary and philosophical works they've read and how these lessons can be applied to their own lives and the lives of others. A history curriculum, for example, should make salient the relationships between history and personally relevant everyday experiences.

Teachers should engage students in dialogical and dialectical thinking, in addition to the reflective thinking described earlier. What is dialogical thinking (Principle 12)? When one is faced with a complex problem involving several points of view, it is often necessary to take into account different frames of reference and various perspectives to find the best possible solution. What may at first appear as the right answer may turn out to be the wrong choice when the long term is considered or when the interests of the community as a whole are taken into account. In dialogical thinking, one uses multiple frames of reference to generate and deliberate about various perspectives on the issue at hand (Kuhn, Shaw, & Felton, 1997; Reznitskaya et al., 2001).

What is dialectical thinking (Principle 11)? Whereas dialogical thinking involves the consideration and weighing of multiple points of view, *dialectical thinking* emphasizes the consideration and *integration* of two opposing perspectives. The first perspective considered is the *thesis*. For example, one can be a radical pacifist and opposed to any military presence or intervention, whatever the circumstances. A second perspective, an *antithesis* (a negation of the original statement) is then considered. For example, one can argue that a people can only live freely and in peace if their borders are protected by armed forces. Finally, a *synthesis* or reconciliation of the two seemingly opposing statements is developed. For example, one might decide that borders under dispute should be protected by a third party, such as an international army, rather than having the opposing countries measure their military strength against each other. The process does not stop when the two opposing views are reconciled; on the contrary, each synthesis becomes a new thesis, which can then be integrated in a new round of dialectical thinking. In the classroom, dialectical thinking can be encouraged through opportunities to study different sources, enabling students to build their own knowledge, or through writing assignments that explicitly call for a thesis, antithesis, and synthesis. Empirical studies have investigated the impact of developing such a fluid and dynamic concept of knowledge, where the source of knowledge is not the authority (the teacher or the book), but rather, the student. Such conceptions of knowledge have been shown to relate to active engagement in learning (e.g., McDevitt, 1990), persistence in performing a task (e.g., Dweck & Leggett, 1988), and deeper comprehension and integration of the material taught (e.g., Qian & Alvermann, 2000; Songer & Linn, 1991).

## Procedure 3: Ethical Values

Encourage students to study not only truth but also ethical values, as developed during their reflective thinking. The problems of major corporate fiascos such as Enron, WorldCom, Global Crossing, and more recently, a series of failed banks beginning with Bear Stearns and continuing through Lehman Brothers and other major banks, began with the rejection of positive ethical values.

## Procedure 4: Flexible Thinking

Place an increased emphasis on critical, creative, and practical thinking in the service of good ends that benefit the common good. In the typical classroom, teachers encourage critical thinking skills in their students. Some teachers also aim to develop creative and practical thinking skills (Sternberg & Grigorenko, 2007; Sternberg, Jarvin, & Grigorenko, 2009) by engaging students in activities that lead them to go beyond the content they have studied (creative thinking) to apply this knowledge to their environment (practical thinking). To enhance wise thinking, however, students should also be encouraged to consider the outcome of their thinking and to keep in mind that the best solution is not the one that benefits only the individual doing the thinking but rather the one that helps others as well. The common good should be the guiding principle in choosing between different possible solutions.

## Procedure 5: Thinking About Ends

Encourage students to think about how almost *any* topic they study might be used for better or worse ends and about how important that final end is. As described under Procedure 4, students should be encouraged to seek different solutions and to choose the one that benefits the common good rather than the individual. They should also be brought to realize that, just as there are different solutions benefiting different people, a given concept or point of knowledge can be used to a good or poor end. A stereotypical example is that the knowledge of nuclear physics can be applied to constructing bombs or to develop sources of energy. The ends to which one chooses to apply one's knowledge matter greatly.

## Procedure 6: Role Modeling

A teacher is a role model. To role model wisdom, the teacher adopts a Socratic approach to teaching and invites students to play a more active role in constructing learning—from their own point of view and from that of others. Wise thinking is not a set of rules or decisions that the teacher can outline for students to copy down; it is a type of thinking that the students themselves need to adopt and master. The most effective way to encourage wise thinking skills is not through memory drills but through student participation and teacher modeling. For example, a teacher can capitalize on a negative event, such as two students getting into a fight, as a way to demonstrate how one can approach a similar situation in a more constructive way. The teacher can model wise thinking by saying: "When I get into situations like this, I try to see the dispute from the perspective of the other person and think about whether my own behavior contributed to the situation. Was there anything I could have done differently to prevent this confrontation? Is there a solution to our disagreement that is acceptable to both of us?" Also, teachers should not miss the opportunity to recognize and praise good judgments made by students, such as when they show consideration for others and their ideas, or when they offer a solution that benefits the class as a whole rather than themselves as individuals.

In science teaching, dialectical thinking can be applied to illustrate to students the notion that scientific facts are not eternal or immutable but rather the state of affairs as we perceive them at this very specific point in time. Indeed, science often is presented as though it represents the end of a process of evolution of thought, rather than one of many midpoints (Sternberg, 1998). Students could scarcely realize from this kind of teaching that the paradigms of today, and thus the theories and findings that emanate from them, will eventually be superseded, much as the paradigms, theories, and findings of yesterday were replaced by those of today. Further, students must learn that, contrary to the way many textbooks are written, the classical scientific method is an ideal rather than a reality, and that scientists are as susceptible to fads as is anyone else. How many scientists in his time considered as scientific evidence the data presented by Galileo Galilei to demonstrate that the Earth revolves around the Sun and not vice versa?

Wise thinking skills can also be applied in the literature classroom. Literature is often taught in terms of the standards and context of the contemporary American scene. Characters often are judged in terms of our contemporary standards rather than in terms of the standards of the time and place in which the events took place. Imagine if students were routinely encouraged to approach the study of literary works with a dialogical mindset, studying literature in the context of history. Censorship and the banning of books often reflect the application of certain contemporary standards to literature, standards of which an author from the past never could have been aware.

The foreign language classroom is another terrain for enhancing students' wise thinking skills. Foreign languages should be taught in the cultural context in which they are embedded, requiring students to engage in reflective and dialogical thinking to truly grasp the foreign culture and to position themselves and their experiences in relation to this culture. It tends to be more common in Europe to speak one or several languages beyond one's mother tongue. Perhaps American students have so much more difficulty learning foreign languages than do children in much of Europe not because they lack the ability but because they lack the motivation and the exposure. An American student would probably much more readily see the need to learn a foreign language if each of the 50 states spoke a different language, much like the member states of the European Union do. We would also do our students a service by teaching them to understand other cultures rather than just to expect people from other cultures to understand them. Learning the language of a culture is a key to understanding it, and the two cannot be taught separately, or by viewing culture as an appendix to language rather than the context in which it is deeply rooted.

Although we have developed our own teaching for wisdom program, as noted earlier (Sternberg et al., 2008; Sternberg et al., 2007), by far the most comprehensively developed and tested program devoted to teaching wise thinking is Philosophy for Children by the late Matthew Lipman (1985). This program, consisting of books for children ranging from elementary-school to high-school age, presents stories of children (like the readers) who in their daily lives encounter philosophical problems, many of them requiring wise decisions. Large numbers of studies (see "Research on Cognitive Skills," n.d.) have supported the usefulness of the program in improving children's philosophical reasoning and wise thinking.

Underlying all wise thinking is ethical reasoning. How do people reason ethically?

# Teaching for Character: Ethical Reasoning

Drawing in part upon the Latané and Darley (1970) model of bystander intervention, I have constructed a model of ethical behavior that would seem to apply to a variety of ethical problems. The model specifies the specific skills students need to reason and then behave ethically. On this view, ethical behavior is at the heart of good character.

The basic premise of the model is that ethical behavior is far harder to display than one would expect simply on the basis of what we learn from our parents, from school, and from our religious training (Sternberg, 2009). To intervene in an ethically challenging situation, individuals must go through a series of steps, and unless all of the steps are completed, the individuals are not likely to behave in an ethical way, regardless of the amount of training they have received in ethics, and regardless of their levels of other types of skills. The example I will draw on most is genocides, such as in Rwanda and Darfur, where there is a potential for outside intervention, but the intervention in fact never happens or happens only to a minor extent.

According to the proposed model, enacting ethical behavior is much harder than it would appear to be because it involves multiple, largely sequential, steps, summarized in Figure 13.3. The model is one of ethical reasoning as it leads to action. It does not, however, ensure that an individual's reasoning will lead to any one uniquely ethical decision. Rather, it ensures that an individual will go through a comprehensive series of steps that will permit him or her to reason through the problem in ethical terms, regardless of what he or she ultimately decides to do. For example, if a student sees another student cheat, and wants to act ethically, there are different solutions he or she could come to: talk to the student about cheating, talk to a professor about the student's cheating, suggest to a group of friends including the student that they all agree not to cheat, and so on. What these solutions might have in common is that they are based on a somewhat comprehensive analysis of the ethical parameters of the situation.

Consider each step in turn:

## 1. Recognize That There Is an Event to Which to React

In cases where there has been an ethical transgression, the transgressors often go out of their way to hide that there is even an event to which to react. For example, many countries hide the deplorable condition of their political prisoners. The Nazis hid the existence of death camps and referred to Jews, Roma, and other peoples merely as being "resettled." The Rwandan government tried to cover up the massacre of the Tutsis and also of those Hutus who were perceived as sympathetic to the Tutsis. The goal of the transgressors is to obscure the fact that anything is going on that is even worth anyone's attention. One has to recognize that the situation as described by the transgressor may be different from the actual situation. Put

### Figure 13.3   Steps in Model of Ethical Reasoning

| |
|---|
| 1. Recognize that there is an event to which to react |
| 2. Define the event as having an ethical dimension |
| 3. Decide that the ethical dimension is of sufficient significance to merit an ethics-guided response |
| 4. Take responsibility for generating an ethical solution to the problem |
| 5. Figure out what abstract ethical rule(s) might apply to the problem |
| 6. Decide how these abstract ethical rules actually apply to the problem so as to suggest a concrete solution |
| 7. Prepare for possible repercussions of having acted in what one considers an ethical manner |
| 8. Act |

Source: Sternberg, R. J. (2009). A new model for teaching ethical behavior. *Chronicle of Higher Education* 55(33), B14–B15.

another way, one has to be creative in contemplating possibilities other than the one presented by those who wish to cover up their transgressions.

When people hear their political, educational, or religious leaders talk, they may not believe there is any reason to question what they hear. After all, they are listening to authority figures. In this way, leaders, and especially cynical and corrupt leaders, may lead their followers to accept corruption and even disappearances as nonevents.

## 2. Define the Event as Having an Ethical Dimension

Given that one acknowledges that there is an event to which to pay attention, one still needs to define it as having an ethical dimension. Given that perpetrators will go out of their way to define the situation otherwise—as a nonevent, a civil war, an internal conflict that is no one else's business, and so on—one must actually redefine the situation to realize that an ethical component is involved.

In the case of the Nazi genocide, the campaign against Jews was defined as a justified campaign against an internal enemy bent upon subversion of the state (Sternberg & Sternberg, 2008). It was of course not defined as genocide. To this day, the Turkish government defines the Armenian genocide as a conflict for which both sides must share the blame (Sternberg & Sternberg, 2008). And in Rwanda, the government defined the genocide as a fight against invading aggressors who came from outside the country and did not belong there in the first place.

## 3. Decide That the Ethical Dimension Is of Sufficient Significance to Merit an Ethics-Guided Response

If one observes a driver going one mile per hour over the speed limit on a highway, one is unlikely to become perturbed about the unethical behavior of the driver, especially if the driver is oneself. A genocide is a far cry from driving one mile per hour over the speed limit. And yet, if one is being told by cynical, dishonest leaders that the events that are transpiring are the unfortunate kinds of events that happen in all countries—didn't America have its own Civil War?—then it may not occur to people that the event is much more serious than its perpetrators are alleging it to be.

## 4. Take Responsibility for Generating an Ethical Solution to the Problem

People may allow leaders to commit wretched acts, including genocide, because they figure it is the leaders' responsibility to determine the ethical dimensions of their actions. Isn't that why they are leaders in the first place? Or people may assume that the leaders, especially if they are religious leaders, are in a uniquely good position to determine what is ethical. If a religious leader encourages someone to become a suicide bomber or to commit genocide, that person may feel that being such a bomber must be ethical. Why else would a religious leader have suggested it?

## 5. Figure Out What Abstract Ethical Rule(s) Might Apply to the Problem

Most of us have learned, in one way or another, ethical rules that we are supposed to apply to our lives. For example, we are supposed to be honest. But who among us can say he or she has not lied at some time, perhaps with the excuse that he or she was protecting someone else's feelings? When we use such an excuse, we insulate ourselves from the effects of our behavior. Perhaps, we can argue, the principle that we should not hurt someone else's feelings takes precedence over not lying. Of course, as the lies grow larger, we can continue to use the same excuse.

When leaders encourage genocide, they clearly violate one of the Ten Commandments, namely, "Thou shalt not murder." This is why the killings, to the extent they are known, are posed by cynical leaders as "justifiable executions" rather than as murders. The individual must analyze the situation carefully to realize whether the term *murder* applies.

## 6. Decide How These Abstract Ethical Rules Actually Apply to the Problem so as to Suggest a Concrete Solution

This kind of translation is, I believe, nontrivial. In our work on practical intelligence, some of which was summarized in Sternberg et al. (2000), we found that there is, at best, a modest correlation between the more academic and abstract aspects of intelligence and its more practical and concrete aspects. Both aspects, though, predicted behavior in everyday life. People may have skills that shine brightly in a classroom, but that they are unable to translate into real-world consequential behavior.

## 7. Prepare for Possible Repercussions of Having Acted in What One Considers an Ethical Manner

When Harry Markopolos (2011) pointed out to regulators that Bernard Madoff's investment returns had to be fraudulent, no one wanted to listen. It was Markopolos who was branded as a problem, not Madoff. In general, when people blow the whistle, they need to be prepared for their bona fides to be questioned, not necessarily those of the person on whom they blew the whistle (as Marianne Gingrich discovered when she was branded a liar by her former husband, upon her revelation that her ex-husband wanted an open marriage when she learned that he was having an affair, later resulting in divorce).

People think creatively when they imagine the possible repercussions of acting ethically—will they lose their friends, will they lose their job, will they lose their reputation? During the Enron scandal, whistleblower Sherron Watkins lost all three. Relatedly, when reports first came in of Nazi genocide, there was a general reaction of disbelief—how could such atrocities possibly be happening? Whistleblowers need to imagine all the things that could go wrong, but they also need to imagine what could go right and how they can maximize the chances of things going right. Such imagination requires creative thinking.

## 8. Act

In ethical reasoning, there may be a large gap between thought and action. Both often involve defying the crowd, and hence, even people who believe a certain course of action to be correct may not follow through on it.

In the Latané and Darley (1970) work, the more bystanders there were, the less likely an individual was to take action to intervene. Why? Because people figured that, if something was really wrong, then someone would have taken responsibility. You are better off having a breakdown on a somewhat lonely country road than on a busy highway, because a driver passing by on the country road may feel that he or she is your only hope.

Sometimes, the problem is not that other people seem oblivious to the ethical implications of the situation, but that they actively encourage you to behave in ways you define as unethical. In the Rwandan genocides, Hutus were encouraged to hate Tutsis and to kill them, even if they were within their own family (see discussion in Sternberg & Sternberg, 2008). Those who were not willing to participate in the massacres risked becoming victims themselves (Gourevitch, 1998). The same applied in Hitler's Germany. Those who tried to save Jews from concentration camps themselves risked going to such camps (Totten, Parsons, & Charny, 2004). It is easier to follow the crowd than to act creatively or, in many instances, ethically. And that is why corruption is so common throughout the world. Even when people know of it, they often re-elect corrupt leaders, allowing the corruption to persist.

It might be argued, as one prepublication reviewer of this chapter did, that even individuals such as Hitler or Stalin or Osama bin Laden might have believed, according to their own system of ethics, that what they did was ethical. On this view, ethics is in the mind of the beholder. However, according to the definition of wisdom presented earlier in the chapter, wisdom is the use of cognitive and other skills in order to promote a common good as mediated by positive ethical principles. What Hitler, Stalin, and bin Laden did fails this test for wise behavior as mediated by positive ethical principles, because their actions did not help to achieve a common good. It is unclear that what they did helped to achieve a good for anyone. But it certainly did not help to achieve a good for those people who were tortured and murdered. The path to wisdom is not through moral relativism.

## Conclusions

In conclusion, schools cannot teach wisdom or ethics, but they can teach for wisdom and ethics. The balance theory provides one of many bases by which teachers can teach for wisdom. The important goal is to teach knowledge not for its own sake but for its use to promote the common good by balancing intrapersonal, interpersonal, and extrapersonal interests over the short and long terms through the mediation of positive ethical values. Individual and group happiness depends far more on the acquisition of wisdom than on the accumulation of knowledge. Knowledge can destroy the world, as the sophistication of terrorist bombs and attacks has shown us; wisdom can only make it better. And ethical behavior is the *sine qua non* for the execution of wise ideas.

What the field of wisdom and ethics needs most, I believe, is material that enhances our teaching and assessment of wisdom and ethics. When I was provost at Oklahoma State University, I tried to realize these two goals in two ways.

The first was through the Panorama Project, described earlier. Because I left Oklahoma State before data were collected, I cannot say what the results were. The second was through the creation of an ethical leadership track. This track was to involve infusing case studies in ethics into curriculum materials across the entire span of subjects taught at Oklahoma State. Students who chose this track would elect specially designated courses with an ethical leadership component, as well as involving themselves in service-learning and student-affairs activities designed to promote wise and ethical thinking. Students who stayed with the program would receive a designation on their transcripts indicating their participation in the track. We would then assess wise and ethical thinking in those who did and did not elect the track to evaluate its effectiveness.

Our society does not lack smart leaders. If we look at recent presidents and presidential candidates, for example—Bill Clinton, John Kerry, George H. W. Bush, George W. Bush, Barack Obama, Mitt Romney, to name just a few—we have lots of top-level politicians with Harvard and Yale degrees. Smart and knowledgeable leaders have made their way into leadership positions throughout the society. But our society lacks wise and ethical leaders. If you try to think of a few notably wise and ethical leaders, you may not find it easy to do. As a society, we have a responsibility to change this situation and educate our young people to be wise and ethical as well as knowledgeable and smart.

# References

Bandura, A. (1999). Moral disengagement in the perpetration of inhumanities. *Personality and Social Psychology Review, 3*, 193–209.

Csikszentmihalyi, M., & Nakamura, J. (2005). The role of emotions in the development of wisdom. In R.J. Sternberg & J. Jordan (Ed.), *A handbook of wisdom: Psychological perspectives* (pp. 220–242). New York, NY: Cambridge University Press.

Csikszentmihalyi, M., & Rathunde, K. (1990). The psychology of wisdom: An evolutionary interpretation. In R. J. Sternberg (Ed.), *Wisdom: Its nature, origins, and development* (pp. 25–51). New York, NY: Cambridge University Press.

Dweck, C. S., & Leggett, E. L. (1988). A social–cognitive approach to motivation and personality. *Psychological Review, 95*, 256–273.

Flavell, J. H. (1987). Speculations about the nature and development of metacognition. In F. E. Wienert & R. H. Kluwe (Eds.), *Metacognition, motivation, and understanding* (pp. 21–29). Hillsdale, NJ: Lawrence Erlbaum.

Gourevitch, P. (1998). *We wish to inform you that tomorrow we will be killed with our families: Stories from Rwanda.* New York, NY: Farrar, Straus & Giroux.

Hyman, R. (1989). *The elusive quarry: A scientific appraisal of psychical research.* Amherst, NY: Prometheus Books.

Kuhn, D., Shaw, V., & Felton, M. (1997). Effects of dyadic interaction on argumentative reasoning. *Cognition and Instruction, 15*, 287–315.

Latané, B., & Darley, J. (1970). *The unresponsive bystander: Why doesn't he help?* Englewood Cliffs, NJ: Prentice Hall.

Lipman, M. (1985). *Harry Stottlemeier's discovery.* Montclair, NJ: First Mountain Foundation.

Markopolos, H. (2011). *No one would listen: A true financial thriller.* New York, NY: Wiley.

McDevitt, T. M. (1990). Mothers' and children's beliefs about listening. *Child Study Journal, 20*, 105–128.

Pascual-Leone, J. (1990). An essay on wisdom: Toward organismic processes that make it possible. In R. J. Sternberg (Ed.), *Wisdom: Its nature, origins, and development* (pp. 244–278). New York, NY: Cambridge University Press.

Qian, G., & Alvermann, D. E. (2000). Relationship between epistemological beliefs and conceptual change learning. *Reading & Writing Quarterly, 16*, 59–74.

Research on cognitive skills. (n.d.). Retrieved from http://www.montclair.edu/cehs/academics/centers-and-institutes/iapc/research/cognitive-skills/

Reznitskaya, A., Anderson, R. C., McNurlen, B., Nguyen-Jahiel, K., Archodidou, A., & Kim, S. (2001). Influence of oral discussion on written argument. *Discourse Processes, 32*, 155–175.

Reznitskaya, A., & Sternberg, R. J. (2004). Teaching students to make wise judgments: The "teaching for wisdom" program. In P. A. Linley & S. Joseph (Eds.), *Positive psychology in practice* (pp. 181–196). New York, NY: Wiley.

Shermer, M. (2002). *Why people believe weird things.* New York, NY: Holt.

Songer, N. B., & Linn, M. C. (1991). How do views of science influence knowledge integration. *Journal of Research in Science Teaching, 28*, 761–784.

Stanovich, K. E. (2009). *What intelligence tests miss: The psychology of rational thought.* New Haven, CT: Yale University Press.

Sternberg, R. J. (1998). A balance theory of wisdom. *Review of General Psychology, 2*, 347–365

Sternberg, R. J. (2001). Why schools should teach for wisdom: The balance theory of wisdom in educational settings. *Educational Psychologist, 36*, 227–245.

Sternberg, R. J. (Ed.). (2002). *Why smart people can be so stupid.* New Haven, CT: Yale University Press.

Sternberg, R. J. (2003). *Wisdom, intelligence, and creativity synthesized.* New York, NY: Cambridge University Press.

Sternberg, R. J. (2004). Teaching for wisdom: What matters is not what students know, but how they use it. In D. R. Walling (Ed.), *Public education, democracy, and the common good* (pp. 121–132). Bloomington, IN: Phi Delta Kappan.

Sternberg, R. J. (2005). Foolishness. In R. J. Sternberg & J. Jordan (Eds.), *Handbook of wisdom: Psychological perspectives* (pp. 331–352). New York, NY: Cambridge University Press.

Sternberg, R. J. (2007). A systems model of leadership: WICS. *American Psychologist, 62*(1), 34–42.

Sternberg, R. J. (2009). Reflections on ethical leadership. In D. Ambrose & T. Cross (Eds.), *Morality, ethics, and gifted minds* (pp. 19–28). New York, NY: Springer.

Sternberg, R. J. (2010). *College admissions for the 21st century.* Cambridge, MA: Harvard University Press.

Sternberg, R. J., Bonney, C. R., Gabora, L, & Merrifield, M. (2012). WICS: A model for college and university admissions. *Educational Psychologist, 47*(1), 30–41.

Sternberg, R. J., Forsythe, G. B., Hedlund, J., Horvath, J., Snook, S., Williams, W. M., . . . Grigorenko, E. L. (2000). *Practical intelligence in everyday life.* New York, NY: Cambridge University Press.

Sternberg, R. J., & Grigorenko, E. L. (2007). *Teaching for successful intelligence* (2nd ed.). Thousand Oaks, CA: Corwin.

Sternberg, R. J., Jarvin, L., & Grigorenko, E. L. (2009). *Teaching for wisdom, intelligence, creativity, and success.* Thousand Oaks, CA: Corwin.

Sternberg, R. J., Jarvin, L., & Reznitskaya, A. (2008). Teaching of wisdom through history: Infusing wise thinking skills in the school curriculum. In M. Ferrari & G. Potworowski (Eds.), *Teaching for wisdom* (pp. 37–57). New York, NY: Springer.

Sternberg, R. J., & Jordan, J. (2005). *Handbook of wisdom: Psychological perspectives.* New York, NY: Cambridge University Press.

Sternberg, R. J., Reznitskaya, A., & Jarvin, L. (2007). Teaching for wisdom: What matters is not just what students know, but how they use it. *London Review of Education, 5*(2), 143–158.

Sternberg, R. J., & Stemler, S. E. (2004). Wisdom as a moral virtue. In T. A. Thorkildsen & H. J. Walberg (Eds.), *Nurturing morality* (pp. 187–197). New York, NY: Kluwer Academic/Plenum.

Sternberg, R. J., & Sternberg, K. (2008). *The nature of hate.* New York, NY: Cambridge University Press.

Totten, S., Parsons, W. S., & Charny, I. W. (Eds.). (2004). *Century of genocide: Critical essays and eyewitness accounts.* New York, NY: Routledge.

# PART V

## Enriching Relationships, Managing Money

# 14

# Making Marriage (and Other Relationships) Work

*Matthew D. Johnson*

Binghamton University

Relationships matter. Of all of the relationships we have, our intimate relationships—close relationships in which there is the potential for sex—matter the most. If I ask you how satisfied you are with your life over-all, your answer will probably be correlated with the satisfaction (or lack thereof) you feel with your intimate relationship more than any other aspect of your life (Heller, Watson, & Ilies, 2004). In fact, the association between the quality of our intimate relationships and our subjective well-being has been replicated many times (e.g., Proulx, Helms, & Buehler, 2007). It is not just the quality of intimate relationships that matters; simply being married is associated with greater levels of life satisfaction compared with people who are cohabiting, single, separated, divorced, or widowed (Diener, Suh, Lucas, & Smith, 1999). Thus, the types and qualities of our intimate relationships appear to go a long way in determining the quality of our lives.

Beyond global measures like life satisfaction, relationship quality and status (e.g., whether one is single, cohabiting, married, divorced) are associated with nearly every aspect of our lives. Relationship dysfunction is the primary reason people experience acute emotional distress in the United States (Swindle, Heller, Pescosolido, & Kikuzawa, 2000; Veroff, Kulka, &

Douvan, 1981). It is associated with suicide (Langhinrichsen-Rohling, Snarr, Slep, Heyman, & Foran, 2011; Stander, Hilton, Kennedy, & Robbins, 2004), increases in substance abuse (Overbeek et al., 2006), and nearly all adult mental illnesses (Whisman, 2007). Beyond mental health, the quality of intimate relationships is associated with cardiovascular functioning (e.g., Nealey-Moore, Smith, Uchino, Hawkins, & Olson-Cerny, 2007), recovery time from cancer (e.g., Datta, Neville, Kawachi, Datta, & Earle, 2009; Yang & Schuler, 2009), and immunity to pathogens (e.g., Cohen et al., 1998; Dopp, Miller, Myers, & Fahey, 2000; Kiecolt-Glaser et al., 1993). In fact, adults who are married live longer than nonmarried adults (Murphy, Xu, & Kochanek, 2013), and the better the marriage the longer the married people will live (e.g., Coyne et al., 2001; Gallo, Troxel, Matthews, & Kuller, 2003).

Intimate relationships matter even beyond the health and well-being of those in them. Children raised in the home of married parents are less likely to experience academic or emotional problems compared with the children of cohabiting parents (e.g., Brown, 2000). Still, parents' relationship quality exerts an even greater impact on children than does their marital status. In particular, the toll of parental conflict on children includes behavioral problems (e.g., Goeke-Morey, Papp, & Cummings, 2013), sleep disturbance (e.g., El-Sheikh, Buckhalt, Keller, Cummings, & Acebo, 2007), compromised health (e.g., Troxel & Matthews, 2004), and hastened pubertal onset (Belsky et al., 2007). Although divorce may have beneficial effects on children if it reduces the conflict between the parents (e.g., Amato, Loomis, & Booth, 1995), it is clear that parents' relationship quality influences children (for reviews, see Davies & Cummings, 1994; Grych & Fincham, 1990).

Finally, intimate relationships have societal implications. Even though our relationships seem like a private matter, there is a public interest in the well-being of intimate relationships. One indication of the societal implications of marriage is that being married is associated with greater wealth (e.g., Chang & Lui, 2010). In fact, this association is so strong that it has led to speculation that the poor quality of intimate relationships could explain poverty (e.g., Schneider, 2011; Wilson, 2009). Yet even beyond the financial implications of marriage and marital quality, society has an interest in promoting marriage because of the stability that it brings. For example, marital stability leads to lower absenteeism (e.g., Forthofer, Markman, Cox, Stanley, & Kessler, 1996), lower rates of alcohol and other drug abuse (e.g., Fleming, White, & Catalano, 2010), lower rates of criminal behavior (e.g., Laub, Nagin, & Sampson, 1998), and greater civic participation (e.g., Kern, 2010). In summary, the cumulative benefits of well-functioning relationships have led societies throughout history to promote and encourage them.

Given that intimate relationships are a fundamental aspect of the infrastructure of our lives, the question then becomes how can we make them work better? In this chapter, I lay out a strategy for making intimate relationships healthier and happier. Although I focus on intimate relationships, like marriage, much of what I discuss can be applied to other relationships, including those with coworkers, children, other family members, friends, and associates.

## The *Intra*personal and *Inter*personal Aspects of Intimate Relationships

In relationships, there are two options: thinking and acting. How people think about and act in their relationships impacts how well their relationships function and how satisfying they are. Of course, thinking and acting are two expansive concepts. In this chapter, I focus on thoughts and actions that predict relationship satisfaction and, therefore, maintain or facilitate intimacy. Another way to conceptualize thoughts and actions in relationships is to consider thoughts as *intra*personal and actions as *inter*personal. Indeed, it is possible to improve relationships by simply thinking about them differently. Yet in my experience, most people skip this step and instead focus either on their communication with their partner or on how their partner should change. Still, the idea of changing our relationships by examining *intra*personal processes is empirically supported and—perhaps more importantly—empowering. Therefore, I focus on thoughts, rather than *inter*personal behaviors, first.

## Thoughts as *Intra*personal Predictors of Relationship Satisfaction

The thoughts people have about their relationships are highly variable. There are cultural (e.g., Goodwin & Gaines, 2004), generational (e.g., Blanchard-Fields, Hertzog, & Horhota, 2012), and individual differences (e.g., Bradbury & Fincham, 1988) in how people construe their relationships. Garth Fletcher and Geoff Thomas (1996) divided relationship thoughts into values and beliefs. These values and beliefs might center on the self, the other, or the relationship. This framework provides a basis for understanding how thoughts may be categorized and considered as *intra*personal predictors of relationship satisfaction.

# Values

Values are expressions of how relationships should function. Examples of values include the following:

- "Divorce is never justifiable unless there is violence in the relationship."
- "I could never stay with a partner who cheated on me."
- "Mothers should take the lead in parenting."

Values can be divided further into values regarding traditions, ideals, and standards.

## Traditional Values

The extent to which people hold traditional values regarding relationships is often reflected in other values, such as whether they think that familial responsibilities are largely defined by gender. For example, people who value more traditional gender roles often feel that men should be responsible for financial and physical security, and that women should be responsible for maintaining the home and raising the children. Traditional values are also related to the acceptability of divorce, premarital cohabitation, same-sex marriage, and having children outside of marriage. Many of these values correlate with one another and may be plotted on a traditional-nontraditional continuum; however, there is reliable evidence that the extent to which people hold traditional values is declining in the United States (e.g., Wang, 2012). In any case, partners who have different ideas about the need to adhere to traditional values may experience conflict based on these differences.

## Ideals

Ideals are values that are typically specific and represent beliefs about what would constitute the perfect relationship or partner. Garth Fletcher and Jeffry Simpson (2001) have developed a model regarding how ideals function in close relationships and, consistent with their predictions, have found that the closer one's partner approximates the "idealized partner," the greater the relationship satisfaction (e.g., Fletcher, Simpson, & Thomas, 2000).

## Standards

Standards are similar to ideals but represent the minimum qualities that a relationship or person must meet to be considered a satisfying relationship.

Violations of standards in marriage tend to be what motivates couples to pursue marital therapy or separation (Overall, Fletcher, & Simpson, 2006).

## Beliefs

Beliefs are ideas about how relationships function. Beliefs drive much of how we act and feel in our relationships. Examples of beliefs include the following:

- "I'm too fat to find a partner."
- "People in good relationships don't argue as much as we do."
- "We were destined to be together."

Substantial research exists on the impact of beliefs on relationship functioning. For example, people who believe in the destiny of relationships (e.g., "Our relationship was meant to be.") are more likely to avoid tackling difficult issues as they arise (Knee, 1998). In this brief review, I focus on beliefs involving expectations, intentions, and attributions.

### Expectations

Expectations are specific beliefs or predictions about the future functioning of a relationship. As with other areas in our lives, when reality does not live up to expectations, we will likely be disappointed. Take a moment and think about a time when you were disappointed with some aspect of your relationship. Notice how the gap between your expectations and the reality you experienced led to the feeling of disappointment. For example, if you were expecting your partner to throw you a party for your birthday, but instead, the two of you went out for a nice dinner, then you might feel sad or angry with your partner. Had you not had the thought, "I expect my partner to throw me a birthday party," you might well have enjoyed the experience of going out to dinner. In other words, unfulfilled positive expectations can lead to frustration and distress.

### Intentions

For the purposes of this chapter, the definition of *intentions* is limited to the reasons that motivate one's actions. Understanding the rationale for such behavior is often difficult and may be especially difficult in the face of strong emotions. For example, if a person stopped talking to his partner following an argument, his therapist might ask why he was withdrawing. He might respond by saying, "I gave my partner the silent treatment to show her that I'm angry." This statement may sound rational. Nevertheless, in that moment, he may simply have been overwhelmed by the emotion and felt the need to retreat until the feelings of anger subsided. It is often difficult to express the rationale for personal behavior, which may partly explain why many of the people I treat in couple therapy prefer to explain the rationale of their partners' behavior rather than their own.

### Attributions

Relationship scientists refer to speculation about the cause of *another* person's behavior as *attributions*. In relationships, people make *maladaptive attributions* when they attribute negative, stable, and intentional causes to their partners' actions that have failed to meet their expectations or standards. For example, a person might believe, "He's just trying to upset me by leaving his dirty dishes in the sink." Notice how this statement is negative and intentional. People's beliefs about the intentions of others are especially powerful predictors of relationship satisfaction. For example, consider the dishes in the sink example: Imagine if the thought was not that "He was trying to upset me," but "He must have been in a big hurry this morning if he left those dishes in the sink." This statement is neither negative nor intentional. These disparate interpretations could engender very different feelings about the relationship.

Attributions are comparatively strong predictors of relationship satisfaction. In their landmark meta-analysis and review of the predictors of marital quality and dissolution, Benjamin Karney and Thomas Bradbury (1995) examined 115 longitudinal studies of marriage. They found that maladaptive attributions predict lower levels of relationship satisfaction for both women and men. This finding has since been replicated repeatedly and is evident even after controlling for other factors such as depression (Karney, Bradbury, Fincham, & Sullivan, 1994). Most importantly, maladaptive attributions clearly predict changes in relationship satisfaction, rather than merely being correlated with satisfaction (Fincham, Harold, & Gano Phillips, 2000; Karney & Bradbury, 2000). In addition, attributions are associated with how people behave in relationships (e.g., Johnson, Karney, Rogge, & Bradbury, 2001). This association between attributions and behavior is also evident in clinical populations (Waldinger & Schulz, 2006) and appears to develop early in intimate relationships (Osterhout, Frame, & Johnson, 2011).

## Summary

The thoughts people have about their intimate relationships predict relationship outcomes and are key to understanding what brings about closeness and conflict in relationships. Focusing on these thoughts may enable individuals to address the underlying issues that lead to relationship discord and dissolution.

# *Inter*personal Behaviors as Predictors of Relationship Satisfaction

As the word *intra*personal suggests, the psychological concepts I have discussed thus far happen within the self. Yet it is only through *inter*personal behaviors that values, beliefs, and information processing methods impact the coparticipant in a relationship. Interpersonal behaviors tend to be the focus of models of relationship development and interventions— and for good reason. How people behave toward each other is easy to observe compared to what people are thinking and provides a tempting point of intervention. The complaints people voice are most often about interpersonal behavior and often boil down to the refrain, "This person did not treat me well." This common complaint is about interpersonal behavior.

In intimate relationships, partners interact in various contexts. For the purposes of this chapter, I have divided the review of interpersonal behaviors into three commonly occurring situations in relationships: discussing a problem in the relationship, discussing a problem outside the relationship (e.g., a problem at work), and discussing a positive event.

## Problem-Solving

When a couple discusses a problem that directly affects both partners they engage in problem solving. For example, in the case of a newlywed couple that discovers they have very different standards for household cleanliness, an important goal of problem solving would be to reconcile their differences in this area of potential conflict.

Research findings regarding the longitudinal effects of problem-solving behavior on relationship satisfaction have varied to a much greater degree than other predictors of satisfaction. Overall, negativity, such as displays of anger or making global (rather than specific) complaints about one's partner and reciprocation of negativity tend to predict lower satisfaction longitudinally, with the opposite being true for positive behaviors, such as expressing affection and carefully listening to one's partner (e.g., Huston & Chorost, 1994; Laurent, Kim, & Capaldi, 2008; Lawrence et al., 2008; Noller, Feeney, Bonnell, & Callan, 1994; Smith, Vivian, & O'Leary, 1990). However, variation in the direction and magnitude of the effects reported in the literature may be due to some studies with counterintuitive findings. For example, Karney and Bradbury (1997) found that wives' negative behavior had a beneficial impact on husbands' and wives' satisfaction over time. Similarly, Heavey, Layne, and Christensen (1993) noted that husbands' negativity and demandingness predicted greater relationship satisfaction in wives (cf. Caughlin, 2002). These surprising and contradictory results imply that the role of problem-solving behavior may be more complicated and variable than first believed (Kenny, Mohr, & Levesque, 2001). For example, the effect of problem-solving behavior appears to change based on contextual stressors (McNulty & Russell, 2010), whether good communication skills were used even in the face of negative affect (Johnson et al., 2005; Kim, Capaldi, & Crosby, 2007), and whether the two people in the relationship are in synchrony during the discussion (Johnson & Bradbury, 1999). These complicated findings have led some relationship scientists to the conclusion that focusing on problem-solving behavior is an ineffective way to improve relationships (e.g., Johnson & Bradbury, 2014).

## Social Support

Social support occurs when one person in the relationship experiences a problematic situation that is largely external to the relationship, and the person providing support assists in solving or alleviating the problem or its consequences. For example, if one spouse is experiencing difficulty with his or her boss, he or she might discuss the situation with his or her partner, who then provides helpful suggestions regarding strategies to mitigate conflict or relieve distress.

Like problem-solving behaviors, the effect of supportive behavior on relationship quality is complex. Some researchers have found that greater social support is associated with increased relationship quality (e.g., Sullivan, Pasch, Johnson, & Bradbury, 2010). However other researchers have determined that the benefits of a supportive spouse are greatest when the recipient of the support is not aware of having received the support (e.g., Bolger, Zuckerman, & Kessler, 2000). Indeed, awareness of the support actually predicted worse individual outcomes (e.g., depressive symptoms) and lower relationship quality. Researchers have replicated this counterintuitive finding and attempted to delineate the boundaries and moderators of the negative effects of visible support. For example, the problematic impact of visible support diminished (a) when it was provided in response to the expressed desire for support (Maisel & Gable, 2009); (b) as the amount of support between spouses approached equity (Gleason, Iida, Bolger, & Shrout, 2003); and (c) for unmarried couples only, when the support was seen as promoting relationship goals, rather than preventing relationship problems (Molden, Lucas, Finkel, Kumashiro, & Rusbult, 2009). In summary, the impact of support on relationships is complicated and is a topic of immense importance for relationship science (for a more detailed review of this literature, see Sullivan & Davila, 2010).

## Capitalization

Discussions in relationships that pivot around problem solving and social support are often generated by problems that emerge either within or outside of the relationship. In contrast, capitalization focuses on how positive events can change a relationship. Specifically, capitalization refers to reactions to positive events that enhance well-being. Such reactions can happen individually or within relationships. For example, the psychological benefits of a job promotion for the individual and for her or his intimate relationship will very much depend on the partner's reaction. Was the news of the promotion shared? And perhaps more importantly, did the partner enthusiastically celebrate the good news?

Shelly Gable and her colleagues reported that people who discuss personal positive events with a partner experience greater personal psychological benefits (e.g., more positive affective states, fewer symptoms of depression). In addition, partners who respond to positive events with constructive enthusiasm further enhance the personal benefits for the discloser and enhance the quality of the relationship (e.g., Gable, Gosnell, Maisel, & Strachman, 2012). In other words, Gable and her colleagues' research underscored the need to attend to the "positives" in life and in relationships, not just the negatives.

## Summary

How we treat each other matters. This fact of life helps to explain why every model of how relationships develop includes the exchange of behaviors between the members of the relationship (Johnson, 2012). Just as dyadic behavior is integral to every etiological model, it is also a key element of every treatment for intimate relationship distress (e.g., Greenberg & Johnson, 1988; Jacobson & Christensen, 1996; Snyder, Wills, & Grady-Fletcher, 1991) and every program designed to prevent intimate relationship dysfunction (e.g., Markman, Renick, Floyd, Stanley, & Clements, 1993; Rogge, Cobb, Johnson, Lawrence, & Bradbury, 2002). By dividing interpersonal behaviors into three relational categories (problem solving, social support, and capitalization), it is possible to recognize that the impact of how we treat each other depends on context. After all, relationships do not happen in a vacuum, so we must consider our *intra*personal and *inter*personal responses to the positive and negative events that arise in our relationships.

## Roles of Thoughts and Behaviors in Preventing and Treating Relationship Discord

It is tempting to translate the research on *intra*personal and *inter*personal variables that impact relationships into interventions that engender better relationships. Indeed, psychologists have been attempting to accomplish this transformation for over 30 years using methods that target individuals and couples. Not surprisingly, the research on *intra*personal variables has mostly been applied to individual psychotherapy and self-help guides, and the research on *inter*personal variables has mostly been applied to conjoint psychotherapy (i.e., treating both members of a relationship together) and self-help guides for couples and families. The research on how thoughts can lead to relationship dysfunction is incorporated in psychotherapies that emphasize restructuring thoughts; this work can be traced to early studies on how cognition mediates behavior change in social situations (Bandura, 1969, 1977) and the cognitive behavioral therapies that followed (e.g., Beck, 1976). Since then, a group of interventions, referred to as "third-wave behavioral therapies" (the first wave being basic behavioral therapies and the second being cognitive behavioral therapies; Hayes, 2004), have focused on mindfulness (i.e., nonjudgmental awareness of present moment experience) and acceptance of the self and others (see Chapters 4 and 7). These therapies encompass acceptance and commitment therapy (Hayes, Strosahl, & Wilson, 1999), dialectical behavior therapy (Linehan, 1993), the cognitive behavioral analysis system of psychotherapy (McCullough, 2000), and functional analytic psychotherapy (Kohlenberg & Tsai, 1991), among others.

Although these treatments have shown promise and demonstrated efficacy across a broad array of disorders and populations, some have argued that they have yet to fulfill the strict criteria needed to meet the definition of "empirically supported treatments" (Öst, 2008; cf. Gaudiano, 2009; for a discussion of these criteria, see Chambless & Ollendick, 2001). Nevertheless, promising research-based findings regarding the effectiveness of these interventions, coupled with empirically based modifications of the treatments, implies that they may prove to be helpful to individuals seeking better interpersonal relationships. Moreover, a number of self-help books dovetail nicely with third-wave interventions. Although few rigorous studies have been conducted on the effectiveness of self-help books, people motivated to improve the *intra*personal aspects of their relationships may find some of them helpful. For example, in her books, Byron Katie (Katie & Katz, 2005; Katie & Mitchell, 2002) focuses on acceptance and mindfulness in relationships of all types. Indeed, viable options for modifying the *intra*personal aspects of relationship problems now include self-directed as well as therapist-guided interventions.

The most rigorously tested third-wave intervention for treating both members of a discordant relationship together (i.e., conjoint therapy) is integrative behavioral couple therapy (IBCT; Jacobson & Christensen, 1996). This treatment combines the research findings on *intra*personal and *inter*personal determinants of relationship functioning in one integrative treatment. In contrast to traditional behavioral marital therapy, which focuses solely on *inter*personal dynamics (e.g., Jacobson & Margolin, 1979; Stuart, 1980), IBCT focuses on acceptance as well as change in the relationship. Couples are asked to think about the issues that create conflict or distance in their relationships and to determine whether they can accept the way things are or whether changes are imperative. Couples often do not anticipate this request because they assume changes are needed (usually changes in the other person) to improve the relationship.

For example, a wife might want her husband to spend more evenings at home, while he may want his wife to go out more often. Both the husband and the wife would likely request that their therapist help them to change the other person's behavior. The wife would ask for help in getting the husband to be home more when he was not working, and the husband would ask for help in getting the wife to agree to go out on the town more often. The tempting solution for the novice therapist is to try to negotiate a compromise. For example, the husband would agree to spend all but one evening a week at home with the family and the wife would agree to get a babysitter and go out on a date with her husband one night a week. On the surface, this strategy seems reasonable and prudent, but in adopting this strategy the therapist bypasses both the opportunity for the partners to discuss why these issues are important to each of them and to work toward acceptance of differences between the partners. IBCT and some other couple therapies (e.g., Greenberg & Johnson, 1988; Snyder, 2002) deemphasize problem solving by first understanding the meaning and importance behind the issues that generate relationship dissatisfaction or dysfunction and evaluating whether acceptance, rather than change or compromise, is a useful strategy.

The therapist's job is to help draw out the links between the *intra*personal and *inter*personal dynamics of the relationship that explain why a particular issue is so important. For example, when a couple is arguing frequently about how one of them never puts his or her dirty dishes in the dishwasher, it is the therapist's task to understand what this act symbolizes to the complaining partner. Together the therapist and couple may work toward the realization that the dirty dishes on the counter have come to represent a lack of respect for the wishes of one partner. From that point, it is a short step to think, if my partner doesn't respect me, how can he or she love me? Thus, the dirty dishes may come to symbolize that the couple is possibly falling out of love. Such a connection is rarely obvious to either partner. After talking through an issue, such as cleaning up dirty dishes, there may be no need to move toward an explicit solution—because the dishes are not the main issue.

IBCT also emphasizes examining what initially attracted the partners to one another. Couples often find that some of the aspects of the partner that "drive them crazy" are the very same ones that they found to be attractive during courtship. In the case of the dirty dishes, we might discover that the partner was attracted to his or her "wild side" and that on occasion he or she threw caution to the wind. An IBCT therapist would help the partner to understand that this come-what-may attitude that was so appealing in the initial stages of their relationship is the same cavalier attitude that today leads him or her to leave dirty dishes on the counter. At the same time, IBCT would help him or her to recognize that the partner feels disrespected and ultimately unloved when he or she does this. So, is a solution necessary? Is there a problem to be solved? Maybe, but answers to these questions require a conversation involving all parties. Can the couple accept each other and their foibles, or do the dishes left on the counter represent a problem that demands a solution? The clients and therapist then work toward an answer to this question collaboratively. By invoking both acceptance and change, IBCT addresses relational problems on the dual levels of the *intra*personal (mindfulness, understanding, and acceptance) and the *inter*personal (communication and, when necessary, change).

## A Case Study Using *Intra*personal and *Inter*personal Interventions in Practice

In their therapist guidebook for IBCT, Neil Jacobson and Andy Christensen (1996, p. x) note that the unofficial motto of their treatment is "dig it, change it, suck it up, or split!" The easiest way to describe how these imperatives work in practice is to describe them in the context of a couple in treatment, so let me introduce a fictional couple similar to various couples I have treated. Tom and Judy consulted me because of multiple issues that impacted their relationship. Tom was a Latino man in his early 30s who worked at a well-paying office job. Judy was a Caucasian woman, also in her early 30s, who was a part-time professional actor, but who earned most of her money doing odd jobs in the home construction business. They had been together for 5 years, were unmarried, had no children, and had recently bought a house together that needed a great deal of work.

## Dig It

During my initial assessment, I learned that Tom admired Judy's "carpentry skills and work ethic" as well as her "movie-star good looks." Judy found Tom sophisticated, smart, stable, and handsome. They both shared a desire to settle down. I also learned that although they co-owned the house, Tom provided most of the money that allowed them to afford their mortgage. In turn, Judy's construction skills and strong work ethic (and her long stretches of not working as an actor) enabled them to buy "more house" than they otherwise could afford, because it needed extensive repair. They both liked their arrangement. As this information was shared, Judy noted that she felt she should work on the house every day because she felt some guilt regarding Tom going to his job each day to be able to pay for their house. In addition, Judy spent many afternoons on auditions, so she devoted all of her free time to working on the house. Despite their agreement regarding buying their house, it had become a major source of concern.

Judy worked on the house each weekend and, on weekdays, she would often start working on the house before Tom was even out of bed. Tom became frustrated with how little time they spent together and commented that he felt he was "in competition with the house" for Judy's attention and time. Tom began to feel unloved and ignored. When Tom expressed these concerns, Judy quickly responded that Tom had spent entire weekends in Las Vegas gambling without Judy (I will return to this point). In addition, she felt that Tom devalued her work on the house. At this point, I tried to get them to "dig it" by noting that the traits in each other that were causing distress were the same traits that they also found attractive.

In session, Judy expressed how important it was to her to contribute to the relationship by improving the house because she did not contribute much financially. Nevertheless, Tom simply missed Judy and wanted to spend more quality time with her. Once they heard each other's perspectives, much of the resentment dissipated. How could Tom be angry because

Judy wanted to do her part for their home? How could Judy be angry because Tom wanted to spend more time with her? Their realizations allowed them to see that some of their distress stemmed from the very traits that they also appreciated (or "dug") in the other. This allowed them to "dig" these traits again.

## Change It

In addition to the issues regarding the house, Tom also expressed great frustration about how little sex they were having. He explained that he had tried accepting that perhaps his libido was stronger than Judy's and that a drop-off in their sex life was normal. However, when he learned that Judy had been masturbating, Tom was hurt and angry. It was one thing not to have sex, but Tom viewed Judy's masturbation as something of a betrayal. As we talked through the issue, each partner expressed feelings about sex. Judy indicated that she was raised in a conservative home, and that she had trouble shedding the idea of sex being shameful. In fact, she was embarrassed and hurt that Tom would even raise the subject of her masturbating. She felt that it was private and not an appropriate topic for conversation. Tom, on the other hand, felt that it was selfish of Judy to masturbate when he had repeatedly requested more sex, and that it was making Judy even less interested in sex. The conversation next turned to the more mundane aspects of the problem with their sexual relationship, such as Judy's habit of falling asleep in the living room while watching television. Tom didn't mind, but when Judy did come to the bedroom she was too tired for anything but sleep. The issues surrounding sex led to mutual feelings of resentment.

It seemed to me that the pressure to have sex (notice the expectation) was—paradoxically—part of what was impeding their ability to achieve a mutually satisfactory sexual relationship. To reduce the pressure they experienced, I banned sex altogether until our next session. The intervention succeeded. At the next session, the couple sheepishly reported that they rarely left their bedroom over the course of an entire weekend. In other words, thought change led to behavior change.

## Suck It Up

As I mentioned previously, Tom travelled to Las Vegas on a number of occasions. When I queried about this further, Tom indicated that he had been gambling most of his adult life, and that he really enjoyed it; he gambled four or five times a year and was adamant that it was not a problem. Judy replied that she didn't mind Tom's gambling, although she personally didn't like to gamble and was not a big fan of Las Vegas. Still, what really hurt was that Tom had recently traveled to Las Vegas straight from work without informing her. Tom stated that this occurred after they had a fight about how much Judy was working on the house, and "we weren't going to spend any time together that weekend anyway" because Judy was intent on replacing the roof. Tom acknowledged that the trip to Las Vegas was a petty move on his part and apologized. Judy said she knew Tom really liked to gamble but emphasized how much she personally found it anxiety inducing and unpleasant. They both noted that Tom was a decent gambler, and that Tom won all of the money for their down payment in one particularly good weekend in Las Vegas. In the end, Judy "sucked it up" (i.e., accepted it), because Tom really seemed to like gambling and did not squander their money doing so.

## Split

Happily, Tom and Judy seemed eager to improve their relationship, and neither of them ever mentioned that they were considering dissolving their relationship. Nevertheless, for some couples this is the most reasonable course of action. One of the most common situations in which couples should carefully consider the wisdom of staying together is when they can no longer control their arguments to the point that their conflicts are affecting their children. As noted previously, children are impacted in the short and long term by parents who frequently exhibit intense emotional conflict. In these cases, divorce—assuming that it reduces parental conflict—may improve children's well-being. On the other hand, divorce among couples in low-conflict marriages can be a shock to the children and may negatively impact their well-being (e.g., Amato et al., 1995).

Finally, there are violent situations in which I urge the dissolution of the relationship. Violence has no place in intimate relationships and is counterproductive. If you are the initiator of violence, you should know that being violent is more likely to result in the end of your relationship (Rogge & Bradbury, 1999). If you are a victim of relationship violence, I recommend considering the risks (to you and your children) of remaining in your current relationship by taking "the Danger Assessment" (Campbell, Webster, & Glass, 2009) at http://www.dangerassessment.org. If you or someone you know is at risk, please call your local domestic violence agency or the National Coalition Against Domestic Violence at 1–800–799-SAFE (7233). If you are neither a perpetrator nor a victim of interpersonal violence, consider supporting your local domestic violence agency so they can help those who are in danger.

## Summary

Mostly through addressing their relationship problems using acceptance and other *intra*personal strategies, Tom and Judy became more satisfied with their relationship and, in turn, experienced improvement in the *inter*personal aspects of their lives together. While I helped to facilitate the process in the context of couple therapy, they did the hard work of examining and changing their thoughts about each other and their relationship.

Certainly, if their relationship had not improved by focusing on *intra*personal changes, I could have employed *inter*personal strategies. One commonly taught interpersonal skill is called active listening, a method in which the two people are designated the roles of *speaker* and *listener*. The speaker's job is to focus on specific events and behaviors and to discuss their emotional impact. One tactic the speaker might use is called an X-Y-Z statement: "When you do [X (a specific behavior)] during [Y (a specific situation)], I feel [Z (an emotion)]." The listener's job is to paraphrase what the speaker said without responding until the speaker feels understood. After the speaker feels that the listener understands his or her point, they switch roles. Many couples find that this technique facilitates the discussion of difficult topics. You will find a more detailed description of this and other *inter*personal techniques in the book *Fighting for Your Marriage* (Markman, Stanley, & Blumberg, 1994).

## Conclusion

Although I have focused on intimate relationships, much of what I have written can be applied to all relationships. To improve relationships of any kind, I suggest that readers begin by examining their values and beliefs regarding relationships: *Intra*personal factors can be powerful tools to make relationships more rewarding. Whether striving to improve a relationship with a spouse, client, or friend, examining thoughts about the person is an excellent place to start. Doing work on oneself may be the best solution to relationship difficulties. As exemplified in the case of Tom and Judy, simply dropping or modifying a conflict-producing or unrealistic expectation or building up tolerance to a partner's behavior can reap benefits in the relationship, including more sex. An example beyond romantic relationships is a classic study in which mothers were more compassionate and understanding in interactions with their children when they stepped back from their parenting duties and spent some time each day talking with friends (Wahler, 1980). In any case, understanding and working on yourself is an excellent starting point for improving your relationships. Changing beliefs about relationships is neither easy nor intuitive; nevertheless, the hard work of *intrapersonal* change can be rewarding because it can improve your intimate relationships and, consequently, your well-being and that of your loved ones.

# References

Amato, P. R., Loomis, L. S., & Booth, A. (1995). Parental divorce, marital conflict, and offspring well-being during early adulthood. *Social Forces, 73*, 895–915. doi:10.2307/2580551

Bandura, A. (1969). *Principles of behavior modification*. New York, NY: Holt, Rinehart and Winston.

Bandura, A. (1977). *Social learning theory*. Englewood Cliffs, NJ: Prentice Hall.

Beck, A. (1976). *Cognitive therapy and emotional disorders*. New York, NY: International Universities Press.

Belsky, J., Steinberg, L. D., Houts, R. M., Friedman, S. L., DeHart, G., Cauffman, E., . . . Susman, E. (2007). Family rearing antecedents of pubertal timing. *Child Development, 78*, 1302–1321. doi:10.1046/j.1467–8624.2003.00637.x

Blanchard-Fields, F., Hertzog, C., & Horhota, M. (2012). Violate my beliefs? Then you're to blame! Belief content as an explanation for causal attribution biases. *Psychology and Aging, 27*, 324–337. doi:10.1037/a0024423

Bolger, N., Zuckerman, A., & Kessler, R. C. (2000). Invisible support and adjustment to stress. *Journal of Personality and Social Psychology, 79*, 953–961. doi: 10.1037/0022–3514.79.6.953

Bradbury, T. N., & Fincham, F. D. (1988). Individual difference variables in close relationships: A contextual model of marriage as an integrative framework. *Journal of Personality and Social Psychology, 54*, 713–721. doi:10.1037/0022–3514.54.4.713

Brown, S. L. (2000). The effect of union type on psychological well-being: Depression among cohabitors versus marrieds. *Journal of Health and Social Behavior*, 241–255. doi:10.2307/2676319

Campbell, J. C., Webster, D. W., & Glass, N. (2009). The Danger Assessment: Validation of a lethality risk assessment instrument for intimate partner femicide. *Journal of Interpersonal Violence, 24*, 653–674. doi: 10.1177/0886260508317180

Caughlin, J. P. (2002). The demand/withdraw pattern of communication as a predictor of marital satisfaction over time. *Human Communication Research, 28*, 49–85. doi:10.1093/hcr/28.1.49

Chambless, D. L., & Ollendick, T. H. (2001). Empirically supported psychological interventions: Controversies and evidence. *Annual Review of Psychology, 52*, 685–716. doi:10.1146/annurev.psych.52.1.685

Chang, M., & Lui, M. (2010). *Lifting as we climb: Women of color, wealth, and America's future*. Oakland, CA: Insight Center for Community Economic Development.

Cohen, S., Frank, E., Doyle, W. J., Skoner, D. P., Rabin, B. S., & Gwaltney, J. M., Jr. (1998). Types of stressors that increase susceptibility to the common cold in healthy adults. *Health Psychology, 17*, 214–223. doi:10.1037/0278–6133.17.3.214

Coyne, J. C., Rohrbaugh, M. J., Shoham, V., Sonnega, J. S., Nicklas, J. M., & Cranford, J. A. (2001). Prognostic importance of marital quality for survival of congestive heart failure. *American Journal of Cardiology, 88*, 526–529. doi: 10.1016/S0002–9149(01)01731–3

Datta, G. D., Neville, B. A., Kawachi, I., Datta, N. S., & Earle, C. C. (2009). Marital status and survival following bladder cancer. *Journal of Epidemiology and Community Health (1979), 63*, 807–813. doi:10.2307/20721062

Davies, P. T., & Cummings, E. M. (1994). Marital conflict and child adjustment: An emotional security hypothesis. *Psychological Bulletin, 116*, 387–411. doi: 10.1037/0033-2909.116.3.387

Diener, E., Suh, E. M., Lucas, R. E., & Smith, H. L. (1999). Subjective well-being: Three decades of progress. *Psychological Bulletin, 125*, 276–302. doi: 10.1037/0033–2909.125.2.276

Dopp, J. M., Miller, G. E., Myers, H. F., & Fahey, J. L. (2000). Increased natural killer-cell mobilization and cytotoxicity during marital conflict. *Brain, Behavior, and Immunity, 14*, 10–26. doi:10.1006/brbi.1999.0567

El-Sheikh, M., Buckhalt, J. A., Keller, P. S., Cummings, E. M., & Acebo, C. (2007). Child emotional insecurity and academic achievement: The role of sleep disruptions. *Journal of Family Psychology, 21*, 29–38. doi:10.1037/0893–3200.21.1.29

Fincham, F. D., Harold, G. T., & Gano Phillips, S. (2000). The longitudinal association between attributions and marital satisfaction: Direction of effects and role of efficacy expectations. *Journal of Family Psychology, 14*, 267–285. doi: 10.1037/0893–3200.14.2.267

Fleming, C. B., White, H. R., & Catalano, R. F. (2010). Romantic relationships and substance use in early adulthood: An examination of the influences of relationship type, partner substance use, and relationship quality. *Journal of Health and Social Behavior, 51*, 153–167. doi:10.1177/0022146510368930

Fletcher, G. J. O., & Simpson, J. A. (2001). *Ideal standards in close relationships*. New York, NY: Cambridge University Press.

Fletcher, G. J. O., Simpson, J. A., & Thomas, G. (2000). Ideals, perceptions, and evaluations in early relationship development. *Journal of Personality and Social Psychology, 79*, 933–940. doi:10.1037/0022–3514.79.6.933

Fletcher, G. J. O., & Thomas, G. (1996). Close relationship lay theories: Their structure and functions. In G. J. O. Fletcher & J. Fitness (Eds.), *Knowledge structures in close relationships: A social psychological approach* (pp. 3–24). Mahwah, NJ: Lawrence Erlbaum.

Forthofer, M. S., Markman, H. J., Cox, M., Stanley, S., & Kessler, R. C. (1996). Associations between marital distress and work loss in a national sample. *Journal of Marriage and the Family, 58*, 597–605. doi:10.2307/353720

Gable, S. L., Gosnell, C. L., Maisel, N. C., & Strachman, A. (2012). Safely testing the alarm: Close others' responses to personal positive events. *Journal of Personality and Social Psychology, 103*, 963–981. doi:10.1037/a0029488

Gallo, L. C., Troxel, W. M., Matthews, K. A., & Kuller, L. H. (2003). Marital status and quality in middle-aged women: Associations with levels and trajectories of cardiovascular risk factors. *Health Psychology, 22*, 453–463. doi:10.1037/0278–6133.22.5.453

Gaudiano, B. A. (2009). Öst's (2008) methodological comparison of clinical trials of acceptance and commitment therapy versus cognitive behavior therapy: Matching apples with oranges? *Behaviour Research and Therapy, 47*, 1066–1070. doi:10.1016/j.brat.2009.07.020

Gleason, M. E. J., Iida, M., Bolger, N., & Shrout, P. E. (2003). Daily supportive equity in close relationships. *Personality & Social Psychology Bulletin, 29*, 1036–1045. doi:10.1177/0146167203253473

Goeke-Morey, M. C., Papp, L. M., & Cummings, E. M. (2013). Changes in marital conflict and youths' responses across childhood and adolescence: A test of sensitization. *Development and Psychopathology, 25*, 241–251. doi:10.1017/s0954579412000995

Goodwin, R., & Gaines, S. O. (2004). Relationships beliefs and relationship quality across cultures: Country as a moderator of dysfunctional beliefs and relationship quality in three former Communist societies. *Personal Relationships, 11*, 267–279. doi:10.1037/0033–2909.118.1.3

Greenberg, L. S., & Johnson, S. M. (1988). *Emotionally focused therapy for couples.* New York, NY: Guilford Press.

Grych, J. H., & Fincham, F. D. (1990). Marital conflict and children's adjustment: A cognitive-contextual framework. *Psychological Bulletin, 108*, 267–290.

Hayes, S. C. (2004). Acceptance and commitment therapy, relational frame theory, and the third wave of behavioral and cognitive therapies. *Behavior Therapy, 35*, 639–665. doi:10.1016/s0005–7894(04)80013–3

Hayes, S. C., Strosahl, K., & Wilson, K. G. (1999). *Acceptance and commitment therapy.* New York, NY: Guilford Press.

Heavey, C. L., Layne, C., & Christensen, A. (1993). Gender and conflict structure in marital interaction: A replication and extension. *Journal of Consulting and Clinical Psychology, 61*, 16–27. doi:10.1037/0022–006X.61.1.16

Heller, D., Watson, D., & Ilies, R. (2004). The role of person versus situation in life satisfaction: A critical examination. *Psychological Bulletin, 130*, 574–600. doi: 10.1037/0033–2909.130.4.574

Huston, T. L., & Chorost, A. F. (1994). Behavioral buffers on the effect of negativity on marital satisfaction: A longitudinal view. *Personal Relationships, 1*, 223–239. doi:10.1111/j.1475–6811.1994.tb00063.x

Jacobson, N. S., & Christensen, A. (1996). *Integrative couple therapy: Promoting acceptance and change.* New York, NY: Norton.

Jacobson, N. S., & Margolin, G. (1979). *Marital therapy: Strategies based on social learning and behavior exchange principles.* New York, NY: Brunner/Mazel.

Johnson, M. D. (2012). Healthy marriage initiatives: On the need for empiricism in policy implementation. *American Psychologist, 67*, 296–308. doi:10.1037/a0027743

Johnson, M. D., & Bradbury, T. N. (1999). Marital satisfaction and topographical assessment of marital interaction: A longitudinal analysis of newlywed couples. *Personal Relationships, 6*, 19–40. doi:10.1111/j.1475–6811.1999.tb00209.x

Johnson, M. D., & Bradbury, T. N. (2014). *A reexamination of social learning theory based on outcome studies of interventions to treat and prevent marital discord.* Manuscript submitted for publication.

Johnson, M. D., Cohan, C. L., Davila, J., Lawrence, E., Rogge, R. D., Kamey, B. R., . . . Bradbury, T. N. (2005). Problem-solving skills and affective expressions as predictors of change in marital satisfaction. *Journal of Consulting and Clinical Psychology, 73*, 15–27. doi:10.1037/0022–006x.73.1.15

Johnson, M. D., Karney, B. R., Rogge, R., & Bradbury, T. N. (2001). The role of marital behavior in the longitudinal association between attributions and marital quality. In V. Manusov & J. H. Harvey (Eds.), *Attribution, communication behavior, and close relationships* (pp. 173–192). New York, NY: Cambridge University Press.

Karney, B. R., & Bradbury, T. N. (1995). The longitudinal course of marital quality and stability: A review of theory, methods, and research. *Psychological Bulletin, 118*, 3–34. doi:10.1037/0033–2909.118.1.3

Karney, B. R., & Bradbury, T. N. (1997). Neuroticism, marital interaction, and the trajectory of marital satisfaction. *Journal of Personality and Social Psychology, 72*, 1075–1092. doi:10.1037/0022–3514.72.5.1075

Karney, B. R., & Bradbury, T. N. (2000). Attributions in marriage: State or trait? A growth curve analysis. *Journal of Personality and Social Psychology, 78*, 295–309. doi:10.1037/0022–3514.78.2.295

Karney, B. R., Bradbury, T. N., Fincham, F. D., & Sullivan, K. T. (1994). The role of negative affectivity in the association between attributions and marital satisfaction. *Journal of Personality and Social Psychology, 66*, 413–424. doi:10.1037/0022–3514.66.2.413

Katie, B., & Katz, M. (2005). *I need your love—is that true? How to stop seeking love, approval, and appreciation and start finding them instead.* New York, NY: Harmony Books.

Katie, B., & Mitchell, S. (2002). *Loving what is: Four questions that can change your life.* New York, NY: Harmony Books.

Kenny, D. A., Mohr, C. D., & Levesque, M. J. (2001). A social relations variance partitioning of dyadic behavior. *Psychological Bulletin, 127*, 128–141. doi:10.1037/0033–2909.127.1.128

Kern, H. L. (2010). The political consequences of transitions out of marriage in Great Britain. *Electoral Studies, 29*, 249–258. doi:10.1016/j.electstud.2010.01.004

Kiecolt-Glaser, J. K., Malarkey, W. B., Chee, M., Newton, T., Cacioppo, J. T., Mao, H.-Y., & Glaser, R. (1993). Negative behavior during marital conflict is associated with immunilogical down-regulation. *Psychosomatic Medicine, 55*, 395–409.

Kim, H. K., Capaldi, D. M., & Crosby, L. (2007). Generalizability of Gottman and colleagues' affective process models of couples' relationship outcomes. *Journal of Marriage and Family, 69*, 55–72. doi:10.1111/ j.1467–9507.1997.tb00101.x

Knee, C. R. (1998). Implicit theories of relationships: Assessment and prediction of romantic relationship initiation, coping, and longevity. *Journal of Personality and Social Psychology, 74*, 360–370. doi:10.1037/0022–3514.74.2.360

Kohlenberg, R. J., & Tsai, M. (1991). *Functional analytic psychotherapy: Creating intense and curative therapeutic relationships.* New York, NY: Plenum.

Langhinrichsen-Rohling, J., Snarr, J. D., Slep, A. M. S., Heyman, R. E., & Foran, H. M. (2011). Risk for suicidal ideation in the U.S. Air Force: An ecological perspective. *Journal of Consulting and Clinical Psychology, 79*, 600–612. doi:10.1037/a0024631

Laub, J. H., Nagin, D. S., & Sampson, R. J. (1998). Trajectories of change in criminal offending: Good marriages and the desistance process. *American Sociological Review, 63*, 225–238. doi:10.2307/2657324

Laurent, H. K., Kim, H. K., & Capaldi, D. M. (2008). Interaction and relationship development in stable young couples: Effects of positive engagement, psychological aggression, and withdrawal. *Journal of Adolescence, 31*, 815–835. doi: 10.1037/08933200.19.1.98

Lawrence, E., Pederson, A., Bunde, M., Barry, R. A., Brock, R. L., Fazio, E., . . . Dzankovic, S. (2008). Objective ratings of relationship skills across multiple domains as predictors of marital satisfaction trajectories. *Journal of Social and Personal Relationships, 25*, 445–466. doi:10.1177/0265407508090868

Linehan, M. M. (1993). *Cognitive-behavioral treatment of borderline personality disorder.* New York, NY: Guilford Press.

Maisel, N. C., & Gable, S. L. (2009). The paradox of received social support: The importance of responsiveness. *Psychological Science, 20*, 928–932. doi:10.11 11/j.1467–9280.2009.02388.x

Markman, H. J., Renick, M. J., Floyd, F., Stanley, S., & Clements, M. (1993). Preventing marital distress through communication and conflict management training: A four and five year follow–up. *Journal of Consulting and Clinical Psychology, 62*, 1–8. doi:10.1037/0022–006X.61.1.70

Markman, H. J., Stanley, S., & Blumberg, S. L. (1994). *Fighting for your marriage.* San Francisco, CA: Jossey-Bass.

McCullough, J. P. (2000). *Treatment for chronic depression: Cognitive Behavioral Analysis System of Psychotherapy.* New York, NY: Guilford Press.

McNulty, J. K., & Russell, V. M. (2010). When "negative" behaviors are positive: A contextual analysis of the long-term effects of problem-solving behaviors on changes in relationship satisfaction. *Journal of Personality and Social Psychology, 98*, 587–604. doi:10.1037/a0017479

Molden, D. C., Lucas, G. M., Finkel, E. J., Kumashiro, M., & Rusbult, C. E. (2009). Perceived support for promotion-focused and prevention-focused goals: Associations with well-being in unmarried and married couples. *Psychological Science, 20*, 787–793. doi:10.1111/j.1467–9280.2009.02362.x

Murphy, S. L., Xu, J., & Kochanek, K. D. (2013). Deaths: Final data for 2010. *National Vital Statistics Reports, 61*, 1–120.

Nealey-Moore, J. B., Smith, T. W., Uchino, B. N., Hawkins, M. W., & Olson-Cerny, C. (2007). Cardiovascular reactivity during positive and negative marital interactions. *Journal of Behavioral Medicine, 30*, 505–519. doi:10.1007/s10865–007–9124–5

Noller, P., Feeney, J. A., Bonnell, D., & Callan, V. J. (1994). A longitudinal study of conflict in early marriage. *Journal of Social and Personal Relationships, 11*, 233–252. doi:10.1177/0265407594112005

Öst, L.-G. (2008). Efficacy of the third wave of behavioral therapies: A systematic review and meta-analysis. *Behaviour Research and Therapy, 46*, 296–321. doi: 10.1016/j.brat.2007.12.005

Osterhout, R. E., Frame, L. E., & Johnson, M. D. (2011). Maladaptive attributions and dyadic behavior are associated in engaged couples. *Journal of Social and Clinical Psychology, 30*, 787–818. doi:10.1521/jscp.2011.30.8.787

Overall, N. C., Fletcher, G. J. O., & Simpson, J. A. (2006). Regulation processes in intimate relationships: The role of ideal standards. *Journal of Personality and Social Psychology, 91*, 662–685. doi:10.1037/0022–3514.91.4.662

Overbeek, G., Vollebergh, W., de Graaf, R., Scholte, R., de Kemp, R., & Engels, R. (2006). Longitudinal associations of marital quality and marital dissolution with the incidence of DSM-III-R disorders. *Journal of Family Psychology, 20*, 284–291. doi:10.1037/0893–3200.20.2.284

Proulx, C. M., Helms, H. M., & Buehler, C. (2007). Marital quality and personal well-being: A meta-analysis. *Journal of Marriage and Family, 69*, 576–593. doi: 10.1111/j.1741–3737.2007.00393.x

Rogge, R. D., & Bradbury, T. N. (1999). Till violence does us part: The differing roles of communication and aggression in predicting adverse marital outcomes. *Journal of Consulting and Clinical Psychology, 67*, 340–351. doi:10.1037/0022–006X.67.3.340

Rogge, R. D., Cobb, R. M., Johnson, M. D., Lawrence, E., & Bradbury, T. N. (2002). The CARE program: A preventative approach to marital intervention. In A. S. Gurman & N. S. Jacobson (Eds.), *Clinical handbook of couple therapy* (3rd ed., pp. 420–435). New York, NY: Guilford Press.

Schneider, D. (2011). Wealth and the marital divide. *American Journal of Sociology, 117*, 627–667. doi:10.1086/661594

Smith, D. A., Vivian, D., & O'Leary, K. D. (1990). Longitudinal prediction of marital discord from premarital expressions of affect. *Journal of Consulting and Clinical Psychology, 58*, 790–798. doi:10.1037/0022–006X.58.6.790

Snyder, D. K. (2002). Integrating insight-oriented techniques into couple therapy. In J. H. Harvey & A. Wenzel (Eds.), *A clinician's guide to maintaining and enhancing close relationships* (pp. 259–275). Mahwah, NJ: Lawrence Erlbaum.

Snyder, D. K., Wills, R. M., & Grady-Fletcher, A. (1991). Long-term effectiveness of behavioral versus insight-oriented marital therapy: A 4-year follow-up study. *Journal of Consulting and Clinical Psychology, 59*, 138–131. doi:10.1037/0022–006X.59.1.138

340 PART V: Enriching Relationships, Managing Money

Stander, V. A., Hilton, S. M., Kennedy, K. R., & Robbins, D. L. (2004). Surveillance of completed suicide in the Department of the Navy. *Military Medicine, 169*, 301–306.

Stuart, R. B. (1980). *Helping couples change: A social learning approach to marital therapy.* New York, NY: Guilford Press.

Sullivan, K. T., & Davila, J. (Eds.). (2010). *Support processes in intimate relationships.* New York, NY: Oxford University Press.

Sullivan, K. T., Pasch, L. A., Johnson, M. D., & Bradbury, T. N. (2010). Social support, problem solving, and the longitudinal course of newlywed marriage. *Journal of Personality and Social Psychology, 98*, 631–644. doi:10.1037/a0017578

Swindle, R., Jr., Heller, K., Pescosolido, B., & Kikuzawa, S. (2000). Responses to nervous breakdowns in America over a 40–year period: Mental health policy implications. *American Psychologist, 55*, 740–749. doi:10.1037/0003–066 x.55.7.740

Troxel, W. M., & Matthews, K. A. (2004). What are the costs of marital conflict and dissolution to children's physical health? *Clinical Child and Family Psychology Review, 7*, 29–57. doi:10.1023/B:CCFP.0000020191.73542.b0

Veroff, J., Kulka, R. A., & Douvan, E. (1981). *Mental health in America: Patterns of help-seeking from 1957 to 1976.* New York, NY: Basic Books.

Wahler, R. G. (1980). The insular mother: Her problems in parent-child treatment. *Journal of Applied Behavior Analysis, 13*, 207–219. doi:10.1901/jaba.1980 .13–207

Waldinger, R. J., & Schulz, M. S. (2006). Linking hearts and minds in couple interactions: Intentions, attributions, and overriding sentiments. *Journal of Family Psychology. Special Issue: Relational Disorders and Relational Processes in Mental Health, 20*, 494–504. doi:10.1037/0893–3200.20.3.494

Wang, W. (2012). *The rise of intermarriage: Rates, characteristics vary by race and gender.* Washington, DC: Pew Research Center.

Whisman, M. A. (2007). Marital distress and DSM-IV psychiatric disorders in a population-based national survey. *Journal of Abnormal Psychology, 116*, 638–643. doi:10.1037/0021-843X.116.3.638

Wilson, W. J. (2009). *More than just race: Being black and poor in the inner city.* New York, NY: Norton.

Yang, H.-C., & Schuler, T. A. (2009). Marital quality and survivorship: Slowed recovery for breast cancer patients in distressed relationships. *Cancer, 115*, 217–228. doi:10.1002/cncr.23964

# 15

# The Joys of Loving

## Enhancing Sexual Experiences

*Rachael Ann Fite*

A s a nation, we are deeply ambivalent about sex. Over the past few decades, we have witnessed our society become saturated with sexual messages, propagated by an unending torrent of sexually explicit movies, music, magazines, and advertising, along with an explosion of websites, online pornography, sexual e-commerce, chat rooms, and special interest blogs. Still, many of us experience inhibition and embarrassment regarding our sexual behaviors, desires, and concerns, and few of us feel comfortable sharing sexual thoughts and performance concerns, even in the context of intimate relationships and in the confines of the physician's office. The reluctance to seek and gain accurate knowledge regarding sexuality deepens ignorance and powerlessness, while drowning in a sea of sexual images fosters inappropriate expectations, rigid cultural scripts about sexuality, and a sense of inadequacy and angst in the bedroom.

Our culture's dominant picture of sexuality, which can be characterized as "everyone is having fabulous sex on a frequent, regular basis," diverges sharply from the reality most of us experience. We are rarely in a position to step back from the river of hype and develop a healthy perspective on sex based on scientific findings. The paucity of readily available science-based knowledge likely (a) increases vulnerability to accepting as fact inaccurate information presented in titillating movies and magazines and other media outlets and (b) contributes to the billions of dollars the American public wastes on useless potions and products that falsely promise to enhance sexual pleasure. This chapter is intended for readers who are interested in human sexuality or would like to improve their own sexual experiences and for therapists interested in treating patients using information and techniques proven to be effective based on scientific research.

As a research-trained clinical psychologist who specializes in sexual health, I have come to deeply appreciate the challenges couples grapple with regarding sexuality, and I have acquired valuable knowledge of what science has to offer to improve their intimate lives. In partnership, we move toward achieving the couples' goal of a healthy, satisfying sexual relationship. On a daily basis, I am impressed with the vital importance of sex in our lives. Sex can make us feel vibrant and wonderfully satisfied. Healthy sexual intimacy can provide or facilitate (a) shared pleasure; (b) a bond that energizes, strengthens, and deepens relationships; (c) a means of reducing stress; (d) a buffer against the aggravations of quotidian life; and (e) sexual release. But when things are not going well, sex can become an arduous chore, a source of psychological pain, resentment, anxiety, self-doubt, and avoidance. Conflicts and misunderstandings about sex can pull couples into their respective corners, awkward and silent, each feeling misunderstood, angry, and hurt. This state of affairs can exact an enormous emotional toll on the individuals involved and can engender a downward spiral of increasingly negative anticipation, performance anxiety, failed experiences, guilt, and blaming, which escalates sexual avoidance and ultimately can jeopardize relationships.

Research on the impact of sexuality in our lives has consistently demonstrated that satisfaction with sexuality is a key factor in marriage satisfaction (Butzer & Campbell, 2008; Byers, 2005; Kisler & Christopher, 2008; Litzinger & Gordon, 2005; Sprecher, 2002; Yeh, Lorenz, Wickrama, Conger, & Elder, 2006). Sexual activities account for approximately 20% of our marital happiness when sex is good, but when there is dysfunction or dissatisfaction in bed, marital *un*happiness can climb to a whopping 70% (McCarthy, 1997). Sexual dissatisfaction not only disrupts enjoyment in the short term, but it can seriously compromise the viability of the marriage itself, particularly in the early years of the union.

## Surveys and Sex in the Laboratory

Unfortunately, most of the best-known studies on human sexuality are poorly designed and therefore provide inaccurate and misleading information. Modern statisticians and social scientists have noted that the Janus

Report, the Kinsey reports, the Playboy survey, and the Hite Report, for example, are seriously flawed methodologically (Hall, 2004; Leonhardt, 2000; Michael, Gagnon, Laumann, & Kolata, 1994; ). Yet the average American, if he or she had ever heard of these studies, would likely believe that their conclusions ring with truth.

*The Janus Report on Sexual Behavior* (Janus & Janus, 1993), for example, attempted to survey Americans in a manner consistent with the population distribution reported in the 1990 census data. The researchers' effort to represent older individuals in the survey was laudable, but their recruitment method exemplifies an all-too-typical and fatal flaw that plagues sex research. More specifically, rather than randomly selecting participants from all adult age groups, the researchers relied on a nonrepresentative, self-selected sample of older participants who sought treatment in sex therapy clinics. In all likelihood, individuals who are willing to pay for and engage in the emotionally taxing process of sex therapy are more interested in having sex and engaging in better or more frequent sex than the average older citizen. Not surprisingly, one of the findings of the Janus Report was that 70% of Americans aged 65 and older reported that they have sex once a week. Other research studies, however, which have used more appropriate sampling techniques, found that for individuals that age, only 7% have sex on a weekly basis (Call, Sprecher, & Schwartz, 1995; Michael et al., 1994).

The Kinsey reports (Kinsey, Pomeroy, & Martin, 1948; Kinsey, Pomeroy, Martin, & Gebhard, 1953) were similarly flawed. The studies described in these reports are based on what is called a *sample of convenience*. Rather than randomly select individuals to be surveyed based on population data, Kinsey recruited participants from specific and non-representative populations (e.g., fraternities, gay groups, group residential settings). For example, of the nearly 12,000 individuals who provided data for the Kinsey reports, no African Americans were among the respondents (Griffitt & Hatfield, 1985). Moreover, Kinsey used a highly problematic sampling technique known as *snowball sampling*, in which participants were encouraged to tell their friends and associates about the research. These individuals then approached Kinsey and provided data that were clearly not representative of the broader population (Michael et al, 1994).

In the absence of other putatively scientific information about sex, Kinsey's work exerted an enormous impact on the public imagination. The information contained in Kinsey's books, *Sexual Behavior in the Human Male* (1948) and *Sexual Behavior in the Human Female* (1953), became the standard of comparison for many individuals to evaluate their sexual behaviors and choices. Unfortunately, these volumes were fonts of erroneous information, much of which continues to be accepted as fact today. For example, Kinsey reported that half of the husbands in America had engaged in extramarital sex, a statistic that since has been contradicted by numerous, well-designed studies indicating the rate to be in the range of 15% to 25% (Laumann, Gagnon, Michael, & Michaels, 1994; Smith, 1994; Michael et al, 1994). One can only speculate about how normalizing infidelity may have influenced the cultural mores and actual decision making of individuals at the time. Similarly misleading high rates of infidelity continue to be propagated by reports on the Internet (Weaver, 2007).

Kinsey's books also set the stage for decades of misinformation about homosexual sex. He reported that one out of three men had engaged sexually with another man some time in his life. Further, he reported that 10% of men engaged exclusively in sexual relationships with men. Unfortunately, the inaccurate statistic that "one person in ten in the United States is gay" continues to be presented as fact (Gates, 2011). Indeed, more recent studies, using more appropriate random sampling methodologies, have found that the percentage of men sexually involved exclusively with other men is approximately 4%, whereas the percentage of women who report exclusive lesbian relationships is approximately 1% (Laumann et al., 1994; Michael et al., 1994).

Researchers have employed different but equally problematic methods in several other popular surveys of sexual behavior in the United States, including the Playboy survey (Hunt, 1974) and the Hite Report (Hite, 1976/1987). These methodological problems include targeted sampling of potentially biased populations (e.g., relying on data provided by Playboy magazine subscribers or National Organization of Women members to represent sexual experiences of the general population; Griffitt & Hatfield, 1985; Michael et al., 1994) and generalizing the conclusions to the American population, despite extraordinarily high refusal rates. For example, the Playboy survey had a 98.7% refusal rate, and the Hite Report had a 97% refusal rate (Michael et al., 1994), which clearly should elicit the reasonable question of who were the individuals who did respond, and what larger population are they, in fact, representative of? Representativeness of these data was further diminished because the researchers allowed self-selected volunteers to provide sexual survey data (e.g., the Kinsey Reports, the Hite Report, the Playboy survey) without any efforts made to determine, and correct for, the relevant differences among the individuals who refused to participate. Unfortunately, although many results from widely circulated research reports are skewed and inaccurate, the public has received them as factual truths, which often jive with misleading portrayals in the media that sex occurs on a frequent basis and is more often than not perfectly executed, varied, active, and rewarding. However, if we consider only methodologically sound studies, a very different picture emerges.

# Myths to Debunk

Education and accurate facts regarding sex and sexual activities are vital to healthy relationships and sexual functioning. In this section, I consider three popular myths of human sexuality as a vehicle for countering inaccurate beliefs about sex and fostering more adaptive and realistic views about personal sexuality.

## Myth #1: Everyone, Except You, Is Having Plenty of Fabulous and Interesting Sex

The music, movie, and advertising industries serve up fantasies of hot, steamy, and flawless sex to sell products and increase profit margins. Accordingly, the public can easily fall prey to misinformation and distortions about sexuality that (a) engender unrealistic expectations that few can realistically hope to attain, (b) form the crux of maladaptive personal sexual scripts, and (c) foster the tendency to make invidious comparisons with people's bodies, behaviors, and experiences with what is seen on screen and in print.

A landmark, well-designed study called the National Health and Social Life Survey (Laumann et al., 1994; Michael et al., 1994) was among the first research endeavors to provide interpretable, extensive, and reliable data on the topic of sex in America. The study meets the gold standard of social research methodology (e.g., large sample randomly selected, representative sample with respect to relevant variables, data lost due to refusals to participate accounted for) and has since been replicated (J. A. Davis & Smith, 1991) with nearly identical results (Laumann et al., 1994; Michael et al., 1994; Smith, 1994).

These first peeks inside the bedrooms of Americans yielded a rich lode of information regarding sex and relationships in our modern culture. For example, 90% of Americans report that they are married by age 30, and the large majority of the population spends their adulthood in a marriage with an average duration of 25 years. Contrary to popular belief, the great majority of couples are faithful, whether they are married or cohabitating, with 85% of women reporting that they have been faithful throughout all their partnerships. Younger women report slightly more fidelity (88.3% of 18- to 29-year-old women), compared with 80.1% of women aged 40 to 49. Of men, 75% report lifetime faithfulness. Like women, younger men report higher rates of fidelity (93% of 18- to 29 year-old-men, compared with 63% of men aged 50 to 59). Only 4% of Americans report they have engaged in extramarital sex in the previous 12 months (Laumann et al., 1994; Thompson, 1983). Although Americans do have more sexual partners than in previous years, only 3% of the adult population report five or more sexual partners in their lifetime, and half of all adults report three or fewer partners in their lifetime. The data on the frequency of sex in America show that the people having the most sex are married couples.

Research shows that three factors largely predict the frequency of sex: age, partnership status, and partnership duration. Newly married young people have the most sex. The frequency of sex is nearly identical across all demographic variables, including level of education, geographic location, ethnicity, race, and religion. Of married people, 40% report they participate in sex two or more times each week, whereas another 50% have sex once every 10 days. Only 10% of couples report that they have sex a few times, or less, each year. The frequency of sex falls off significantly in one's 30s, and continues to decrease with each decade of life.

Research on what specifically takes place in bedrooms shows that Americans do not engage in a great deal of variation, sexually speaking (Laumann et al., 1994; Michael et al., 1994; ). For example, nearly every adult surveyed (95%) who is sexually active reported that the most recent sexual encounter consisted of, and culminated in, vaginal sex. The majority of Americans have tried oral sex at some point in their lives (80% of men and 70% of women), but oral sex only occurs in one out of five sexual encounters.

When there is variation outside the very prevalent norm (i.e., mutual manual stimulation followed by vaginal sex), the specific sexual practices are linked to three specific social variables: education, age, and race. Considering how education is related to oral sex practices, for example, twice as many women who have attended college have experienced oral sex (giving and receiving) compared with women who have not finished high school. With regard to age, 33% of men in their 20s reported having engaged in giving and receiving oral sex during their last sexual interaction, compared to only 13% of men in their 50s. The same age disparity is reported for women. The impact of race is reflected in reported lifetime experience giving oral sex: 75% of White women have engaged in it, compared to only 34% of African American women.

Similar trends exist for anal sex practices in America. Approximately one quarter of men and women reported having tried anal sex during their lifetime, and nearly 10% had engaged in it during the previous 12 months. Only 2% of people reported having had anal sex during their most recent encounter, however. There is a greater likelihood of having had anal sex one or more times if people are younger, White, and better educated.

Over 80% of individuals report that their sexual activities typically last one hour or less, and the older respondents were far more likely than the younger ones to have sexual encounters lasting 15 minutes or less. Whereas the typical lovemaking encounter lasts from 15 to 45 minutes, only 2 to 7 minutes of that time is spent having intercourse (Leiblum & Rosen, 1989).

In addition to less impressive sexual norms than might be expected based on media portrayals, sexual problems are more widespread than many people may realize (McCarthy, 1997; Michael et al., 1994). Although estimates vary across studies, the prevalence of sexual dysfunction is reported to be 10% to 52% for men and 25% to 63% for women (Laumann, Paik, & Rosen, 1999; Lewis et al., 2004; Rosen, Taylor, Leiblum, & Bachmann, 1993; Spector & Carey, 1990). The four most prevalent sexual problems include erectile disorder (ED), premature ejaculation (PE), lack of desire for women, and difficulties achieving climax for women.

Many studies have reported estimates of moderate to complete ED (Feldman, Goldstein, Hatzichristou, Krane, & McKinlay, 1994; Laumann et al., 1999; Selvin, Burnett, & Platz, 2007) in the range of 18% to 30% of adult men, varying from about 2% in men younger than 40 years to 86% in men 80 years and older (Prins, Blanker, Bohnen, Thomas, & Bosch, 2002). Prevalence studies on ED have prompted the National Institutes of Health Consensus Panel on Impotence (1993) to deem ED an important national problem and to suggest further study and treatment development as an urgent need for our population. Depending on the population studied, 20% to 40% of men report premature ejaculation (Althof et al., 2010; Laumann, Paik, & Rosen, 1999; Laumann et al., 2005; Trudel, 2002), and many more than that complain that they are unable to sustain sexual activity as long as they would like.

Low sexual desire is the most frequent sexual complaint among women (Davison, 2012). In a nationally representative sample of adult American women, the rate of low or hypoactive sexual desire was estimated to range from 26.7% in premenopausal women to 52.4% in naturally postmenopausal women (West et al., 2008). In adult men, the rates of hypoactive sexual desire are lower, and typically hover around 15% (Laumann et al., 1999).

Research shows that only 29% of American women who engage in sex have orgasms consistently, although 44% of men report that their partners do so (Laumann et al., 1994; Michael et al., 1994). Nonclinical population surveys find that 30% percent of women report that they are unable to achieve orgasm (Michael et al., 1994; Trudel, 2002). In contrast, orgasms on a consistent basis are reported by 75% of men, whereas only 5% of men report coming to a climax "sometimes, rarely, or never."

A stunning statistic is that between one third and one half of the population experiences sexual difficulties. These statistics paint a sobering picture counter to the myth that "everyone except for you" is having more and better sex.

## Myth #2: Vaginal Intercourse Is the Most Effective Way to Get the Female to Orgasm

As noted above, in our culture, vaginal intercourse is the goal of nearly all sexual activity. Data show that 95% of adult Americans report having engaged in vaginal intercourse in their most recent sexual encounter. Of men, 95% name this specific act as their preferred method of climaxing, and most couples view the sexual interaction as over when the man climaxes (Laumann et al., 1994; Michael et al., 1994). Unfortunately, the great majority of women are unable to reach orgasm with vaginal intercourse alone. Even among women who report that they are regularly orgasmic, one third state that they are never able to reach climax during intercourse (Foley, Kope, & Sugrue, 2012). Moreover, for those women who can achieve climax during intercourse, most can do so only if they either receive the necessary clitoral stimulation by the incidental or intentional rubbing action caused by penile thrusting or if they are adequately aroused prior to the penetration by effective, nonpenetrative stimulation (Foley et al., 2012).

Women report that they experience the most physical pleasure from nongenital and genital nonintercourse stimulation (Basson 2000, 2001; Foley et al., 2012). Both genders hold the misconception that vaginal intercourse is "as good for her as it is for him." Although this contention, generally speaking, is not correct, it persists despite the fact that it contributes to many missed orgasms for women and considerable discontent for both men and women as they struggle in the dark, figuratively and literally, to achieve the elusive female climax.

Misunderstanding of the anatomical aspect of female arousal is propagated by the cultural embrace of a very narrow definition of sex. That is, many people in our culture wrongly equate sex with vaginal intercourse. There are many reasons for this view. Evolutionarily speaking, vaginal intercourse is what truly matters: If the sole purpose of sex is to procreate, then intercourse is all that is required. Additionally, several major religions dictate that vaginal intercourse occurs only in the marital context and constitutes the only acceptable sexual act. Moreover, television, movies, and music vividly portray sex as a passionate, intense crescendo of breathless kissing and speedy clothing removal, followed by a flawless, fabulous act of penetration. Viewers rarely witness extended scenes of sensual pleasuring or nonpenetrative, genital stimulation. These influences shape our expectations and personal sexual scripts, which largely dictate our behaviors (Irvine, 2003; Zea, Reisen, & Diaz, 2003). Unfortunately, the popular script that vaginal penetration is the ultimate goal, and the narrow definition of sex that supports it, is truly a disservice, if not harmful, to men and women alike (McCarthy & Fucito, 2005).

The good news is that most women can orgasm, when provided with the proper stimulation. Researchers have shown that 75% of women are capable of reaching orgasm with clitoral stimulation (Foley et al., 2012). Although many specific sexual acts allow each partner to reach orgasm, even simultaneously, for most women, clitoral stimulation is required.

Clitoral stimulation provided orally appears to be the most reliable means for women to reach orgasm (Dodson, 2002; Leiblum & Sachs, 2003). However, as noted above, only 20% of male-female sexual interactions include oral sex. Manual clitoral stimulation is always available during intercourse, provided the partners choose sexual positions that allow the female to receive adequate stimulation. Still, the most common way for couples to consistently reach orgasm is the method called "taking turns," with "first her, then him," being the recipient of effective sexual stimulation.

## Myth #3: Women Experience Sex Like Men Do

Masters and Johnson (1966) developed the original, science-based model of the sexual response cycle, which Helen Singer Kaplan (1979) further elaborated. This traditional conceptualization focuses on biological indicators of desire, including genital responses, conscious sexual thoughts, sexual fantasies, and the wish to self-stimulate. Masters and Johnson's research, which established the first scientific account of human sexual responses, was based on laboratory studies of men and women who were able to achieve orgasm during intercourse and who consented to be observed in a laboratory, while hooked up to various monitors and recording devices (Tiefer, 1991). Unfortunately, willingness to participate in such research set the female participants squarely apart from most women in the population. As a result, researchers have increasingly criticized the portrayal of the female sexual response cycle depicted through this research as inaccurate. The Masters and Johnson description of the male sexual response, however, has generally held up to the scrutiny of modern research.

The model that has emerged as a more accurate description of female sexuality is based on findings that women's motivation to engage in sexual interactions (i.e., sexual desire) is not strictly sexual; in fact, most often, it is not even primarily sexual (Basson 2000, 2001; Hall, 2004). For women (particularly in their 30s or older, and not in a new relationship) sexual arousal and desire and sexual receptiveness is *not* about biological urges for sexual release. Instead, it pivots more on the emotional and interpersonal context and wish to be intimate, which are far more influential for women in determining the outcome of any given sexual opportunity (Basson 2000, 2001; Hall, 2004; Regan & Berscheid, 1999). Women in long-term relationships reliably report that their drive to be sexual is linked to feeling emotionally connected, respected, and able to talk to their partner. These aspects of emotional intimacy are what turn women's neutral feelings about sex into desire and receptivity, and combined with effective sexual stimulation, a physical state of sexual arousal (Christopher & Sprecher, 2000; Cohen & Shotland, 1996; Hill & Preston, 1996). Clearly, this perspective of female sexual arousal and responses diverges sharply from the traditional male model.

Male and female sexual responses also differ substantially in terms of arousal awareness. Women, in general, have a poor and unreliable awareness of their own sexual responses. The female arousal response, equivalent to the male erection, is vaginal vasocongestion, which involves characteristic responses of genital swelling and flushing, lubrication, and increased clitoral sensitivity. Researchers have shown that women generally fail to perceive these physiological changes when they occur (Basson, 2001; Laan & Everaerd, 1995, 1998; Laan, Everaerd, van der Velde, & Geer, 1995).

Of course, awareness of arousal is much more apparent in the case of men insofar as their erection is visible. The awareness of the physical response itself provides feedback that contributes to sexual arousal & further promotes sexual behaviors and desire in a recursive manner (Barlow, 1986; Metz & McCarthy, 2004). In contrast, women's physical responses do not provide sensory feedback to promote further interest in, or motivation for, more sexual interaction. Indeed, women often are unaware of their bodies' responses to stimulation or sexual images and thoughts. Due to the relative absence of clear biological urges and awareness of sexual arousal, women rely more on the interpersonal context to assess and recognize their desire.

A notable exception to this pattern is women in their 20s, who tend to have more biologically driven sexual responses (Basson, 2001). Another exception occurs in long-term relationships following a physical separation, when women of all ages tend to have more sex-drive-based sexual responses that are not so dependent on relational factors (Basson, 2001). Clearly, even apart from these exceptions, some women of all ages (like those in the Masters and Johnson research) experience sexual responses that are more biologically based, and similar to the more typical male responses. The average woman's sexual response, however, is not well reflected in the original Masters and Johnson depiction and is instead more accurately understood within the relational context.

It bears emphasis that men also have important intimacy needs in relationships that clearly play a role in sexual desire and arousal. However, generally speaking, compared with women, men's arousal responses tend to be instigated more by biological than relational factors (Metz & McCarthy, 2003; Shabsigh, 2007).

# Healthy Concepts to Set the Stage for Enhancement

## Healthy Sexuality Is Your Own Responsibility

A healthy, satisfying sex life starts in a person's mind as well as body, often beginning with the understanding that (a) sexual functioning cannot be divorced from physical functioning, (b) sex is a natural and good part of life, and (c) individuals have as much right to pursue enhanced sexual experiences as they do to pursue a healthy marital relationship or a fit and healthy body. When people take responsibility for their own pleasure, sexual skill development, and body and sexual responses, they begin to acquire the mindset necessary to build a satisfying sexual relationship.

As a clinical psychologist specializing in treating patients with ongoing sexual difficulties, I frequently hear people make complaints that reflect their misunderstanding of personal responsibility: "My boyfriend can't get me off," "My wife still doesn't know what turns me on," and "My husband is terrible in bed." Invariably, when I inquire about the person's efforts to teach their partners the specific methods to improve their sexual relationship, they typically report that they have not done so. Additionally, given the inhibition and emotion most people feel about sex, the statements partners make are often anxiety laden, accusatory, dismissive, and pessimistic. People rarely share with their partners how they would like sex to be initiated, what type of kissing is most arousing, what they would like to try, or any other aspect of their sexual desires or preferences. Unfortunately, when their partners don't know what they prefer, they're often disappointed, hurt, angry, and resentful. If people don't think about, explore, and discuss their likes and dislikes and needs and wants with their partners, they deprive themselves of opportunities to experience and share sexual satisfaction.

## Good Sex Does Not Happen Magically

Pleasurable sexual activity, however, is more than a mindset or the product of good communication: it is a physical act. Like learning to be good at any physical activity, it requires skills to be honed, accompanied by the motivation to practice and excel. Pleasure giving and receiving are physical at their core and mental at the level of receptivity, decision making, focus, and perseverance. These mental and physical skills can be taught and learned, practiced, and improved. People are not born great skilled athletes or great lovers; both talents require a set of skills and the ability to master teachable concepts that can be learned on a mutual basis.

Setting appropriate goals is important. When the basics and mechanics of good, consistent sexual responding are in place, the couple can discuss other goals, such as more variation and frequency in sexual activities and simultaneous orgasms. Regardless of the specific goal a couple identifies, what is key is that each partner takes equal ownership of achieving the goal. The challenge for the male is to establish an emotional, relational, and sexual context for the woman to achieve climax and feel satisfied, while managing his arousal level to sustain an erection or sexual activity until he and his partner are ready to climax. The challenge for the woman is to become comfortable with her sexual responses, facilitating her ability to become more sexually responsive, reaching orgasm reliably and effectively. To achieve these goals requires communication, self-knowledge, and a set of requisite skills.

Before proceeding further, it is important to note that individuals for whom sexual dysfunction is not psychogenic in origin may experience few or no skill deficits. In cases of any functional loss, sexual or otherwise, it is prudent to first consult a physician to determine whether a change in functioning is caused by a medical issue. Many medications, therapies, and procedures are available for individuals with biologically based sexual dysfunctions (Metz & McCarthy, 2003, 2004; Shabsigh, 2007). Many sexual difficulties do not have biological origins and are directly amenable to improvement through mental and behavioral changes. However, it is also true that some sexual difficulties arise as the result of a temporary physical problem (e.g., urinary tract infection, side effect of a medication, upswing of stress) but can be maintained for psychological reasons, after the physical source of the difficulty is no longer present (Metz & McCarthy, 2003, 2004). Many individuals could benefit from expert psychological and medical evaluation of their sexual difficulties and from making a commitment to improve aspects of their intimate life that are amenable to change.

Importantly, dysfunction and enhancement range on a single continuum. Accordingly, the same skill-based interventions used to treat erectile dysfunction, premature ejaculation, and low desire and problematic orgasm for women can also be employed to enhance sexual pleasure. Individuals who want more sex, more intense orgasms, longer mutually satisfying interactions, and a better understanding of how to satisfy their partner, can consult the steadily accumulating body of empirical research that, while based on ameliorating dysfunction, can also be applied to the enhancement of sexual activities.

## The Tone of the Lovemaking is Crucial

The manner in which we choose to complete life tasks determines what we ultimately accomplish. When we are generous, relaxed, empathic, nonjudgmental, and patient, we set the tone for emotionally satisfying and intimate interactions, sexual or otherwise. As discussed above, when women feel connected and close to their partner, their natural set point of neutral interest in sex is more likely to morph into desire and receptiveness to sexual engagement. Importantly, most women experience the most physical pleasure from nongenital and genital nonintercourse stimulation (Basson 2000, 2001; Foley et al., 2012). Women frequently describe their partners as "rushing" toward vaginal sex, at the expense of their ability to relax and enjoy and slowly build up the physical arousal that allows them to climax. Women are benefitted, and therefore men as well, when both partners conceive of foreplay as central to lovemaking. Interestingly, men also request that their female partners proceed more slowly (Dodson, 2002; McCarthy & Fucito, 2005). Partners would do well to openly acknowledge that sensual, non-penetrative pleasuring is the main course for most women and proactively engage in sexual interactions that facilitate female orgasms. Each partner should relax his or her body and create the relational environment for the partner to relax, as people function better sexually when they are relaxed and calm (Metz & McCarthy, 2003). Asking gentle, information-based questions about what is especially pleasurable is a helpful way both to communicate interest in better ways to enjoy sexual activities and to gauge sexual preferences. For women, and no doubt many men, researchers have garnered support for the old adage that "sex doesn't start in the bedroom." Men who are interested in having more sex and satisfied and receptive partners should take heed from this research and apply the findings with gusto.

## Empirically Supported Skill Enhancement

### Pay Attention: The Problems of Distraction

If a man participates in sex and worries about losing his erection or not pleasing his partner, what he is *not* doing is enjoying the intimate encounter. Consider the analogy of sexual arousal as being like water coursing through a pipe. As the flow of arousal travels through the pipe, it represents the attention devoted to pleasurable physical sensations. If the arousal information in the pipe has to share its space with performance anxiety, or other distracting thoughts, it can interrupt, diminish, or preclude the flow of sexual excitement and pleasure, producing erectile problems in men or delayed or absent orgasm in women.

The difference between enhancing sexual enjoyment for individuals without significant arousal issues and treating an arousal dysfunction is often merely a matter of degree. Learning to pay attention and focus on moment-to-moment experience is an exceptionally helpful means of enhancing sexual experiences for all individuals. The ancient art of tantric sex, famous for the intensity and duration of mutual orgasms, is based on achieving the same proactive mental focus.

Paying attention in this concerted way is more important and more difficult than many people realize. Indeed, in my clinical practice, many people express surprise when they observe their thoughts in the midst of sexual encounters and discover that they habitually fail to pay attention to erotic sensations and, instead, become aware of thoughts that range from completely counterproductive (e.g., "Is my partner seeing the flab on my belly?", "I hope I don't lose my erection") to unhelpful and distracting (e.g., "I have got to remember to take the chicken out of the freezer," "I should have sent that email to my boss today"). When errant thoughts compete for attention with sexual arousal, predictable outcomes are a less-than-satisfactory sexual experience, a waning erection, or an elusive orgasm.

The first step for many individuals with performance concerns is to realize that being fully present in the sexual moment is a worthwhile skill and an important goal to achieve. Clinicians have succeeded in teaching patients seeking treatment for erectile dysfunction and orgasm issues to practice focusing on sexual sensations and thereby minimize competing stimuli and increase the ability to function better sexually (Dove & Wiederman, 2000; Meana & Nunnink, 2006; Metz & McCarthy, 2004).

Decades ago, Masters and Johnson (1970) developed the sexual exercise called sensate focus that continues to be useful and effective today (Meston, Hull, Levin, & Sipski, 2004; Ribner, 2003; Rosen, 2001). In sensate focus, sexual action is slowed way down, and the focus is on the sensual sensations of caressing and touching, often with the explicit directive to not proceed to intercourse. This exercise teaches the couple skills of sensual focus and creates an interaction conducive to acquiring new patterns of mutual pleasuring. When the focus is on pleasure and not intercourse, both men and women experience a significant increase in intimacy and closeness and develop a new script for mutually pleasurable sexual encounters (Foley et al., 2012; McCarthy & Fucito, 2005; Metz & McCarthy, 2004).

## The Role of Masturbation for Sexual Enhancement

Masturbation is at the core of two extremely important aspects of good sex: the timing of ejaculation for men and the path to orgasm for women. A man's self-control over the timing of his orgasm is called ejaculatory control, and it is best learned in the context of masturbation (Perelman, 2006; Metz & McCarthy, 2004).

The problem of the male climaxing too soon is very often simply his lack of understanding and knowing how to control his sexual responses. In order for a couple to have control over the duration of their love making, it is key for a man to learn and practice ejaculatory control. Through masturbation, a man can learn his unique bodily response to arousal and develop the ability to recognize the space between imminent and inevitable sexual release. It is in this space where he can learn through self-knowledge and self-control to maintain his arousal at a peak level, without ejaculating until he and his partner are ready.

When a man learns to recognize that he is in the arousal gap (between imminent and inevitable), he can then develop a personal strategy to maintain control until he and his partner are ready to move to climax. To do so, he needs to learn how to relax his body, become aware and consciously able to control and strengthen his pelvic muscle, through various exercises of stopping and starting flow of urine, and learn to tolerate increasingly higher levels of arousal without ejaculating. Arousal tolerance can be developed by establishing a graded list (0 to 100) of increasingly arousing stimuli (e.g., images, actions, sensations, fantasies, techniques) and starting at the bottom of the list, slowly working up and down the list, allowing for an erection to develop, then recede, each time focusing on and staying within the space between imminent and inevitable ejaculation. Over time, the man is able to move further up the list, as he develops more control while delaying orgasm. Metz and McCarthy (2003) have written an excellent book intended for the public on the specific methods to tolerate increasing arousal, not just stopping the arousal or distracting oneself from it. Practicing relaxation, self-awareness, arousal tolerance, and self-control techniques can facilitate the ability to inhibit ejaculations. Men who delay ejaculation also report stronger and more intense orgasms (Dodson, 2002), a lovely bonus for this generous act of self-control.

The second aspect of enhancement through masturbation is that it is the most effective way for a woman to learn how her body responds to sexual stimulation and what type of stimulation is most pleasurable and likely to produce an orgasm, with or without a partner. Clitoral stimulation is the most effective and reliable means for most women to reach climax (Dodson, 2002; Metz & McCarthy, 2003; Nairne & Hemsley, 2011), but women are quite individual in how the specific stimulation is best provided. Many women like very light, indirect touch, but others prefer more intense pressure. Some women prefer very little movement, whereas other women prefer the opposite. Some women achieve orgasm most easily with circular motions, whereas others report that use of a vibrator provides the most effective stimulation for orgasm (Herbenick et al., 2010). Learning what works is best done, at least initially, by a woman alone, in nonpartnered activity, with the woman then in a position to either teach her partner how to stimulate her to orgasm or provide self-stimulation to accompany the pleasure that her partner provides. Because many people are uncomfortable with the practice of masturbation (Dodson, 2002; Foley et al., 2012), this discomfort is best handled directly and openly. Each partner should work toward an explicit behavioral acceptance of masturbation and its important role in mutually satisfying partnered sex.

While on the topic of masturbation, there is one important issue that requires a brief digression. Known in the medical community as an increasingly prevalent problem called sexual compulsivity, it is more commonly known as "sex compulsivity." Public awareness continues to increase on this topic, despite the fact that those individuals affected by it are generally extremely ashamed and rarely admit or discuss the problem openly. Still, sexual compulsivity is a real problem that significantly impairs and damages both the individual (usually the man) and his spouse. Because most Americans have come to understand the problem of sexual compulsivity by reading gossip magazines and viewing titillating television shows on the topic, there is considerable misinformation that bears correction. Sexual compulsivity is not about having unabashed endless sex in the Don Juan style often assumed. The majority of people with sexual compulsions operate in complete isolation, where they excessively masturbate and use pornography as their central behaviors (Carnes, 2001). They live generally in a state of denial, avoiding their increasing fears of being caught and their intense feelings of shame and self-disgust at their inability to stop. Quickly or slowly, people with sexual compulsions often escalate into additional problematic behaviors such as web chatting, phone sex, and anonymous sex partner matching sites (Carnes, 2001, 2008). Continued familiarity with these environments may lead to escalation to increasingly more direct, in-person sexual encounters. Each escalation triggers more intense feelings of fear and shame, which in turn brings on more intense secrecy and denial (Collins & Adleman, 2011). An extremely wide variety of sexual compulsions include compulsive prostitution use, massage parlor use, chronic affairs, anonymous sex, transgender behaviors, and cross dressing. At its core, however, the excessive, out-of-control use of masturbation (often with pornography) is typically the foundational behavioral problem. Individuals seeking treatment for this problem often are also suffering from depression, various anxiety disorders, or other disorders of impulse control (e.g., gambling, spending, eating compulsions).

The cycle of sexual acting out is often triggered by overwhelming negative emotions. Once the decision is made to engage in the sexual behaviors, there is an intense anticipation of pleasure and unrealistic expectations during the pursuit or planning of an encounter. Once the sexual encounter occurs, individuals report a crushing revulsion and intense feelings of shame and self-hate, often vowing to never engage in the behaviors again (Collins & Adleman, 2011). These cycles repeat over years and very often the secret sex life is addressed only when it has been discovered and exposed by an irate and shattered spouse. Individuals and couples devastated by this problem can and do recover. There is a growing body of helpful books for those affected (and their spouses), particularly those written by Patrick Carnes, Stephanie Carnes, and Pia Mellody. Also, there are a surprising number of available support meetings (in person, online, or via telephone), in the 12-step tradition, which are viewed by many as absolutely critical to their continuing progress (go to saa-recovery.org or sa.org for information). Finally, there are a growing number of therapists specifically trained to address this problem and its aftermath. These therapists generally carry the qualification of CSAT (certified sex addiction therapist) and can be located by searching for the term *certified sex addiction therapist.*

## How to Choose More Desire

Desire is the crucial foundation for change and action in our intimate lives. Sexual desire is the force that attracts two people toward intimacy and sparks the motivation to overcome fatigue, boredom, fear, shyness, insecurity, and innumerable potential obstacles that stand in the way of positive sexual relations. Without desire, there is no self-generated motivation to act. In short, desire is essential to a rewarding sex life.

Researchers have shown that for the great majority of people who report low sexual desire, the cause is rarely biological (Hall, 2004; Leiblum & Sachs, 2003), rendering useless the aggressively marketed pharmaceutical agents, potions, and panaceas touted as cures for low desire. Ironically, inhibited desire is a side effect of many medications, including those developed to treat high blood pressure, anxiety, and depression. Accordingly, consumers concerned about sexual side effects are well advised to discuss alternatives with prescribing physicians. Kathryn Hall's *Reclaiming Your Sexual Self* (2004, for women) and Shabsigh's *Sensational Sex in 7 Easy Steps* (2007, for men) offer comprehensive lists of medications known to decrease libido. However, for the majority of people who experience low desire, the problem is far more likely to be the product of their psychological makeup, life stresses, body image problems, fatigue, depression, a history of sexual abuse or trauma, and relationship issues (Hall, 2004; Leiblum & Sachs, 2003). Couples' issues that diminish desire include the inability to resolve marital conflict, lack of physical attraction, poor-quality love-making, fear of closeness or intimacy, and discomfort over power disparity in the relationship (Pridal & LoPiccolo, 2000).

Gaining insight regarding impediments to more intense or frequent sexual desire can be extremely useful. It is often important that couples discuss low sexual desire in an open and honest manner, and view it as a couple issue, rather than the sole problem of the partner with lower desire. Fortunately, people who choose to bring more desire into their lives can take action to realize their goal.

In most couples, one partner wants more sex than the other, which can lead to the partner feeling rejected or sexually deprived, while the other partner experiences anger about being pressured to engage in unwanted sex. Accordingly, both partners experience the disparity in desire negatively. Often couples stuck in this quagmire lose mutual physical affection when the lower-desire partner withdraws due to the fear that any expression of affection will be misinterpreted as an attempt to initiate sexual activity.

Given this common consequence of a desire imbalance, the first step is to re establish a comfortable level of loving nonsexual, physical affection between the partners. Each individual needs to understand that actions intended to achieve closeness (e.g., hugging, cuddling, holding hands) are *not* invitations to sexual interactions. Touch elicits feelings of attachment for both partners, and for women, often an increase in sexual desire.

In the next step, I encourage frank discussions in which each partner discusses preferred methods of interacting on a sexual basis. It is imperative that the individual with lower desire teaches his or her partner the methods of sexual initiation, and the circumstances around initiation, that most inspire receptivity. Likewise, the greater-desire partner needs to teach his or her partner how best to decline a sexual initiation. Aggressive or insensitive interactions surrounding initiating and declining sexual activity are to be specifically avoided.

Research has shown that individuals with low desire tend to be unaware of sexually relevant environmental cues (Pridal & LoPiccolo, 2000). Similar to the common experience of recognizing that you are hungry when you smell or see food, sexual interest is increased with awareness of sexual cues. Individuals who purposefully become more aware of sexual elements or stimuli in their lives report that these efforts increase spontaneous sexual thoughts and increased receptivity (Pridal & LoPiccolo, 2000; Schover & LoPiccolo, 1982). Increasing awareness of sexual cues can be accomplished in many ways, for example, by paying attention and keeping a log of sexual scenes in movies and on television, reading books or stories with romantic or erotic content, and making an intentional point to tell these stories to the partner, talking and thinking about sex generally, and constructing and sharing fantasies of sexual or sensual interactions.

The next step is to create an environment conducive to sex. The daily conversations between spouses are often limited to establishing who will take the dog to the vet and whether the dishwasher is working as well as it once did. This hardly inspires passion. Instead, people can be encouraged to act affectionate, sexual, and flirtatious in private settings, including sending an occasional sexy text or email that is brief, positive, and promising, and to tease and be teased. Moreover, partners can leave notes, buy sexual toys, and express wishes that are sensual and sexual, even if these gestures are outside the person's typical comfort zone. If the partner is not in the mood to be playful, individuals are advised to choose to interpret it generously and to try again at a more opportune time.

The final component to increasing desire is addressing and improving actual love-making skills. Good sex provides positive feedback, creates strong memories, promotes self-confidence, prompts creative suggestions, and increases desire for future encounters. Learning to be a good lover is important and typically very much appreciated. Several excellent sex manuals are available, which provide specific and explicit instructions. *Becoming Orgasmic* (Heiman & LoPiccolo, 1988) is written by two eminent sex research psychologists and has an accompanying video. The act of finding and reading sex manuals together and discussing the various topics can also bring sexuality back to the forefront of attention, thus increasing desire.

## Communication Is Essential

The ability to talk openly and safely about sexual topics consistently predicts both marital and sexual satisfaction (D. Davis et al., 2006; Litzinger & Gordon, 2005). Research indicates that those couples that do not have the necessary skills to communicate, and instead act defensively and withdraw from each other, are more likely to end up divorced (Carr'ere & Gottman, 1999; Gottman & Levenson, 1992; Rogge & Bradbury, 1999). Couples and sex therapists report that sexual issues are among the most difficult topics to discuss (Sanford, 2003). Moreover, the more difficult it is for a couple to talk about a topic, the more likely that they will participate in damaging and negative communication tactics (e.g., expressing contempt or disgust, being critical nonconstructively; Carr'ere & Gottman, 1999; Litzinger & Gordon, 2005).

Sharing sexual desires and preferences, making sexual requests, and providing feedback to partners about intimate interactions is typically very challenging. Metts and Cupach (1989) examined the uniquely difficult aspects of sexual communication and identified the main reasons for reluctance to communicate as feeling vulnerable; exposing private identity, embarrassment, shame, and fear of ridicule; and being hurt. Despite the difficulties inherent in sexual communication, it is extremely helpful for couples to push through their inhibitions and learn to communicate effectively. Many couples have managed through nonverbal communication to be in sync and satisfied with each other sexually. Most couples, however, are often not in perfect interpersonal harmony and would experience greater intimacy, feelings of safety, and sexual satisfaction if they were able to exchange sexual information verbally.

Generally speaking, it is reassuring and confidence building to know with certainty how to please a sexual partner, but this is particularly true for men. Purnine, Carey, and Jorgensen (1997) found that in couples in which the man accurately understood his partner's sexual needs and desires, the woman's and the man's sexual satisfaction was significantly and positively related. The researchers found that it was less important for a woman to possess specific information about her partner's needs and desires for both to report satisfaction. Purnine, Carey, and Jorgensen's research further indicated that men's satisfaction with their sexuality may be based more on their performance and pleasing their partners and less on their being effectively stimulated themselves. Communication clearly helps each partner know how to provide effective and sexually satisfying stimulation. As Kaplan (1974) observed decades ago, providing effective stimulation may be central to men's sexual satisfaction, whereas receiving effective stimulation may be central to women's sexual satisfaction.

Rosen and Leiblum (1988) have promoted the importance of sexual scripts that develop in relationships. A comfortable sexual script implies agreement between partners regarding specific sexual acts, how and who initiates sexual encounters, and the frequency of sexual interactions. Significant difficulties can arise when a previously comfortable script is disrupted by life changes (e.g., arrival of children, aging, illness, sexual difficulty), and the couple does not possess the necessary communication skills to effectively handle such changes and negotiate a new script. Agreement on the patterning of sexual activities predicts both sexual and marital satisfaction (Purnine, Carey & Jorgenson, 1997).

## Case Example

The case study that follows illustrates the pitfalls of not communicating about sexual topics. My patients Mike and Jen sought treatment after 5 years of marriage. Both in their late 30s, they embarked on therapy in significant marital distress. Mike had learned and absorbed as a young man a variety of unhelpful, unrealistic expectations about men's desire and performance from his boastful friends and through watching porn videos. He believed that men were supposed to be ready and happy to have sex at any time, regardless of the situation, and he held rigid beliefs about what "real men" do, feel, and don't talk about.

One year before Mike and Jen came for therapy, Mike had experienced several episodes during sex in which he lost his erection and was unable to continue having intercourse. Mike interpreted these incidents as a dramatic loss of masculinity and a harbinger of a complete loss of sexual functioning. Accordingly, he experienced a particularly strong emotional reaction to those incidents of fear and defensiveness, acted angry at the time, and refused to speak to Jen about it. Instead, he decided to "handle" his concerns about erection loss by purposely ejaculating quickly, so he wouldn't lose his erection. Soon the nature of their intimacy changed and became one-sided and strained. The couple had managed up to that point to have a sexual relationship without any verbal communication about sexual needs and preferences. During these weeks of sexual difficulty, Mike and Jen felt awkward and distant and became concerned about the growing tension, but neither felt able to talk about the situation openly. Because of her own strong negative emotional reactions, Jen began to make critical, sarcastic remarks regarding the abruptness and brevity of their sexual interactions. As the strain worsened, Mike not only stopped having sex with Jen but also avoided all physical contact with her because he worried that she would misinterpret his affection as a sexual invitation. Jen, who had always been sensitive about her weight, personalized Mike's rejection of her and felt hurt and humiliated. She did not express any of these feelings, and as time passed and nothing changed, she became increasingly angry.

When Jen finally spoke up about the topic, she was nervous and resentful and did not express herself very well. Mike was defensive and overreacted because he felt guilty, anxious, and angry. During their brief but heated talk, Mike ended up saying the problem was Jen's fault. She was hurt by his words and then began to experience a downward spiral characteristic of many couples that are not skilled at communication. They became increasingly distant, avoided each other, and began to interpret each other's behaviors in a negative way. Mike and Jen began to quarrel openly about sex, and because they were both prone to making thoughtless and blaming remarks, they soon transitioned into arguing about the things said in anger during their verbal battles, which included in-laws, character deficits, driving habits, and so forth. What began as a sexual misstep morphed into a serious threat to their marriage due to an inability to communicate effectively. Not surprisingly,

Mike and Jen came to treatment expressing high levels of hurt and anger, spanning a broad range of topics.

After I assisted in de-escalating the relationship crisis and provided the couple with education on sexuality, Mike and Jen began to learn and practice basic communication skills in session. We began to address their sexual relationship to get it back on track. Mike expressed feeling inadequate sexually, and he was able to explain the connection between his sexual performance and his views of himself as a worthy man. He shared that he had felt less desire for sex than he had in the past, which made him feel like a failure. Jen was very surprised to learn about Mike's feelings and began to feel less angry. She disclosed her own feelings of inadequacy regarding her weight and described feeling shame that she was apparently not attractive to Mike anymore. She was able to explain to Mike how his distancing and emotional withdrawal was far more devastating than anything that could possibly go wrong between them sexually.

Mike and Jen were ready to re-engage with each other sexually, and the final part of their therapy work was to learn to communicate with each other about sex. They were instructed on the value of shifting their goal from performance to pleasure, and they initiated a series of sexual homework assignments of regular sensual touching. Additionally, they had weekly assignments to participate in specific sexual communication tasks to complete during the sensual touching exercises. Their first was to make unsolicited positive statements, in the midst of the sexual interaction or shortly afterward, regarding what they specifically enjoyed during the current encounter. For example, "I love it when you caress my breasts with your mouth," or "It makes me really turned on when you undress me slowly before we get into bed." They were required to verbalize specific, instructive, and positive information.

The second exercise was to communicate and ask positive, information-seeking questions about their partner's sexual preferences in a positive, respectful, and reassuring manner. Doing so in the moment is often easiest for people, as it was for Mike and Jen. They were instructed to ask questions gently and kindly, for example, "Do you like it when I do this really lightly or when I exert more pressure?" or "Does this feel better when I go slowly or do you like it faster?" They soon graduated to asking questions more broadly and open-endedly, which requires more of the person answering, such as inquiring about fantasies during or after a sexual encounter and asking the partner about what they liked best or what they may have wanted to change. As with most every couple I have guided through these exercises, to their pleasant surprise, Mike and Jen reported they discovered that they did not know their partner's preferences as well as they had assumed. They began to experience improved sexual compatibility, more trust and emotional safety, and greater mutual desire.

This case illustrates that effective communication is the primary tool for negotiating the ongoing challenges couples face. Good communication is also extremely helpful in developing sexual skills by creating a specific road map to achieve pleasure and intimacy. Committing to making at least one statement and asking at least one question during each encounter typically contributes to developing a more satisfactory sexual relationship.

## Conclusions and Future Research

Researchers have only recently begun to examine the enhancement of sexual interactions. The work of Rosemary Basson (2000, 2001) in particular, has moved the field forward in terms of understanding women's sexual responses and illuminating the fact that women's sexuality is not simply a variation of men's sexuality. At this early stage of scientific inquiry, with few exceptions, the great majority of studies on sexuality focus on alleviating or "correcting" dysfunction, rather than the enhancement of human sexual experiences more generally. Although there is a slowly accumulating body of exceptional research that has begun to shed light on the central components of sexual enhancement, there is a paucity of scientific research that evaluates sexual techniques, thinking patterns, beliefs, and interpersonal skills specific to promoting and enhancing sexual experiences. Moreover, there are few well-controlled randomized trials that compare different approaches to treating diverse sexual dysfunctions and enhancing sexual pleasure in nonclinical populations. Finally, there is a pressing need to translate extant research findings into readily accessible, science-based how-to books and manuals dedicated to sexual enhancement and intended specifically for those who are not experiencing dysfunction of any kind.

## References

Althof, S. E., Abdo, C. H., Dean, J., Hackett, G., McCabe, M., McMahon, C. G., & Tan, H. M. (2010). International Society for Sexual Medicine's guidelines for the diagnosis and treatment of premature ejaculation. *Journal of Sexual Medicine, 7*(9), 2947–2969.

Barlow, D. H. (1986). Causes of sexual dysfunction: The role of anxiety and cognitive interference. *Journal of Consulting and Clinical Psychology, 54*(2), 140.

Basson, R. (2000). The female sexual response: A different model. *Journal of Sex & Marital Therapy, 26* (1), 51–65.

Basson, R. (2001). Using a different model for female sexual response to address women's problematic low sexual desire. *Journal of Sex & Marital Therapy, 27,* 395–403.

Butzer, B., & Campbell, L. (2008). Adult attachment, sexual satisfaction, and relationship satisfaction: A study of married couples. *Personal Relationships, 15,* 141–154.

Byers, E. (2005). Relationship satisfaction and sexual satisfaction: A longitudinal study of individuals in long-term relationships. *Journal of Sex Research, 42,* 113–118.

Call, V., Sprecher, S., & Schwartz, P. (1995). The incidence and frequency of marital sex in a national sample. *Journal of Marriage and Family, 57(3).*

Carnes, P. J. (2001). *Out of the shadows.* Center City, MN: Hazelden.

Carnes, P. J. (2008). *Facing the shadow: Starting sexual and relationship recovery.* Carefree, AZ: Gentle Path Press.

Carr'ere, S., & Gottman, J. M. (1999). Predicting divorce among newlyweds from the first three minutes of a marital conflict discussion. *Family Process, 38,* 293–301.

Christopher, S. F., & Sprecher, S. (2000). Sexuality in marriage, dating, and other relationships: A decade review. *Journal of Marriage and Family, 62,* 999-1017.

Cohen, L. L., & Shotland, R. L. (1996). Timing of first sexual intercourse in a relationship: Expectations, experiences, and perceptions of others. *Journal of Sex Research, 33,* 291–299.

Collins, G., & Adleman, A. (2011). *Breaking the cycle: Free yourself from sex addiction, porn obsession and shame.* Oakland, CA: New Harbinger.

Davis, D., Shaver, P. R., Widaman, K. F., Vernon, M. L., Follette, W. C., & Beitz, K. (2006). I can't get no satisfaction: Insecure attachment, inhibited sexual communication, and sexual dissatisfaction. *Personal Relationships, 13,* 465–483.

Davis, J. A., & Smith, T. W. (1991). *General social surveys, 1972–1991: Cumulative codebook (No. 12).* Chicago, IL: National Opinion Research Center.

Davison, S. L. (2012). Hypoactive sexual desire disorder. *Current Opinion in Obstetrics and Gynecology, 24(4),* 215–220.

Dodson, B. (2002). *Orgasms for two: The joy of partner sex.* New York, NY: Harmony Books.

Dove, N. L., & Wiederman, M. W. (2000). Cognitive distraction and women's sexual functioning. *Journal of Sex & Marital Therapy, 26,* 67–78.

Feldman, H. A., Goldstein, I., Hatzichristou, D. G., Krane, R. J., & McKinlay, J. B. (1994). Impotence and its medical and psychosocial correlates: Results of the Massachusetts Male Aging Study. *Journal of Urology, 151,* 54–61.

Foley, S., Kope, S., & Sugrue, D. (2012). *Sex matters for women: A complete guide to taking care of your sexual self* (2nd ed.). New York, NY: Guilford Press.

Gates, G., (2011, April 8). Gay people count, so why not count them correctly? *Washington Post.* Retrieved from http://www.washingtonpost.com

Gottman, J. M., & Levenson, R. W. (1992). Marital processes predictive of later dissolution behavior, physiology, and health. *Journal of Personality and Social Psychology, 63,* 221–233.

Griffitt, W., & Hatfield, E. J. (1985). *Human sexual behavior.* Glenview, IL: Scott, Foresman.

Hall, K. (2004). *Reclaiming your sexual self: How you can bring desire back into your life.* Hoboken, NJ: John Wiley & Sons.

Heiman, J., & LoPiccolo, J. (1988). *Becoming orgasmic.* Englewood Cliffs, NJ: Prentice Hall.

Herbenick, D., Reece, M., Sanders, S. A., Dodge, B., Ghassemi, A., & Fortenberry, J. D. (2010). Women's vibrator use in sexual partnerships: Results from a nationally representative survey in the United States. *Journal of Sex & Marital Therapy, 36*(1), 49–65.

Hill, C. A., & Preston, L. K. (1996). Individual differences in the experience of sexual motivation: Theory and measurement of dispositional sexual motives. *Journal of Sex Research, 33,* 27–45.

Hite, S. (1976/1987). *The Hite report.* New York, NY: Dell.

Hunt, M. (1974). *Sexual behavior in the 1970s.* Chicago, IL: Playboy Press.

Irvine, J. M. (2003). Introduction to "Sexual Scripts: Origins, Influences and Changes." *Qualitative Sociology, 26,* 489–490.

Janus, S. S., & Janis, C. L. (1993). *The Janus Report on Sexual Behavior.* New York, NY: John Wiley & Sons.

Kaplan, H. S. (1974). *The new sex therapy: Active treatment of sexual dysfunctions.* New York, NY: Times Books

Kaplan, H. S. (1979). Hypoactive sexual desire. *Journal of Sex & Marital Therapy, 3,* 3–9.

Kinsey, A., Pomeroy, W., & Martin, C. (1948). *Sexual behavior in the human male.* Philadelphia, PA: Saunders.

Kinsey, A., Pomeroy, W., Martin, C., & Gebhard, P. (1953). *Sexual behavior in the human female.* Philadelphia, PA: Saunders.

Kisler, T. S., & Christopher, F. (2008). Sexual exchanges and relationship satisfaction: Testing the role of sexual satisfaction as a mediator and gender as a moderator. *Journal of Social and Personal Relationships, 25,* 587–602.

Laan, E., & Everaerd, W. (1995). Determinants of female sexual arousal: Psycho-physiological theory and data. *Annual Review of Sex Research, 6,* 32–76.

Laan, E., & Everaerd, W. (1998). Physiological measures of vaginal vasocongestion. *International Journal of Impotence Research, 10,* S107–S110.

Laan, E., Everaerd, W., van der Velde, J., & Geer, J. H. (1995). Determinants of subjective experience of sexual arousal in women: Feedback from genital arousal and erotic stimulus content. *Psychophysiology, 32,* 444–451.

Laumann, E. O., Gagnon, J. H., Michael, R. T., & Michaels, S. (1994). *The social organization of sexuality: Sexual practices in the United States.* Chicago, IL: University of Chicago Press.

Laumann, E. O., Nicolosi, A., Glasser, D. B., Paik, A., Gingell, C., Moreira, E., & Wang, T. (2005). Sexual problems among women and men aged 40–80 y: Prevalence and correlates identified in the Global Study of Sexual Attitudes and Behaviors. *International Journal of Impotence Research, 17*(1), 39–57.

Laumann, E. O., Paik, A., & Rosen, R. C. (1999). Sexual dysfunction in the United States prevalence and predictors. *Journal of the American Medical Association, 281*, 537–544.

Leiblum, S., & Rosen, R. (Eds.). (1989). *Principles and practice of sex therapy: Update for the 1990s.* New York, NY: Guilford Press.

Leiblum, S. R., & Sachs, J. (2003). *Getting the sex you want.* New York, NY: ASJA Press.

Leonhardt, D. (2000, July 28). John Tukey, 85, statistician. *New York Times.* Retrieved from http://www.nytimes.com

Lewis, R. W., Fugl-Meyer, K. S., Bosch, R., Fugl-Meyer, A. R., Laumann, E. O., Lizza, E., & Martin-Morales, A. (2004). Epidemiology/risk factors of sexual dysfunction. *Journal of Sexual Medicine, 1*(1), 35–39.

Litzinger, S., & Gordon, K. C. (2005). Exploring relationships among communication, sexual satisfaction, and marital Satisfaction. *Journal of Sex & Marital Therapy, 31*, 409–424.

Masters, W. H., & Johnson, V. E. (1966). *Human sexual response.* Boston, MA: Little, Brown.

Masters, W. H., & Johnson, V. E. (1970). *Human sexual inadequacy.* Boston, MA: Little, Brown.

McCarthy, B. W. (1997). Strategies and techniques for revitalizing a nonsexual marriage. *Journal of Sex & Marital Therapy, 23* (3), 231–240.

McCarthy, B. W., & Fucito, L. M. (2005). Integrating education, realistic expectations, and therapeutic interventions in the treatment of male sexual dysfunction. *Journal of Sex & Marital Therapy, 31* (4), 319–328.

Meana, M., & Nunnink, S. E. (2006). Gender differences in the content of cognitive distraction during sex. *Journal of Sex Research, 43*, 59–67.

Meston, C. M., Hull, E., Levin, R. J., & Sipski, M. (2004). Disorders of orgasm in women. *Journal of Sexual Medicine, 1*, 66–68.

Metts, S., & Cupach, R. W. (1989). The role of communication in sexuality. In K. McKinney & S. Sprecher (Eds.), *Human sexuality: The societal and Interpersonal context* (pp. 139–161). Norwood, NJ: Ablex.

Metz, M. E., & McCarthy, B. W. (2003). *Coping with Premature Ejaculation.* Oakland: New Harbinger Publications.

Metz, M. E., & McCarthy, B. W. (2004). *Coping with erectile dysfunction.* Oakland, CA: New Harbinger.

Michael, R. T., Gagnon, J. H., Laumann, E. O., & Kolata, G., (1994). *Sex in America: A definitive survey.* Boston, MA: Little, Brown.

Nairne, K. D., & Hemsley, D. R. (2011). The use of directed masturbation training in the treatment of primary anorgasmia. *British Journal of Clinical Psychology, 22*(4), 283–294.

National Institutes of Health Consensus Development Panel on Impotence. (1993). *Journal of the American Medical Association, 270*, 83–90.

Perelman, M. A. (2006). A new combination treatment for premature ejaculation: A sex therapist's perspective. *Journal of Sexual Medicine, 3*, 1004–1112.

Pridal, C. G., & LoPiccolo, J. (2000). Multielement treatment of desire disorders. In S. R. Leiblum & R. C. Rosen (Eds.), *Principles and practice of sex therapy*. New York, NY: Guilford Press.

Prins, J., Blanker, M. H., Bohnen, A. M., Thomas, S., & Bosch, J. L. (2002). Prevalence of erectile dysfunction: A systematic review of population-based studies. *International Journal of Impotence Research, 14*(6), 422.

Purnine, D. M., Carey, M. P., & Jorgensen, R. S. (1997). Inventory of dyadic heterosexual preferences and inventory of dyadic geterosexual preferences-other. In C. M. Davis, W. L. Yarber, R. Bauseman, G. Schreer, & S. L. Davis (Eds.), *Sexually-related measures: A Compendium*. Thousand Oaks, CA: Sage.

Regan, P. C., & Berscheid, E. (1999). *Lust: What we know about human sexual desire*. Thousand Oaks, CA: Sage.

Ribner, D. S. (2003). Modifying sensate focus for use with Jewish couples. *Journal of Sex & Marital Therapy, 29*, 165–171.

Rogge, R. D., & Bradbury, T. N. (1999). Till violence do us part: The differing roles of communication and aggression in predicting adverse marital outcomes. *Journal of Consulting and Clinical Psychology, 67*, 340–351.

Rosen, R. C. (2001). Psychogenic erectile dysfunction. *Urologic Clinics of North America, 28*, 269–278.

Rosen, R. C., Taylor, J. F., Leiblum, S. R., &Bachmann, G. A. (1993). Prevalence of sexual dysfunction in women: Results of a survey study of 329 women in an outpatient gynecological clinic. *Journal of Sex & Marital Therapy, 19*, 171–188.

Rosen, R. C., & Leiblum, S. R. (1988). A sexual scripting approach to problems of desire. In S. R. Leiblum & R. C. Rosen (Eds.), *Sexual desire disorders* (pp. 168–191). New York, NY: Guilford Press.

Sanford, K. (2003). Expectancies and communication behavior in marriage: Distinguishing proximal-level effects from distal-level effects. *Journal of Social and Personal Relationships, 20*, 391–402.

Schover, L. R., & LoPiccolo, J. (1982). Treatment effectiveness for dysfunctions of sexual desire. *Journal of Sex & Marital Therapy, 8*(3), 179–197.

Selvin, E., Burnett, A. L., & Platz, E. A. (2007). Prevalence and risk factors for erectile dysfunction in the US. *American Journal of Medicine, 120*(2), 151.

Shabsigh, R. (2007). *Sensational sex in 7 easy steps*. New York, NY: Rodale.

Smith, T. W. (1994). *The demography of sexual behavior*. Menlo Park, CA: Kaiser Family Foundation.

Spector, I. P., & Carey, M. P. (1990). Incidence and prevalence of the sexual dysfunctions: A critical review of the empirical literature. *Archives of Sexual Behavior, 19*, 389–408.

Sprecher, S. (2002). Sexual satisfaction in premarital relationships: Associations with satisfaction, love, commitment, and stability. *Journal of Sex Research, 39*, 190–196.

Tavris, C., & Sadd, S. (1975). *The Redbook report on female sexuality*. New York, NY: Delacorte.

Thompson, A. P. (1983). Extramarital sex: A review of the research literature. *Journal of Sex Research, 19*(1), 1–22.

Tiefer, L. (1991). Historical, scientific, clinical and feminist criticisms of "the human sexual response cycle." *Annual Review of Sex Research, 2,* 1–23.

Trudel, G. (2002). Sexuality and marital life: Results of a survey. *Journal of Sex & Marital Therapy, 28,* 229–249.

Weaver, J. (2007, April 16). Many cheat for a thrill, more stay true for love. *MSNBC. com.* Retrieved from http://www.msnbc.msn

West, S. L., D'Aloisio, A. A., Agans, R. P., Kalsbeek, W. D., Borisov, N. N., & Thorp, J. M. (2008). Prevalence of low sexual desire and hypoactive sexual desire disorder in a nationally representative sample of U.S. women. *Archives of Internal Medicine, 168*(13), 1441.

Yeh, H. C., Lorenz, F. O., Wickrama, K., Conger, R. D., & Elder, G. H., Jr. (2006). Relationships among sexual satisfaction, marital quality, and marital instability at midlife. *Journal of Family Psychology, 20,* 339–343.

Zea, M. C., Reisen, C. A., & Diaz, R. M. (2003). Methodological issues in research on sexual behavior with Latino gay and bisexual men. *American Journal of Community Psychology, 31,* 281–291.

# 16

# Raising Our Kids Well

## Guidelines for Positive Parenting

*Keith D. Allen*

*Mark D. Shriver*

Munroe Meyer Institute

University of Nebraska Medical Center

*Cy Nadler*

Children's Mercy Hospital

School of Medicine: University of Missouri-Kansas City

## Positive Parenting: Definitions and Key Concepts

People take parenting seriously and have done so for a very long time. Indeed, ideas about how parents should treat children have been expressed through writings in religion, philosophy, and law throughout history. Some of the earliest known systematic theorizing about parenting occurred as long ago as the fourth century BCE. Plato and Aristotle wrote that parents should attend closely to the care of infants and should be involved in structuring children's play activities to encourage the most positive or useful social traits (French, 2002). To a large extent, early writings with parenting advice were dominated primarily by philosophers, religious leaders, and physicians (Holden, 1997).

That changed most dramatically with the advent of psychology as a science and as a discipline distinct from philosophy in the late 19th and early 20th centuries. As psychology developed, theory and research about parenting directly influenced conceptualizations of what constitutes effective parenting and the interest has not waned. A recent search of professional literature with the PsychInfo keyword *parenting* produced 25,000 hits. In just the first 3 months of 2012, there were scholarly articles on topics ranging from "vegetable parenting" to "grandparent parenting." In addition, there were myriad articles on the impact of parenting on behavioral health issues such as obesity, smoking, depression, asthma, stuttering, dating violence, social phobia, attention deficit hyperactivity disorder (ADHD), sleep problems, attachment, job satisfaction, delinquency, injury, aggression, perfectionism, and Internet risks.

## Parenting Matters

This long-held interest in parenting stems, at least in part, from the considerable body of evidence, both in science and in practice, suggesting that parenting matters (e.g., Bornstein, 2005). Parenting practices have been clearly linked to the health and well-being of children and adolescents (e.g., Dishion & McMahon, 1998), and some have suggested that it may be the most important public health issue facing our society (Hoghughi, 1998). For example, studies have found that positive parenting fosters the child's sense of basic security, thereby enabling attachment, which is essential for subsequent mental health and self-esteem (Hoghughi & Speight, 1998). In addition, parenting has been found to have an important role in a child's development of social and cognitive skills (Landry, Smith, & Swank, 2003).

Nevertheless, not everyone agrees on how much parenting matters. The last decade has brought increased attention to the role of factors such as genetics and peers in accounting for how children turn out (e.g., Cowan, 2005; Mekertichian & Bowes, 1996; Plomin, 1999; Wright & Beaver, 2005; ). In addition, a number of provocative books have questioned the influence of families in general and parenting in particular (Harris, 2009; Rowe, 1994). Yet although twin and adoption studies have shown, for example, that a wide range of children's attributes are clearly influenced by the genes they inherit from their parents, this does not mean that the influence of parenting style must be weak (Maccoby, 2000). Evidence suggests that the expression of heritable traits often depends on experience with specific parental behaviors (Collins, Maccoby, Steinberg, Hetherington, & Bornstein, 2000). Indeed, there is still substantial evidence that parenting is linked to psychological well-being (e.g., Ceballo, Ramirez, Hearn, & Maltese, 2003), and that it contributes in important ways to psychological development and emotional health (Bjorklund, Yunger, & Pellegrini, 2002). In fact, children exposed to emotional support from parents early in life have been found to have better mental health outcomes throughout adulthood (Chronis et al., 2007; Shaw, Krause, Chatters, Connell, & Ingersoll-Dayton, 2004; ). Finally, it is clear that parenting matters because it is linked to negative outcomes as well as good ones. Parenting is the single largest variable implicated in childhood accidents, child abuse, underachievement in school, drug abuse, truancy, and teen pregnancy (Hoghughi, 1998).

## When Parenting Matters Most

Although parenting is clearly linked to the well-being of children in general, it is even more critical to the health and well-being of a child who is challenging or difficult. Of course, many parents experience the challenges of occasional noncompliance and disobedience (Sanders et al., 1999). Studies have found that almost half of all parents of nonreferred children report problems with disobedience (Achenbach & Edelbrock, 1981; Campbell, 1995). Indeed, a certain level of disobedience in early childhood is not only normal but considered necessary for children to develop autonomy and assertiveness (Dix, Stewart, Gershoff, & Day, 2007). Nevertheless, when disobedience is perceived by a parent to be unusual in its frequency or intensity, it needs to be addressed to prevent future problems (Kalb & Loeber, 2003). Although acting-out behavior is often a normal stage of development that eventually will remit, there is a subset of children who present ongoing management problems for parents (Kerr, Lopez, Olson, & Sameroff, 2004). For this subset of children, behavioral problems identified in the preschool years persist (e.g., S. B. Campbell & Ewing, 1990; Keenan, Shaw, Delliquardi, Giovannelli, & Walsh, 1998) and place these children at a greater risk for later negative outcomes such as poor educational attainment, psychiatric disorders, and even juvenile delinquency (Mesman & Koot, 2001; Moffitt, 1993). Equally concerning is the fact that these early behavior problems can interfere with overall family functioning as well as a child's health and well-being (Fossum, Morch, Hadegard, & Drugli, 2007).

Unfortunately, ineffective parenting can exacerbate rather than resolve these early problems. Indeed, children who are exposed to harsh and punitive parenting during early development are likely to have more negative outcomes, such as fighting with peers, stealing, and anxiety (e.g., McKee et al., 2007). Furthermore, ineffective discipline strategies such as scolding and lack of monitoring have been found to increase behavior problems in children and antisocial behaviors in adolescents (Patterson, Reid, & Dishion, 1992).

## Positive Parenting as a Solution

Fortunately, there are excellent sources of guidance to help parents improve their parenting. These sources of guidance are grounded in science and have substantial empirical support. During the 1960s and 1970s, researchers began studying the best ways to train parents to manage challenging children (e.g., Walter & Gilmore, 1973; Wiltz & Patterson, 1974). The idea to use parents as agents of change made sense because parents have the greatest amount of contact with their child on a day-to-day basis and are clearly in a position to have a great amount of control and influence. As a result, researchers targeted parents and began developing programmatic approaches to positive parenting. Positive parenting has been defined, in general, as the appropriate contingent responsiveness of parents (whether positive, neutral, or disciplinary) to a wide range of child behavior and, in particular, as the appropriate use of contingent reinforcement to strengthen prosocial behavior (Wahler & Meginnis, 1997). Both elements (i.e., relationship-building and intentional reinforcement of prosocial behaviors) are thought to be important to fostering the harmony and synchrony necessary for a good parent-child relationship, and both elements are consistently present in the parenting programs that were developed.

Now, some 40 years later, the accumulated evidence in support of the positive benefits of these programs is substantial (for a review, see Eyberg, Nelson, & Boggs, 2008). Indeed, the Child and Adolescent Psychology Division (53) of the American Psychological Association (2012) has examined which parenting programs are backed by science and found five well-established empirically supported approaches to training parents. These programs are Parent Management Training (PMT; Patterson, Reid, Jones, & Conger, 1975), Helping the Noncompliant Child (HNC; McMahon & Forehand, 2003), Triple P (PPP; Sanders, 1999), The Incredible Years (TIY; Webster-Stratton & Reid, 2003), and Parent-Child Interaction Therapy (PCIT; McNeil & Hembree-Kigin, 2010). What follows is an overview of each program and a brief summary of the empirical evidence in support of these positive parenting approaches.

# Positive Parenting and Science: A Review of the Evidence

## Parent Management Training

PMT was developed by Gerald Patterson who, along with his associates at the Oregon Research Institute, helped pioneer behavioral parent training in the late 1960s and early 1970s. As they looked to address problems such as noncompliance, tantrums, crying, arguing, and teasing in children, Patterson and his colleagues were some of the first to conduct studies showing that parents could be taught the importance of consequences and how to use consequences to change behavior in a positive way. In PMT, parents are taught to view themselves as agents of behavior change in children from 3 to 14 years of age. Parents learn the importance of rewarding appropriate ways of behaving using praise and privileges as well as point systems, in which children can earn points that are later exchanged for more privileges, activities, and prizes. Parents are then taught how to use discipline for inappropriate behavior in the form of loss of points (on the point chart) or timeout.

The approach places a strong emphasis on teaching parents to understand the behavior theory behind the parenting techniques with the thought that parents who understand the basic principles of behavior change may be able to develop their own programs in response to new problems. The program also places a relatively strong emphasis on the use of point systems to help change behavior. These point systems offer flexibility in addressing a variety of different behaviors in children across a wide range of ages, and the point system charts help remind parents to monitor behavior. Perhaps most importantly, extensive research has demonstrated that their approach works. Studies have found that this parent training program produces significant improvements in child behavior (e.g., Patterson, Chamberlain, & Reid, 1982), with benefits that maintain for up to a year after parent training is complete (e.g., DeGarmo, Patterson, & Forgatch, 2004). In addition, the core elements of the program have been incorporated into training packages for parents of adolescents (Dishion & Kavanagh, 2003), foster parents (Chamberlain, Fisher, & Moore, 2002), divorced mothers (Forgatch &DeGarmo, 2002), and school prevention programs (J. B. Reid & Eddy, 2002).

## The Incredible Years

TIY was developed by Carolyn Webster-Stratton, director of the Parenting Clinic at the University of Washington. Like PMT, TIY emphasizes the critical role that parent-child interactions play in the development of child behavior (Webster-Stratton & Hancock, 1998). Nevertheless, the program places relatively greater emphasis on teaching parents how to use interactive play skills and modeling positive communication as well as how to use reinforcement and nonphysical discipline. The program originally was designed to target common childhood problems in children ranging from 2 to 8 years of age, such as tantrums and noncompliance, but has been expanded to address broader topics such as self-confidence, homework completion, and self-advocacy in children as old as 12 years old.

Parents meet weekly during training, in groups, to watch videotapes of parents modeling effective (and not so effective) parenting skills. Parents learn to focus on their child and to follow their child's lead during play by describing and commenting on what they see, by modeling cooperative play, by praising and approving of creative and appropriate actions, and by imitating what their child does. During play, parents are asked to resist urges to direct, command, organize, teach, and question.

Parents are also taught, outside the context of play, to "catch 'em being good," using specific and immediate praise and positive touch. In addition, TIY program encourages parents to model behaviors they want to see in their children and to use an incentive program, arguing that praise alone may not be enough to change behavior. The incentive program typically involves the delivery of stickers or points to children for appropriate or desired behavior, with the idea that the stickers or points can later be exchanged for other rewards, such as treats, privileges, or tangibles. The parent groups discuss and prepare for limit testing that will occur and then observe, discuss, and practice selective ignoring for inappropriate behavior and timeout or point losses for behaviors that cannot be ignored.

Numerous well-controlled, peer-reviewed studies have demonstrated that parents trained in TIY program have more positive parenting practices, improved parent-child interactions, and more prosocial behavior in their children (e.g., Webster-Stratton, 1994). When training has been offered in a prevention context, parents have also shown significant improvements in positive parent techniques (e.g., Webster-Stratton, 1998). Finally, studies with multiethnic parents have found that parenting techniques are also effective for and valued by diverse populations (e.g., M. J. Reid, Webster-Stratton, Beauchaine, 2002).

## Helping the Noncompliant Child

**HNC,** developed by Rex Forehand and Robert McMahon, uses a two-phase training model in which parents (typically of children between ages 2 to 8 years) are first taught to use their attention to establish positive, prosocial interaction patterns during "free play" and then use compliance training to reduce misbehavior during a "command" condition (McMahon & Forehand, 2003). During the free play, the child is permitted to lead and direct the activity while the parents provide a running commentary describing any appropriate play behavior or activity and using immediate and specific praise as well as physical touch to reward improved or desired behavior.

Parents are encouraged to eliminate questions or commands and to avoid any attempts at teaching the child. In the command phase, parents learn and practice how to communicate commands clearly, how to reward compliance, and how to use time-out or loss of privileges for noncompliance.

The 12-week training relies heavily on parents practicing skills with their child, who is typically present in every session. The training encourages parents to have standing rules about what is expected in the home and includes numerous handouts to help parents remember and use important positive parenting skills.

The supporting science behind this program is impressive, in part because the developers have empirically demonstrated the efficacy of important components of parent training such as praise (Bernhardt & Forehand, 1975), clear instruction giving (Roberts, McMahon, Forehand, & Humphreys, 1978), and time-out (e.g., Hobbs, Forehand, & Murray, 1978). Subsequent studies have shown that combining these techniques resulted in parents who were more positive (e.g., Wells & Egan, 1988), who had better feelings about their children (e.g., Forehand, Griest, & Wells, 1979), and who had children who were, even after many years, more well adjusted (e.g., Long, Forehand, Wierson, & Morgan, 1994). More recent studies suggest that these parenting strategies can be successfully adapted for community prevention efforts (Conduct Problems Prevention Research Group, 2002).

## Triple P—Positive Parenting Program

Triple P was developed by Matthew Sanders and his colleagues at The University of Queensland. The parent training component of Triple P is just one part of a "multilevel, preventively oriented parenting support strategy" targeting parents of children between the ages of 0 to 16 years (Sanders, 1999, p. 72). Parent training is embedded in a continuum of intervention levels that range from nationally executed media and information campaigns about raising healthy children (Level 1) to enhanced intensive family therapy that targets family stressors and other barriers to treatment in addition to severe child behavior problems (Level 5). There are also adaptations for group treatment (similar to TIY program), self-directed treatment (i.e., a parent workbook), and telephone-assisted treatment (i.e., telehealth). The Level 4 parent training program is called Standard Triple P.

Standard Triple P (Level 4) is designed to educate parents about how to foster child development and manage child misbehavior. Parents are taught how to deliver their attention contingent upon desirable behavior, purposefully ignore misbehavior, deliver clear instructions, and discipline children effectively. Discipline strategies include the use of logical consequences, quiet time (i.e., nonexclusionary timeout), and time-out. Parents are taught basic learning principles such as modeling and reinforcement and receive coaching and then practice how to apply this knowledge to solve novel problems in home and community settings. Families who do not see sufficient improvement at Level 4 are referred to the Enhanced Level 5 intervention which includes home visits to practice parenting skills and problem-solve, parent psychoeducation on coping with stress and mental illness using cognitive behavioral strategies, and a module for couples to improve their communication and mutual support of applying positive parenting skills.

Evaluations of the Triple P approach have demonstrated that parents who participate in the training are able to use the positive parenting strategies to produce positive changes in their children (e.g., Sanders & Dadds, 1982; Sanders & Glynn, 1981). Sanders and colleagues continue an ambitious research program and have extended their work to multiple continents and a wide range of populations, including families affected by maltreatment and abuse (Prinz, Sanders, Shapiro, Whitaker, & Lutzker, 2009), obesity (West, Sanders, Cleghorn & Savies, 2010), and developmental disabilities and autism (Sanders, Mazzucchelli, & Studman, 2004; Whittingham, Sonfronoff, Sheffield, & Sanders, 2009). A recent meta-analysis of 25 studies on the Level 4 program support its overall effectiveness in helping promote positive parenting and improve the behavioral health of children (de Graaf, Speetjens, Smit, de Wolff, & Tavecchio, 2008).

## Parent-Child Interaction Therapy

PCIT was developed by Sheila Eyberg and embraces attachment theory and the notion that sensitive and responsive parenting helps children develop more secure and effective emotional and behavioral self-regulation (Eyberg & Robinson, 1982; McNeil & Hembree-Kilgin, 2010). With this in mind, the program encourages parents to use play as a means of helping children between the ages of 2 to 8 years learn problem-solving skills as well as develop secure attachments. Thus, play itself is considered to be developmentally therapeutic.

In spite of this emphasis on attachment, the skills parents are taught are remarkably similar to those offered by the previously described programs. Parents learn to follow the child's lead, describe the action, and avoid questions and commands during play. Parents learn to both model and imitate appropriate behavior and also learn to selectively encourage good behavior and discourage inappropriate behavior by combining praise and touch with systematic ignoring of inappropriate child behavior. Finally, they learn to use time-out or loss of privileges when children misbehave and are asked to practice all of the skills with their child, both during training and in child-directed and parent-directed homework sessions.

Numerous well-controlled investigations have demonstrated that the positive parenting skills learned during the program training can produce parents who are more positive and attentive, as well as children who are less demanding and difficult (e.g., McNeil, Capage, Bahl, & Blanc, 1999; Nixon, Sweeney, Erickson, & Touyz, 2003). These benefits have been found to extend to school settings (McNeil, Eyberg, Eisenstadt, Newcomb, & Funder-burk, 1991) and to culturally diverse parents (e.g., Capage, Bennett, & McNeil, 2001). In addition, researchers are continuing to explore cultural, socioeconomic, and therapist variables that may impact outcome and main-tenance of outcome (Herschell, Calzada, Eyberg, & McNeil, 2002).

## Positive Parenting Techniques

Although the parent training programs described above were initially devel-oped to address early behavioral challenges such as noncompliance and tem-per tantrums, the parenting skills identified emphasize positive approaches to the development of prosocial behavior in children. As a result, they are equally important to those who simply want to know how to improve the health and well-being of a child (Biglan, Flay, Embry, & Sandler, 2012). Fortunately, because these programs evolved from the same basic behavioral and develop-mental foundations (see Roberts, 2008, for a more extensive history of behav-ioral parent training), they overlap substantially in terms of what parents are taught (Shriver & Allen, 2008). Furthermore, a recent meta-analytic review of these and many other published parent training programs has provided addi-tional validation of the components consistently associated with parenting effectiveness (Kaminski, Valle, Filene, & Boyle, 2008). Accordingly, it is pos-sible to recommend the "best-supported practices" for parents who want to enhance the health and well-being of a child (see Table 16.1).

### Best Practices

#### Build a Positive Relationship

A primary component of improving and maintaining child behavioral health involves building a positive relationship between parents and children by teaching parents how to increase positive interactions with their children, especially during play. This often involves intentionally scheduling opportuni-ties to play with a child and, during that time, trying to increase attentive responsiveness to the child's activities while trying to decrease the parental

**Table 16.1**    Positive Parenting Handout: What Parents Should Do

### Promoting Behavioral Health and Well-Being in Children: What Parents Should Do

Most parents want to nurture and care for their children in a way that promotes healthy development and emotional well-being. This means helping a child develop a sense of self-worth and self-discipline as well as teaching them to be responsible, independent, and well-adjusted. Decades of study and investigation have demonstrated six core components of effective parenting which are listed below.

1. Build a Positive Relationship: This means intentionally arranging to have many warm, affirming, nondemanding interactions with your child.

   a. Show interest in your child: notice and talk about what they do
   b. Follow their interests when you can
   c. Reduce criticisms and efforts to teach during every interaction
   d. Show affection with positive physical touch
   e. Use active listening/reflect comments and emotions

2. Nurture and Reward Desired Social Behavior: Place a greater emphasis on catching and rewarding good behavior than catching and disciplining bad.

   a. Catch child being good and use positive attention and labeled praise
   b. Use planned tangible rewards
   c. Allow kids to earn privileges for good behavior
   d. Use point charts and happy faces for success

3. Monitor and Supervise: Do you know where your children are and what they are doing? Achieving #1 and #2 will require that you do and will reduce or prevent likelihood of bad choices.

4. Use Effective Communication: Show and tell which behaviors are desirable.

   a. Model behaviors that you would like to see
   b. Clarify rules and expectations
   c. Give clear, direct commands

5. Practice: Parents and children both benefit from practicing positive, healthy behavior.

   a. Practice provides more opportunity to reinforce
   b. Practice helps a child learn basic skills they will need for success.

6. **Discourage Misbehavior:** Discipline is important but works best when there is a proportionately greater emphasis on positive rewarding and relating.
   a. Use planned ignoring
   b. Use time-out or natural/logical consequences
   c. Avoid spanking as a primary method of discipline

*Sources:* Biglan et al. (2012); Kaminski et al. (2008); Shriver & Allen (2008).

demands on a child during play. For example, parents are often coached to use reflective listening when a child is talking during play and to use imitation of child actions to create a responsive environment and to communicate positive regard for the child. In addition, parents are commonly encouraged to follow the child's lead during play interactions and to resist the temptation to repeatedly ask questions or to try to teach during play. The parenting programs universally recommend using praise for appropriate and cooperative play behavior as well as physical affection to increase the value of parent-child interactions. Finally, parents are often explicitly discouraged from criticizing child behaviors (even if the child is being mildly inappropriate), as well as issuing commands that limit and restrict a child's imaginative play.

### Reinforce Desired Child Behaviors

Each of the empirically supported programs emphasizes that parents should take specific steps to nurture, encourage, and reinforce behaviors that they like to see in their children. Desired child behaviors can include sharing with siblings or peers, following directions the first time without a reminder, cleaning up after play, making polite requests, getting ready for bed without a fuss, and coming when called. Strategies for parents to encourage or reinforce a child's behavior can range from offering descriptive praise, to delivering affectionate touch, to providing small treats, to arranging for special privileges. At a minimum, parents are asked to attempt to "catch your child being good," which typically involves immediate delivery of the rewards whenever desired behaviors are observed. Several of the programs encourage parents to even interrupt their adult-centered activities and conversations periodically to attend to children when desired child behavior is occurring. Examples might include a child who is quiet while the parent is on the phone, a child who waits patiently for food at a restaurant, or a child who stays in bed when the parent walks out of the room. This "catch 'em being good" approach asks parents to look for naturally occurring opportunities to reinforce desired behavior, but the empirically supported parenting programs do not leave it to chance that parents will actually remember to do this. Almost as difficult as remembering to catch a child being good is to recognize when a child is, in fact, being good. Thus, parents are often asked to also use a more structured point system to prompt themselves to remember to look and to remind themselves what to look for. For example, a point chart would provide a specific list of good behaviors as well as a specific amount of points that can be earned for using those behaviors. The earned points are typically then traded for planned rewards or privileges.

### Effectively Communicate Expectations

Although parents can and should look to frequently reward their children for positive behavior, parents who use effective communication can increase the odds that their children will make good choices in the first place. This often begins with modeling for a child the behaviors that are expected but can also include establishing straightforward standing rules about what is expected (e.g., keep hands and feet to self) and the consequences for rule violations (e.g., hitting or kicking means no TV today). Effective communication of rules involves reviewing the rules with a child, modeling for them what rule following looks like, posting the rules in a prominent place, and even practicing following the rules. Effective communication also involves being very intentional about how expectations are communicated to children on a moment-to-moment basis. For example, children sometimes have trouble identifying whether a statement by a parent is a question, a suggestion, or a command. This might occur when the command is actually phrased as a question or when the command itself is vague. Not surprisingly, children do not respond as well when it is not clear what behavior is expected. As a result, all the empirically supported programs teach parents to use a firm voice when giving a command, to use direct statements about what is expected rather than questions or requests (e.g., "It's time to pick up the toys" rather than "Can you pick up the toys?"), to be specific rather than vague, and to be simple rather than complex.

### Monitor Your Child

Clear commands and expectations will be of little use if the child rarely experiences encouragement and reinforcement for cooperation. For this reason, the empirically supported parenting programs place a primary emphasis on positive parent practices. Above all else, the programs focus on teaching parents to actively and consistently reinforce children for desired behavior. Accomplishing this requires, almost by default, an increased level of monitoring of what children are doing. That is, to be able to catch a child being good, to implement a point system, or to follow through consistently with consequences, whether positive or negative, requires that parents monitor children more closely. In addition, the importance of this relationship between monitoring and well-being continues throughout childhood and into adolescence, when lack of parental monitoring is one of the best predictors of children engaging in risky behaviors that can negatively impact health (see Dishion & McMahon, 1998, for a review).

### Practice

All of the programs emphasize the importance of intentionally arranging for opportunities for the parent and child to practice desired behaviors. This is probably most important in situations where a child may not understand what he or she is expected to do or is missing basic skills necessary to succeed. In these situations, combining instruction and modeling about what is expected along with practice will create more opportunities for a child to succeed and, therefore, create more opportunities for encouragement and reinforcement. As a result of an emphasis on practice, parents are not only in a position to encourage and support emerging behavior, but they are also in a position to teach new ones.

### Discourage Misbehavior

Finally, to compliment the emphasis on encouraging and reinforcing appropriate and healthy behaviors, proven parent training programs invariably include recommendations for parents to discourage inappropriate or unhealthy child behavior. There is wide consensus that these types of discouraging practices by parents should be implemented as consistently as possible. Indeed, predictability of consequences has been positively associated with child behavioral health (e.g., Patterson & Stouthamer-Loeber, 1984).

One of the most common and well-supported techniques for discouraging misbehavior involves ignoring misbehavior combined with an effort to focus attention instead on behaviors that one would prefer to see. In cases in which misbehavior cannot be ignored, there is strong empirical support for a planned consequence such as time-out. Time-out for misbehavior is recommended by all of the parent training programs and usually involves brief

(2 to 10 minutes, depending on age) placement in an area that removes a child's access to things he or she values, such as toys, electronics, activities, and parental attention. Time-out also serves the important function of allowing children (as well as parents) an opportunity to calm down. Finally, time-out can serve as an effective alternative to physical discipline strategies that are not recommended and are, in fact, discouraged by the empirically supported programs. In fact, overly harsh, intense, or punitive discipline strategies are seen as modeling hostile and coercive behaviors for children. Parents are encouraged to administer consequences such as time-out as unemotionally as possible, reserving emotional reactions for positive responses directed at appropriate and prosocial child behavior.

Although time-out is the most prominent discipline component, the empirically supported parent training programs also recommend a range of other brief and predictable consequences for misbehavior, including time-limited privilege losses that maximize the child's opportunity to try again as well as small response costs (allowance fines and token losses). Nevertheless, with the exception of time-out, these disciplinary strategies have rarely been investigated as independent parenting techniques (for a review of time-out research, see Everett, Hupp, & Olmi, 2010).

## Applying Best Practices in Positive Parenting

The six positive parenting principles presented in Table 16.1 were derived from research targeting young children with challenging behavior. However, there is every reason for parents to feel comfortable applying these same principles to raising typical children, with an eye toward preventing problem behaviors from emerging in the first place (Biglan et al., 2012). Indeed, this is exactly the approach being taken by the Triple P program in Australia, in which the core elements of positive parenting are being disseminated to all parents in a nationally executed media and information campaign about raising healthy children (Sanders, 1999). These core principles are also being disseminated to parents of children with a diverse group of clinical disorders, such as ADHD, anxiety disorders, oppositional defiant disorder, and even autism spectrum disorders (e.g., McNeil & Hembree-Kilgin, 2010). Ultimately, the core principles of positive parenting have applicability with a broad spectrum of children.

These positive parenting practices have also been determined to be valuable in promoting healthy outcomes with adolescents and in the prevention of adolescent problems such as drug and alcohol use, antisocial behavior, and risky sexual behavior (Biglan, Brennan, Foster, & Holder, 2004). For example, Patterson and Forgatch (2005) developed a program for parents of adolescents that derived directly from their original work in parent management training and is designed to address typical problems encountered by parents and includes each of the core principles in Table 16.1. Likewise, Dishion and Kavanagh (2003) developed a family-centered program focused on preventing and treating common adolescent problems. In this program, they specifically identify key parenting practices for promoting positive youth development that include: "relationship building, limit-setting, positive reinforcement, monitoring, and conflict resolution" (Dishion & Kavanagh, 2003, p. 13). Note, however, that parenting an adolescent often requires an appreciation for and sensitivity to their more advanced cognitive and social development, their strong desire for independence, and the increasing influence of peers. As a result, programs for parents of adolescents commonly incorporate additional strategies to improve parent-adolescent communication, negotiation, and problem solving.

## Applied Controversies

While decades of research has made it increasingly clear what parents can do to promote the behavioral health and well-being of their children, it is not always so clear what parents should avoid. Interestingly, although all of the empirically supported parenting programs support rewarding children, there are some experts who consider this to be detrimental to children. Likewise, while time-out is one of the most widely disseminated and recommended methods for discouraging misbehavior, it is not universally accepted as an appropriate parenting technique. Finally, although it never appears as a recommended practice in parent training programs, spanking is a commonly used discipline strategy that generates considerable controversy in regard to whether it is harmful or counterproductive. A review of the empirical evidence regarding each of these issues should prove helpful in guiding practice.

### Spanking

Spanking is a common practice in the United States. In 1994 to 1995, 94% of parents reported spanking their preschool-aged child (Straus & Stewart, 1999). By 2002, reflecting a decline, almost 80% of parents still reported spanking or slapping their preschool-aged child (Zolotor, Theodore, Runyan, Chang, & Laskey, 2011). Over half of parents surveyed in 2002 reported spanking or slapping their school-aged child (ages 6 to 11 years; Zolotor et al., 2011). Spanking is also commonly used in many other countries (Runyan et al., 2010). In spite of its apparent widespread use, spanking is not universally embraced and, in some countries, spanking is even outlawed (Smith,

2012; Zolotor et al., 2011). Indeed, the United Nations has adopted a statement on child rights that describes spanking as a form of child violence and advocates that countries take all appropriate measures to protect children from violence such as spanking (UNICEF, 1989, 2006). To date, the United States and Somalia are the only two countries that have not signed on to this convention (Smith, 2012; Zolotor et al., 2011).

Certainly part of the debate about spanking is rooted in whether spanking is morally justifiable rather than whether spanking is effective at discoursing misbehavior. Morals are largely ingrained within cultural and religious traditions and are not readily changed based on what science may proclaim. To many experts, the empirical evidence is clear that spanking is not effective and may in fact be detrimental to children's development (e.g., Berlin et al., 2009; Gershoff, 2002; Lansford et al., 2009; Zolotor, Theodore, Chang, Berkoff, & Runyan, 2008). Spanking is thought to increase the propensity for aggression in a child's relations with others (Taylor, Manganello, Lee, & Rice, 2010) and to increase his or her likelihood of behavior problems at school (Slade & Wissow, 2004).

However, other experts have found numerous methodological problems with much of the research on spanking, raising questions about what we think we know. For example, in a review of the literature, Hicks-Pass (2009) found definitional problems (e.g., spanking was conflated with more abusive physical punishment), sample limitations, research design limitations, measurement problems (e.g., self-report, retrospective report, rating scales with questionable reliability and validity), and a general lack of controlling for confounding variables. Ultimately, Hicks-Pass asked, "If 94 percent of parents spank, and spanking is correlated with aggression, suicide, and psychiatric symptoms, what factor or factors could explain why 94 percent of the population is not suicidal, aggressive, or depressed?" (p. 77). Larzelere and Kuhn (2005) suggested that the answer to questions such as the one posed by Hicks-Pass may lie, at least in part, in understanding the manner in which spanking is used. Larzalere and Kuhn described concerns that much of the previous research on spanking is correlational and typically failed to discriminate among different types of spanking, including what they defined as conditional, customary, or abusive spanking. Moreover, their meta-analysis of the literature suggested that *conditional* spanking (e.g., spanking limited to when a 2- to 6-year-old child refuses to sit in time-out) was actually superior to most alternative nonphysical disciplinary methods. They also found that *customary* spanking (e.g., how parents typically use spanking) was equally effective to alternative disciplinary methods. Only overly severe physical punishment was more likely to lead to negative child outcomes relative to alternative discipline methods (Larzelere & Kuhn, 2005).

Still other researchers have suggested that understanding the risks and benefits of spanking requires knowing something about the context in which it is used. This notion comes from research suggesting that spanking may not be detrimental to children's development at all. Spanking may in fact be effective when it is done in proper context, such as when there is a positive parent-child relationship, when it is used as an enforcement of other discipline, or when it is implemented within the context of accepted cultural norms (Gunnoe & Mariner, 1997; Larzelere, 2000; McLoyd & Smith, 2002; Simons & Johnson, 1994). For example, some researchers have suggested that race may mitigate any negative effects of spanking because spanking in some cultural groups is commonly accepted (e.g., Deater-Deckard & Dodge, 1997; Lansford, Deater-Deckard, Dodge, Bates, & Pettit, 2004). In contrast, other studies have found no differences relative to race/ethnicity regarding the negative outcomes of spanking (Gershoff, Lansford, Sexton, Davis-Kean, & Sameroff, 2012; Lorber, O'Leary, & Smith Slep, 2011).

### Guidance

From the perspective of science, whether spanking is bad and should be avoided is simply not clear. For this reason alone, it seems important to avoid harsh judgment of those that spank, especially when used in the context of a positive parent-child relationship, a key element in positive parenting. What is clear, however, is that none of the empirically supported parent training programs recommend spanking, nor do any of the numerous parenting programs on the federal government's National Registry of Evidence-Based Programs and Practices (Substance Abuse and Mental Health Service Administration, 2012). Thus, one must consider it risky to recommend a practice that is not widely endorsed within one's profession and does not appear to fall within the general standard of practice. However, refusing to recommend a practice is not the same as discouraging a practice. Should parents be discouraged from spanking? We think so. Even though there are some experts who have suggested that the literature supports the use of spanking in the right controlled context, there are no studies demonstrating that parents can be counted on to use spanking in this way. At the same time, there are reasonable alternatives that do have empirical support, not just in effectiveness but also in the appropriate use by parents. Recommendations should focus there.

### Time-out

In spite of considerable support for time-out as an effective technique for reducing problem behaviors, the practice has critics. Particularly in popular media outlets, the criticisms consistently center on declarations that time-out does not work (e.g., Gregory, 2012), is detrimental to the child (Haiman, 2012; Markham, 2012), or perhaps even leads to separation anxiety (e.g., Stiffelman, 2011). Still others have complained that time-out is too easily misused (Batcha, 2012), is an authoritarian approach that teaches children that they are not loved (e.g., N. Campbell, 2011), or is an approach that teaches that negative emotions are not acceptable and should be bottled up, breeding anger and resentment (Thompson, 2012). These criticisms are largely based on philosophical differences about what constitutes good parenting or perhaps on personal experiences or anecdotal reports. Many popular parenting websites provide commentaries or host blogs that promote particular parenting strategies or attempt to sell parenting books. A search of the peer-reviewed literature finds no empirical evidence that time-out has harmful or negative side effects and no data-based evidence questioning its effectiveness. Indeed, the evidence from 40 to 50 years of research involving this particular technique supports a conclusion that time-out works well, particularly in the context of a reinforcing environment in which there is a positive parent-child relationship (Morawska & Sanders, 2011).

### Guidance

The criticism that time-out can be misused or ineffective if implemented incorrectly could easily be dismissed as a truism, but that would be a mistake. Frankly, time-out can be difficult to implement, particularly for a parent who finds ignoring to be difficult or who has a child who is resistant. Nevertheless, most of the empirically supported parenting programs rely heavily on time-out as the primary technique for discouraging misbehavior. Thus, time-out is well established as an effective parenting technique and could be recommended to parents with confidence, especially in the context of providing guidance about how to implement it.

### Rewards

Since the mid-1970s there has been much research suggesting that the use of rewards may have detrimental effects on children, sabotaging their natural desire and producing other untoward side effects (e.g., Condry, 1977; Deci, Koestner, & Ryan, 1999; Kohn, 1993; Lepper & Green, 1978). This research has led some experts to go as far as discouraging any programs that involve attempts to reinforce child behavior (Kohn, 2005). Yet there is also considerable evidence that rewards do not have bad side effects (e.g., Dickinson,

1989; Pierce, Cameron, Banko, & So, 2003; Strain & Joseph, 2004). Nevertheless, concerns persist and the issue continues to be debated, both in the scientific literature (e.g., Cameron & Pierce, 2002; Urdan, 2003) and in the blogosphere (e.g., Topham, 2012).

The debate is fueled, in large part, by differing assumptions about the importance of the environment in shaping behavior and, more specifically, assumptions about how reinforcement affects intrinsic motivation (e.g., Deci & Ryan, 1985; Reiss, 2005). Intrinsic motivation is typically described as motivation to act without needing external rewards. Some claim that there is empirical evidence that reinforcement can undermine natural or intrinsic motivation (e.g., Henderlong & Lepper, 2002). However, continued research on this subject has revealed that detrimental effects of reinforcement are largely a function of the research methods used to study it (Akin-Little & Little, 2004; Bright & Penrod, 2009). In a meta-analysis of 145 studies on this topic, Cameron, Banko, and Pierce (2011) found "no evidence for detrimental effects of reward on measures of intrinsic motivation" (p. 21). In fact, the evidence suggested that on tasks that individuals initially find to be of low interest (e.g., low task engagement), both verbal and tangible rewards were found to have positive effects. Even on high-interest tasks, verbal rewards, such as praise, were found to have positive effects on task engagement/performance as well as self-reported interest in the task. The only detrimental effects of rewards were observed when tangible rewards were used to encourage engagement with tasks already of high interest, and even then, the detrimental effects were observed only if the participants received less than the maximum reward available (Cameron et al., 2001). Interestingly, there is some research suggesting that when praise is used, it is most beneficial if it is directed toward the child's behavior and effort (e.g., "You're working hard!") and not to some ability or quality of the child (e.g., "You're so smart!"). This research on the differential effects of praising ability relative to effort is largely correlational, but it appears that while praising a child's ability and effort can be equally effective in conditions of success, praising effort may show more benefit under conditions of failure. In other words, when children fail, they persist with behavior longer if their effort has been praised relative to children whose ability was praised (Burnett, 2002; Dweck, 2002; Henderlong & Lepper, 2002; Mueller & Dweck, 1998).

## Guidance

Broad assertions that reinforcement has adverse side effects are simply not supported, and calls for abandoning the systematic use of reinforcement in applied settings are unwarranted. While it is possible, in some cases, to show that rewarding a child for doing something he or she already does often can reduce a child's interest or engagement with that activity, the effect is limited to contrived situations and even then is usually temporary. Moreover, rarely would someone offer tangible rewards to a child for doing something he or she already does a lot or does well. On the other hand, the judicious and targeted use of rewards for teaching and promoting the use of prosocial behaviors is now widely recognized as a core feature of positive parenting and an important part of raising healthy children (Biglan et al., 2012).

## Faithful Applications of Positive Parenting: Self-help

For individuals who are interested in educating themselves about parenting by reading a book, there is a dizzying array of choices. A recent Internet search of self-help books on parenting found a staggering 70,000 hits for those seeking advice from Amazon and over 115,000 hits for those trolling at Barnes & Noble. There is advice on active parenting, commonsense parenting, confident parenting, positive parenting, effective parenting, loving parenting, and logical parenting, to name just a few. Some authors make rather extraordinary claims about their proven methods and their successes or offer vivid testimonials from readers and sometimes themselves. Others offer anecdotes from their own successes (and failures) as a parent. Faced with many choices and an abundance of supporting evidence, it can be confusing and difficult to know where to begin when seeking self-help advice about how to parent. Fortunately, others have already done that work. As we have seen previously, rather extensive evaluations of the empirical, peer-reviewed literature can provide relatively clear guidance on the principles and practices that have been found by scientists to directly benefit the health and well-being of children and the parent-child relationship (Shriver & Allen, 2008). As such, one way to approach the search for a valuable self-help book is to find those that rely on those same principles and practices. Toward that end, the most logical place to begin the search for good self-help books is to return to the empirically supported parenting programs themselves. Forehand, Webster-Stratton, Patterson, and Sanders, each highly respected and prominent researchers who developed and evaluated one of the empirically supported parenting programs, have also written a corresponding self-help book. To guide the selection process, we cross-referenced these four books on Amazon with those at Barnes and Noble. Forehand's book is currently the best-selling of the four.

## Parenting the Strong-Willed Child

Forehand and Long's (2010) *Parenting the Strong-Willed Child*, is a parent-friendly, 5-week version of their formal 12-session program described earlier. The book is true to its programmatic origins and in some ways is like a clinician's manual simplified for parents. As such, it walks the parent through the 5-week program with quite a bit more structure than most other self-help books. Each step builds upon the previous step, and readers are encouraged to track their progress in building the core foundational skills. These skills are then applied later in the book to solving a list of specific problems (e.g., managing mealtime, sibling rivalry, bedtime struggles, getting dressed, problems in the car). There is a strong reliance on behavioral concepts and terms throughout. The book is also realistic about the challenges of being a parent and the many social, cultural, health, and relationship variables that influence success. Perhaps as important as its scientific foundations is the fact that the authors have recently subjected their parent self-help book to a controlled empirical test (Forehand, Merchant, Long, & Garai, 2010). They found that parents who read their *Parenting the Strong-Willed Child* book (in comparison to those who read a parenting book with a developmental focus) had more well-adjusted children and found the book useful and easy to implement. Overall, this is an easy book to recommend.

Several other choices could be considered strong competitors of the Forehand and Long book because of their direct connection to an empirically supported program, including Webster Stratton's (2004) *The Incredible Years: A Trouble-Shooting Guide for Parents* and Sanders's (1998) *Every Parent: A Positive Approach to Children's Behaviour*. Both of these books are less structured and may be appealing for that reason. In addition, they address a larger number and wider variety of common childhood problems than *Parenting the Strong-Willed Child*. For example, *The Incredible Years* book includes advice about dawdling, divorce, short attention spans, TV addicts, and managing children in public, while the *Every Parent* book includes advice about handling child fears, sportsmanship, bullying, and homework. In addition, Sanders has also conducted a number of evaluations of his *Every Parent* book as a self-help guide but with mixed results (Markie-Dadds & Sanders, 2006a, 2006b Sanders, Markie-Dadds, Tully, & Bor, 2000;). Finally, each of these books includes an inordinate number of recommendations for successful implementation of each component of good parenting. To some parents, that approach might seem overwhelming. Nevertheless, these books have the same strong foundation in scientifically validated and positive approaches to parenting that are found in *Parenting the Strong-Willed Child*.

To help in evaluating the remaining self-help books, we decided to use the same empirically derived principles and practices previously discussed as a standard against which to compare the content of the most popular parenting books currently available. To guide the selection process, we cross-referenced the top books on Amazon with those at Barnes & Noble using *parenting* and *parenting-discipline* as the search terms and then sorting by *popular* or *best seller*. The top three books that appeared on both lists were *1-2-3 Magic*, by Thomas Phelan (2010), *Have a New Kid by Friday: How to Change Your Child's Attitude, Behavior and Character in 5 Days* by Kevin Leman (2008), and *Setting Limits With Your Strong-Willed Child* by Robert MacKenzie (2001). Phelan's book is currently the bestselling of the three.

## 1-2-3 Magic

The recommendations proffered in *1-2-3 Magic* are based on the five well-validated core components of good parenting described previously. A section on relationship building encourages parents to play with their children using reflections and descriptions while minimizing questions and criticisms. Another section emphasizes rewarding good behavior using praise and reward programs with sticker charts and both natural and arbitrary reinforcers. Finally, recommendations for discouraging misbehavior center on setting limits, using effective communication, and relying on nonharsh consequences such as time-out. The *1-2-3 Magic* program (including a video and group sessions but not the book alone) has been subjected to a controlled evaluation itself. Results showed that parents reported improved skills and had fewer child behavior problems than those who did not receive the program (Bradley et al., 2003). In spite of the name of the book, Phelan emphasizes that good parenting is not, in fact, magic, but hard work. This highly readable and engaging book could be comfortably recommended to parents. The remaining two popular books that emerged from our search include some important elements of empirically supported recommendations. Both *Setting Limits* and *Have a New Kid by Friday* discuss the importance of praising children, setting limits, using effective communication, and consistent and nonharsh discipline. However, *Setting Limits* is openly opposed to tangible rewards in clear contrast to the empirical literature. In addition, there is a stronger emphasis on waiting for misbehavior to occur to cue parents to intervene rather than on catching children being good. *Have a New Kid*, like each of these popular books, emphasizes discipline and recommends implementation in a structured Monday-through-Friday format that may be attractive to some. Of greater concern with this book, however, is the promise of seeing changes in relationships within a very short time period (i.e., 1 week) and the stated guarantee of success. Both practices (promising quick and guaranteed success) are often considered hallmarks of pseudoscience.

## Case Study

Bill is a psychologist in a primary care setting, working alongside several pediatricians, providing behavioral health services to their patients. A family has been referred to Bill with some questions about their 4-year-old preschooler named Josh. They report that Josh seems developmentally on target, has good language and social skills, is liked by his peers, and in many ways seems intellectually advanced, but he has begun showing some stubbornness that is starting to frustrate his parents. They note that, at times, Josh acts as if he doesn't hear them when they give simple commands like "It's time to eat," "Can you find your shoes?," or "Can you pick up?" They can get him to respond if they remind him repeatedly but feel like they should not need to ask him so many times. Increasingly, they end up doing the task themselves. They have tried reasoning with Josh and explaining why he should obey but to no avail.

Bill is well acquainted with the empirically supported parenting programs but thinks taking the parents through a full 8- to 12-week program may not be necessary at this point. He is familiar with the core components of positive parenting that can be derived from the empirically supported programs and feels he can use those to get the parents pointed in the right direction. Consistent with the best programs, he starts by recommending that they focus initially on relationship-building activities. He models for them in session how to engage Josh in low-demand, child-led play activities, and then they practice both in session and at home during the following week. Bill also encourages the parents to look for opportunities to catch Josh being good, using behavior-specific praise and affirming touch, especially when Josh cooperates with following simple directions like coming to dinner when called, putting away toys, and following simple commands. Bill encourages them to not take these successes for granted and reminds them that they will need to be more vigilant to "catch Josh being good." Finally, he suggests that, for now, they minimize their responses to his noncompliance, focusing instead on successes. During the session, Bill models praising Josh when he complies with simple commands, and he has the parents practice as well. When it is time to go, the parents prompt Josh to get his coat and Josh immediately complies. His parents, already thinking about scheduling the next appointment, nearly miss an opportunity to praise good behavior, but Josh's mother does catch the opportunity and praises Josh. Bill makes sure to use behavior-specific praise himself to acknowledge the mother's success at noticing and commenting on Josh's good behavior. When they return, the parents are pleased to note that they have all enjoyed the low-demand play activities, but they are most excited to report that since they have shifted their strategies to praising success and minimizing their response to failure, Josh is beginning to show more cooperation with basic requests. Bill notices that when the family enters the treatment room, Josh is prompted to hang up his coat, which he does, and his parents immediately praise his coopera-tion and give him a hug. They acknowledge that it has been difficult to remain vigilant and catch Josh's successes, but they admit that Josh has more successes than they realized, and they are pleased with his progress.

Bill now recommends that another way they can help Josh with his listen-ing skill is to make sure they clearly communicate their expectations. Bill points out that this does not mean pestering Josh over and over to do as he is told. Instead, he asks the parents to shift their communication style so that the commands they give are clear and direct and, when possible, they specify expectations in advance. He shows them how to make their expectations and their commands clear and direct, telling Josh what is expected rather than asking or suggesting. He models, and then the parents practice, using specific praise and affirming hugs when Josh is cooperative. When it is nearly time to go, Bill prompts Josh's parents to get close to Josh and then tell Josh clearly and firmly that in just a few minutes, it will be time to put the trains away. Josh complains and indicates that he does not want to comply, but Bill asks Josh's parents to ignore Josh's complaints, offering no threats or expla-nations. Then, in about 3 minutes, they issue a clear command, telling him, "OK, Josh, now it is time to start cleaning up. Put this train (parent points) in the toy box." Josh grumbles and complains but complies with the com-mand, and his parents praise and hug him enthusiastically. Bill decides to not recommend time-out at this point because Josh has responded well to a positive approach combined with clearer communication. However, he does give them a handout (Table 16.1) that provides some guidelines for addi-tional positive parenting ideas that they could use as a guide. Bill also sug-gests that they can consider buying *1-2-3 Magic* as an additional resource if they like, because it is based on sound positive parenting principles. Finally, he tells them they can return to the clinic for more coaching if desired.

## Conclusions and Future Directions

The evidence is strong that we have a good understanding about how par-ents can best promote healthy development and emotional well-being in their children as well as discourage problem behaviors. Parents who invest time and effort to nurture the parent-child relationship, reward and encourage appropriate behaviors, monitor their children, communicate clearly, and have predictable, nonharsh discipline will be more likely to have emotionally secure, well-adjusted children. In addition, there are well-written, easily accessible books that can guide the way for both clinicians and parents alike. Yet our knowledge about parenting is incomplete. For example, each of the empirically supported parenting programs was developed to solve behavior problems such as tantrums, noncompliance, and arguing in children who may be demanding, temperamental, or stubborn. As such, the six core components are important to successful outcomes. Nevertheless, we do not know whether children who are less challenging may require proportionately fewer of the recommended components or whether there is a dose-response relation between the amount of each core component that is used and the strength of the outcome. In addition, although there is wide support for the importance of relying on positive approaches to parenting, we also do not know the best ratio of positive to limit-setting components. Studies that address these types of issues will be important, because getting parents to adhere to all of the core elements is a continuing challenge (Allen & Warzak, 2000) and perhaps an unnecessary challenge for parents of more typical children.

In addition, there is an increasing need to acknowledge that all of the current parenting recommendations are culturally derived (Shriver & Allen, 2008). Although there is some preliminary research on the effectiveness of the parent training programs with other cultural groups, there are certain assumptions, values, and expectations within the core parenting recommendations that derive from the dominant culture and may not fit well with the values and expectations of other cultural, ethnic, or minority groups. With the growing diversity among families and children in the United States, it will be important for behavioral health providers to incorporate culturally sensitive practices into parenting recommendations. To aid this process, parenting researchers will need to evaluate both the effectiveness and acceptability of established parenting approaches to parents from minority cultures. This is important because parents will not use positive parenting approaches that are not seen by them as valued or acceptable.

Finally, while we know that some self-help books are based on sound principles and include core positive parenting recommendations, we do not have adequate evaluations on the effectiveness of self-help books alone. Initial attempts have relied on parent report rather than direct measures of changes in parenting practices, changes in parent-child relationships, or changes in child well-being. Of course, these types of studies will not be easy to do because they must be done in the home, where experimental control is more difficult to establish and having observers in the home is invasive. Yet that is exactly where research on parent training began (Patterson, Reid, & Dishion, 1992), and the home may be where we need to return again.

# References

Achenbach, T. M., & Edelbrock, C. S. (1981). Behavioral problems and competencies reported by parents of normal and disturbed children aged four through sixteen. *Monographs of the Society for Research in Child Development, 46*(1), 1–82. doi:10.2307/1165983

Akin-Little, K. A., & Little, S. G. (2004). Re-examining the overjustification effect. *Journal of Behavioral Education, 13*, 179–192. doi:10.1023/B:JOBE.00000 37628.81867.69

Allen, K. D., & Warzak, W. J. (2000). The problem of parental nonadherence in clinical behavior analysis: Effective treatment is not enough. *Journal of Applied Behavior Analysis, 33*, 373–391. doi:10.1901/jaba.2000.33–373

American Psychological Association, Division 53. (2012). *Effective child therapy: Evidence-based mental health treatment for children and adolescents.* Retrieved from http://www.effectivechildtherapy.com/sccap/?m=sPro&fa=pro_ESTopt ions#sec8

Batcha, B (2012). Why time-out is out. *Parents.* Retrieved from http://www.parents .com/toddlers-preschoolers/discipline/time-out/why-time-out-is-out/

Berlin, L. J., Ispa, J. M., Fine, M. A., Malone, P. S., Brooks-Gunn, J., Brady-Smith, C., . . . Bai, Y. (2009). Correlates and consequences of spanking and verbal punishment for low-income white, African American, and Mexican American toddlers. *Child Development, 80*, 1403–1420. doi:10.1111/j.1467–8624.2009.01341.x

Bernhardt, A. J., & Forehand, R. (1975). The effects of labeled and unlabeled praise upon lower and middle class children. *Journal of Experimental Child Psychology, 19*, 536–543.

Biglan, A., Brennan, P. A., Foster, S. L., & Holder, H. D. (2004). *Helping adolescents at risk: Prevention of multiple problem behaviors.* New York, NY: Guilford Press.

Biglan, A., Flay, B., Embry, D., & Sandler, I. (2012). The critical role of nurturing environments for promoting human well-being. *American Psychologist, 67*(4), 257–271. doi:10.1037/a0026796

Bjorklund, D. F., Yunger, J. L., & Pellegrini, A. D. (2002). The evolution of parenting and evolutionary approaches to childrearing. In M. H. Bornstein (Ed.), *Handbook of parenting: Vol. 2: Biology and ecology of parenting* (2nd ed.; pp. 3–30). Mahwah, NJ: Lawrence Erlbaum.

Bornstein, M. H. (2005). Parenting matters. *Infant and Child Development, 14*, 311–314.

Bradley, S. J., Jadaa, D. A., Brody, J., Landy, S., Tallett, S. E., Watson, W., . . . Stephens, D. (2003). Brief psychoeducational parenting program: An evaluation and 1-year follow-up. *Journal of the American Academy of Child and Adolescent Psychology, 42*, 1171–1178. doi:10.1097/00004583–200310000–00007

Bright, C. N., & Penrod, B. (2009). An evaluation of the overjustification effect across multiple contingency arrangements. *Behavioral Interventions, 24*, 185–194. doi:10.1002/bin.284

Burnett, P. C. (2002). Teacher praise and feedback and students' perceptions of the classroom environment. *Educational Psychology, 22*, 5–16. doi:10.1080/014 43410120101215

Cameron, J., Banko, K. M., & Pierce, W. D. (2001). Pervasive negative effects of rewards on intrinsic motivation: The myth continues. *The Behavior Analyst, 24*, 1–44.

Cameron, J., & Pierce, W. D. (2002). *Rewards and intrinsic motivation: Resolving the controversy.* Westport, CT: Bergin & Garvey.

Campbell, S. B. (1995). Behavior problems in preschool children: A review of recent research. *Journal of Child Psychology and Psychiatry, 36*(1), 113–149. doi:10.1111/j.1469–7610.1995.tb01657.x

Campbell, N. (2011, April 26). The disadvantages of using time out as a child punishment. Retrieved from http://www.livestrong.com/article/95688-disadvantages-using-time-out-child/

Campbell S. B., & Ewing, L. J. (1990). Follow-up of hard-to-manage preschoolers: Adjustment at age 9 and predictors of continuing symptoms. *Journal of Child Psychology and Psychiatry, 31*, 871–889. doi:10.1111/j.1469–7610.1990.tb00831.x

Campbell, S.B. (1995). Behavior problems in preschool children: A review of recent research. *Journal of Child Psychology and Psychiatry, 36*(1), 113-149. doi:10.1111/j .1469-7610.1995.tb01657.x

Capage, L. C., Bennett, G. M., & McNeil, C. B (2001). A comparison between African American and Caucasian children referred for treatment of disruptive behavior disorders. *Child & Family Behavior Therapy, 23*(1), 1–14.

Ceballo, R., Ramirez, C., Hearn, K., & Maltese, K. (2003). Community violence and children's psychological well-being: Does parental monitoring matter? *Journal of Clinical Child and Adolescent Psychology, 32*(4), 586–592.

Chamberlain, P., Fisher, P. A., & Moore, K. (2002). Multidimensional treatment foster care: Applications of the OSLC intervention model to high-risk youth and their families. In J. B. Reid, G. R. Patterson, & J. Snyder (Eds.), *Antisocial behavior in children and adolescents: A developmental analysis and model for intervention* (pp. 203–218). Washington, DC: American Psychological Association.

Chronis, A. M., Lahey, B. B., Pelham, W. E., Williams, S. H., Baumann, B. L., Kipp, H., . . . Rathouz, P. J. (2007). Maternal depression and early positive parenting predict future conduct problems in young children with attention-deficit/hyperactivity disorder. *Developmental Psychology, 43*, 70–82. doi:10.103 7/0012–1649.43.1.70

Collins, W. A., Maccoby, E., Steinberg, L., Hetherington, E., & Bornstein, M. (2000). Contemporary research on parenting: The case for nature and nurture. *American Psychologist, 55*(2), 218–232.

Condry, J. (1977). Enemies of exploration: Self-initiated versus other-initiated learning. *Journal of Personality and Social Psychology, 35,* 459–477. doi:10.10 37//0022–3514.35.7.459

Conduct Problems Prevention Research Group. (2002). Evaluation of the first three years of the Fast Track prevention trial with children at high risk for adolescent conduct problems. *Journal of Abnormal Child Psychology, 30,* 19–35.

Cowan, P. A. (2005). Reflections on "Parenting Matters" by Marc Bornstein. *Infant and Child Development, 14*(3), 315–319.

de Graaf, I., Speetjens, P., Smit, F., de Wolff, M., & Tavecchio, L. (2008). Effectiveness of the Triple P Positive Parenting Program on behavioral problems in children: A meta-analysis. *Behavior Modification, 32,* 714–735. doi:10.1177/01454455 08317134

Deater-Deckard, K., & Dodge, K. A. (1997). Externalizing behavior problems and discipline revisited: Nonlinear effects and variation by culture, context, and gender. *Psychological Inquiry, 8*(3), 161–175.

DeGarmo, D. S., Patterson, G. R., & Forgatch, M. S. (2004). How do outcomes in a specified parent training intervention maintain or wane over time? *Prevention Science, 5,* 73–89.

Deci, E. L., Koestner, R., & Ryan, R. M. (1999). A meta-analytic review of experiments examining the effects of extrinsic rewards on intrinsic motivation. *Psychological Bulletin, 125,* 627–668. doi:10.1037//0033–2909.125.6.627

Deci, E. L., & Ryan, R. M. (1985). *Intrinsic motivation and self-determination in human behavior.* New York, NY: Plenum Press.

Dickinson, A. M. (1989). The detrimental effects of extrinsic reinforcement on "intrinsic motivation." *The Behavior Analyst, 12,* 1–15.

Dishion, T. J., & Kavanagh, K. (2003). *Intervening in adolescent problem behavior: A family-centered approach.* New York, NY: Guilford Press.

Dishion, T. J., & McMahon, R. J. (1998). Parental monitoring and the prevention of child and adolescent problem behavior: A conceptual and empirical formulation. *Clinical Child and Family Psychology Review, 1,* 61–75.

Dix, T., Stewart, A. D., Gershoff, E. T., & Day, W. H. (2007). Autonomy and children's reactions to being controlled: Evidence that both compliance and defiance may be positive markers in early development. *Child Development, 78,* 1204–1221. doi:10.1111/j.1467–8624.2007.01061.x

Dweck, C. S. (2002). Messages that motivate: How praise motivates students' beliefs, motivation, and performance (in surprising ways). In J. Aronson (Ed.), *Improving academic achievement: Impact of psychological factors on education* (pp. 37–60). San Diego, CA: Academic Press.

Everett, G. E., Hupp, S. D. A, & Olmi, D. J. (2010). Time-out with parents: A descriptive analysis of 30 years of research. *Education and Treatment of Children, 33,* 235–259.

Eyberg, S. M., Nelson, M. M., & Boggs, S. R. (2008). Evidence-based treatments for child and adolescent disruptive behavior disorders. *Journal of Clinical Child and Adolescent Psychology, 37*(1), 215–237.

Eyberg, S. M., & Robinson E. A. (1982). Parent-child interaction training: Effects on family functioning. *Journal of Clinical Child Psychology, 11,* 130–137.

Forehand, R. L., Griest, D. L., & Wells, K. C. (1979). Parent behavioral training: An analysis of the relationship among multiple outcome measures. *Journal of Abnormal Child Psychology, 7,* 229–242.

Forehand, R., & Long, N. (2010). *Parenting the strong-willed child: The clinically proven five-week program for parents of two- to six-year-olds* (3rd ed.). New York, NY: McGraw-Hill.

Forehand, R. L., Merchant, M. J., Long, N., & Garai, E. (2010). An examination of parenting the strong-willed child as bibliotherapy for parents. *Behavior Modification, 34,* 57–76. doi:10.1177/0145445509356351

Forgatch, M., & DeGarmo, D. (2002). Extending and testing the social interaction learning model with divorce samples. In J. B. Reid, G. R. Patterson, & J. Snyder (Eds.), *Antisocial behavior in children and adolescents: A developmental analysis and model for intervention* (pp. 235–256). Washington, DC: American Psychological Association.

Forgatch, M.S., & Patterson, G. R. (2005). *Parents and adolescents living together: Part 2: Family problem solving,* (2nd ed.). Champaign, IL: Research Press.

Fossum, S., Morch, W., Hadegard, B. H., & Drugli, M. B. (2007). Childhood disruptive behaviors and family functioning in clinically referred children: Are girls different from boys? *Scandinavian Journal of Psychology, 48,* 375–382. doi:10.1111/j.1467–9450.2007.00617.x

French, V. (2002). History of parenting: The ancient Mediterranean world. In M. Bornstein (Ed.), *Handbook of parenting: Volume 2 biology and ecology of parenting* (2nd ed., pp. 345–376). Mahwah, NJ: Lawrence Erlbaum.

Gershoff, E. T. (2002). Corporal punishment by parents and associated child behaviors and experiences: A meta-analytic and theoretical review. *Psychological Bulletin, 128,* 539–579. doi:10.1037//0033–2909.128.4.539

Gershoff, E. T., Lansford, J. E., Sexton, H. R., Davis-Kean, P., & Sameroff, A. J. (2012). Longitudinal links between spanking and children's externalizing behaviors in a national sample of white, black, Hispanic, and Asian American families. *Child Development, 83,* 838–843.

Gregory, N (2012). Why timeouts are bad. *New Parent.* Retrieved from http://www.newparent.com/grow/time-outs/

Gunnoe, M. L., & Mariner, C. L. (1997). Toward a developmental-contextual model of the effects of parental spanking on children's aggression. *Archives of Pediatrics and Adolescent Medicine, 151,* 768–775.

Haiman, P. (2012). The case against timeout. *The Natural Child Project.* Retrieved from http://www.naturalchild.org/guest/peter_haiman.html

Harris, J. R. (2009). *The nurture assumption: Why children turn out the way they do, revised and updated.* New York, NY: Free Press.

Henderlong, J., & Lepper, M. R. (2002). The effects of praise on children's intrinsic motivation: A review and synthesis. *Psychological Bulletin, 128,* 774–795. doi:10.1037//0033–2909.128.5.774

Herschell, A. D., Calzada, E., Eyberg, S., & McNeil, C. (2002). Parent-child interaction therapy: New directions in research. *Cognitive and Behavioral Practice, 9,* 9–16.

Hicks-Pass, S. (2009). Corporal punishment in America today: Spare the rod, spoil the child? A systematic review of the literature. *Best Practices in Mental Health, 5,* 71–88.

Hobbs, S. A., Forehand, R. L., & Murray, R. G. (1978). Effects of various durations of time-out on the noncompliant behavior of children. *Behavior Therapy, 9,* 652–656.

Hoghughi, M. (1998). The importance of parenting in child health. *British Medical Journal, 316,* 1545. doi:10.1136/bmj.316.7144.1545

Hoghughi, M., & Speight, A. (1998). Good enough parenting for all children—A strategy for a healthier society. *Archives of Disease in Childhood, 78,* 293–300. doi:10.1136/adc.78.4.293

Holden, G. W. (1997). *Parents and the dynamics of child rearing.* Boulder, CO: Westview Press.

Kalb, L. M., & Loeber R. (2003). Child disobedience and noncompliance: A review. *Pediatrics, 111,* 641–652. doi:10.1542/peds.111.3.641

Kaminski, J. W., Valle, L.A., Filene, J. H., & Boyle, C. L. (2008). A meta-analytic review of components associated with parent training program effectiveness. *Journal of Abnormal Child Psychology, 36,* 567–589.

Keenan, K., Shaw, D., Delliquadri, E., Giovannelli, J., & Walsh, B. (1998). Evidence for the continuity of early problem behaviors: Application of a developmental model. *Journal of Abnormal Child Psychology, 26,* 441–445.

Kerr, D. R., Lopez, N. L., Olson, S. L., & Sameroff, A. J. (2004). Parental discipline and externalizing behavior problems in early childhood: The roles of moral regulation and child gender. *Journal of Abnormal Child Psychology, 32,* 369–383. doi:10.1023/B:JACP.0000030291.72775.96

Kohn, A. (1993). *Punished by rewards.* Boston, MA: Houghton Mifflin.

Kohn, A. (2005). *Unconditional parenting: Moving from rewards and punishment to love and reason.* New York, NY: Simon and Schuster.

Landry, S. H., Smith, K. E., & Swank, P. R. (2003). The importance of parenting during early childhood for school-age development. *Developmental Neuropsychology, 24,* 559–591. doi:10.1207/S15326942DN242&3_04

Lansford, J. E., Criss, M. M., Dodge, K. A., Shaw, D. S., Pettit, G. S., & Bates, J. E. (2009). Trajectories of physical discipline: Early childhood antecedents and developmental outcomes. *Child Development, 80,* 1385–1402. doi:10.1111/j.1467–8624.2009.01340.x

Lansford, J. E., Deater-Deckard, K., Dodge, K. A., Bates, J. E., & Pettit, G. S. (2004). Ethnic differences in the link between physical discipline and later adolescent externalizing behaviors. *Journal of Child Psychology and Psychiatry, 45,* 801–812.

Larzelere, R. E. (2000). Child outcomes of nonabusive and customary physical punishment by parents: An updated literature review. *Clinical Child and Family Psychology Review, 3,* 199–221.

Larzelere, R. E., & Kuhn, B. R. (2005). Comparing child outcomes of physical punishment and alternative disciplinary tactics: A meta-analysis. *Clinical Child and Family Psychology Review, 8,* 1–37. doi:10.1007/s10567–005–2340-z

Leman, K. (2008). *Have a new kid by Friday: How to change your child's attitude, behavior and character in 5 days.* Grand Rapids, MI: Revell.

Lepper, M. R., & Greene, D. (Eds.). (1978). *The hidden costs of reward: New perspectives on the psychology of human motivation.* Hillsdale, NJ: Lawrence Erlbaum.

Long, P., Forehand, R., Wierson, M., & Morgan, A. (1994). Does parent training with young noncompliant children have long-term effects? *Behaviour Research and Therapy, 32,* 101–107. doi:10.1016/0005–7967(94)90088–4

Lorber, M. F., O'Leary, S. G., & Smith Slep, A. M. (2011). An initial evaluation of the role of emotion and impulsivity in explaining racial/ethnic differences in the use of corporal punishment. *Developmental Psychology, 47,* 1744–1749.

Maccoby, E. E. (2000). Parenting and its effects on children: On reading and misreading behavior genetics. *Annual Review of Psychology, 51,* 1–27.

MacKenzie, R. J. (2001). *Setting limits with your strong-willed child: Eliminating conflict by establishing clear, firm, and respectful boundaries.* Roseville, CA: Prima.

Markham, L. (2012). What's wrong with timeouts? *Aha! Parenting.* Retrieved from http://www.ahaparenting.com/parenting-tools/positive-discipline/timeouts

Markie-Dadds, C., & Sanders, M. R. (2006a). A controlled evaluation of an enhanced self-directed behavioural family intervention for parents of children with conduct problems in rural and remote areas. *Behaviour Change, 23,* 55–72.

Markie-Dadds, C., & Sanders, M. R. (2006b). Self-directed Triple P (Positive Parenting Program) for mothers with children at-risk of developing conduct problems. *Behavioural and Cognitive Psychotherapy, 34,* 259–275.

McKee, L., Roland, E., Coffelt, N., Olson, A. L., Forehand, R., Massari, C., . . . Zens, M. S. (2007). Harsh discipline and child problem behaviors: The roles of positive parenting and gender. *Journal of Family Violence, 22,* 187–196. doi:10.1007/s10896–007–9070–6

McLoyd, V. C., & Smith, J. (2002). Physical discipline and behavior problems in African American, European American, and Hispanic children: Emotional support as a moderator. *Journal of Marriage and Family, 64,* 40–53.

McMahon, R. J., & Forehand, R. L. (2003). *Helping the noncompliant child: Family-based treatment for oppositional behavior* (2nd ed.). New York, NY: Guilford Press.

McNeil, C., Capage, L., Bahl, A., & Blanc, H. (1999). Importance of early intervention for disruptive behavior problems: Comparison of treatment and waitlist-control groups. *Early Education and Development, 10*(4), 445–454.

McNeil, C., Eyberg, S., Eisenstadt, T., Newcomb, K., & Funderburk, B. (1991). Parent-child interaction therapy with behavior problem children: Generalization of treatment effects to the school setting. *Journal of Clinical Child Psychology, 20*(2), 140–151.

McNeil, C., & Hembree-Kilgin, T. (2010). *Parent-child interaction therapy* (2nd ed.). New York, NY: Springer.

Mekertichian, L. K., & Bowes, J. M. (1996). Does parenting matter? The challenge of the behavioural geneticists. *Journal of Family Studies, 2*(2), 131–145.

Mesman, J., & Koot, H. M. (2001). Early preschool predictors of preadolescent internalizing and externalizing DSM-IV diagnoses. *Journal of the American Academy of Child and Adolescent Psychiatry, 40,* 1029–1036. doi:10.1097/00004583–200109000–00011

Moffitt, T. E. (1993). Adolescent-limited and life-course persistent antisocial behavior: A developmental taxonomy. *Psychological Review, 100,* 674–701. doi:10.1037//0033–295X.100.4.674

Morawska, A., & Sanders, M. (2011). Parental use of time out revisited: A useful or harmful parenting strategy? *Journal of Child and Family Studies, 20,* 1–8. doi:10.1007/s10826–010–9371-x

Mueller, C. M., & Dweck, C. S. (1998). Praise for intelligence can undermine children's motivation and performance. *Journal of Personality and Social Psychology, 75,* 33–52. doi:10.1037//0022–3514.75.1.33

Nixon, R., Sweeney, L., Erickson, D., & Touyz, S. (2003). Parent-child interaction therapy: A comparison of standard and abbreviated treatments for oppositional defiant preschoolers. *Journal of Consulting and Clinical Psychology, 71*(2), 251–260.

Patterson, G. R., Chamberlain, P., & Reid, J. B. (1982). A comparative evaluation of a parent-training program. *Behavior Therapy, 13,* 638–650.

Patterson, G. R., & Forgatch, M. S. (2005). *Parents and adolescents living together: Part I: The basics* (2nd ed.). Champaign, IL: Research Press.

Patterson, G. R., Reid, J. B., & Dishion, T. J. (1992). *A social interactional approach: Vol. 4: Antisocial boys.* Eugene, OR: Castalia.

Patterson, G. R., Reid, J. B., Jones, R. R., & Conger, R. E. (1975). *A social learning approach to family intervention: Vol. 1: Families with aggressive children.* Eugene, OR: Castalia.

Patterson, G. R., & Stouthamer-Loeber, M. (1984). The correlation of family management practices and delinquency. *Child Development, 55,*1299–1307.

Phelan, T. (2010). *1–2–3 Magic: Effective discipline for children 2–12* (4th ed.). Glen Ellyn, IL: ParentMagic.

Pierce, W. D., Cameron, J., Banko, K. M., & So, S. (2003). Positive effects of rewards and performance standards on intrinsic motivation. *Psychological Record, 53*(4), 561–578.

Plomin, R. (1999). Two views about the nurture assumption, *PsycCRITIQUES, 44* (4), 269–271.

Prinz, R. J., Sanders, M. R., Shapiro, C. J., Whitaker, D. J., & Lutzker, J. R. (2009). Population-based prevention of child maltreatment: The U.S. Triple P system population trial. *Prevention Science, 10,* 1–12. doi:10.1007/s11121–009–0123–3

Reid, J. B., & Eddy, J. M. (2002). Preventive efforts during the elementary school years: The linking the interests of families and teachers project. In J. B. Reid, G. R. Patterson, & J. Snyder (Eds.), *Antisocial behavior in children and adolescents: A developmental analysis and model for intervention* (pp. 219–234). Washington, DC: American Psychological Association.

Reid, M. J., Webster-Stratton, C., & Beauchaine, T. (2002). Parent training in Head Start: A comparison of program response among African American, Asian American, Caucasian, and Hispanic mothers. *Prevention Science, 2*(4), 209–227.

Reiss, S. (2005). Extrinsic and intrinsic motivation at 30: Unresolved scientific issues. *The Behavior Analyst, 28,* 1–14.

Roberts, M. W. (2008). Parent training. In M. Hersen & A. M. Gross (Eds.), *Handbook of clinical psychology* (Vol. 2, pp. 653–693). Hoboken, NJ: John Wiley & Sons.

Roberts, M. W., McMahon, R., Forehand, R., & Humphreys, L. (1978). The effects of parental instruction giving on child compliance. *Behavior Therapy, 9,* 793–798.

Rowe, D. (1994). *The limits of family influence: Genes, experience, and behavior.* New York, NY: Guilford Press.

Runyan, D. K., Shankar, V., Hassan, F., Hunter, W. M., Jain, D., Paula, C. S., . . . Bordin, I. A. (2010). International variations in harsh child discipline. *Pediatrics, 126*(3), e701-e711. doi: 10.1542/peds.2008–2374

Sanders, M. R. (1998). *Every parent: A positive approach to children's behaviour.* Sydney, New South Wales, Australia: Addison-Wesley.

Sanders, M. R. (1999). Triple p-positive parenting program: Towards an empirically validated multilevel parenting and family support strategy for the prevention of behavior and emotional problems in children. *Clinical Child and Family Psychology Review, 2,* 71–90.

Sanders, M. R., & Dadds, M. R. (1982). The effects of planned activities and child management training: An analysis of setting generality. *Behavior Therapy, 13,* 1–11.

Sanders, M. R., & Glynn, E. L. (1981). Training parents in behavioural self-management: An analysis of generalization and maintenance effects. *Journal of Applied Behavior Analysis, 14,* 223–237.

Sanders, M. R., Markie-Dadds, M. R., Tully, L., & Bor, W. (2000). The Triple P-Positive Parenting Program: A comparison of enhanced, standard, and self-directed behavioral family intervention for parents of children with early onset conduct problems. *Journal of Consulting and Clinical Psychology, 68*(4), 624–640.

Sanders, M. R., Mazzucchelli, T. G., & Studman, L. J. (2004). Stepping Stones Triple P: The theoretical basis and development of an evidence-based positive parenting program for families with a child who has a disability. *Journal of Intellectual and Developmental Disability, 29,* 265–283.

Sanders, M. R., Tully, L. A., Baade, P. D., Lynch, M. E., Heywood, A. H., Pollard, G. E., & Youlden, D. R. (1999). A survey of parenting practices in Queensland: Implications for mental health promotion. *Health Promotion Journal of Australia, 9,* 112–121.

Shaw, B. A., Krause, N., Chatters, L. M., Connell, C. M., & Ingersoll-Dayton, B. (2004). Emotional support from parents early in life, aging, and health. *Psychology and Aging, 19*(1), 4–12. doi:10.1037/0882–7974.19.1.4

Shriver, M. D., & Allen, K. D. (2008). *Working with parents of noncompliant children: A guide to evidence-based parent training for practitioners and students.* Washington, DC: American Psychological Association.

Simons, R. L., & Johnson, C. (1994). Harsh corporal punishment versus quality of parental involvement as an explanation for adolescent maladjustment. *Journal of Marriage and Family, 56,* 591–607.

Slade, E. P., & Wissow, L. S (2004). Spanking in early childhood and later behavior problems: A prospective study of infants and young toddlers. *Pediatrics, 113,* 1321–1330. doi:10.1542/peds.113.5.1321

Smith, B. L. (2012). The case against spanking. *American Psychologist, 43*(4), 60.

Stiffelman, S. (2011, September 22). Positive discipline: Why time-outs don't work. Retrieved from http://www.sheknows.com/parenting/articles/805746/positive-discipline-why-timeouts-dont-work

Strain, P. S., & Joseph, G. E. (2004). A not so good job with "Good Job": A response to Kohn (2001). *Journal of Positive Behavior Interventions, 6*(1), 55–59. doi:10.1177/10983007040060010801

Strauss, M. A., & Stewart, J. H. (1999). Corporal punishment by American parents: National data on prevalence, chronicity, severity, and duration in relation to child and family characteristics. *Clinical Child and Family Psychology Review, 2,* 55–70.

Substance Abuse and Mental Health Service Administration. (2012). *National registry of evidence-based programs and practices.* Retrieved from http://www.nrepp.samhsa.gov/

Taylor, C. A., Manganello, J. A., Lee, S. J., & Rice, J. C. (2010). Mothers' spanking of 3-year-old children and subsequent risk of children's aggressive behavior. *Pediatrics, 125,* e1057. doi:10.1542/ped.2009–2678

Thompson, S. (2012, March 11). *No more time-outs.* Retrieved from http://www.babble.com/kid/child-development/no-time-outs-child-disciplining-punishment/

Topham, T. (2012, September 2). *Why extrinsic rewards are so bad for motivation.* Retrieved from http://timtopham.com/2012/02/09/why-extrinsic-rewards-are-so-bad-for-motivation/

UNICEF, (1989). *Convention on the Rights of the Child.* Geneva, Switzerland: Author.

UNICEF. (2006). *Convention on the Rights of the Child: General Comment No. 8.* Geneva, Switzerland: Author.

Urdan, T. (2003). Book review: Intrinsic motivation, extrinsic rewards, and divergent views of reality. *Educational Psychology Review, 15*(3), 311–325. doi: 10.1023/A:1024652318828

Wahler, R. G., & Meginnis, K. L. (1997). Strengthening child compliance through positive parenting practices: What works? *Journal of Clinical Child Psychology, 26*(4), 433–440.

Walter, H. I., & Gilmore, S. K. (1973). Placebo versus social learning effects in parent training procedures designed to alter the behaviors of aggressive boys. *Behavior Therapy, 4,* 361–377.

Webster-Stratton, C. (1994). Advancing videotape parent training: A comparison study. *Journal of Consulting and Clinical Psychology, 62,* 583–593.

Webster-Stratton, C. (1998). Preventing conduct problems in Head Start children: Strengthening parenting competencies. *Journal of Consulting and Clinical Psychology, 66,* 715–730.

Webster-Stratton, C. (2004). *The incredible years: A trouble-shooting guide for parents of children aged 3 to 8.* London, UK: Umbrella Press.

Webster-Stratton, C., & Hancock, L. (1998). Training for parents of young children with conduct problems: Content, methods, and therapeutic processes. In C. E. Schaefer & J. M. Briesmeister (Eds.), *Handbook of parent training* (pp. 98–152). New York, NY: John Wiley & Sons.

Webster-Stratton, C., & Reid, M. (2003). The Incredible Years parents, teachers, and children training series: A multifaceted treatment approach for young children with conduct problems. In A. E. Kazdin & J. R. Weisz (Eds.), *Evidenced-based psychotherapies for children and adolescents* (pp. 224–240). New York, NY: Guilford Press.

Wells, K. C., & Egan, J. (1988). Social learning and systems family therapy for childhood oppositional disorder: Comparative treatment outcome. *Comprehensive Psychiatry, 29,* 138–146.

West, F., Sanders, M. R., Cleghorn, G. J., & Savies, P. S. W. (2010). Randomized clinical trial of a family-based lifestyle intervention for childhood obesity. *Behaviour Research and Therapy, 48,* 1170–1179.

Whittingham, K., Sonfronoff, K., Sheffield, J., & Sanders, M. R. (2009). Stepping Stones Triple P: An RCT of a parenting program with parents of children diagnosed with autism spectrum disorder. *Journal of Abnormal Child Psychology, 37,* 469–480.

Wiltz, N. A., & Patterson, G. R. (1974). An evaluation of parent training procedures designed to alter inappropriate aggressive behavior of boys. *Behavior Therapy, 5,* 215–221.

Wright, J. P., & Beaver, K. M. (2005). Do parents matter in creating self-control in their children? A genetically informed test of Gottfredson and Hirschi's theory of low self-control. *Criminology: An Interdisciplinary Journal, 43*(4), 1169–1202.

Zolotor, A. J., Theodore, A. D., Chang, J. J., Berkoff, M. C., & Runyan, D. K. (2008). Speak softly—and forget the stick: Corporal punishment and child physical abuse. *American Journal of Preventive Medicine, 35,* 364–369. doi:10.1016/j. amepre.2008.06.031

Zolotor, A. J., Theodore, A. D., Runyan, D. K., Chang, J. J., & Laskey, A. L. (2011). Corporal punishment and physical abuse: Population-based trends for three-to-11-year-old children in the United States. *Child Abuse Review, 20,* 57–66. doi:10 .1002/car.1128

# 17

# Financial Skills

*William O'Donohue*
*Alexandros Maragakis*
University of Nevada, Reno

## Overview of Socioeconomic Status and Its Correlation With Quality of Life

In the psychological, medical, and economic literature, socioeconomic status (SES) is a consistent predictor of several important quality-of-life variables, including overall life satisfaction, ability to obtain access to medical care, quality of romantic relationships, and even numbers of maladaptive behaviors (Amato, Booth, Johnson, & Rogers, 2007; Kahneman & Deaton, 2010; Maisel & Karney, 2012; Smith, 1999). The differences between the lowest and highest group of SES in regard to these outcomes are extremely robust and are consistent throughout the world across a number of cultures (Ibrahim, Kelly, & Glazebrook, 2012; Kosidou et al., 2011; Walsh, Levine, & Levav, 2012). Although SES is a general indicator of one's financial position, studies have examined more specific financial factors, such as annual income, and how these affect quality of life.

Although the relation between these important outcomes and SES is fairly robust, the studies that have examined SES are necessarily correlational. It would be ethically and practically problematic to randomly assign individuals to SES levels—although quite pleasant for some of the subjects. Therefore, even though SES is highly correlated with many aspects of one's quality of life, this finding does not imply that SES *causes* these differences in an individual's quality of life. First, the direction of the relationship is unclear: These outcomes may in fact have a causal role in SES. Second, SES may be a proxy variable for underlying mechanisms that effect both SES and quality of life, such as intelligence, health, ability to delay gratification, familial support, or even demographics (e.g., whether one is a member of a group that typically experiences discrimination). However, while the current state of the literature does not allow for causal inferences, it is important to note that SES may in fact have a causal relationship with quality of life. In this section of the chapter, we review the literature on how SES and other financial variables may play an important role in an individual's overall quality of life. We also explore alternative hypotheses for why SES is highly correlated with one's quality of life. The chapter then will discuss certain basic financial skills (e.g., compound interest, the role of inflation, risk diversification) and the importance of these basic skills for financial well-being. The chapter concludes with possible implications for therapy in regard to financial skills.

## Defining Socioeconomic Status

The construct of socioeconomic status is commonly used in the literature. However, there is little consensus on how to measure it (Maisel & Karney, 2012). The most common parameters of SES—as the name would imply—include both the dimensions of income and education. However, others have indicated that this analysis of SES is incomplete (Drentea & Reynolds, 2012), and additional important parameters such as debt, subjective financial strain, and relative financial standing to one's area code have been suggested as additions to SES.

Because this chapter focuses on financial issues and skills as these potentially affect health, particularly psychological health, the minimum requirement for a study to be included in this review is specific mention of measuring income. Although financial well-being is more than just income, income is the fundamental component of it. For example, other key variables such as net assets (assets minus liabilities) may also display interesting relationships with physical and psychological health. Therefore, studies that examine other aspects along with income will broaden the analysis of how finances may affect overall quality of life.

## Money and Physical Health

An individual's financial position is correlated with both short- and long-term physical health outcomes. Low SES is associated with premature mortality and poor general physical health in comparison with high SES (Marmot, 2005; Smith, 1999). Some studies indicate that there is a 6-year difference in life expectancy between individuals of low and high SES (Braveman, Cubbin, Egerter, Williams, & Pamuk, 2010; Smith, 1999). The fact that SES is correlated with one's longevity obviously makes it an important issue that cannot be overlooked.

Individuals of low SES have a higher prevalence of chronic diseases compared with individuals of high SES (Smith, 1999), and this may be a partial explanation for shorter lifespan. These chronic health problems are compounded by the fact that individuals who are classified as lower SES are also especially likely to engage in health risk behaviors like smoking, drinking, and lack of proper diet and exercise (Smith, 1999). There is also evidence that if a mother who is of low SES is pregnant or has young children, this is predictive of long-term negative effects on the children. Children born into low SES families are more likely to have a low birth weight, and in turn are more likely to develop chronic diseases as adults (Johnson & Schoeni, 2011). Even born with normal weight, children who are exposed to an environment with characteristics associated with negative financial status, such as limited access to healthcare, neighborhood poverty, or inadequate nutrition, are more likely to develop chronic diseases, such as obesity, diabetes, and asthma (Johnson & Schoeni, 2011). With the exponential rise of chronic diseases and the burden it has on the healthcare system, the fact that low SES is associated with poorer health outcomes is alarming because low SES individuals are less likely than others to seek out medical attention.

## Money and Mental Health

People's financial situations also have a long-standing and enduring relationship with mental health. In general, individuals of higher SES also have better overall mental health than their lower SES counterparts; this is especially true for extremely poor people (Drentea & Reynolds, 2012).

Individuals of low SES report more acute stressful life events than their high SES counterparts (Maisel & Karney, 2012). These stressful events may in turn cause more practical and psychological difficulties for low SES individuals, because they are not able to obtain a wide variety of supports that could have been available if they had the finances to obtain the support (e.g., healthcare, babysitting, stress-reducing leisure activities). The inability to properly handle acute stressful events may in turn lead to an increased likelihood of mental health problems.

The most prevalent mental disorder associated with low SES is depression (Muntaner, Eaton, & Miech, 2004). Depression is strongly associated with SES, even after controlling for gender and race (Walsh et al., 2012).

Preliminary results also suggest a correlation between low SES and a wide range of anxiety disorders (e.g., panic disorder, specific phobic, general anxiety disorder; Muntaner et al., 2004). Studies also indicate an association between low SES and the likelihood of schizophrenia (Muntaner et al., 2004).

There is also a correlation between age and financial stress. For example, economic hardship during childhood appears to have lifelong effects on an individual's mental health. In one study, economic hardship, defined as the inability to obtain proper food, shelter, and healthcare during childhood, predicted the onset of 20 DSM-IV disorders throughout the individual's life (McLaughlin et al., 2011). Adolescents of low SES families are more likely to have both externalizing problems (e.g., aggression, delinquency) and internalizing problems (e.g., depression, anxiety; Amone-P'Olak et al., 2009; Walsh et al., 2012). Elderly individuals who have a high amount of debt are more likely to report problems with depression, anxiety, and anger than elderly individuals without debt (Drentea & Reynolds, 2012).

## Money and Personal Relations

Personal relationships, both romantic and personal, are also correlated with one's financial position. Individuals in lower SES groups have higher divorce rates and lower overall relationship satisfaction than their high SES counterparts (Conger, Conger, & Martin, 2010; Maisel & Karney, 2012). Preliminary data further indicate that as low SES families experience economic gains, they experience marital gains (Duncan, Huston, & Weisner, 2007). Income in general is directly related to reports of martial quality (Amato et al., 2007).

Financial stress is also related to general family well-being. As indicated earlier, children and adolescents of low SES families have more mental health problems and a higher likelihood of ending up in the correctional system (Amone-P'Olak et al., 2009). Improvement in family income is associated with parents' well-being and beneficial developmental outcomes for children and adolescents (Conger et al., 2010).

## Possible Reasons for These Relationships With Financial Variables

Finances may therefore bear significant implications for many aspects of life. However, it is important to further understand and analyze how finances would have such a widespread effect over quality of life. One explanation for why finances are so highly correlated with SES is the negative aspects of the environments associated with low SES families. These families usually live in neighborhoods that have lower access to healthcare, quality education, and leisure activities, and higher crime rates. Interesting analyses show, for example, that supermarkets in lower SES neighborhoods, compared with higher SES neighborhoods, stocked fewer fresh vegetables and more unhealthy snacks such as potato chips—thus contributing to increased rates of obesity (Flegal, Carroll, Kit, & Ogden, 2010). The First Lady, Michelle Obama, has called these areas "food deserts." This environmental hypothesis provides a potential behavioral explanation for why poor finances are associated with such negative effects, because the environment is associated with more stress, fewer preventative pathways, and less support to help when acute stress events occur.

Another explanation is a perpetuating cycle—a positive feedback loop—between poor health and low SES. As one suffers from poor health, one's ability to obtain gainful employment is hindered due to health problems. Due to the difficulties associated with obtaining employment, one cannot earn sufficient money to balance basic and medical needs. In turn, acute stressful events produce increased psychological problems, due to one's inability to allocate funds to alleviate the situation (e.g., engage in therapy, find a babysitter, take time off from work). This cycle perpetuates itself since the increased stress produces worse health outcomes, in turn hindering an individual's ability to earn money.

A final hypothesis is these effects are due to a third variable that is confounded with income: education. Education is highly correlated with income and martial satisfaction (Conger et al., 2010). Education is also associated with higher likelihood of seeking and obtaining medical attention. Also, education allows for more employment options and higher likelihood for occupational advancement—perhaps allowing for periodic improvements in salary or job requirements that can combat burnout and hedonic adaptation. In addition, education may provide either increased information or cognitive skills to improve one's financial condition. It is a goal of liberal arts education to teach critical thinking; this skill may provide individuals with improved problem-solving skills that can improve financial decisions and options. In addition, some curricula, such as those in business, even teach directly relevant skills such as accounting and investing. Therefore, according to this hypothesis, education rather than finances per se is the underlying causal factor.

## Where the Buck Stops

Although lack of sufficient finances has obvious deleterious effects, research suggests that the benefits of being financially stable plateaus at a certain point. The most important factor influencing one's happiness in relation to money is being able to meet one's basic physical needs (e.g., clothing, housing, food, medical care). Kahneman and Deaton (2010) showed that one's life evaluation increases steadily as income increases. However, there is minimal benefit to emotional well-being after an income of approximately $75,000 per household (Kahneman & Deaton, 2010). Individuals who make more than $75,000 can purchase more, but presumably they lose some happiness in the smaller activities in life (perhaps because they are working longer hours to achieve this superior income). Therefore, although the effects of poor finances have serious implications, the emotional benefits seen after a household makes $75,000 are minimal, making money only beneficial to a certain degree. A limitation with this research, though, is that it focuses on yearly income and does not directly examine the influence of net assets at key developmental stages in one's life, such as a down payment for a home, financing a child's education, paying for medical bills, or financing retirement. Most individuals would rather have incomes of only $50,000 but assets of a couple of million dollars.

## Financial Literacy: What It Is, Why It Is Important, and Some Key Data

Many pathways impact financial status. Obviously, some individuals simply inherit assets or win a lottery that places them in a positive financial category. However, for most individuals the pathway is more complex (i.e., they must earn their financial status). This pathway is complex for two reasons: (1) this pathway can involve other routes, such as long-term educational commitments, skill and luck at finding a job, advancing in one's career, saving, investing wisely, levels of consumption that are warranted by income and assets, luck at not experiencing adverse events that affect financial status; and (2) it is a myth that one's financial status is relatively fixed (Sowell, 2010). First, financial status tends to change across the lifespan, with many individuals meeting poverty guidelines when they first leave the home, and often becoming wealthier as they age, sometimes quite significantly. Second, for many individuals, including small business owners but also those with investments, general economic factors can result in rapid increases or decreases in total assets. For example, many individuals recently lost significant assets in the housing bust. The University of Michigan Panel Survey on Income Dynamics showed that, among people who were in the bottom 20% income bracket in 1975, only 5% were still in that category in 1991 (Sowell, 2010). Nearly six times as many of them were in the top 20% in 1991.

Thus, although it is clear that financial status is affected by a variety of factors over which the individual has no control (e.g., financial status of parents, intelligence, genetic influences on health, state of general economy, gender, race), most individuals can control additional variables. These variables offer some hope for improved financial status and improved outcomes correlated with financial status.

With the increased use of computers and electronics, marketing tools and strategies have become more effective at targeting consumers to purchase certain products. This change in turn may lead to targeting vulnerable groups that may engage in financial decisions (e.g., inappropriate use of high-interest credit cards to purchase these items) that have detrimental long-term effects. The premise operating in this view is that by being more financially literate, one's improved financial decision making will decrease the likelihood for negative outcomes and increase the likelihood of positive outcome for both short- and long-term goals. Such financial literacy should hopefully also prevent harm that results from succumbing to marketing gimmicks and other poor financial decisions. Some have argued that financial literacy is not only important on an individual level but the essence of having an efficient and healthy national economy (Braunstein & Welch, 2002). This section of the chapter briefly describes the basics of financial literacy, discusses why it is important, and provides references to practical materials on financial literacy.

## Basics on What Financial Literacy Is and Why It Is Important

Financial literacy, in broad terms, is the ability to use knowledge and skills to manage financial resources effectively for a lifetime of financial well-being. It is one's basic knowledge of key information about how to solve financial problems. Although financial literacy encompasses a wide range of financial issues and domains, three topics in particular are typically stressed: compound interest, the role of inflation, and risk diversification. Nevertheless, others have suggested that financial literacy includes the basic understanding of credit and savings, an understanding of how to invest, how to accrue enough money for retirement, and other goals such as financing children's education. In addition, financial literacy can also focus on such issues such as homeownership, debt reduction, and how specialty groups (e.g., military personnel, students, labor workers) accrue assets or wealth in their special circumstances.

When examining the literature on financial literacy, the most common way of assessing this construct is multiple-choice tests that assess knowledge of a wide range of financial matters, with the most common being compound interest, the role of inflation, and risk diversification (Lusardi & Mitchell, 2005). Compound interest is defined as the calculated interest that is based off of the principal value of an investment and the accrued interest already earned from an investment. Compound interest is important to understand, because as an investment is left to grow, the amount of money it earns accelerates with the passage of time. Therefore, the longer an investment is left to collect interest, the more interest it will collect every year. For example, a $5,000 investment that collects 7% interest per year left for 40 years will not be worth $19,000 ($5,000 plus $14,000) but will be valued at $74,872 due to compound interest. The most important practical point is that one should begin to save early in one's life. Savings for one's child's education when the child is born allows compound interest to have a large effect, as does savings for retirement in one's 20s.

Inflation is defined as the rate at which the level of prices for goods rise and, subsequently, purchasing power falls. Although inflation rises at different rates every year, most central banks try to keep inflation between 1% to 2% annually. This is important to understand, because what you can buy for $100 today will not be the same as what it can buy you 15 to 20 years from now. Therefore, we must keep inflation in mind when deciding how much money we would like to have saved for retirement as the buying power of the dollar systematically decreases or what kind of return on investments would be adequate for them. Understanding inflation is also important to understanding the real return on investments. For example, if the inflation rate is around 3% and a bank is offering 3% interest—the principal is not growing but simply being protected against the eroding effects of inflation (a situation that is fairly typical today).

Risk diversification is a strategy in which one makes a wide variety of uncorrelated investments. By investing in a wide variety of vehicles that tend to move somewhat independently (e.g., large cap stocks, small cap stocks, international stocks, short-term bonds, long-term bonds), risk is minimized by having unsystematic positive and negative performances of investments be neutralized by one another. In addition, a key principle is that one can assume more risk (e.g., have a portfolio weighted toward small cap stocks) when one's financial goals are more distal but one needs to assume less risk when one's financial goals are more proximal. Although these may seem to be basic principles of financial planning, many adults are still unaware of them.

When given this test, the average adult earns a C, and the average high school student who is about to graduate earns an F (Lusardi & Mitchell, 2007). This financial illiteracy among youth is of great concern because financial decisions made in youth have long-term implications (Lusardi,

Mitchell, & Curto, 2010). For example, when asked about debt, 30% of young adults report that they worried about it frequently; 29% had to put off or not continue their education due to it; and 22% took a job they would otherwise not have if they had not been in debt (Lusardi et al., 2010). Also, individuals 25 and under are the fastest growing group of bankruptcy filers (U.S. Congress Senate Committee on Banking, Housing, and Urban Affairs, 2002, as cited by Lusardi et al., 2010).

Financial literacy bears obvious implications for retirement as well. For example, in a review of the literature, financial literacy was found to be related to successfully planning for retirement (Lusardi & Mitchell, 2005). Financial literacy is also correlated with acquiring professional assistance in planning for retirement, which in turn is correlated with higher confidence in one's retirement plan (Lusardi & Mitchell, 2005).

Some argue that financial literacy is not just a proxy variable for education, marital status, race, or sex. Even when these variables are held constant, financial literacy continues to be an important predictor of financial planning and financial well-being (Lusardi, 2008). Also, throughout the literature, certain social groups consistently perform poorly on financial literacy tests. They include the young and old, women, individuals with low SES, and racial minorities, particularly African American and Hispanic (Lusardi, 2008; Lusardi & Mitchell, 2007). These groups are also particularly vulnerable to financial problems.

Because financial literacy is highly correlated with financial well-being, it merits utmost attention. Young adults are often unable to continue school due to poor financial decisions, and the elderly have often not saved enough money for retirement.

## The Data on Increasing Financial Literacy

Because financial literacy is highly correlated with sound financial decision making, does improving financial literacy actually produce behavior change in how individuals handle finances? This question has been the topic of discussion for government agencies, business corporations, and special interest groups. Nevertheless, data on the effects of increasing financial literacy are mixed (Braunstein & Welch, 2002; Lusardi, 2008).

Some education programs that target specific financial behaviors, such as homeownership and savings, have yielded positive effects. When examining the effects of financial literacy on homeownership, different forms of financial advice had different ranges of success. For example, individuals in group counseling on homeownership had a 19% lower 90-day delinquency rate than those who did not, whereas those who received individual counseling or received financial training in a class format had 34% and 26% lower delinquency rates, respectively (Braunstein & Welch, 2002). Also, individuals who took a class about the importance of saving and managing debt averaged having saved about $1,600 and reduced debt by $1,200 within a 1-month period (Braunstein & Welch, 2002). Effects of seminars and financial help have been particularly strong with individuals of low income and education. Some reports indicate that improving financial literacy in low-income families increases wealth by about 18% (Lusardi, 2008).

At the same time, other data are negative; financial behavior does not always change. For example, after seminars that were intended to change retirement goals and increase retirement income, only 12% of attendees reported wanting to change their retirement goals, and 30% reported wanting to change their retirement income. Moreover, during a follow-up, very few had actually made changes in their retirement planning behavior (Lusardi, 2008). Also, many of the studies assessing whether financial literacy affects behavior do not use random assignment and therefore may recruit individuals who may already have some interest in their financial well-being.

Although improving financial literacy has had mixed results, it is an important first step that is particularly important for young adults. Understanding how to spend one's money in a manner that will allow that money to grow over time is necessary to accrue sufficient funds when retiring. The remainder of this chapter provides the reader ways that one can build and maintain a healthy financial life. See Table 17.1 for more details.

## Implications for Research and Therapy

There has been scant attention to whether an assessment of financial issues can help to produce positive psychological outcomes for clients. We know that financial issues are on the list of most common worries for clients (deRoiste, 1996) as well as a variable associated with negative mood in such conditions as depression (Leahy, 2009). In addition, financial problems are among the top issues that result in marital disagreements and conflict (Papp, Cummings, & Goeke-Morey, 2009). Financial problems can also contribute to sleep disorders (Jansson-Frojmark & Rikard, 2012) and occur in such problems as pathological gambling and binge spending in bipolar disorder. Also, we know that certain severe psychological problems such as substance abuse and schizophrenia can cause downward social, occupational, and financial drift, which can result in a myriad of financial problems. It also seems prudent to review financial issues when evaluating somatic complaints

**Table 17.1**   Institute for Financial Literacy

### Standard I: Money Management

Recognize how cash flow management and net worth analysis can be used as tools to achieve financial goals.

**Money Management Benchmarks:**

Cash Flow Management

Adults can:

- Identify the components of a budget
- Create personalized budget document
- Revise their budgets to reflect current cash flow

Personal Net Worth

Adults can:

- Identify the components of a personal net worth statement
- Create personalized net worth statements
- Understand that their net worth will fluctuate as the values of their assets and liabilities change.

Financial Goal Setting

Adults can:

- Differentiate between short- and long-term financial goals
- Prioritize their financial goals
- Construct a realistic financial goal action plan
- Revise their financial goals as life circumstances change

### Standard II: Credit

Know how and where to obtain credit and the implications of using and misusing credit.

**Credit Benchmarks:**

Obtaining Credit

Adults can:

- Differentiate among the types of credit.
- Understand which types of credit are better suited for particular purposes than other types
- Identify types of financial institutions where credit can be obtained
- Understand how the credit application process works

*(Continued)*

(Continued)

Utilization of Credit

Adults can:

- Comprehend the legal implications of using credit
- Understand what a credit report is, how to dispute errors in credit reports, and what a consumer's rights are regarding credit reports
- Understand what credit scores mean and the significance of their use in modern life
- Recognize what precautions can be taken to prevent identity theft and fraud, and what to do if victimized

### Standard III: Debt Management

Recognize how using debt can be a tool in asset building.

### Debt Management Benchmarks:

Debt Measurement

Adults can:

- Know what tools are available to them to measure their debt load
- Determine what their appropriate debt load is
- Understand the difference between good debt and bad debt

Debt Resolution

Adults can:

- Recognize the warning signs of excessive consumer debt
- Understand options available to assist with excessive debt loads
- Evaluate which professionals can assist in dealing with excessive debt issues

### Standard IV: Risk Management

Use appropriate risk management strategies to protect assets and quality of life.

### Risk Management Benchmarks:

Insurance

Adults can:

- Differentiate among the types of insurance products
- Understand their insurance needs
- Comprehend the implications of being insured or uninsured

**Risk Management**

Adults can:

- Evaluate the effectiveness of risk management tools in protecting against financial loss
- Assess their risk tolerance level
- Use risk tolerance levels in developing risk management strategies

**Standard V: Investing and Retirement Planning**

Implement investment and retirement strategies to achieve financial goals.

**Investing and Retirement Planning Benchmarks:**

Planning

Adults can:

- Differentiate among the types of investment vehicles
- Identify the types of financial institutions where investment products can be purchased
- Understand the differences between retirement and nonretirement and qualified and nonqualified investments
- Recognize the importance of planning for retirement

Strategies

Adults can:

- Evaluate the risks and rewards associated with investment options
- Understand the role risk tolerance plays when choosing investment vehicles
- Comprehend the legal implications of investing
- Assess their overall financial situation in determining retirement needs

*Source*: https://financiallit.org/resources/national-standards/.

seen in primary care settings, such as headaches, stomach problems, and general complaints about stress. Such an assessment is especially warranted in times of prolonged and widespread national economic problems and for key populations such as the unemployed.

What would this financial assessment or screening look like? At the level of screening it would simply involve placing one or a few items in all general screens—such as "I worry about my financial situation," "My partner and I generally do not disagree about money," "I have a good understanding of money and financial planning," or "I believe my finances are in good order."

Responses to these issues may indicate that further assessment is needed and may allow the clinician to form and explore hypotheses about the relationships between the client's presenting problems and financial variables.

In addition, more research is needed to explore pathways regarding how the identification of negative attitudes and beliefs may be related to financial illiteracy, which in turn is related to psychological stress or other psychological problems. In cognitive therapy, the therapist looks for irrational beliefs about self, the world, and the future (Beck & Beck, 2011), and certainly finances can be a component of any part of this triad. More research is needed into the detection and identification of beliefs such as those that follow:

## 25 Irrational or Problematic Thoughts About Finances

1. If I avoid thinking about my debt, or my failure to save, or my general ignorance about financial matters, I can still be financially healthy.

2. Buying things is the best way that I regulate my emotions.

3. It is OK to hide or keep secret my spending or our financial problems from my partner.

4. Saving is something I can do later.

5. My income is inadequate, but I don't know what to do about it.

6. I don't know my financial goals, so I just avoid thinking about finances.

7. I am counting on someone else to support me.

8. It is OK that I have no savings for any kind of emergency.

9. I don't really have any sort of budget because it is too complex, scary, or confining.

10. People who know me say I am very cheap.

11. Gambling or very high-risk investments are a good way for me to quickly generate assets so I can catch up.

12. It is important to buy my children all the things they want; otherwise, I will be a failure as a parent.

13. It is important for me to impress others by my conspicuous consumption of things like cars, houses, vacations, and clothes.

14. If I can borrow the money for something, that means I can afford it.

15. Do I have about enough saved for all my financial goals, like an emergency fund, retirement, buying a house, or my children's college?

16. I do not need to buy key types of insurance (e.g., medical, disability, car, rental, homeowners, life).

17. I do not care about or understand the risks of my investments or possible investments.

18. I do not care about or understand my tax situation and the tax implications of my behavior.

19. Terms like stocks, bonds, compound interest, and mortgages are confusing to me.

20. If I care about financial matters, that means I am a shallow or bad person.

21. I do not deserve to become financially secure.

22. The rich or financially secure are not good people.

23. Someone else will take care of me financially.

24. I do not need to shop for the best value or deal.

25. I don't really care or know how to figure out the true cost of something (for example, commuting to work).

Perhaps even listing beliefs such as these and having the client endorse the extent to which he or she agrees or disagrees with each might be useful. In addition, it may be useful to raise questions about the role of money in most psychological complaints. For example, it could be useful to ask questions such as, "You told me that one of the issues that brought you in is $x$. Do money or finances have any role in $x$?" For example, if the client comes in presenting with depression, this question would be asked about his or her dysphoric affect.

It is also interesting to note the possible roles of financial dysfunction in diagnosis. Most Diagnostic and Statistical Manual of Mental Disorders (DSM) diagnoses require that the presenting problem interfere with functioning, including occupational and social functioning. However, there are not clear methods for assessing this functioning. Certainly, it would be clear that a parent who stays in bed and does not care for young children is experiencing problems in functioning. But what about a person who is underemployed, perhaps due to irrational thinking about his or her employment possibilities? What about a person who due to his or her lack of financial literacy is not saving for an emergency or insurance or his or her child's education? Perhaps there is a need to develop valid models of healthy financial functioning and use these in overall assessments of the quality of adult functioning.

The focus of this book is on prevention of problems and psychological health. The key question then becomes, "What sort of activities by the clinical psychologist related to financial variables can serve a preventative function regarding psychological problems and a facilitative function regarding positive psychological states?" It does not seem reasonable that the psychologist actually teach financial skills, as there is a large body of knowledge, all of which is beyond the scope of a psychologist's usual training and competence. However, it does not seem reasonable that a clinical psychologist ignore this domain of variables, as it can have significant implications for a client's psychological state.

Therefore, it would seem that the following can be a prudent course of action for therapists:

1. Screen for financial stress, particularly in the problems listed earlier. Be sensitive to possible signs of problematic financial attitudes (e.g., avoidance), emotions (e.g., fear, depression), or behaviors (e.g., spending that seems out of line with reported job or income; buying and consuming to manage negative emotions).

2. Screen for an acceptable level of financial literacy, especially regarding key developmental financial events (e.g., saving for college and buying life insurance for new parents, retirement planning for all, saving for a house for newlyweds).

3. Refer clients to resources that can help them increase their financial literacy and improve their financial behavior. These resources should be sound and relatively objective. It would be an advantage if they have some "edutainment" value, such as Suze Orman on CNBC (see Table 17.2 for possibilities).

However, the major limitation of this approach is that Issue 2 of the Irrational or Problematic Thoughts About Finances, buying things is the best way that I regulate my emotions, may indicate problematic attitudes and emotions as the root of the financial problems, rather than educational deficits. Clients may need to have more rational, open, honest, and healthy attitudes and emotions regarding money, spending, and their current financial situation and goals than they currently have. Currently, there are no special clinical tools to apply to these problems, but we need more outcome research to determine if generic tools such as cognitive restructuring of irrational beliefs (Leahy, 2009), generic problem-solving skills (Nezu, & Ricelli, this volume), exposure to reduce anxiety (Zalta & Foa, 2012), and even emotional acceptance skills (Wilson et al., 2012) can help clients deal with them. Clearly, more research is needed to evaluate the effectiveness of these interventions for the problems in the financial domain.

**Table 17.2**    Resources That Can Be Used to Help Clients Gain Improved Financial Literacy

1. The large investment companies such as Fidelity (fidelity.com) and Vanguard (vanguard.com) offer a variety of free instructional information regarding general investing advice and more specific information on options like mutual funds, insurance, and college and retirement savings programs.

2. Khanacademy.org provides an entire series of free short instructional videos on finances and economics covering issues such as bonds versus stocks, shorting stocks, mortgages, compound interest, exchange-traded funds, hedge funds, tax deductions, and life insurance.

3. There are classic books on financial planning such as *Personal Financial Planning,* 12th edition by Gitman, Joehnk, & Billingsley (2010); *Get a Financial Life: Personal Finance in Your Twenties and Thirties* by Kobliner (2009); *The Motley Fool Personal Finance Workbook* (Gardner, Gardner, & Yochim, 2002); *Your Money or Your Life* (Dominquez & Robin, 2002); *The Bogleheads' Guide to Investing* (Larimore, Lindauer, & LeBoeuf, 2008).

4. Suze Orman has a fairly entertaining, sound, and wide-ranging CNBC television show.

5. Local banks should have advisors and materials; look for large banks such as Bank of America.

6. There are government resources such as my money.gov, which has information on developing a spending plan; managing debt and credit; dealing with mortgages; planning for retirement; savings and investing; getting a loan; getting insurance; and detecting scams and fraud. Also the Small Business Association (sba.gov) is oriented toward starting and growing a small business.

7. Local community colleges often have courses on finance for beginners.

8. Seek some mentorship from successful people you may know. There is also SCORE (Service Corps of Retired Executives; score.org), which has information and online or face-to-face mentoring free on accounting and budgeting, cash flow management, financing, and business planning.

# References

Amato, P. R., Booth, A., Johnson, D. R., & Rogers, S. (2007). *Alone together: How marriage in America is changing.* Camridge, MA: Harvard University Press.

Amone-P'Olak, K., Burger, H., Ormel, J., Huisman, M., Verhulst, F. C., & Oldehinkel, A. J. (2009). Socioeconmic position and mental health problems in pre- and early-adolescents: The TRIALS study. *Social Psychiatry & Psychiatric Epidemiology, 44,* 231–238.

Braunstein, S., & Welch., S. C. (2002 November). Financial literacy: An overview of practice, research, and policy. *Federal Reserve Bulletin, 445–457.*

Braveman, P. A., Cubbin, C., Egerter, S., Williams, D. R., & Pamuk, E. (2010). Socioeconomic disparities in health in the United States: What the patterns tell us. *American Journal of Public Health, 100,* S186–S196.

Beck, J., & Beck, A. (2011). *Cognitive behavior therapy: Basics and beyond.* New York, NY: Guilford Press.

Conger, R. D., Conger, K. J., & Martin, M. J. (2010). Socioeconomic status, family processes, and individual development. *Journal of Marriage and Family, 72,* 685–704.

deRoiste, A, (1996). Sources of worry and happiness in Ireland. *Irish Journal of Psychology, 17,* 193–212.

Drentea, P., & Reynolds, J. R. (2012). Neither a borrower nor a lender be: The relative importance of debt and SES for mental health among older adults. *Journal of Aging and Health, 24*(4), 673–695.

Duncan, G., Huston, A., & Weisner, T. (2007). *Higher ground: New hope for the working poor and thier children.* New York, NY: Russell Sage.

Flegal, K. M., Carroll, M. D., Kit B. K., Ogden, C. L. (2012). *Prevalence of obesity and trends in the distribution of body mass index among U.S. adults, 1999–2010. Journal of the American Medical Association, 307*(5), 491–497. doi:10.1001/jama.2012.39

Ibrahim, A. K., Kelly, S. J., & Glazebrook, C. (2012). Analysis of an Egyptian study on the socioeconmic distribution of depressive symptoms among undergraduates. *Social Psychiatry and Psychiatric Epidemiology, 47*(6), 927–937.

Jansson-Frojmark, M. L., & Rikard, M. (2012). Don't worry, be constructive: A randomized controlled feasibility study comparing behavior therapy singly and combined with constructive worry for insomnia. *British Journal of Clinical Psychology, 5,* 142–157.

Johnson, R. C., & Schoeni, R. F. (2011). Early-life origins of adult disease: National longitudinal population-based study of the United States. *American Journal of Public Health, 101*(12), 2317–2324.

Kahneman, D., & Deaton, A. (2010). High income improves evaluation of life but not emotional well-being. *Proceedings of the National Academy of Sciences.* doi:10.1073/pnas.1011492107

Kosidou, K., Dalman, C., Lundberg, M., Hallqvist, J., Isacsson, G., & Magnusson, C. (2011). Socioeconomic status and risk of psychological distress and depression in the Stockhold Public Health Cohort: A population-based study. *Journal of Affective Disorders, 134*(1–3), 160–167.

Leahy, R. L. (2009). Financial anxieties: Nine steps for coping with your worries. *The Behavior Therapist, 32*(2), 29–31.

Lusardi, A. (2008). Household saving behavior: The role of financial literacy, information, and financial education programs. *NBER Working Paper No. 13824.*

Lusardi, A., & Mitchell, O. S. (2005). *Financial literacy and planning: Implications for retirement wellbeing.* Ann Arbor: University of Michigan Retirement Research Center.

Lusardi, A., & Mitchell, O. S. (2007). Financial literacy and retirement preparedness: Evidence and implications for financial education. *Business Economics, 35–44.*

Lusardi, A., Mitchell, O. S., & Curto, V. (2010). Financial literacy among the young. *Journal of Consumer Affairs, 44*(2), 358–380.

Maisel, N. C., & Karney, B. R. (2012). Socioeconomic status moderates associations among stressful events, mental health, and relationship satisfaction. *Journal of Family Psychology, 26*(4), 654–660.

Marmot, M. (2005). Social determinants of health inequalities. *Lancet, 365,* 1099–1104.

McLaughlin, K. A., Breslau, J., Green, J. G., Sampson, N. A., Zaslvsky, A. M., & Kessler, R. C. (2011). Childhood socio-economic status and the onset, persistence, and serverity of DSM-IV mental disorders in a U.S. national sample. *Social Science & Medicine, 73,* 1088–1096.

Muntaner, C., Eaton, W. W., & Miech, R. O. (2004). Socioeconomic position and major mental disorders. *Epidemiologic Reviews, 26,* 53–62.

Papp, L. M., Cummings, E. M., & Goeke-Morey, M. C. (2009). For richer and poorer: Money as a topic of marital conflict in the home. *Family Relations, 58,* 91–103.

Smith, J. P. (1999). Healthy bodies and thick wallets: The dual relation between health and economic status. *Journal of Econmic Perspectives, 13*(2), 145–166.

Sowell, T. (2010). *Basic economics.* New York, NY: Basic Books.

Walsh, S. D., Levine, S. Z., & Levav, I. (2012). The association between depression and parental ethnic affiliation and socioeconic status: A 27-year longitudinal U.S. community study. *Social Psychiatry and Psychiatric Epidemiology, 47,* 1153–1158.

Wilson, K. G., Flynn, M. K., Bordieri, M., Nassar, S., Lucas, N., & Whiteman, K. (2012). Acceptance and cognitive behavior therapy. In W. O'Donohue & J. E. Fisher (Eds.), *Cognitive behavior therapy: Core principles for practice.* Hoboken, NJ: John Wiley & Sons.

Zalta, A. K., & Foa, E. B. (2012). Exposure therapy: Promoting emotional processing of pathological anxiety. In W. O'Donohue & J. E. Fisher (Eds.), *Cognitive behavior therapy: Core principles for practice.* Hoboken, NJ: John Wiley & Sons.

# Author Index

Aarsland, D., 227, 228
Abad, N., 252, 256
Abdel, A., 148
Abdo, C. H., 347
Abildso, C., 151
Abraído-Lanza, A. F., 277
Abramowitz, J. S., 21
Abrams, R., 32
Abrantes, A. M., 236, 237, 238, 239
Acebo, C., 169, 319
Achenbach, T. M., 371
Adame, D. D., 152
Adamson, B., 123
Addis, M., 106
Addis, M. E., 21, 29, 78, 81
Adleman, A., 356, 357
Adler, A. B., 103, 104
Afari, N., 133
Affleck, G., 123
Aganoff, J. A., 233
Agans, R. P., 347
Agras, W. S., 79
Aguillard, R. N., 182
Ai, A. L., 277
Akin-Little, K. A., 387
Aknin, L. B., 254, 260
Aks, D. J., 230
Aldridge, A. A., 31
Alexopoulas, G. S., 32
Alfano, S., 63
Alfieri, T., 124
Algoe, S. B., 260
Allen, K. D., 377, 388, 393
Allen, S. S., 239
Allmon, D., 76
Allport, G. W., 276
Almeida, D. M., 42
Almeida, O. P., 228
Alonso, J., 119

Alsten, C., 182
Alter, J., 170
Althof, S. E., 347
Alvermann, D. E., 306
Alzheimer's Society Systematic Review Group, 227, 228
Amato, P. R., 219, 332, 405, 408
Ambady, N., 14
American Academy of Sleep Medicine, 148, 176
American Psychiatric Association, 105
American Psychological Association, 142
Amone-P'Olak, K., 408
Ancoli-Israel, S., 172
Andersen, M. B., 233
Anderson, C. L., 261
Anderson, J. R., 31
Anderson, L. A., 232
Anderson, R. C., 305
Anderson, T. L., 277
Anderssen, S., 227, 228
Andersson, H. I., 119
Anderzen-Carlsson, A., 155
Andreasen, T., 62
Angermeyer, M. C., 119
Annesi, J. J., 233
Ano, G. G., 277, 278, 285
Ansley, T. N., 273
Antonuccio, D. O., 2, 76, 79
Appel, L. J., 2
Arand, D. L., 171
Archodidou, A., 305
Arent, S., 232
Arigo, D., 18
Armeli, S., 123
Armstrong, H. E., 76

Armstrong, R. B., 236
Arnow, B. A., 120
Ashby, D., 120
Ashton, J., 205
Astrup, A, 196, 197, 210
Aten, J. D., 281
Atkins, C. J., 124
Atkins, D. C., 76, 77
Atkins, P. W. B., 77
Atkinson, J. H., 133
Auchterlonie, J. L., 95
Audiffren, M., 228
Avants, S. K., 283
Aydin, T., 226
Aziz, S., 277

Baade, P. D., 371, 375
Babcock, J. C., 146
Bach, P., 79
Bachmann, G. A., 347
Bacon, L., 208
Baer, R. A., 65, 68, 74, 149
Bahl, A., 377
Bai, Y., 384
Bailey, T. C., 31
Baisden, J., 122
Baker, S. R., 16
Bakken, H., 227
Ballard, C., 227, 228
Bandelow, B., 236
Bandura, A., 301, 327
Banich, M. T., 225
Banko, K. M., 387, 397
Barber, C. R., 282
Barlow, D. H., 25, 27, 28, 350
Barnes, P. M., 3, 143, 145
Barnes, V. A., 144
Barnes-Holmes, D., 77
Barnett, R. C., 93

Baron, R. M., 79
Barrera M. Jr., 92, 95
Barrett, B., 147
Barrett, L., 18
Barrios, V., 74
Barry, R. A., 325
Bartley, C. A., 237
Bartmann, U., 236
Bartz, J., 282
Baruch, D. E., 76
Baruch, G. K., 93
Basak, C., 232
Bassaine, L., 62
Basson, R., 348, 349, 350, 353, 363
Batcha, B., 386
Bates, J. E., 384, 385
Bathon, J., 123
Baucom, D. H., 76
Bauer, J. J., 91, 94
Bauer-Wu, S. M., 101
Baum, A., 41
Bauman, A., 240
Baumann, B. L., 371
Bays, J. C., 211
Beach, S. R. H., 283
Beale, M., 135
Beauchaine, T., 374
Beaver, K. M., 370
Beck, A. T., 16, 21, 28, 65, 99, 100, 327, 418
Beck, J., 16, 418
Beebe, L. H., 239
Beevers, C. G., 205
Begue, L., 99
Beitel, M., 283
Beitz, K., 359
Belavich, T. G., 274
Belendink, K.A., 197
Bell, A. C., 47, 48
Bell, I., 102, 147, 148
Belsky, J., 319
Belyea, M. J., 181
Ben Cheikh, R., 173
Benish, S. G., 104
Benjet, C., 94
Bennett, G. M., 377
Bennett, K., 208
Benson, H., 181
Benson, R., 182
Benzinger, T., 232
Berg, C. J., 31
Berger, R., 170
Berghoff, C. R., 80
Berglund, P., 123
Bergsma, A., 261
Berkoff, M. C., 383, 384

Berlin, K. S., 76
Berlin, L. J., 384
Berlyne, D. E., 257
Berman, M. E., 236
Berman, M. I., 203
Berndt, E. R., 109
Bernert, R. A., 186
Bernhardt, A. J., 375
Berns, S., 76
Berntson, G. G., 170
Berrett, M. E., 282, 283
Berry, E. V., 25
Berscheid, E., 349
Betrisey, C., 277
Bhasin, M., 181
Biddle, G. F. S., 239
Bigal, M. E., 120
Biglan, A., 81, 377, 382, 388
Bijlani, R. L., 152
Biklen, D., 2
Bilicp, M., 226
Billington, E., 31
Bingham, C. O., 123
Birch, L. L., 196, 197, 210
Bissett, R. T., 75, 76, 77, 102
Bisson, J. I., 104
Biswas-Diener, R., 260
Bjorklund, D. F., 371
Black, D. S., 155
Blair, S. N., 3, 240
Blanc, H., 377
Blanchard, E. B., 154
Blanchard-Fields, F., 320
Blanker, M. H., 347
Blasey, C. M., 120
Blechert, J., 64
Bliese, P. D., 103
Bloch, M. H., 237
Bloch, W., 233
Bloom, B., 3, 143, 145
Blum, C. M., 145, 148, 150, 156, 182
Blumberg, S. L., 333
Blumenthal, J. A., 225, 231, 236
Boah, A. R., 152
Bockow, T. B., 123
Boden, M. T., 64
Boehm, J. K., 254, 256, 257, 258
Boelen, P. A., 96
Bogan, R. K., 170
Boggs, S. R., 372
Bohlmeijer, E., 103
Bohnen, A. M., 347
Bohus, M., 17
Bolger, N., 325, 326

Bolling, M. Y., 76
Bolling, S. F., 277
Bombardier, C., 130
Bonanno, G. A., 91, 92, 93, 94, 95, 102, 103
Bond, F. W., 74, 79, 203
Bonnell, D., 325
Bonnet, M. H., 170, 171
Bonney, C. R., 298
Booth, A., 219, 332, 405, 408
Boothby, J. L., 135
Bootzin, R. R., 146, 148, 168, 169, 179, 180, 181, 182, 183
Bor, W., 389
Bordieri, M., 420
Bordin, I. A., 383
Borges, G., 94
Borisov, N. N., 347
Bornstein, M. H., 370
Borras, L., 277
Boscarino, J. A., 102
Bosch, J. L., 347
Bosch, R., 347
Bostrom, A., 92, 94
Boswell, W. R., 260
Bouchard, C., 3
Boudreau, J. W., 260
Boulanger, J., 75, 77, 79
Boutelle, K. N., 203
Bowden, A., 148
Bowen, S., 146
Bowes, J. M., 370
Bowman, P. J., 288
Boyle, C. L., 377
Boyle, G. J., 233
Braams, B. R., 64
Bradbury, T. N., 320, 323, 325, 327, 332, 359
Bradley, L. A., 123
Bradley, S. J., 390
Brady-Smith, C., 384
Brand, S., 183, 233
Brandsma, L. L., 75
Brandt, P., 277
Brannon, L., 145, 224, 225
Branstetter, A. D., 79
Braunstein, S., 411, 413, 414
Braveman, P. A., 407
Bray, D., 31
Bredin, S. S., 151
Breen, A., 120
Breitenstein, C., 225
Breivik, H., 119
Brennan, P. A., 382
Breslau, J., 408

Breslau, N., 173
Breus, M. J., 173
Brickman, P., 260
Bright, C. N., 390
Brinks, J., 227
Britton, W. B., 146, 183
Broch, L., 177
Brock, R. L., 325
Broderick, P. C., 158
Brody, J., 390
Broman-Fulks, J. J., 236
Broocks, A., 236
Brooks, A. J., 172
Brooks-Gunn, J., 384
Brosse, A. L., 236
Broughton, R. J., 171
Browman, K. E., 172
Brown, A., 27
Brown, A. W., 196, 197, 210
Brown, C. A., 132
Brown, G., 93
Brown, G. K., 123
Brown, J. S., 93
Brown, K. W., 65, 67
Brown, R. A., 236, 237,
    238, 239
Brown, S. L., 319
Brown, T., 238
Brown, T. D., 152
Brownell, K. D., 201
Bryant, F. B., 24
Bryant, R. A., 103, 104
Bryngelsson, I., 155
Bucci, D. J., 230
Buchbinder, R., 129
Buchowski, M. S., 239
Buck, S., 234
Buckhalt, J. A., 319
Buehler, C., 318
Bugg, J. M., 232
Bullen, C., 238
Bunce, D., 68, 74, 79
Bunde, M., 325
Bunting K., 203
Burger, H., 408
Burke, L. B., 135
Burnett, A. L., 347
Burnett, P. C., 387
Burney, R., 132
Burns, A. B., 93
Burns, D. D., 100
Burton, C. L., 102
Buscemi, J., 119
Busch, A. M., 76
Buschkuehl, M., 233
Bush, A. L., 282
Bussing, A., 145, 151

Butler, A., 100
Butler, A. C., 21, 28
Butler, J., 4
Butryn, M., 203
Butryn, M. L., 75, 79, 197
Butter, E. M., 274
Butzer, B., 342
Buysse, D. J., 148, 171, 172,
    177, 180, 182
Byers, E., 342
Bynum, D., 272
Byrne, G. J., 149, 182
Byrne, R., 261
Bzdewka, T. M., 152

Cacioppo, J. T., 170, 319
Cahana, A., 121, 135
Cahill, S. P., 104
Cairns, J., 174
Cakirbay, H., 226
Calamaro, C. J., 174
Calhoun, L. G., 42
Calkins, D. R., 134
Call, V., 343
Callaghan, G. M., 76
Callaghan, P., 234
Callahan, J., 103
Callahan, R., 103
Callan, V. J., 325
Calzada, E., 377
Cameron, A. Y., 237
Cameron, J., 387, 397
Camp, M. E., 282
Campbell, J. C., 332
Campbell, L., 342
Campbell, N., 386
Campbell, S. B., 371
Campbell-Sills, L., 25, 27, 28
Canter, P. H., 146, 153, 157
Capage, L. C., 377
Capaldi, D. M., 231, 325
Capranica, L., 229
Cardaciotto, L., 65
Carels, R. A., 274
Carey, M. P., 347, 360
Carlson, L. E., 183
Carmody, J., 153
Carnes, D., 120
Carnes, P. J., 356, 357
Carpenter, K. C., 68, 74
Carpenter, R. W., 27
Carragee, E. J., 122
Carr'ere, S., 359
Carrigan R. D., 172
Carroll, M. D., 409
Carskadon, M. A., 169
Carson, J. W., 151, 152

Carson, V. B., 272
Carson Wong, A., 29
Carter, S., 21, 75
Carter S. R., 205
Casazza, K., 196, 197, 210
Casella, R., 229, 230
Casey, C. Y., 120
Caspi, A., 92
Castelnuovo, G., 145
Castro, C., 103
Catalano, R. F., 319
Cauffman, E., 319
Caughlin, J. P., 325
Cavanagh, J. F., 18
Cavera, R. S., 236
Ceballo, R., 370
Cella, D., 135
Cella, M., 135
Centers for Disease Control
    and Prevention, 224
Cepeda, N. J., 258
Cereatti, L., 230
Cerrada, C., 152
Chaddock, L., 232
Chamberlain, P., 373
Chambless, D. L., 28, 78,
    100, 327
Chambliss, H. O., 232, 241
Chan, C. W., 122
Chan, R. C., 230
Chancellor, J., 254
Chang, E. C., 31
Chang, J. J., 383, 384
Chang, M., 319
Chaouloff, F., 236
Chapman, J., 100
Chapman, J. E., 21, 28
Chapman, K. L., 151
Charboneau, E., 239
Charles, S. T., 42
Charlson, F. J., 227
Charny, I. W., 313
Chatters, L. M., 371
Chawla, N., 146
Cheavens, J. S., 21, 31, 32
Chee, M., 319
Chen, E. Y., 230
Chen, K. M., 156
Chen, K. W., 149
Cheng, C., 92, 94
Cherkin D. C., 151
Cheung, L., 211
Chiesa, A., 132
Chin, A., 227
Chmielewski, M., 74
Choi, I., 254
Choi, P. Y., 233

Choi, T. K., 146
Chorost, A. F., 325
Chou, R., 122
Christensen, A., 76, 77, 146, 325, 328, 329
Christianson, T. J., 232
Christopher, F., 342
Christopher, S. F., 350
Chronis, A, M, 371
Chtourou, H., 173
Ciccolo, J. T., 238
Cisler, J. M., 96
Clark, C. G., 232, 241
Clark, D. A., 21
Clark, D. M., 92
Clarke, A., 205
Clarkin, J. F., 32
Claus, D., 129
Cleghorn, G. J., 376
Clements, M., 327
Cloitre, M., 97
Clough, P. J., 233
Coates, A., 100
Coates, D., 260
Cobb, R. M., 327
Coe, C. L., 147
Coelho, H. F., 146, 157
Coffelt, N., 371
Coffey, K. A., 101, 144, 147, 254
Coghill, R. C., 132
Cohan, C. L., 325
Cohen, J., 146, 155
Cohen, L. L., 350
Cohen, N. J., 225
Cohen, R., 119
Cohen, S., 93, 124, 263, 319
Cohn, A., 237
Cohn, M. A., 144, 147, 254
Coifman, K., 102
Colcombe, A., 225
Colcombe, S. J., 232
Colditz, G. A., 227
Cole, B., 274
Cole, S. P., 152
Colecchi, C., 180
Collett, B., 119
Collier, C. D., 226
Collins, G., 356, 357
Collins, W. A., 370
Comerford, A., 149
Condry, J., 386
Conger, K. J., 408, 409
Conger, R. D., 342, 408, 409
Conger, R. E., 372
Congleton, C., 153
Connell, C. M., 371

Conner, T. S., 123
Constantino, M., 120
Contrada, R. J., 41
Cooper, H., 231
Cooper, L., 151
Cope, J. G., 277
Cordain, L., 199
Córdova, C., 225
Cordray, D. S., 224
Costa, P. T., 253
Côté, S., 21
Coudeyre, E., 129
Covic, T., 123
Cowan, P. A., 370
Cowan, R. L., 239
Cox, K. L., 228
Cox, M., 319
Coyne, J. C., 124, 319
Craft, L. L., 234
Craig, G., 103
Craig, I. W., 92
Craighead, L. W., 217
Craighead, W. E., 29
Craigie, M. A., 183
Cranford, J. A., 124, 319
Craske, M. G., 156
Criss, M. M., 384
Critchley, H. D., 16
Crocker, J., 91
Cronk, R., 261
Crosby, L., 325
Crow, S. J., 203
Csikszentmihalyi, M., 6, 251, 262, 298
Cubbin, C., 407
Cuijpers, P., 47, 103, 104
Cullen, M., 18
Cully, J. A., 282
Culpepper, L., 152
Cummings, E. M., 319, 414
Cupach, R. W., 359
Currier, J. M., 91
Curry, L. A., 31
Curtis, J. T., 93
Curto, V., 412, 413, 414
Cushing, C., 79
Cykert, S., 272
Czerniecki, J. M., 124, 128

Dadds, M. R., 376
Dahl, J., 79
Dahn, J. R., 226, 234
Dalal, D., 2
Daley, A., 233, 234, 235
Dalgleish, T., 91
Dalman, C., 405
D'Aloisio, A. A., 347

Daniel, S. S., 278
Danton, W. G., 2
Darley, J., 308, 313
Das, L. S., 144
Da Silva Prado, J., 173
Datta, G. D., 319
Datta, N. S., 319
Daughters, S. B., 21, 32
Davidson, J. R., 109
Davidson, R. J., 15, 16, 27, 150
Davies, P. T., 319
Davila, J., 325, 326
Davis, C. L., 231
Davis, D., 359
Davis, D. E., 273
Davis, D. M., 155
Davis, F. C., 230
Davis, J. A., 345
Davis, M., 97
Davis, M. C., 123
Davis, R. B., 152
Davis-Kean, P., 385
Davison, G. C., 75
Davison, S. L., 347
Dawson, D., 175
Day, W. H., 371
Deacon, B. J., 96
Deak, T., 95
Dean, J., 347
Deater-Deckard, K., 385
Deaton, A., 405, 410
Deci, E. L., 251, 252, 256, 386, 387
Deckx, S., 148
De Garmo, D. S., 373
de Graaf, I., 376
de Graaf, R., 319
De Grazia, J. M., 171
de Greiff, A., 147
De Hart, G., 319
De Hert, M., 148, 239
de Jongh, A., 104
Dekel, S., 93
de Kemp, R., 319
Delbanco, T. L., 134
Della Porta, M. D., 252, 254, 256, 259
Delliquadri, E., 371
De Mello, M., 173
Demler, O., 123
DeNelsky, G. Y., 2
De Queiroz, S., 173
de Roiste, A, 414
Derry, S., 121
De Rubeis, R. J., 21
Deshpande, S., 129

De Simone, S. L., 31
Deslandes, A., 235
Detweiler, M., 203
Devilly, G. J., 103
Dew, R. E., 278
de Wolff, M., 376
Deyo, R. A., 151
Diaz, A. B., 236
Diaz, R. M., 348
Dickerhoof, R., 254, 255,
    256, 259
Dickinson, A. M., 386–387
Diener, E., 250, 251, 252,
    253, 254, 260,
    262, 318
Diener, M., 251, 252
Dietrich, M. S., 239
Dillworth, T. M., 146
DiMatteo, M. R., 254
Dimeo, F., 236
Dimidjian, S., 21, 29, 78,
    92, 95
Di Napoli, E., 97
Dinges, D. F., 172
DiPaolo, M., 18
Dishion, T. J., 370, 371, 373,
    381, 383, 394
Dishman, R. K., 236
Dix, T., 371
Dixon, J., 154
Dobson, K. S., 21, 28, 29,
    50, 78
Dodge, B., 355
Dodge, K. A., 384, 385
Dodson, B., 349, 353,
    355, 356
Dogui, M., 173
Dolan, R., 16
Donahue, M. J., 276
Dopp, J. M., 319
Doppelt, O., 93
Dorsey, C., 177
Doss, B. D., 77
Dostoevsky, F., 75
Dougherty, J., 124
Douleh, T., 79
Douvan, E., 318
Dove, N. L., 354
Doyle, E. J., 151
Doyle, W. J., 319
Drentea, P., 406, 407, 408
Drobes, D. J., 238
Drugli, M. B., 371
Duangado, K. M., 31
Duggan, J., 285
Duguid, J. E., 77
Dunayevich, E., 197, 211

Duncan, G., 408
Dunmore, E., 92
Dunn, A. L., 232, 236, 241
Dunn, E. W., 254, 260
Dunsiger, S., 238
Dupeyron, A., 129
Dupuis, P., 30
Durkheim, E., 279
Dusek, J.A., 181
Dweck, C. S., 306, 387
Dworkin, R. H., 119, 135
Dyas, J. V., 178
Dzankovic, S., 325
D'Zurilla, T. J., 42, 43, 44,
    45, 46, 47, 48, 52, 53

Earle, C. C., 319
Eaton, W. W., 407, 408
Eberth, J., 143, 146, 155
Eccleston, C., 79, 130,
    133, 151
Echeverría, S. E., 277
Eddy, J. M., 373
Edelbrock, C., 371
Edelmann, R. J., 16
Edinger, J. D., 148, 171,
    180, 182
Edwards, R. R., 123
Egan, J., 375
Egerter, S., 407
Eggett, D. L., 283
Ehde, D. M., 123, 124, 128
Ehlers. A., 92
Ehlers, A., 103, 104
Eifert, G. H., 81, 203
Eisenberg, D. M., 134, 152
Eisenstadt, T., 377
Eissler-Russo, J. L., 152
Ejlertsson, G., 119
Ekeberg, Ø., 96
Ekholm, J., 226
Ekman, P., 15, 16, 18
Elder, G. H. Jr., 342
Eldridge, K., 77
Elfenbein, H. A., 14
Elibero, A., 238
Elliot, C., 233
Ellis, A., 50
Ellison, C. G., 277
Ellsworth, P., 15
El-Sheikh, M., 319
Embry, D., 377, 382, 388
Emery, E., 277
Emery, G., 16, 28, 65
Emmelkamp, P. M. G.,
    77, 78
Emmons, R. A., 254, 263

Enevoldsen, L., 62
Eng, W., 31
Engel, G. L., 122
Engel, J. M., 123
Engels, R., 319
Ennett, S. T., 2
Epstein, B., 151
Epstein, D. R., 168, 180, 181
Erickson, D., 377
Erickson, K. I., 232
Eriksen, K., 273
Ernst, E., 2, 146, 153, 157
Ernst, J. M., 170
Erro J., 151
Esch, T., 182
Eshelman, E. R, 97
Espie, C. A., 148, 171, 180,
    181, 182
Esquivel, G., 236
Esteve-Zarazaga, R., 124, 128
Everaerd, W., 350
Everett, G. E., 382
Everly, G. S., 92
Everly, G.S. Jr., 2
Ewing, L. J., 371
Exline, J., 274, 278, 284
Eyberg, S. M., 372, 376, 377

Fagan, A. M., 232
Fahey, J. L., 319
Faigin, C. A., 284
Fairburn, C. G., 79
Falvo, D., 122, 124
Fan, J. T., 156
Farooqi, I. S., 201
Farrar, J. T., 152
Farrow, V., 65
Fasman, R., 123
Faulkner, G., 238, 239
Fazio, E., 325
Feeney, J. A., 325
Feist, J., 145, 224, 225
Feldman, D. B., 30, 31
Feldman, H. A., 347
Feldman Barrett, L., 30
Feller, C., 236
Felton, M., 305
Feng, S., 153
Ferenschak, M. P., 96
Ferguson, M. J., 119
Ferguson, S. A., 175
Ferguson, Y., 252, 256
Ferrari, A. J., 227
Ferraro, K. F., 288
Feske, U., 78
Field, N. P., 95
Fifield, J., 123

Figley, C. R., 102
Filene, J. H., 377
Fincham, F. D., 283, 319,
    320, 323
Fine, M. A., 384
Finkel, E. J., 326
Finkel, S. M., 144, 147, 254
Finkelstein, S. N., 109
Finlon, K. J., 32
Fireman, B., 120
Fisher, P. A., 373
Flaherty, K. N., 176
Flannery, R. B., 149
Flausino, N., 173
Flavell, J. H., 304
Flay, B., 377, 382, 388
Flegal, K. M., 409
Fleming, C. B., 319
Flessner, C. A., 79
Fletcher, G. J. O., 320, 321,
    322, 326
Fletcher, K. E., 150
Fletcher, P. C., 201
Flewelling, R. L., 2
Flicker, L., 228
Floerke, V. A., 261
Flor, H., 128
Floyd, F., 327
Flynn, M. K., 420
Foa, E., 97
Foa, E. B., 92, 95, 96, 101,
    104, 420
Fobker, M., 225
Foley, K. M., 123
Foley, S., 348, 349, 353,
    354, 356
Folkman, S., 18, 19, 20, 92,
    94, 98
Follette, V. M., 203, 205, 207
Follette, W. C., 359
Foltz, C., 18
Fontaine, K. R., 196, 197, 210
Foran, H. M., 319
Ford, B. Q., 261
Forehand, R., 371, 372, 374,
    375, 388, 389
Forehand, R. L., 372, 374,
    375, 389
Foreyt, J. P., 197, 211
Forfylow, A. L., 149
Forgatch, M., 373, 382
Forgatch, M. S., 373, 382
Forgatch, M.S., 383
Forman, E., 100
Forman, E. M., 21, 28, 63,
    65, 67, 68, 75, 76, 79,
    80, 203

Forsting, M., 147
Forsyth, J. P., 74, 80, 81
Forsythe, G. B., 312
Fortenberry, J. D., 355
Forthofer, M. S., 319
Fossum, S., 371
Foster, C., 134
Foster, G. D., 197, 211
Foster, J. K., 228
Foster, M., 80
Foster, N. E., 120
Foster, S. L., 382
Fox, A., 27
Fraley, R. C., 93
Frame, L. E., 323
Franco, M., 272
Frank, E., 92, 93, 95, 319
Franklin, B. A., 227, 240
Franzen, P. L., 180
Frazier, P. A., 183
Frederick, S., 253, 257, 260
Fredrickson, B. L., 24, 25,
    30, 93, 101, 144, 147,
    254, 258
Freedman, G., 227
French, V., 369
Freud, S., 279
Fricchione, G. L., 182
Fridel, K. W., 146, 183
Friedman, H., 227
Friedman, S. L., 319
Friesen, W. V., 15, 16
Frisch, M. B., 31
Froh, J. J., 254
Frutchey, R. M., 274
Fryer, C.S., 4
Fucito, L. M., 348, 353, 354
Fugl-Meyer, A. R., 347
Fugl-Meyer, K. S., 347
Fujita, F., 253
Fuller, I., 120
Fuller, J. A. K., 254
Fulton, P. R., 63
Fyer, A. J., 109

Gable, S. L., 260, 326
Gabora, L, 298
Gagnon, J. H., 343, 344,
    345, 346, 347, 348
Gaines, S. O., 320
Gajebasia, K. S., 152
Gajebasia, N. K., 152
Galantino, M. L., 152
Galatzer-Levy, I. R., 102
Gall, T. L., 277
Gallacher, D., 119
Gallagher, M. W., 31

Gallo, L. C., 319
Gálvez, G., 229, 230
Gamez, W., 74
Gano Phillips, S., 323
Gappmaier, E., 233
Garai, E., 389
Gard, T., 153
Garland, S. N., 183
Garofalo, A., 103
Garrison-Diehn, C., 97
Gartner, A. L., 273
Garza, M.A., 4
Gaskin, D. J., 119, 120
Gatchel, R. J., 133
Gater, R., 120
Gates, G., 344
Gaudiano, B. A., 75, 79,
    80, 327
Gauntlett-Gilbert, J., 132
Gaylord-King, C., 153
Gebhard, P., 343
Geda, Y. E., 232
Geigle, P., 152
Gelis, A., 129
Geller, P. A., 75
Genty, M., 129
Geoghegan, P., 174
George, A., 236
George, C. J., 93
George, S. Z., 131
George, W. H., 76
Gerber, M., 233
Gerbode, F., 103
Germer, C. K., 63
Gershkovich, M., 68
Gershoff, E. T., 371, 384, 385
Ghassemi, A., 355
Gibbel, M. R., 284
Gibbs, A. C., 170
Giese-Davis, J., 18
Gifford, E. V., 79, 203, 205
Gilbert, D. T., 101, 250, 260,
    261, 265
Gilbert, M., 31
Giles, D., 31
Gill, D., 121
Gillieron, C., 277
Gillihan, S. J., 96
Gilmore, S. K., 372
Gilovich, T., 261
Gingell, C., 347
Giordano, L. A., 123
Giovannelli, J., 371
Gizewski, E. R., 147
Glajchen, M., 124
Glaser, R., 263, 319
Glass, N., 332

Glasser, D. B., 347
Glazebrook, C., 405
Gleason, M. E. J., 326
Glenn, N. D., 277
Gleser, J., 236
Glovinsky, P. B., 181
Glynn, E. L., 376
Goate, A. M., 232
Godemann, F., 236
Goeke-Morey, M. C., 319, 414
Gold, M. S., 201
Goldfried, M. R., 44
Goldin, P. R., 224
Goldstein, E., 103
Goldstein, I., 347
Goldston, D. B., 278
Gollan, J. K., 78
Golledge, J., 91
Gomez, S., 171
Goodman, M. J., 154
Goodwin, A., 239
Goodwin, R., 320
Goolkasian, P., 150, 151
Gorczynski, P., 239
Gordon, A. A., 238, 239
Gordon, J. S., 148
Gordon, K. C., 342, 359
Gordon, N. F., 3
Gordon, N. S., 150, 151
Gorman, P., 31
Gortner, E. T., 78
Gosnell, C. L., 326
Gotlib, I. H., 100, 233
Goto, F., 150
Gottman, J. M., 359
Gould, D., 31
Gourevitch, P., 313
Grady-Fletcher, A., 326
Graham, C., 131
Graham, J., 279
Gramann, K., 16
Grant, J. A., 132
Gray, M. J., 103, 104
Graydon, J., 228
Grayman-Simpson, N. A., 285
Green, J. G., 408
Greenberg, B. D., 236, 237
Greenberg, L. S., 326, 328
Greenberg, M. A., 120
Greenberg, P. E., 100, 109
Greene, D., 386
Gregory, N., 386
Grewal, D., 18
Griest, D. L., 375
Griez, E., 236
Griffiths, R., 279, 283

Griffitt, W., 343, 344
Grigorenko, E. L., 306, 312
Griskevicius, V., 263
Grodstein, F., 232
Gross, C. R., 183
Gross, D. P., 129
Gross, G., 68
Gross, J. J., 15, 16, 18, 19, 21, 22, 27, 64, 224
Grossman, P., 101, 103, 143, 146, 147, 150, 158
Grossman, S. R., 32
Grosswald, S., 153
Gruber, J., 18, 261, 262
Grych, J. H., 319
Guallar, E., 2
Gualtieri, T., 231
Guenole, N., 68, 74
Guereje, O., 120
Guerrero, F., 77
Guiney, H., 230, 231
Gujna, N., 178
Guler, M., 226
Gunnoe, M. L., 385
Gunz, A., 252, 256
Gurin, G., 288
Gustavsson, C., 131
Gwaltney, J. M. Jr., 319
Gyurak, A., 21

Haaga, D. A., 153
Haarig, F., 143, 146, 155
Haas, G., 120
Hackett, G., 347
Hadegard, B. H., 371
Hafer, C. L., 99
Hahn, J., 277, 278, 279
Hahn, S., 225
Haidt, J., 260, 279
Haiman, P., 386
Halgin, R. P., 236
Hall, E. M. L., 277
Hall, K., 343, 349, 357
Hallqvist, J., 405
Halpern, J. M., 96
Hamer, M., 227
Hamilton, J. P., 100
Hamilton, K. E., 50
Hamilton, N., 31
Han, M., 173
Hancock, L., 373
Hanh, T. N., 211
Hans, E., 100
Hansenne, M., 25, 30
Hanson, A., 100
Hardie, E. A., 90
Harding, G., 135

Hardman, R. K., 282, 283
Haring, M., 93, 95
Harkrider, K. E., 277
Harney, P., 31
Harold, G. T., 323
Harpin, R. E., 120
Harrington, H., 92
Harris, C., 31
Harris, J. R., 253, 370
Harrison, C. R., 225
Harstall, C., 118, 119
Hartman, M., 101
Harvey, L., 171
Haskell, W. L., 3, 240
Hassan, F., 383
Hatfield, C., 175
Hatfield, E. J., 343, 344
Hatzenbuehler, M. L., 18
Hatzichristou, D. G., 347
Haugen, M. R. G., 284
Hauri, P. J., 148, 169, 173
Havik, O. E., 182
Hawkins, H. L., 231
Hawkins, M. W., 319
Hawkley, L. C., 170
Hay, M., 237
Hayashi, M., 171, 172
Hayes, A. J., 171
Hayes, A. M., 205
Hayes, J. A., 155
Hayes, L., 77
Hayes, S. C., 65, 68, 74, 75, 76, 77, 79, 80, 81, 101, 102, 103, 146, 203, 205, 207, 327
Haynes, P. L., 146, 183
Hayney, M. S., 147
Haythornthwaite, J. A., 123
Hayward, C., 120
Hazlett-Stevens, H., 156
He, J., 227
Head, D., 232
Heard, H. L., 76
Hearn, K., 370
Heavey, C. L., 325
Hedlund, J., 312
Heffner, H., 207
Heffner, M., 203
Heiman, J., 359
Heinz, A., 236
Helgeson, V. S., 24
Heller, D., 318
Heller, K., 318
Helms, H. M., 318
Helson, H., 253, 257
Hembree, E. A., 97, 104

Hembree-Kilgin, T., 372, 376, 382
Hemsley, D. R., 355
Henderlong, J., 387
Henderson, A. K., 277
Henkens, K., 91
Hennekens, C. H., 227
Herbenick, D., 355
Herbert, J. D., 63, 65, 67, 68, 75, 76, 79, 80, 203
Herisson, C., 129
Hermann, C., 154
Hernandez, B., 175
Hernandez, K. M., 277
Herrera, A. P., 288
Herschell, A. D., 377
Hertz, M. I., 183
Hertzog, C., 320
Hetherington, E., 370
Heyman, R. E., 319
Heywood, A. H., 371, 375
Hickling, E. J., 80
Hicks, B. M., 254
Hicks, R. W., 233
Hicks-Pass, S., 384
Hildebrandt, M. J., 76, 77
Hill, A. J., 203
Hill, C. A., 350
Hill, J. O., 197, 211
Hiller, W., 100
Hilton, S. M., 319
Himelstein, S., 154
Hinshaw, S. P., 27
Hinton, D. E., 147, 158
Hitchcock, P., 75, 76, 80
Hite, S., 344
Hobbs, S. A., 375
Hobson, J. A., 170
Hoelscher, T. J., 171
Hoffman, A. J., 124, 128
Hoffman, B. M., 231
Hoffman, K. L., 75, 79, 203
Hofmann, S. G., 77, 146, 147, 149, 158
Hofstetter, M., 175
Hoftun, G. B., 120
Hoge, C. W., 95, 103
Hoghughi, M., 370, 371
Holahan, C. J., 122
Holbrook, M. L., 152
Holden, G. W., 369
Holder, H. D., 382
Hole, T., 227
Holland, J. M., 91
Holleran, S. A., 31
Hollmann, W., 233

Hollon, S. D., 21, 29, 78, 100, 102
Holsboer-Tachsler, E., 183
Holttum, S., 148
Hölzel, B. K., 153
Hood, C. J., 145, 148, 150, 156, 182
Hooff, B., 15
Hook, J. N., 273
Hook, J. P., 273
Hooper, N., 205
Hopkins, J., 65
Hopkins, M. E., 230
Hopko, D., 97
Horhota, M., 320
Hori, T., 171, 172
Horne, J. A., 171
Horvath, J., 312
Houck, P., 92, 95
Hougaard, E., 102, 146
Houser-Marko, L., 252, 256
Houston, B. K., 224
Houts, R. M., 319
Howe, G., 123
Hu, F. B., 227
Hubbard, D., 120
Huebner, E. S., 31
Huedo-Medina, T. B., 179
Huertas, F., 229, 230
Huguelet, P., 277
Huisman, M., 408
Hull, E., 354
Humphreys, L., 375
Hunkeler, E. M., 120
Hunt, M., 344
Hunt, S., 97
Hunter, W. M., 383
Hupp, S. D, A., 382
Hupp, S. D. A., 382
Hurt, T. R., 283
Huston, A., 408
Huston, T. L., 325
Hyman, R., 297

IASP Newsletter, 120
Ibrahim, A. K., 405
Iida, M., 326
Ilardi, S. S., 234
Ilies, R., 318
Ilsley, J., 203
Imel, Z. E., 104
Indredavik, M. S., 120
Ingersoll-Dayton, B., 371
Inglis, S. J., 171
Ionescu-Pioggia, M., 171
Ironson, G., 277
Irvine, J. M., 348

Irving, L. M., 31
Isacsson, G., 405
Ispa, J. M., 384
Ito, S., 171, 172
Ivers, H., 181
Ivnik, R. J., 232
Izard, C. E., 32

Jackson, J. S., 288
Jacobs, E., 257
Jacobs Bao, K., 254, 260
Jacobson, E., 145, 182
Jacobson, N. S., 21, 29, 78, 146, 328, 329
Jadaa, D. A., 390
Jaeger, S., 143, 146, 155
Jaeggi, S. M., 233
Jahnke, R., 150
Jain, D., 383
Jain, S., 102, 147, 148
Jakicic, J., 238, 239
Jakupcak, M., 97
James, W., 273
Jameson, J. P., 282
Jamil, A., 148
Janis, C. L., 343
Janoff-Bulman, R., 260
Jansson-Frojmark, M. L., 414
Janus, S. S., 343
Jarvin, L., 297, 298, 306
Jasnoski, M. L., 224
Jay, S. M, 175
Jazaieri, H., 224
Jeffcoat, T., 80, 103
Jennings, D. J. II., 273
Jennings, E. G., 238
Jennings, P., 18
Jensen, B., 239
Jensen, J. E., 149
Jensen, M. P., 123, 124, 125, 128, 129, 131, 132, 135
Jesse, R., 279, 283
Jewell, T., 277
Jin, P., 144
Jin, R., 123
Johannes, C. B., 119
Johansen, K., 96
John, O. P., 21, 22
John P. J., 152
Johnsen, B. H., 182
Johnson, A., 80
Johnson, C., 385
Johnson, D. R., 405, 408
Johnson, E. O., 173
Johnson, J. D., 95
Johnson, M. D., 323, 325, 326, 327

Johnson, R. C., 407
Johnson, S. K., 150
Johnson, S. M., 326, 328
Johnston, J. A., 119
Johnston, M., 80
Joiner, T., 24, 258
Joiner, T. E., 93
Jones, C., 253
Jones, J., 77, 274
Jones, M., 29
Jones, M. N., 277
Jones, R. R., 372
Jonides, J., 233
Jordan, J., 297
Jorgensen, R. S., 360
Joseph, G. E., 387
Juarascio, A. S., 75, 203
Jungquist, C., 179

Kaasboll, J., 120
Kabat-Zinn, J., 65, 76,
    100, 103, 132, 146,
    150, 182
Kabeya, M., 150
Kadar, J. L., 274
Kahl, K. G., 78
Kahneman, D., 405, 410
Kalak, N., 233
Kalb, L. M., 371
Kalin, N. H., 27
Kalsbeek, W. D., 347
Kaltman, S., 93, 95
Kamey, B. R., 325
Kaminski, J. W., 377
Kampert, J. B., 232, 241
Kane, R. T., 29, 97
Kankane, A., 152
Kanter, J. W., 76
Kaplan, H. S., 349, 360
Kaplan, R. M., 124
Kaplar, L. E., 274
Karam, E., 119
Karney, B. R., 323, 325, 405,
    406, 407, 408
Karri, S. K., 149
Kashdan, T. B., 74, 94
Kashima, E. S., 90
Kashima, Y., 90
Katie, B., 328
Katz, M., 328
Kavanagh, K., 373, 383
Kawachi, I., 319
Kaysen, D., 97
Keefe, F., 123
Keefe, F. J., 123, 151, 152
Keenan, K., 371
Keller, P. S., 319

Kelly, S. J., 405
Keltner, D., 102
Kemeny, M. E., 18
Kemppainen, P., 226
Keng, S. L., 74
Kennedy, K. R., 319
Kennedy, K. S., 170
Kennedy-Moore, E., 16
Kenny, D. A., 79, 325
Kenrick, D.T., 263
Keosaian, J., 152
Kern, H. L., 319
Kerns, R. D., 124, 128
Kerr, D. R., 371
Kesper, U., 146
Kessler, R. C., 109, 123, 134,
    319, 325, 408
Kiecolt-Glaser, J. K., 263, 319
Kikuzawa, S., 318
Killingsworth, M. A., 101
Kim, B., 146
Kim, H. K., 325
Kim, J. S., 232
Kim, M., 154
Kim, S., 305
Kim, Y. H., 22
Kim, Y. W., 146
King, D. E., 272
King, E. A., 31
King, K., 276
King, L. A., 254, 260
Kinsey, A., 343
Kipp, H., 371
Kirkehei, I., 96
Kirkpatrick, K. L., 254
Kirkpatrick, L. A., 279
Kirsch, I., 179
Kisler, T. S., 342
Kit B. K., 409
Kitchens, J., 73
Klausen, J., 77
Klausner, E. J., 32
Klein, S., 197, 211
Kleinert, J., 233
Kliem, S., 29
Kline, L. E., 178
Klipper, H. Z., 181
Klonizakis, M., 179
Knapen, J., 148, 239
Knee, C. R., 322
Knopman, D. S., 232
Koch, E. J., 93
Koch, J. R., 288
Kochanek, K. D., 319
Koenig, H. G., 272, 277,
    278–279
Koerner, K., 78

Koes, B., 130
Koestner, R., 386
Kohl, H. W., 3
Kohlenberg, B. S., 76, 79
Kohlenberg, R. J., 21, 29,
    76, 78, 327
Kohn, A., 386
Kohn, M., 155
Kolata, G., 344, 345, 346,
    347, 348
Kolodner, K., 120
Koltyn, K. F., 226
Koniak-Griffin, D., 224
Koocher, G. P., 103
Koole, S. L., 23
Koot, H. M., 371
Kope, S., 348, 349, 353,
    354, 356
Koretz, D., 123
Kornør, H., 96
Koroglu, M. A., 226
Kortte, K. B., 31
Kosciulek, J. F., 124
Kosek, E., 226
Kosfelder, J., 29
Kosidou, K., 405
Kosson, D., 21, 32
Kotov, R., 74
Kotsou, I., 30
Kovacevic, A., 95
Kozak, M. J., 92, 101
Kozak, N., 170
Kraemer, H. C., 79
Kramer, A. F., 225, 231, 232
Krane, R. J., 347
Krause, N., 371
Krauthamer-Ewing, E. S., 32
Kreitzer, M. J., 183
Kremer, H., 277
Krietemeyer, J., 65
Kripke, D. F., 178
Krisanaprakornkit, T., 153
Kristeller, J., 150
Kröger, C., 29
Krogh, J., 234, 235
Krueger, R. F., 254
Krumrei, E. J., 277, 284
Krystal, A. D., 177
Kubitz, K. A., 173
Kubzansky, L. D., 27, 28
Kuchera, A. M., 197
Kuchibhatla, M., 278
Kuhn, B. R., 384
Kuhn, D., 305
Kuipers, H., 236
Kuldau, J., 239
Kulka, R. A., 318

Kuller, L. H., 319
Kumari, V., 152
Kumashiro, M., 326
Kunze, S., 143, 146, 155
Kupfer, D. J., 93, 171
Kupper, S., 148
Kvale, G., 182
Kwan, V. S. Y., 253

Laan, E., 350
Lack, L. C., 172
Lahey, B. B., 371
Laippala, P., 154
Laks, J., 235
Lambourne, K., 228, 230
Lamond, N., 175
Lancer, D., 237
Lancer, R., 237
Landers, D. M., 173, 234, 237
Landers, M., 232
Landry, S. H., 370
Landy, S., 390
Lane, M., 109
Langer, E. J., 64
Langer, R. D., 178
Langhinrichsen-Rohling,
    J., 319
Lansford, J. E., 384, 385
Larson, C. L., 230
Larzelere, R. E., 384, 385
Laskey, A. L., 383, 384
Latané, B., 308, 313
Lau, M. A., 101, 146, 158
Laub, J. H., 319
Laufman, L. E., 288
Laumann, E. O., 343, 344,
    345, 346, 347, 348
Laurent, H. K., 325
Lautenschlager, N. T., 228
Lavie, P., 171
Lawlor, B. A., 174
Lawlor, D. A., 234, 235
Lawrence, E., 325, 327
Layne, C., 325
Layous, K., 252, 254,
    255, 259
Lazar, S. W., 153
Lazarus, R. S., 18, 19, 20, 98
Le, T. K., 119
Leahy, R. L., 414, 450
Lechtermann, A., 225
Leden, I., 119
Lee, C. W., 104
Lee, E. A., 22
Lee, H. C., 254
Lee, I., 240
Lee, J., 120, 146

Lee, J. W., 288
Lee, S., 119, 146
Lee, S. J., 384
Lefebvre, J. C., 123
Leggett, E. L., 306
Lehman, D. R., 93, 95
Lehrbach, M. P., 80
Leiblum, S., 347
Leiblum, S. R., 347, 349,
    357, 360
Lejuez, C. W., 21, 32, 97
Leman, K., 390
Lemola, S., 233
Leonhardt, D., 343
Lepper, M. R., 386, 387
Lester, K. W., 182
Lett, H. S., 236
Levav, I., 405, 407, 408
Levenson, R. W., 15, 16,
    21, 359
Levesque, M. J., 325
Levin, M. E., 75, 76, 77, 79
Levin, R. J., 354
Levine, J. D., 118
Levine, S. Z., 405, 407, 408
Lewinsohn, P. M., 92, 95
Lewis, R. W., 347
Liberman, J. N., 120
Lichstein, K. L., 148, 180, 182
Lilienfeld, S. O., 103
Lillis, J., 74, 76, 203
Linehan, M. M., 17, 27, 29,
    30, 76, 146, 327
Linn, M. C., 306
Linnoila, M., 174
Linville, P. W., 93
Lipman, M., 308
Lipper, S., 171
Lipton, R. B., 120
Lipworth, L., 132
Little, S. G., 387
Litz, B. T., 104
Litz, V. T., 103, 104
Litzinger, S., 342, 359
Lizza, E., 347
Loeber R., 371
Loeser, J. D., 122, 125
Loewenstein, G., 253,
    257, 260
Lohr, J. M., 103
Long, N., 375, 389
Long, P., 375
Longmore, R. J., 21, 79
Loomis, L. S., 219, 332
Lopez, M., 182
Lopez, N. L., 371
Lopez, S. J., 31

Lopez-Martinez, A. E.,
    124, 128
LoPiccolo, J., 358, 359
Lorber, M. F., 385
Lorenc, A., 148
Lorenz, F. O., 342
Losada, M. F., 258
Lowe, M. R., 75
Lucas, G. M., 326
Lucas, N., 420
Lucas, R. E., 251, 252, 253,
    254, 260, 262, 318
Ludtke, R., 145, 151
Lui, M., 319
Lundberg, M., 405
Lundgren, T., 79
Lundholm, U. P., 155
Luoma, J. B., 74, 205
Luoma, J. L., 77
Lupiáñez, J., 229, 230
Luque, A., 229, 230
Lusardi, A., 412, 413, 414
Lutzker, J. R., 376
Luxton, D. D., 158
Lydersen, S., 120
Lykken, D., 252, 253
Lynch, J. E., 208
Lynch, M. E., 371, 375
Lynch, T. R., 17, 21, 32
Lynn, S. J., 64, 157
Lyons, R., 124
Lyubomirsky, S., 100, 101,
    252, 253, 254, 255,
    256, 257, 258, 259,
    260, 261

Ma, Y., 153
Maccoby, E. E., 370
Macera, C. A., 3
Machado, L., 230, 231
MacKenzie, R. J., 390
MacLean, A. W., 174
MacLean, C. D., 272
MacLeod, C., 100
Madden, D. J., 225
Maddison, R., 238
Magaletta, P. R., 31
Magnusson, C., 405
Magyar, G. M., 278
Mahoney, A., 274, 277,
    278, 289
Maier, S. F., 95
Maisel, N. C., 326, 405,
    406, 407, 408
Maitoza, R., 91
Malarkey, W. B., 319
Malmivaara, A., 154

Malone, P. S., 384
Malouff, J. M., 23, 47
Maltese, K., 370
Manber, R., 158, 169, 182, 183, 186
Mancebo, M. C., 236, 237
Manes, R. R., 23
Manganelli, M., 230
Manganello, J. A., 384
Manger, T. A., 236
Maniar, S. D., 31
Manne, S. L., 124
Manson, J. E., 227
Manzi, C., 91
Manzoni, G. M., 145
Mao, H.-Y., 319
Marcus, B. H., 238, 239
Margolin, G., 328
Mariner, C. L., 385
Markham, L., 386
Markie-Dadds, C., 389
Markie-Dadds, M. R., 389
Markman, H. J., 319, 327, 333
Markopolos, H., 312
Marlatt, G. A., 146, 236, 238
Marmot, M., 407
Marsh, G. R., 171, 182
Martell, C. R., 81, 92, 95, 106
Marti, C. N., 233
Martin, C., 343
Martin, M., 123
Martin, M. J., 408, 409
Martin, P. R., 239
Martin-Morales, A., 347
Marx, B. P., 74
Marzolini, S., 239
Mascaro, N., 31
Masley, S., 231
Maslow, A. H., 262
Mason, T. B., 174
Massari, C., 371
Massion, A. O., 150
Masters, W. H., 349, 354
Masuda, A., 74, 77, 171, 203
Mata, J., 233
Mathews, A., 100
Mathias, C. J., 16
Matsumoto, D., 39n 1
Matthews, K. A., 319
Matthews, R., 104
Mattis, J. S., 285
Maurissen, K., 148, 239
Mauss, I. B., 15, 16, 261, 262

Maydeu-Olivares, A., 44, 53
Mayer, J. D., 18
Mazzucchelli, T. G., 29, 97, 376
McAuley, E., 225, 232
McCabe, M., 347
McCall, W. V., 177, 278
McCallie, M. S., 145, 148, 150, 156, 182
McCann, U., 279, 283
McCarter, L., 15, 16
McCarthy, B. W., 342, 347, 348, 350, 352, 353, 354, 355.354
McCarthy, S., 285
McCorkle, R., 154
McCracken, L. M., 74, 79, 132, 133, 151
McCrae, R. R., 253
McCullagh, P., 234
McCullough, J. P., 327
McCullough, M. E., 254, 263, 282
McCurry, S. M., 75, 76, 102
McDermott, M. J., 97
McDevitt, T. M., 306
McEntee, D. J., 236
McEwan, B. S., 95
McGrath, K. B., 75
McGue, M., 254
McGuire L., 263
McGurk, D., 103
McHaffie, J. G., 132
McHugh, L., 205
McKay, M., 97
McKee, L., 371
McKinlay, J. B., 347
McLaughlin, K. A., 18, 408
McLoyd, V. C., 385
McMahon, C. G., 347
McMahon, R. J., 370, 372, 374, 375, 381
McMorris, T., 228
McNair, L. M., 283
McNally, R., 103
McNeil, C. B., 372, 376, 377, 382
McNulty, J. K., 325
McNurlen, B., 305
McWilliams, M. E., 236
Meade, N. N., 239
Meana, M., 354
Medina-Mora, M. E., 94
Meginnis, K. L., 372
Meichenbaum, D., 97
Mekertichian, L. K., 370
Melhem, N., 92, 95

Mellinger, D., 157
Melnikova, I., 117
Melville, P., 239
Menard, J., 236, 237
Mendelberg, H., 236
Mendelson, W. B., 179
Mennin, D. S., 18
Merchant, J., 151
Merchant, M. J., 389
Merikangas, K. R., 123
Merrick, J., 62
Merrifield, M., 298
Mesman, J., 371
Meston, C. M., 354
Mets, M. A., 178
Metts, S., 359
Metz, M. E., 350, 352, 353, 355.354
Meyer, T., 236
Michael, J. C., 197
Michael, R. T., 343, 344, 345, 346, 347, 348
Michael, S. T., 31
Michaels, S., 343, 344, 345, 346, 347, 348
Michalowski K. R., 172
Michalsen, A., 145, 151
Miciak, M. A., 129
Mickelson, K., 124
Middlemass, J., 179
Middleton, H., 178
Middleton, L., 228
Miech, R. O., 407, 408
Miglioretti, D. L., 151
Mikolajczak, M., 25, 30
Milam, J., 155
Miller, D. L., 232
Miller, E. R., 2
Miller, G. E., 95, 319
Miller, P. H., 231
Milliken, C. S., 95
Mills, P. J., 102, 147, 148
Minnick, M. R., 22
Mino, L., 233
Mintun, M. A., 232
Mishra, R. C., 18, 21, 22
Mitchell, J. T., 2, 92
Mitchell, O. S., 412, 413, 414
Mitchell, S., 328
Mitchell, T. R., 261
Mochan, K., 232
Moffitt, T. E., 92, 371
Mogck, E. P., 152
Mogle, J., 42
Mohan, A., 152
Moholdt, T., 227
Mohr, C. D., 325

Mohr, S., 277
Moitra, E., 65, 75
Molden, D. C., 326
Molinari, E., 145
Mølstad, P., 227
Molton, I. R., 131
Monk, T., 92, 95
Monk, T. H., 170, 171, 172
Monsell, S., 49
Moore, K., 373
Moore, L., 203
Moore, M. R., 123
Moore, R. A., 121
Mooren, F.C., 225
Moos, R. H., 122
Moraes, C. F., 225
Moraes, H., 235
Morales, E., 229, 230
Morawska, A., 396
Morch, W., 371
Moreira, E., 347
Morgan, A., 375
Morin, C. M., 148, 180, 181, 182
Morley, S., 130
Morris, J. C., 232
Morris, N., 239
Moss, K., 97
Motoyoshi, N., 171
Motta, R. W., 236, 237
Mueller, C. M., 387
Muller, D., 147, 150
Mullin, B. C., 27
Muñoz, R. F., 92, 95
Muntaner, C., 407, 408
Murphy, S. L., 319
Murphy, T. J., 236, 238
Murray, C. J., 227
Murray, R. G., 375
Murray-Swank, A., 277
Murray-Swank, N. A., 277, 278, 284
Muto, T., 80
Myers, H. F., 319
Myers, J., 227

Nagai, Y., 16
Nagendra, H. R., 152
Nagin, D. S., 319
Naglatzki, R., 147
Naglieri, J. A., 231
Nahin, R. L., 3, 143, 145
Nairne, K. D., 355
Naitoh, P., 171
Nakamura, J., 298
Nanyonjo, R. D., 288

Nassar, S., 420
National Center for Health Statistics, 119
National Institutes of Health, 179, 196, 347
Nealey-Moore, J. B., 319
Neff, K. D., 254
Negi, L. T., 152
Neighbors, H. W., 288
Neimeyer, R. A., 91
Nelis, D., 30
Nelson, M. M., 372
Nelson, S. K., 254, 259
Nes, R. B., 253
Nesse, R. M., 93, 95
Neubauer, D. N., 176
Neuberg, S.L., 263
Neville, B. A., 319
Newcomb, K., 377
Newman, C. F., 50
Newman, C. L., 236
Newton, T., 319
Nezu, A. M., 42, 43, 44, 45, 46, 47, 48, 49, 52, 53, 54, 56
Nezu, C. M., 43, 46, 48, 52
Ngamjarus, C., 153
Nguyen-Jahiel, K., 305
Nicassio, P. M., 120, 123, 182
Nichols, C. P., 252, 256
Nicklas, J. M., 124, 319
Nicolosi, A., 347
Nidich, S. I., 153
Nielsen, G. H., 76, 182
Niemann, L., 101, 103, 143, 146, 150
Nixon, R., 377
Nóbrega, O. T., 225
Nolen-Hoeksema, S., 18, 25, 26, 100
Noller, P., 325
Norcross, J. C., 103
Nordentoft, M., 234, 235
Nordhus, I. H., 182
Norlock, F. E., 134
Norman, R. E., 227
Norris, R. L., 101
North, T. C., 234
Norton, M. I., 254, 260, 261
Nova, P., 175
Nowak, J., 21, 32
Nowakowski, S., 186
Nranjo, J. R., 183
Nunnink, S. E., 354

Oates, K. L. M., 277
Obasi, C. N., 147
Oberle, E., 254
O'Brien, J. Z., 133
O'Connor, K. A., 95
O'Connor, P. J., 173
O'Doherty, J., 16
O'Donovan, M. T., 174
Oemig Dworsky, C. K., 284
Ogawa, K., 150
Ogden, C. L., 409
O'Grady, K., 281
Oh, D., 77, 146, 149
Oishi, S., 251, 262
Okie, S., 210
Okifuji, A., 118, 130, 133
Okumura, M. S., 230
Olatunji, B. O., 96, 103
Oldehinkel, A. J., 408
O'Leary, K. D., 325
O'Leary, S. G., 385
Olfson, M., 109
Oliveira, N., 235
Oliver, J. M., 31
Olivier, B., 178
Ollendick, T. H., 28, 327
Olmi, D. J., 382
Olson, A. L., 371
Olson, S. L., 371
Olson-Cerny, C., 319
O'Neal, K. K., 2
O'Neil, P. M., 197, 211
Ones, D. S., 233
Ong, J. C., 158, 182, 183, 186
Onken, M., 236
Orcutt, H. K., 68, 74
Orme-Johnson, D. W., 144
Ormel, J., 408
Orne, E. C., 172
Orne, M. T., 172
Orner, R., 178
Orsillo, S. M., 146
Osness, W. H., 224
Ospina, M., 118, 119
Öst, L. G., 77, 327
Ostafin, B. D., 146
Osterhout, R. E., 323
Ostermann, T., 145, 151
Otis, J. D., 124, 128
Ott M. J., 101
Otu, H. H., 181
Overall, N. C., 322
Overbeek, G., 319
Owen, L., 149

Paalasmaa, P., 226
Pace, T. W. W., 152
Padesky, C. A., 100
Paffenbarger, R. S. Jr., 3
Pagano, R. R., 236, 238
Pagnini, F., 145
Pagoto, S. L., 238
Paik, A., 347
Pallensen, S., 182
Palm, K. M., 76, 79
Palmroos, P., 154
Pamuk, E., 407
Pankratz, V. S., 232
Papa, A., 91, 97, 102, 104
Papineau, K. L., 174
Papp, L. M., 319, 414
Parducci, A., 257
Pargament, K. I., 272,
    273, 274, 276, 277,
    278–279, 280, 281,
    284, 285, 289, 290
Parish, B. P., 123
Parish, T. S., 154
Park, C. L., 92, 94
Park, L. E., 91
Park, N., 252, 254, 263
Park, S., 239
Parker, C. R., 76
Parks, A. C., 252, 263
Parsons, S., 120
Parsons, W. S., 313
Pasch, L. A., 325
Pascual-Leone, J., 298
Pashler, H., 258
Pastor-Barriuso, R., 2
Pate, R. R., 3, 240
Pat-Horenczyk, R., 93
Patil, S. G., 132
Patten, S. B., 227
Patterson, D. R., 124, 125,
    128, 129
Patterson, G. R., 371, 372,
    373, 381, 382,
    383, 394
Patterson, R., 183
Paula, C. S., 383
Pbert, L., 150
Pearce, M. J., 287
Pearson, A. N., 203, 207
Pederson, A., 325
Pek, J., 144, 147, 254
Pekrun, G., 236
Pelham, W. E., 371
Penedo, F. J., 226, 234
Peng, P., 122
Penrod, B., 390

Perelman, M. A., 354
Perez, C. R., 22
Perez, L., 278–279
Pergolizzi, J. V., Jr., 118
Perlis, M. L., 179
Perri, L. M., 123
Perri, M. G., 44
Persinger, M. A., 279
Pertovaara, A., 226
Pesce, C., 229, 230
Pescosolido, B., 318
Petajan, J. H., 233
Peterson, C., 252, 254,
    263, 277
Peterson, E., 261
Peterson, L. G., 150
Petkus, A. J., 133
Petrie, S. R., 171
Petrilli, R. M., 175
Petrucelli, N., 174
Petruzzello, S. J., 173
Pettit, G. S., 384, 385
Pew Research Center, 63
Phelan, T., 390
Phifer, N., 272
Phillips, L. L., 282
Phillips, R. S., 152
Phillips, T., 121
Piasecki, M. M., 79
Piasecki, M. P., 76
Piazza, J. J., 42
Pierce, R. S., 252
Pierce, W. D., 387, 397
Pierson, H. M., 76
Piet, J., 102, 146
Pilcher J. J., 172
Pilling, S., 104
Pincus, H. A., 109
Pincus, T., 120
Pirritano, M., 229
Pistorello, J., 75, 76, 77, 79,
    81, 102
Piyavhatkul, N., 153
Plant, E. A., 93
Platz, E. A., 347
Plomin, R., 370
Plumb, J., 75, 77, 79
Pollard, G. E., 371, 375
Pollatos, O., 16
Pomeroy, W., 343
Ponniah, K., 100, 102
Portenoy, R. K., 120
Posner, D., 179
Posner, M. I., 153
Poulton, R., 92
Powell, K. E., 240

Powers, M. B., 77, 78, 96
Praissman, S., 157
Prakash, R., 232
Prakash, R. S., 232
Prapavessis, H., 238
Pratt, M., 3
Prenger, R., 103
Prentice, A. M., 224
Presnell, A., 97
Pressman, S. D., 263
Preston, L. K., 350
Pridal, C. G., 358
Prigerson, H. G., 93
Prins, J., 347
Prinz, P. N., 174
Prinz, R. J., 376
Probst, M., 148, 239
Prohaska, T. R., 232
Pronin, E., 257
Proulx, C. M., 318
Pryor, K., 214
Ptolemy, A. S., 175
Pühse, U., 233
Pull, C. B., 77
Pupo, C., 32
Purnine, D. M., 360

Qian, G., 306
Quillian, R. E., 171, 182
Quinn, S.C., 4
Quoidbach, J., 25, 30
Qureshi, M. Z., 178

Rabian, B. A., 236
Rabin, B. S., 319
Rabin, R. C., 176
Radtke, R. A., 171, 182
Raedeke, T. D., 233
Raepsaet, J., 148
Rafaeli, E., 93
Raffa, R. B., 118
Raghuram, N., 152
Rainforth, M., 153
Raingruber, B., 154
Raison, C. L., 152
Rakel, D., 147
Ramirez, C., 370
Ramirez, C. L., 29
Ramirez-Maestre, C.,
    124, 128
Rand, K. L., 31
Rappaport, B. A., 135
Rappaport, J., 3
Rashid, T., 263
Rasid, Z. M., 154
Rasmussen, S. A., 236, 237

Rasmussen-Hall, M. L., 79
Ratcliffe, S. J., 174
Ratey, J. J., 198
Rathouz, P. J., 371
Rathunde, K., 298
Rauer, A. J., 277
Raysz, A., 146
Read, J. P., 238, 239
Redding, R. E., 80
Ree, M. J., 183
Reece, M., 355
Reed, J., 233, 234
Rees, C. S., 29, 97
Regalia, C., 91
Regan, P. C., 349
Reichborn-Kjennerud, T., 253
Reichling, D. B., 118
Reid, J. B., 371, 372,
    373, 394
Reid, K. J., 177
Reid, M. J., 374
Reigle, T. G., 236
Reilly-Spong, M., 183
Rein, T., 149
Reisen, C. A., 348
Reiss, S., 387
Reneman, M. F., 129
Renick, M. J., 327
Rennicke, C., 93
Resnick, D. K., 122
Rethorst, C. D., 237
Revicki, D., 135
Reyner, L. A., 171
Reynolds, C. F., 92, 93, 95,
    171, 172
Reynolds, G., 230
Reynolds, J. R.,
    406, 407, 408
Reynolds, K. A., 24
Reznitskaya, A., 297, 298,
    302, 305
Ribinik, P., 129
Ribner, D. S., 354
Rice, J. C., 384
Richard, P., 119, 120
Richards, D., 104
Richards, J. M., 22
Richards, P. S.,
    279, 282, 283
Richards, W., 279
Richardson, G. S., 176
Rich-Edwards, J. W., 227
Ridgeway, V. A.,
    101, 146, 158
Rieben, I., 277
Riedel, B. W., 182
Riemersma, R. A., 2

Rigby, S., 276
Rikard, M., 414
Ringwalt, C. L., 2
Rinne, M., 154
Ritschel, L. A., 29, 31
Rizvi, S. L., 30
Robbins, D. L., 319
Roberts, B. W., 253
Roberts, M. W., 375, 377
Roberts, R. O., 232
Roberts, V., 238
Robins, C. J., 74
Robinson, C., 154
Robinson, L. R., 124, 128
Robinson, N., 148
Robinson E. A., 372, 376
Robles T., 263
Rocca, W. A., 232
Roche, B., 77
Rockwood, K., 228
Rodgers, W., 277
Rodriguez, S., 181
Roecklein, K. A., 232
Roehrs, T., 173, 177
Roehrs, T. A., 174, 176
Roemer, L., 146
Roesch, S. C., 31, 102,
    147, 148
Roetzheim, R., 231
Rofey, D. L., 197
Rogers, R., 49
Rogers, S., 405, 408
Rogge, R. D., 323, 325,
    327, 332, 359
Rognmo, Ø., 227
Rohrbaugh, M. J., 124, 319
Rohrer, D., 258
Rojas Vega, S., 233
Roland, E., 371
Rollings, K. H., 130
Rolls, B. J., 200, 257
Rolls, E. T., 257
Rolo, C., 31
Romano, J. M., 123, 128
Romundstad, P. R., 120
Rosa, K. R., 145
Rose, E. M., 273, 284
Rosen, D. H., 31
Rosen, G. M., 75
Rosen, R. C., 347, 354, 360
Rosenberg, A., 97
Rosenberg, R., 124, 128
Rosenkranz, M., 150
Rosenthal, L. D., 174, 176
Rosenthal, M. Z., 21, 32
Rosenthal, R., 256
Rosnow, R. L., 256

Ross, J. M., 276
Rössner, S., 224
Rostant, L., 238
Roth, T., 173, 174, 177
Rothbart, M. K., 153
Rothbaum, B., 95, 96, 97
Rotshtein, P., 16
Rottenberg, J., 94
Rowe, D., 370
Rowe, E. A., 257
Roysamb, E., 253
Rozanski, A., 27, 28
Rude, S. S., 254
Rudy, T. E., 128
Ruggero, C., 74
Ruiz, F. J., 77
Rumble, M. E., 123
Rummel, C., 97
Runyan, D. K., 383, 384
Rusbult, C. E., 326
Rush, A. J., 16, 28, 65
Russas, V., 183
Russell, J. A., 15
Russell, V. M., 325
Russo, A. R., 80
Rüther, E., 236
Rutledge, T., 133
Ryan, L., 175
Ryan, R. M., 65, 67, 251,
    252, 256, 276,
    386, 387
Rybarczyk, B., 182
Rye, M. S., 274, 277
Ryff, C. D., 251
Rygg, M., 120

Sachs, J., 349, 357
Sachs-Ericsson, N., 93
Safran, J. D., 158
Salerno, J. W., 153
Salmon, P., 233
Salovey, P., 18
Salters-Pedneault, K., 146
Salzberg, S., 70, 183
Sameroff, A. J., 371, 385
Sampson, N. A., 408
Sampson, R. J., 319
Sampson, W. S., 171
Sanabria, D., 229, 230
Sanders, M. R., 275, 371,
    372, 375, 376, 382,
    389, 396
Sanders, S. A., 355
Sanders, S. H., 124
Sandler, I., 377, 382, 388
Sandoz, E. K., 73, 205
Sandstedt, S., 31

Sandvik, E., 252
Sanford, K., 359
Santorelli, S. F., 150
Saper, R. B., 152
Sapolsky, R. M., 17, 27, 28
Sarang, P. S., 145
Sardahaee, F. S., 227, 228
Sareen, S., 152
Sarris, J., 149, 182
Saskin, P., 180
Sateia, M., 177
Saul, S., 176
Savies, P. S. W., 376
Savino, N. S., 261
Sawyer, A. T., 77, 146, 149
Sayers, W. M., 75
Sayette, M. A., 75
Scabini, E., 91
Scalf, P. E., 232
Schaller, M., 263
Schandry, R., 16
Schersten, B., 119
Schiff, M., 93
Schkade, D., 252
Schlamann, M., 147
Schleifer, C., 278
Schmaling, K. B., 21, 29, 78
Schmidt, S., 101, 103, 143,
    146, 150, 183
Schneider, D., 319
Schneider, D. J., 21, 75, 205
Schneider, K. L., 238
Schneider, R., 27
Schneider, R. H., 153
Schoeni, R. F., 407
Scholte, R., 319
Schonert-Reichl, K. A., 254
Schooler, J. W., 262
Schorling, J. B., 154
Schouten, A. P., 15
Schover, L. R., 358
Schruers, K., 236
Schubert, A., 2
Schueller, S. M., 259
Schuler, T. A., 319
Schultz, L., 272
Schulz, M. S., 323
Schumacher, J., 150
Schutte, N. S., 23, 47
Schutte-Rodin, S., 177
Schwartz, G. E. R.,
    102, 147, 148
Schwartz, J. T., 236
Schwartz, L., 128
Schwartz, P., 343
Schwarz, M., 143, 146, 155
Schweiger, U., 78

Scipio, C. D., 123
Scogin, F., 97, 100
Scott, E., 277
Scott, W. D., 205
Sedlmeier, P., 143, 146, 155
Sefick, W. J., 254
Segal, Z. V., 66, 76, 101,
    146, 157, 158
Segerstrom, S. C., 95
Seidenfeld, A., 32
Seidlitz, L., 252
Selby, A., 103
Seligman, M. E., 6
Seligman, M. E. P., 251, 252,
    254, 262, 263
Selvin, E., 347
Semple, R. J., 146
Seraganian, P., 238
Serretti, A., 132
Sevier, M., 77
Sewell, M. T., 97
Sexton, H. R., 385
Shabsigh, R., 350, 352
Shaffer, W. O., 122
Shafranske, E., 274
Shah, P., 285
Shallcross, A. J., 261
Shankar, V., 383
Shapiro, C. J., 376
Shapiro, D. A., 100
Shapiro, F., 104
Shapiro, R., 104
Shapiro, S. L., 102, 147,
    148, 158, 180,
    182, 183
Sharma, R., 152
Sharma C. M., 152
Sharma N., 152
Shaver, P. R., 359
Shaw, B. A., 371
Shaw, B. F., 16, 28, 65
Shaw, C., 203
Shaw, D., 371
Shaw, D. S., 384
Shaw, S., 305
Shear, K., 92, 95
Shear, M. K., 93
Sheffield, J., 376
Sheldon, K. M., 101, 252,
    253, 254, 256, 257,
    258, 259
Shennan, J., 80
Sheppard, S. C., 80
Shepperd, J. A., 93
Sherman, K. J., 151, 152
Shermer, M., 297
Shields, M. R., 230

Shinnick, P., 149
Shipman, K., 27
Shirota, A. I., 172
Shoham, V., 124, 319
Shotland, R. L., 350
Shriver, M. D.,
    377, 388, 393
Shrout, P. E., 326
Shum, D., 230
Sidani, S., 181
Siebern, A. T., 186
Siegel, R. D., 63
Sigmarsson, S. R., 78
Sigmon, D. S., 31
Sigmon, S. T., 31
Sikkema, K. J., 287
Sillowash, R., 92, 95
Silva, V. C., 225
Silveira, H., 235
Simões, H. G., 225
Simon, G. E., 120
Simonovski, S., 15
Simons, R. L., 385
Simpson, C., 238
Simpson, J., 31
Simpson, J. A., 321, 322
Simpson, K. H., 119
Simpson, L. E., 76
Simpson, T., 97
Simpson, T. L., 146
Sin, N. L., 253, 259
Singh, S. S., 18, 21, 22
Singphow, C., 152
Sinyor, D., 238
Sipski, M., 354
Siriwardena, A. N., 179
Siriwardena, N. A., 178
Sisitsky, T., 109
Sivilli, T. I., 152
Skinner, M., 119
Skjotskift, S., 182
Skoner, D. P., 319
Slade, E. P., 384
Slep, A. M. S., 319
Sliwinski, M. J., 42
Sloan, D. M., 74
Smit, F., 376
Smith, B. L., 383–384
Smith, B. W., 31, 278–279
Smith, D., 151
Smith, D. A., 325
Smith, G., 65
Smith, H. L., 251, 318
Smith, J., 385
Smith, J. C., 230
Smith, J. P., 405, 407
Smith, K. E., 370

Smith, L. J., 180
Smith, M. T., 179
Smith, P. J., 231
Smith, S., 81, 103, 170
Smith, T. B., 282
Smith, T. W., 319, 344, 345
Smith-Osborne, A., 103
Smith Slep, A. M., 385
Smoski, M. J., 74
Smout, M. F., 77, 103
Smyth, J. M., 18
Snarr, J. D., 319
Snook, S., 312
Snowden, M., 232
Snyder, C. R., 30, 31
Snyder, D. K., 326, 328
So, S., 397
Soehner, A. M., 170
Sondag, K. A., 31
Sonfronoff, K., 376
Songer, N. B., 306
Sonnega, J., 93, 95
Sonnega, J. S., 124, 319
Sood, R., 180
Sorrell, J. T., 133
Soto, J. A., 22
Souissi, M., 173
Souissi, N., 173
Soulby, J. M., 101
Soulsby, J. M., 146, 158
Sowell, T., 410
Spector, I. P., 347
Speetjens, P., 376
Speight, A., 370
Spencer, D., 123
Spencer, M. K., 233
Spencer, R. L., 95
Sperry, J., 203
Spielman, A. J.,
      148, 180, 181
Spielman, L., 32
Sprecher, S., 342, 343, 350
Spring, B., 238
Stahl, B., 103
Stampfer, M. J., 227
Stander, V. A., 319
Stanley, M. A., 282
Stanley, S., 319, 327, 333
Stanley, S. M., 283
Stanovich, K. E., 296
Staples, J. K., 148
Starkey, N. J., 80
Steen, T. A., 252, 254, 263
Stefano, G. B., 182
Steffel, L. M., 29
Steffen, L. E., 31
Steger, M. F., 74

Steglitz, J., 119
Stegner, A. J., 226
Steinberg, L., 151, 370
Steinberg, L. D., 319
Steiner, T. J., 120
Steinman, L., 232
Steiro, A., 96
Stemler, S. E., 298
Stepanski, E., 182
Stephens, D., 390
Steptoe, A., 227
Sternberg, K., 313
Sternberg, R. J., 297, 298,
      299, 300, 302, 306,
      307, 308, 309, 310,
      312, 313, 321
Sterne, J. A., 234, 235
Stetter, F., 148
Stevens, R., 208
Stewart, A. D., 371
Stewart, J. M., 62
Stewart, R. E., 100
Stewart, W. F., 120
Stickgold, R., 170
Stiffelman, S., 386
Stoddard, J. A., 133
Stoelb, B. L., 131
Stone, B. M., 174
Stone, J., 180
Storey, K. M., 236
Stouthamer-Loeber, M., 381
Strachman, A., 326
Strain, P. S., 387
Strauman, T. A., 231
Street, G. P., 21
Streeter, C. C., 149
Ströhle, A., 234, 236
Strong, D. R., 236, 237,
      238, 239
Strosahl, K. D., 65, 75, 76,
      101, 102, 146, 203,
      205, 207, 327
Stroud, M. W., 135
Strüder, H. K., 233
Strussman, B. J., 3
Struve, F., 62
Stuart, R. B., 328
Studman, L. J., 376
Stump, J., 100
Sturmey, P., 29
Suarez, A., 76
Substance Abuse and
      Mental Health Services
      Administration, 109
Sugden, K., 92
Sugrue, D., 348, 349, 353,
      354, 356

Suh, E. M., 251, 254, 318
Suh, S., 186
Suldo, S. M., 31
Sullilvan, M., 124
Sullivan, K., 170
Sullivan, K. T.,
      323, 325, 326
Sullivan, M. J., 123
Sulprizio, M., 233
Susi, B., 272
Sussman, S., 155
Sutherland, G., 233
Swanick, S., 102, 147, 148
Swank, A. B., 277
Swank, P. R., 370
Swartz, A. M., 230
Sweeney, K., 257
Sweeney, L., 377
Sweers, K., 239
Swindle, R. Jr., 318
Szabo, A., 232

Taal, E., 103
Tabka, Z., 173
Tallett, S. E., 390
Tamaki, M., 172
Tambs, K., 253
Tamir, M., 262
Tan, H. M., 347
Tan, U., 226
Tanaka, H., 172
Tang, K. C., 144
Tang, T. Z., 21
Tang, Y., 153
Tanner, M., 153
Tapper, K., 203
Tarakeshwar, N., 277, 278,
      279, 285, 287
Taub, J., 170
Tavecchio, L., 376
Taylor, A., 92, 227, 238
Taylor, A. H., 238
Taylor, C. A., 384
Taylor, J. F., 347
Taylor, K. L., 124
Taylor, R. J.r., 118
Teasdale, J. D., 66, 76, 101,
      146, 157, 158
Tedeschi, R. G., 42
Tekur, P., 152
Tellegen, A., 252, 253
Telles, S., 145
Ten Broeke, E., 104
Tennen, H., 123
Tessier, S., 171
Tessitore, A., 229
Thegler, S., 62

Theodore, A. D., 383, 384
Thomas, G., 320, 321
Thomas, S., 347
Thomas, S. B., 4
Thompson, A. P., 345
Thompson, L., 261
Thompson, R. A., 15, 16
Thompson, R. J., 233
Thompson, S., 386
Thorn, B., 123
Thorn, B. E., 135
Thorp, J. M., 347
Thorpy, M. J., 169, 170, 180
Thorsteinsson, E. B., 47
Thum, Y. M., 77
Thurman, D. J., 232
Tian, L., 239
Tian, Q., 230
Tichy, J., 260
Tiefenthaler-Gilmer, U., 146
Tiefer, L., 349
Tietzel, A. J., 172
Tiggemann, M., 208
Tkach, C., 254
Toarmino, D., 75, 76, 102
Tobar, D. A., 226
Tobler, N. S., 2
Tolin, D. F., 21
Tomich, P. L., 24
Tomporowski, P. D.,
    228, 230, 231
Toney, L., 65
Topham, T., 387
Törneke, N., 77
Torres-Vigil, I., 288
Toshima, M. T., 124
Tosun, M., 226
Totten, S., 313
Toulopoulou, T., 230
Touyz, S., 377
Tran, Z. V., 234
Travis, F., 153
Treesak, C., 183
Trine, M. R., 226
Trivedi, M. H., 232, 241
Troxel, W. M., 319
Truax, P. A., 78
Trudel, G., 347
Trull, T. J., 27
Tryon, W. W., 26
Tsai, M., 76, 327
Tsang, A., 119
Tsang, J.-A., 254
Tsutsumi, T., 150
Tufik, S., 173
Tugade, M. M., 24, 30
Tull, M. T., 97

Tully, L. A., 371, 375, 389
Turk, D. C., 118, 119, 121,
    125, 128, 135
Turner, J. A., 123
Turner, S., 104
Tweed, R. G., 93, 95

Uchino, B. N., 319
Ugarte, C., 120
Uitti, J., 154
UNICEF, 384
Unwin, J., 31
Urdan, T., 387
Ussher, M. H., 238

Valle, L.A., 377
Valle, M. F., 31
Van Bockxmeer, F. M., 228
Van Boven, L., 261
Vancampfort, D., 148, 239
van den Bout, J., 96
Van den Bulck, J., 170
Van der Velde, J., 350
Vangel, M., 153
Van Middendorp, H., 28
Van Ness, P., 154
Van Rensburg, K. J., 238
van Solinge, H., 91
van Straten, A., 47
Vantieghem, M. R., 230
van Tulder, M., 130
Vasconcelles, E. B.,
    277, 278
Vásquez, E., 277
Vaughn, A. A., 31
Ventafridda, V., 119
Ventegodt, S., 62
Verhulst, F. C., 408
Vernon, M. L., 359
Veroff, J., 318
Verster, J. C., 178
Viechtbauer, W., 253
Vignoles, V. L., 91
Viljanen, M., 154
Villatte, M., 77
Villodas, F., 31
Vitaliano, P. P., 174
Vivian, D., 325
Voelker, K., 225
Volkerts, E. R., 178
Vollebergh, W., 319
Vøllestad, J., 76
Volling, B. L., 277
Von Koch, L., 131
Von Korff, M., 119, 120
Vörding, M. B. Z. S., 77
Voss, M. W., 232

Vowles, K. E., 79, 132,
    133, 151
Vul, E., 258

Waccholtz, A. L., 274, 285
Wadden, T. A., 197, 211
Wagner, M. C., 226
Wahler, R. G., 333, 372
Wakimoto, R., 90
Walach, H., 101, 103, 143,
    146, 150
Waldinger, R. J., 323
Walker, A. G., 277
Wall, M., 183
Wallston, K. A., 123
Walser, R. D., 205
Walsh, B., 371
Walsh, R., 253
Walsh, S. D., 405, 407, 408
Walter, H. I., 372
Walton, K. E., 253
Walton, K. G., 153
Wampold, B. E., 104
Wang, J., 153
Wang, P. S., 109
Wang, T., 347
Wang, W., 321
Ward, A., 147
Warmerdam, L., 47
Warzak, W. J., 393
Watanabe, M., 119, 171
Watkins, L. R., 95
Watson, D., 74, 80, 318
Watson, J. C., 16
Watson, W., 390
Weaver, J., 344
Webb, V., 197
Webster, D. W., 332
Webster, M. J., 236
Webster-Stratton, C.,
    372, 373, 374
Weeks, C. E., 76
Wegener, S. T., 31
Wegner, D. M., 21, 75, 205
Weinberg, J., 152
Weiner, J., 204
Weisæth, L., 96
Weisner, T., 408
Weitzman, E. D., 174
Welch. S. C., 411, 413, 414
Weld, C., 273
Weler, B., 171
Wells, A., 66, 76
Wells, K. B., 109
Wells, K. C., 375
Welsh, D., 100
Welsh-Bohmer, K., 231

Wenk-Sormaz, H., 153
Wenzlaff, R. M., 158, 205
Werner, E. L., 129
Werner, K., 224
West, F., 376
West, S. L., 2, 347
Westefeld, J. S., 273
Westerdahl, E., 155
Wetherell, J. L., 133
Wetterneck, C. T., 79
Weytens, F., 30
Whalen, P. J., 230
Wheeler, J., 76
Whelton, S. P., 227
Whisman, M. A., 319
Whitaker, D. J., 376
White, A. T., 233
White, H. R., 319
White, T., 21, 75
White, T. L., 205
Whitehouse, W. G., 172
Whiteley, J. A., 238
Whiteman, K., 420
Whitfield, G. E., 100
Whitfield, T. H., 149
Whittingham, K., 376
Wickrama, K., 342
Widaman, K. F., 359
Wiederman, M. W., 354
Wierson, M., 375
Wilhelm, F. H., 15, 16
Wilkins, V. M., 46
Willett, W. C., 227
Williams, A., 130, 154
Williams, A. C., 135
Williams, C. J., 100
Williams, D. L., 174
Williams, D. M., 238
Williams, D. R., 407
Williams, J. C., 64
Williams, J. M., 146, 158
Williams, J. M. G.,
    66, 76, 101
Williams, K. A., 151
Williams, S., 146, 157

Williams, S. H., 371
Williams, W. M., 312
Willingham, M. W., 277
Wills, R. M., 326
Wills, T. A., 124
Wilmore, J. H., 3
Wilson, G. T., 79, 201
Wilson, H. D., 119, 121, 135
Wilson, K. G., 65, 73, 75,
    76, 101, 102, 146, 203,
    205, 207, 327, 420
Wilson, N. M., 182
Wilson, T. D., 250, 260,
    261, 265
Wilson, W. J., 319
Wiltz, N. A., 372
Winbush, N. Y., 183
Winfrey, O., 143, 203
Winje, D., 96
Winter, B., 225
Winter, L., 78
Wipfli, B. M., 237
Wirth, O., 171
Wisco, B. E., 100
Wisløff, U., 227
Wissow, L. S., 384
Witkiewitz, K., 146
Witoonchart, C., 153
Witt, A. A., 77, 146, 149
Wixted, J. T., 258
Wohlgemuth, W. K.,
    171, 182
Wohlhueter, A. L., 181
Wolpe, J., 95, 96
Woodburn, E. M., 32
Woods, D. W., 79
Woodward, J. T., 31
Worrell, M., 21, 79
Worthington, E. L. Jr.,
    273, 281
Wortman, C. B., 93, 95
Wranik, T., 18
Wren, A. A., 151, 152
Wright, J. P., 370
Wright, K. R., 170

Wright, M. A., 151, 152
Wrobleski, K. K., 31
Wuensch, K. L., 277
Wyatt, J. K., 170

Xiao, J., 228
Xin, X., 227
Xu, J., 319

Yakhkind, A., 149
Yang, C. M., 181
Yang, H.-C., 319
Yeh, H. C., 342
Yeomans, P. D., 75
Yerramsetti, S. M., 153
Yi, J., 76
Yook, K., 146
Youlden, D. R., 371, 375
Youngstedt, S. D., 173, 236
Yu, Q., 153
Yurdakul, L., 148

Zahonero, J., 229
Zalta, A. K., 420
Zaslvsky, A. M., 408
Zautra, A. J., 123
Zea, M. C., 348
Zee, P. C., 177
Zeidan, F., 132, 150, 151
Zeitzer, J. M., 175
Zens, M. S., 371
Zeppieri, G., 131
Zerbini, L. F., 181
Zettle, R. D., 68, 74, 79
Zhou, X., 119
Ziauddeen, H, 201
Ziedonis, D. M., 149
Zilca, R., 252
Zimmermann, D.,
    143, 146, 155
Zinnbauer, B. J., 273, 274
Ziv, M., 224
Zolotor, A. J., 383, 384
Zrane, A., 173
Zuckerman, A., 325

# Subject Index

Note: In page references, f indicates figures and t indicates tables.

ABC Model of Healthy Thinking, 50, 54
Absenteeism, 109, 319
*A Cancer Patient's Guide to Overcoming Depression and Anxiety,* 97
Acceptance and Action Questionnaire (AAQ), 73–74
Acceptance and Commitment Therapy (ACT):
  body image dissatisfaction and, 207
  chronic pain and, 132–133
  clinical trials and, 77–78
  cognitive defusion/ psychological acceptance and, 71
  main goal of, 102
  maladaptive responses to stressors and, 101–102
  mental/physical distress and, 102–103
  MM and, 69–70, 146
  overeating/weight loss and, 203, 217
  pain and, 79
  psychological acceptance and, 69
  values clarification and, 215–216
Activity theories, 251, 252
Acupressure, 182
Acupuncture, 3
Acute pain, 118–119
  *See also* Pain

Acute stress disorder, 96
Addiction:
  obesity and, 201–202
  positive psychological and, 262
  regulating emotions and, 29
  *See also* Substance abuse/use
Adjustment disorder, 94–95
Adolescents:
  aerobic exercise and, 233
  SES and, 408
  teaching wisdom to, 299–301
  *See also* Children; Positive parenting
Ad populum reversal, 63
Aerobic exercise, 225, 226–227, 240–241
  anxiety and, 236–237, 239
  cognitive functioning and, 228–232
  depression and, 234–236, 239
  drug/alcohol use and, 238–239
  heart disease and, 227
  menstruating women and, 233
  mood and, 232–234
  neurodegenerative diseases and, 227–228
  schizophrenia and, 239–240
  visual attention and, 230
  *See also* Exercise
Affordable Care Act (ACA), 4–5

African Americans:
  financial literacy and, 413
  religion/spirituality and, 288
  *See also* Minorities
African American women, 282, 283, 285–287
Aggression:
  regulating emotions and, 27
  stress and, 94–95
Alcohol abuse/use:
  aerobic exercise and, 238–239
  alcoholism and, 46
  emotions and, 17
  intimate relationships and, 319
  managing emotions and, 92
  OTC sleep aids and, 176
  positive parenting and, 382
  preventive behavioral health and, 59
  problem solving and, 46
  regulating emotions and, 27, 28
  religion/spirituality and, 275
  SES and, 407
  sleep and, 173–174
  TM and, 153
  *See also* Drug abuse/use; Substance abuse/use
Altruism, 275
Alzheimer's disease, 228
Amenorrhea, 206
American Academy of Sleep Medicine, 148, 176

American College of Sports
   Medicine, 240
American Heart
   Association, 240
American Psychological
   Association (APA),
   78, 142, 372
*A mindfulness meditation-*
   *Based Stress Reduction*
   *Workbook,* 103
Anaerobic exercise, 225
Anal sex, 346
Anger:
   aerobic exercise and, 233
   chronic pain and,
      122, 123
   healthcare religion/
      spirituality and, 286
   healthy human sexuality
      and, 351
   pre-event beliefs and,
      91–92
   problem solving and, 46
   PST and, 55
   psychopathology and,
      45–46
   regulating emotions
      and, 18
   SES and, 408
   sexual communication
      and, 361, 362
   sexual desire and, 358
   sexual intimacy and, 342
   stress and, 142–143
   suppressing, 22
   time-out and, 386
Anorexia nervosa, 206
Antidepressant medication,
   47–48, 177
   *See also* Medications
Antihistamines, 175–176
Anxiety:
   AT and, 150
   about appearance, 207
   ACT and, 77, 133
   aerobic exercise and,
      230, 233,
      236–237, 239
   associated with memories
      of traumatic
      events, 104
   chronic pain and, 120,
      122, 123, 126–127,
      129, 135
   diaphragmatic breathing
      and, 156
   EA and, 203–204

effective treatment for, 100
effective treatment of
   social, 78–79
experiential acceptance
   and, 66–67
experimental avoidance
   and, 79
exposures, 72
extreme social, 68
financial literacy and, 420
healthy human sexuality
   and, 351, 353
hope and, 32
insomnia and, 184
intimate relationships
   and, 332
MBSR and, 150
meditation and, 143
mindful awareness/
   psychological
   acceptance and, 64
mindfulness training
   and, 155
MM and, 74, 132, 146,
   183, 212, 213
PMR and, 148, 154
positive parenting and,
   371, 382
positive psychological
   and, 262
prescription sleeping pills
   and, 176–177
problem solving and, 46
PST and, 47, 56
psychological acceptance
   and, 79–80
psychopathology and,
   45–46
qi gong, 149
regulating emotions and,
   25–26, 27, 29
religion/spirituality and,
   275, 276, 278, 279
SCT and, 180
SES and, 408
sexual communication
   and, 361
sexual compulsivity
   and, 356
sexual desire and, 357
sexual intimacy and, 342
sleep and, 186
social, 72
SPS and, 47
stress and, 92, 94–95
successful treatment of,
   28, 97

time-out and, 386
AT training and, 148
treating chronic pain
   and, 151
treatment for, 28–29
weight loss and, 214–215
yoga and, 149
Appetite Awareness Training
   (AAT), 217, 218–219t
Argumentum ad
   populum, 63
Arthritis:
   biological factors
      associated with, 126
   depression and, 123
   MM and, 132
   religion/spirituality
      and, 277
   rheumatoid, 123
Asthma, 407
Attachment theory, 376
Attention-control
   conditions, 47–48
Attention Deficit
   Hyperactivity Disorder
   (ADHD):
   positive parenting and,
      370, 382
   regulating emotions
      and, 27
   TM and, 153
Autism, 376, 382
Autogenic Training (AT),
   144–145, 147–148
Autonomy, 252, 256
Avoidant problem solving,
   45, 53
   *See also* Problem solving

Back pain, 119, 120, 122
   PST and, 47
   yoga and, 151–152
Balance theory, 298, 303f,
   304f, 313
Bankruptcy, 413
*Becoming Orgasmic,* 359
Behavior:
   changing eating, 216–217
   emotions and, 15–16
   ethical, 314
   ethical reasoning and,
      297, 312
   financial literacy and,
      413, 420
   happiness and, 254, 261
   interpersonal, 324–327
   model of ethical, 308–313

negative/positive,
    324–325
obesity and, 210
overeating and, 219–220
positive, 255, 256
positive parenting and,
    371, 372, 373, 374,
    375, 376, 377, 378t,
    379–380, 381, 382,
    387, 388
positive reinforcement
    and, 213
regulating emotions
    and, 29
religion/spirituality
    and, 273
repetitive, 212
vaginal intercourse and,
    348, 353
wise, 313
Behavioral Activation (BA),
    95–96, 98
grief and, 104–108
psychological acceptance
    and, 69
treating depression
    and, 29
Behavioral disorders, 28–29
Behavioral health, 4, 6
Behavioral Weight Loss
    (BWL), 197
Behavior therapy:
EA and, 203–205
goal of, 95–96
MM and, 64–65
Beliefs:
body image dissatisfaction
    and, 207–208
chronic pain and, 134
CT and, 98–99
financial literacy and,
    418, 419
healthcare religion/
    spirituality and,
    281, 289
human sexuality and, 363
negative, 99–100, 101
political, 300
positive ethical values
    and, 297–298
reflective thinking
    and, 304
relationships and,
    322, 324, 333, 334
religion/spirituality and,
    273, 275
stress and, 91

thoughts/relationships
    and, 320
See also Religion;
    Thoughts
Benzodiazepines, 177
The Biggest Loser, 210
Bipolar disorder, 18, 414
Blood pressure:
exercise and, 226, 227
qi gong/tai chi and, 150
religion/spirituality
    and, 275
sexual desire and, 357
TM and, 153
yoga and, 151, 155–156
Body dysmorphic
    disorder, 104
Bone health, 150
Borderline Personality
    Disorder (BPD), 27, 29
Brain issues:
aerobic exercise and,
    227–228, 232, 240
chronic pain and, 129
exercise and, 198
hypnosis and, 131–132
MM and, 132, 150
obesity and, 201–202
pain and, 118
religion/spirituality
    and, 279
AT training and, 147–148
Breast-feeding, 197
Breathing:
retraining, 156
techniques, 145
Buddhism:
healthcare religion/
    spirituality and, 283
meditation and, 143
MM and, 64
religion/spirituality
    and, 275
yoga and, 145
Bulimia, 206
Bullying, 389
Bureau of Labor Statistics
    Inflation Calculator, 109

Caffeine, 171, 174–175
Cancer:
MBSR and, 150
meditation and,
    101, 143, 154
MM and, 183
preventive behavioral
    health and, 59

problem solving and, 46
PST and, 47
relationships and, 319
religion/spirituality and,
    275–276, 277, 278
sleeping pills and, 178
Cannabis, 239
Cardiovascular disease:
preventive behavioral
    health and, 59
regulating emotions and,
    27–28
relationships and, 319
religion/spirituality
    and, 278
stress and, 95
TM and, 153
See also Heart disease
Cerebrovascular disease,
    27–28
Certified Sex Addiction
    Therapist (CSAT), 357
Chamomile tea, 175–176
Character, 297
building, 9
teaching for, 308–313
Chemotherapy, 101
Child abuse, 371
Children:
financial literacy and,
    411, 412–413
monitoring, 380–381
raising, 369
regulating emotions
    and, 27
SES and, 407, 408
spanking, 383–385
See also Adolescents;
    Positive parenting
Chinese medicine, 144
Chiropractic medicine, 3
Cholesterol, 151
Christians:
meditation and, 143
religion/spirituality
    and, 288
Chronic health conditions:
chronic pain and,
    120, 121
goals and, 92
happiness and, 263
meditation and, 143
obesity and, 198–199
PST and, 59
SES and, 407
yoga and, 151
See also Physical health

Chronic pain, 117–119
  ACT and, 77, 132–133
  biological factors
      associated with, 126
  biomedical models of,
      121–122
  biopsychosocial
      approaches to,
      134–135
  biopsychosocial assessment
      of, 126, 129
  biopsychosocial model
      and, 122–125
  catastrophizing and, 123
  cognitive behavioral
      strategies for,
      129, 130
  cognitive behavioral
      therapy and, 130
  coping with, 123–124
  costs of, 119–120
  counseling for, 129
  diagnosis of, 125–126
  educational approaches
      to, 129
  emotional stress and, 131
  experimental avoidance
      and, 79
  hypnosis and, 131–132
  illness conviction and,
      127
  MM and, 132
  negative consequences
      of, 124
  preventing, 133–134
  psychological factors of,
      126–127
  psychological
      interventions for, 129
  quota system for,
      130–131
  religion/spirituality and,
      276, 278
  social aspects of, 123–125
  social/environmental
      factors of, 128–129
  surgery for, 122
  treatment of, 129,
      151–152
  weight loss and, 215
  yoga and, 151
  See also Pain
Chronification priming, 118
Churches:
  BA and, 106, 107
  stress and, 93
  See also Religion

Coaching:
  positive parenting and,
      376, 379
  problem solving and, 49
Cognitive Behavioral
      Treatment for Insomnia
      (CBT-I), 179–186
Cognitive Behavior Therapy
      (CBT), 77, 130, 197
  aerobic exercise and, 236
  body image dissatisfaction
      and, 207
  for chronic pain, 130, 133
  emotions and, 16–17,
      28–29
  insomnia and, 158
  PMR and, 148
  psychological acceptance
      and, 69
  relationships and, 327
  third-generation models
      of, 78
Cognitive defusion, 65–66
  psychological acceptance
      and, 70–72
Cognitive distancing,
      64, 65–66, 67
  psychological acceptance
      and, 76
Cognitive fusion, 204, 205
Cognitive mediation, 79
Cognitive reappraisal, 23,
      28, 29, 75
  regulating emotions
      and, 21
Cognitive restructuring:
  body image dissatisfaction
      and, 207
  depression and, 78
  financial skills and, 420
  metacognition and, 66
  "second generation"
      models and, 76
  useful guides to, 100
Cognitive skills:
  positive parenting and, 370
  SES and, 409
  teaching for wisdom
      and, 302
Cognitive Therapy (CT),
      98–100
  ACT and, 77
  cognitive distancing and,
      65–66
  financial literacy and, 418
  MM and, 66, 101
  PST and, 47–48

Communication:
  healthcare religion/
      spirituality and, 283
  healthy human sexuality
      and, 351, 352, 353,
      359–363
  positive parenting and,
      373–374, 375, 376,
      378t, 379, 380, 390,
      392, 393
  relationships and, 325
Communication
      technologies, 59–60
Comorbid psychological
      disorders, 183–186
Complementary And
      Alternative Medicine
      (CAM), 3, 145, 149
Compound interest,
      411–412
Conduct disorder, 27
Conjoint therapy, 328
Consciousness:
  cognitive defusion and,
      65–66
  MM and, 144
  psychological acceptance
      and, 71–72
Consumer Reports,
      209–210
Cosmetic surgery, 207–208
Counseling:
  chronic pain and, 129
  healthcare religion/
      spirituality and, 282
  HHWB and, 6
Crime:
  problem solving and, 46
  SES and, 409
Critical Incident Stress
      Debriefing (CISD),
      2, 103
Critical thinking, 306, 409
Culture:
  Asian, 22–23
  chronic pain and, 122
  positive parenting and,
      377, 393
  regulating emotions and,
      22–23
  sexual behaviors and,
      341, 345
  spanking and, 385
  teaching foreign
      languages and, 308
  teaching for wisdom and,
      299–300

thoughts/relationships and, 320

vaginal intercourse and, 348

values and, 298

*See also* Western culture

10-day Vipassana, 154

Death. *See* Mortality

Debriefing interventions, 103

Decision making:
ethical behavior and, 309
financial, 411, 413
healthy human sexuality and, 351
positive ethical values and, 298
problem solving and, 45, 51
PST and, 57
reflective thinking and, 304
religion/spirituality and, 276
stress and, 95
teaching for wisdom and, 302, 303f

Deep breathing, 50, 54, 144

Defusion, 205–207, 212

Delayed sleep phase disorder, 175–176

Dementia:
aerobic exercise and, 227–228
yoga and, 155–156

Demographics, 406

Depression:
ACT and, 77, 133
aerobic exercise and, 230, 233, 234–236, 239
attributions/relationships and, 323
BA and, 104–108, 106
chronic pain and, 120, 122–123, 124, 126–127, 129, 135
effective treatment for, 100
EMDR and, 104
emotions and, 16–17
exercise and, 226
experiential avoidance and, 74
financial literacy and, 419, 420
financial problems and, 414

healthcare religion/ spirituality and, 287

hope and, 32

major disorders of, 94–95

MBCT and, 157–158

MBSR and, 150

meditation and, 143

mindful awareness/ psychological acceptance and, 64

MM and, 74, 132, 146, 150, 183

PMR and, 148

positive experience and, 261–262

positive parenting and, 370

positive psychological and, 262, 263

problem solving and, 46

PST and, 47–48, 56, 59

psychological acceptance and, 79–80

psychopathology and, 45–46

recurrent, 76

regulating emotions and, 22, 24, 25–26

relationships and, 326

religion/spirituality and, 275, 276, 278

SES and, 407, 408

sexual compulsivity and, 356

sexual desire and, 357

sleep and, 184, 186

sleeping pills and, 177–178

SPS and, 47

stress and, 92

successful treatment of, 97

treating chronic pain and, 151

treatment of major, 28–29

yoga and, 149, 155–156

*See also* Happiness

*The Depression Cure,* 234

Despair:
healthcare religion/ spirituality and, 281
religion/spirituality and, 279

Developmental disabilities, 376

Diabetes:
ACT and, 77
obesity and, 197

PST and, 47

regulating emotions and, 27–28

religion/spirituality and, 278

SES and, 407

Diagnostic and Statistical Manual of Mental Disorders (DSM), 419

Dialectical Behavior Therapy (DBT), 76, 146
regulating emotions and, 29–30

Dialogical thinking, 305, 308

Diaphragmatic breathing, 144, 147, 156

Diazepam, 176–177, 184

Diet:
aerobic exercise and, 233
body image dissatisfaction and, 207–208
chronic pain and, 122
happiness and, 264
healthcare religion/ spirituality and, 285
highly rated, 200
low-fat, 202
mindful awareness/ psychological acceptance and, 64
obesity and, 195–196, 197–198
Paleo, 199–200
religion/spirituality and, 275, 276
SES and, 407, 408, 410
*See also* Nutrition

Dieting:
most common paradox of, 199–202
pitfalls associated with, 216–219, 218–219t
yo-yo, 199
*See also* Weight loss

Diphenhydramine, 176

Disabilities:
developmental, 376
religion/spirituality and, 276

Disease:
Alzheimer's, 2, 227–228
cerebrovascular, 27–28
exercise and, 224
lung, 278
neurodegenerative, 227–228

physiological, 28
*See also* Cardiovascular
disease; Diabetes;
Heart disease
Disease Control and
Prevention (CDC), 224
Distress:
EA and, 204
experiential acceptance
and, 66–67
exposure therapy and,
100–101
healthcare religion/
spirituality and, 283
insomnia and, 184, 185
intimate relationships
and, 326, 330–331
marital, 360–361
MBCT and, 158
MM and, 64, 147,
212, 213
overeating and, 207
PST and, 48
psychological acceptance
and, 80
reducing the intensity
of, 100–101
relationships and,
318–319
religion/spirituality and,
275, 276
social support/relationships
and, 325
yoga and, 152
*See also* Stress/stressors
Divorce:
children and, 332
chronic pain and, 120
communication and, 359
ethical reasoning and, 312
positive parenting
and, 389
PST and, 52
relationships and, 318–319
religion/spirituality and,
277, 278
SES and, 408
values and, 321
*See also* Marriage
Dreams, 286–287
Drug abuse/use:
aerobic exercise and,
238–239
for chronic pain, 121
emotions and, 17
healthcare religion/
spirituality and, 283

intimate relationships
and, 319
managing emotions
and, 92
positive parenting and,
371, 382
regulating emotions and,
27, 29
religion/spirituality and,
275, 277
*See also* Alcohol abuse/
use; Nicotine
addiction; Substance
abuse/use
Dual attention
techniques, 104
Dysrationalia, 296–297
Dysthymia, 47

Eating disorders:
ACT and, 203
aerobic exercise and, 240
EMDR and, 104
healthcare religion/
spirituality and, 282
obesity and, 199
*See also* Diet
Education:
chronic pain and, 120, 129
financial literacy and,
411, 412, 413, 414
positive parenting
and, 371
SES and, 409
sexual behaviors and, 346
*See also* Schools; Teachers
Ejaculatory control,
354–355
Emergency room visits, 121
Emotional distress. *See*
Distress
Emotional dysregulation, 59
Emotional eating, 203–204
Emotional freedom
therapy, 103
Emotion-focused goals, 43
Emotions, 14–15
chronic pain and, 120,
122, 131, 135
contempt and, 39n 1
deep breathing and, 54
down regulation of
negative, 24
effective ways to regulate,
28–32
facial expressions and,
14–15, 16, 25

financial literacy and,
418, 420
functions served by, 16
habitual avoidance
of, 93
happiness and,
24, 255–256, 257,
258, 262
healthcare religion/
spirituality and, 280,
284, 285
healthy human sexuality
and, 351, 352–353,
356–357
hedonic adaptation and,
260–261
intensity of, 15
intimate relationships
and, 319
loving-kindness and
compassion
meditation and, 147
managing, 18, 92
meditation and, 143
MM and, 146, 212
obesity and, 209
overeating and, 202–207
pain and, 118
positive, 24, 255, 257,
258, 262
positive/negative,
22, 24–25, 29
positive parenting and,
370–371, 376, 378t,
392–393
problem solving and,
44, 50
PST and, 48, 53, 54, 56
reducing unwanted, 25
reflective thinking and,
304
religion/spirituality and,
275, 277, 290
savoring, 24
SES and, 410
sexual communication
and, 361, 362–363
sexual intimacy and,
342, 354
stress and, 91, 142
suppressing, 21–23
time-out and, 386
weight loss and, 209–210,
211, 215, 216,
217, 220
women/human sexuality
and, 349–350

*See also* Anger; Anxiety;
    Depression; Distress;
    Fear; Feelings; Grief;
    Guilt; Happiness;
    Regulating emotions
Empathy:
    loving-kindness and
        compassion
        meditation and, 147
    meditation and, 70
    mindfulness training
        and, 155
Employment:
    financial literacy and, 419
    religion/spirituality
        and, 277
    SES and, 409
    unemployment and, 417
Energy drinks, 174–175
Equanimity, 182–183
Equine-assisted therapies, 103
Erectile Disorder (ED),
    347, 354
Eszopiclone, 183
Ethical reasoning, 308–313
    steps in model of, 310f
Ethics:
    ethical thinking and, 297
    teaching for wisdom and,
        301–302
Ethnicity. *See* Race/ethnicity
*Every Parent,* 389
Evidence-based care, 5
Executive functioning,
    225, 230–231, 237
Exercise, 223–224, 240–241
    aerobic, 225
    anaerobic, 225
    BA and, 98
    EA and, 204
    experts on, 2–3
    happiness and, 253
    isokinetic, 225–226
    isometric, 224–225,
        225–226
    isotonic, 225
    long-term plan for, 216
    motivation and, 214
    obesity and, 198
    preventive behavioral
        health and, 59
    regulating emotions and,
        27, 29
    religion/spirituality
        and, 276
    running, 231–232
    SES and, 407

short/long-term effects
    of, 8
sleep and, 172–173
taxonomy of, 224–227
types of, 224–225
walking, 227, 228,
    230, 231–232, 237,
    238, 240
weight loss and, 217
yoga and, 152
*See also* Aerobic exercise
Experiential acceptance,
    63, 66–67, 73
Experiential avoidance,
    64, 73–74
    controlling unwanted/
        intrusive thoughts
        and emotions
        through, 101–102
    obesity and, 203–205,
        205–206, 207, 209,
        214, 215, 217
    prevention programs
        and, 81
    psychological acceptance
        and, 67, 73
    psychopathology and, 74
Exposure therapy, 95–96
    emotional distress and,
        100–101
Expressive writing, 23
Externalization multitasking
    strategy, 48
Extramarital sex, 343–344
Extrapersonal interests, 297
Eye Movement Desensitization
    and Reprocessing
    (EMDR), 104

Facial expressions, 14–15,
    16, 25
Family:
    chronic pain and,
        120, 123
    coping with, 124
    religion/spirituality
        and, 289
    stress and, 93
    *See also* Children; Positive
        parenting
Family therapy, 289, 375
Fantasies, sexual, 349, 355,
    358–359
Fatigue:
    aerobic exercise and, 233
    caffeine/energy drinks
        and, 174

MM and, 150
napping and, 172
sleep schedules and, 170
Fear:
    chronic pain and, 122
    pre-event beliefs and,
        91–92
    regulating emotions
        and, 26
    suppressing, 22–23
Feedback:
    emotions and, 16
    performance, 49
*Feeling Good Handbook,*
    100
Feelings:
    MM and, 64
    negative, 275
    religion/spirituality and,
        273
    stress and, 91
    weight loss and, 211–212
    *See also* Thoughts
*Fighting for Your
    Marriage,* 333
Financial literacy, 410–414
    compound interest and,
        411–412
    credit and, 411
    data on increasing,
        413–414
    debt and, 411, 413,
        414, 418
    homeownership and,
        411, 413–414
    inflation and, 411–412
    institute for, 415–417t
    resources for, 421t
    risk diversification and,
        411–412
    savings and, 411,
        413–414, 418
    *See also* Money;
        Socioeconomic
        Status (SES)
Financial security, 122
Financial skills, 405–406
Food and Drug
    Administration
    (FDA), 175
    antihistamines and, 176
    hypnotics and, 178
Forgiveness:
    relationships and, 3
    religion/spirituality and,
        276, 283, 286, 288
    well-being and, 253

Free association
   techniques, 104
*Full Catastrophe Living,* 103
Functional Analytic
   Psychotherapy
   (FAP), 76
Functional Magnetic
   Resonance Imaging
   (fMRI), 147–148

Gambling, 414, 418
Gamma Amino Butyric Acid
   (GABA), 176–177
Gastrointestinal
   symptoms, 52
Generation of alternatives,
   45, 51, 56
Genetic factors:
   exercise and, 240–241
   financial literacy
      and, 411
   happiness and, 253
   obesity and, 197, 210
   positive parenting
      and, 370
Genetic predisposition
   theories, 251, 252, 253
Genocide, 309, 310, 311,
   312, 313
*Get Out of Your Mind
   and Into Your Life,*
   80–81, 103
Goals:
   ACT and, 77
   BA and, 98, 107, 108
   body image dissatisfaction
      and, 208
   financial literacy and,
      411, 412, 420
   happiness and, 256, 258
   healthy human sexuality
      and, 352, 358
   identity and, 90
   meaningful, 215–216
   problem solving and,
      43, 51
   PST and, 55–56, 59–60
   psychological flexibility
      and, 68
   stress and, 91, 92, 93,
      108–109
   teaching for wisdom
      and, 302
   values and, 69
   for weight loss, 216, 217
Goal satisfaction theories,
   251–252

Grants, community
   transformation, 5
Gratitude:
   happiness and, 253–254,
      255–256, 257, 260,
      262, 265
   religion/spirituality
      and, 288
Grief:
   BA and, 104–108
   chronic pain and, 122
   effective treatment for, 96
   effective treatment for
      pathological, 97
   insomnia and, 185
   religion/spirituality
      and, 278
   stress and, 92
Guilt:
   chronic pain and, 123
   healthcare religion/
      spirituality and, 286
   pre-event beliefs and,
      91–92

Happiness, 250–251
   achieving, 9
   autonomy and, 252, 256
   body image dissatisfaction
      and, 207–208
   competence and, 252, 256
   counting blessings
      and, 258
   definition of, 251
   dieting and, 199
   empirically supported
      ways to, 253–254
   improving, 253–254
   increasing practices for,
      263–265
   kindness and, 253, 254,
      255, 256,
      257–258, 262
   mediating factors that
      lead to greater, 255
   mental health and,
      262–263
   money and, 259–261
   motivation/effort
      and, 257
   obesity and, 199
   positive activities and,
      255, 256–259
   positive experiences and,
      261–262
   positive memories and,
      260–261

potential costs of actively
   pursuing, 261–262
psychological science
   and, 265
regulating emotions and,
   25, 30
religion/spirituality and,
   275, 277
self-help literature
   and, 261
SES and, 410
sexual behaviors
   and, 342
teaching for wisdom
   and, 300
values and, 72–73
variety and, 257–258
wisdom and, 313–314
*See also* Well-being
Hatha yoga, 151–152, 238
*Have a New Kid by Friday,*
   390, 390–391
Health. *See* Physical health
*Health, Happiness, and
   Well-Being* (HHWB),
   3, 6
Health at every size
   movement, 208
Healthcare:
   chronic pain and, 124
   religion/spirituality and,
      279–287, 289
   SES and, 407, 408, 409
Health insurance, 109
Health psychology, 6
Health survey, 144–145
Healthy thinking/positive
   imagery, 48–49,
   50–51, 54, 55
Heart disease:
   aerobic exercise and, 227
   MBSR and, 150
   meditation and, 143
   sleep apnea and, 178
   AT training and, 148
   *See also* Cardiovascular
      disease
Heart rate:
   MM and, 150
   qi gong/tai chi and, 150
Hedonic adaptation,
   260–261
Helping the Noncompliant
   Child (HNC), 372,
   374–375
Herbal remedies, 3, 175–176
Heroin addiction, 282, 283

Hinduism:
  meditation and, 143, 144
  MM and, 64
  yoga and, 145
Hispanics:
  financial literacy and, 413
  religion/spirituality
    and, 288
  See also Minorities
Hite Report, 342–343, 344
Homeopathic products, 3
Homeownership, 411,
    413–414
Homosexual sex, 344
Hope:
  chronic pain and, 123
  healthcare religion/
    spirituality and, 281,
    286–287
  problem solving and, 42
  regulating emotions and,
    24, 30–31, 31–32,
    39–40n 2, 40n 3
  religion/spirituality
    and, 275
Hopelessness:
  healthy thinking/positive
    imagery and, 54, 55
  positive visualization to
    overcome, 55
  problem solving and,
    46, 50–51
  PST and, 48, 52
  regulating emotions
    and, 24
  rumination and, 100
Human Immunodeficiency
    Virus (HIV):
  healthcare religion/
    spirituality and, 282,
    285–287
  PST and, 47
  religion/spirituality and,
    277, 278
Human sexuality,
    341–342, 347
  aerobic exercise and, 233
  anal sex and, 346
  chronic pain and,
    120, 122
  communication and, 351,
    352, 359–363
  debunking myths about,
    345–350
  definition of, 348
  ejaculatory control and,
    354–355

erectile dysfunction
    and, 354
  extramarital sex and,
    343–344
  good sex and, 351–352
  healthy, 9–10, 351–353
  homosexual sex and, 344
  intimate relationships
    and, 331
  lesbian relationships
    and, 344
  lovemaking and, 352–353
  masturbation and, 331,
    354–357
  paying attention and,
    353–354
  relationships and,
    318, 333
  religion/spirituality and,
    276, 277
  sensate focus and, 354
  sex manuals and, 359
  sexual compulsivity and,
    356–357
  sexual desire and,
    357–359
  sexual dysfunction and,
    347, 352, 354, 363
  sexual fantasies and, 349,
    355, 358–359
  sexual practices and,
    346–347
  skills and, 353–354, 359
  sleep and, 179, 180
  surveys on, 342–345
  vaginal intercourse and,
    348–349, 353
  vaginal vasocongestion
    and, 350
  women and, 348–350
  See also Intimacy;
    Orgasms; Sexual
    abuse
Hygiene, definition of, 169
Hyperactivity, 27, 153, 370
Hyperalgesic priming, 118
Hypertension:
  obesity and, 197
  PST and, 47
  stress and, 95
  AT training and, 148
Hyperventilation, 156
Hypnosis, 176, 177, 178–179
  chronic pain and,
    131–132
  cognitive behavioral
    strategies for, 129

Identity:
  coping and, 92
  exposing private,
    359–360
  intrapersonal interests
    and, 297
  stressors and, 91
  values/goals and, 90
Illness conviction, 127
Impulsive-careless problem
    solving, 45, 53
  See also Problem solving
Impulsivity:
  regulating emotions
    and, 27
  stress and, 94–95
The Incredible Years, 389
Infidelity, 343–344
Inflation, 411–412
Insomnia:
  alcohol and, 174
  antihistamines and, 176
  case study on, 183–186
  CBT and, 158
  cognitive behavioral
    treatment for,
    179–186
  meditation and,
    143, 146, 183
  napping and, 172
  PMR and, 148, 182
  SCT and, 179–180
  sleep diaries and,
    180–181, 184
  sleeping pills and,
    177–178
  SRT and, 180–181
  stress and, 181
  AT training and, 148
  yoga and, 149
  See also Sleep
Integrative Behavioral
    Couples Therapy
    (IBCT), 76–77, 146,
    328–329
Intelligence, 296–297
  financial literacy and, 411
  regulating emotions
    and, 18
  SES and, 406
Interoceptive awareness, 16
Interpersonal difficulties:
  psychopathology and,
    45–46
  regulating emotions
    and, 18
Interpersonal satisfaction, 21

Intimacy:
    anger and, 342
    anxiety and, 342
    emotional issues and,
        342, 354
    healthcare religion/
        spirituality and, 286
    sexual communication
        and, 360, 361, 363
    sexual desire and,
        357–358
    stress and, 342
    *See also* Human sexuality
Intrapersonal interests, 297
Introverts, 254, 264
Islam, 143
Isokinetic exercise, 225–226
Isometric exercise, 224–225,
    225–226
Isotonic exercise, 225–226
Iyengar yoga, 151

Jainism, 145
Janus Report, 342–343
*The Janus Report on Sexual
    Behavior,* 343
Journals:
    meditation and, 143
    psychological acceptance
        and, 70
    self-help literature
        and, 261
Juvenile delinquency, 371

Kaleidoscope program,
    298–299
Kindness, 253, 254, 255,
    256, 257–258, 262
Kinsey reports, 342–343
Knowledge:
    positive ethical values
        and, 313
    teaching for wisdom and,
        300, 302
    wisdom and, 313–314

Leadership:
    ethical, 314
    wisdom and, 299
Lesbian relationships, 344
Life satisfaction, 22, 23,
    24, 31
Lifestyle changes:
    happiness and, 253, 257
    obesity and, 198
    weight loss and, 211, 220

Love, 24
Loving-kindness and
    compassion
    meditation, 147
Low income:
    chronic pain and, 120
    financial literacy and, 414
    *See also* Poverty
L-Tryptophan, 175–176
Lung disease, 278

1-2-3 *Magic,* 390–391
Magnetic resonance
    spectroscopy, 149
Major Depressive Disorder
    (MDD), 226
Marijuana, 239
Marriage:
    change in, 328, 329, 333
    chronic pain and, 120
    enriching, 9
    financial literacy and, 413
    financial problems and, 414
    healthcare religion/
        spirituality and, 283
    healthy human sexuality
        and, 351
    infidelity and,
        343–344, 345
    PST and, 52, 53, 55
    religion/spirituality and,
        275, 277–278
    satisfaction with, 318, 360
    SES and, 408, 409
    sexual behaviors and,
        342, 345–346
    sexual communication
        and, 359–363
    stability, 319
    stress and, 92
    therapies for, 328
    vaginal intercourse
        and, 348
    *See also* Divorce
Martial arts, 70, 144
Masturbation, 331, 354–357
Meaning:
    BA and, 98, 106, 107
    bereavement and, 93
    goal of behavioral
        therapies and, 95–96
    regulating emotions
        and, 24
Media:
    body image dissatisfaction
        and, 207–208

emotional overeating and,
        202–203
    exercise and, 224
    positive parenting and,
        375, 382
    sexual behaviors and,
        341–342, 344,
        345, 347
    stress and, 142
    time-out and, 386
    vaginal intercourse
        and, 348
    weight loss and, 210, 220
Medical Expenditure Panel
    Survey (MEPS), 119
Medications:
    antidepressant, 47–48
    chronic pain and,
        117, 121, 135
    half-life of, 177
    healthcare religion/
        spirituality and, 285
    historians of medicine
        and, 4
    obesity and, 197
    prescription, 29
    psychiatric, 48
    psychotropic, 2
    sexual desire and, 357
    sexual dysfunctions
        and, 352
    for weight loss, 211
Meditation, 68–69
    chronic pain and,
        151–152
    definition of, 144
    empirical basis for
        using, 8
    examined by healthcare
        providers, 154–155
    happiness and, 254, 255
    healthcare religion/
        spirituality and, 282,
        283, 284, 289
    loving-kindness, 70, 147
    loving-kindness/
        compassion, 144, 158
    qi gong, 149
    religion/spirituality and,
        274–275
    sleep and, 181–183
    stress and, 101, 143
    variants of, 70
    yoga and, 145
    *See also* Mindfulness
        Meditation (MM)

Melatonin, 175–176
Melatonin agonists, 177
Memory:
  aerobic exercise and,
    228–229, 230,
    231, 232
  antihistamines and, 176
  caffeine use and, 175
  hypnotics and, 179
  MM and, 64
Mental health:
  ACA and, 5
  aerobic exercise and, 239
  community health
    changes on, 4
  community psychologists
    and, 3–4
  happiness and, 262–263
  healthcare religion/
    spirituality
    and, 285
  HHWB and, 6
  positive parenting and,
    370, 371
  regulating emotions
    and, 21
  religion/spirituality and,
    272, 276, 277,
    278, 279
  resilience and, 92
  SES and, 407–408
  stress and, 42
  values/goals and, 90
  See also Physical health
Mental illness:
  positive parenting
    and, 376
  positive psychological
    perspectives on,
    262–265
  regulating emotions and,
    18, 30
  relationships and,
    318–319
  religion/spirituality
    and, 278
Meta-analytic studies, 282
Metacognition, 66
  psychological acceptance
    and, 62, 64
  reflective thinking
    and, 304
Meta-cognitive therapy, 76
Method of approaching
    problems, 48–49
Migraines, 152, 154

Mindful awareness,
    64, 69–70, 101
  literature on, 76
  meditation and, 144
  problem orientation
    and, 44
  psychological acceptance
    and, 76
  thought suppression
    and, 75
Mindful Eating, 211
Mindfulness:
  breathing and, 213
  obesity and, 197
  religion/spirituality and, 288
  third-wave behavioral
    therapies and,
    327, 328
  weight loss and, 211, 217
  See also Mindfulness
    Meditation (MM)
Mindfulness-Based
    Cognitive Therapy
    (MBCT), 146
Mindfulness-Based Stress
    Reduction (MBSR),
    132, 146, 150
  prisoners and, 154
  review of, 157–158
Mindfulness Meditation
    (MM), 64–65, 146–147
  chronic pain and, 132
  cognitive behavioral
    strategies for, 129
  cognitive therapy and, 101
  definition of, 65
  exercises, 102
  psychological acceptance
    and, 62, 63–69
  psychological variables
    and, 74
  regulating emotions
    and, 23
  sleep and, 182–183
  stress and, 101
  theory behind, 212
  training for, 156
  treating chronic pain
    with, 151
  for weight loss, 211–213
  See also Meditation;
    Mindfulness
The mindfulness meditation
    and Acceptance
    Workbook for
    Anxiety, 81

Mindfulness Meditation-
    based Cognitive
    Therapy (MBCT), 76,
    77, 101
  depressive disorders
    and, 102
Mindfulness Meditation-
    based Stress Reduction
    (MBSR), 76, 101
  mental/physical distress
    and, 102–103
Mind Over Mood, 100
Minorities:
  African Americans,
    288, 413
  African American women,
    282, 283, 285–287
  financial literacy and, 413
  Hispanics, 288, 413
  positive parenting
    and, 393
  religion/spirituality
    and, 288
  See also Women
Modeling. See Role
    modeling
Money:
  happiness and, 259–261
  managing, 9
  stress and, 142
  See also Financial literacy
Monkey mind, 204
Mood:
  aerobic exercise and,
    232–234, 237
  BA and, 98
  chronic pain and, 129
  financial problems
    and, 414
  MM and, 150
  napping and, 171
  pain and, 118
  regulating emotions
    and, 23
  resilience and, 92
  sleep schedules and, 170
  yoga and, 149
  See also Depression;
    Happiness
Mood disorders:
  effective treatment of
    social, 78–79
  MM and, 146
  regulating emotions
    and, 27
  treatment for, 28–29

Morality:
    religion/spirituality
        and, 279
    spanking and, 385
    teaching for wisdom
        and, 302
Mortality:
    BA and, 104–108
    religion/spirituality
        and, 278
    SES and, 406–407
    sleeping pills and,
        177–178
    stress and, 95
Motivation:
    created through three
        processes, 213
    happiness and, 257, 258
    healthy human sexuality
        and, 351
    intrinsic, 387
    obesity and, 197
    problem solving and,
        44, 50–51
    PST and, 48, 55–56, 57
    sexual desire and, 357
    weight loss and,
        213–216, 217
    women/human sexuality
        and, 349–350
Multidimensional
    Experiential Avoidance
    Questionnaire, 74
Multiple sclerosis:
    aerobic exercise and, 233
    biological factors
        associated with, 126
Multitasking, 48–49

Napping, 170–172, 180
    See also Sleep
National Coalition Against
    Domestic Violence, 332
National Health and Social
    Life Survey, 345
National Health Interview
    Survey, 3
National Health Statistics
    Report, 145
National Institute of Health
    (NIH), 196, 210
National Institutes of
    Health Consensus
    Panel, 347
National Organization of
    Women, 344

National Prevention, Health
    Promotion, and Public
    Health Council, 5
National Sleep
    Foundation, 169
Neck pain, 151–152, 154
Need satisfaction theories,
    251–252
Negative problem
    orientation, 44
Neurodegenerative diseases,
    227–228
Neuroticism, 30, 253
Nicotine addiction:
    ACA and, 5
    ACT and, 77
    aerobic exercise and, 238
    exercise and, 225–226
    experimental avoidance
        and, 79
    medications for, 211
    positive parenting
        and, 370
    preventive behavioral
        health and, 59
    SES and, 407
Nonbenzodiazepine, 177
Nonjudgmental awareness:
    emotional reactions
        and, 54
    MBCT and, 157–158
    MBSR and, 157
    meditation and, 70
    stress and, 101, 102
Nonverbal behaviors, 25
Nutrition:
    ACA and, 5
    BA and, 98
    happiness and, 253
    historians of medicine
        and, 4
    regulating emotions
        and, 29
    SES and, 407
    stress and, 142
    See also Diet

Obama Care, 4–5
Obesity, 195–196, 220
    ACT and, 77
    addiction and, 201–202
    aerobic exercise and, 233
    best way to prevent, 198
    body image dissatisfaction
        and, 207
    breast-feeding and, 197

childhood, 210
    emotional overeating and,
        202–207
    exercise and, 224
    experiential avoidance
        and, 203–205,
        205–206, 207, 209,
        214, 215, 217
    experimental avoidance
        and, 79
    genetic factors and, 210
    overeating and, 199–202
    positive parenting
        and, 370
    preventing the development
        of, 198–199
    PST and, 47
    regulating emotions and,
        27–28
    SES and, 407, 409
    yoga and, 151
    See also Weight loss
Obsessive-Compulsive
    Disorder (OCD),
    77, 236–237
Oklahoma City bombing,
    278–279
Oklahoma State University,
    299, 314
Opioid use, 133, 134
Oppositional defiant
    disorder, 27, 382
Optimism:
    happiness and, 254,
        255–256, 257, 262,
        263, 265
    problem solving and, 44
    regulating emotions and,
        22, 24, 30–31
    religion/spirituality and,
        275, 277
Oregon Research Institute,
    372–373
Orgasms:
    healthy human sexuality
        and, 352, 353, 354
    masturbation and, 355–356
    vaginal intercourse and,
        348–349
    women and, 347,
        348–349, 352, 353,
        354, 355–356
    See also Human sexuality
Overcoming Depression
    One Step at a Time, 81,
    97, 106

Overeating:
  EA and, 204
  emotional, 202–207
  guilt/shame associated
    with, 206
  obesity and, 199–202
  thoughts and, 205–207
Over-The-Counter (OTC)
  substances, 173,
  175–176

Pain:
  back, 47, 119, 120, 122,
    151, 152
  cognitions, 127
  coping with chronic, 7
  definitions/overview of,
    118–119
  limiting activity for,
    130–131
  long-term solution for
    managing, 127
  MBSR and, 150
  meditation and, 143
  multidisciplinary
    treatment of, 133
  neck, 151–152, 154
  problem solving and, 46
  psychological avoidance
    and, 74
  somatoform, 148
  thinking about, 130
  treatment of, 151–152
  See also Chronic pain
Panic disorder:
  aerobic exercise and,
    236, 237
  effective treatment
    for, 100
  PMR and, 148
Panorama program, 299, 314
Paranoia, 278
Parent-Child Interaction
    Therapy (PCIT),
    372, 376–377
Parenting. See Positive
    parenting
Parenting the Strong-Willed
    Child, 389–390
Parent Management
    Training (PMT),
    372–373
Parents. See Positive
    parenting
Patient-Centered Medical
    Homes (PCMHs), 5

Person-activity fit, 258
Personality:
  chronic pain and, 124
  disorders, 47
  happiness and,
    251, 252, 253,
    255, 258, 264
  pathology, 27
  predisposition theories,
    251, 252, 253
  problem solving and,
    44–45, 46
  regulating emotions and,
    30
  religion/spirituality
    and, 275
  resilience and, 92–93
Philadelphia mindfulness
    meditation scale, 65
Physical fitness. See Exercise
Physical health:
  aerobic exercise and, 239
  behavioral health
    and, 4, 6
  bone health and, 150
  exercise and, 224
  financial literacy
    and, 411
  financial problems and,
    415, 417
  healthcare religion/
    spirituality
    and, 285
  health promotion
    strategies and, 5
  health surveys and,
    144–145
  HHWB and, 6
  improving, 149–151
  intimate relationships
    and, 319
  meditation and, 143
  obesity and, 199
  positive parenting and,
    370, 371, 377,
    378–379t
  problem solving and, 46
  promoting psychological,
    145–149
  regulating emotions and,
    21, 27, 28, 30, 31
  religion/spirituality and,
    272, 276, 277, 278,
    279, 288
  SES and, 406–407, 409
  stress and, 42, 94–95, 142

  See also Chronic health
    conditions; Diabetes;
    Healthcare; Mental
    health; Psychological
    health
Physical illness:
  regulating emotions and,
    18, 27, 29
  stress and, 95
  See also Disease
Physical therapy, 129
Physiological disease, 28
Physiology:
  chronic pain and, 121
  emotions and, 15–16
Planful problem solving, 45,
    48–49, 51, 53, 56
  See also Problem solving
Playboy survey,
    342–343, 344
Pornography, 341, 356, 361
Positive-Activated Affect
    (PAA), 233–234
Positive parenting, 369
  autism and, 376, 382
  best practices in, 377,
    379, 382–383
  building positive
    relationships and,
    377, 379
  communicating
    expectations
    and, 380
  discourage misbehavior
    and, 381–382
  disobedience and, 371
  faithful applications of,
    388–392
  guidance and, 385, 386,
    387–388
  guidelines for, 10
  modeling, 374, 376, 378t,
    380, 381, 382
  monitoring children and,
    380–381
  promoting behavioral
    health and,
    378–379t
  reinforcing desired child
    behaviors and,
    379–380
  relationship-building
    activities
    and, 391
  rewards and, 379, 380,
    386–387, 388

self-help books on,
    388–392
spanking and, 383–385
techniques, 377–388,
    378–379t
time-out and, 375, 376,
    379t, 381–382, 383,
    384, 385–386,
    390, 392
Positive problem
    orientation, 44
Positive psychology,
    251, 262–263
HHWB and, 6
Post-bereavement pathology,
    103–104
Posttraumatic Stress
    Disorder (PTSD), 109
aerobic exercise and, 236
diaphragmatic breathing
    and, 156
effective treatment for,
    96, 97, 100
EMDR and, 104
experiential avoidance
    and, 74
PMR and, 148
pre-event beliefs and,
    91–92
preventing the onset
    of, 103
PST and, 47
regulating emotions
    and, 29
religion/spirituality
    and, 278
sleep and, 186
stress and, 94–95
AT training and, 148
See also Stress/stressors
Poverty:
financial literacy
    and, 410
intimate relationships
    and, 319
SES and, 407
See also Low income
Prayer:
healthcare religion/
    spirituality and,
    282, 283, 284,
    285, 287
religion/spirituality and,
    272–273, 276
sleep and, 181–182
See also Religion

Pregnancy, teen, 371
Prejudice:
obesity and, 196–197
religion/spirituality
    and, 276
Premature Ejaculation
    (PE), 347
Prescription medication.
    See Medications
Prescription sleeping pills,
    176–179
Preventative care, 4–5
Prevention and Public
    Health Fund, 5
Prevention and Relationship
    Enhancement Program
    (PREP), 283
Prisoners:
exercise and, 226
meditation and, 154
Problem definition,
    45, 51, 56
Problem-focused goals,
    43, 56
Problem orientation,
    44, 46, 47, 48, 50, 53
Problem solving:
avoidant, 45, 53
BA and, 105, 107
business/financial, 46
chronic pain and, 129
DBT and, 30
defining effective, 48
definition of a problem
    and, 43
dialogical/dialectical
    thinking and, 305
effective, 7, 41–43
effective/ineffective, 46
emotions and, 17
financial literacy and, 420
goals and, 43
happiness and, 261–262
healthcare religion/
    spirituality and, 283
healthy thinking/positive
    imagery and, 48–49,
    50–51, 54, 55
impulsive-careless, 45, 53
multitasking, 48–49, 53
planful, 45, 48–49, 51,
    53, 56
positive parenting
    and, 376
regulating emotions and,
    18, 23, 24–25

relationships and,
    324–325, 326
rumination and, 100
SES and, 409
stress and, 46–47, 95
styles, 45
theory, 44
See also Social Problem
    Solving (SPS)
Problem-Solving Therapy
    (PST), 42–43
case example of, 51–58
comprehensive version
    of, 53
effectiveness of, 47
exploration of new
    methods for
    implementing of,
    59–60
goals of, 48
misconception
    regarding, 45
for positive
    functioning, 59
prevention training
    for vulnerable
    populations and, 59
preventive behavioral
    health and, 59
studies that evaluate the
    efficacy of, 47–48
training, 48–50
Process theories, 251, 252
Productivity:
chronic pain and, 119–120
problem solving and, 49
regulating emotions
    and, 21
stress and, 109
Productivity, workplace, 77
Progressive Muscle
    Relaxation (PMR),
    144–145, 148, 182
conclusions from review
    of research evidence
    on, 154
Project Dare, 2
Prostitution, 356
Pseudoscience, 196
Psychiatric disorders, 371
Psychiatric medication, 48
    See also Medications
Psychoanalytic
    psychotherapy, 62
Psychoeducation,
    77, 152, 376

adjunctive techniques
  of, 49
Psychological acceptance,
  62–63, 66–67, 80–81
  cognitive defusion and,
    70–72
  experiential exercise
    targeting, 71–72
  fostering, 69–73
  interventions designed to
    foster, 75–76
  and MM explained,
    63–69
  research on, 73–80
  suppression and, 75
Psychological avoidance, 74
Psychological Debriefing
  (PD), 103
Psychological disorders:
  healthcare religion/
    spirituality and, 282
  stress and, 94–95
Psychological flexibility,
  67–68
  ACT and, 77, 102
  psychological acceptance
    and, 64
  treating chronic pain
    and, 151
Psychological health:
  financial literacy and,
    419, 420
  HHWB and, 6
  promoting, 145–149
  regulating emotions and,
    22, 27
  See also Physical health
Psychological problems:
  aerobic exercise and, 240
  financial skills and, 409,
    414, 418, 420
  PST and, 48
  psychological acceptance
    and, 80, 81
  SES and, 409, 419
Psychological resilience, 30
Psychological stress:
  aerobic exercise
    and, 239
  financial illiteracy
    and, 418
  ineffective emotion
    regulation and, 27
  meditation and, 152
  PMR and, 148
  See also Stress/stressors

Psychopathology, 45–46
  ACT and, 77
  experiential avoidance
    and, 74
  healthcare religion/
    spirituality and, 289
  PST and, 48
  regulating emotions and,
    18, 26–27
  social problem solving
    and, 46
  stress and, 46–47
Psychosis, 79, 80, 239
Psychosocial stress, 152, 153
Psychosocial therapies,
  47–48
Psychotic disorders, 77
Psychotic experiences, 64
Psychotropic medications, 2
  See also Medications

Qi gong, 144, 149
  health benefits of,
    150–151
  sleep and, 181–182

Race/ethnicity:
  financial literacy and,
    411, 413
  sexual behaviors and, 346
  spanking and, 385
Radical acceptance, 102
Randomized Controlled
  Trials (RCTs):
  aerobic exercise and,
    231–232, 237, 239
  conclusions from review
    of research evidence
    on, 153, 154
  exercise and, 226
  exercise/depression and,
    234–235
  happiness and, 252
  MM and, 147, 150
  PST and, 47–48
  AT training and, 148
  yoga and, 149, 152
Rape victims, 148
Rational thought, 296–297
Recession, 296
Reclaiming Your Sexual
  Self, 357
Regulating emotions,
  6–7, 17–18
  antecedent-focused, 23
  benefit finding and, 24

cognitive strategies for,
    23–24
  DBT and, 29–30
  effective strategies for,
    21–25
  hope and, 24, 30–31,
    31–32, 39–40n 2,
    40n 3
  identifying effective, 23
  ineffective, 25–28
  process model of, 18–21
  rumination and, 25–26
  savoring strategies
    for, 24, 25
  strategies for, 23–24
  successfully, 28
  See also Emotions
Relationships, 318–320,
  333–334
  attributions and, 323
  beliefs and, 322
  body image dissatisfaction
    and, 207, 208
  capitalization and, 326
  change and, 328, 329,
    333, 334
  chronic pain and,
    120, 124
  communication and, 325
  depression and, 326
  emotions and, 16
  enriching, 9
  expectations about, 322
  healthcare religion/
    spirituality and, 283
  healthy sexual, 351–353
  intentions and, 322–323
  interpersonal behaviors
    and, 324–327
  intimate, 318–320
  intrapersonal interests
    and, 297
  intrapersonal/
    interpersonal aspects
    of intimate, 320–334
  lesbian, 344
  loss of, 93
  obesity and, 198, 199
  positive parenting and,
    372, 377, 379, 385
  problem solving and,
    324–325, 326
  regulating emotions
    and, 22
  religion/spirituality and,
    272, 274, 275, 278

satisfaction, 320–324, 360
self-help guides and,
    327, 328
SES and, 405, 408
sexual behaviors and,
    342, 345
sexual desire and,
    357–358
sexual intimacy and,
    342, 354
social support and,
    325–326
stress and, 142
thinking/acting and, 320
third-wave behavioral
    therapies and,
    327–328
thoughts and, 320–324
violence in intimate, 332
women/human sexuality
    and, 349–350
Relaxation:
    attention-switching
        techniques
        and, 157
    chronic pain and, 131,
        151–152
    cue-controlled, 156
    empirical basis for
        using, 8
    examined by healthcare
        providers, 154–155
    introduction to, 144–145
    MM and, 183
    sleep and, 181–183
    stress and, 143
    techniques, 23–24
    training, 185
Religion, 272–273
    definition of, 274
    ethical behavior and,
        309, 310
    ethical reasoning
        and, 311
    healthcare and, 279–287
    importance of, 9
    Islam, 143
    Jainism, 145
    meaning of, 273–275
    meditation and, 154
    positive parenting
        and, 369
    Scientology, 103
    sexual behaviors
        and, 346
    spanking and, 385

vaginal intercourse
    and, 348
See also Buddhism;
    Christians;
    Churches; Hinduism;
    Prayer; Spirituality
Resilience:
    ACT and, 102
    definition of, 92–93
    promoting, 93–94
    regulating emotions and,
        30–31
Respect:
    healthcare religion/
        spirituality and,
        279–280
    relationships and, 329
    sexual communication
        and, 362
Respiratory infections, 147
Response coherence theory,
    15–16
Retirement:
    financial literacy and,
        411, 412, 413,
        414, 418
    SES and, 410
Reversed Advocacy Role-
    Play, 50
Rheumatoid arthritis, 123
    See also Arthritis
Risk diversification,
    411–412
Rituals, 284
Role modeling, 307
    positive parenting and,
        374, 376, 378t, 380,
        381, 382, 392
    problem solving and, 49
Rumination:
    BA and, 107, 108
    regulating emotions
        and, 25–26

Safety:
    healthcare religion/
        spirituality and, 279
    OTC sleep aids and, 176
    sexual communication
        and, 360
Savassana, 211–212
Savor, 211
Schizoaffective disorder, 277
Schizophrenia:
    aerobic exercise and,
        239–240

financial problems
    and, 414
PMR and, 148
PST and, 47
religion/spirituality
    and, 277
Schools:
    curriculum and, 299–300
    ethical behavior and, 309
    positive parenting and,
        371, 377
    teaching for wisdom and,
        299–302, 303f, 304f
    teaching wisdom/ethics
        in, 313
    See also Education
Scientology, 103
Selective Serotonin Reuptake
    Inhibitors (SSRIs), 226
Self-determination
    theory, 252
Self-doubt:
    experiential acceptance
        and, 66–67
    sexual intimacy and, 342
Self-efficacy:
    BA and, 98
    regulating emotions and,
        30–31
    unresolved stressors
        and, 99
    values/goals and, 90
Self-esteem:
    body image dissatisfaction
        and, 208
    healthcare religion/
        spirituality
        and, 287
    MM and, 74
    positive parenting
        and, 370
    problem solving and, 46
    regulating emotions and,
        22, 24, 30–31
    religion/spirituality and,
        275, 276, 277
    undermining, 93
    values/goals and, 90
Self-harm:
    problem solving and, 46
    regulating emotions and,
        29
Self-help books, 80–81
Sensate focus, 354
Sensational Sex in 7 Easy
    Steps, 357

Serotonin And
  Norepinephrine
  Reuptake Inhibitors
  (SNRIs), 121
*Setting Limits With Your
  Strong-Willed Child,*
  390–391
Sex. *See* Human sexuality
Sexual abuse:
  healthcare religion/
    spirituality
    and, 284
  religion/spirituality
    and, 278
  sexual desire and, 357
*Sexual Behavior in the
  Human Female,*
  343–344
*Sexual Behavior in the
  Human Male,* 343–344
Sexual compulsivity,
  356–357
Sexual desire, 357–359
Sexual dysfunction, 347,
  352, 354, 363
Shame:
  healthcare religion/
    spirituality
    and, 286
  healthy human sexuality
    and, 356–357
  pre-event beliefs and,
    91–92
  regulating emotions
    and, 18
  sexual communication
    and, 360, 362
  sexual compulsivity
    and, 356
  stress and, 109
Simplification multitasking
  strategy, 48
Sitting meditation,
  154, 155, 157
Situation avoidance, 26
Sleep, 168–169, 186
  apnea, 178
  BA and, 98, 107, 108
  chronic pain and,
    126–127, 129, 135
  diaries, 180–181, 184
  disorders, 148, 414
  disorders center, 184
  emotions and, 17
  exercise/depression
    and, 234

hygiene, 169–175,
    184–185
  inertia, 172
  intimate relationships
    and, 319
  popular myths about, 8
  positive parenting
    and, 370
  regulating emotions and,
    27, 29
  schedules, 169–170
  stress and, 95, 142
  *See also* Hypnosis;
    Insomnia
Sleeping pills, 176–179
Sleep Restriction Therapy
  (SRT), 180–181
Smoking. *See* Nicotine
  addiction
Snowball sampling, 343
Social anxiety disorder:
  adolescent pregnancy
    and, 224
  aerobic exercise
    and, 237
  anxiety-provoking
    conversations
    and, 72
  cognitive restructuring
    and, 78
  effective treatment
    for, 100
Social phobia, 224, 370
  PMR and, 148
  PST and, 47
Social Problem Solving
  (SPS), 42–43
  psychopathology/stress
    and, 46–47
  social problem solving/
    psychopathology
    and, 46
  *See also* Problem solving
Social Problem Solving
  Inventory-Revised
  (SPSI-R), 53
Social support:
  chronic pain and,
    128–129
  happiness and, 256
  obesity and, 197
  relationships and,
    325–326
  religion/spirituality
    and, 288
  weight loss and, 217

Socioeconomic Status (SES),
    405–406
  financial literacy and,
    410–414
  health and, 406–407
  housing and, 408, 410
  mental health and,
    407–408
  relationships and, 408
  *See also* Financial literacy
Solution implementation/
  verification, 51
Somatoform pain
  disorder, 148
Spinal cord injuries:
  hope and, 31
  pain and, 118
  problem solving and, 46
Spirituality, 272–273
  definition of, 274
  healthcare and, 279–287
  importance of, 9
  meaning of, 273–275
  psychological acceptance
    and, 69
  *See also* Religion
Spiritually integrated
  couples treatment, 283
Spiritual self-schema
  therapy, 283
St. John's Wort, 175–176
Statistical mediation, 79
Stimulus Control Therapy
  (SCT), 179–180
"Stop, Slow Down, Think,
  and Act" (S.S.T.A.),
  48–50, 54, 58
Stress in America report,
  142–143
Stress Inoculation Training
  (SIT), 97
Stress Management and
  Relaxation Training
  (SMART), 149
Stress/stressors, 108–110
  actions and, 91
  acute stress disorder
    and, 96
  adjustment disorder and,
    94–95
  aerobic exercise
    and, 233
  alleviating, 92
  avoidance of, 95–96
  causes of, 142
  chronic, 93

chronic pain and,
    126–127
coping with, 92, 94,
    98–99, 102–103
cultivating resilience to,
    96–97
dealing with, 93
definition of, 91
depression and, 92
effective ways to cope
    with, 7
EMDR and, 104
emotions are not, 15
financial literacy and,
    418, 420
financial problems
    and, 417
insomnia and, 181, 185
job related, 96
loving-kindness and
    compassion
    meditation and, 147
meditation and, 101, 143
mindfulness training
    and, 155
positive parenting and,
    375, 376
prevention training
    for vulnerable
    populations and, 59
preventive behavioral
    health and, 59
problem solving and, 41,
    42, 44, 45. See also
    Problem solving
problem solving model of,
    46–47
promoting resilience
    to, 93
PST and, 51–58
psychosocial treatments
    for, 95
reducing, 152
regulating emotions and,
    24, 27
religion/spirituality and,
    272, 277, 278
resilient to, 93
schizophrenia and, 239
SES and, 407, 408, 409
severe, 95
sexual desire and, 357
sexual intimacy and, 342
sleep and, 181–183, 182
AT training and, 148
values and, 101

workbooks on, 97
worksite stress
    and, 79
See also Distress;
    Posttraumatic Stress
    Disorder (PTSD);
    Psychological stress
Subjective well-being. See
    Happiness
Substance abuse/use:
    caffeine and, 171,
        174–175
    cannabis and, 239
    financial problems
        and, 414
    heroin and, 282, 283
    MM and, 146
    opioids and, 133, 134
    PST and, 47
    qi gong and, 149
    regulating emotions
        and, 26
    relationships and,
        318–319
    religion/spirituality
        and, 278
    sleep and, 186
    stress and, 94–95
    See also Addiction;
        Alcohol abuse/use;
        Drug abuse/use;
        Nicotine addiction
Suicide:
    problem solving and, 46
    PST and, 47, 59
    regulating emotions and,
        29, 30
    relationships and,
        318–319
    religion/spirituality
        and, 275
    spanking and, 384
Supportive therapy, 47–48
Surgery:
    body image dissatisfaction
        and, 207–208
    for chronic pain, 122
    obesity and, 197
    religion/spirituality
        and, 277
    for weight loss, 211
Survival:
    DBT and, 30
    regulating emotions
        and, 27
    survivor guilt and, 105

Symbols:
    healthcare religion/
        spirituality and, 287
    relationships and, 329
Symptomatology, 45–46
Systematic Desensitization
    (SD), 95–96

Tai chi, 144
    chronic pain and, 134
    examined by healthcare
        providers, 154–155
    health benefits of,
        150–151
    mindful awareness and, 70
    sleep and, 181–182
    yoga and, 149
    See also Yoga
Tea, chamomile, 175–176
Teachers:
    ethical reasoning and,
        308–313
    as role models, 307
    teaching for wisdom and,
        299–302, 303f, 304f
    See also Education;
        Schools
Ten Commandments,
    311–312
10-day Vipassana, 154
Terrorism, 93, 278–279
The Incredible Years (TIY),
    372, 373–374
Therapy:
    sexual communication
        and, 360–363
    sexual dysfunctions
        and, 352
The Secret, 261
Third-wave behavioral
    therapies, 327–328
Thought Field therapy, 103
Thoughts:
    body image dissatisfaction
        and, 207–208
    critical thinking and,
        306, 409
    dialogical, 305, 308
    emotions and, 15–16
    ethical, 314
    happiness and, 254
    healthy human sexuality
        and, 351, 353–354
    human sexuality and, 363
    negative, 100
    obesity and, 209

overeating and, 205–207
pain and, 118
positive, 255, 256
rational, 296–297
reflective, 304
relationship dysfunction
    and, 327
relationships and, 333
relationship satisfaction
    and, 320–324
religion/spirituality
    and, 273
sexual, 349, 358–359
stress and, 91
teaching for wisdom and,
    299–302, 300
thin ideal and, 207–208
weight loss and,
    211–212, 217
women/human sexuality
    and, 349–350
See also Beliefs; Feelings;
    Mindfulness
    Meditation (MM)
Tobacco smoking. See
    Nicotine addiction
Training:
    ethical behavior and, 309
    financial literacy and, 420
    healthcare religion/
        spirituality and, 289
    parent management,
        382–383
    positive parenting and,
        372–373, 374, 375,
        376, 377, 385,
        393, 394
    prevention, 59
Transcendental Meditation
    (TM), 144
    conclusions from review
        of research evidence
        on, 153
    prisoners and, 154
Transgender behaviors, 356
Trauma:
    pain and, 118
    sexual desire and, 357
Traumatic Incident
    Reduction, 103
Treatment As Usual
    (TAU), 152
Trichotillomania, 79
Triple P (PPP), 372,
    375–376, 382
Tufts University, 299

Ulcers, 27–28
Unemployment,
    3–4, 296, 417
    See also Employment
Unipolar depression, 28–29
University of Michigan
    Panel Survey on
    Income Dynamics, 410
University of
    Queensland, 375
University of
    Washington, 373
U.S. Bureau of Labor
    Statistics Inflation
    Calculator, 109
U.S. Department of Health
    and Human Services, 5
U.S. News & World
    Report, 200

Vaginal intercourse,
    348–349, 353
Vaginal vasocongestion, 350
Valerian root, 175–176
Valium, 184, 185
Valued Living
    Questionnaire, 73
Values:
    ACT and, 77
    definition of a problem
        and, 43
    ethical, 306
    goals and, 69
    happiness and, 72–73,
        254, 258
    healthcare religion/
        spirituality and, 280
    identity and, 90
    positive ethical, 297–298
    positive parenting
        and, 393
    psychological flexibility
        and, 68
    reflective thinking
        and, 304
    relationships and,
        324, 333
    stress and, 91, 101
    teaching for wisdom and,
        300, 303f, 304f
    thoughts/relationships
        and, 320, 321–322
    traditional, 321
    wisdom and, 299
Values clarification,
    72–73, 215–216

Vascular dementia, 227–228
Viniyoga, 151
Vision:
    healthcare religion/
        spirituality and, 282
    wisdom and, 299
Visualization multitasking
    strategy, 48
Vitamin supplements, 3
Vocational counseling, 129
Volumetrics, 200–201

Walking meditation,
    154, 155
Weight loss, 219–220
    aerobic exercise and,
        227, 233
    emotions and, 216, 220
    lifestyle changes and, 198,
        211, 220
    MM and, 211–213
    motivation and, 213–216
    preventive behavioral
        health and, 59
    psychosocial interventions
        for, 211
    successful, 8, 209–210
    worry and, 215
    See also Dieting; Obesity
Well-being:
    chronic pain and, 120
    healthcare religion/
        spirituality
        and, 284
    HHWB and, 6
    improving, 149–151
    regulating emotions
        and, 25
    religion/spirituality and,
        272, 273, 276, 277,
        279, 288
    review of research
        on, 253
    theories, 251, 252
Western culture:
    body image dissatisfaction
        and, 207–208
    meditation and, 143
    regulating emotions
        and, 22–23
    See also Culture
Whistleblowering, 312
Wisdom, 297–298
    building, 9
    definition of, 313
    happiness and, 313–314

measuring, 298–299
teaching for, 299–308,
    303f, 304f
theory of, 303f, 304f
Wisdom, Intelligence,
    Creativity, Synthesized
    (WICS) theory, 299
Women:
    African American, 282,
        283, 285–287
    chronic pain and, 119
    financial literacy
        and, 413
    healthcare religion/
        spirituality and,
        282–283, 284
    healthy human sexuality
        and, 352, 353
    human sexuality and,
        349–350, 363

masturbation and,
    355–356
orgasms and, 347,
    348–349, 352, 353,
    354, 355–356
sexual communication
    and, 360
sexual desire and, 358
vaginal intercourse and,
    348–349
Worksite stress, 79
World Health Organization
    (WHO), 119
World Mental Health
    Surveys, 119

Yoga, 149
    chronic pain and, 134
    empirical basis for
        using, 8

examined by healthcare
    providers, 154–155
Hatha, 151–152
healthcare religion/
    spirituality
    and, 289
introduction to, 144–145
Iyengar, 151
mindful awareness
    and, 70
schizophrenia and, 239
sleep and, 181–182
stress and, 143
treating chronic pain
    with, 151
Viniyoga, 151
for weight loss, 211–212
See also Qi gong; Tai chi

Zolpidem, 177, 178

# ⑤SAGE research**methods**

The essential online tool for researchers from the world's leading methods publisher

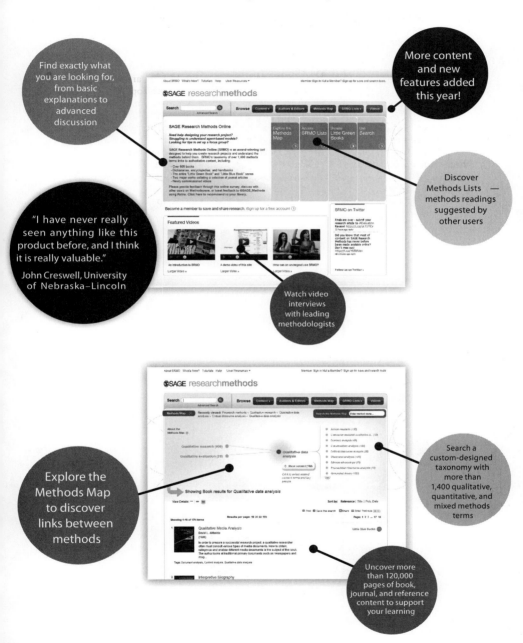

More content and new features added this year!

Find exactly what you are looking for, from basic explanations to advanced discussion

Discover Methods Lists — methods readings suggested by other users

"I have never really seen anything like this product before, and I think it is really valuable."
John Creswell, University of Nebraska–Lincoln

Watch video interviews with leading methodologists

Search a custom-designed taxonomy with more than 1,400 qualitative, quantitative, and mixed methods terms

Explore the Methods Map to discover links between methods

Uncover more than 120,000 pages of book, journal, and reference content to support your learning

# Find out more at
# www.sageresearchmethods.com